Restrictions on the Right to Strike

Bulletin of Comparative Labour Relations

VOLUME 120

Founding Editor

The series started in 1970 under the dynamic editorship of Professor Roger Blanpain (Belgium), former President of the International Industrial Relations Association. Professor Blanpain, Professor Emeritus of Labour Law, Universities of Leuven and Tilburg, was also General Editor of the International Encyclopedia of Laws (with more than 1,600 collaborators worldwide) and President of the Association of Educative and Scientific Authors Authors. He passed away in October 2016.

General Editor

In 2015 Frank Hendrickx, Professor of labour law at the Faculty of Law of the University of Leuven (Belgium) joined as a co-Editor. Frank Hendrickx has published numerous articles and books and regularly advises governments, international institutions and private organisations in the area of labour law as well as in sports law. He is the Editor-in-Chief of the European Labour Law Journal and General Editor of the International Encyclopaedia of Laws.

Introduction

The Bulletins constitute a unique source of information and thought-provoking discussion, laying the groundwork for studies of employment relations in the 21st century, involving among much else the effects of globalization, new technologies, migration, and the greying of the population.

Contents/Subjects

Amongst other subjects the Bulletins frequently include the proceedings of international or regional conferences; reports from comparative projects devoted to salient issues in industrial relations, human resources management, and/or labour law; and specific issues underlying the multicultural aspects of our industrial societies.

Objective

The Bulletins offer a platform of expression and discussion on labour relations to scholars and practitioners worldwide, often featuring special guest editors.

The titles published in this series are listed at the end of this volume.

Restrictions on the Right to Strike

International Law and National Laws in Europe

Editor

Bernd Waas

José João Abrantes
Edoardo Ales
Diego Álvarez Alonso
Kadriye Bakirci
Catherine Barnard
Lorna Mifsud Cachia
Iván Antonio Rodríguez Cardo
Tomas Davulis
Isabel Valente Dias
Luminita Dima
Raluca Dimitriu
Kristīne Dupate
Ivana Grgurev
Martin Gruber-Risak
Tamás Gyulavári
Mehmed Hadžić
Mette Søsted Hemme
Andreas Inghammar
Senad Jašarević
Todor Kalamatiev
Suzanne Kali
Annija Kārkliņa
Anthony Kerr
Francis Kessler
Miriam Kullmann
Ulla Liukkunen
Nikita Lyutov
Leszek Mitrus
Joaquín García Murcia
Sascha Obrecht
Costas Papadimitriou
Wolfgang Portmann
Jean-Luc Putz
Nataša Randlová
Wilfried Rauws
Christoph Reusser
Aleksandar Ristovski
Robert Schronk
Eneida Sema
Mykhailo Shumylo
Vesna Simović-Zvicer
Yana Simutina
Erik Sinander
Ioannis Skandalis
Alexander Sønderland Skjønberg
Krassimira Sredkova
Albena Velikova – Stoyanova
Gaabriel Tavits
Nicos Trimikliniotis
Ivana Vukorepa

General Editor

Frank Hendrickx

Founding Editor

Roger Blanpain

Wolters Kluwer

Published by:
Kluwer Law International B.V.
PO Box 316
2400 AH Alphen aan den Rijn
The Netherlands
E-mail: lrs-sales@wolterskluwer.com
Website: www.wolterskluwer.com/en/solutions/kluwerlawinternational

Sold and distributed by:
Wolters Kluwer Legal & Regulatory U.S.
920 Links Avenue
Landisville, PA 17538
United States of America
E-mail: customer.service@wolterskluwer.com

ISBN 978-94-035-2519-8

e-Book: ISBN 978-94-035-2529-7
web-PDF: ISBN 978-94-035-2539-6

Notes on Contributors

José João Abrantes is Full Professor at the NOVA School of Law. He has been President of the Constitutional Court since April 2023.

Specialist in Labour Law, he is a member of several scientific associations and networks. In particular, he is the Portuguese national expert of the European Labour Law Network, which assists the Directorate General for Employment, Social Affairs and Equal Opportunities of the European Commission. For seven years, he was Vice-President of APODIT – Portuguese Association of Labour Law.

He has many years of national and international experience as a specialist and consultant in the labour area, namely in matters of European and international law, having provided consultancy and technical assistance to ministries (e.g., the Ministry of Labour) and other public institutions. He is fluent in English, French, German, Spanish and Italian and has more than one hundred publications, especially in the labour area, in Portugal and many other countries.

Edoardo Ales is Full Professor of Labour Law and Industrial Relations at the University of Naples 'Parthenope' (Italy). He also teaches Social and Labour Market Regulation at LUISS in Rome (Italy). He is Invited Professor of International and Comparative Labour Law at the Pontifical Lateran University (Vatican State). He is currently Member of the Board of the Italian Labour Law and Social Security Association (AIDLaSS). He is Member of the *International Advisory Board of the International Journal of Comparative Labour Law and Industrial Relations*, of the Board of Directors of *Giornale del Diritto del Lavoro e delle Relazioni Industriali* and of the *Rivista del Diritto della Sicurezza Sociale*. He is Associate Editor of the *Italian Labour Law e-Journal* and Co-editor of *DLM.int*. He is Member of the Scientific Committee of the Marco Biagi Foundation of the University of Modena and Reggio Emilia (Italy). Since 2006, he has been the National Expert for Italy in the ICF-ECE and since 2019 serving in that quality also for the MoveS Network, supporting the EU Commission in the field of labour law and free movement of workers.

Diego Álvarez Alonso Associate Professor of Labour Law and Social Security and Vice-Dean of the Faculty of Law at the University of Oviedo (Spain). 'European

Doctorate', with PhD Extraordinary Award. National research award 'Premio Estudios Financieros' (2005). Member of the Social Law Research Group (GDS) of the University of Oviedo, distinguished with the 'Alicia Salcedo' Equality Award of Oviedo's Legal Bar Association. Member of diverse legal associations, academic societies and networks, and participant in various research projects and contracts financed by the national government or the EU.

Kadriye Bakirci is Law Professor, certified lawyer; Council of Europe Certified Tutor for the Training of the Trainers for the COE Programme on Human Rights Education for Legal Professionals; National Expert for the European Labour Law Network; and National Expert for the European Network of Legal Experts in Gender Equality and Non-Discrimination. Currently, she is a visiting fellow at Kellogg College Oxford University (England).

Professor Catherine Barnard, FBA, FLSW, FRSA, is Professor of EU Law and Employment Law. She is the author of two leading texts, *The Substantive Law of the EU: The Four Freedoms* (Oxford, OUP, 2022, 7th ed.) and (with Peers ed.), *European Union Law* (Oxford, OUP, 2023, 4th ed.), and is doing ground-breaking empirical work (with Costello and Fraser Butlin) on the realities of the operation of EU law (and now Withdrawal Agreement Law) in Great Yarmouth. She has written extensively on labour law (e.g., EU Employment Law (Oxford, OUP, 2012, 5th ed.)).

Lorna Mifsud Cachia is a lawyer working in Malta and Managing Partner in Dingli & Dingli Law Firm, a law firm based in Valletta, Malta. She has worked and works extensively in Maltese and EU Labour Law and lectures EU Labour Law at the University of Malta (Malta).

Lorna was admitted to the bar in 2002 and has, since then, represented and advised clients across a vast array of industries in both the private and public spheres. Lorna is one of the founding members of the Malta Employment Lawyers Association and has been a member since 2012 of the European Labour Law Network.

Iván Antonio Rodríguez Cardo is Professor of Labour and Social Security Law at the University of Oviedo (Spain). He is a member of several legal associations and scientific networks, as well as a member of research teams on numerous labour law projects funded by the Government of Spain and the European Union. He is the author of 15 books and more than a hundred papers published in leading labour law journals. He has been a member of the ELLN since its establishment in 2005 and has served as a national expert in several tenders reporting to the European Commission on the implementation of EU Directives.

Prof. Dr Tomas Davulis, LLM, is Law Professor at Vilnius University (Lithuania) and serves as Justice at the Constitutional Court of the Republic of Lithuania. His main research areas include European Union law, labour law, anti-discrimination law, and human rights. Tomas Davulis is also a member of the European Labour Law Network and the European Network of Legal Experts in gender equality and anti-discrimination.

Isabel Valente Dias is Guest Professor at NOVA School of Law in Lisbon (Portugal). She is concluding her PhD at NOVA School of Law in Labour Law. She is also a senior lawyer at Morais Leitão, Galvão Teles, Soares da Silva & Associados, developing her professional activity in the field of labour and social security law. She is also a Portuguese expert at ELLN – European Labour Law Network.

Luminiţa Dima is a professor at the Faculty of Law, University of Bucharest (Romania) and a PhD coordinator. She is a member of the European Centre of Expertise in the field of labour law, employment, and labour policies, and she has served as a national expert in various projects for the European Commission in this area. Ms Dima is also a lawyer in the Bucharest Bar Association, specializing in the field of labour and employment law.

Raluca Dimitriu is a professor at the Faculty of Law, University of Economic Studies, Bucharest, and a PhD coordinator. She is a member of the European Centre of Expertise in the field of labour law, employment, and labour policies; MoveS in the area of free movement of workers; and the CEE Labour Experts Network. Dimitriu has served as an ILO expert and a Eurofound national expert.

Kristīne Dupate is an associate professor at the University of Latvia (Latvia), Faculty of Law, Department of International and European Law Sciences. Her main field of expertise and scientific research is international and national human rights, especially labour, gender equality and non-discrimination law. Since 2008 she has been a member (national expert) of the European Networks for the EU Commission in the fields of gender equality, labour law and free movement of workers and social security coordination. Since January 2017 she has been a member of the Committee of Social Rights of the Council of Europe, re-elected in 2022 with the term of the office until 2028. In 2023, she was elected as General Rapporteur of the Committee of Social Rights of the Council of Europe.

Ivana Grgurev is Tenured Professor and the Head of the Department of Labour and Social Security Law at the University of Zagreb (Croatia). She is a national expert in the European Labour Law Network. Ivana was a visiting lecturer at the University College Dublin (Ireland) and the University of Trento (Italy). She has published several books and articles in the field of labour law (non-discrimination law, collective agreements, managerial contracts, etc.).

Dr Martin Gruber-Risak is an associate professor at the Department for Labour and Social Security Law of the University of Vienna (Austria) and the academic director of the LLM in Labour Law at this university. With a rich career spanning domestic and international legal stages, including the University of Passau (Germany) and the University of Otago (New Zealand), Dr Gruber-Risak's expertise encompasses both Austrian and European labour law. He is also a national expert with the 'European centre of expertise in the field of labour law, employment and labour market policies (ECE)' that advises the European Commission.

Tamás Gyulavári is Professor of Labour Law and Chair of Labour Law Department at Pázmány Péter Catholic University in Budapest (Hungary). He has been a visiting professor at Porto, Bologna, Santiago de Compostela, Vienna, Quito, Jakarta and Loyola Chicago Universities. He has published and edited 13 books and over 60 articles in Hungarian, and over 15 articles in English, including top journals. He has been working on a dozen of EU projects. He is the Chair of the Labour Law Research Network and also a member of the European Labour Law Network and the European Disability Expertise.

Dr Mehmed Hadžić is Professor of Labour Law and Social Security Law at the Department for State and International Public Law at the University of Sarajevo – Faculty of Law (Bosnia and Herzegovina) since 2002. He obtained her PhD at the Faculty of Law, the University of Sarajevo (Bosnia and Herzegovina) in 2013. His research focuses primarily on labour law and social security law. Through his work, the following topics are covered: individual and collective labour rights, individual labour disputes, mediation, flexicurity, prohibition of discrimination, active and passive labour market policies.

Mette Søsted Hemme is Associate Professor, PhD, of Labour Law at Aarhus University. Her expertise covers individual and collective labour law, including public-sector employment. She is the author of multiple publications on national and EU labour law topics; *inter alia*, she is the co-author of a textbook on the legal framework of public employment ('Forvaltningspersonalet'). She also serves as a national expert (Denmark) for the ELLN network.

Dr Andreas Inghammar is the Deputy Dean of Lund University School of Economics and Management (Sweden) and Associate Professor in Business Law. He holds an LLD from Lund University, Faculty of Law (Sweden). His main focus is comparative and international labour law.

Senad Jašarević was born on 5 January 1963 in Novi Sad, Serbia. He graduated from the Faculty of Law in Novi Sad in 1986 where he currently holds the position of Full Professor, specializing in Labour Law and Social Security Law. He is Vice-president of the Serbian Association for Labour Law and Social Security. Senad Jašarević is a mediator of the Republic Agency for Settlement of Labour Disputes. He is the author of numerous articles, books, studies in the field of labour and social security law.

Todor Kalamatiev is Full Professor (retired) at the Ss. Cyril and Methodius University in Skopje (Iustinianus Primus Faculty of Law – Skopje, North Macedonia). He was a long-time head of the Department of Labour Law at the Faculty of Law in Skopje. He was also a president of the Macedonian Bar Examination Commission. Professor Kalamatiev has participated in several international scientific projects, including the European Labour Law Network project on restatement of labour law in Europe, where he was the representative for North Macedonia. Currently, he holds the position of president of the Association for Labour and Social Law of North Macedonia.

Suzanne Kali is an experienced researcher and lecturer. Her research for Leiden University and Radboud University Nijmegen is mainly focused on the fields of labour law, equality law and pension law.

Dr iur. Annija Kārkliņa is a professor at the Faculty of Law of the University of Latvia (Latvia) and the Head of the Constitutional and Administrative Law Department. She has almost 20 years of experience in the academic field. By decision of the Latvian Council of Science, she has been granted expert status in legal science. A. Kārkliņa has provided expert opinions to various state institutions. In addition to her academic work, she practices as a sworn attorney.

Anthony Kerr is a Senior Counsel at the Bar of Ireland and an adjunct associate professor at the UCD Sutherland School of Law. He is an executive committee member of the Institute of Employment Rights, a National Reporter for the International Labour Law Reports and the Ireland representative on the European Labour Law Network and the European Centre of Expertise in the field of labour law, employment and labour market policies.

Francis Kessler is an emeritus assistant professor at the Sorbonne Law School at University Paris 1 (France) where he teaches Social Security, Labour Law and European Social Law and a member of the European Centre of Expertise in the field of labour law, employment and labour market policies (ECE). He is also an attorney at the Paris bar.

Miriam Kullmann is Professor of Labour and Social Security Law at Utrecht University (The Netherlands). She is also an independent member of the European Committee of Social Rights (Council of Europe).

Ulla Liukkunen is Professor of Labour Law and Private International Law at the University of Helsinki (Finland). Her research interests include labour law, private international law and transnational law.

Leszek Mitrus is professor at the Chair of Labour Law and Social Policy at the Jagiellonian University in Kraków (Poland), member of the European Labour Law Network and author of more than 150 publications on Polish and European labour law and social security law; *inter alia*, he is the author of the monograph on termination with notice of an employment contract due to reasons concerning an employee, and co-author of commentaries to the Polish Labour Code and the Charter of Fundamental Rights of the European Union. From 2016 to 2018, he has been a member of the Commission for Codification of Labour Law.

Nikita Lyutov, Dr Jur., Prof., Head of Department of Labour at Kutafin Moscow State Law University, MSAL (Russia). In 2022, he moved to Kazakhstan and currently works at Maqsut Narikbayev University (MNU). Prof. Lyutov is a frequent external collaborator with the ILO. Since 2001 Prof. Lyutov has authored more than 220 articles, monographs and conference presentations.

Joaquín García Murcia is Professor of Labour Law and Social Security at the Complutense University of Madrid (Spain). He has co-authored several leading books on Labour and Employment Law in Spain, such as Labour Law and Practical Treatise on Labour Law. He has published numerous papers in Labour Law and Social Security Law journals, led multiple research projects, supervised numerous doctoral theses, and coordinated the *Labour Law Journal* published by the Spanish Ministry of Employment. He has also served as a legal adviser at the Spanish Constitutional Court.

Dr Sascha Obrecht is a university assistant at the Department for Labour and Social Security Law of the University of Vienna (Austria). As a former staff member of the Minister of Social Affairs, he was responsible for labour law and occupational health and safety. He also worked as an associate in a law firm, has published numerous papers in the field of labour and social security law and is a regular lecturer in those fields.

Costas Papadimitriou is emeritus Professor of Labour Law at the Law School of Athens. He is a Supreme Court Attorney at Law and President of the Greek Organization for Mediation and Arbitration. He is also a member of the Department of Studies of the Greek Parliament since 1994 and a national expert for different international networks.

Wolfgang Portmann, Professor of Private and Labour Law at the University of Zurich (Switzerland), is the author and editor of numerous publications focusing on Swiss, comparative, European, and international labour law. He is also the Chairman of the publishing board of the *Swiss Journal for Labour Law and Unemployment Insurance* (ARV) and a member of the European Labour Law Network (ELLN). In addition, Wolfgang Portmann acts as a consultant for a law firm and is responsible for training lawyers specializing in labour law on behalf of the Swiss Bar Association. From 2010 to 2014, Wolfgang Portmann served as Director of the Institute of Law at the University of Zurich.

Jean-Luc Putz became a lawyer and partner at Arendt & Medernach, after serving for 15 years as a judge in Luxembourg. Specializing in labour law and business crime, he teaches Labour Law at the University of Luxembourg (Luxembourg). He is the author of numerous books, case law collections, and articles, including a two-volume treatise on collective labour law.

Nataša Randlová is a founding partner of Randl Partners, attorneys-at-law, and a lecturer at Randls Training educational agency. She is also teaching Labour Law at Charles University in Prague (The Czech Republic). She mainly specializes in collective bargaining, transfer of rights and obligations, temporary assignment of employees and HR. She is the author of several labour law commentaries and also a lot of articles on employment and labour law. She is a mediator of collective bargaining claims registered at the Ministry of Labor.

Wilfried Rauws was a Full Professor Emeritus at the Free University of Brussels from 2001 until 2021, where he taught Belgian Labour Law and Social Security Law,

EU-Employment Law, and Comparative Labour Law. He was the elected Dean of the Faculty of Law and Criminology from 2015 to 2019. Previously, he has been sixteen years attorney at the Antwerp Bar (1986-2000), and again after his retirement in 2021 at the University dealing with labour law cases, and a part-time senior lecturer professor at the Law Faculty of the University of Maastricht in the Netherlands from 2001 to 2019. Wilfried Rauws is currently deputy judge in the Court of Appeal. Wilfried Rauws is member of the chief editor of the main Belgian legal periodical *Rechtskundig Weekblad* (Weekly Journal of Law), and member of the editorial board of the *Tijdschrift voor Privaatrecht* (Journal of Private Law). Wilfried Rauws is the national expert for Belgium of the European Labour Law Network (ELLN), which is headed by Prof. Dr Bernd Waas, Goethe Universität Frankfurt, Germany. Wilfried Rauws was the President of the Belgian Association for Labour Relations.

Christoph Reusser, Mlaw, attorney at law, is a research assistant at the chair of Professor Roger Rudolph for labour and private law at the University of Zurich (Switzerland).

Aleksandar Ristovski is Full Professor of Labour Law at the Ss. Cyril and Methodius University in Skopje (Iustinianus Primus Faculty of Law - Skopje, North Macedonia). Professor Ristovski has participated in several international scientific projects, including the European Labour Law Network project on restatement of labour law in Europe, where he was the representative for North Macedonia. He is a national expert for North Macedonia in the CEElex network of national legal experts on labour and industrial relations in Central and Eastern Europe and a vice-president of the Association for Labour and Social Law of North Macedonia.

Prof. Asoc. Dr Eneida Sema is a pedagogue in the Civil Department, Faculty of Law, Tirana University (Albania), since 2004. She is a lecturer of 'Labour Law' and 'International Labour Law'. Eneida was conferred the degree 'Doctor of Juridical Sciences' in 2010 and was conferred the title 'Associate Professor' in 2013 with a special focus on her research in the field of labour law. She is the author and co-author of many scientific articles considering labour law issues. She was conferred the title 'Attorney at Law' in July 2005.

Prof. JUDr Robert Schronk, CSc (PhD). He worked at two universities (Comenius University, Bratislava, Faculty of Law 1991-2022; Matej Bel University, Faculty of Law, Banská Bystrica 1996-2014), where he led lectures and seminars on labour law, international and European labour Law. He was a responsible solver or co-solver of scientific research projects and grants and also worked in academic functions. He is an author of publications on Slovak and European labour law. Since 2003 he has been registered in the list of lawyers maintained by the Slovak Bar Association and is a member of the European Labour Law Network - ELLN (2007-present).

Mykhailo Shumylo, DSc (Law), is the Head of the Secretariat of the High Council of Justice and a professor in the Department of International, Civil and Commercial Law at the State University of Trade and Economics. He has been an expert in the working group for drafting the Labour Code of Ukraine and a national expert for the Council of Europe. He has authored over hundred academic publications on social rights and labour law.

Vesna Simović-Zvicer is a professor at the University of Montenegro (subjects: Labour Law, European Labour Law and Social Law). She is a member of the following international associations/professional associations: national expert at the European Network for Gender Equality (since June 2018); national expert at the European Center for Expertise (since 2016); a member of the research team at the European Network for Labor Law (since 2014).

Yana Simutina, D.Sc.(Law), is a Professor in Labour Law and a senior research fellow at the Koretsky Institute of State and Law of the National Academy of Sciences of Ukraine. She has over 20 years of teaching and research experience in Ukrainian labour and employment law, human rights and EU labour law. She has been a national consultant to the Council of Europe and provided academic expertise in parliamentary working groups on drafting the Ukrainian Labour Code, laws on Collective Labour Disputes and on Social Dialogue. She was awarded a British Academy and CARA Fellowship in 2022 and is currently a visiting professor at the University of Bristol Law School.

Erik Sinander is an associate professor at Stockholm University. He is also an expert for Swedish law in the European Labour Law Network.

Ioannis Skandalis is Assistant Professor of Labour Law at the Law School of the National and Kapodistrian University of Athens (Greece). He is a Supreme Court Attorney at Law, as well as a non-practising Solicitor of England and Wales. He is the author of three monographs, as well as a large number of articles and contributions to collective titles. He is a national expert in different networks and has participated as a speaker in many national and international conferences.

Dr Alexander Sønderland Skjønberg is Full Professor in Law at the Department of Law and Governance, BI Norwegian Business School. Additionally, he holds a position as Professor II at the Faculty of Law, University of Oslo (Norway). Skjønberg's legal expertise primarily lies in collective and individual labour law. Skjønberg holds several national and international positions and serves as a deputy judge in the National Labour Court of Norway.

Albena Velikova-Stoyanova has graduated from the Law Faculty of Sofia University 'St. Kliment Ochridski' (Bulgaria). She is Assistant Professor in Labour Law and Social Security at Sofia University. She is a member of the Management Board of the Bulgarian Association for Labour Law and Social Security. She participates as an expert in the implementation of projects funded by the European Union and has publications in Bulgaria and in several European countries.

Krassimira Sredkova is Professor in Labour Law and Social Security, PhD in Law, Attorney at Law in Sofia Bar Association, President of the Bulgarian Association for

Labour Law and Social Security and a member of the International Association for Legislation. From 2015 to 2020, she was a member of the European Committee of Social Rights in the Council of Europe. She has more than 250 publications in Bulgaria and abroad in the fields of labour law, social security, international labour law and the EC law.

Gaabriel Tavits graduated from the Faculty of Law of the University of Tartu (Estonia) in 1994. Since then, he has been researching and teaching Labour Law and Social Security Law. Both areas of law include both a European and an international dimension. His research is also related to the problems of discrimination (on different grounds).

His research activity of the last five years is related to the analysis of new forms of employment and the legal problems of atypical employment relationships.

In the last three years, his research has been devoted to collective labour relations within new forms of employment including also aspects of social security protection.

Dr Nicos Trimikliniotis is a barrister and Professor of Sociology Sciences and Law and heads the Centre for Fundamental Rights and Digital Transitions & Society (DIGITS) at the University of Nicosia (Cyprus). He is the National Expert for the European Labour Law Network, Odysseus Network, and the Global Citizenship Observatory. He has researched labour law, fundamental rights, migration and asylum law, citizenship, and social transformation/borders. He has authored numerous international reports on Cyprus.

Ivana Vukorepa is Professor of Labour and Social Security Law at the University of Zagreb (Croatia). She has collaborated on several national and international research projects, as well as in the European experts' networks such as: ESPN in the field of social policy (from 2014 to 2018), MoveS in the field of free movement of workers and social security coordination (since 2018) and ECE in the field of labour law, employment and labour market policies (since 2020).

Bernd Waas is Professor of Labour Law and Civil Law at Goethe University Frankfurt (Germany). He is the Coordinator of the European Labor Law Network (ELLN), a network of labour law experts that advises the European Commission's Directorate-General (DG) for Employment, Social Affairs and Inclusion. He is a member of the ILO Committee of Experts on the Application of Conventions and Recommendations (CEACR). He is also Chairman of the German Section of the International Society for Labor and Social Security Law (ISLSSL) and a member of the ISLLS Executive Committee. He is also a member of the Advisory Board of the Labor Law Research Network (LLRN).

Summary of Contents

Table of Contents

Acknowledgements

My thanks go to the colleagues from the European Labour Law Network who participated in this enterprise. My thanks also go to former and current members of staff at the Chair, without whose efforts this book could not have been published: Faiqa Ahmad, Robyn Albrecht, Emiliano Maran, Miriam Koelges, Magdalena Schröer and Sophie Weil. You have done a fantastic job. Thank you very much indeed.

Frankfurt, March 2025

Introduction

Bernd Waas

The existence of a right to strike has long been disputed at ILO level. As is well known, the issue is pending before the International Court of Justice in The Hague. The question of whether a right to strike exists under international law has occasionally been overshadowed by the fact that the ILO supervisory bodies do not assume an unlimited right to strike but consider certain restrictions to be permissible. This book addresses the question of what limits exist in this respect for the right to strike under international law. To this end, Part I contains two presentations: on the one hand, a look at the ILO law, on the other, a discussion of the European Convention on Human Rights and the European Social Charter.

In Part II, the focus will then shift from international law to national legal systems in Europe. In particular, the annual reports of the ILO Committee of Experts show that the Member States of the organisation often fail to observe the limits of permissible restrictions on the right to strike. For this reason alone, it makes sense to take a closer look at the legal systems in Europe from this perspective.

The immediate reason for the book was the efforts of the legislator in the United Kingdom to regulate the right to strike in the area of essential services. This legislative initiative led to heated discussions about the admissibility of restrictions on the right to strike far beyond the United Kingdom and even far beyond Europe. At the same time, there was renewed interest in regulations in other countries in many places. Accordingly, questions were frequently asked not only about the position of international law but also about how other states view restrictions on the right to strike (both within and outside the area of essential services).

In the United Kingdom itself, the original legislative plans have come to nothing due to the change of government that has occurred in the meantime, but this does not affect the importance of the issue. Developments at the international level and at the level of individual states continue to be of great interest. The aim of this book is to satisfy this interest as much as possible and to give the reader access to the current law.

Part I International Law

CHAPTER 1

Restrictions on the Right to Strike under the Law of the ILO

Bernd Waas

1 GENERAL INFORMATION

1.1 Legal Basis of the Right to Strike

Whether and to what extent a right to strike is recognised under Convention No. 87 has been a matter of dispute among the ILO Constituents for some time and has now also reached the International Court of Justice.[1] This dispute, which continues to this day, is not to be glossed over here, but neither is it to be examined in detail. It is true that whether there is a right to strike is a preliminary question for the question of limitations on this right. This does not change the fact, however, that the subject of this chapter is not the right to strike as such, including its legal justification, but only the question of which limitations of this right are to be recognised under Convention No. 87.

The following presentation is based on the observations of the ILO Committee of Experts (CEACR). In addition, reference is also made to the 'case law' of the Committee on Freedom of Association (CFA), which also plays an important role with regard to freedom of association.[2] On the question of the CEACR's power of interpretation and the effect of its decisions, which is also frequently discussed in connection with the

1. *See* the Request for Advisory Opinion of 16 November 2023 (Right to Strike under ILO Convention No. 87).
2. Though the two Committees work independently of each other, they take account of each other's work. *See* in this respect, in particular, General Survey on the fundamental Conventions, 2012, para. 52, where the CEACR acknowledges 'the legitimacy of the recommendations and principles of the Committee on Freedom of Association [which] is accentuated by the consensus that prevails in its work and the expertise in industrial relations provided by the Government, Employer and Worker members who sit on the Committee in their individual capacity'. *See also* Bellace, *The Committee on Freedom of Association: Making Freedom of Association a Reality*, in:

recognition of the right to strike, reference should be made here to a formula that the Committee has been using for some time in its annual reports. It reads (in part): 'The Committee of Experts undertakes an impartial and technical analysis of how the Conventions are applied in law and practice by Member States, while cognizant of different national realities and legal systems. In doing so, it must determine the legal scope, content and meaning of the provisions of the Conventions. Its opinions and recommendations are non-binding, being intended to guide the actions of national authorities. They derive their persuasive value from the legitimacy and rationality of the Committee's work based on its impartiality, experience and expertise.'[3]

2 PERMITTED RESTRICTIONS

It is recognised that the right to strike under Convention No. 87 'is not absolute and may be restricted in exceptional circumstances, or even prohibited'.[4] More specifically, according to the ILO supervisory bodies, there are three acceptable restrictions: First, States may restrict or even prohibit the right to strike of public servants 'exercising authority in the name of the State'. Second, restrictions are acceptable as far as 'essential services' are concerned. Third, the right to strike can be restricted in situations of acute national or local crisis. In the following, all three limitations will be examined in more detail.[5]

2.1 Certain Categories of Public Servants

2.1.1 Armed Forces and Police

Convention No. 87 contains an explicit provision for members of the army and the police. In this respect, Article 9(1) of the Convention stipulates that 'the extent to which the guarantees provided for in this Convention shall apply to the armed forces and the police shall be determined by national laws or regulations'. Members of the armed forces and the police form the only explicitly recognised exceptions from the scope of application of the Convention. These exceptions are justified on the basis of the responsibility of these two categories of workers for the external and internal security of the State.[6] It should be noted, however, that Article 9(1) must be construed in a restrictive manner. For example, the exceptions laid down here do not include civilian personnel in the armed forces, fire service personnel, prison staff, customs and excise officials, civilian employees in the industrial establishments of the armed forces and

---

Curtis/Wolfson (eds), 70 Years of the ILO Committee on Freedom of Association: A Reliable Compass in Any Weather, p. 5 (16) (2022).

3. Application of International Labour Standards 2025, Report of the Committee of Experts on the Application of Conventions and Recommendations, International Labour Conference 113th Session, para. 14 (2025).
4. General Survey on the fundamental Conventions, para. 127 (2012).
5. Cf. also Novitz, *The Restricted Right to Strike: 'Far-Reaching' ILO Jurisprudence on the Public Sector and Essential Services*. Comparative Labor Law and Policy Journal 38(3), pp. 353-374.
6. General Survey on the fundamental Conventions, para. 67 (2012).

civilian employees in the intelligence services.[7] Nor do they automatically apply to all employees who may carry a weapon in the course of their duties.[8] Furthermore, the CEACR recognises that it is not always easy to determine whether workers belong to the military or the police. In this respect, it considers that in case of doubt, the right to strike should be deemed to exist.[9]

2.1.2 Public Servants Exercising Authority in the Name of the State

Irrespective of this, the ILO supervisory bodies are of the opinion that the right to strike may also be restricted for public servants, provided that these 'exercise authority in the name of the State'.[10] This exception is justified by 'the importance of ensuring the continuity of the functions of the three branches of the State (the legislative, executive and judicial authorities) and of essential services'.[11] In this context, the CEACR has paid particular attention to the legal status of teachers.[12] In the view of the Committee,

7. *See* in this regard, for instance, *Comoros* - Direct Request (CEACR) - adopted 2022, published 111th ILC session (2023): Exceptions do not include 'civilian personnel of the armed forces, firefighters, prison personnel, customs and tax officers, and civilian employees from industrial establishments of the armed forces'. *See also* Compilation of decisions of the Committee on Freedom of Association (6th ed. 2018), para. 350.
8. General Survey on the fundamental Conventions, para. 67 (2012). As a recent example, *see* Latvia - Direct Request (CEACR) - adopted 2021, published 110th ILC session (2022).
9. *See* General Survey on the fundamental Conventions, para. 68 (2012). *See also* Ecuador - Observation (CEACR) - adopted 2001, published 90th ILC session (2002).
10. General Survey on Freedom of Association and Collective Bargaining, para. 158 (1994); General Survey on the fundamental Conventions, para. 129 (2012). *See also* Compilation of decisions of the Committee on Freedom of Association, para. 828.
11. General Survey on the fundamental Conventions, para. 129 (2012).
12. This applies, for example, with regard to the legal situation in Germany, where the Federal Constitutional Court expressly denied a right to strike for civil servants (including teachers) in its decision of 12 June 2018 - 2 BvR 1738/12 ao. *See* in this regard Germany - Observation (CEACR) - adopted 2021, published 110th ILC session (2022): 'The Committee takes due note of the ruling of the Federal Constitutional Court that for civil servants, irrespective of their duties, the strike ban amounts to an independent traditional principle of the career civil service system within the meaning of section 33(5) of the Basic Law, which justifies an overriding of freedom of association. Moreover, the Committee wishes to make clear that its task is not to judge the validity of the Court decision of 12 Jun. 2018 (Case No. 2 BvR 1738/12), which is based upon issues of German national law and precedents. The Committee's task is to examine the outcome of this decision on the recognition and exercise of the workers' fundamental right to freedom of association. In this regard, the Committee observes with regret that the result of the Court's decision is not in keeping with the Convention, inasmuch as it amounts to a general ban on the right to strike of civil servants based on their status, irrespective of their duties and responsibilities, and in particular a ban on the right of civil servants who are not exercising authority in the name of the State (such as teachers, postal workers and railway employees) to have recourse to strike action.' On 14 December 2023, the ECHR held that the ban on strikes by civil servants' teachers did not take away the core of their freedom of association and did not violate the right of association as guaranteed by Art. 11 of the ECHR; ECHR *Humpert and others v. Germany* (14 December 2023) (Applications Nos 59433/18, 59477/18, 59481/18 and 59494/18). In this regard, the CEACR stated the following: 'The ECtHR's judgment concerns the interpretation of the European Convention on Human Rights. Just as the ECtHR's "jurisdiction is limited to the [European Convention on Human Rights], [with] no competence to assess a respondent State's compliance with the relevant standards of the ILO" (paragraph 101 of the judgment), the Committee has no competence to pronounce itself on the Courts' interpretation of the European Convention on Human Rights or Germany's compliance therewith. Rather, the mandate of the

public sector teachers are not included in the category of public servants 'exercising authority in the name of the State' even though,[13] 'under certain circumstances, the maintenance of a minimum service may be envisaged in this sector'.[14]

2.2 Essential Services in the Strict Sense of the Term

The second applicable restriction on the right to strike concerns 'essential services'. The ILO supervisory bodies assume that the term is to be interpreted restrictively. Accordingly, 'essential services' in this context are only those 'the interruption of which would endanger the life, personal safety or health of the whole of part of the population'.[15] Furthermore, it is recognised that the concept of 'essential services' must not be understood in absolute terms. Instead, a non-essential service may become essential if, for instance, the strike exceeds a certain duration or extent.[16]

The ILO supervisory bodies have repeatedly been confronted with the task of deciding whether certain activities are 'essential services'. These do not include, for example: the banking sector, railways, transport services and public transport, air transport services and civil aviation, teachers and the public education service, postal services, municipal services, road cleaning and refuse collection and radio and television.[17] In contrast, essential services in the strict sense of the term may include air traffic control services, telephone services, firefighting services, health and ambulance services, prison services, security forces and water and electricity services.[18] The CEACR has also considered that other services (such as meteorological services and social security services) include certain components which are essential and others

Committee consists in undertaking an impartial and technical analysis of how the Conventions are applied in law and practice by Member States; in doing so, it must determine the legal scope, content and meaning of the provisions of the Conventions (...). In this respect, the Committee recalls that it has always considered that the right to strike is one of the essential means available to workers and their organizations for the promotion and protection of their economic and social interests. While it has recognized that the right to strike may be restricted or even prohibited in the public service, the Committee has established that such a limitation may be applied only in the case of public servants exercising authority in the name of the State'; Observation (CEACR) - adopted 2024, published 113th ILC session (2025).

13. General Survey on the fundamental Conventions, para. 129 with references (2012).
14. General Survey on the fundamental Conventions, para. 130 (2012).
15. General Survey on the fundamental Conventions, para. 131 (2012). *See also* Compilation of decisions of the Committee on Freedom of Association, paras 830 et seqq.
16. General Survey on the fundamental Conventions, para. 131 (2012). *See also* Compilation of decisions of the Committee on Freedom of Association, para. 837.
17. General Survey on the fundamental Conventions, para. 134 (2012). With regard to the position of the CFA, *see also* Compilation of decisions of the Committee on Freedom of Association, para. 842.
18. General Survey on the fundamental Conventions, para. 135 (2012). The CFA, in contrast, considered to be essential services: the hospital sector, electricity services, water supply services, the telephone service, the police and the armed forces, the firefighting services, public or private prison services, the provision of food to pupils of school age and the cleaning of schools and air traffic control. *See* Compilation of decisions of the Committee on Freedom of Association, para. 840.

that are not.[19] Whether an 'essential service' exists can therefore be answered differently for individual areas within a particular activity.

National provisions in which 'essential services' are either defined too broadly from the outset or in which authorities are given too much discretion to unilaterally declare a service essential are not in line with Convention No. 87.[20] Furthermore, regulations are not in conformity with the Convention if they are not designed to avoid endangering 'the life, personal safety or health of the whole of part of the population' but are guided by completely different standards. These include, in particular, possible adverse economic consequences of a strike or the possible impairment of public order or of the general or national interest.[21] In the past, the CEACR has occasionally noted that the classification as an 'essential service' is often left to the courts in individual cases or even based on an agreement between the social partners. With regard to the former, however, the Committee has expressly pointed out that the judicial decision power does not change the fact that the specifications for determining 'essential services' must always be observed.[22] With regard to the latter, it appears that the CFA considers the social partners to have some authority to define the term 'essential services' independently.[23]

In the view of the CEACR, in the area of 'essential services', the less severe means of a negotiated minimum service should always be considered, as opposed to a total ban on strikes.[24] However, the parties to an industrial dispute should only be obliged to establish a minimum service in certain situations, namely: '(i) in services the interruption of which would endanger the life, personal safety or health of the whole or part of the population (or essential services "in the strict sense of the term"); (ii) in services which are not essential in the strict sense of the term, but in which strikes of a certain magnitude and duration could cause an acute crisis threatening the normal conditions of existence of the population; and (iii) in public services of fundamental

19. General Survey on the fundamental Conventions, para. 135 (2012).
20. General Survey on the fundamental Conventions, para. 132 (2012).
21. General Survey on the fundamental Conventions, para. 132 (2012). As for the former *see also* Compilation of decisions of the Committee on Freedom of Association, para. 848: 'By linking restrictions on strike action to interference with trade and commerce, a broad range of legitimate strike action could be impeded. While the economic impact of industrial action and its effect on trade and commerce may be regrettable, such consequences in and of themselves do not render a service essential, and thus the right to strike should be maintained.'
22. *See*, for instance, *Colombia* – Observation (CEACR) – adopted 2009, published 99th ILC session (2010): 'the Committee hopes that the highest judicial authority will take into account the principles of the supervisory bodies in relation to essential services, in which the right to strike may be prohibited or restricted (...)'.
23. *See* Compilation of decisions of the Committee on Freedom of Association, para. 852: 'In a case in which a collective agreement included the classification of several services as essential, the Committee observed that, generally speaking, the list in the collective agreement (...) corresponded to its notion of essential services. Although some of the services set out in the agreement (...) fell outside the scope of essential services in the strict sense of the term, these restrictions on the right to strike were the result of an agreement freely entered into by the two parties.'
24. *See* in this regard also General Survey on Freedom of Association and Collective Bargaining, para. 162 (1994). *See also* Compilation of decisions of the Committee on Freedom of Association, para. 867.

importance'.[25] At the same time, the Committee ties the establishment of such a minimum service to two preconditions. First, it must 'genuinely and exclusively be a minimum service, that is one which is limited to the operations which are strictly necessary to meet the basic needs of the population or the minimum requirements of the service, while maintaining the effectiveness of the pressure brought to bear'.[26] Second, 'since this system restricts one of the essential means of pressure available to workers to defend their interests, their organizations should be able, if they so wish, to participate in defining such a service, along with employers and the public authorities'.[27] In this context, the Committee makes two demands: On the one hand, the participation of the social partners in defining minimum services should be enshrined in law. On the other hand, differences of opinion between the social partners should not be decided by state authorities 'but by a joint or independent body which has the confidence of the parties, responsible for examining rapidly and without formalities the difficulties raised and empowered to issue enforceable decisions'.[28] With regard to the former, the CFA holds the view that 'it would be desirable for actions to be taken wherever convenient so that the negotiations on the definition and organization of the minimum service not be held during a labour dispute so that all parties can examine the matters with the necessary full frankness and objectivity'.[29] Regarding the latter, the CFA is of the opinion that 'a definitive ruling on whether the level of minimum services was indispensable or not made in full knowledge of the facts can be pronounced only by the judicial authorities, in so far as it depends, in particular, upon a thorough

25. General Survey on the fundamental Conventions, para. 136 (2012). *See also* Compilation of decisions of the Committee on Freedom of Association, para. 866.
26. General Survey on the fundamental Conventions, para. 137 (2012). *See also* Togo – Observation (CEACR) – adopted 2022, published 111st ILC session (2023). *See also* Compilation of decisions of the Committee on Freedom of Association, para. 874: 'Minimum service should be restricted to the operations which are necessary to satisfy the basic needs of the population or the minimum requirements of the service, while ensuring that the scope of the minimum service does not render the strike ineffective.'
27. General Survey on the fundamental Conventions, para. 136 (2012). *See*, for instance, most recently Chad – Direct Request (CEACR) – adopted 2022, published 111st ILC session (2023). Apart from this, the CEACR considers the establishment of a negotiated minimum service to be justified if it aims 'to ensure the security of facilities and the maintenance of equipment'. As for the position of the CFA, *see* Compilation of decisions of the Committee on Freedom of Association, paras 871, 873 and, in particular, 881 which reads as follows: 'The determination of minimum services and the minimum number of workers providing them should involve not only the public authorities, but also the relevant employers and workers organizations. This not only allows a careful exchange of viewpoints on what in a given situation can be considered to be the minimum services that are strictly necessary, but also contributes to guaranteeing that the scope of the minimum service does not result in the strike becoming ineffective in practice because of its limited impact, and to dissipating possible impressions in the trade union organizations that a strike has come to nothing because of overgenerous and unilaterally fixed minimum services.'
28. General Survey on the fundamental Conventions, para. 138 (2012). *See also* for example Timor-Leste – Direct Request (CEACR) – adopted 2022, published 111st ILC session (2023). *See also* Compilation of decisions of the Committee on Freedom of Association, paras 882 et seqq.
29. *See* Compilation of decisions of the Committee on Freedom of Association, para. 875. *See also ibid.*, para. 876: 'Negotiations over the minimum service should be ideally held prior to a labour dispute, so that all parties can examine the matter with the necessary objectivity and detachment.'

knowledge of the structure and functioning of the enterprises and establishments concerned and of the real impact of the strike action'.[30]

2.3 Situations of Acute National or Local Crisis

The third restriction on the right to strike relates to situations of acute national or local crisis. The CEACR understands this to mean 'genuine crisis situations, such as those arising as a result of a serious conflict, insurrection or natural, sanitary or humanitarian disaster, in which the normal conditions for the functioning of society are absent'.[31] However, restrictions on the right to strike can only be considered to the extent that they are necessary due to the crisis situation. In particular, the right to strike may only be restricted 'for a limited period and to the extent necessary to meet the requirements of the situation'.[32] According to the CFA, the responsibility for suspending a strike on the grounds of national security or public health should not lie with the Government but with an independent body which has the confidence of all parties concerned.[33]

3 COMPENSATORY GUARANTEES FOR WORKERS DEPRIVED OF THE RIGHT TO STRIKE

As seen above, the right to strike can be restricted in certain cases. However, it is recognised that this cannot be done without 'compensatory guarantees'.[34] Rather, workers who are (at least partially) deprived of the right to strike must be compensated for the restrictions imposed on their freedom of action. In the view of the CEACR, 'such protection should include, for example, impartial conciliation and eventually arbitration procedures which have the confidence of the parties, in which workers and their organizations could be associated'. Moreover, such arbitration awards 'should be binding on both parties and once issued should be implemented rapidly and completely'.[35]

4 CONCLUSION

A closer look at Convention No. 87 shows that restrictions of the right to strike are subject to strict requirements. The fact that these are formulated in some detail in the 'jurisprudence' of the ILO supervisory bodies may surprise some external observers.

30. *See* Compilation of decisions of the Committee on Freedom of Association, para. 875. *See also ibid.*, para. 885.
31. General Survey on the fundamental Conventions, para. 329 (2012). *See also* for example Seychelles – Direct Request (CEACR) – adopted 1995, published 82nd ILC session (1995).
32. General Survey on the fundamental Conventions, para. 140 (2012).
33. *See* Compilation of decisions of the Committee on Freedom of Association, para. 825.
34. General Survey on the fundamental Conventions, para. 141 (2012). *See also* Compilation of decisions of the Committee on Freedom of Association, para. 853.
35. General Survey on the fundamental Conventions, para. 141 (2012). *See also* Compilation of decisions of the Committee on Freedom of Association, para. 856.

CHAPTER 2

Restrictions on the Right to Strike under the ECHR and the ESC

Kristīne Dupate

1 GENERAL INFORMATION

The right to strike is explicitly and implicitly provided by numerous international agreements. The right to strike is provided by Article 8(1)(d) of the International Covenant on Economic, Social and Cultural Rights (ICESCR) and Article 6(4) of the European Social Charter (ESC) – two international agreements dealing with social and economic rights.[1]

Meanwhile, two international agreements dedicated to civil and political rights do not provide the right to strike explicitly as they provide the right to freedom of association in general. Those, in particular, are the International Covenant on the Civil and Political Rights (ICCPR) – Article 22 and of the European Convention for the Protection of Human Rights and Fundamental Freedoms (ECHR) – Article 11(1). While the European Court of Human Rights (ECtHR) 'has on several occasions held that strike action is protected by Article 11',[2] the Human Right Committee has clearly stated 'that the right to strike cannot be considered as an implicit component of the right to form and join trade unions' because the drafters of the ICCPR had not intended to include such right within the scope of Article 22.[3]

1. Provided by both – 1961 and Revised European Social Charter.
2. *See*, for example, ECHR decisions in the cases *Ognevenko v. Russia* (20 November 2018), Application No. 44873/09, para. 57 and *National Union of Rail, maritime and Transport Workers v. United Kingdom* (8 April 2014), Application No. 31045/10, para. 84.
3. European Center for Not-for-Profit Law and International Center for Not-for-Profit Law, Relevant Sources of Law on Article ICCPR: Right to Freedom of Association (2023), p. 7, available at https://ecnl.org/publications/relevant-sources-law-article-22-iccpr.

Interestingly the right to strike is not explicitly provided by any ILO conventions; however, as it has been recognized by the ILO Committee on Freedom of Association (CFA), 'The right to strike is an intrinsic corollary to the right to organize protected by Convention No. 87.'[4]

The right to strike is also explicitly provided by Article 28 of the Charter of Fundamental Rights of the European Union (CFREU), though according to Article 153(5) of the Treaty on the Functioning of the European Union the EU does not have competence to legislate on this right as right to strike is explicitly excluded from the EU's competence. Nevertheless, as right to strike is provided by the FCREU, it must be respected by the EU, the EU Member States and private persons when they act within the EU competence.[5]

1.1 Legal Basis of the Right to Strike

The CFA 'has always regarded the right to strike as constituting a fundamental right of workers and of their organizations'.[6] It has stressed that it 'has always regarded the right to strike by workers and their organizations as a legitimate and essential means of defending their economic and social interests'.[7] In addition, 'the occupational and economic interests which workers defend through the exercise of the right to strike do not only concern better working conditions or collective claims of an occupational nature, but also the seeking of solutions to economic and social policy questions and problems'.[8]

As recognized by the ECtHR, the right to strike 'without any doubt' is the most important means to secure a trade union's freedom to protect the occupational interests of its members[9] because it constitutes an important instrument to make its voice heard.[10]

Also, the ECSR has stated 'that the right to strike is intrinsically linked to the right to collective bargaining, as it represents the most effective means to achieve a

4. Compilation of decisions of the Committee on Freedom of Association, Freedom of association, International Labour Office Geneva (6th ed. 2018), para. 754, available at https://www.ilo.org/publications/freedom-association-compilation-decisions-committee-freedom-association-pdf.
5. Article 51(1) of the CFREU; *see also* the CJEU, *Fact Sheet Field of Application of the Charter of Fundamental Rights of the European Union* (2021), available at https://curia.europa.eu/jcms/jcms/p1_1043199/fr/.
6. Compilation of decisions of the Committee on Freedom of Association, Freedom of association, International Labour Office Geneva (6th ed. 2018), para. 751, available at https://www.ilo.org/publications/freedom-association-compilation-decisions-committee-freedom-association-pdf.
7. Compilation of decisions of the Committee on Freedom of Association, Freedom of association, International Labour Office Geneva (6th ed. 2018), paras 751-752, available at https://www.ilo.org/publications/freedom-association-compilation-decisions-committee-freedom-association-pdf.
8. Compilation of decisions of the Committee on Freedom of Association, Freedom of association, International Labour Office Geneva (6th ed. 2018), para. 758, available at https://www.ilo.org/publications/freedom-association-compilation-decisions-committee-freedom-association-pdf.
9. ECHR decision in the cases *Ognevenko v. Russia* (20 November 2018), Application No. 44873/09, para. 57.
10. ECHR decision in the case *Humpert and others v. Germany* (14 December 2023), Application Nos 59433/18, 59477/18 and 59494/18, para. 104.

favourable result from a bargaining process'.[11] The ECSR has stressed that the right to strike 'represents an essential basis for the fulfilment of other fundamental rights guaranteed by the Charter'.[12]

As to the EU law, the CJEU has affirmed that 'the right to take collective action, including the right to strike, must therefore be recognised as a fundamental right which forms an integral part of the general principles' of EU law, and the CJEU is an institution which supervises its observance.[13]

2 PERMITTED RESTRICTIONS

Though the right to strike is recognized as the fundamental right of workers and their organizations because this right provides them the essential means to secure and promote not only better working conditions and occupational interests but also economic and social interests, it is not absolute. According to international law, the right to strike may be restricted or even prohibited.

Article 8(1)(d) of ICESCR allows strikes but only if 'exercised in conformity with the laws of the particular country', and Article 8(2) allows imposition of restrictions on the exercise of the right to strike on members of the armed forces or of the police or of the administration of the State.

The CFA does not provide the formula under which right to strike may be restricted because CFA in principle does not allow prohibition of the strikes.[14] However, the CFA defines the situations allowing restrictions or ban on the right to strike. First, 'general prohibition of strikes can only be justified in the event of an acute national emergency and for a limited period of time'.[15] Second, this right may be restricted or prohibited in the public service and only for public servants exercising authority in the name of the State and in essential services in the strict sense of the term (i.e., services the interruption of which would endanger the life, personal safety or health of the whole or part of the population).[16]

Article 11(2) of ECHR and Article G of ESC[17] provides for explicit right to restrict the right to strike to the States, however, under several conditions.

Under Article 11(2) of ECHR, the restrictions, first, must comply with the general formula for restriction of the freedom of association, covering also the right to strike. According to ECHR Article 11(2), it is required that restrictions which are prescribed by law 'are necessary in a democratic society in the interests of national security or public

11. The decision of the ECSR in the case *European Organisation of Military Associations (EUROMIL) v. Ireland* (12 September 2017), Complaint No. 112/2014, para. 111.
12. The decision of ECSR in the case *Swedish Trade Union Confederation (LO) and Swedish Confederation of Professional Employees (TCO) v. Sweden* (3 July 2013), Complaint No. 85/2012, para. 109.
13. The CJEU decision in case C-438/05 *International Transport Workers' Federation and Finnish Seamen's Union v. Viking Line ABP and OÜ Viking Line Eesti* (11 December 2007), para. 44.
14. Paragraph 757.
15. Paragraph 824.
16. Paragraph 830.
17. *See*, for example, decision of ECSR in the case *Confédération générale du travail* (CGT) *v. France* (14 September 2022), Complaint No. 155/2017, para. 56.

safety, for the prevention of disorder or crime, for the protection of health or morals or for the protection of the rights and freedoms of others'. In other words, the restrictions have to be prescribed by law, have to serve one of the legitimate aims provided by Article 11(2) and have to be necessary in democratic society for the achievement of respective aims.[18] As regards the notion 'necessary in democratic society', a State must demonstrate 'that the interference corresponded to a "pressing social need", that the reasons given by the national authorities to justify it were relevant and sufficient and that the interference was proportionate to the legitimate aim pursued. It means, as the ECtHR has recognized that in assessing whether "pressing social need" exists and what measures should be adopted to deal with it, States have only a limited margin of appreciation.[19] In addition, the fair balance to be struck between the competing interests of the individual and of the community as a whole'.[20]

Second, under Article 11(2) of ECHR, the States have a narrow margin of appreciation or 'margin of appreciation is to be reduced' in applying restrictions in the following cases:

(1) where measures affect an essential element of trade-union freedom;
(2) where restrictions strike at the core of trade-union activity, which include severe restrictions on 'primary' or direct industrial action by public-sector employees who are neither exercising public authority in the name of the State nor providing essential services to the population.[21]

Third, ECHR has recognized specific fields of activity – public administration, armed forces and police – where right to strike might be enjoyed under specific conditions. However, the ECtHR has held that even though the second sentence of Article 11(2) does not expressly refer to the requirement of necessity, the lawful restrictions imposed on members of the armed forces, of the police or of the administration of the State must also meet a pressing social need and be 'necessary in a democratic society'.[22]

Fourth, as regards restriction of the right to strike of workers providing essential services to the population, the ECtHR has held that a complete ban requires the State to put forward solid reasons to justify the necessity of such ban.[23]

18. *See*, for example, ECHR decision in the case *Vyerentsov v. Ukraine* (11 April 2013), Application No. 20372/11, para. 51.
19. ECHR decision in the case *Humpert and others v. Germany* (14 December 2023), Application Nos 59433/18, 59477/18 and 59494/18, para. 67.
20. *See*, for example, ECHR decision in the case *Humpert and others v. Germany* (14 December 2023), Application Nos 59433/18, 59477/18 and 59494/18.
21. ECHR decision in the case *Humpert and others v. Germany* (14 December 2023), Application Nos 59433/18, 59477/18 and 59494/18, para. 111.
22. Registry of the ECtHR, Guide on Art. 11 of the European Convention on Human Rights, paras 293-294 (31 August 2024), available at https://ks.echr.coe.int/documents/d/echr-ks/guide_art_11_eng.
23. Registry of the ECtHR, Guide on Art. 11 of the European Convention on Human Rights, para. 278 (31 August 2024), available at https://ks.echr.coe.int/documents/d/echr-ks/guide_art_11_eng; *see also* ECHR decision in the cases *Ognevenko v. Russia* (20 November 2018), Application No. 44873/09, paras 72-73.

Fifth, as regards the scope of Article 11(2), the ECtHR has ruled that this provision 'is not limited to bans and refusals to authorise the exercise of Convention rights, but also embraces punitive measures taken after such rights have been exercised, including various disciplinary measures'.[24]

The restriction conditions on the rights stipulated by ESC are set by Article G. As elaborated by the ECSR, 'Pursuant to Article G, a restriction on the exercise of a right recognised by the Charter can be seen as compatible with the Charter if it fulfils the following conditions:

- it must be prescribed by law;
- it must pursue one of the aims set out in Article G;
- it must be proportionate to the aims pursued.'[25]

In other words, proportionality in exercising the right to strike requires that the balance is to be stroked between the rights and freedoms, on the one side, and the responsibilities, on the other.[26] The ECSR has not explicitly ruled on the nature of margin of appreciation of the State in putting restrictions on the right to strike in general. It, however, has specified that a wide margin of appreciation is enjoyed by the States regarding restrictions in specific fields - in armed forces and police.[27]

Though, as explained above, right to strike is explicitly excluded from the competence of the EU, the right to strike may come into play when colliding with other rights - especially economic freedoms of the EU. In the light of this, the right to strike as provided by Article 28 of the CFREU may be restricted according to Article 52(1) under the condition that the restriction must be provided by the law and must respect the essence of the respective right. In addition, restrictions are subject to proportionality, which means that 'limitations may be made only if they are necessary and genuinely meet objectives of general interest recognised by the Union or the need to protect the rights and freedoms of others'. In particular, the CJEU has held with regard to restriction of the right to strike that although it is a fundamental right, it may 'none the less be subject to certain restrictions'.[28]

It follows that ESC and ECHR require observance of the strict test in case of prohibition or restriction of the right to strike. The same conclusion seems to be the case regarding legal regulation under the CFREU. In contrast, Article 8(1)(d) of ICESCR

24. ECHR decision in the case *Ognevenko v. Russia* (20 November 2018), Application No. 44873/09, para. 61.
25. Decision of the ECSR in the case *European Trade Union Confederation (ETUC)/Centrale Générale des Syndicats Libéraux de Belgique (CGSLB)/Fédération Générale du Travail de Belgique* (FGTB) *v. Belgium* (13 September 2011), Complaint No. 59/2009, para. 40.
26. Decision of the ECSR in the case *European Trade Union Confederation (ETUC)/Centrale Générale des Syndicats Libéraux de Belgique (CGSLB)/Fédération Générale du Travail de Belgique* (FGTB) *v. Belgium* (13 September 2011), Complaint No. 59/2009, para. 34.
27. The decision of the ECSR in the case *European Organisation of Military Associations (EUROMIL) v. Ireland* (12 September 2017), Complaint No. 112/2014, para. 116.
28. The CJEU decision in the case C-438/05 *International Transport Workers' Federation and Finnish Seamen's Union v. Viking Line ABP and OÜ Viking Line Eesti* (11 December 2007), para. 44.

refers to national law 'as prima facie unconditional limitation the exercise of the right to strike'; thus, it does not offer the tools to assess national laws.[29]

2.1 Restriction on the Right to Strike in Essential Services

2.1.1 Essential Services in the Strict Sense of the Term

It could be argued that international legal regulation between 'essential services in strict sense' and 'services which are not to be considered as essential in the strict sense' is not clearly cut.

The Essential Services (To Be Considered as Essential Services in the Strict Sense)

As it has been defined by FCA, the 'essential services in strict sense are services the interruption of which would endanger the life, personal safety or health of the whole or part of the population'.[30]

In addition, FCA has explained what is meant by essential services in more detail. It has held that whether a particular service should be considered essential in the strict sense of the term depends to a large extent on the particular circumstances prevailing in a country. Further, 'this concept is not absolute, in the sense that a non-essential service may become essential if a strike lasts beyond a certain time or extends beyond a certain scope, thus endangering the life, personal safety or health of the whole or part of the population'.[31]

There are three sectors in which the restriction on the right to organize, including right to strike, is explicitly permitted. In this regard, Article 8(2) of the ICESCR lists allowed the following sectors: armed forces, police and administration of the State, while Article 5 of the ESC stipulates only armed forces and police. The ECSR has recognized, based on the FCA categorization of employment sectors, that armed forces should be considered as an essential service in the strict sense.[32] And indeed, the CFA considers only one exceptional sector where right to strike may be restricted – it is public service,[33] while armed forces and police are categorized as 'essential services in the strict sense'.[34] If follows that main international agreements in principle recognize

29. Niklas Bruun, Klaus Locher, Isabelle Schomann and Stefan Clauwaert (eds), *The European Social Charter and the Employment Relation*, Bloomsbury, pp. 266-267 (2017).
30. Compilation of decisions of the Committee on Freedom of Association, Freedom of association, International Labour Office Geneva (6th ed. 2018), para. 830, available at https://www.ilo.org/publications/freedom-association-compilation-decisions-committee-freedom-association-pdf.
31. Compilation of decisions of the Committee on Freedom of Association, Freedom of association, International Labour Office Geneva (6th ed. 2018), para. 837, available at https://www.ilo.org/publications/freedom-association-compilation-decisions-committee-freedom-association-pdf.
32. The decision of the ECSR in the case *Confederazione Generale Italiana del Lavoro* (CGIL) *v. Italy* (22 January 2019), Complaint No. 140/2016, para. 151.
33. Compilation of decisions of the Committee on Freedom of Association, Freedom of association, International Labour Office Geneva (6th ed. 2018), paras 826-835, available at https://www.ilo.org/publications/freedom-association-compilation-decisions-committee-freedom-association-pdf.
34. Compilation of decisions of the Committee on Freedom of Association, Freedom of association, International Labour Office Geneva (6th ed. 2018), para. 840, available at https://www.ilo.org/publications/freedom-association-compilation-decisions-committee-freedom-association-pdf.

public service, armed forces and police as essential services in the strict sense. However, taking into account the specific characteristics of each of the three sectors listed, they will be discussed in a separate section of this chapter.

Apart from public service, police and armed forces, the CFA considers far more sectors as essential services in the strict sense, in particular, air traffic control, public and private prison services, fire-fighting services, telephone service, water supply services, electricity and hospital services, and the provision of food to pupils of school age and the cleaning of schools.[35]

The Essential Services Not to Be Considered as Essential Services in the Strict Sense

There is no separate definition in which essential services should not be considered essential services in the strict sense; however, it is logical because there is definition on what essential service is in the strict sense; thus, all other essential services should be considered as essential services which are not essential services in the strict sense.

CFA has decided on a number of essential sectors, recognizing many of them as essential services not in the strict sense, for example, the education sector, rail, airline and postal services, aircraft repairs, radio and television.[36] Based on CFA standard, also ECtHR has ruled that, for example, railway services are not to be considered as essential services in the strict sense since there is 'international consensus' on which services are essential in the strict sense. In the light of this finding, the ECtHR referred not only to ILO (CFA) standards but also to ESC (ECSR) standards, taking into account that the latter also follow ILO in categorising essential services.[37]

However, it should be borne in mind that in certain circumstances the right to strike in services, which are not considered as essential services in the strict sense, may be restricted under the same conditions as essential services in the strict sense, in particular, where 'the extent and duration of a strike might be such as to result in acute national crisis endangering normal living conditions of the population'.[38]

2.1.2 Restrictions on the Right to Strike in Essential Services in General[39]

(a) Restriction of the Right to Strike in Essential Services in the Strict Sense

No international agreement provides explicit legal regulation on how, when and under which conditions the right to strike in the essential services in the strict sense may be

35. Compilation of decisions of the Committee on Freedom of Association, Freedom of association, International Labour Office Geneva (6th ed. 2018), para. 842, available at https://www.ilo.org/publications/freedom-association-compilation-decisions-committee-freedom-association-pdf.
36. Compilation of decisions of the Committee on Freedom of Association, Freedom of association, International Labour Office Geneva (6th ed. 2018), para. 842, available at https://www.ilo.org/publications/freedom-association-compilation-decisions-committee-freedom-association-pdf.
37. ECHR decision in the case *Ognevenko v. Russia* (20 November 2018), Application No. 44873/09, para. 72.
38. Compilation of decisions of the Committee on Freedom of Association, Freedom of association, International Labour Office Geneva (6th ed. 2018), para. 866, available at https://www.ilo.org/publications/freedom-association-compilation-decisions-committee-freedom-association-pdf.
39. Note that restriction on the right to strike in public service armed forces and police is discussed in a separate section below.

restricted by the States. Such conditions may be found in interpretative documents only.

The FCA has recognized that right to strike may be restricted or prohibited in essential services in the strict sense, which means services the interruption of which would endanger the life, personal safety or health of the whole or part of the population.[40]

The ECtHR has ruled that restrictions on the right to strike may be imposed on workers providing essential services (in the strict sense) for the population and that with regard to this, there is international consensus as both the FCA and ECSR have recognized it.[41] As to restrictions, the ECtHR has held that the notion of 'essential service' (in the strict sense) must be construed narrowly, and only convincing and compelling reasons can justify the restrictions.[42]

In case where substantial restrictions or total ban on the right to strike are not appropriate, there could be imposed conditions on the obligation to provide minimum services.[43]

(b) Restriction of the Right to Strike in Essential Services Not to Be Considered as Essential Services in the Strict Sense

According to the CFA, the strike could be prohibited if it is established that there is 'imminent threat to the life, personal safety or heath of the whole or part of the population'.[44] However, as it follows from the above, if an interruption of service may constitute 'imminent threat to the life, personal safety or health of the whole or part of the population', it becomes an essential service in the strict sense. Thus, prohibition of the right to strike in essential services not in the strict sense is not permissible.

It also follows that, as regards the restrictions, the usual restriction conditions apply. However, in addition, in the essential service not in the strict term, the obligation to provide minimum services might be imposed 'where the extent and duration of a strike might be such as to result in acute national crisis endangering the normal living conditions of the population'.[45]

It also follows that for the ban or restriction of the right to strike in essential services in the strict sense, the States must be able to demonstrate compelling reasons to justify it. The prohibition of the right to strike is not permissible in essential services

40. Paragraph 830.
41. ECHR decision in the case *Ognevenko v. Russia* (20 November 2018), Application No. 44873/09, para. 65.
42. ECHR decision in the case *Ognevenko v. Russia* (20 November 2018), Application No. 44873/09, paras 72 and 73.
43. Compilation of decisions of the Committee on Freedom of Association, Freedom of association, International Labour Office Geneva (6th ed. 2018), paras 866-867, available at https://www.ilo.org/publications/freedom-association-compilation-decisions-committee-freedom-association-pdf.
44. Compilation of decisions of the Committee on Freedom of Association, Freedom of association, International Labour Office Geneva (6th ed. 2018), para. 836, available at https://www.ilo.org/publications/freedom-association-compilation-decisions-committee-freedom-association-pdf.
45. Compilation of decisions of the Committee on Freedom of Association, Freedom of association, International Labour Office Geneva (6th ed. 2018), para. 866, available at https://www.ilo.org/publications/freedom-association-compilation-decisions-committee-freedom-association-pdf.

not in the strict sense. And in all essential services in case of a strike might be imposed obligation to provide minimum services.

2.2 Certain Categories of Public Servants

Article 8(2) of ICESCR allows imposition of restrictions on the exercise of the right to strike on members of the armed forces or of the police or of the administration of the State.

Similarly, the right to put restrictions on right to strike on members of armed forces, police and on persons in charge of administration of the State is explicitly provided by Article 11(2) of ECHR.

Meanwhile Article 6(4) of the ESC does not distinguish any specific sector of employment where right to strike may be restricted. However, Article 5 of the ESC provides the right to restrict right to organize in armed forces and police. In this context, the ECSR has held that since Article 6(4) does not make a distinction neither between public and private sector nor police and armed forces, it is for the ECSR to provide interpretation on how limitations to right to strike should be applicable in latter two sectors.[46]

ILO conventions do not contain an explicit right to put restrictions in these sectors; however, the FCA has recognized that right to strike may be restricted in public service as well as in armed forces and police as the latter two are to be considered as essential services in the strict sense.[47]

2.2.1 Public Service

(a) The Notion of the Public Service

As recognized by the FCA, the right to strike may be restricted or prohibited 'in the public service only for public servants exercising the authority in the name of the State'.[48] Otherwise, too broad definition of the concept of public servant might result in a very wide restriction for workers of a public sector.[49] According to the FCA, the public servants who exercise the authority of the State are, for example, those working in the administration of justice and judiciary, customs officers and servants who perform the tasks related to the administration, audit and collection of internal revenues. While

46. The decision of the ECSR in the case *Confederazione Generale Italiana del Lavoro (CGIL) v. Italy* (22 January 2019), Complaint No. 140/2016, para. 145.
47. Compilation of decisions of the Committee on Freedom of Association, Freedom of association, International Labour Office Geneva (6th ed. 2018), paras 828; 840, available at https://www.ilo.org/publications/freedom-association-compilation-decisions-committee-freedom-association-pdf.
48. Compilation of decisions of the Committee on Freedom of Association, Freedom of association, International Labour Office Geneva (6th ed. 2018), para. 830, available at https://www.ilo.org/publications/freedom-association-compilation-decisions-committee-freedom-association-pdf.
49. Compilation of decisions of the Committee on Freedom of Association, Freedom of association, International Labour Office Geneva (6th ed. 2018), para. 829, available at https://www.ilo.org/publications/freedom-association-compilation-decisions-committee-freedom-association-pdf.

public servants in state-owned commercial enterprises must be allowed to strike under the condition that interruption of respective services does not endanger the life, personal safety or health of the whole or part of the population.[50]

Also, ECtHR has held that the notion of '"administration of the state" should be construed narrowly'. It means that it should be assessed in the light of the post held by the official concerned.[51] Also the freedom of association may be restricted in case there is a need to ensure political neutrality.[52] The ECtHR has acknowledged that 'administration of the state' does not include municipal servants, as well as public servants or employees of the state-run commercial or industrial undertakings.[53] The reason for restriction on the right to strike in public sector is necessary because employees in public service owe to their employer a duty of loyalty, reserve and discretion. 'Since the role of civil servants in a democratic society is to assist the government in discharging its functions, the duty of loyalty and reserve assumes special significance for them.'[54]

(b) The Restrictions on the Right to Strike in Public Service

The FCA has recognized that the right to strike in public service may be restricted or prohibited.[55] The ECtHR has stated the same by adding that 'the States have wide margin of appreciation in putting the restrictions on civil servants exercising public authority of the State'.[56] The ECSR considers that 'the right to strike of certain categories of public servants may be restricted'; however, 'these restrictions should be limited to public officials whose duties and functions, given their nature or level of responsibility, are directly related to national security, general interest'.[57]

In the light of this, the criticism deserves the recent ECtHR decision in the case *Humpert v. Germany*.[58] In this case, the applicants were teachers with civil servant status who were subject to disciplinary measures against them for having participated, during their working hours, in strikes which had been organized by the trade union of which they were members. The applicants considered that such disciplinary measures were in breach of their right to freedom of association as provided for in Article 11 of the Convention.

50. Compilation of decisions of the Committee on Freedom of Association, Freedom of association, International Labour Office Geneva (6th ed. 2018), para. 831, available at https://www.ilo.org/publications/freedom-association-compilation-decisions-committee-freedom-association-pdf.
51. Registry of the ECtHR, Guide on Art. 11 of the European Convention on Human Rights, para. 295 (31 August 2024), available at https://ks.echr.coe.int/documents/d/echr-ks/guide_art_11_eng.
52. Registry of the ECtHR, Guide on Art. 11 of the European Convention on Human Rights, para. 297 (31 August 2024), available at https://ks.echr.coe.int/documents/d/echr-ks/guide_art_11_eng.
53. Registry of the ECtHR, Guide on Art. 11 of the European Convention on Human Rights, paras 296, 299 (31 August 2024), available at https://ks.echr.coe.int/documents/d/echr-ks/guide_art_11_eng.
54. The decision of the ECtHR in the case *Trade Union of the Police in the Slovak Republic and Others v. Slovakia* (25 September 2012), Application No. 11828/08, para. 57.
55. Paragraph 830.
56. ECHR decision in the case *Humpert and others v. Germany* (14 December 2023), Application Nos 59433/18, 59477/18 and 59494/18, para. 112.
57. The decision of the ECSR in the case *European Organisation of Military Associations (EUROMIL) v. Ireland* (12 September 2017), Complaint No. 112/2014, para. 113.
58. ECHR decision in the case *Humpert and others v. Germany* (14 December 2023), Application Nos 59433/18, 59477/18 and 59494/18.

In this case, the ECtHR (Grand Chamber) has ruled with 16 voted to one that there has been no violation of Article 11 of ECHR with respect to applicants.

The decision was criticized because it goes against, first, the general position of other international bodies with regard to the status of schoolteachers, in particular, to what extent they could be considered civil servants in charge of the administration of the State. The FCA has stated that the education sector does not constitute an essential service. At the same time the FCA recognized that the principal and vice-principal of the schools may be restricted or prohibited from striking.[59] Second, such decision goes against the conclusions of international bodies with respect to a total ban on the right to strike for civil servants in Germany. Respective ban has been found as incompatible with ICCPR, ICESCR, ILO standards and ESC.[60]

Such a decision of the ECtHR is explained by the unwillingness of the ECtHR to go against the German Constitutional Court which in the same case before the ECtHR ruled that there was no violation of freedom of association.[61]

2.2.2 Police

Already on 2013 the ECSR took a note of the evolution towards the expansion of the right to strike to police officers in national legal systems.[62] It means that total ban on the right to strike of members of police is not acceptable anymore. However, in case of total ban, the 'states must demonstrate compelling reasons as to why an absolute prohibition on the right to strike is justified in the specific national context in question'.[63]

However, when it comes to restriction of the right to strike – 'as to the mode and form of strike action' – the ECSR considers that the States have a wide margin of appreciation.[64] The ECSR has also recognized in this context that the States have a

59. Compilation of decisions of the Committee on Freedom of Association, Freedom of association, International Labour Office Geneva (6th ed. 2018), paras 844-846, available at https://www.ilo.org/publications/freedom-association-compilation-decisions-committee-freedom-association-pdf.
60. ECHR decision in the case *Humpert and others v. Germany* (14 December 2023), Application Nos 59433/18, 59477/18 and 59494/18, paras 53-60.
61. *See*, Ignatius Yordan Nugraha, *Defusing a Brewing Conflict With the Constitution: Humpert and Others v Germany, Procedural Rationality, and the Right of Civil Servants to Strike*, Strasburg Observers (2024), available at https://strasbourgobservers.com/2024/02/06/defusing-a-brewing-conflict-with-the-constitution-humpert-and-others-v-germany-procedural-rationality-and-the-right-of-civil-servants-to-strike/; Justine Batura, *A European Dialogue on Strike Action: The Strike Ban for German Civil Servants Between Karlsruhe and Strasbourg*, Verfassungsblog (2023), available at https://verfassungsblog.de/a-european-dialogue-on-strike-action/.
62. The decision of the ECSR in the case *European Confederation of Police (EuroCOP) v. Ireland* (2 December 2013), Complaint No. 83/2012, para. 203.
63. The decision of the ECSR in the case *European Confederation of Police (EuroCOP) v. Ireland* (2 December 2013), Complaint No. 83/2012, paras 211-212; the decision of the ECSR in the case *Confederazione Generale Italiana del Lavoro (CGIL) v. Italy* (22 January 2019), Complaint No. 140/2016, para. 145.
64. The decision of the ECSR in the case *European Confederation of Police (EuroCOP) v. Ireland* (2 December 2013), Complaint No. 83/2012, para. 202; the decision of the ECSR in the case *Confederazione Generale Italiana del Lavoro (CGIL) v. Italy* (22 January 2019), Complaint No. 140/2016, para. 145.

narrower margin of appreciation when restricting the right to strike in police than in armed forces.[65]

The ECtHR has stated that the States have a wide margin of appreciation in restricting the right to strike of members of the police.[66] However, such restrictions are to be construed strictly, and they should be justified by convincing and compelling reasons.[67] As regards the restrictions put on the member of the police, the ECtHR considers that they are armed and represent 'law-enforcement agents' which distinguish them from other persons employed in the public service, like, for example, medical doctors or judges; thus, more stringent restrictions imposed on the members of the police does not exceed what is necessary in democratic society because they serve for the protection of the State's general interests, i.e., to ensure national security, public safety and the prevention of the disorder.[68]

2.2.3 Armed Forces

Similarly to the restrictions on the right to strike in public administration and police, also in case of armed forces the States have a wide margin of appreciation. At the same time also in this sector the restrictions are to be construed strictly; they must be justified by convincing and compelling reasons. As a result, the restrictions must be such as not to impair the very essence of the right.[69]

The ECSR considers that the States have a wide margin of appreciation on how they restrict the right to strike in armed forces by taking into account the national system. It means that the States may, for example, decide upon the mode and form of collective action or establishment of the minimum service.[70]

No case has been detected where any of the international supervisory bodies would have ruled on the permissibility of right to strike in armed forces as such. In the case *Confederazione Generale Italiana del Lavoro (CGIL) v. Italy*, the ECSR ruled that a complete ban on Guardia di Finanza – the military police in charge of economic and financial matters – is not proportionate; however, the reason for such conclusion was the lack of compensatory measures in case of complete ban on the right to strike.[71]

---

65. The decision of the ECSR in the case *European Organisation of Military Associations (EUROMIL) v. Ireland* (12 September 2017), Complaint No. 112/2014, para. 116.
66. ECHR decision in the case *Humpert and others v. Germany* (14 December 2023), Application Nos 59433/18, 59477/18 and 59494/18, para. 112.
67. ECHR decision in the case *Ognevenko v. Russia* (20 November 2018), Application No. 44873/09, para. 59.
68. The ECtHR decision in the case *Junta Rectora Del Ertzainen Nazional Elkartasuna (ER.N.E.) v. Spain* (21 April 2015), Application No. 45892/09, para. 38.
69. ECHR decision in the case *Ognevenko v. Russia* (20 November 2018), Application No. 44873/09, para. 59; ECHR decision in the case *Humpert and others v. Germany* (14 December 2023), Application Nos 59433/18, 59477/18 and 59494/18, para. 112.
70. The decision of the ECSR in the case *Confederazione Generale Italiana del Lavoro (CGIL) v. Italy* (22 January 2019), Complaint No. 140/2016, para. 148.
71. The decision of the ECSR in the case *Confederazione Generale Italiana del Lavoro (CGIL) v. Italy* (22 January 2019), Complaint No. 140/2016, para. 152.

3 COMPENSATORY GUARANTEES FOR WORKERS DEPRIVED OF THE RIGHT TO STRIKE

The international supervisory bodies have the same standards as to the entitlement of compensatory measures in case of restriction or prohibition on the right to strike.

Since the right to strike is a primordial instrument in collective bargaining process, in case of restrictions on the right to strike, the workers affected should be provided with other effective means to ensure that they continue enjoying their rights to act in order to improve employment conditions. The CFA stresses that restrictions on the right to strike should be accompanied by adequate, impartial and speedy conciliation and arbitration proceedings.[72]

The ECSR also mentions, among compensatory measures, an effective and regular procedure of negotiation at the highest level between the employees and an employer regarding not only the material and salary conditions but also the work organization, conciliation or arbitration procedure. In addition, the ECSR considers as compensatory measure requirement on establishment of minimum service.[73]

4 CONCLUSION

The right to strike is explicitly and implicitly provided by numerous international agreements.

The purpose of the right to strike is obvious – it represents the most effective tool for the defence of occupational and economic interests of workers, and it facilitates not only improvement of working conditions or collective claims of occupational nature but also serves for the solutions to economic and social policy problems.

Restrictions on the right to strike could be applied only in accordance with a general formula for the restriction of human rights; in particular, restrictions must be provided by the law and it must have a legitimate aim and be proportionate to the aim pursued.

Since the right to strike is essential for the enjoyment of the right of association in general, the States have a narrow margin of appreciation in restricting them.

The situation is different regarding restriction of the right to strike in essential services in the strict sense, public service, police and armed forces.

Because the States have the right to restrict or even ban the right to strike in the mentioned sectors, the notion of those sectors themselves must be construed strictly. The notion of 'essential services in the strict sense' means services the interruption of which would endanger the life, personal safety or health of the whole or part of the

72. Compilation of decisions of the Committee on Freedom of Association, Freedom of association, International Labour Office Geneva (6th ed. 2018), paras 853-856, available at https://www.ilo.org/publications/freedom-association-compilation-decisions-committee-freedom-association-pdf.
73. The decision of the ECSR in the case *Confederazione Generale Italiana del Lavoro (CGIL) v. Italy* (22 January 2019), Complaint No. 140/2016, para. 152.

population. Also, the notion of 'public service' applies only to public servants exercising authority in the name of the State.

The States enjoy a wide margin of appreciation in restricting the rights to strike in essential services in the strict sense, public service, police and armed forces; however, restrictions are to be construed strictly and they must be justified by convincing and compelling reasons. In case of restriction or total ban on the rights to strike in these sectors, effective compensatory measures must be put in place to ensure that respective workers effectively enjoy their right of freedom of association and, in particular, the right to collective bargaining.

PART II Country Reports

CHAPTER 3

Restrictions on the Right to Strike in Albania

Eneida Sema

1 GENERAL INFORMATION

1.1 Legal Basis of the Right to Strike

In the history of the development of industrial relations, Albania is a country that recognized these relations relatively late. After the Turkish invasion and the declaration of independence in 1912, the governments of that time tried to improve the economic and legal situation, taking into consideration that part of the positive developments of neighbouring Western European countries.

After the political developments in 1929, despite the adoption of the Civil Code which was an approach to the Italian civil legislation of that time, industrial relations were still weak in terms of their development.

But the isolation of Albania after 1945, with the installation of a dictatorial regime that lasted for almost a period of five decades, finally removed the possibility of the approach of Albanian legislation to work with that of Western European countries. Just like in the countries of the eastern camp at that time, that period in Albania not only recognized a political regime that severely violated human rights and the rights of employees as well but also installed new economic and social relations which gradually recognized the state as the sole owner of everything.

Thus, the labour legislation recognized in a superficial way some rights of employees, including the right to join and organize workers in the Professional Union of that time.

In 1957, Albania ratified the two Labour Organization Conventions regarding trade union freedom and the right to organize.[1] We must say that even though the government of that time 'per page' recognized the basic rights at work, these rights were not implemented and were seriously violated. At that time, the right to organize meant the opposite of its purpose, precisely the obligation to be part of a structure, the creation of which facilitated the control of the mass of workers by the regime's structures.

The overthrow of the communist regime in 1990 brought about a series of major changes in terms of the functioning of political, economic, and social relations and freedoms. Albania has ratified important acts related to human rights, especially in the field of labour relations as well, such as the Convention on Fundamental Human Rights and the European Social Charter.[2]

1.2 Main Features of the Regulation

The freedom of association, one of the important principles of labour law, is the foundation of labour legislation, thus recognizing the right of every employee or employer to be or not be a member of trade union structures or organizations whose purpose is to protect interests and legitimate professional, economic, and social rights of their members. It is understood that at the centre of trade union rights is the right to organize, which means the right of every employee or employer to organize in organizations in the form of associations that are created and function independently to protect the legitimate interests of theirs.

After the 1990s, Albania embraced without hesitation the principles and basic rights at work, now internationally recognized, including trade union rights. Throughout the post-communist period, the culture of rights at work and the right to organize has been the subject of discussion regarding the necessity of developing policies to raise awareness among employees about the importance of trade union rights.

There are a lot of trade union organizations of employees and organizations of employers as well in Albania, but apparently, these structures seem to survive under the shadow of a mentality of 'being' and not for 'functionality and improving'.

In the framework of the various problems that may exist in the country, taking into account the fact that Albania is now seeking to be a member of the European Union, the implementation of the law related to the exercise of trade union rights thus plays a major role in the further improvement of policies of employment, labour market, working conditions, and social dialogue as well. But, if we refer to the strike as an important legal instrument, although it is the last legal instrument to meet the

1. C087 – Freedom of Association and Protection of the Right to Organize Convention, 1948, and C098 – Right to Organize and Collective Bargaining Convention, 1949 (No. 98).
2. The ratification of the ECHR by Albania was made in 1996 with the approval of Law No. 8137, dated 31 July 1996.
   The Republic of Albania has ratified the European Social Charter with Law No. 8960, dated 24 October 2002, published in Official Gazette No. 75, dated 22 November 2002 (*see* p. 2087).

demands of trade union organizations of employees, it is practically not properly used by the trade unions.

In Albania, the right to strike is a constitutional right.[3] Thus, the right to strike is sanctioned and guaranteed, qualifying and specifically linking the exercise of this right to the labour relationship. But we must also say that in this constitutional provision, the establishment of legal restrictions is expressly allowed in cases where these restrictions are considered necessary to provide society with the necessary services.

Just as the Declaration of Philadelphia declares that: 'freedom of expression and organization is a necessary condition for continuous progress', the Conventions of the International Labour Organization ratified in Albania[4] aim to protect trade union freedoms and rights, as well as guarantee their implementation. The guarantees provided by Convention No. 98 are recognized by employees and employers in all sectors of activity while regarding the exercise of trade union rights by the Armed Forces and the police, the Convention states that the level of implementation of the guarantees is determined by the provisions of national legislation.

The protection of rights at work and the improvement of working conditions are the main goals aimed at the right and freedom of organization; thus, the exercise of important instruments such as the right to strike as a means to achieve the legal goal takes on special importance. The right to organize, guaranteeing the freedom to create trade unions and the freedom to participate in them, is protected by the European Convention on Human Rights[5] which allows the restrictions that are necessary in a democratic society such as cases of protection of national security, public safety, for the protection of order and crime prevention, for the preservation of health or morality, or the protection of the rights and freedoms of others. In terms of the relevant provision, in the internal legislation, legal restrictions can be set for employees of the state administration, police employees, as well as the Armed Forces.

In the European Social Charter[6] the rights of employees are protected, such as the right to organize and the right to negotiate collectively, where, among other things, the right of workers and employers to act is protected, including the right to strike. In this sense, the provisions of the International Covenant on Economic, Social and Cultural Rights (ICESCR) approved by the General Assembly of the United Nations on 16 December 1966, ratified by Albania on 4 October 1991, reinforce the standards established in Convention No. 87 'On Freedom of Association and Protection of the Right to Organize', and also explicitly sanction the right to strike. Limitations are defined in this act in cases where national security and public order can be at risk, and

3. *See* Constitution of the Republic of Albania, A.51: 'The employee's right to strike, which is related to labour relations, is guaranteed. Restrictions for special categories of employees can be established by law to ensure society essential services.' http//web: qbz.gov.al.
4. Respectively C087 – Freedom of Association and Protection of the Right to Organize Convention, 1948, and C098 – Right to Organize and Collective Bargaining Convention, 1949.
5. The European Convention of Human Rights was ratified by Law No. 8137 dated 31 July 1996, announced by Decree No. 1573, dated 2 August 1996 of the President of the Republic.
6. *See* Law No. 8960, dated 24 October 2002, 'For the Ratification of the European Social Charter', Official Gazette No. 75, dated 22 November 2002.

also these limitations intend to protect the rights and freedoms of other persons in a wider context.

1.3 The Right to Strike in Legal Regulations

Taking into consideration the fact that the right to strike is a constitutional right, as well as the fact that Albania has ratified important international acts that guarantee the right to organize and trade union freedom, the strike represents a special institute regulated in a section, especially in the Albanian Labour Code.[7]

The provisions of this code guarantee the freedom of participation in a legal strike; and regulate the exercise of the strike, the cases of restrictions, the conditions of the legality of the strike, its effects, minimum services, and services of vital importance. General strikes and solidarity strikes are also regulated by the provisions of this code. The trade unions exercise the right to strike to resolve their economic and social demands.

Participation in strikes is voluntary and freedom of participation is guaranteed against any oppression or discrimination due to participation or not. In terms of the provisions of the code,[8] the use of force is not allowed to stop a legal strike, but the law obliges union representatives to use tools peacefully to convince employees to participate in strikes.

For a strike to be legal in Albania, several legal conditions must be met in the sense of the regulations in the Labour Code,[9] such as:

- It is organized by a trade union that enjoys legal personality according to the law.
- It aims to achieve the signing or implementation of a collective labour contract or if one exists, the fulfilment of requirements arising from labour relations and not regulated by this contract, except in cases where the latter provides for the absolute obligation of peace.
- The union or unions, on the one hand, and the employers' organization or organizations, on the other hand, have tried to agree, subject to the mediation and conciliation procedure.
- It is not contrary to the legislation in force.

During the development of a legal strike, the parties make the necessary efforts to talk among themselves to find suitable solutions to the created situation.

The provisions of the Labour Code also regulate the solidarity strike. A solidarity strike is a strike that is organized in support of a legal strike. The representatives of the

7. The Labour Code of the Republic of Albania was approved by Law No. 7961, dated 12 July 1995; amended by Law No. 8085, dated 13 March 1996; amended by Law No. 9125, dated 29 July 2003; amended by Law No. 10 053, dated 29 December 2008; amended by Law No. 136/2015, dated 5 December 2015.
8. *See* A.197/2/1-A.197/2/2, Albanian Labour Code.
9. *See* A.197/3, Labour Code.

union organization notify the employer of the place, time, and reasons two days before the strike.[10]

In terms of the regulatory provisions in this code,[11] the general strike at the national or regional level is legal if it does not conflict with the requirements of the provisions of this code regarding minimum services, services of vital importance and special situations, as well as when the general strike is organized to oppose the policies, social and economic measures of the government or local government, which conflict with the interests of the employees.

The strike is legally permitted for civil service employees, whose employment relationship is regulated by a separate law,[12] with exceptions expressly defined in the provisions of this law. The civil servant has the right to create and join trade unions and professional associations which aim to protect his interests, as well as the right to be a member of the governing bodies of the trade union. The provision of this law prohibits the election of civil servants who belong to the senior management category in the civil service in the senior management bodies of the union or professional association.

We must say that in terms of the provisions of the above-mentioned law, this law applies to any employee who exercises a public function in a state administration institution, independent institution or local government unit, with the exception certain as the elect; the minister and deputy minister; officials appointed by the Assembly, the President of the Republic or the Council of Ministers; the judge and the prosecutor; the military of the Armed Forces; the personnel of the State Information Service; personnel of direct public service units; the member and the chairman of the collegial governing bodies of the committees or institutions subordinate to the Prime Minister or a ministry; administrative employees; cabinet functionaries; employees who perform the attributes of the agent/officer of the Judicial Police and those who according to the law are allowed to carry weapons; civilians in the structures of the Armed Forces; employees of the Financial Supervision Authority; drainage board employees; lawyers at the State Attorney's Office.

Union organizations of public employees must enjoy complete independence from public authorities, as well as they must enjoy full protection against all intervention actions of public authorities in matters of their creation, operation, and administration.

Police officers and foreign service officers are considered 'civil servants'[13] according to the Law on Civil Servants, but other specific rights or obligations are regulated in the relevant special laws.[14]

In terms of the provisions of Law No. 108/2014, 'For the State Police', every police employee, except the Director of the State Police, has the right to be a member of the trade union, but during the development of trade union activities, police

10. *See* A.197/7, Labour Code.
11. *See* A.197/8/a, Labour Code.
12. Law No. 152/2013 For the Civil Servant (amended by Law No. 178/2014 and Law No. 41/2017), *see* A.35, http//web:qbz.gov.al.
13. *See* A.3, Law No. 152/2013 'On Civil Servants'.
14. Law No. 108/2014, For the State Police, Official Journal, Year 2014 - Number 137, A.83/4, A.92, http//web: qbz.gov.al; and Law No. 152/2015 For fire protection and rescue services, A.20.

employees are prohibited from wearing the uniform, or to use police tools and symbols. In the law, there are no other definitions regarding the definition of trade union activity. The relations between the police unions and the State Police Director are regulated in the collective agreement.

However, regarding the conflict of interest, the special law provides that the police officer must avoid any conflict between his private interest and the public interest in the performance of his duties according to the legislation in force.

If we consider the employees of the fire protection service,[15] we can say that they have the right to form and join unions. They have the right to participate in the activities of their union, but they are prohibited from striking.

2 PERMITTED RESTRICTIONS

2.1 Certain Categories of Public Servants

The establishment of legal restrictions, necessary to provide society with the necessary services, is provided for in the constitutional provisions.

It is forbidden to strike in vital services. In terms of the provision of the Labour Code[16] those services whose interruption endangers the life, personal safety, or health of a part or the whole population are considered vital services. Specifically, services of vital importance are:

- necessary medical and hospital services;
- air traffic control services;
- essential fire protection services;
- essential services in prisons.

For the categories of employees of vital services, categorized as necessary for the safety and health guarantee of a part or the entire population, collective conflicts are resolved in a final and mandatory manner.[17]

The Labour Code is an important legal act as it remains the most important basic legal structure in the hierarchy of legal sources of labour legislation, ranked after the constitution and ratified international acts, and it is the law that carries the main weight of the labour law principles, as well as basic rights at work. But apart from this law, we should consider the special legal treatment of the categories of 'civil servants'. These categories are recognized with the right to strike, except when otherwise provided by law. Thus, in terms of the relevant provision[18] the exercise of the right to strike is not allowed in the field of essential services of state actors such as: transport, public television, water, gas, and electricity supply, prison administration, justice system administration, national defence services, emergency health services, food supply services, or air traffic control services.

15. Law No. 152/2015 'On fire protection and rescue services'.
16. *See* A.197/5, Albanian Labour Code.
17. *See* A.196, Albanian Labour Code.
18. *See* A.35 Law No. 152/2013 'On Civil Servants'.

2.2 Legal Restrictions Imposed on the Exercise of the Right to Strike in Minimum Services

Due to the importance of the provision of certain services for a part or the entire population of a country, the strike cannot be exercised if the performance of the minimum service is not ensured. In terms of the legal regulations in the Labour Code[19] minimum services can be requested in:

- water supply sectors;
- electricity supply; and
- other service sectors, to meet the basic needs of the population; and to ensure that these needs are met.

The trade union organizations that organize the strike must appoint the necessary employees for the provision of services in these activities. The representatives of the employees' union and the employers appoint the employees who will offer the service by agreement. When the agreement for the appointment of these employees is not reached, the parties turn to the court, which conducts the lottery for the appointment of the arbitrator of the case, who decides within 24 hours of his appointment.

2.3 Situations of Acute National or Local Crisis

The strike represents one of the constitutional rights for employees, but just as this right is limited to major interests for the benefit of a part or the entire population of the country, the law also considers the exercise of the right to strike in cases of special situations.

In terms of the regulatory provisions of the Labour Code[20] special situations are considered:

- natural disasters;
- state of war;
- state of emergency;
- cases where the freedom of elections is put at risk.

If the strike has started and during this operation they are faced with any of the above conditions, the strike must be suspended, and if any of the conditions occur and as long as it has not passed, the strike cannot be exercised.

3 COMPENSATORY GUARANTEES FOR WORKERS DEPRIVED OF THE RIGHT TO STRIKE

In Albania, employees employed in vital services are prohibited from striking. Conflicts that arise between the parties in the employment relationship are resolved in a

19. *See* A.197/6, Albanian Labour Code.
20. *See* A.197/4, Albanian Labour Code.

mandatory and final manner by an arbitration court.[21] During the dispute, in these services, at first, the parties turn to the procedure of mediation and reconciliation. The mediation process is activated with the request of the interested parties addressed to the relevant minister for the resolution of the collective conflict that has arisen. The mediator, who in each case is appointed by the minister, intervenes immediately to help the parties find the right solution. This procedure lasts 10 days.[22]

If the mediation process is not successful in resolving the conflict, the relevant minister moves to the state office of reconciliation which works with the central national office and the relevant offices in the districts. Depending on the dimensions of the collective conflict, reconciliation offices are also activated, the purpose of which is to reconcile the parties by calling them to a special session to listen to them regarding their conflict. Then the conciliation office proposes a solution to the parties, which is left up to the parties to decide on.[23] The conciliation procedure lasts 10 days, and if this process turns out to be unsuccessful in resolving the conflict, the parties refer to the arbitration court. The parties agree to choose three arbitrators to resolve the case, and if the parties do not agree on the appointment of arbitrators, the court appoints the arbitrators.[24] The arbitration process lasts three weeks and the decision is an executive title.

4 CONCLUSION

The strike is an important institution in Albanian Labour Legislation. The right to strike represents one of the constitutional rights and its exercise is regulated by law. The main regulations related to the strike can be found in the Albanian Labour Code, which stipulates the conditions for the legality of the strike, the effects of an illegal strike, and the rights of employees related to the strike. Employees who are employed in vital services are exempted from the right to strike, while in services that are considered essential for the population, the strike is allowed after ensuring the number of employees who will continue to provide the services properly. For services whose employees are excluded from the right to strike, collective conflicts are resolved in a binding and final manner by the arbitration court, the decision of which constitutes executive title according to the provisions of the Albanian Civil Procedure code.

In principle, not only the collective conflict but also the right to strike when it is exercised for the fulfilment of the legal demands of the employees represents the confrontation with the requests for improvement. Thus, the limitation of the right to strike must be based on the absolute and vital importance of services for a part or all of the population of a country.

Regardless of the wide range of problems relating to employment, working conditions, or the need for labour law improvements, in Albania after the 1990s and even nowadays, we should admit that the lack of exercising basic labour rights

21. *See* A.197/4, Albanian Labour Code.
22. *See* A.188/a; A.192, Labour Code.
23. *See* A.193, Albanian Labour Code.
24. *See* A.196, Albanian Labour Code.

including the right to strike as necessary practices to improve working conditions is unfortunately evident. I think that practically Albanian trade unions and their activities should be more independent from other actors' interference and need a 'true revitalization process' in order to play their crucial role.

CHAPTER 4

Restrictions on the Right to Strike in Austria

Martin Gruber-Risak & Sascha Obrecht

1 GENERAL INFORMATION

Austria is not a strike country. The annual average for the period 2008 to 2016 was two working days lost per thousand workers.[1] For comparison: in France, this figure was 123 working days.[2] In the years 2005-2010 and 2015-2017, there was not even a single hour of strike action in Austria.[3] This is in particular due to the role of the Austrian system of social partnership: The representatives of the workers' interest groups (Chambers of Labour and Austrian Trade Union Federation) and employers (Economic Chamber of Austria and the Austrian Chamber of Agriculture) rely on formal and informal negotiations to resolve conflicts without industrial action.[4] This model permeates Austrian industrial relations, provides considerable stability in the world of work – as can be seen from the strike statistics – and ensures that the major interest groups sometimes have a considerable say in social policy. Thus, numerous representatives of the interest groups that make up social partnership can be found directly in Parliament. Furthermore, the statutory interest groups, the Chamber of Labour and the

1. Hagen Lesch, *Internationaler Arbeitskampfvergleich: Studie des Instituts der deutschen Wirtschaft Köln*, IW-Kurzbericht 71.2017, p. 2 (2017).
2. Lesch, *Arbeitskampfvergleich*, p. 2.
3. Austrian Trade Union Federation, *Österreichische Streikstatistik seit 1945*, p. 2, https://www.google.com/url?sa=t&rct=j&q=&esrc=s&source=web&cd=&ved=2ahUKEwiDmevkqeSOAxV6hv0HHcYKBXwQFnoECBkQAQ&url=https%3A%2F%2Fwww.oegb.at%2Fcontent%2Fdam%2Foegb%2Fdownloads%2Fder-%25C3%25B6gb%2FOeGB_Streikstatistik_2023.pdf&usg=AOvVaw0cURN8GWgESBvmPNV4cQoE&opi=89978449 (accessed 30 July 2025); Economic Chamber of Austria, *Streiks in Österreich*, p. 2, https://wko.at/statistik/Extranet/Langzeit/Lang-Streiks.pdf (accessed 30 July 2025).
4. Christoph Kietaibl, *Arbeitsrecht I*[10], p. 381 (2022).

Chamber of Commerce, have a selective role in certain areas of the executive, especially in the administration of social security, and are involved in the judiciary in labour and social law cases through the participation of expert lay judges.

This mostly informal yet efficient setup of Austrian industrial relations also explains the most conspicuous phenomenon surrounding industrial action in this country: the total lack of a legal framework for industrial action. On the one hand, the very limited practical relevance may be one of the reasons for the reluctance of the legislature.[5] On the other hand, however, it is mainly due to the Social Partners' lack of interest in formalizing the rules of industrial action, which explains the legislator's passive attitude. Both the workers' and employers' interest groups consider the efficient promotion of their members' interests more related to factual organizational strength than better legal standing.[6]

It is therefore not surprising that the current President of the Constitutional Court, Christoph Grabenwarter, still describes the right to strike as something of a blank spot almost one hundred years after the entry into force of the Austrian Constitution:[7] There is no comprehensive legal regulation, and, even more so, case law is extremely limited. For a long time, and until recently, it was a standard tenet of constitutional law that no (fundamental) individual right to strike was guaranteed under the Austrian Constitution. However, according to Grabenwarter, this can no longer be upheld today. In the meantime, this is also the view of the majority of voices in the literature[8] and will be discussed in the following chapters.

1.1 Legal Basis of the Right to Strike

As already indicated, the Austrian legislator restrained from formally regulating either the right to strike generally or the details for exercising it. In addition to a few historical provisions, which are mainly aimed at prohibiting the coercive use of coalitions against individuals for the purpose of organizing or participating in collective action (*see* section 2.1 below), there are only a few more recent regulations. These oblige the state administration to take a neutral position towards the parties to an industrial conflict and not to unilaterally influence the outcome of it (*see* section 2.2 below).[9]

Beyond this, however, the Austrian legislator does not provide for any further provisions, in particular, no prohibition or restrictions regarding participation in strikes, regulations on the admissibility of industrial action or potentially adverse consequences for participating workers. It was therefore left to the scholars to make

5. Different Opinion: Andreas Mair, *Arbeitskampf und Arbeitsvertrag: zum Verhältnis von kollektivem Kampf und individualrechtlicher Bindung*, p. 34 (2008).
6. Heinz Krejci, *Lohnzahlung bei Teilstreik*, p. 34 (1988).
7. Christoph Grabenwarter, *Recht auf Streik. Ein Paradigmenwechsel mit Folgen im Arbeitskampfrecht Österreichs*, von Krejci, JBl 2015, p. 743 (2015).
8. *See* Heinz Krejci, *Recht auf Streik* (2015); Franz Marhold, *Die Koalitionsfreiheit im österreichischen Recht*, DRdA 5a/2015, p. 413 (2015); Elisabeth Kohlbacher, *Grundrecht auf Streik: Rechtsgrundlagen und Rechtsfolgen*, ecolex 2015, p. 690 (2015); *and previously also* Martin Risak, *3,65 oder 5,5%, das ist hier die Frage: Grundsätzliches zum 'Metaller*innen-Oktoberstreik' 2011*, juridikum 2012, p. 23 (2012).
9. Mair, *Arbeitskampf*, pp. 45 et seq.; Kietaibl, *Arbeitsrecht I*, p. 384.

more fundamental considerations. They developed the so-called separation theory, which until a few years ago was considered the prevailing opinion.[10] According to this theory, the actions of the coalitions involved in the industrial dispute must be considered separately from the individual contractual consequences of workers' participation in the industrial dispute.[11] In such a view, participation in the strike is permissible for the individual employee, but at the same time, it constitutes a breach of his/her contractual obligations – the provision of his/her work in person. Therefore, it was predominantly argued in the literature that even the participation of an employee in a justified strike entitled the employer to dismiss him without notice for a breach of contract.[12] However, this theory has been increasingly questioned in recent years and has now lost its position as the prevailing opinion.[13]

The basis for this is the case law of the ECtHR, which now derives a right to strike from the freedom of association under Article 11 ECHR (*see* section 2.2 below). This is of major relevance in Austria as the ECHR is directly applicable and has the status of constitutional law. Individuals can therefore directly base a claim on it, and it has to be taken into account when interpreting labour law provisions.

2 MAIN FEATURES OF THE REGULATION

2.1 Historical Beginnings

There are a few historical legal remnants that are applicable until now: For example, the Coalition Act 1870[14] decrees that agreements on planning of industrial action are not binding; intimidation or the use of force to achieve participation in industrial action are to be punished (section 2f Coalition Act 1870).[15] According to the Anti-Terror Act 1930,[16] provisions in collective agreements are invalid if they aim to make membership or non-membership of a trade union a prerequisite for working in an establishment (section 1 leg cit). Likewise, the attempt to achieve the same goal through one's own actions is also forbidden (section 4 leg cit).

2.2 Neutrality of the State Administration During Industrial Action

The few existing provisions in connection with industrial action are primarily aimed at the state not interfering in the conflict and thus influencing the outcome.

10. *With further evidence* Krejci, *Recht auf Streik*, p. 59 *and* Marhold, *Koalitionsfreiheit*, p. 415.
11. *With further evidence* Mair, *Arbeitskampf*, p. 62.
12. *With further evidence* Krejci, *Recht auf Streik*, p. 293.
13. Krejci, *Recht auf Streik*, p. 278.
14. Gesetz vom 7 April 1870, wodurch unter Aufhebung der §§ 479, 480 und 481 des allgemeinen Strafgesetzes in Betreff der Verabredungen von Arbeitgebern oder Arbeitnehmern zur Erzwingung von Arbeitsbedingungen, und von Gewerbsleuten zur Erhöhung des Preises einer Waare zum Nachtheile des Publikums besondere Bestimmungen erlassen werden RGBl 1870/43.
15. Marhold, *Die Koalitionsfreiheit im österreichischen Recht*, p. 412.
16. Bundesgesetz vom 5 April 1930 zum Schutz der Arbeits- und der Versammlungsfreiheit BGBl 1930/113.

Section 3(10) AMFG[17] can be seen as an almost exemplary case in point: It declares the placement of workers by the Public Employment Service in an establishment on strike or of striking workers to a different establishment to be inadmissible. Closely linked to this is the regulation that it is not expected of an unemployed person to accept a job in a company that is on strike. The rejection of such a job offer therefore does not lead to the loss of entitlement to unemployment benefits according to section 9(2) AlVG.[18] Conversely, according to section 13 AlVG, there is also no entitlement to unemployment benefit if unemployment results from a company shutdown caused by a strike.

Finally, a number of provisions make it hard to find replacement workers in cases of strike: Section 9 of the AÜG[19] prohibits the assignment of temporary agency workers to establishments on strike; section 8(5) ZDG,[20] the assignment of persons carrying out alternate civilian service to such establishments; and section 10 of the AuslBG,[21] the granting of employment permits to foreigners to work in an establishment on strike.

2.3 Article 11 ECHR as the Basis for Industrial Action in Austria

According to Article 11 ECHR, 'Everyone has the right to freedom of peaceful assembly and to freedom of association with others, including the right to form and to join trade unions for the protection of his interests.' The ECtHR has now ruled in numerous decisions that the right to strike is an inseparable consequence of freedom of association, even if it does not have an absolute character.[22] The starting point was the decision in the *Enerji Yapi-Yol Sen/TUR*[23] case of 21 April 2009, whereby an explicit recognition of the right to strike had already been indicated in previous decisions. In the *Karacay* case of 27 June 2007, for example, the ECtHR considered the warning of a civil servant for taking part in a strike to be a violation of the freedom of association. In the *Demir and Baykara* case of 12 November 2008, the ECtHR interpreted the freedom of association under Article 11 ECHR in the light of both Article 28 CFR and other sources of international law. In the above-mentioned *Enerji Yapi-Yol Sen* case, the Court then referred to ILO Convention No. 87 and the freedom of association protected therein and held that the right to strike follows directly and inseparably from the freedom of association.

Subsequently, the ECtHR has continued and further refined its case law.[24] In *RMT/VK*,[25] for example, the ECtHR found that the (legal) ban on sympathy strikes in

17. Bundesgesetz vom 12 December 1968 betreffend die Arbeitsmarktförderung (*Arbeitsmarktförderungsgesetz – AMFG*) BGBl 1969/31.
18. Arbeitslosenversicherungsgesetz 1977 (AlVG) BGBl 1977/609.
19. Bundesgesetz vom 23. März 1988, mit dem die Überlassung von Arbeitskräften geregelt wird (*Arbeitskräfteüberlassungsgesetz* – AÜG) BGBl 1988/196.
20. Bundesgesetz über den Zivildienst (*Zivildienstgesetz 1986 – ZDG*) BGBl 1986/679.
21. Bundesgesetz vom 20. März 1975, mit dem die Beschäftigung von Ausländern geregelt wird (*Ausländerbeschäftigungsgesetz – AuslBG*) BGBl 1975/218.
22. Kohlbacher, *Streik*, p. 690.
23. *Enerji Yapi-Yol Sen/TUR*, No. 68959/01, Marginal No. 24, Eur. Ct. H.R.
24. *Kaya und Seyhan*, No. 30946/04, Eur. Ct. H.R.
25. *RMT/VK*, No. 31045/10, Eur. Ct. H.R.

the United Kingdom fundamentally restricted the freedom of association guaranteed by Article 11 ECHR but then, in a second step, found it to be proportionate and necessary in a democratic society.

According to the correct and overwhelmingly prevailing view in recent literature, in the light of developments in ECtHR case law, the 'separation theory' previously advocated in Austria can no longer be upheld. Based on this, the prevailing doctrine now follows the approach that the legitimacy of a strike also has effects at the individual contractual level.[26] Accordingly, if a strike is lawful, the main contractual obligations are suspended. In this case, striking workers are exercising a constitutionally guaranteed right, and consequently they are not in breach of their contractual obligation to perform their services. Therefore, participation in strike action does not constitute grounds for dismissal (anymore).[27] Furthermore, a lawful strike does not make the worker liable for damages.[28]

As mentioned, the ECHR has constitutional status in Austria. Individuals can directly invoke it and thus their right to strike. The fundamental right to collective action thus has (at least indirect) third-party effect;[29] i.e., it also has an effect between private individuals in the interpretation of the law.

2.4 Entitlement to Strike

The right to strike is conferred on individual workers as well as on coalitions, i.e., voluntary associations of workers (trade unions) when they organize industrial action. This means that the Austrian Trade Union Federation is invested with such a fundamental right.

The basis of the right to strike in European law without any national restrictions has the effect that not only workers' interest groups formally established as trade unions in the form of associations are protected but also so-called ad hoc associations.[30] This means that workers in a company or establishment can also strike[31] without the 'approval' of the union.[32] In particular, ad hoc coalitions can demand changes to employment contracts (or other permissible strike objectives).

The statutory representations of interest, the so-called chambers (such as the Chambers of Labour and the Chambers for Doctors), are not invested with the right to strike as they are not coalitions based on voluntary membership. They are thus not voluntary associations for the promotion of common interests of their members that are protected by Article 11 ECHR, but legally established representations of interests with compulsory membership. Even if these are vested with the right to collective bargaining according to section 4(1) Labour Constitution Act (ArbVG), it does not

26. Krejci, *Recht auf Streik*, p. 271.
27. Kohlbacher, *Streik*, p. 692.
28. Krejci, *Recht auf Streik*, pp. 319 et seq.
29. *See* Kohlbacher, *Streik*, p. 692 with further evidence.
30. Elias Felten, *Koalitionsfreiheit und Arbeitsverfassungsrecht*, p. 389 (2017).
31. Felten, *Koalitionsfreiheit*, p. 408.
32. Robert Rebhahn, *in ZellKomm*^{2} § 1151 ABGB Marginal No. 253/1.

necessarily follow that they have the right to strike. In any case, this cannot be argued on the basis of freedom of association and is therefore not constitutionally protected.

Moreover, works council members not only have no right to strike but also are even prohibited from organizing industrial action in this role.[33] This is justified by the so-called peace obligation under works constitution law, which is derived from section 39 ArbVG, and also results from the fact that compulsory arbitration is possible for individual works agreement matters to compensate for the ban on industrial action. However, this obligation to keep the peace does not preclude individual works council members from organizing industrial action in another capacity (e.g., as trade union officials).[34]

2.5 Permissible Objectives of Strikes

It is undisputed that the conclusion or amendment of a collective agreement can be a permissible objective of a strike; this is in any case the core of the right to strike (so-called core area doctrine).[35] The only restriction here is that for the duration of a collective agreement, there is a so-called peace obligation; i.e., in this case, an (unwritten) ban on industrial action applies to both contracting parties.[36] However, if the collective agreement has expired, in particular due to the expiry of a time limit or termination, then industrial action is permissible.

However, in our opinion, the right to strike goes beyond negotiations for the conclusion of a collective agreement and can be directed at all measures that contribute to an improvement of working conditions, i.e., that can be chosen as an objective by the workers' association. This results from the autonomy of the coalition, i.e., that coalitions can determine their own goals and the ways to achieve them.[37] Thus, apart from the conclusion or amendment of a collective agreement, compliance with laws (e.g., in the area of worker protection such as the provision of personal protective equipment) or the refraining from unlawful measures such as structural discrimination can be enforced by means of industrial action. It is also arguable that better equipment in workplaces, additional jobs to relieve the workload of those already employed or the like may be the subject of industrial action. In addition, a change in employment contracts can also be achieved through industrial action.[38] What is essential is the relationship to the employment relationship and that the opponent of the strike action is at least theoretically able to meet the demand. Therefore, only strikes that pursue objectives that have nothing to do with the tasks of workers' and employers' organizations are inadmissible.[39]

---

33. *See* Austrian Supreme Court, No. 9 ObA 125/03b, DRdA 2005/6 (critical Rebhahn).
34. Rebhahn, *in ZellKomm*[2] § 1151 ABGB para. 252 *with further evidence.*
35. Krejci, *Recht auf Streik*, p. 221.
36. *See* Wolfgang Brodil & Martin Gruber-Risak, *Arbeitsrecht in Grundzügen*[11] Marginal No. 113 (2022).
37. So insb Krejci, *Recht auf Streik*, p. 236.
38. Rebhahn, *in ZellKomm*[2] § 1151 ABGB Marginal No. 25.
39. *See* Krejci, *Recht auf Streik*, p. 236.

Even if one were to follow the restrictive views in the doctrine, which considers a restriction of the right to strike to the effect that it is only permissible to fight for goals that can be regulated by collective agreements,[40] it must be noted that such restrictions have not explicitly been imposed in Austria.

3 PERMITTED RESTRICTIONS

In connection with Article 11 ECHR, it should be noted that restrictions on the freedom of association and the right to organize under Article 11(2) ECHR must be provided for by law. As there are no explicit legal restrictions on the right to strike in Austria, the full scope of the right to strike is guaranteed. The legislator has simply not provided for any restrictions. For the purposes of this chapter, we must therefore resort to more fundamental considerations and have to point out that such questions have not been decided by the courts yet.

3.1 Proportionality Test

The right to strike may be enshrined in Article 11 ECHR, but the unanimous view is that it is not unlimited and that its exercise must remain proportionate.

To this end, it must be weighed against other rights, such as the right to property of employers, although it is not clear whether this is merely a matter of gross disproportion[41] or whether the general principle of proportionality should be applied and thus a finer test.[42] Ultimately, this limitation results from the consideration that strikes can also be impermissible if they threaten to cause or subsequently actually cause disadvantages that are disproportionate to those advantages that are to be achieved with the help of industrial action.[43] In detail, much is disputed in the literature, and there is no case law. In any case, the examination concerns the objective, timing, nature, and extent of the means of industrial action.[44]

3.2 Certain Categories of Public Servants

The strike as a means of industrial action aims to improve the working conditions of the strikers, i.e., to achieve a permissible strike objective. This implies that the opponent of the strike is also in a position to make corresponding concessions and can thus fulfil the demand of the striking party. It follows from this that in the course of collective bargaining an employers' association and its members can be the addressee of strike action. If the strike objective only concerns individual employers, e.g., preventing the relocation of a company, they can also be opponents of the industrial action. All that

40. *See* Elisabeth Kohlbacher, *Streikrecht und Europarecht*, p. 231 (2014); Kohlbacher, *Streik*, p. 692.
41. *See* Rebhahn, in *ZellKomm*^{2} § 1151 ABGB Marginal No. 257.
42. Krejci, *Recht auf Streik*, p. 252.
43. Krejci, *Recht auf Streik*, p. 252.
44. Krejci, *Recht auf Streik*, p. 253.

matters is the potential fulfilment of the industrial action demand. However, it is unlawful and thus immoral under civil law if the strike objective does not affect the strikers.[45]

Public employees can also go on strike, and not only if the working conditions are regulated by collective agreements. Even in the case of statutory regulation of working conditions, as is the case with contractual public employees and civil servants in Austria, it must be possible for them to influence their working conditions through collective action as a consequence of the right of association. This is a conflict of interests inherent in the employment relationship and not a so-called political strike to enforce a generally applicable law. In such situations, the law also has the function of a collective agreement, and the idea of equal treatment argues for granting workers the same means of influencing their employers as in the case of a collective agreement.[46]

3.3 Essential Services in the Strict Sense of the Term

The question of whether a strike is proportionate is more difficult to assess, especially in the case of strikes in establishments providing essential services of general interest (e.g., hospitals). According to Krejci's correct view,[47] what is special in such cases is that the activity carried out is of particular importance for the general public. In this respect, the assessment of the permissibility of a strike action depends on weighing the importance of the activity for the community and the extent or intensity of the disruption of this activity by the strike. The more important the activity is for the community, the quicker the strike leads to the unacceptability of the interference in this activity, the quicker the disproportionality is reached. Krejci[48] therefore rightly points out that especially in the public service and the necessary provision of services of general interest, there are areas where even minor interference cannot be tolerated by the community. In such cases, even in the event of a strike, the necessary minimum level of service must be maintained, and the necessary emergency, maintenance and rescue work must be carried out. This applies in particular to hospitals, rescue services or the police.

It is rightly pointed out that the examination of the gross disproportion or the principle of proportionality can cause considerable difficulties in individual cases. In any case, it leaves the courts with a considerable margin of appreciation in the event of a dispute and thus makes their decisions difficult to predict, especially if one advocates a finer standard of review. This is further reinforced by the fact that there is virtually no case law on the issue of strikes in Austria. As Krejci pointedly puts it: 'You have to live with it.'[49]

---

45. Krejci, *Recht auf Streik*, p. 250; Elisabeth Brameshuber, *Rahmenbedingungen des Streikrechts*, ASoK 2023, p. 74 (2023).
46. Robert Rebhahn, *Der Arbeitskampf bei weitgehend gesetzlicher Regelung der Arbeitsbedingungen (Teil II)*, DRdA 2004, p. 503 (2004); Krejci, *Recht auf Streik*, pp. 242 et seq.
47. Krejci, *Recht auf Streik*, p. 250.
48. Krejci, *Recht auf Streik*, p. 250.
49. Krejci, *Recht auf Streik*, p. 255.

3.4 Situations of Acute National or Local Crisis

In this regard, reference can essentially be made to the explanations in section 2.3. In situations of acute national or local crisis, the proportionality test described above for workers who plan to go on strike but are indispensable for dealing with the crisis will regularly result in the inadmissibility of such industrial action. The test will also have to take into account whether the entire group of workers is really needed for the settlement of the crisis or whether a certain part of the group is still entitled to the right to strike. This will be difficult to assess in individual cases in such exceptional situations, and a legal regulation for such situations would be desirable.

4 COMPENSATORY GUARANTEES FOR WORKERS DEPRIVED OF THE RIGHT TO STRIKE

As already explained, there are hardly any provisions on the right to strike in Austrian law. The remarks on the permitted restrictions on the right to strike are therefore derived solely from the considerations of the academic literature and not from legal provisions. Consequently, there is even less in the literature on compensatory guarantees, as they exist in other countries, *inter alia*, through mediation-like procedures. It must therefore be stated that the Austrian legislator has not made any provisions for this case and that scholars in Austria have not yet approached the topic due to the lack of a starting point.

5 CONCLUSION

Within certain limits, strikes are not only legally permissible but also constitutionally protected, in particular by Article 11 ECHR that applies directly in Austria. This concerns both the organization of strikes and individual participation in strikes.

It is undisputed that the conclusion and amendment of collective agreements can be a permissible strike objective. If the working conditions are regulated by law, strikes can also be called for a corresponding amendment to the law since in this case the law fulfils the function of a collective agreement. Strike opponents can be all persons who can at least theoretically fulfil the strike objectives. Therefore, not only private but also public employers, in particular local authorities, can be the addressee of strike action. Accordingly, public servants also have the right to strike.

The right to strike is not unlimited though but must be weighed against other constitutionally protected rights, such as the right to property. However, it is not clear whether this is merely a question of gross disproportion or whether the general principle of proportionality should be applied.

In the case of strike action against establishments providing essential services of general interest, a finer examination must be carried out, as the interests of third parties and the general public must also be taken into account. Therefore, in a hospital, for example, an emergency operation will usually have to be set up also in the case of a strike.

The Austrian legislator has so far exercised extreme restraint in regulating the right to strike. At least in the case of an acute national or local crisis, a legal regulation seems to be welcome from a legal policy point of view. *De lege lata*, a proportionality test must also be applied here, weighing up the interests of the general public, whereby they must be given even greater emphasis in such crisis situations.

CHAPTER 5

Restrictions on the Right to Strike in Belgium

Wilfried Rauws

1 GENERAL INFORMATION

1.1 Legal Basis of the Right to Strike

In historical perspective, the right to collective action in the private branch of industry was derived by the Belgian Cour de cassation indirectly (*a contrario* reasoning) from the Belgian Essential Services Law of 19 August 1948.[1] The Law of 19 August 1948 does not apply to the public sector, so there was not yet a basis for the right of collective action for public sector workers accepted.

Afterwards, European legal sources came to the forefront.

Article 6(4) of the European Social Charter (further ESC) provides that the contracting parties recognize the right of workers and employers to take collective action in cases of conflicts of interest, including the right to strike, subject to obligations that might arise out of collective bargaining agreements previously enter to.

The annex of the ESC adds that each contracting party may itself regulate by law the right to strike, provided that any further restriction on this right is justified by the requirement that it is necessary in a democratic society for the protection of the rights and freedoms of others and for the protection of public order, national security, public health, or morality.[2]

1. Cass. 21 December 1981, *Rechtskundig Weekblad* (1981-1982), p. 2525 with opinion of Advocate-General Lenaerts, and case note M. Rigaux.
2. Article G; *infra* s. 2.3.2.

Following the Dutch Supreme Court's ('Hoge Raad') ruling of 30 May 1986, the so-called Dutch Railway ruling,[3] it was also fairly generally accepted in Belgium that Article 6(4) on the right to take collective action has a direct effect in the Belgian legal order. Since the European Social Charter was ratified by Belgium, Article 6(4) is then considered to be the basis of the right to strike in Belgium.[4] But recently the criminal division of the Cour de cassation re-opened the discussion over the self-executing character of Article 6 and ruled that Articles 6(4) and G of the European Social Charter are not sufficiently clear and precise to confer them direct effect. Accordingly, those provisions grant strikers no subjective right which they can invoke against the criminal punishments because of the malicious obstruction of traffic as punishable under Article 406 Penal Code.[5] The European Committee of Social Rights evaluated this criminal case law in its Report on Belgium, 'Conclusions 2022', and found that 'the situation in Belgium is in conformity with Article 6 (4) of the Charter'.[6] As regards the denial of the direct application of Article 6(4) ESH, it is important to note that a later cassation judgment of 12 December 2022 corrects its previous mistake that Article 6(4) would not have a direct effect. This decision of the Belgian Cour de cassation rules that the right to strike is based on Article 6(4) of the Revised European Social Charter of 3 May 1996, approved by the Law of 15 March 2002. In doing so, the court aligns itself with the opinion of Advocate-General H. Mormont, who clearly assumes that Article 6(4) has a direct effect in the Belgian legal order.[7]

Important in view of the legal protection afforded by the judgments of the European Court of Human Rights in Strasbourg is Article 11 of the European Convention on Human Rights. Several ECtHR judgments derive the right to collective action of employees from the private sector *and* public sector civil servant officials from the freedom of association and trade union. Taking union action is an inseparable part of the right to association.[8]

---

3. *Nederlandse Jurisprudentie* (1986), No. 226.
4. Appeal Labour Court Brussels, 5 November 2009, *Journal des tribunaux de travail* (2010), p. 139; p. 12; Council of State, *Sociaalrechtelijke Kronieken* (2014), p. 44.
5. Cass. 23 March 2022, P.21.1500.F, *Sociaalrechtelijke Kronieken* (2023), 1 with opinion Advocate-General Vandermeersch and case note; *see also* J. Clesse, 'Conflit collectif du travail et entrave méchante à la circulation', case note on Cass. 23 mars 2022, *Jurisprudence de Liège, Mons et Bruxelles* (2022), p. 1312; A. De Becker, 'De draagwijdte van de directe werking van artikel 6, lid 4 van het Europees Sociaal Handvest in rechtsvergelijkend perspectief', *Tijdschrift Sociaal Recht* (2022), pp. 503-525. Compare also on malicious obstruction of traffic Cour de cassation, 7 January 2020, *Rechtskundig Weekblad* (2020-2021), p. 1342, with opinion Advocate-General De Smet.
6. European Committee of Social Rights. Conclusions (2022), Belgium, pp. 31-32, https:rm.coe.int /conclusions-2022-belgium-e/1680aa9865.
7. Cass. 12 December 2022, *Jurisprudence de Liège, Mons et Bruxelles* (2023), p. 736, with the opinion of General-Advocate H. Mormont and case note M. Duchesne and J. Clesse, 'Grève: droit, faute et responsabilité d'autrui', *Rechtskundig Weekblad* (2023-2024), p. 1462, case note W. Rauws.
8. ECtHR 21 April 2009, No. 68959/01, *Enerji Yapi-Yol Sen/Turkey*; ECtHR 8 April 2014, No. 31045/10, *National Union of Rail, Maritime and Transport Workers v. UK;* ECtHR 20 November 2018, *Ognevenko v. Russia,* § 54, 55, 60, www.echr.coe.int.; Constitutional Court 15 July 2021, No. 107/2021, point 57.2; opinion of Advocate-General De Smet on the judgment of the Cour of cassation of 7 January 2020, *Rechtskundig Weekblad* (2020-2021), p. 1342; M. Merino, 'Le

In Belgium, the fundamental right to collective action is finally based on the general legal principles of European Union law.[9]

2 RESTRICTIONS TO THE RIGHT OF COLLECTIVE ACTION IN INTERNATIONAL LAW

2.1 UN Treaty on Economic, Cultural and Social Rights

International public law also recognizes the right to collective action. For example, Article 8 of the UN Covenant on Economic, Cultural and Social Rights of 19 December 1966, approved by the Law of 15 May 1981, imposes an obligation on the signatory states to guarantee the right to strike. This provision, which only contains obligations for the States Parties to the Convention, in the absence of lack of sufficient clarity and completeness, does not have a self-executing effect in the Belgian legal order nor private-law horizontal effect.[10]

No convention concluded in the lap of the International Labour Organization explicitly recognizes the right to collective action according to the UN Committee on Freedom of Association, the right to strike and to organize union meetings are essential aspects of trade union rights as protected by the ILO Convention No. 87 on the freedom of association.[11]

The ILO Convention No. 87 is particularly interesting with regard to the limitation of the right to collective action and, in particular, the limits of those limitations. For example, Article 9 of the ILO Convention No. 87 allows the police and armed forces to be completely excluded from the personal scope of the Convention. The ILO Convention No. 87 has no self-executing character.[12]

2.2 Monitoring by the UN Committee on the Freedom of Association

Compliance with the ILO Convention is monitored by a number of ILO monitoring bodies, such as the UN Committee on the Freedom of Association. The decisions of this committee have authoritative moral value but are not binding like the rulings of a law court.[13]

---

renforcement de la protection de la liberté syndicale par la Cour européenne des droits de l'homme', *Revue trimestrielle des droits de l'homme* (2007), pp. 463-492.

9. European Court of Justice (ECJ), No. C-341/05 *Laval*, point 91; Art. 28 EU Charter of Fundamental Rights.
10. Council of State, 30 December 1993, *Sociaalrechtelijke Kronieken* (1994), p. 244, case note J. Jacqmain; *see also* Cour de cassation 20 December 1990, *Pasicrisie* (1990), p. 392, No. 215; V. Vannes, *Le droit de grève. Concilier le droit de grève et les autres droits fondamentaux: recours au principe de proportionnalité?* Brussels, Larcier (2015), p. 187.
11. International Labour Office, *Compilation of Decisions of the Committee on Freedom of Association*, hereinafter '*ILO Digest 2018*', Geneva, 6th ed. (2018), p. 39, No. 204 and p. 143, No. 754.
12. V. Vannes, *Le droit de grève. Concilier le droit de grève et les autres droits fondamentaux: recours au principe de proportionnalité?* Brussels, Larcier (2015), p. 205.
13. J.M. Servais, *Droit international du travail*, Brussels, Larcier (2015), p. 71; L. Nissen, 'Stakingsrecht en minimumdienstverlening: waar liggen nu de grenzen?', in E. Alofs & G. Van Limberghen (eds), *Juridische Meesterwerken VUB 2018-2019*, Brussels, Intersentia (2021) pp. 265-266.

The UN Committee on the Freedom of Association considers restrictions on the right to strike legitimate in three cases:

(1) A general prohibition of strikes can only be justified in the event of an acute national emergency and for a limited period of time.[14]
(2) The right to strike may be restricted or prohibited in **the public service** only for public servants exercising authority in the name of the State, or in **essential services** in the strict sense of the term (*infra*).[15] Essential services whose interruption would endanger the life, personal safety or health of the whole or part of the population.[16]
(3) The right to collective action might be restricted, also in the private sector of industry, to guarantee 'essential services in the strict sense of the term, that is, services the interruption of which would endanger the life, personal safety or health of the whole or part of the population'.[17]

The following may be considered to be essential services:

- the police and the armed forces;
- the fire-fighting services;
- public or private prison services;[18]
- the hospital sector;
- air traffic control.[19]

In the opinion of the UN Committee on the Freedom of Association, rail services do not constitute essential services in the strict sense of the term.[20]

2.3 Permitted Restrictions

2.3.1 Possible Restrictions of the Right to Collective Action under the European Social Charter and the European Convention on Human Rights

2.3.1.1 Article 11(2) of the European Convention on Human Rights

From the standpoint of enforceable positive law, the limitation system of fundamental rights, and in particular the right of collective action, is more important. The limitation system is roughly the same for the limitation of the right to collective action derived

14. *ILO Digest 2018*, p. 154.
15. *ILO Digest 2018*, p. 154.
16. *ILO Digest 2018*, p. 156, No. 838.
17. *ILO Digest 2018*, pp. 154-155.
18. *ILO Digest 2018*, p. 156, No. 840.
19. *ILO Digest 2018*, pp. 156-157.
20. *ILO Digest 2018*, p. 158.

from Article 11 of the European Convention on Human Rights (further ECHR) on trade union freedom and Article 6(4) European Social Charter (further ESH).

Under Article 11(2) ECHR, the exercise of freedom of association, including trade union freedom, may not be subjected to any restrictions other than those prescribed by law and necessary in a democratic society in the interests of national security, public safety, the prevention of disorder or crime, for the protection of health or morals or the protection of the rights and freedoms of others.

2.3.2 Article G of the Revised European Social Charter (ESC)

Part V, Article G of the European Social Charter, Revised Version, provides that certain restrictions may be prescribed by law on the right to strike in order to collectively promote the interests of workers to the extent that such restrictions are necessary in a democratic society and are aimed at a legitimate objective, which is to protect the rights of freedoms of others or to protect public order, national security, public health or morals. The permissible limitations on fundamental social rights, elaborated in national law, may be applied only for the purpose for which they are intended.[21]

The European Social Charter does not require that the restrictions must necessarily be imposed solely through provisions of statutory law. Instead, case law of domestic courts can also comply with this requirement, provided that it is sufficiently stable and foreseeable to provide legal certainty for the parties concerned.[22]

According to the European Committee of Social Rights, the right to strike can be limited: 'However, a limitation of that right is possible only if it falls within the limits set by Article G, which provides that the limitations on the rights guaranteed by the Charter, if prescribed by law, pursue a legitimate aim and are necessary in a democratic society to ensure respect for the rights and freedoms of others or to protect public policy, national security, public health and morals.'[23] The European Committee of Social Rights gives a few examples. Excessive or abusive forms of collective action, such as extended blockades, which would put at risk the maintenance of public order or unduly limit the rights and freedoms of others (such as the right of other workers to work or the right of employers to engage in a gainful occupation) may be limited or prohibited by law.[24]

Most legal disputes occur in relation to striking posts. The striking workers who are part of a strike post have the right to peacefully call for solidarity from workers in order to participate in collective action. However, they may not use coercive means to

21. J. Peeters, 'Wegblokkades, grondrechten en de strafwet: een merkwaardige (én delicate) triade. Commentaar onder Antwerpen 28 oktober 2004', *Sociaalrechtelijke Kronieken* (2006), pp. 370-373; P. Pecinovsky, *EU Economic Governance and the Right to Collective Bargaining*, Bruges, Die Keure (2019) pp. 237-238.
22. ECSR 13 September 2011, *Belgian trade unions CGSLB, CSC and FGTB v. Belgium*, Complaint No. 59/2009, §§ 43-44; *Digest de jurisprudence du Comité européen des droits sociaux* (December 2018), p. 103; A. Koukiadaki, 'Restrictions Article G' in N. Bruun (ed.), *The European Social Charter and the Employment Relation*, Oxford and Portland, Bloomsbury (2017) p. 89.
23. *Digest de jurisprudence du Comité européen des droits sociaux* (2018), p. 103.
24. *Digest of the Case Law of the European Committee of Social Rights* (2022), p. 91.

block the company and prevent non-strikers from going to work. There is no obligation to strike. It is very difficult to take action against picket liners in court. The trade union that in practice usually organizes the collective action and the picket line cannot be summoned due to the lack of legal personality. Sometimes the identity of a blocking union leader or of some employees of the company can be determined, and they can be summoned in summary proceedings, for example. But such a judicial decision has only limited authority of res judicata and therefore only has effect with regard to the summoned activists. Usually, many unknown activists participate in the blocking picket line. The only way to take action against them is to initiate summary proceedings with a unilateral request. This procedure led to a lot of case law.[25] In 2011, the European Committee of Social Rights ruled that the Belgian case law of some interim injunctions judges, who prohibit blocking pickets on a unilateral application, violates the right to collective action guaranteed by Article 6(4) of the European Social Charter, first because Belgian case law on the matter is divided and therefore case law is not prescribed by law and second because the procedure for unilateral applications does not guarantee procedural fairness.[26] However, judicial law allows parties who are not involved in the summary proceedings based on a unilateral application to file a third-party objection with the court against the decision made on a unilateral application. Critics of the use of the unilateral application,[27] including the European Committee in its decision in 2011, wrongly lose sight of Article 6 of the European Convention of Human Rights, which guarantees the fundamental right of access to justice. The right of access to a court must be 'practical and effective'.[28] For the right of access to be effective, an individual must have a clear, practical opportunity to challenge an act that is an interference with his rights. Article 6 is applicable to interim proceedings, where the interim injunction is immediately enforceable.[29] The unilateral petition procedure against the non-peaceful protesters at the picket line is the only way to guarantee the fundamental right to access to justice, as it was often not possible to identify all the persons against whom the ban on blocking access to the company was imposed. The Court of Appeal of Ghent rightly legitimized in a recent injunction the summary proceedings on a unilateral application on the ground of access to justice in Article 6 ECHR against the unknown and unidentifiable occupiers of Ghent University who protested against Israel's war in Gaza.[30] The European Committee of Social Rights has not taken into account in its decision of 13 September 2011 the meaning of Article 6

25. *See* recently *See* W. Van Eeckhoutte, *Sociaal Compendium Arbeidsrecht 2023-24*, Mechelen, Wolters Kluwer (2023), pp. 2229-2230. *See* more over: Summary Proceedings Court Brussels, 17 October 2013, *Sociaalrechtelijke Kronieken* (2014), p. 28, case note situerende noot I. Van Hiel; 'Summary Proceedings Court East Flanders Court', *Rechtspraak Antwerpen Brussel Gent* (14 June 2023), p. 1467; 'Summary Proceedings Court Brussels', *Rechtspraak Antwerpen Brussel Gent* (19 April 2023), p. 1472, case note B. Lietaert.
26. ECSR, 13 September 2011 No. 59/2009, *Sociaalrechtelijke Kronieken* (2014), p. 10.
27. For instance, F. Dorssemont, 'Collectieve conflicten', *Nieuw Juridisch Weekblad* (2024), pp. 300-306.
28. ECtHR, 4 December 1995, No. 23805/94, *Bellet v. France*, § 38.
29. ECtHR, 29 March 2011, *RTBF v. Belgium*, §§ 64-65, in Council of Europe, *Guide on Article 6 of the European Convention on Human Rights Right to a fair trial (civil limb)*, 2017, p. 14.
30. Court of Appeal Ghent, 13 June 2024, No. 2024/EV/17, *Universiteit Gent v. unknown*, pp. 14-15.

ECHR in its evaluation of Article 6(4) ESC in Belgium and thus neglected that there was a problem of conflict of fundamental rights. It is noteworthy that the European Committee on Social Rights concluded in its last report 'Conclusions 2022 Belgium' 'that the situation in Belgium is in conformity with Article 6 (4) of the Charter', notwithstanding the lament of the Belgian trade unions that the practice of unilateral applications is less frequent but is still used.[31]

3 THE MARGIN OF APPRECIATION OF THE DOMESTIC AUTHORITIES

The ECtHR ruled that the domestic authorities and the domestic courts have a wide margin of appreciation to justify the restrictions of fundamental rights in the context of industrial and economic policies of the State.[32]

It is useful to note that compliance with the ESC at European level is verified by the European Committee of Social Rights (ECSR). The ECSR does not possess judicial or quasi-judicial status. The 'decisions' of this committee of experts are not legally binding but are particularly authoritative because they are given by a particular qualified body.[33] This becomes clear in a recent ruling of the European Court of Human Rights in the German Humpert case on the ban of all strikes of civil servants in Germany. The ECSR repeatedly found the prohibition of strikes by all civil servants in Germany not to be in conformity with Article 6(4) of the European Social Charter.[34] Nevertheless, the ECtHR judged that the prohibition of strikes for civil servants, as it results from the German Grundgesetz, does not violate the guaranteed right to strike based on Article 11 of the ECHR on trade union freedom as interpreted by the ECtHR on 21 April 2009 in the famous *Enerji Yapi-Yol Sen/Turkey* case.[35]

Also, the ECSR accepts that the Contracting States have a margin of appreciation to justify restrictions on Charter rights, such as upon the right to strike.[36]

4 LIMITATIONS ON THE RIGHT OF COLLECTIVE ACTION IN BELGIAN LABOUR LAW IN A NUTSHELL

Restrictions on the right of collective action arise under Belgian Law on the following grounds:[37]

31. European Committee of Social Rights. Conclusions (2022), Belgium, p. 32, https:rm.coe.int/conclusions-2022-belgium-e/1680aa9865.
32. ECtHR, 8 April 2014, *RMT v. UK*, §§ 86-88 on the prohibition of solidarity (sympathy) strikes under UK law; ECtHR (Grand Chamber), 9 July 2013, *Sindicatul Pastorul cel Bun v. Romania*, §133.
33. ECtHR, 8 April 2014, *RMT v. UK*, §94, *Labour Law Reports* 2014/128; Y. Donders, 'Europa's voorvechter van economische en sociale Rechten', *Ars Aequi* (2014), pp. 253-261.
34. ECtHR, 14 December 2023, No. 59433/18, *Humpert and others v. Germany*.
35. ECtHR 21 April 2009, No. 68959/01, *Enerji Yapi-Yol Sen/Turkey, supra* n. 8.
36. ECSR 9 September 2009, *CFDT v. France*, Complaint No. 50/2008, §39; ECSR 2 December 2013, Complaint 83/2012; A. Koukiadaki, 'Restrictions Article G' in N. Bruun (ed.), *The European Social Charter and the Employment Relation*, Oxford and Portland, Bloomsbury (2017) pp. 94-97.
37. *See* W. Van Eeckhoutte, *Sociaal Compendium Arbeidsrecht 2023-24*, Mechelen, Wolters Kluwer (2023), pp. 2203-2205, 2211-2217, 2220-2225.

(1) Relevant mandatory or normative provisions in collective bargaining agreements, at least in the private sector (Article 6(4) ESC). It follows from the finality of the right to negotiate collective bargaining agreements that purely political strikes by workers and their unions are not permissible and fall out of the scope of Article 6.[38]
(2) The general legal principle of the prohibition of the abuse of rights.[39]
(3) According to the *Viking* and *Laval* rulings of the ECJ, a restriction on the free movement of services or the right to establishment can be accepted only if justified by overriding reasons of public interest and if it is proportional; that is, the measure is suitable for securing the attainment of the objective pursued and must not go beyond what is necessary in order to attain it. The cross-border collective actions are subject to the proportionality test, subjecting the right to strike to the restrictions on the free movement of services and freedom of establishment within the European Union.[40]
(4) Certain forms of collective action such as malicious obstruction of traffic that make the use of means of transport dangerous or can cause accidents are punishable (Article 406 Criminal Code). Other examples of forms of collective action that are legally subject to the limitations in criminal law are theft, illegal possession of a weapon, arson or hostage taking.[41]
(5) Collective conflicts can have very detrimental effects on the public interest, for example, when they would cause damage to the production apparatus or supply, endanger public health or public safety. A legal system was therefore

38. Appeal Court Mons, 5 February 2014, *Sociaalrechtelijke Kronieken* (2014), p. 23. The European Social Rights Committee also decided political strikes fall outside the scope of Art. 6 ESC, *Conclusions*, II, 1971, Council of Europe Press (1995), p. 27.
39. Belgian Constitutional Court 26 July 2017, No. 101/2017, Regarding minimum services at the Belgian Railways, point B.23.6, https://www.const-court.be/public/n/2017/2017-101n.pdf; Belgian Constitutional Court 18 May 2017, No. 64/2017, point B.29.6; Council of State 5 February 2009, No. 190.223, *Mortier v. TEC*, https://www.raadvst-consetat.be/Arrets/190000/200/190223.pdf#xml = http://www.raadvst-consetat.be/apps/dtsearch/getpdf.asp?DocId = 13655&Index = c%3a%5csoftware%5cdtsearch%5cindex%5carrets%5ffr%5c&HitCount = 2&hits = a7a + a80 + &0856482025215; Ph. Gosseries, 'Confrontation des droits de propriété et d'entreprise au droit de travail y compris de grève', in Ph. Gosseries en M. Morsa (ed.), *L'humanisme juridique*, Brussels, Larcier (2013), p. 50 e.v.; W. Van Eeckhoutte, 2019, *Sociaal Compendium Arbeidsrecht 2023-2024*, Mechelen, Wolters Kluwer (2023), pp. 2214-2015, No. 3919.
40. ECJ 18 December 2007, No. C-341/05, *Laval;* ECJ 1 December 2007, No. C-438/05 *Viking;* V. Skouris, 'Das Verhältnis der Grundfreiheiten zu den Gemeinschaftsgrundrechten', *Recht der Arbeit* (2009) (Beilage), pp. 25-30; J. Malmberg, *The Impact of the ECJ Judgements on Viking, Laval, Rüffert and Luxemburg on the Practice of Collective Bargaining and the Effectiveness of Social Action*, European Parliament, Brussels (2010), p. 6, https://www.europarl.europa.eu/RegData/etudes/etudes/join/2010/440275/IPOL-EMPL_ET(2010)440275_EN.pdf; Constitutional Court, 26 July 2017, No. 101/2017, points B.23.5.1-B.23.5.2; Constitutional Court 15 July 2021, No. 107/2021, point B.57.2.
41. *See* Cour de cassation, 7 January 2020, *Rechtskundig Weekblad* (2020-2021), p. 1342, with opinion Advocate-General De Smet; read also A. De Becker, 'De draagwijdte van de directe werking van artikel 6, lid 4 van het Europees Sociaal Handvest in rechtsvergelijkend perspectief', *Tijdschrift Sociaal Recht* (2022) pp. 503-525.
European Committee of Social Rights. Conclusions (2022), Belgium, p. 32, https:rm.coe.int/conclusions-2022-belgium-e/1680aa9865.

devised which, in the event of a strike or lockout, ensures essential services. When it comes to the public sector in particular, the accent is placed on a certain form of 'minimum service' or 'continuity of public service'.

The remainder of this chapter will focus exclusively on the limitations on workers' and employers' right of collective action from the last point of the guarantee of essential services in Belgium.

5 LAW OF 19 AUGUST 1948 RELATING TO ESSENTIAL SERVICES (ESSENTIAL SERVICES LAW) IN THE PRIVATE SECTOR

5.1 General

Shortly after World War II, the Belgian legislator realized that certain activities were of such general interest that they could not be unconditionally and suddenly halted, but without the intention of fundamentally affecting the right to strike. The starting point of the Essential Services Law of 19 August 1948 is that the social partners should jointly agree on the extent to which the right to take collective action should be restricted in order to safeguard the general interest.[42]

5.2 Scope

From the fact that the Essential Services Law relies essentially on the functioning of joint committees, it may be inferred that the law applies only to the private sector. The personal scope of this Essential Services Law completely coincides with that of the Collective Bargaining Agreement Law of 5 December 1968. As a result, the Essential Services Law applies only to the private sector. Public employers are as a rule, with a few exceptions, excluded from the scope of the CBA Law and thus also from the Essential Services. Therefore, not only civil servants but also employees with employment contracts with the public law employer fall outside the personal scope of the Essential Services Law.

Thus, although the law does not apply to the public sector, the federal government had applied the Essential Services Law in respect of public services:[43]

- On 13 May 1975, the Minister of Transport 'requisitioned' the pilotage staff of the maritime and inland ports.
- On 22 December 1982, the Minister of Economic Affairs did the same with the personnel of the installations of the port services in Antwerp.
- On 27 January 1988, the Minister of Transport imposed the personnel in charge of the traffic control services to perform their work.

42. Memory of Understanding, *Parliamentary Documents*, Chamber of Representatives (1947-1948), pp. 1-2, No. 414.
43. W. Van Eeckhoutte, *Sociaal Compendium Arbeidsrecht 2023-24*, Wolters Kluwer (2023), p. 2114, No. 3930.

However, the latter Ministerial Decree was annulled by the Council of State on the grounds that the Essential Services Law only covers strikes and lockouts in the private sector and not in the public sector.[44]

5.3 Description of the Essential Services

The sectoral social partners have a central role in the Essential Services Law. They should first of all identify vital needs in the joint committees, and then define public interest and minimum services. Joint committees' decisions can be declared generally binding by royal decree. The decision of the joint committee, defining the services of general interest and vital needs, becomes enforceable only through the declaration of universal applicability by royal decree.[45] In derogation from Article 47 of the Collective Bargaining Agreement Law of 5 December 1968, general principle, the joint committees' decisions can be given legal force if they obtained at least 75 % of the votes of each party labour and capital in the joint committee.

Such royal decrees were issued in the following sectors:[46]

- Royal Decree of 29 January 1949, *Moniteur belge* of 30 January 1949, on the generation, distribution and consumption of electricity.
- Royal Decree of 29 January 1949, *Moniteur belge* of 30 January 1949 on the production, distribution and consumption of gas.
- Royal Decree of 31 December 1960, *Moniteur belge* of 2 January 1961 on the collection of household waste.
- Royal Decree of 12 April 1964, *Moniteur belge* of 12 April 1964 on medical care.
- Royal Decree of 23 June 1995, *Moniteur belge* of 1 August 1995 regarding the petroleum sector.
- Royal Decree of 13 June 1999, *Moniteur belge* of 9 December 1999 regarding the hotel sector.
- Royal Decree of 21 June 1999, *Moniteur belge* of 9 December 1999, regarding the educational and housing establishments of the Flemish Community.
- Royal Decree of 21 June 1999, *Moniteur belge* of 9 December 1999 regarding the educational and accommodation establishments of the French Community.
- Royal Decree of 10 September 2010, *Moniteur belge* of 11 October 2010 on the health establishments and services.

It is generally assumed that the decisions taken by the Belgian joint committees are in line with the decisions of the ILO supervisory bodies.[47]

44. Council of State 28 February 1990, *Sociaalrechtelijke Kronieken* (1990), p. 343, No. 34.252, case note V. Pertry.
45. Articles 1 and 2 Essential Services Law.
46. *See* W. Van Eeckhoutte, *Sociaal Compendium Arbeidsrecht 2024-25*, Wolters Kluwer (2024), p. 2262, No. 4011.
47. C. Deneve, 'Staking en IAO-normen en: rechtspraak', in M. Rigaux & F. Dossemont (eds) *Vitale behoeften, essentiële diensten, minimumprestaties en stakingsrecht. Naar een amendering van de Prestatiewet?*, Antwerp, Intersentia (2003), pp. 79-80; *supra* n. 3.

5.4 Deprivation of a Decision of the Joint Committee[48]

When a joint committee has not made the decisions, it may, if it appears necessary, be requested by the federal Minister of Labour to determine the vital needs, as well as the measures and services which must be ensured.

If the joint committee has not so determined within six months of the request to the committee by the federal Minister of Labour or because it has neglected to take a decision, or because the committee has not been able to reach the required quorum of 75% to take a decision, the King himself shall determine the vital needs, as well as the goods, measures, or services. The same applies when there is no joint committee.[49]

5.5 Designation of Employees for the Performances of the Essential Services[50]

After the essential services have been determined in the case of a strike, the important question arises as to which workers are to perform those services. The first hypothesis is that there are work-ready workers. Workers and employers decide after mutual consultation which workers will have to ensure the vital goods and services.

Where there are work willing workers, in particular workers employed in the enterprise concerned, the employer shall be obliged to cooperate with these workers to ensure the provision of services of general interest.

Another situation arises in case of default of an agreement. In the absence of agreement between employers and employees, a restricted select committee of the joint committee is authorized to designate the employees in the undertakings which are indispensable to perform the essential services of general interest. According to the Essential Services Law, the joint committees may indeed delegate certain members in a joint subcommittee, which has the authority to designate the employees in the enterprises who are needed in order to ensure the essential services.

If the select committee is not composed or has not appointed those employees, the latter shall be designated by the Minister of Labour or by the Minister of Economy.

5.6 Effects of the Performance of Employees of the Essential Services[51]

The performance of the essential services of general interest does not alter either the nature or the terms of the employment contract between the employer and the employee. Except with a dismissal permission granted by a restricted select committee of the joint committee or, in its absence, by the Minister of Labour, current employment contracts may not be terminated, and the notice periods are suspended for the duration of the essential services.

48. Article 2bis Essential Services Law.
49. Article 2bis Essential Services Law.
50. Article 3 Essential Services Law.
51. Article 6 Essential Services Law.

5.7 Sanctions

Violations of the provisions of the Essential Services Law and its implementing decrees are established and punished in accordance with the Social Criminal Code of 6 June 2010, as amended by the Law of 15 May 2024.[52]

With a Level 3 sanction, the employers and/or the employees are punished who, in violation of the Essential Services Law:

- refuse to carry out, or cause to be carried out, the measures, performances or services to be secured in the event of a strike or lockout in order to cope with certain vital needs and essential services;
- refuse to carry out some urgent work on machinery or equipment or to complete some tasks required by a case of force majeure or unforeseen necessity (Article 207 Social Criminal Code).

The penal sanctions of Level 3 consist of administrative fines between EUR 100 and 1,000 or a criminal fine between EUR 200 and 2,000, whereas all these fines have to be multiplied with legal surcharges, currently standing at eight.

The employer who knowingly and intentionally refuses the joint committees any information necessary for the preparation, implementation and monitoring of the above measures or knowingly provides them with false information is also punishable by a Level 3 sanction.[53]

6 RESTRICTIONS OF THE RIGHT TO COLLECTIVE ACTION IN THE PUBLIC SECTOR

6.1 Missing of a Legal General Safeguard of Essential Services in the Public Sector

In Belgian public law, the right of civil servants to strike is currently recognized indirectly by Article 18 of the Royal Decree of 22 December 2000, regulating the general legal principles for the staff of the Communities and Regions. This article provides that the civil servants' participation in the strike can only result in the loss of their salary. At the European level, the right to collective action is grounded upon Article 11 ECHR (*supra* No. 1). Article 6 of the ESC is mute relating to the right to strike of civil servants.[54] The ECSR seems nevertheless to accept in principle the right to strike of civil servants. So, the Committee of Social Rights considered that a strike ban in sectors such as public administration ('internal affairs'), state security sectors and national defence could serve a legitimate purpose since work stoppages in these sectors could pose threats to public order and national security. However, simply

52. Article 7 Essential Services Law.
53. Article 208 Social Criminal Code. *See also* Art. 101 Social Criminal Code.
54. F. Dorssemont, 'The Right to bargain Collectively', in N. Bruun (ed.), *The European Social Charter and the Employment Relation*, Oxford and Portland, Bloomsbury (2017), p. 270.

prohibiting all employees in the aforementioned sectors from striking, without any distinction as to function, could not be considered proportionate.[55]

It should also be noted that striking is a fundamental right, but this does not mean that this right is absolute, nor that no restrictions are possible, as it appears in Article 6(4) and Article G of the Revised European Social Charter of 3 May 1996. Article G of this convention allows for legal restrictions, among other things, to protect the rights and freedoms of 'others'. Importantly, a recent case law of the European Court of Human Rights, which rules on the limitations of the right to strike derived from the trade union freedom enshrined in Article 11 ECHR, grants a wide autonomous margin of appreciation when imposing restrictions on States Parties, e.g., with regard to the domestic banning of sympathy strikes.[56]

Unlike for the private sector, there is no general law to safeguarding the essential services of general interest in the public sector.[57] The question was then raised as to whether a modern application of the 'principle of continuity of public service' from the administrative law could provide practical relief as a basis for ensuring minimum service in the event of a strike in public law entities. This question was rightly answered in the affirmative, but the basis proved too vague to achieve an effective safeguarding of essential services in the public sector.[58]

However, in some public companies or public services, there are voluntary strike protocols concluded between the trade unions and the government that may impose a binding limitation on the right to strike of the public servants concerned to the extent that such strike protocols are included in the administrative personnel statute.[59]

The fact that the previous federal government planned in 2014 some important guaranteed service, which should be considered a synonym for guaranteed minimum service, relating to parts of the public sector is by no means a coincidence since the Essential Services Law of 19 August 1948 safeguarding vital needs applies only to the private sector.[60] Enforced restrictions on the right to strike therefore had until recently no legal basis in Belgium. Earlier legislative proposals to create similar legislation have been tabled but were not accepted.[61] Minimal service legislation exists in countries such as France and Germany.[62]

---

55. ECSR, December 2010, Conclusions 2010 Moldova, https://www.ohchr.org/sites/default/files/lib-docs/HRBodies/UPR/Documents/session12.
56. ECHR 8 April 2014, No. 31045/10, *RMT v. U.K.*, *Labour Law Reports* 2014/128; *supra* n. 6.
57. L. Nissen, 'Stakingsrecht en minimumdienstverlening: waar liggen de grenzen', in E. Alofs & G. Van Limberghen (eds), *Juridische Meesterwerken VUB 2018-2019*, Brussels, Intersentia (2021), p. 285.
58. A. De Becker, *De overheid en haar personeel. Juridische grondslagen van de grondslagen van de ambtenaar*, Brugge, Die Keure (2007), pp. 573-575.
59. *See, e.g.*, for the railways, Council of State 6 November 2012, No. 221.273, *Ivens v. SNCB*.
60. Coalition agreement Government Michel 2014, https://emnbelgium.be/sites/default/files/attachments/4793_regeerakkoord_federale_regering_2015_2019.pdf; *supra* n. 9.
61. *See* Bellot Proposition, *Parl. Documents*, Senate (2010-2011), No. 5-422/1; *see also* the Vastersavendts Report, *Parl. Documents*, Senate (2013-2014), No. 5-422/4, p. 2 and No. 5-422/5, p. 2.
62. L. Nissen, 'Stakingsrecht en minimumdienstverlening: waar liggen de grenzen', *supra* n. 13, pp. 286-287.

    More rigorous restrictions in Germany where there is a constitutional ban on strikes for civil servants: Bundesverfassungsgericht 12 June 2018, 2 BvR 1738/12, 2 BvR 646/15, 2 BvR 1068/14, 2 BvR 1395/13, https://www.bundesverfassungsgericht.de/SharedDocs/Entscheidu

In an important advisory opinion on a proposal of law of the liberal party of December 2003 to guarantee a minimum service in the context of public services of general interest, the Legislative Section of the Council of State addresses the issue of a minimum service with reference to the International Labour Organization (ILO).[63] According to the monitoring bodies within the ILO, the right to strike in the ILO Convention No. 87, 'essential services' can justify the restrictions on the right to strike. They define those services restrictively: They are those 'dont l'interruption mettrait en danger, dans l'ensemble ou dans une partie de la population, la vie, la sécurité ou la santé de la personne'. According to the Council of State, the right to strike may also be limited for services that are **not** strictly speaking essential when strikes of any size and duration are likely to cause an acute crisis threatening the normal living conditions of the population.[64] The Council of State noted that in guaranteeing minimum services, the proposed bill went beyond those related to vital needs within the meaning of the Law of 19 August 1948. The ILO Trade Union Freedom Committee ruled that the scope of minimum services should be determined with the participation of workers' and employers' organizations.[65]

The conclusion is relatively straightforward: Legislation on guaranteed minimum services in the public sector seems to be compatible with the right to strike insofar as the guarantee is limited to essential services by analogy with the 1948 Essential Services Law, with Belgian domestic authorities having a wide margin of appreciation of its own.[66]

For army and police personnel, statutory restrictions on their right to collective action (*infra*) had long existed. But for other public sector personnel, any legal safety for essential services net was lacking. In the coalition agreement of 9 October 2014, the previous federal government planned to establish guaranteed service in a number of very important public services, notably in the prison system, the railways and the air navigation service Belgocontrol, in each case after and in consultation with the social partners (*infra*).

6.2 Far-Reaching Legal Ban on Strikes for Military and Police Officers

There is an absolute ban on strikes for military personnel of the Belgian army and members of the secret services.[67] In Belgium, staff members of the police may unite in trade unions in order to negotiate collectively.[68]

ngen/EN/2018/06/rs20180612_2bvr173812en.html. W. Linsenmaier, 'Artikel 9 Grunggesetz Vereinigungsfreiheit', *Erfurter Kommmentar zum Arbeitsrecht*, Munich, Beck (2017), pp. 125-126.

63. *Parl. Documents*, Chamber of Representatives (2003-2004), p. 5, No. 51-604/3.
64. *Parl. Documents*, Chamber of Representatives (2003-2004), p. 5, No. 51-604/3.
65. ILO, *Recueil des principes du Comité de la liberté syndical du BIT*, Geneva (1996), § 560.
66. W. Rauws, 'Gegarandeerde dienstverlening en het stakingsrecht', *Rechtskundig Weekblad* (2014-2015), p. 1642.
67. Article of the 175 Law 28 February 2007 on the legal status of army service men; Art. 17 of the Law of 17 March 2004 on the personnel of the State Security.
68. *See* L. Nissen, 'Stakingsrecht en minimumdienstverlening: waar liggen de grenzen', *supra* n. 13, p. 287.

Members of the police are not subject to an absolute ban on strikes but to a conditional right to strike. Article 126 of the Integrated Police Law of 7 December 1989 provides that the exercise of the right to strike by federal and local police officers is subject to the following conditions:

(1) 12 days' prior notice of the strike by a recognized trade union organization.
(2) The prior discussion with the competent authority of the matter on the occasion of which the strike is contemplated in the Police Services Negotiating Committee.

Taking into account Article 9 of the ILO Convention No. 87, limitations on the armed forces' right to strike are not problematic.[69] Moreover, since the monitoring bodies consider the police and army to be essential services, a blanket ban or minimum service provision does not seem problematic in the light of ILO conventions.[70]

At the European level, the ECSR is more critical of an absolute ban on the right to strike for military and police officers.[71] But more important is that the ECtHR is less critical in the way that it recently ruled that the margin of appreciation afforded to the State will be wide if a substantial restriction on the right to strike concerns civil servants exercising public authority in the name of the State, such as members of the police force.[72]

6.3 Semi-continuity of Passenger Public Transport Services

Railway staff are among those most likely to revert to the strike weapon, leading to a political drive for minimum service on a voluntary basis.

This drive led to statutory interference with the right to strike in public transport:

- The Federal Law of 23 July 1926 concerning SNCB and the staff of the Belgian Railways, as amended by the Law of 29 November 2017 on the continuity of service for rail passenger transport services in the event of a strike.
- The Decree of 31 July 1990 of the Flemisch Region on the public law externally autonomous agency 'Vlaamse Vervoermaatschappij – De Lijn' as amended by the Decree of the Flemish Region of 28 May 2021 regarding the continuity of services in case of strike.
- The Decree of 26 October 2017 of the Walloon Region on the minimum services for public transport by the 'TEC'.

6.4 The Federal Railway Personnel Law of 29 November 2017

This law regulates the continuity of rail passenger transport services in the event of a strike based on available personnel. The law does not question the right to strike but

69. *Supra* n. 2.
70. *Supra* n. 3.
71. *Supra* n. 15; ECSR 12 December 2017, Complaint 112/2014, *EUROMIL v. Ireland*.
72. ECtHR 14 December 2023, No. 59433/18, *Humpert and others v. Germany*, § 112.

aims to provide a minimum service with adapted transport supply, organized on the basis of the non-striking staff. Thus, the law does **not** provide for a requisitioning of staff members to ensure minimum service. The minimum service provision therefore has no binding character. Therefore, the amending law introduces a minimum service sui generis. By appealing to staff not participating in the strike, an adapted transport offer can possibly be organized. The aim is to protect everyone's freedom to travel without restrictions, including to work or school, as well as the right of free movement of persons.[73]

That law stipulates that a minimum period of eight working days must be respected between the submission of the strike notice and the start of the strike.[74] An adapted transport offer according to one of the transport plans will be provided only if there are sufficient personnel in the essential professional categories available.

Unless there is a duly proven valid reason, railway personnel in the essential job categories must, no later than 72 hours before the start of the strike day, communicate their final intention of whether or not participating in the strike day.[75] The legislator therefore does not start from basic needs or essential services but rather from essential professional categories.[76] Staff members who fail to declare their intention or who fail to honour their intention not to participate in the strike expose themselves to disciplinary sanctions.

Finally, Article 4(5) of the amending Law of 29 November 2017 stipulates importantly that the striking staff must refrain from taking any measures that impede the provision of transport services. Specifically, they must not block access to the workplace for staff members wishing to work, nor shall they use physical, trains, for example, or material force of any kind whatsoever, against them or the users, nor use the work equipment and the infrastructure. The prohibition contained in the law prevents the striking railway workers not to organize peaceful pickets in order to protect the other to convince workers to join the ongoing strike action.[77]

The aforementioned law aims to protect the rights of railway users, at least at a minimum level. With regard to the Railway Law, the Constitutional Court ruled that the measures it contains in that regard are relevant and proportionate in relation to the objective pursued and, in particular, considered individually or together, do not affect

73. Memory of Understanding, *Parl. Documents*, Chamber of Representatives (2017-2018), No. 2650/001, pp. 7-9.
74. Article 2 of the Law of 29 November 2017.
75. Article 4 of the Law of 29 November 2017.
76. *See* L. Nissen, 'Stakingsrecht en minimumdienstverlening: waar liggen de grenzen', *supra* n. 13, p. 291.
77. Belgian Constitutional Court 26 July 2017, No. 101/2017, Regarding minimum services at the Belgian Railways, point B.23.6, https://www.const-court.be/public/n/2017/2017-101n.pdf; Council of State 5 February 2009, No. 190.223, Mortier *v. TEC*, https://www.raadvst-consetat.be/Arrets/190000/200/190223.pdf#xml=http://www.raadvst-consetat.be/apps/dtsearch/getpdf.asp?DocId=13655&Index=c%3a%5csoftware%5cdtsearch%5cindex%5carrets%5ffr%5c&HitCount=2&hits=a7a+a80+&0856482025215; Ph. Gosseries, 'Confrontation des droits de propriété et d'entreprise au droit de travail y compris de grève', in Ph. Gosseries & M. Morsa (eds), *L'humanisme juridique*, Brussels, Larcier (2013), p. 50 e.v.; W. Van Eeckhoutte, 2019, *Sociaal Compendium Arbeidsrecht 2023-2024*, Mechelen, Wolters Kluwer (2023), p. 2213, No. 3917.

the core of trade union freedom or the right to collective bargaining and is therefore not infringing Article 11(2) ECHR nor Article G Revised ESC.[78] Moreover, the European Committee of Social Rights concluded in its report 'Conclusions 2022 Belgium' that also the Law of 29 November 2017 'is in conformity with Article 6 (4) of the Charter'.[79]

The government also considered, and rightly so, that the judgments of the ILO supervisory bodies should not be tested since the legislature does not organize a real mandatory minimum service provision.[80]

Be that as it may, the new law has actually increased a minimum service supply of transport in case of rail strikes.

6.5 The Decree of the Flemish Region of 28 May 2021 Regarding the Continuity of Services in Case of Strike in the Flemish Regional Public Transport

This Decree amends an earlier Decree on regional public transport and mirrors more or less the rules of the Federal Railway Personnel Law.[81]

The Decree imposes on strikes, initiated under the procedure of notice following social conflicts in accordance with collective bargaining agreements, a minimum waiting period of eight working days between the submission of the strike notice and the start of the strike.[82]

Unless there is a duly proven valid reason, staff members of professional categories essential to public transport shall give final notice of their participation in the strike day no later than 72 hours before the start of the strike day. Staff members of the Flemish public transport Company 'De Lijn' who fail to declare their intention on whether or not to participate in the strike or who fail to honour their intention not to participate in the strike expose themselves to disciplinary sanctions.[83]

Finally, as in the mentioned Federal Rail Traffic Law, the amending Decree prohibits:

(1) staff members of 'De Lijn' to block access to the workplace for staff members who want to work;
(2) to use physical or material violence of any kind against the staff members who want to work or against the users;
(3) in addition, the striking employees may not prevent the use of the work equipment and infrastructure.

78. Constitutional Court 14 May 2020, *Rechtskundig Weekblad* (2021-2022), p. 581, No. 67/2020.
79. European Committee of Social Rights, Conclusions (2022), Belgium, p. 32, https:rm.coe.int/conclusions-2022-belgium-e/1680aa9865.
80. Memory of Understanding, *Parl. Documents*, Chamber of Representatives (2017-2018), p. 11, No. 2650/001; *see* L. Nissen, 'Stakingsrecht en minimumdienstverlening: waar liggen de grenzen', *supra* n. 13, p. 291; *see also* F. Lievens, 'De la cogestion au "service minimum": un siècle de concertation sociale au sein des chemins de fer belges', *Tijdschrift Sociaal Recht* (2019), pp. 213-263.
81. *Supra* n. 17.
82. Article 3 of the amending Decree of 28 May 2021.
83. Article 4 of the Decree of 28 May 2021.

The amending Decree does not prevent the striking workers from organizing peaceful strike action to persuade other workers to join the ongoing strike action.[84]

On entirely analogous grounds to the judgment 67/2020 on the railway transport, the Constitutional Court dismissed, as one could expected, the unions' annulation appeal against the Flemish Decree of 28 May 2021. The constitutional dispute over competence between the federal government and the Regions is not relevant here.[85]

6.6 The Decree of the Walloon Region on Public Transport

The first modest push for a minimum service at the Walloon public transport company TEC to introduce a minimum service for the buses and trams was made with the Walloon Decree of 26 October 2017, which amends the Decree of 21 December 1989 on the public passenger transport service in the Walloon Region, with a view to guaranteeing the continuity of the public service within the TEC. Article 1 of the Decree stipulates that the next management agreement between the Walloon Government and the TEC must include modalities to ensure continuity of the public transport service.

Article 32 of the Agreement 'Contrat de service public entre la Wallonie et l'Opérateur de Transport de Wallonie 2019-2023' of 31 January 2019 stipulates that in the event of a strike action resulting in the interruption of service, the TEC shall undertake to give priority to the allocation of available staff in order to ensure continuity of public service on as many essential lines as possible according to pre-established priorities.[86]

6.7 Continuity of Penitentiary Services During a Strike

The functioning of the prison system in Belgium has been more than problematic for many years due to prisoner overcrowding and the shortage of warders. Moreover, prison staff have been on frequent strikes for a long time. This also compromised the fundamental rights of prisoners in terms of food distribution, hygiene and the right to legal aid. When prison guards go on strike, the police force and sometimes the army were and still are called in to take over the duties of prison staff during strikes, but this is, according to Parliament, clearly no longer of this time. Indeed, guarding and supervising detainees within a prison environment is not part of their normal duties, and consequently the rights of detainees are severely affected during periods of social conflict. Indirectly, this also disservices public security since these police officers cannot be deployed on their normal police assignments.[87] The European Committee for the Prevention of Torture and Inhuman or Degrading Treatment or Punishment of the

84. Constitutional Court, 17 May 2023, No. 78/2023, point B.60, https://www.const-court.be/public/n/2023/2023-078n.pdf.
85. Read Constitutional Court, 17 May 2023, No. 78/2023, point B.7-B.18.
86. L. Nissen, 'Stakingsrecht en minimumdienstverlening: waar liggen de grenzen', *supra* n. 13, pp. 293-294.
87. Memory of Understanding, *Parl. Documents*, Chamber of Representatives (2018-2019), No. 54-3351/001, p. 14.

Council of Europe did not notice during the seventh visit of the Belgian prisons from 27 March 2017 to 6 April 2017 any concrete progress towards the establishment of a viable system enabling prisoners' basic rights to be respected in all circumstances, particularly in the context of the many collective actions led by prison staff.[88] In a public statement on 13 July 2017, the CPT even advised the Belgian government to enact the necessary legislation on guaranteed service in the event of a strike.[89]

On 28 May 2019, the ECtHR condemned Belgium for the infringement of Article 3 of the ECHR on inhuman or degrading treatment in the Belgian prisons because of the consequences of strike of the warders.[90] Unlike the fundamental right to strike, the ban on inhuman and degrading treatment has an absolute character.[91] Not surprisingly, in the coalition agreement, the previous federal government inserted the aspiration to introduce a minimum service regulation in the prison system, as in the other European countries, except Albania. The Law of 23 March 2019 on the organization of penitentiary institutions and the status of penitentiary staff finally introduced a minimum service provision in the prison system.

The legislator's starting point was the recognition that penitentiary services should be recognized as essential services in the strict sense as their absence threatens to endanger the life, safety and health of detainees.[92] The legislator therefore intended to create a framework for maintaining the proper functioning of penitentiary institutions by imposing an obligation to initiate consultation procedures without delay as soon as collective conflict arises. Article 15 of the Law of 23 March 2019 on the organization of penitentiary services stipulates that in the event of a social conflict within the penitentiary services, social consultation with the representative trade unions shall be immediately initiated within the competent concertation committee established within the Ministry of Justice. The Royal Decree of 19 November 2019, implementing Articles 15 and 16 of the Law of 23 March 2019 on the organization of penitentiary services in relation to the status of penitentiary staff, defines the terms of the procedures in order to regulate consultation with the trade unions in the event of a social conflict.[93]

This Royal Decree stipulates, among other things, that at least a 10-day waiting period must be respected between the strike notification and the start of the strike.[94] The European Social Rights Committee considers that notice periods in conciliation

88. https://www.coe.int/en/web/cpt/belgium.
89. Comité européen pour la prévention de la torture et des peines ou traitements inhumains ou dégradants (CPT). Déclaration publique relative à la Belgique, https://rm.coe.int/pdf/1680731787, also quoted in the ruling of the Constitutional Court of 15 July 2021, No. 107/2021, point B.64.2.
90. ECtHR 28 May 2019, *Clasens v. Belgium*, application 26.564/16.
91. ECtHR 21 April 2009, No. 68959/01, *Enerji Yapi-Yol Sen/Turkey*, point 32; Constitutional Court 15 July 2021, No. 107/2021, point B.57.2.
92. Memory of Understanding, *Parl. Documents*, Chamber of Representatives (2018-2019), No. 3351/001, 10; *supra* n. 3; Constitutional Court 15 July 2021, No. 107/2021, point B.59.3.
93. Constitutional Court 15 July 2021, No. 107/2021, points B.63.1 and 63.2.
94. Article 8 Law 23 March 2019.

procedures preceding a strike are in line with Article 6(4) of the Revised European Social Charter, provided their duration is reasonable.[95]

What is also important is that the legislator has listed what are the nine essential services that must remain assured at all times.[96] The essential services are derived directly from the CPT's reports and public statement. At the time of the strike, access to the prison should be guaranteed, e.g., for doctors and nurses and lawyers of the detainees.[97]

In case of a strike, the prison director should take necessary measures to prepare a plan to ensure the provision of services.[98] Organizing the continuity of essential services is done by completing a plan, to be discussed between the prison management and staff, and calculating staffing needs for each prison. If there is no concrete operational plan within three months of the entry into force of the Law of 23 March 2019, the Minister of Justice will determine the necessary measures and performance.[99] Among other things, the scheme provides for the establishment of a plan that defines the performance that must be ensured at least daily throughout the strike to ensure the safety and health of the detained persons.

The prison director draws up a list of work-willing prison guards.[100] Prison guards have the obligation to communicate no later than 72 hours before the start of the first day of strike their final intention on whether or not they will participate in the strike day.[101]

If a strike lasts more than two days and the list of staff members who are willing to work during the strike does not cover the needs defined in the plan referred to in Article 19, and if no solution is reached with the representative trade unions, the provincial governor or in the Brussels Region the Minister-President of the Brussels Government, in consultation with the prison director and the leaders of the representative trade unions, can proceed to the requisition of the necessary striking staff members and command staff members to go to their place of employment in order to provide the services necessary to ensure the essential services.[102] The requisitioning of strikers does not in itself constitute a violation of the trade union freedom when its purpose is to ensure essential services, which include penitentiary services.[103]

Staff members who have communicated their intention not to participate in the strike day or who have not confirmed their intention to participate in the strike day within the set deadlines, and who, except for a duly proven valid reason, do not present themselves at their place of work, shall expose themselves to an administrative

95. *Digest de jurisprudence du Comité européen des droits sociaux* (December 2018), p. 106.
96. Article 17; L. Nissen, 'Stakingsrecht en minimumdienstverlening: waar liggen de grenzen', *supra* n. 13, p. 300.
97. Article 18.
98. Article 16 para. 1.
99. Article 19 Law 23 March 2019.
100. Article 16 para. 1.
101. Article 16 para. 1.
102. Article 16 para. 2.
103. Constitutional Court 15 July 2021, No. 107/2021, point B.77.1; *see a contrario* the *ILO Digest 2018*, p. 173, No. 921.

measure. That measure 'may in no case have the character of a disciplinary penalty'.[104] Article 16 of the Royal Decree implementing Articles 15 and 16 of the Law of 23 March 2019 on the organization of penitentiary services establishes the administrative measure imposed on staff members who fail to appear at their place of work despite having either notified their intention to come to work or failed to notify (and thus implicitly indicating their intention not to strike), or having been called in. This civil servant is placed on non-active status for the duration of the unauthorized absence, in accordance with the statute for government employees.

Those staff members, as well as those who participate in the strike day, will not receive pay for the duration of the work stoppage. The same applies to prison staff members who have been ordered by the governor to come to work and ignore the order.[105]

Unlike the railways, the regulation of minimum services in prisons has a binding character, as then also results in a real restriction of the right to strike and the right to collective bargaining. But the Belgian Constitutional Court,[106] following the opinion of the Legislation Section of the Council of State, considers that the legal regulation on minimum services essential for the health and safety of detainees is admissible in the light of the principles of the ILO supervisory bodies.

By seeking to ensure the continuity of penitentiary services in the event of a strike, the Law of 23 March 2019 pursues the purpose of that Law which is to promote the guarantee of the fundamental rights of the detainees, seeking a balance with the right to strike of the staff of penitentiary institutions. That balance was not violated, according to the Constitutional Court. In conclusion, the Belgian Constitutional Court ruled that the minimum service provision for prisons, as regulated by the Law of 23 March 2019, does not lead to a disproportionate interference with the right to strike, does not prevent social dialogue and collective bargaining, and does not undermine trade union freedom and the right to bargain collectively. There is no disregard of Article 11 ECHR, Article G ESH, nor of the principles established by the ILO supervisory bodies with regard to the ILO Convention No. 87 on the freedom of trade union.[107]

In line with this assessment, the European Committee of Social Rights concluded its report 'Conclusions 2022 Belgium' that also the Law of 29 November 2017 'is in conformity with Article 6 (4) of the Charter'.[108]

7 CONCLUSION

Belgium has always recognized a fairly liberal right of collective action, without this fundamental right being absolute. Domestic law established, shortly after World War

104. Article 16 para. 3; Constitutional Court 15 July 2021, No. 107/2021, points B.72. and 72.4.
105. Article 16 para. 3.
106. Constitutional Court 15 July 2021, No. 107/2021, point B.61.1.
107. Constitutional Court 15 July 2021, No. 107/2021, points B.66, 70, 73 and 78.
108. European Committee of Social Rights, Conclusions (2022), Belgium, p. 32, https:rm.coe.int/conclusions-2022-belgium-e/1680aa9865.

II in 1948, in order to safeguard essential services in the private sector, a reasonably well-functioning law on Essential Services of General Interest.

Safeguarding essential services in the public sector has long remained problematic. Longtime there was no legal basis at all to guarantee essential services in the public sector. The general legal principle of continuity of public service from administrative law proved too contestable as a legal basis to ensure a continuous minimum service of essential services in the public sector. Apart from the traditional restrictions on the right to strike among public law enforcement and defence personnel, in particular the military and police forces, it is only in the second decade of the 21st century that the legislator has taken action to implement the essential safeguard in two public sectors with frequent strikes, namely public rail transport and the prison system. The long strikes in 2016 by prison guards in French-speaking Belgium led to downright dramatic situations of inhuman and degrading treatment of prisoners. During that period, two types of laws were introduced to ensure essential services in parts of the public sector. The legal system in public transport is based on workers willing to work as best as possible and prevents strikers from frustrating the work of those willing to work through blockades. The legislation to safeguard essential services in penitentiary institutions also relies on the deployment of willing staff members, but in the event of insufficient deployment, staff members can be compulsorily requisitioned.

In general, it is considered that Belgian legislation on essential services does not disproportionately restrict the fundamental right of private sector employees and public sector civil servants employees to participate in collective action.

CHAPTER 6

Restrictions on the Right to Strike in Bosnia and Herzegovina

Mehmed Hadžić

1 GENERAL INFORMATION

The right to strike is one of the pillars without which the development of collective labour relations would be unimaginable. Freedom of association would remain limited only to expressing dissatisfaction with employers and competent public authorities. Only with the possibility of exercising the right to strike, not only employers but also competent public authorities become much more willing to compromise within social dialogue, which results in concluding collective agreements guaranteeing a certain level of rights to workers and stability and predictability of business to employers. A strike is always a collective work stoppage by workers in order to exert economic pressure on the employer to agree to, in principle, very precise demands by workers to improve their socio-economic status. In relation to this initial definition of a strike, different variations arise in practice, and then such a strike is perceived and defined differently. Given that various interests of both the employer and the broader society can potentially be endangered by the conduct of a strike, it is necessary to regulate the strike by law or other legal provisions. Except for a general strike that inevitably includes political protests and demands, all other strikes not in line with the national legislative framework are perceived as illegal and can be prohibited. Holding a strike in Bosnia and Herzegovina (BiH) has a long tradition. The wave of strikes during 1905 while the Austro-Hungarian monarchy ruled the territory of BiH evolved into a movement for the establishment of unions and the forming of the Main Labor Union Alliance and requests for freedom and free assembly and association. During the strikes in July and August 1905 workers demanded better wages and shorter working time.[1]

1. Belma Buljubašić, *Sindikalne organizacije u Bosni i Hercegovini: između radničke klase i političkih*

Due to the specific state structure, there are several normative frameworks in Bosnia and Herzegovina regulating the right to strike. This chapter will analyse the legal basis and framework for exercising the right to strike, as well as the limitations on the right to strike in certain sectors in Bosnia and Herzegovina, in accordance with the International Labour Organization standards.

1.1 Legal Basis for Exercising the Right to Strike

After the dissolution of the Socialist Federal Republic of Yugoslavia (SFRY) and the signing of the Dayton Peace Agreement in 1995, labour legislation in Bosnia and Herzegovina was adopted according to its constitutional establishment. Specifically, labour legislation in Bosnia and Herzegovina consists of the legislation adopted and applied in the Federation of Bosnia and Herzegovina (FBiH), Republika Srpska (RS), Brčko District of Bosnia and Herzegovina (BD BiH), and the labour law applicable to the level of BiH Institutions.[2]

Trade union rights and freedoms, from which the right to strike in Bosnia and Herzegovina is derived, are mainly based on International Labour Organization (ILO) Conventions No. 87 on Freedom of Association and Protection of the Right to Organize and No. 98 on the Right to Organize and Collective Bargaining, which are integral parts of the legal system of Bosnia and Herzegovina.[3] Furthermore, Bosnia and Herzegovina ratified the Revised European Social Charter of 1996,[4] which, in Article 6 (the right to collective bargaining) paragraph 4, prescribes 'the right of workers and employers to collective action in cases of a conflict of interests, including the right to strike'.

Furthermore, the legal basis for the exercise of the right to strike can be found in the constitutions of Bosnia and Herzegovina, the Federation of Bosnia and Herzegovina, and Republika Srpska. The text of the Constitution of Bosnia and Herzegovina does not explicitly recognize the right to strike. As an annex and integral part of the constitutional law, 15 international agreements are listed, including the International Covenant on Civil and Political Rights of 1966 and the optional protocols of 1966 and 1989, as well as the International Covenant on Economic, Social, and Cultural Rights of 1966. These covenants recognize the freedom of association, establishment, and operation of trade unions to protect the interests of workers. The right to strike is explicitly recognized in Article 8 of the International Covenant on Economic, Social, and Cultural Rights, provided it is exercised in accordance with the laws of each individual country. These two covenants, as annexes, are an integral part of the Constitution of the Federation of Bosnia and Herzegovina, which additionally mentions in Part II, Article 2(1), point l, among other freedoms and rights, 'the freedom of association, including the freedom to establish and join unions and the freedom not to

elita, in Alfredo Saso & Nrmin Kujović (eds), *Socijalna demokratija u BiH- Historijski pregled i razmatranja za budućnost*, Friedrich-Ebert-Stiftung BiH, Sarajevo, 2020, p. 45.

2. Jasminka Gradaščević-Sijerčić, *Aktuelni izazovi u razvoju radnog prava*, Yearbook of the Faculty of Law in Sarajevo, XLVIII, 2005, p. 195.
3. In force as of 2 June 1993.
4. Ratification: 7 October 2008; entry into force: 1 December 2008.

join unions'. In the Constitution of Republika Srpska, Article 42 explicitly states that 'Employees have the right to strike, under conditions determined by law.'

1.2 Main Features of the Regulation

As a right, strike in Bosnia and Herzegovina is established by labour laws as *lex generalis* regulations.[5] The procedure for conducting a strike is governed by *lex specialis* regulations, namely the Law on Strike of the Federation of Bosnia and Herzegovina[6] (hereinafter 'the FBiH Law on Strike'), the Law on Strike of Republika Srpska[7] (hereinafter 'the RS Law on Strike'), the Law on Strike of Brčko District of Bosnia and Herzegovina[8] (hereinafter 'the BD BiH Law on Strike'), and the Law on Strike of Employees in Institutions of Bosnia and Herzegovina.[9]

These laws specify the phases that the strike organizer needs to go through, such as announcing the strike, mediation process, specificities of holding strikes in industries of special interest, consequences of participating in the strike, and so on. If any of these phases are omitted or improperly carried out during the process of organizing and conducting the strike, the legality of the strike is usually reviewed by competent judicial authorities.

1.3 Decision to Go on Strike and Notice of Strike

In the Federation of Bosnia and Herzegovina and at the level of BiH Institutions, only a trade union can adopt a decision to go on strike. In Republika Srpska and Brčko District of Bosnia and Herzegovina, the decision to go on strike at the employer level is adopted by the trade union or the majority of employees at the employer. In Republika Srpska, the union must have representative status. The basic characteristic of representativeness in both the Federation of Bosnia and Herzegovina and Republika Srpska is the required number of members of a particular union at the employer level, in a particular industry or activity, or at the entity level, for that union to be a party to collective bargaining. At the level of an industry or activity in Republika Srpska, only a representative union can adopt a decision to go on strike.[10] The provision in the

5. *See* the following provisions: Article 156 and Article 157 of the FBiH Law on Labour published in the *Official Gazette of FBiH*, 26/2016, 89/2018, 44/2022 and 39/2024; Article 258 of the RS Law on Labour published in the *Official Gazette of RS*, 1/2016, 66/2018, 91/2021 – Decision of the Constitutional Court of RS, 119/2021, 112/2023 and 39/2024; Article 162 and Article 163 of the BD BiH Law on Labour published in the *Official Gazette of BD BiH*, 34/2019, 2/2021, 6/2021 and 15/2022; Articles 95 through 97 of the Law on Labour in the Institutions of BiH published in the *Official Gazette of BiH*, 26/2004, 7/2005, 48/2005, 60/2010, 32/2013, 93/2017, 59/2022, and 88/2023.
6. Published in the *Official Gazette of FBiH*, 14/2000.
7. Published in the *Official Gazette of RS*, 111/2008 and 23/2020.
8. Published in the *Official Gazette of BD BiH*, 3/2006.
9. Published in the *Official Gazette of BiH*, 41/2016.
10. *See* provisions of Article 2 of the FBiH Law on Strike, Article 4 of the RS Law on Strike, Article 3 of the BD BiH Law on Strike, Article 3, para. 1, point c) of the Law on Strike of the Employees in the Institutions of BiH.

Federation of Bosnia and Herzegovina that only a union can organize a strike is very problematic because it prevents the organization of strikes in those employers where a union is not organized. In the new draft of the FBiH Law on Strike from 2018, workers will be able to organize a strike in those employers where there is no union.

In all four legislations, the decision to go on strike or a written notice of strike must indicate the reasons for going on strike or workers' demands, the day of commencement, and the location of the strike. The reasons for going on strike must be legally permissible, and the union, as the organizer of the strike, must have a legal interest to go on strike. If there is no legal interest, the strike in the Federation of Bosnia and Herzegovina can be prohibited by filing a lawsuit with the competent court.[11] The strike is announced to the employer by providing a written decision to go on strike or a special written notice of strike at least 10 days before the start of the strike in the Federation of Bosnia and Herzegovina, 7 days in Republika Srpska, 5 days in the Brčko District of Bosnia and Herzegovina, and 17 days at the level of BiH Institutions.[12] In addition, in Republika Srpska, the decision to go on strike in a particular sector or industry is communicated to the representative association of employers in that sector, industry, or field, or to the Government of Republika Srpska, if the strike is organized in sectors, domains or industries within:

- public administration and defence, mandatory social security;
- education;
- health care and social work activities, in accordance with the regulation governing the classification of activities.[13]

The purpose of a written notice is to inform the employer of the reasons for the strike but at the same time warned of the determination of strike organizers to try to fulfil their demands through this means.

1.4 Peaceful Dispute Resolution

In all four legislations, there is an obligation to attempt peaceful dispute resolution. In the Federation of Bosnia and Herzegovina, Brčko District of Bosnia and Herzegovina, and at the level of BiH Institutions, parties in a dispute must attempt to resolve the

11. In the reasoning of the judgment of the Supreme Court of the Federation of Bosnia and Herzegovina No. 65 0 Rs 872389 21 Rev of 26 October 2021, which confirms the decision of the second instance court to prohibit the strike organized by the BH Telecom Union, it is stated that if there was no conflict of interest between the parties, such a strike is not legally permissible. Justifying this position, the court further states that 'from the written correspondence of the parties it follows that the process of collective bargaining was not in any way obstructed by the plaintiff, as the employer, who participated in negotiations and in all phases of the strike (conciliation, arbitration), showed a willingness to promote workers' rights, supported the defendant Union, and that workers' rights were not in any way threatened or reduced, but the plaintiff offered the conclusion of individual and collective agreements'.
12. *See* provisions of Article 4 of the FBiH Law on Strike, Article 6 of the RS Law on Strike, Article 5 of the BD BiH Law on Strike, and Article 13 of the Law on Strike of Employees in the Institutions of BiH.
13. *See* provisions of Article 6, para. 2 of the RS Law on Strike.

dispute peacefully before a strike can commence.[14] In the Federation of Bosnia and Herzegovina, if from the moment a written notice of strike is issued the parties do not agree on a method for peaceful dispute resolution, they must apply the procedure prescribed in the Law on Peaceful Settlement of Labour Disputes.[15] Mediation under this law is conducted by a conciliation board. According to the FBiH Law on Strike, the procedure for peaceful dispute resolution cannot last longer than five days from the day of submission of the proposal to the conciliation board. The implementation of the procedure for peaceful dispute resolution is a precondition for the legality of the strike. Similar provisions are prescribed in the labour legislation of the Republic of Croatia.[16]

In Republika Srpska, the parties in dispute are also obliged to attempt to resolve the dispute amicably from the day of delivery of the decision to commence the strike or to submit the dispute to a special mediation body agreed upon by the parties. If the dispute is not settled amicably within eight days from the start of the strike, the parties may invite a representative of Republika Srpska's authority or a representative of a representative union at the level of Republika Srpska, provided the union is not the organizer of the strike, as well as experts in various fields to participate in resolving the dispute. The parties may also present the dispute to a special mediation body in accordance with the *lex specialis*, the Law on the Peaceful Settlement of Disputes.[17]

2 PERMITTED RESTRICTIONS

In industries of special interest, such as healthcare, water supply, electricity production, postal and international transport, public radio and television services, and communal services, strike laws, except in the Brčko District of Bosnia and Herzegovina, prescribe special conditions for holding a strike. These are the industries in which the strike can cause consequences for the life, health, or safety of the population, the property of citizens or legal persons, or the occurrence of large-scale damage due to the interruption of the production process.

In the Federation of Bosnia and Herzegovina, Article 1 states that strikes in the armed forces, ministries of internal affairs, and administration and service bodies in the Federation of Bosnia and Herzegovina will be regulated by a special law. However, as of 2024, this special law has not yet been enacted.

The specificity of conducting strikes in industries of special interest is that a list of jobs and the number of employees who will be performing during the strike must be determined.

In the Federation of Bosnia and Herzegovina, at the employer's proposal, the union and the employer shall mutually determine the jobs that will not be interrupted during the strike. If the union and the employer do not reach this agreement within five

14. *See* provisions of Article 6 of the FBiH Law on Strike, Article 6 of the BD BiH Law on Strike, and Article 9 of the Law on Strike of Employees in the Institutions of BiH.
15. Published in the *Official Gazette of FBiH*, 49/2021.
16. For more details, *see* Andrijana Bilić & Trpimir Perkušić, *Zakonitost štrajka: Qui, Quid, Quando et Quamodo?* Pravni vjesnik, Nos 3-4, 2018, p. 121.
17. Published in the *Official Gazette of RS*, 91/16.

days from the start of negotiations, the resolution of the dispute shall be entrusted to arbitration. The arbitration consists of one representative from the union and one from the employer, as well as an independent chairman appointed by mutual agreement of the union and the employer. If the union and the employer cannot agree on the appointment of the chairman from the arbitration and these issues are not regulated by a collective agreement or an agreement between the union and the employer, the competent municipal court shall appoint the chairman at the request of the union or the employer within five days.

The arbitration shall give a decision within five days from the start of the arbitration proceedings. At the latest on the day of announcing the strike, the union is obligated to publish the agreement on the jobs where work cannot be interrupted during the strike. These jobs can be determined in advance by a collective agreement.[18]

In Republika Srpska, the minimum work processes and the way of ensuring it shall be determined by the founder's act or the employer's director, depending on the nature of the activity, the degree of endangerment of life and health, and other circumstances significant for fulfilling the needs of the employers, citizens, and other subjects. In determining the minimum work processes, the employer is obligated to seek the opinion of the union or the workers' council or the authorized representative of the workers. The director and the strike committee shall determine the workers who are required to work during the strike to ensure the minimum work processes, no later than five days before the strike.[19]

At the level of BiH Institutions, the employer can reassign employees to appropriate work positions to ensure the minimum work processes during the strike. Members of the strike committee cannot perform these tasks without the consent of the strike committee.[20]

In their 2018 conclusions, the European Committee of Social Rights consider that organizing a strike in sectors of special importance is not in accordance with Article 6(4) of the Revised European Social Charter, on the grounds that the sectors in which the right to strike may be restricted are overly extensive and the restrictions do not satisfy the conditions laid down in Article G of the Charter. In accordance with Article G of the Charter, essential services are activities that are necessary for a democratic society to protect the rights and freedoms of others or to protect the public interest, national security, public health, or morals.

3 THE RIGHT TO LOCK OUT

The right to lock out as an employer's response to the initiation of a strike is only prescribed in the Federation of Bosnia and Herzegovina. Lockout, i.e., exclusion from the work process by the employer of those workers who do not participate in the strike in the Federation of Bosnia and Herzegovina, is possible only as a defensive lockout in the sense that the employer can exclude workers who do not participate in the strike

18. *See* provisions of Article 5 of the FBiH Law on Strike.
19. *See* provisions of Article 12 of the RS Law on Strike.
20. *See* provisions of Article 15, para. 3 and para. 4 of the Law on Strike in the Institutions of BiH.

only after eight days from the day of the beginning of the strike. The employer cannot exclude from the work process all workers who do not participate in the strike but only half of the total number of workers who participate in the strike. For example, if 50 workers participate in the strike, the employer can exclude a maximum of 25 workers who do not participate in the strike from the work process. In addition, the employer is obligated to pay contributions for the minimum wage for the workers who have been excluded from the work process. A lockout can last up to the end of the strike at the longest.[21]

4 LEGAL CONSEQUENCES OF HOLDING A STRIKE

An employee who participates in a strike organized in accordance with the law does not violate the employment contract, and disciplinary proceedings cannot be initiated against them. In the Federation of Bosnia and Herzegovina and the Brčko District of Bosnia and Herzegovina, the employer may reduce the salary of an employee for the time they spent on strike. In Republika Srpska and at the level of BiH Institutions, employees do not have the right to a salary for the time they spent on strike. An exception is provided for in the RS Law on Strike, which states that employees will be entitled to compensation for lost wages if they participated in a strike organized for the purpose of paying wages and which did not last longer than 12 days.

In the Federation of Bosnia and Herzegovina and the Brčko District of Bosnia and Herzegovina, the employer cannot hire new workers to replace workers who are participating in the strike. A similar ban exists in Republika Srpska and at the level of BiH Institutions, with legally prescribed exceptions. In Republika Srpska, the employer can hire new workers if:

(1) the safety of people and property is threatened;
(2) the maintenance of the minimum work process that ensures the safety of people and property is threatened; and
(3) international obligations must be fulfilled.

At the level of BiH Institutions, the employer can hire new workers if the minimum work process and international obligations are threatened.

Here, the question arises as to whether employees who participated in a strike not organized in accordance with the law violate the employment contract and whether they can be held liable. The answer is affirmative because employees are legally protected only if they participated in a strike organized in accordance with the laws on strike, which is explicitly stated in the Laws on Strike of Republika Srpska and at the level of BiH Institutions, and indirectly in the Laws on Strike of the Federation of Bosnia

21. *See* provisions of Article 7 of the FBiH Law on Strike.

and Herzegovina and the Brčko District of Bosnia and Herzegovina.[22] It is indisputable that organizers of a strike not organized in accordance with the law should bear the appropriate legal consequences, but the question arises as to whether participants in the strike should also bear the same consequences. Namely, participants in the strike may not necessarily know whether the strike was organized in accordance with the law or not, as they may not have been informed whether all the prescribed steps were taken in accordance with the law. This is possible, especially in cases where many workers have taken part in the strike.

5 STRIKE BAN

In the Federation of Bosnia and Herzegovina and at the level of BiH Institutions, an employer who holds that a strike is not organized in accordance with the law may file a lawsuit with the competent court to prohibit such a strike. At the level of BiH Institutions, it is stated that such a procedure before the BiH court is urgent. In the Federation of Bosnia and Herzegovina, the competent court is obligated to give a decision on the employer's request to ban the strike within five days. Similarly, a union organizing a strike in the Federation of Bosnia and Herzegovina can file a lawsuit with the competent court to prohibit a lockout by the employer, i.e., the exclusion from the work process of those workers who do not participate in the strike, if they believe such a procedure was illegal. In this case, as well, the competent court is obligated to give a decision within five days of the request. Unions and employers may seek compensation from the other party through the competent court due to strikes or lockouts not organized in accordance with the law on strike.

In Republika Srpska and the Brčko District of Bosnia and Herzegovina, supervision and application of the law on strike are carried out by the competent inspection. In Republika Srpska, it is the Republic Inspection Administration, and in the Brčko District of Bosnia and Herzegovina, it is the labour inspection.

In Republika Srpska, if the competent inspection determines that the employer has violated the law or other regulations by an act or action, it is authorized, in addition to obligations and authorizations determined by the law, to postpone the execution of the employer's decision on termination of an employment contract or removal of the worker, the organizer of the strike, or the participant in the strike from work, until a final court decision is made.

6 CONCLUSION

The constitutional basis for organizing and conducting a strike in Bosnia and Herzegovina is found in international agreements that are an integral part of the Constitution of Bosnia and Herzegovina and the Federation of Bosnia and Herzegovina and have

22. *See* provisions of Article 3 of the FBiH Law on Strike, Article 16 and Article 17 of the RS Law on Strike, Article 2 of the BD BiH Law on Strike, Article 18, and Article 21 of the Law on Strike of Employees in the Institutions of BiH.

constitutional force. The Constitution of the entity of Republika Srpska explicitly states that workers have the right to strike under conditions determined by law. In addition, the right to strike is established in ratified international documents such as the Revised European Social Charter of 1996 and specifically the International Labour Organization Conventions Nos 87 and 98.

The legal framework for organizing and conducting a strike is regulated by the labour laws and *lex specialis* laws on strike of the Federation of Bosnia and Herzegovina, Republika Srpska, Brčko District of Bosnia and Herzegovina, and at the level of BiH Institutions. These laws on strike provide detailed standards for the steps or previous actions that must be taken by the strike organizers to make the strike lawful. The most significant previous actions are voting on a strike, a written notice of strike, the procedure of conciliation, and the identification of jobs that cannot be interrupted during a strike.

Organizing and conducting a strike is additionally regulated in activities of special social interest, in which the maintenance of the strike without any limitations could lead to endangering the lives and health of the population, as well as causing significant material damage. The basic legal limitation of conducting a strike in these activities is reflected in the obligation to determine the jobs that cannot be interrupted during the strike and the number of employees who are required to perform these jobs. Organizing and conducting a strike in activities of special interest has also been the subject of criticism by the European Committee of Social Rights, which, in their conclusions from 2018, state that these activities are too broadly defined and do not correspond to the standard established in Article G of the European Social Charter.

The possibility of a lockout by the employer as a response to a strike is only prescribed in the Federation of Bosnia and Herzegovina.

Supervision of organizing and conducting a strike is carried out through the competent court in the Federation of Bosnia and Herzegovina and at the level of BiH Institutions, or through the competent inspection in Republika Srpska and the Brčko District of Bosnia and Herzegovina. The competent court in the Federation of Bosnia and Herzegovina and at the level of BiH Institutions may prohibit the further maintenance of the strike if it is not organized and conducted in accordance with the law on strike.

By creating four normative frameworks for organizing and conducting a strike, the conditions have been created for different levels of enjoyment of workers' collective rights in Bosnia and Herzegovina. This issue is particularly important for workers of those employers who have their facilities in both entities and the Brčko District of Bosnia and Herzegovina because they cannot exercise their constitutionally and legally established right to strike in a unified manner.

CHAPTER 7

Restrictions on the Right to Strike in Bulgaria

Krassimira Sredkova & Albena Velikova-Stoyanova

1 GENERAL INFORMATION

As is well known, strike is a means of compulsory settlement of a collective labour dispute. This is a dispute between employees and employers on issues of labour relationships, social insurance relationships and standard of living (Article 1(1) of the Law on Settlement of Collective Labour Disputes (LSCLD)). The strike is intended as a last resort to reach a solution to the dispute where other (voluntary) methods fail.

The legal concept of a strike according to the Bulgarian legislation is derived from the provision of Article 11(1) LSCLD. This is a temporary suspension of work by employees in order to resolve a certain collective labour dispute. During the strike, they stay at their workplaces but do not perform their jobs. Thus, they put pressure on the employer to accept their demands under the dispute.

2 LEGAL BASIS OF THE RIGHT TO STRIKE

The Bulgarian legal framework of the right to strike is based on the current international acts that are in force for Bulgaria: Article 8, paragraph 1, (e) of the International Covenant on Economic, Social and Cultural Rights (ICESCR); ILO Convention No. 87 on Freedom of Association and Protection of the Right to Organize; Article 6, item 4 of the European Social Charter (ESC) and Article 28 of the Charter of Fundamental Rights of the European Union (CFR).

Unlike many other countries, the right to strike is expressly recognized in Article 50 of the Bulgarian Constitution 1991. The current legislation is contained in Chapter III of the Law on Settlement of Collective Labour Disputes 1990; Article 194, paragraph 3 of the Labour Code (LC) 1986; Article 5 and Article 47 of the Civil Servants Act (CSA).

According to the current regulation, the strike is carried out in the exercise of the subjective transformative right of the employees to suspend the performance of their work under the employment relationship in order to settle a collective labour dispute. This right is exercised through the collective of all employees under a special procedure. During a strike, the employees are only required to be present at their workplaces but are exempt from the obligation to perform tasks assigned to them by the employer. The consequences of participating in a strike depend on whether the strike is legal; however, in all cases, the employee on strike is not owed remuneration because he/she has voluntarily stopped work for which he/she would have received remuneration.

3 PERMITTED RESTRICTIONS

3.1 General Requirements for Admissibility of the Strike

For a strike to be held, it must be admissible. The admissibility of the strike is derived by argument to the contrary from the provisions of Article 16 LSCLD. Any strike that is not expressly forbidden by law is admissible.

Bulgarian legislation determines the admissibility of a strike based on several sets of criteria.

In view of the demands made through the strike, a strike shall only be admissible if *economic and social demands by a community of employees* are made with the said strike (argument Article 1, paragraph 1 LSCLD). Therefore, the law prohibits a strike that makes:

(1) *Demands contrary to the Constitution* (Article 16, item 1 LSCLD). This refers to demands that are contrary to specific provisions of the Constitution – e.g., for the conduct of political activity by trade union organizations. The requirements of the legal order do not allow to violate the Constitution or make demands to amend the Constitution through strikes because these are matters beyond the competence of the parties to the collective labour relationships.

(2) *Political demands* (Article 16, item 7 LSCLD). These are demands to change the government system established in the Constitution or the public bodies that exercise the state authority. Such demands cannot be the subject of a collective labour dispute within the meaning of Article 1, paragraph 1 LSCLD. The implementation of such demands (e.g., for resignation of government) is beyond the competence of the employer as such. Therefore, even with the best will in the world, he/she cannot satisfy them. The means for making such demands are the elections for public bodies, the activities of political parties, political rallies, etc., regulated in the Constitution, the Electoral Code, the Law on Political Parties, the Law on Assemblies, Rallies and Demonstrations, etc.

(3) *Demands under individual labour disputes* (Article 16, item 5 LSCLD). The individual labour dispute within the meaning of Article 357 LC does not

possess one of the essential features of collective labour dispute – commonality of interests. Therefore, the means for settling collective labour disputes, such as a strike, cannot be used for its settlement. For the settlement of individual labour disputes according to Chapter XVIII LC, a judicial procedure is applied. The Supreme Court has also expressly ruled on strikes with such a subject, declaring them illegal (decisions No. 380 – 1991 – III c.d., No. 35 – 1992 – III c.d., etc.).

3.2 Prohibition of a Strike in View of the Time of Its Holding

It is inadmissible to conduct a strike *during a natural disaster and the related urgent rescue and restoration works* (Article 16, item 3 LSCLD). These works are regulated by the Disaster Protection Act. The reason for the inadmissibility of strike in such cases is the extraordinary nature of the situation created by the natural disaster – flood, fire, etc. The interests affected by the disaster are much higher than the interest that may be the subject of any collective labour dispute, in order to complicate the situation further by stoppage of work due to a possible strike. Therefore, a strike in such a situation is inadmissible.

3.3 Certain Categories of Public Servants

Along with the general inadmissibility of strikes, inadmissibility in certain spheres of activity is additionally established. These are as follows:

(1) Activities related to *the state security* (Article 16, item 6 LSCLD). The protection of the national security of the Bulgarian state justifies the inadmissibility of strikes in the systems of the Ministry of Defence, the Ministry of Internal Affairs, the State Intelligence Agency and the National Security Service (Article 16, item 6 LSCLD). The general wording of the ban – 'in the system of … ' – means that it applies to both military and civilian employees of defence industry enterprises who are employed by these departments.

(2) Activities related to *the protection of public and legal order* (Article 16, item 6 LSCLD). This group includes the bodies of the Ministry of the Interior and the judiciary (judicial, prosecutorial and investigative bodies). The crucial importance of the activity of these bodies both for the whole society and for the individuals and the irreparable individual and social consequences its suspension (even if temporary) may lead to justify the prohibition of strikes in them.

(3) Activities related to the *management of administration and performance of a senior position at the central or local government office.* Civil servants who hold the position of chief secretary, secretary of a municipality, general director of a general directorate, director of a directorate and head of an inspectorate have no right to strike (Article 47 in conjunction with Article 5,

paragraph 2 CSA). The prohibition is related to the managerial functions of these persons.

The Constitutional Court also ruled on the inadmissibility of strike for the above-mentioned activities in its Decision No. 14 of 1996 under civil case No. 15 of 1996. It stated that 'the armed forces are obliged to guarantee the sovereignty, security and independence of the country and protect its territorial integrity - Article 9 of the Constitution, and the defence of the fatherland is the duty of every Bulgarian citizen' - Article 59, paragraph 1 of the Basic Law. This constitutional purpose of the national defence system excludes the suspension of all or part of its activity, including through a strike of the civilians working in it under an employment relationship under the Labour Code (military personnel are not employees within the meaning of Article 50 of the Constitution). The activity in the system of the Ministry of Internal Affairs is exclusively related to the protection of national security, the protection of the state border, the protection of public order, the life and health of citizens and the fight against crime. It concerns an essential, particularly important activity, the suspension of which through a strike would endanger the lives, security and health of citizens.

As for the bodies of the court, the prosecutor's office and the investigation, all form one of the three state authorities - the judiciary (Article 8 of the Constitution). The judiciary is called to protect the rights and legitimate interests of citizens - Article 117, paragraph 1 of the Constitution in conjunction with Article 56 of the same. The suspension of the activities of the judicial authorities will endanger the functioning of the state itself.

3.4 Inadmissibility of a Specific Strike

The law shall establish the inadmissibility of a strike on a specific labour dispute. It is related to *non-compliance with the procedure for holding strikes*. On this basis, a strike cannot be held if:

(1) *No direct negotiations were held between the employer and the representatives of the employees* (Article 16, item 2 LSCLD). In the event where the employees have not fulfilled their obligation under Article 3, paragraph 2 LSCLD to submit their demands in writing to the employer and have not sent an invitation for direct negotiations in which they wish to participate through their chosen representatives.

(2) *Violated requirements for the majority when adopting a decision to announce a strike and to notify the employer in advance* (Article 16, item 2 LSCLD). According to Article 11 LSCLD the decision to declare a strike is adopted by a simple majority of all employees in the relevant enterprise or division. Employees or their representatives are obliged to notify the employer or his/her representative in writing at least seven days before the start of the strike and to specify its duration and the body that will lead the strike.

(3) With the strike, demands are placed for the settlement of issues on which there is an agreement or an arbitration decision (Article 16, item 2 LSCLD).

4 MINIMUM SERVICE

4.1 Minimum Required Activities During a Strike

The law provides for certain activities that are of particular importance both to the employer and to third parties and the suspension of which would lead to substantial adverse, and sometimes irreparable, consequences. Therefore, it prescribes mandatory implementation of these activities during a strike. The aim is to limit the adverse consequences of the suspension of the relevant activities and thus protect the common interest. These are the minimum required activities. The term 'minimum service' is also used for them.

The minimum required activities that must also be carried out during a strike are exhaustively listed in Article 14, paragraph 1 LSCLD. They are listed depending on their purpose – that their suspension does not create a certain danger. The minimum necessary activities are related to:

(1) *Prevention of danger to the life and health of citizens* (Article 14, paragraph 1, item 1 LSCLD). These activities are: First, *urgent medical care*. Which medical assistance is urgent is defined in the Health Act and in medical standards. Second, *inpatient treatment*. Inpatient treatment is a treatment in medical facilities where the patient stays overnight. The medical facilities are defined in the Health Act.
The Constitutional Court of the Republic of Bulgaria had the opportunity to rule on the establishment of the minimum required activities, incl. in healthcare. In Decision No. 14 of 1996 under civil case No. 15 of 1996, it states that 'the state guarantees the lives of citizens and protects their health – Article 4, para. 2, Article 28 and Article 52, para. 3 of the Constitution. The International Covenant on Economic, Social and Cultural Rights, to which Bulgaria is a party, recognizes the right of every person to achieve the best possible state of physical and mental health (Article 12, item 1). That is why the suspension of work by the employees in state and municipal health facilities through an effective strike would endanger the life and health of large parts of the population, which is inadmissible in view of the above provisions and Article 57, para. 2 of the Constitution'.

(2) *Satisfactory public utilities to the population* (Article 14, paragraph 1, item 2(1) LSCLD). It includes the distribution, transmission and supply of gas, electricity and heat energy, and communal services (cleaning of settlements, collection of household waste, etc.). According to the decision of the Constitutional Court cited above, the production, distribution and supply of electricity, as well as communications, are essential, particularly important activities, the blocking of which by suspending work in them shall create an

obvious and immediate danger to the safety, health and life of people, which will be contrary to the constitutional requirement that the exercise of rights does not lead to harming the rights or legitimate interests of others. The Constitutional Court accepts that the inadmissibility of suspending the work of the employees in the above-mentioned operations does not exclude their right to protest actions to protect their collective economic and social interests through symbolic strikes, protest meetings, rallies, etc., not leading to suspension of their work.

(3) *Satisfactory transport services to the population* (Article 14, paragraph 1, item 2(2) LSCLD). This includes the operation of public and private transport for common use in and between settlements. According to Article 51 of the Law on Railway Transport, for example, the employees and their employers–carriers during a strike are obliged to provide satisfactory transport service to the population, but not less than 50% of the volume of the transport services before the start of the strike.

(4) *Radio and television broadcasts and telephone services* (Article 14, paragraph 1, item 2(3) LSCLD). This group includes the activities of TV stations, radio stations and telephone stations. They may not be stopped because of a strike.

(5) *Protection of public property, personal property and the natural environment* (Article 14, paragraph 1, item 3 LSCLD). Irreparable damage must not be allowed to them. On this basis, activities cannot be suspended if such suspension would lead to the wastage of perishable raw materials and materials, to environmental pollution, to collapsing of buildings, etc. - for example, to suspend the operation of the wastewater treatment plant in steelworks.

(6) *Observance of public order* (Article 14, paragraph 1, item 4 LSCLD). For example, parking of vehicles on streets outside of designated areas may not be allowed.

4.2 Ensuring the Implementation of the Minimum Required Activities

For the implementation of the minimum required activities during the strike, the employees and the employer must provide the necessary conditions. For this purpose, they must enter into a *written agreement* (Article 14, paragraph 1 LSCLD). It must define the activities and the employees who will carry them out. The agreement must be concluded no later than three days before the planned start of the strike (Article 14, paragraph 2 LSCLD).

If no agreement could be reached, the issue goes to *mandatory labour arbitration* (Article 14, paragraph 3 LSCLD).

The legal regulation of collective labour dispute arbitration is currently contained in Articles 4a-8 LSCLD, Rules of the National Institute for Conciliation and Arbitration (NICA) for mediation and arbitration for the settlement of collective labour disputes (RMA), and Ethical Code of Conduct for mediators and arbitrators of NICA.

The law does not set special requirements for persons who can act as arbitrators in a collective labour dispute. This was done by NICA on the basis of Article 4a, paragraph 7, item 5 LSCLD in the Rules for appointing mediators and arbitrators in collective labour disputes. In general terms, these requirements are reduced to appropriate professional qualifications, experience in the field of labour relationships, personal qualities and abilities to make contact with many and different people, tolerance, firmness in defending a position, etc. Linked to the functions of the arbitrator are the incompatibility rules. They are expressed in the prohibition of the capacity of an arbitrator in a specific collective labour dispute to be acquired by a person for whom certain circumstances are present. These circumstances are specified in Article 16, paragraph 3 RMA. Grounds for incompatibility may be combined in three groups:

> First, concerning the relationships between the arbitrator and the disputing parties in general. This group includes one reason for incompatibility – hierarchical relationship with a party to the dispute (Article 16, paragraph 2, item 1 RMA). The consideration here is that the impartiality of the arbitrator cannot be guaranteed – he/she shall be interested to a certain extent in the settlement of the collective labour dispute.
> Second, related to the specific collective labour dispute. Two grounds are included in this group. One is participation in the settlement of the dispute as a mediator or conciliator (Article 16, paragraph 2, item 2 RMA). In this scenario, the mediator or arbitrator has made efforts to settle the dispute, but they have been unsuccessful. It cannot be expected that in his/her new capacity he/she will achieve any success. The other ground for incompatibility is that the person did not consent to participate in the settlement of the dispute (Article 16, paragraph 2, item 3 POPA). The reasons for doing so are irrelevant.
> Third, related to the personal situation of the arbitrator. This is the reasonable doubt in his/her impartiality and independence (Article 16, paragraph 2, item 4 POPA). It may be due to various reasons. The doubt must be 'reasonable'; i.e., the party that has expressed it should provide the reasons for it, and those reasons should be convincing.

Acquiring the quality of 'arbitrator' occurs upon the inclusion of the individual in the List of Arbitrators under Article 5, paragraph 4 LSCLD. It is decided by the Supervisory Board of NICA at the proposal of the state in the person of the Minister of Labour and Social Policy and the representative trade union and employer organizations. The list is published in the State Gazette. Pursuant to Article 14, paragraph 3 LSCLD, the arbitration body for mandatory labour arbitration is determined by the Director of NICA.

Arbitration proceedings under the mandatory arbitration shall be initiated by the Director of NICA. These proceedings function at their sessions. Several rules have been established for the sessions. The sessions are open (Article 6, paragraph 2 LSCLD) with mandatory summoning of the parties. The number of sessions in which the dispute must be clarified is relatively limited – two sessions. The limitation is relative because it can be overcome by mutual agreement of the parties. The period between two (or a greater number decided by the parties) sessions is also relatively limited. It is limited in its maximum duration – seven days. Minutes are kept for each session (Article 22, paragraph 2 RMA). Explanations of the parties or their representatives are allowed as evidence in the dispute as well as: written documents; opinions of third parties to the dispute; conclusions of experts; other materials. The costs of gathering the evidence and of the arbitration proceedings in general are borne by the parties to the dispute (Article 8, paragraph 2 LSCLD).

In view of the timely settlement of relationships between the disputing parties, Article 7 LSCLD establishes a maximum term for the arbitration body's ruling. It is three days from the day of the last session.

Pursuant to Article 7, paragraphs 1 and 3 LSCLD, the arbitration body shall give its ruling by way of decision. It must be motivated. The arbitration body decides the disputes on legality and not on expediency – it makes its decision based on the current legislation (Article 7, paragraph 1 LSCLD).

However, it is possible that the arbitration procedure will end with an agreement rather than a decision. This possibility is derived from the provision of Article 1, paragraph 1 SFP LSCLD, which stipulates that 'any agreement between the parties reached during ... arbitration ... shall be binding on them'. The agreement, like the arbitration decision, is final. And it is subject to immediate execution.

4.3 Consequences of the Failure to Fulfil the Obligation to Implement the Minimum Required Activities

Failure to fulfil the obligation to carry out the minimum required activities during a strike is a violation of labour legislation. It has been declared an administrative violation (Article 22, paragraph 1 in conjunction with Article 14 LSCLD). This violation implies starting a strike without an agreement to implement the activities under Article 14, paragraph 1 LSCLD, the non-fulfilment of the latter in accordance with an arbitration decision under Article 14, paragraph 3 LSCLD and others. The penalty imposed for this violation is a *fine* of BGN 200 to 500. The penalty is imposed according to the general procedure for imposing administrative criminal liability for violation of labour legislation (argument Article 22, paragraphs 2-3 LSCLD).

5 COMPENSATORY GUARANTEES FOR WORKERS DEPRIVED OF THE RIGHT TO STRIKE

5.1 Direct Negotiations

In the event of a collective labour dispute, workers whose right to strike is prohibited or limited have at their disposal voluntary means provided for in the Law on Settlement of Collective Labour Disputes – Articles 3-8.[1] These are direct negotiations of the parties to the dispute, mediation, voluntary arbitration.

Negotiations between disputing parties (direct negotiations) are the most desirable means of settling a collective labour dispute. With them, the settlement of the dispute is carried out through discussion, concessions and coordination of common interests in an environment of social peace in the enterprise. The parties to the disputed legal relationship smooth out the disputed issues and reach mutually acceptable solutions all by themselves. Direct negotiations are expressed in settling the disputed issue and achieving its solution by the parties to the dispute themselves, by their *mutual agreement*. They are conducted by the protesting employees and their employer. The participation of the parties can be direct or through a representative (Article 1, paragraph 2 LSCLD). The procedure for conducting the negotiations is succinctly regulated in Article 3 LSCLD. It is generally free, determined by the disputing and respectively negotiating parties. The law sets only two mandatory requirements for clarity in the dispute and in the final decision. One requirement is that employees shall submit their requests in writing to the employer. The other requirement is that the workers shall inform the employer of the names of their representatives in the negotiations. Negotiations may lead to a resolution of the dispute – this is desirable. It takes the form of an agreement, which is objectified in writing and signed by the parties. If the agreement does not specify terms for its implementation, it is subject to immediate implementation (argument Article 1, paragraph 1 SFP LSCLD). The law gives it the meaning of a collective labour agreement (Article 1, paragraph 2 SFP LSCLD). If a mutually acceptable solution is not found during the negotiations (the duration of which is not limited), no agreement can be reached, and the dispute remains pending. Other methods for its settlement are made available to the parties.

1. *See* Васил Мръчков, *Колективни трудови спорове и правото на стачка* (Университетско издателство Климент Охридски 1992), (Vassil Mrachkov, *Collective Labour Disputes and the Right to Strike* (University Publishing House Kliment Ochridki 1992)); Васил Мръчков, *Коментар на Закона за уреждане на колективни трудови спорове* (Сиела 1993), (Vassil Mrachkov, *Commentary to the Law on Settlement of Collective Labour Disputes* (Siela 1993)); Васил Мръчков, *Трудово право* (Сиби 10. изд. 2017), (Vassil Mrachkov, *Labour Law* (Sibi 10. Edd. 2017)); Красимра Средкова, *Посредничество за уреждане на колективни трудови спорове*. – Информационен бюлетин по труда, 2012, No. 11 (Krassimira Sredkova, *Mediation for Settlement of Collective Labour Disputes* (Informational Labour Bulletin, 2012, No. 11)); *Арбитраж за уреждане на колективни трудови спорове. Информационен бюлетин по труда*, No. 12 (2012), (*Arbitration for Settlement of Collective Labour Disputes* (Informational Labour Bulletin, 2012, No. 12)); Емилия Банова, *Непосредствени преговори за уреждане на колективните трудови спорове*, *in* Трудови отношения (Труд и право 2014), (Emilia Banova, *Direct Negotiations for Settlement of Collective Labour Disputes, in Labour relations* (Trud i pravo 2014)); Жасмина Саръиванова, Марияна Иванова & Катя Стоянова, *Правомощия на Националния институт за помирение и арбитраж и развитието на помирението и арбитража в Република България, В Актуални проблеми на трудовото и осигурителното право*, Т. IX (Университетско издателство Св. Климент Охридски 2017), (Jasmina Saraivanova, Mariana Ivanova & Katja Stoyanova, *Competences of the National Institute for Mediation and Arbitration and Development of the Conciliation and Arbitration in the Republic of Bulgaria, in Contemporary Problems of the Labour and Social Insurance Law*, Vol. IX (University Publishing House St. Kliment Ochridski 2017)).

5.2 Negotiations with the Participation of a Mediator (Mediation)

The foundations of the legal regulation of mediation as a means of settling a collective labour dispute are contained in Article 4-4a and paragraph 1 SFP LSCLD. Pursuant to Article 4a, paragraph 7, item 4 LSCLD, the Supervisory Board of NICA has adopted the Rules of the National Institute for Conciliation and Arbitration (NICA) for mediation and arbitration for the settlement of collective labour disputes and the Ethical Code of Conduct for mediators and arbitrators of NICA.

There are two prerequisites for starting a mediation procedure. These are alternative prerequisites. One is failure to reach an agreement on the collective labour dispute in the course of direct negotiations between the disputing parties. The other is a refusal to negotiate. This is a hypothesis when one of the parties has refused to participate in the settlement of the dispute through direct negotiations with the other party. Refusal can be either express or tacit.

Each of the parties to the dispute has the right to seek assistance in settling the dispute from a mediator. The other is obliged to accept the assistance. The body from which it was requested is also obliged to provide assistance.

Mediators in collective labour disputes are trade unions, employers' organizations and the National Institute for Conciliation and Arbitration. The NICA mediates through mediators approved by its Supervisory Board. These are natural persons proposed by the representative organizations of employees, the representative organizations of employers and the Minister of Labour and Social Policy as a representative of the state.

The Law on Settlement of Collective Labour Disputes does not establish mandatory rules for conducting the mediation procedure. These are established in the Rules of the National Institute for Conciliation and Arbitration (NICA) for mediation and arbitration for the settlement of collective labour disputes and the Ethical Code of Conduct for mediators and arbitrators of NICA. The law establishes only a recommended period for conducting the procedure – 14 days (Article 4, paragraph 2 LSCLD). The term is recommended – by agreement of the parties to the dispute, a longer term may be established. Upon the expiration of the term for carrying it out, the mediation procedure may end:

(1) First, by reaching an agreement. It is objectified in the agreement between the parties. The mediator only assists in achieving it.
(2) Second, with failure to reach agreement. This means that the dispute could not have been settled with the assistance of a third party. It continues to be pending. The parties have other options to settle it – labour arbitration, means of public impact.

5.3 Labour Arbitration

Another method of voluntary settlement of collective labour disputes is labour arbitration. However, practice rarely uses this method. Among the reasons for this should be mentioned the lack of traditions, the financial difficulties for the parties, and the insufficient knowledge of the possibilities offered by this method.

Labour arbitration is a means of voluntary settlement of collective labour disputes together with direct negotiations, conciliation and mediation. It is a procedure in which a third party (arbitrator, arbitration panel) is empowered to make a decision that settles the collective labour dispute. If the decision is on a legal dispute and concerns the rights and obligations of the parties, it is similar to a court decision. If it concerns disputes of interest (economic disputes), it replaces the failed negotiations with a solution that the third party considers appropriate.

Arbitration differs from other methods of voluntary settlement of collective labour disputes for the reason that through it the dispute is *finally decided by a third party to the disputing parties*. Voluntary arbitration can be carried out by trade union and employers' organizations and/or by the National Institute for Conciliation and Arbitration. The current legal framework is mainly contained in Articles 4a-9 and paragraph 1 SFP LSCLD. It has been further developed in the Rules of the National Institute for Conciliation and Arbitration (NICA) for mediation and arbitration for the settlement of collective labour disputes.

Unlike the mandatory arbitration discussed above regarding minimum activities during a strike, voluntary arbitration is formed at the will of the disputing parties. They reach a decision to refer the dispute to arbitration and appoint the arbitration body. Thus, they are voluntarily bound by the decision of the arbitration body. Voluntary arbitration is a form of social dialogue in labour relationships (Article 2 LC).

Each arbitration procedure shall be conducted by an *arbitration body*. It may be a single-person or collegial body, as stated above (*see* section 4.2). The requirements for the arbitrators are the same as for the mandatory arbitration discussed above.

Arbitration proceedings shall be initiated in the presence of alternative prerequisites established by law. They are specified in Article 4, paragraph 1 and Article 5, paragraph 1 LSCLD and are: failure to reach an agreement on the basis of direct negotiations; refusal to negotiate; failure to reach an agreement with the help of a mediator. Proceedings shall be initiated at the will of the parties to the dispute. It must be objectified in writing. The parties' agreement to refer the dispute to arbitration must necessarily cover several elements – the numerical composition of the arbitration body (single-person or collegial); the personal composition of the arbitration body (if the arbitrator is a single person, he/she must be appointed by both parties by mutual agreement; if an arbitration panel is provided for, each party must specify in the agreement the arbitrators appointed by them). The parties must state precisely, clearly and unequivocally what the disputed issues are; what the employees' demands are; what the employer's position is; and other issues relevant to the resolution of the dispute.

Like anybody that resolves disputes, labour arbitration also functions at its sessions. In principle to them apply the above-mentioned rules regarding mandatory arbitration (*see* section 4.2).

Unlike other methods of voluntary settlement of collective labour disputes, when the dispute is referred to arbitration, it (the dispute) always ends. When the dispute is decided by a single-person body, the decision on it is made by the relevant arbitrator. When decided by an arbitration panel, the decision is taken by a simple majority. Pursuant to Article 7, paragraphs 1 and 3 LSCLD, the arbitration body renders a decision (*see also* Article 24bb POPA). The arbitration body decides the disputes according to legality and not according to expediency – it bases its decision on the current legislation (Article 7, paragraph 1 LSCLD). An arbitration decision can be defined in its nature as an act of a judicial body similar to a court decision.[2] This act is final. It can neither be contested before a national court nor before any other authority. This also follows from the rule pursuant to Article 1, paragraph 1 SFP LSCLD that the arbitration decision is subject to immediate execution. However, it is possible that the arbitration procedure will end with an agreement rather than a decision. This is admissible in both legal and non-legal disputes. The arbitration agreement reflects the common will of the parties to the dispute, reached with the participation of the arbitration body. Therefore, it must be signed by both parties and the arbitration body. This is a manifestation of social dialogue, which Bulgarian labour law made a basic principle in Article 2 LC. If the settled dispute is legal, the settlement will be similar in nature to a court agreement. If it is non-legal, the agreement will have the nature of a collective labour agreement. With it, the parties will assume (establish between themselves) certain rights and obligations.[3] The agreement, like the arbitration decision, is also final. And it is subject to immediate execution.

5.4 Means of Public Impact

Apart from those discussed above, the law regulates also ways to settle collective labour disputes, including where a strike is inadmissible, by attracting public attention. They are carried out without suspending the work under employment or civil service relationships. Their purpose is to draw public attention to the developing collective labour dispute and thus to influence the will of the employer or the appointing authority to accept the employees' demands or to convince the employees that their demands are unacceptable. These methods are regulated in Articles 9-10 LSCLD.

The parties to the collective labour dispute may organize mass public events such as *meetings, rallies, demonstrations, etc.* (Article 9 LSCLD). It is a general requirement that they take place outside the working hours since during working hours employees are obliged to perform their work under the employment relationships. These events can be held both in the enterprise and outside it. When holding rallies and meetings at

2. *See* more on arbitration decision and its nature in Vassil Mrachkov, *Collective Labour Disputes*, 112-113; *Commentary*, 87-88.
3. *See* for the agreement as an act finalizing the arbitration proceedings in Vassil Mrachkov, *Collective Labour Disputes*, 113-114; *Commentary*, 88-90.

the workplace, employees must comply with the Law on Settlement of Collective Labour Disputes and the internal working regulations. When holding rallies, assemblies and demonstrations outside the enterprise, they must comply with the Law on Assemblies, Rallies and Demonstrations since, on the basis of Article 1 of the Supplementary Provisions, this law also applies to events 'provided for in other legal acts'. Such other legal act in this case is the Law on Settlement of Collective Labour Disputes.

A means of influence for the settlement of a collective labour dispute without a strike is also provided for in Article 9 LSCLD, informing the public. The law provides that the parties to the collective labour dispute may inform the public about the disputed matter through *the media*. They can express their opinions in the press, radio, television, etc., in order to thereby influence the opinion of the other party to the dispute.

Article 10 LSCLD also provides for *a symbolic strike*. In it, workers wear external symbols - badges, bands, etc., which express their protest. In this way, they aim to draw attention to the disputed subject of any third parties present in the enterprise. Most often, this tool is used in medical facilities.

CHAPTER 8

Restrictions on the Right to Strike in Croatia

Ivana Grgurev & Ivana Vukorepa

1 GENERAL INFORMATION

1.1 Legal Basis of the Right to Strike

The right to strike in Croatia and thereto related restrictions are regulated by the Constitution, some international and several domestic sources of law consisting mainly of state-enacted legislation. In practice, although rarely, more detailed elaboration of the legislative restrictions on the right to strike can also be found in the collective agreements.

The right to strike is a constitutional right guaranteed by Article 60(1) of the Constitution of the Republic of Croatia.[1] The provision simply states that 'the right to strike shall be guaranteed'. Nevertheless, the following provision of Article 60(2) of the Constitution prescribes that the right to strike 'may be restricted in the armed forces, the police, state administration and public services as specified by law'.

Since Article 134 of the Croatian Constitution prescribes that international treaties concluded and ratified in accordance with the Constitution and duly published, and which have entered into force, are part of domestic legal order and have primacy over domestic law, it is first appropriate to mention the relevant international sources of law that oblige Croatia. In that context, it is worth mentioning that Croatia has ratified ILO Convention No. 87 on Freedom of Association and Protection of the Right to Organize and Convention No. 98 on the Right to Organize and Collective Bargaining

1. The Constitution of the Republic of Croatia, *Ustav Republike Hrvatske* (Official Gazette Nos 56/1990, 135/1997, 113/2000, 28/2001, 76/2010, 5/2014).

Convention[2] and has accepted Article 6 of the European Social Charter of 1961 on the right to strike.[3]

Regarding domestic law, right to strike has been regulated since the first Croatian Labour Act of 1995.[4] Nowadays, the general regulation of the right to strike one finds in the Labour Act of 2014,[5] which contains provisions on the strike and solidarity strike (Article 205), is prescribing also prerequisites for legality of strikes and lockouts (Articles 206-213), providing rules on the determination of essential activities and maintenance of production activities which must not be stopped during a strike or a lockout (Article 214), enumerating consequences of organizing or participating in a strike including proportional reduction of remuneration (Article 215-2016), and prescribing rules on judicial prohibition of an illegal strike or lockout and thereto related indemnity rights (Article 217-2019).[6] Furthermore, in line with the constitutional provision of Article 60(2) on allowed restriction to the right of strike in the Armed Forces, police, public administration and public services, Article 220 of the Labour Act contains no detailed regulation but only confirms that in these four areas the right to strike shall be regulated by separate legislation. Hence, the specific laws that limit the right to strike in Croatia are as follows.

Regarding Armed Forces right to strike is restricted by Article 15 of the Act on Armed Forces of the Republic of Croatia,[7] prescribing an absolute ban of strike for active military personnel while limiting right to strike for other civil servants and employees in that sector during war and other prescribed circumstances.

In the police sector, right to strike is restricted only in specific situations regulated by Article 39 of the Police Act, such as war, armed rebellions, and natural disasters.[8]

Further on, although right to strike could be limited in the state administration sector (based on Article 60(2) of the Constitution and Article 220 of the Labour Act, as described above), no such restrictive provision can be found neither in the Act on Civil Servants[9] nor in the Act on Officials and Employees in the Local and Regional

2. Official Gazette, International Agreements No. 2/1994. About the mandate of the ILO Committee of Experts to interpret ILO Conventions, *see*: Jeffrey Vogt et al., *The Right to Strike in International Law* (Hart 2020).
3. Act on the Ratification of the European Social Charter, the Additional Protocol to the European Social Charter, the Protocol on Amendments to the European Social Charter and the Additional Protocol to the European Social Charter Providing for a System of Collective Complaints (Official Gazette, International Agreements No. 15/2022).
4. Labour Act of 1995, *Zakon o radu* (Official Gazette Nos 38/1995, 54/1995, 65/1995, 102/1998, 17/2001, 82/2001, 114/2003, 142/2003, 123/2003, 30/2004, 68/2005, 94/2009).
5. Labour Act of 2014, *Zakon o radu* (Official Gazette Nos 93/2014, 127/2017, 98/2019, 151/2022, 46/2023, 64/2023).
6. For more details *see*: Viktor Gotovac, *Pravno uređenje štrajka i rješavanja kolektivnih radnih sporova u Republici Hrvatskoj (II. dio)* pp. 18-26, Radno pravo, 14, 11 (2017).
7. Act on Armed Forces of the Republic of Croatia, *Zakon o službi u Oružanim snagama Republike Hrvatske* (Official Gazette Nos 73/2013, 75/2015, 50/2016, 30/2018, 125/2019, 158/2023, 14/2024).
8. Police Act, *Zakon o policiji* (Official Gazette Nos 34/2011, 130/2012, 89/2014, 151/2014, 33/2015, 121/2016, 66/2019, 155/2023).
9. Act on Civil Servants, *Zakon o državnim službenicima* (Official Gazette Nos 155/2023, 85/2024).

Self-Government.[10] Therefore, it can be concluded that strike is allowed under general rules of the Labour Act in the state and local administration.[11]

Regarding public service sector, strike is limited by law only for certain employees in some sensitive sectors, i.e., healthcare sector, firefighting sector, postal service, kindergartens and public information service provided by Croatian Radio-Television. Regarding healthcare sector, relevant is Article 198 of the Health Care Act[12] which as a protective healthcare measure absolutely bans strike to employees in charge of emergency medicine services, while Article 199 implies right to strike to all other employees in healthcare institutions provided that a special prior procedure has been followed. Regarding firefighters' sector, Article 66 of the Firefighting Act[13] restricts right to strike in specific situations such as war, military rebellions, extraordinary events, and disasters. In the postal service sector and preschool educational sector, strike is very limitedly restricted based on Article 4 of the Act on Postal Services[14] and Article 43 of the Act on Preschool Education,[15] respectively. Finally, regarding information service sector, right to strike has been until recently limited to the employees of the Croatian Radio-Television when performing activities as public service. Legal foundation was found in Article 43 of the Act on Croatian Radio-Television[16] and was further elaborated by collective agreement until the Constitutional Court of the Republic of Croatia abolished Article 43(3) of the Act on Croatian Radio-Television in February 2024.[17] More specificities regarding restrictions to the right to strike in the above-mentioned categories of public sectors will be explained later in this chapter.

1.2 Main Features of the Regulation

From the above overview of the legal basis, it can be concluded that the right to strike is a constitutional right which is by Constitution (Article 60(2)) and by law (Article 220 of the Labour Act) allowed to be restricted in four public sectors: Armed Forces, the police, state administration and public services. Restrictions are allowed only by law, which emphasizes the strike as 'the most powerful instrument of trade unions to protect the occupational interests of its members'.[18] The constitutional provision

10. Act on Officials and Employees in the Local and Regional Self-government, *Zakon o službenicima i namještenicima u lokalnoj i područnoj (regionalnoj) samoupravi* (Official Gazette Nos 86/2008, 61/2011, 4/2018, 96/2018, 112/2019, 17/2025).
11. Conclusions on Art. 6(4) of the ECSR, Conclusions XXI-3(2018), Croatia. *See also*: Diana Balenescu, *The Right to Strike in the Public Sector: Croatia* 17 (EPSU and ETUI 2021).
12. Health Care Act, *Zakon o zdravstvenoj zaštiti* (Official Gazette Nos 100/2018, 125/2019, 133/2020, 147/2020, 136/2021, 119/2022, 156/2022, 33/2023, 36/2024).
13. Firefighting Act, *Zakon o vatrogastvu* (Official Gazette Nos 125/2019, 114/2022, 155/2023).
14. Act on Postal Services, *Zakon o poštanskim uslugama* (Official Gazette Nos 144/2012, 153/2013, 78/201, 110/2019).
15. Act on Preschool Education, *Zakon o predškolskom odgoju* i *obrazovanju* (Official Gazette Nos 10/1997, 107/2007, 94/2013, 98/2019, 57/2022, 101/2023).
16. Act on Croatian Radio-Television, *Zakon o Hrvatskoj radioteleviziji* (Official Gazette Nos 137/2010, 76/2012, 78/2016, 46/2017, 73/2017, 94/2018, 114/2022, 20/2023, 18/2024).
17. Constitutional Court of the Republic of Croatia, U-I-1621/2023, 6 February 2024.
18. *Hrvatski liječnički sindikat v. Croatia*, No. 3670/09, Eur Ct. H. R. (2014).

should be interpreted as authorizing the legislator to regulate by law the conditions under which employees in the mentioned segments of the public sector can exercise their right to strike. More specifically, Potočnjak is of the opinion that prescribed conditions for exercising this right may be more restrictive than the conditions under which other workers will use the right to strike, but that these special laws, due to the way the constitutional provision is styled, cannot prohibit right to strike completely.[19]

Further on, based on the legal analyses, several features regarding limitation to the right to strike can be pinpointed. First, legislator has chosen to use its right to restrict right to strike only in three out of four allowed public sectors, i.e., in Armed Forces, police and five areas of public services (healthcare, firefighting, postal service, kindergartens and public information service provided by Croatian Radio-Television), leaving public administration specifically unregulated (hence with no allowed restriction to the right to strike).

Second, laws prescribe two main levels of restriction on the right to strike:

(1) absolute ban; and
(2) relative ban (specific limitations).

The absolute ban of the right to strike is prescribed only for active military personnel and employees in charge of emergency medicine services. We are of the opinion that more nuanced relative limitations to the right to strike can be categorized into three groups:

(1) ban of strike in certain specific situations of danger, such as war, military rebellions, and natural disasters prescribed by special laws (it has been prescribed for firefighters, police, employees in Armed Forces and workers in Croatian Radio-Television);
(2) limitation to the right to strike by imposing regular performance of some services within a specific public sector prescribed by special laws (in healthcare services other than emergency medicine services, in postal services it has been prescribed for delivery of postal items of the fastest category and in preschool sector for nutrition, healthcare and other care for children in kindergartens); and
(3) possibility to agree upon 'essential activities' and 'maintenance of production activities' which must not be stopped during strike pursuant to the rules of Article 214 of the Labour Act.

Labour Act defines 'essential activities' as activities that are aimed at performance of work which is essential for the prevention of risks to life, personal safety, or health of the population, while 'maintenance of production activities' are activities enabling the restoration of regular work immediately after the strike has ended. Both activities are to be agreed before the strike, based on employer's initiative; however,

19. Željko Potočnjak, *Pravo na štrajk* 255 (Pravni fakultet u Zagrebu and SSSH 1992).

the scope of the defined activities must not deny or substantially restrict the right to strike.[20] If the trade union and the employer do not reach an agreement within 15 days of the day of the employer's proposal, the employer or the trade union may, within the next 15 days, request that these activities be defined by an arbitration body consisting of three persons: one representative of the trade union, one representative of the employer and an independent chairperson who is appointed subject to an agreement between the trade union, and the employer.[21] If one of the parties refuses to participate in the arbitration procedure, the procedure shall nevertheless be completed without the participation of that party[22] (hence, it is a type of forced arbitration).[23] The arbitration body must render a decision within 15 days following the initiation of the arbitration procedure.[24] If the employer proposed the definition of 'essential activities' and 'maintenance of production activities' after the day when the mediation procedure had commenced, the procedure for defining these activities may not be initiated until the end of the strike (Article 214(9) of the Labour Act). Considering the complexity of Labour Act provisions regarding 'essential activities' and 'maintenance of production activities' which must not be stopped during strike, criticism appears to be justified. Namely, Bilić and Perkušić criticize the too-long procedure which is, in their opinion, especially problematic in case of strike undertaken on the ground of non-payment of remuneration. They suggest that the employer and the trade union should immediately upon registration of the trade union that operates with it agree on jobs that must not be interrupted in the event of a strike.[25]

2 PERMITTED RESTRICTIONS

2.1 Certain Categories of Public Servants

As indicated in the previous section, certain categories of employees in the public sector are absolutely prohibited from striking, and others are limited in their right to strike. Absolute ban and restrictions of the right to strike in the Armed Forces and the police, as well as the ban and restrictions of the right to strike in emergency medicine services, will be explained in the section on Essential Services in the Strict Sense of the Term.

Right to strike of fire service personnel, employees employed by postal service providers and employees in kindergartens is restricted by law, as will be explained in this section.

20. Article 214(2) and (3) of the Labour Act.
21. In case parties do not agree about the chairperson, the chairperson shall be appointed by the president of the court which, according to the provisions of this Act, has first-instance jurisdiction to hear cases related to the prohibition of a strike or a lockout (Art. 214(6) of the Labour Act).
22. Article 214(7) of the Labour Act.
23. Mihajlo Dika, Željko Potočnjak & Viktor Gotovac, *Radni sporovi*, in Radni odnosi u Republici Hrvatskoj 738 (Željko Potočnjak ed., Pravni fakultet u Zagrebu, Organizator 2007).
24. Article 214(8) of the Labour Act.
25. Andrijana Bilić & Trpimir Perkušić, *Zakonitost štrajka: qui, quid, quando et quomodo?*, 34(3-4) Pravni vjesnik 126-127 (2018) https://doi.org/10.25234/pv/6160 (accessed 10 June 2025).

As regards the right to strike of fire service personnel, Article 66 of the Firefighting Act[26] states:

> A strike in the firefighting service is not allowed in the event of: 1. a state of war or an immediate threat to the independence and unity of the state; 2. armed rebellion, uprising and other forms of violent threat to the constitutional order of the Republic of Croatia or the fundamental freedoms and rights of man and citizens; 3. extraordinary event, accident or disaster; 4. other extraordinary events that interfere with the normal development of life and threaten the safety of people and property.

Concerning postal service, Article 4 of the Act on Postal Services[27] contains certain restrictions on the right to strike of employees employed by postal service providers. It states:

> (1) In the event of a strike, the universal service provider is obliged to carry out the transfer and delivery of postal items of the fastest category that were received before the start of the strike.
> (2) In the event of a strike, the universal service provider is obliged to ensure the reception, routing, transfer and delivery of the fastest category shipments and other shipments that, with the prior opinion of the trade union, are determined by the minister responsible for postal services.

It is worth emphasizing that in case of restrictions on right to strike of employees employed by postal service providers, when determining the activities which must not be stopped during a strike, the minister needs to consider the prior opinion of the trade union.

In the field of education, limitation to the right to strike is only prescribed in preschool education (other levels of education contain no special limitations). Namely, Article 43(2) of the Act on Preschool Education[28] prescribes that 'in the event of a strike, the strike committee, the director of the kindergarten and the administrative council are obliged to provide adequate care, nutrition, health care, as well as other care for the children attending the kindergarten program during the strike'.

The ILO supervisory bodies have considered that it should be possible for strikes to be organized by workers, among others, employed by radio and television. Until recently, the right to strike of the employees of Croatian Radio-Television (HRT) has been restricted. Namely, Article 43(3) of the Act on Croatian Radio-Television[29] stated: 'When HRT performs activities as a public service in accordance with this Law, HRT employees do not have the right to strike, which is regulated in more detail by the general act of HRT or the collective agreement.' The Collective Agreement for Employees of the Croatian Radio and Television concluded on 31 March 2023 gave details on the restriction of the right to strike (Articles 86-88). Article 86 specified extraordinary

26. Firefighting Act, *Zakon o vatrogastvu* (Official Gazette Nos 125/2019, 114/2022, 155/2023).
27. Act on Postal Services, *Zakon o poštanskim uslugama* (Official Gazette Nos 144/2012, 153/2013, 78/201, 110/2019).
28. Act on Preschool Education, *Zakon o predškolskom odgoju i obrazovanju* (Official Gazette Nos 10/1997, 107/2007, 94/2013, 98/2019, 57/2022, 101/2023).
29. Act on Croatian Radio-Television, *Zakon o Hrvatskoj radioteleviziji* (Official Gazette Nos 137/2010, 76/2012, 78/2016, 46/2017, 73/2017, 94/2018, 114/2022, 20/2023, 18/2024).

situations in which the employees of HRT had no right to strike: in cases of natural disasters, epidemics, state of emergency or war, workers had no right to strike. The fact that the restriction of the right to strike applied to all union members (Article 86(2)) and not only to those who perform public service activities *stricto sensu* (such as those who were employed in the news programme) was problematic. This meant, for example, that all employees in charge of the entertainment programme and cultural programme or cleaning personnel would not be allowed to strike in the mentioned situations, which is considered an overly broad restriction of the right to strike. According to Article 88 of the Collective Agreement for Employees of Croatian Radio and Television, during the restriction of the right to strike, the employer was obliged to use all methods of peaceful settlement of collective labour disputes in order to remove all reasons for dissatisfaction of employees. The provision prohibiting strikes by employees of Croatian Radio and Television when they perform their work as a public service has been in force continuously for more than 20 years. However, previously it was specified by law when the employees of Croatian Radio and Television performed their work as a public service. Namely, in Article 3(4) of the Act on Croatian Radio and Television of 2001 (Official Gazette No. 17/2001) it was stated: 'Croatian Radio and Television performs its activities as a public service only in cases of natural disasters, epidemics, state of emergency or war.' By its Decision of 6 February 2024, the Constitutional Court of the Republic of Croatia abolished Article 43(3) of the Act on Croatian Radio-Television. Namely, 'this provision does not meet the requirements of legal certainty', the legitimate aim of restricting the strike is not clearly visible, and the means used are not adequate and proportionate to the need to restrict that right.[30]

Regarding judicial authorities, judges are not entitled to strike since they are not in an employment relationship but represent judicial power, one of the three (legislative, executive, and judicial) levels of power in the state. Nevertheless, due to their remuneration dissatisfaction, judges in Croatia were slowing down their work (go-slow; in Italian: *sciopero bianco*) in May 2023, as a pressure method to get higher salaries.[31] They did not stop working entirely but did minimum work; i.e., they worked only on urgent cases. Views prevailed that the go-slow of work by judges was illegal, among others, because it was contrary to Article 10(1) of the Civil Procedure Act,[32] according to which the civil procedure must be carried out without delay, within a reasonable time and with as few costs as possible.[33]

30. Paragraphs 15 and 16 of the Decision of the Constitutional Court of the Republic of Croatia U-I-1621/2023, 6 February 2024 (Official Gazette No. 18/2024).
31. *Od 8. do 19. svibnja suci u bijelom štrajku: rade samo na hitnim predmetima* (*Informator* 4 May 2023), https://informator.hr/vijesti/od-8-do-19-svibnja-suci-u-bijelom-strajku-rade-samo-na-hitnim-predmetima (accessed 10 June 2025).
32. Civil Procedure Act, *Zakon o parničnom postupku* (Official Gazette Nos 4/1977, 36/1977, 36/1980, 6/1980, 69/1982, 43/1982, 58/1984, 74/1987, 57/1989, 20/1990, 27/1990, 35/1991, 53/1991, 91/1992, 112/1999, 129/2000, 88/2001, 117/2003, 88/2005, 2/2007, 96/2008, 84/2008, 123/2008, 57/2011, 25/2013, 89/2014, 70/2019, 80/2022, 114/2022, 155/2023).
33. *Ugledni profesori pravnih fakulteta tvrde da je štrajk sudaca posve nezakonit: 'Ovo što rade je nakaradno'* (*Telegram* 9 May 2023), https://www.telegram.hr/politika-kriminal/ugledni-profesori-pravnih-fakulteta-tvrde-da-je-strajk-sudaca-posve-nezakonit-ovo-sto-rade-je-nakaradno/ (accessed 10 June 2025).

2.2 Essential Services in the Strict Sense of the Term

In Croatia, the minimum service levels in the public sector at the time of strike are regulated by separate pieces of legislation, based on Article 60(2) of the Constitution of the Republic of Croatia.

As regards the absolute ban and restrictions of the right to strike of the employees in the healthcare sector, the Health Care Act[34] is relevant. More precisely, Article 198 of the Health Care Act prescribes: 'A strike is not allowed in the Croatian Institute for Emergency Medicine, the institutes for emergency medicine of regional self-government units, i.e., the City of Zagreb, and contracted emergency medicine services of health institutions.' Apart from the prohibition of strike in emergency medicine services, regarding the other health activities of health institutions, at the proposal of the Ministry, the Ministry and the trade union determine by agreement the most necessary tasks that must be performed continuously in order to prevent endangering the life or the occurrence of disability of the patient. If the Ministry and the union do not reach an agreement within 15 days from the date of delivery of the Ministry's proposal, the Ministry or the union may, within a further 15 days, ask for arbitration to decide on these matters. If the Ministry has not proposed determining those tasks by the day the conciliation procedure ends, the procedure for determining those tasks cannot be started until the day the strike ends (Article 199 of the Health Care Act). Hence, these provisions are, *mutatis mutandis*, in line with the Labour Act provisions on the establishment of essential activities that cannot be stopped during a strike.

Active military personnel in Croatia are not allowed to strike (Article 15(2) of the Act on Armed Forces of the Republic of Croatia);[35] i.e., they are forbidden to strike without exceptions. However, other civil servants and employees employed by the Armed Forces of Croatia are allowed to strike, except in certain statutorily defined situations. Namely, they are not allowed to strike in a state of war or in a state of immediate threat to the independence, unity and existence of the Republic of Croatia; in case of strike which is directly related to preparedness measure; in case when strike is directly related to the combat readiness of the Armed Force and in case of strike which threatens the vital functions of the Armed Forces (Article 15(6) of the Act on Armed Forces of the Republic of Croatia). There was an attempt to challenge the same provision which prohibited unionization of the active military personnel and right to strike of active military personnel contained in the 2002 Act on Armed Forces in the Republic of Croatia before the Constitutional Court of the Republic of Croatia.[36] However, the Constitutional Court of the Republic of Croatia has concluded that this provision was in line with the Constitution of the Republic of Croatia; i.e., in its opinion, 'unionization of active military personnel is limited in accordance with the

34. Health Care Act, *Zakon o zdravstvenoj zaštiti* (Official Gazette Nos 100/2018, 125/2019, 133/2020, 147/2020, 136/2021, 119/2022, 156/2022, 33/2023, 36/2024).
35. Act on Armed Forces of the Republic of Croatia, *Zakon o službi u Oružanim snagama Republike Hrvatske* (Official Gazette Nos 73/2013, 75/2015, 50/2016, 30/2018, 125/2019, 158/2023, 14/2024).
36. The Constitutional Court of the Republic of Croatia, U-I/3776/2013, 26 November 2015.

principle of proportionality due to a legitimate goal provided for by the Constitution'.[37] Nevertheless, in the legal doctrine, there is an opinion that the statutory restriction of the right to strike of active military personnel is overly wide and not in line with the Constitution. Namely, Potočnjak thinks that in line with the above-cited Article 60(2), the Constitution allows solely for the restriction of the right to strike to certain categories of workers or in certain situations, including the ones employed by the Armed Forces, and no way absolute ban on the right to strike in the whole sector.[38] Similarly, in 2018, the European Committee of Social Rights concluded that it had not been demonstrated that the sectors in which the right to strike may be restricted in Croatia are not overly wide and that these restrictions satisfy the conditions laid down in Article 31 of the 1961 Charter.[39]

Police officers in Croatia are entitled to strike, except in the statutorily defined exceptional situations. Namely, they are not allowed to strike in case of: a state of war or an immediate threat to the independence and unity of the state; armed rebellion, uprising and other forms of violent endangerment of the constitutional order of the Republic of Croatia or fundamental freedoms and rights of man and citizens; declared natural disasters or direct threats of their occurrence in the territory of two or more counties or in the entire territory of the Republic of Croatia; and other disasters and accidents that interfere with the normal course of life and threaten the safety of people and property. Furthermore, a police officer is also obliged to use police powers while participating in a strike if necessary for: protection of life and safety of people; the arrest and bringing to the competent authority of a person caught in a criminal offense for which s/he is being prosecuted ex officio; preventing the commission and detection of the perpetrator of a criminal offense for which s/he is prosecuted ex officio (Article 39 of the Police Act).[40]

It is worth mentioning that in the Croatian modern legal history, several statutory provisions on restrictions on the right to strike were considered unconstitutional by the Constitutional Court of the Republic of Croatia. More precisely, the statutory provisions limiting the right to strike of workers employed by the providers of electricity services, the public postal and telecommunications company, Croatian Railways and Croatian Air Traffic Control were in the late 1990s abolished as unconstitutional.[41] Those provisions were declared unconstitutional due to the fact that in case of strike the sectoral ministers were in charge of defining the necessary volume of service functioning by their unilateral decisions in order to protect the vital interests of the social community, or to protect the special interests of the Republic of Croatia, other legal

37. *Ibid.*
38. Potočnjak, *supra* n. 19, at 156 and 257.
39. ECSR Conclusions XXI-3 (2018) – Croatia – Art. 6(4). *See also*: Natalia Delgado, *The Right to Strike in the Public Sector: Croatia* 15-16 (EPSU and ETUI 2019).
40. Police Act, *Zakon o policiji* (Official Gazette Nos 34/2011, 130/2012, 89/2014, 151/2014, 33/2015, 121/2016, 66/2019, 155/2023).
41. For more details, *see*: Renata Gerkman Rudec, *Pravo na štrajk i ograničenje tog prava u svjetlu prakse Ustavnog suda Republike Hrvatske,* 40(4) Pravo u gospodarstvu 291-301 (2001). *See also*: Zlatan Turčić, *Mogućnost ograničenja ustavnog prava na štrajk: praksa Ustavnog suda Republike Hrvatske*, Aktualnosti hrvatskog zakonodavstva i pravne prakse: građansko, trgovačko, (6) radno i procesno pravo u praksi 411-419 (1999).

entities or citizens. The Constitutional Court considered that the trade unions had to be allowed to participate equally with the relevant ministers in the process of determining the necessary minimum provision of services in these activities during the strike.[42]

2.3 Situations of Acute National or Local Crisis

As explained above, it is statutorily prescribed that police officers, firefighters and civil servants and employees employed by the Armed Forces of Croatia are not entitled to strike in extraordinary situations such as war, catastrophes, or other extraordinary events that disrupt the normal course of life and threaten the safety of people and property.

Furthermore, the Constitution of the Republic of Croatia, Article 17(1) and 17(2) states:

> Individual constitutionally guaranteed freedoms and rights may be curtailed during a state of war or any clear and present danger to the independence and unity of the Republic of Croatia or in the event of any natural disaster. Such curtailment shall be decided upon by the Croatian Parliament by a two-thirds majority of all representatives or, if the Croatian Parliament is unable to convene, by the President of the Republic. The extent of such restrictions must be adequate to the nature of the threat and may not result in the inequality of citizens with respect to race, colour, gender, language, religion, national or social origin.

Apart from the statutorily prescribed restrictions of right to strike of the above-mentioned categories of workers, it derives from Article 17(1) and 17(2) of the Constitution of the Republic of Croatia that the right to strike as one of the constitutionally guaranteed rights can be restricted during a state of war or any clear and present danger to the independence and unity of the Republic of Croatia or in the event of any natural disaster, even to other categories of workers when the Croatian Parliament so decides.

3 COMPENSATORY GUARANTEES FOR WORKERS DEPRIVED OF THE RIGHT TO STRIKE

The workers who are deprived of the right to strike need to be compensated,[43] in line with the decision of the ILO Freedom of Association Committee.[44] As regards the nature of appropriate guarantees in cases where restrictions are placed on the right to strike in essential services and public service, the ILO Freedom of Association Committee considers that 'restrictions on the right to strike should be accompanied by adequate,

42. *Ibid.*
43. Same: Bilić & Perkušić, *supra* n. 25, at 129-130.
44. For more details, *see*: *Freedom of Association International Labour Office Geneva Digest of Decisions and Principles of the Freedom of Association Committee of the Governing Body of the ILO Fifth (Revised) Edition*, paras 595-603 (ILO 2006), https://www.ilo.org/wcmsp5/groups/public/---ed_norm/---normes/documents/publication/wcms_090632.pdf (accessed 10 June 2025).

impartial and speedy conciliation and arbitration proceedings in which the parties concerned can take part at every stage and in which the awards, once made, are fully and promptly implemented'.[45]

Taking these opinions into account, it can be concluded that neither of the special laws banning or restricting right to strike does not provide specific compensatory guarantees in the form of speedy conciliation or arbitration proceedings in exchange of the restriction to the right to strike.

However, it is worth pointing out that nevertheless we are of the opinion that Article 206 of the Labour Act is applicable because it prescribes that in case of dispute which could result in a strike or other form of industrial action, the mediation procedure must be conducted, except when the parties have reached an agreement on an alternative amicable method for its resolution. Furthermore, based on Article 210 of the Labour Act, parties to a dispute may agree to bring their collective labour dispute before an arbitration body. If a dispute concerns the application of laws and regulations or collective agreement, an arbitration body shall base its decision on such law, another regulation or collective agreement, but if a dispute concerns the conclusion, amendment or renewal of a collective agreement, an arbitration body shall base its decision on equitable grounds. Moreover, in that case, an arbitration award shall have the legal force and effects of the collective agreement (Article 212 of the Labour Act), hence preventing the possibility of strike.

Further on, as described above under section 1.2, when determining essential activities and maintenance of production activities which must not be stopped during a strike or a lockout, Article 214 of the Labour Act prescribes even mandatory arbitration in the case of lack of agreement between employer and trade union. A similar provision is contained in the Health Care Act regarding limitations to the right to strike in health institutions (apart from emergency medicine services where strike is banned).

4 CONCLUSION

The right to strike is a constitutional right which is by the Constitution (Article 60(2)) and by law (Article 220 of the Labour Act) allowed to be restricted in four public sectors: the Armed Forces, the police, the state administration and public services. Restrictions are allowed only by law. Croatian legislator has chosen to use its right to restrict right to strike only in three out of four allowed public sectors, i.e., in the Armed Forces, the police and four areas of public services (healthcare, firefighting, postal service and kindergartens), leaving public administration specifically unregulated (hence with no allowed restriction to the right to strike).

It can be identified that laws prescribe two main levels of restriction of the right to strike:

45. *Ibid.*, para. 596.

(1) absolute ban (for active military personnel and employees in charge of emergency medicine services); and
(2) relative limitations which can be further categorized into three groups:
   (i) ban of strike in certain specific situations of danger, such as war, military rebellions, and natural disasters prescribed by special laws (it has been prescribed for firefighters, police, and employees in Armed Forces);
   (ii) limitation to the right to strike by imposing regular performance of some services within a specific public sector prescribed by special laws (in healthcare services other than emergency medicine services, in postal services for delivery of postal items of the fastest category and in preschool sector for nutrition, healthcare and other care for children in kindergartens); and
   (iii) possibility to agree upon 'essential activities' and 'maintenance of production activities' which must not be stopped during strike pursuant to the rules of Article 214 of the Labour Act.

In private sector, the trade union and the employer may prepare and adopt an agreement on rules applicable to the maintenance of production activities and essential activities which must not be stopped during a strike or lockout which works well in practice. In this context, it should be mentioned that there are not many strikes in Croatia.

It can be concluded that the restrictions to the right to strike have been regulated adequately since the statutory provision on the right to strike of the employees of the public information service provided by Croatian Radio-Television has been abolished by the Constitutional Court of the Republic of Croatia as too restrictive.

CHAPTER 9

Restrictions on the Right to Strike in Cyprus

Nicos Trimikliniotis

1 GENERAL INFORMATION

1.1 Legal Basis of the Right to Strike

The Constitution of the Republic of Cyprus protects the right to collective bargaining (Article 26), and the right to strike is explicitly protected (Article 27). The Public Service Law 1990, Article 63, under the heading 'trade union rights' provides that 'freedom of trade unionism and the free exercise of the rights attaching thereto shall be guaranteed to employees'.[1] The Law on Trade Unions 1965 (71/65) provides the procedure for a strike to place. The Republic has also ratified ILO Conventions, such as No. 105, No. 87 on trade union freedoms, and No. 98 on the right to organize trade unions and collective bargaining. Also, beyond the EU Charter for Fundamental Rights, which specifically provides the right to strike under Article 28, important, and regularly cited in Cyprus is the European Social Charter.[2] In particular, regularly cited is Article 6(4) on the right for collective action to defend their interest, including the right to strike and Article 31 which stipulates the kind of acceptable restrictions to the right to strike. Until 1960, Cyprus was a British Colony, but the colonial legislation is saved and continues to be in force, as per Article 188 of the Constitution. When it comes to essential services, colonial legislation is often cited. During World War II, Britain enacted the Supplies and Services Law (Transitional Powers Continuation), Cap 175A, which maintains in force Defence Regulations 79A and 79B and the Essential Services

1. The Greek text reads: 'Συνδικαλιστικό δικαίωμα. Η συνδικαλιστική ελευθερία και η ανεμπόδιστη άσκηση των συναφών με αυτή δικαιωμάτων διασφαλίζονται στους υπαλλήλους'.
2. Ratified with Laws 64/1967 and 5/1976. The revised Social Charter 1996 was ratified with Law 27(III)/2000.

Order.[3] This legislation, British case law and other British colonial legislation which were repealed are used for the interpretation of the right to strike and possible restrictions. As there is no definition of 'strike' in the Constitution, courts have interpreted this as a practice of cessation of work as 'a collective action' which is 'a right of workers, which is recognized in most countries as a legitimate weapon of trade unions to promote the interests of their members'.[4]

1.2 Main Features of the Regulation

The constitutional provisions set the frame for the right to strike, including those in essential services. However, the constitutional prohibition of strikes for the army and the police is framed in such absolute terms that it is disputed by legal scholars, lawyers, and judges whether the absolute prohibition is permitted. These matters have not been decided in court.

Article 26(1) provides: 'Every person has the right to enter freely into any contract subject to such conditions, limitations or restrictions as are laid down by the general principles of the law of contract. A law shall provide for the prevention of exploitation by persons who are commanding economic power.'

Also, Article 26(2) provides that legislation may be enacted to regulate collective bargaining, which may affect the right to strike: 'A law may provide for collective labour contracts of obligatory fulfilment by employers and workers with adequate protection of the rights of any person, whether or not represented at the conclusion of such contract.' Despite occasional threats by different governments in the past, so far, no law has been enacted based on Article 26(2).

The right to strike provided: '27 (1) The right to strike is recognized and its exercise may be regulated by law for the purposes only of safeguarding the security of the Republic or the constitutional order or the public order or the public safety or the maintenance of supplies and services essential to the life of the inhabitants or the protection of the rights and liberties guaranteed by this Constitution to any person.' However, there is explicit absolute prohibition of the right to strike under Article 27(2) for the armed forces, the police, and the gendarmerie, with the opportunity for legislation to extend such prohibition to the public service. '27 (2). The members of the armed forces, of the police and of the gendarmerie shall not have the right to strike. A law may extend such prohibition to the members of the public service.' Again, no law based on Article 27(2) has been enacted so far.

The absolute prohibition of 27(2) is disputed by some legal scholars and judges in Cyprus, as will be discussed below.

3. C. Tornaritis, 'Η Φύσις της Νομοθεσίας περί Ουσιωδών Υπηρεσιών και Έργων' [The Nature of the Legislation on Essential Services and Works], *Κυπριακό Νομικό Βήμα* 3, 9-12 (1975); A. Loizou, *Σύνταγμα της Κυπριακής Δημοκρατίας* (Kailas, Nicosia), 169-173 (2000).
4. *Ship Panayia Myrtiotissa v. Sidiropoulou and another* (1998) 1 CLR 1000 (in Greek), available at: https://www.cylaw.org/cgi-bin/open.pl?file=/apofaseis/aad/meros_1/1998/rep/1998_1_1000.htm (accessed June 2025).

On occasions, the Government threatened to make such a law as part of its bargaining tactics, but this was never even put before parliament. There is however little public support to restrict the right to strike, as Cyprus has a strong tripartite tradition with few strikes, and there is no party support to get such as law through parliament. The unions in the public sector have traditionally been strong with a large number of employees in the public sector. A large number of public sector workers have permanent positions and enjoy better pay and working conditions than those working in the private sector. Therefore, they were not militant. However, recently, particularly after the financial crisis and the Troika memorandum, there is a new militancy among some segments of public sector workers who do not enjoy what they consider to be acceptable conditions of pay and working conditions, some of them in essential services, such as nurses and doctors. There have been stoppages of work and strikes in these.

The matter is regulated by voluntary tripartite agreements as the opportunity to legislate to regulate collective bargaining in the public sector, including the right to strike, has not been taken up. Instead, collective bargaining is generally regulated by the voluntary Industrial Relations Code (IRC),[5] with a specific agreement on labour disputes in essential service signed by trade unions, employers' associations and the Minister of Labour in March 2004, as an extension of the IRC.[6]

The Agreement on the Settlement of Labour Disputes in Essential Services entered into force on 16 March 2004. The Agreement complements the Industrial Relations Code and is therefore fully consistent with the voluntary nature of the industrial relations system applied in Cyprus. The Agreement was signed by the social partners and the Ministry of Labour and Social Insurance. In order to uniformly regulate the resolution of labour disputes in essential services and in the public sector, in November 2005, by a decision of the Council of Ministers, the Agreement on the Labour Dispute Resolution Procedure was extended to the public sector. Under the Agreement, essential services are defined as those services whose interruption would endanger the life, personal safety or health of all or part of the population. In the Agreement, there are specific services which are defined as 'Designated Essential Services' which relate to works or activities that are necessary for the following:

(1) The provision of a continuous supply of electricity.
(2) The provision of water supply for water supply purposes.
(3) Ensuring the operation of telecommunications.
(4) The safe operation of air transport and air traffic control.
(5) The operation of hospitals.

5. J.H. Slocum, *The Development of Labour Relations in Cyprus* (PIO, Nicosia) (1972); Trimiklinitis, N., 'Recent Trends of Collective Bargaining in Cyprus', Papademetriou, C. (ed.), *Recent Trends of Collective Bargaining in Balkan and Southeastern European States*, Sakkoulas, Athens, 21-34.
6. Συμφωνία για την διαδικασία διευθέτησης εργατικών διαφορών στις ουσιώδεις υπηρεσίες, https://www.mlsi.gov.cy/mlsi/dlr/dlr.nsf/All/5275C97BEF460B4DC22586E90041F30A/$file/%CE%A3%CF%85%CE%BC%CF%86%CF%89%CE%BD%CE%AF%CE%B1.pdf?OpenElement (accessed 27 June 2025).

(6) The operation of prisons.
(7) The repair or maintenance of the equipment and electromechanical installations of the National Guard and the police, including the Fire Brigade.
(8) The safe operation of port traffic.

2 PERMITTED RESTRICTIONS

Limitations to the right to strike are permitted, but these must be strictly limited and of such nature and practice that must not undermine or negate the right. Since the 1960s, numerous lawyers (some of whom have become Supreme Court judges later),[7] the attorney general,[8] the deputy attorney general[9] and other scholars have debated the extent and limitations to the right to strike.[10] This debate continues with calls for regulation by employers whenever there is a strike in any essential or strategic service with the employers' associations calling for legislative regulation of strikes in essential services.[11] This is strongly opposed by trade unions.[12] There are no immediate plans to proceed with legislation.

The wording of Article 27(2) contains an absolute denial of the existence of this right which is a subject that has not been decided in court.[13] It is disputed whether this

7. A. Loizou, *Σύνταγμα* της Κυπριακής *Δημ*οκρατίας (Nicosia, Kailas), 169-173 (2001); T. Eliades, 'The Termination of Employment Law: A Halting Point over Wrongful Dismissals' Κυπριακό Νο*μικό* Βή*μα* 1, 225-228 (1972).
8. C.G. Tornaritis, 'Η Φύσις της Νομοθεσίας περί Ουσιωδών Υπηρεσιών και Έργων' Κυπριακό Νο*μικό* Βή*μα* 3, 9-12 (1975); C.G. Tornaritis, 'Συλλογική Σύμβασις Εργασίας' Κυπριακό Νο*μικό* Βή*μα* 1-2, 14-17 (1972); C.G. Tornaritis, Πολιτειακόν Δίκαιον της Κυπριακής *Δημ*οκρατίας (Nicosia, Kentron Epistimonikon Erevnon) 199-201 (1982).
9. L. Loukaides, 'Νομική Προστασία της Συνδικαλιστικής Ελευθερίας στην Κύπρο/Legal Protection of the Freedom of Trade Unionism in Cyprus', Επιθεώρηση Κυπριακού Δικαίου 15, 2346-2359 (1986); 'Νομική Προστασία της Συνδικαλιστικής Ελευθερίας στην Κύπρο/Legal Protection of the Freedom of Trade Unionism in Cyprus', Θέ*μα*τα Κυπριακού Δικαίου II, 117-125 (Nicosia, 1988).
10. P. Polyviou, Το Κυπριακό Εργατικό Δίκαιο Κύπρου. Θεωρία και Πράξη (Nicosia, Chryssafinis & Polyviou) 73-78 (2018); S. Yiannakourou, Κυπριακό Εργατικό Δίκαιο (Athens, Nomiki Bibliothiki), 78 (2022).
A. Emilianides & C. Ioannou, *Labour Law in Cyprus* (Alphen aan den Rijn: Wolters Kluwer International), 258-261 (2024).
11. 'OEB: Όχι σε απεργιακά μέτρα στα δημόσια νοσηλευτήρια', *InBusinessNews*, 28 June 2024.
'OEB: Απαράδεκτη η απεργία στο λιμάνι Λάρνακας-"Η κατάσταση έφθασε στο απροχώρητο"', *InBusinessNews*, 8 May 2024, https://inbusinessnews.reporter.com.cy/article/2024/5/8/773814/oeb-aparadekte-e-apergia-sto-limani-larnakas-e-katastase-ephthase-sto-aprokhoreto/.
'Σταύρος Σταύρου: Νομοθετική ρύθμιση των απεργιών στις ουσιώδεις υπηρεσίες', *InBusinessNews*, 8 January 2024, https://inbusinessnews.reporter.com.cy/article/2024/1/8/751927/stauros-staurou-nomothetike-ruthmise-ton-apergion-stis-ousiodeis-uperesies/.
12. C. Apostolides, Δικαίω*μα* στα *μέ*λη της Αστυνο*μ*ίας να απεργούν (ASDYK 19 April 2024), https://asdyk.org/dikaioma-sta-meli-tis-astynomias-na-apergoun/.
13. C. Christodoulou, *A Study of Labour Law in Cyprus* (Doctoral Dissertation University of Wales), 216-258 (1992); C. Christodoulou, Εγχειρίδιο Κυπριακού Εργατικού Δικαίου (Nicosia, Epifaniou) 79-92 (2009).

is in compliance with the ILO International Conventions, the Social Charter and the EU Charter for Fundamental Rights.[14]

2.1 Certain Categories of Public Servants

The issue of strikes in essential services has been in issue very soon after the establishment of the Republic of Cyprus. Since 1962 the Committee of Independent Experts of the ILO persistently required clarifications about the colonial legislation Supplies and Services Law (Transitional Powers Continuation), Cap 175A, including the Defence Regulations 79A and 79B and the Essential Services Order.[15] The matter is still debated. Most lawyers today agree that the absolute prohibition of the right to strike of the army and police is problematic and must violate the relevant ILO Conventions, the EU Charter for Fundamental Rights and the European Social Charter.

In the 1960s up to the early 1980s, the attorney general of the Republic was of the view that there was no problem with the non-existence of the right to strike for these groups. The then attorney general[16] was a proponent of the absolute prohibition on strikes in essential services, based on the continuing operation of the colonial legislation, strongly countering the view that such absolute prohibition must be contrary to the ILO and international conventions. To justify his view,[17] the Attorney General, Tornaritis, argued that the provisions of the colonial law he construed as being in force are akin to the British Industrial Relations Act 1971.[18] In another influential text, where he comments on the right to strike as a fundamental right, the attorney general acknowledges that 'the power to regulate does not include the power to totally prohibition'.[19] Nonetheless, he concluded that the Republic of Cyprus is empowered to entirely ban strikes for the army and the police. He considers the prohibition permissible as 'this is a matter of degree'.[20] Moreover, he considered that the nature of the function of the army and police is such that it is inconceivable that these forces can proceed to a strike which is essentially 'a cessation of work'. Hence, he saw no contradiction, despite the prima facie antithesis of the two positions. This is not

14. C. Apostolides, *Δικαίωμα στα μέλη της Αστυνομίας να απεργούν* (ASDYK 19 April 2024), https://asdyk.org/dikaioma-sta-meli-tis-astynomias-na-apergoun/.
15. C.G. Tornaritis, 'Η Φύσις της Νομοθεσίας περί Ουσιωδών Υπηρεσιών και Έργων' [The Nature of the Legislation on Essential Services and Works], *Κυπριακό Νομικό Βήμα* 3, 9-12 (1975); A. Loizou, *Σύνταγμα της Κυπριακής Δημοκρατίας* (Kailas, Nicosia), 169-173 (2000).
16. Criton G. Tornaritis (1902-1997) was the longest serving attorney general in Cyprus. He served as AG during British colonial times between 1952 and 1956 and with the founding of the Republic between 1960 and his retirement in 1984. He was succeeded by Stella Soulioti, who was the attorney general from 1984 to 1988.
17. C.G. Tornaritis, 'Η Φύσις της Νομοθεσίας περί Ουσιωδών Υπηρεσιών και Έργων' [The Nature of the Legislation on Essential Services and Works], *Κυπριακό Νομικό Βήμα* 3, 9-12, 12 (1975).
18. The law limited wildcat strikes and prohibited limitations on legitimate strikes. It also established the National Industrial Relations Court, which was empowered to grant injunctions as necessary to prevent injurious strikes and settle a variety of labour disputes.
19. He cites G. Burdeu, *Les Liberteus publiques Les libertés publiques* (Librairie générale de droit et de jurisprudence) (1961).
20. He cites D. Das Basu, *Commentary on the Constitution of India* (Calcutta, S.C. Sarkar and Son), 578 (1956).

surprising given Tornaritis' broader philosophy regarding state necessity, as he was probably the brain behind the 'doctrine of necessity', i.e., a state of exception that would allow the state to operate despite breaches of basic constitutional provisions in 1964.[21]

The view of the former attorney general is not accepted by most lawyers and scholars. Another lawyer suggests that similar prohibitions exist in most constitutions of the world, but police strikes do take place in most Western countries, rendering the position of the former attorney general doubtful.[22]

Most lawyers dispute the above *absolute prohibition* and non-existence of the right to strike for the army, police and gendarmerie contained in the Constitution. They reject the argument that the nature of the services of these forces whose function is to maintain law and order and the safety of the Republic renders the right to strike as 'wholly inconsistent with their status'. From the 1970s, Eliades pointed out that there appears certain inconsistency between Article 27(2) and Article 8 of the International Covenant on Economic, Social and Cultural Rights of the United Nations: Article 8(2) provides that 'this article shall not prevent the imposition of lawful restrictions on the exercise of these rights by members of the Armed Forces or the Police, or of the administration of the states'.[23] Some argue that the complete constitutional denial of the existence of the right to strike to members of the armed forces and the police is contrary to ICESCR which recognizes the existence of such a right and gives only powers to impose lawful restrictions on the exercise of the right: 'However, provided that a strike presupposes the cessation of work in relation to a trade dispute and the existence of relationship of Employer and Employee it cannot be resorted to by members of the Armed Forces in spite of the apparent inconsistency of the Constitution and the Covenant on Economic, Social and Cultural Rights.'[24]

Even though under Convention No. 87, members of the police and the armed forces are the only authorized exceptions from the scope of application of the Convention and this is provided in Article 27 of the Constitution, these exceptions had been construed by the former attorney general in a rather broad manner to deny their rights to strike altogether. Most lawyers in Cyprus today however consider that the absolute prohibition of the right to strike contravenes Article 8 of the International Covenant on Economic, Social and Cultural Rights of the United Nations.[25]

21. C. Combos & A. Constatinides, Κρίτων Τορναρίτης: *Επιλεγμένες Γνωματεύσεις Συνταγματικού* Δικαίου (Athens, Νομική Βιβλιοθήκη) (2019); and N. Trimikliniotis, 'The Proliferation of the Cypriot States of Exception', *The Cyprus Review*, 30(2), 43-84, October 2018.
22. C. Christodoulou, *A Study of Labour Law in Cyprus* (Doctoral Dissertation University of Wales) 221 (1992); C. Christodoulou, Εγχειρίδιο Κυπριακού Εργατικού Δικαίου (Nicosia, Epifaniou) 79-92 (2009).
23. Signed by the Republic on 9 January 1967 and ratified on 2 April 1969.
24. T. Eliades, 'The Termination of Employment Law: A Halting Point over Wrongful Dismissals' *Cyprus Law Tribune* 1, 225-228 (1972).
25. A. Loizou, 'Ο Περιορισμός του Δικαιώματος της Απεργίας κάτω από το Κυπριακό Σύνταγμα και τις Διεθνείς Συμβάσεις' Λυσίας 11, 23-30 (1995); A. Loizou, *Σύνταγμα της* Κυπριακής *Δημοκρατίας* (Nicosia, Kailas), 169-173 (2001). C. Paraskeva, Κυπριακό *Συνταγματικό* Δίκαιο (Athens, Nomiki Vivliothiki), 444 (2015).

In Cyprus, there has been no debate or commentary on the right to strike of the fire service personnel and prison staff who are administratively under the command and structure of the police. The Police Regulations[26] also cover special police officers[27] and fire officers.[28] Police, fire brigadiers and prison guards have unions but there has never been a strike action.

Another relevant matter involving public officials is the case which involves the right of advocates and judges to strike.[29] In this case, the court examined the right to strike of advocates, including those representing the attorney general's office and judges, following the Cyprus Bar Council's invitation to advocates to abstain from appearing before the courts on 21 December 1984. The Bar protested certain decisions of the Supreme Court unconnected with the facts of the above or any particular case, and when the above recourse was called, both the applicant and his counsel, as well as the Counsel of the Republic, were absent. The judge, obiter, stated that while the right to strike is fundamental and must be respected, as 'both judges and advocates play a part in the administration of justice', their right to strike is somehow limited and subordinated to their superior duty for the administration of justice. It would be, he said, 'a flagrant violation of the constitutional duty of Judges to safeguard unimpeded access to Courts of law and breach of the constitutional right of audience of the litigant and his advocate before the Court'. He considered judges as 'dutybound to administer justice according to law', given that in the exercise of this power 'they are the mouthpiece of the law itself': 'It is the responsibility of Judges to uphold the judicial process not only for the protection of the rights of individual litigants but also those of the public in the due administration of the law. For, it is through the efficacy of the judicial process that the rule of law can be sustained. Advocates, too, have an important part to play in the administration of justice.'

2.2 Essential Services in the Strict Sense of the Term

The nature of essential services has been a matter of legal debate in Cyprus since the 1940s when the British colonial authorities passed special legislation during the war; this legislation has not been repealed ever since. In 1983, the Committee issued an opinion that the colonial provisions are not in line with Article 1(b) and 1(c) of Convention No. 105 (Abolition of Forced Labour, 1957) and Convention No. 87 (Freedom of Association and Protection of the Right to Organize, 1948): 'The Committee points out that a prohibition of the right to strike must be limited to essential services in the strict sense of the term, that is those whose interruption would endanger life, persona safety or health of the whole or part of the population.' Therefore, the relevant Regulations issued in the 1940s do not conform with 8(2) of Convention No.

26. Issued under Art. 13, the Law on Police, 73(I)/2004 (Ο Περί Αστυνομίας Νόμος του) (2004).
27. Under the Law on Police, 73(I)/2004 (Ο Περί Αστυνομίας Νόμος του 2004), Art. 13(2)(i).
28. Article 13(2)(j) of the Law on Police, 73(I)/2004.
29. *Rousos V the Republic* (1984) 3 CLR 1437, 22 December 1984.

105 and they are too wide.[30] The Government's response in 1987 was that it is unnecessary to repeal these because the attorney general has reconsidered anew the matter and that the new reading is that the provisions contained in the Essential Works order of 1943 and Defence Regulations 79A and 79B ca only be applied to the extent that they are not inconsistent with the Constitution, including the prohibition of forced or compulsory labour (Article 10) and the right to strike (Article 27). So far, the sole occasion where Regulations 79A and 79B were used were when strike action was threatened by employees in Electricity Authority which could have resulted in the discontinuation of electricity to the whole population. The discontinuation of electricity service would entail the kind of action that could be construed as falling within the meaning of Article 27 of the Constitution. Moreover, no person or organization has challenged in court to claim any violation of the right to strike on this matter.[31]

The Employers Federation OEB has been concisely lobbying that the IRC be amended with regard to strikes in essential services, proposing that this be regulated by compulsory arbitration, but this is strongly opposed by the trade unions. The threats by the Government in 1995 that it would introduce legislation regulating strikes in essential services were beaten off by the unions.[32]

2.3 Situations of Acute National or Local Crisis

The question of acute national or local crisis is important given that Cyprus has been in a permanent state of emergency and exception since late 1963. However, there has never been proclamation of state of emergency as provided by Article 183 of the Constitution. Article 183 provides:

> In case of war or other public danger threatening the life of the Republic or any part thereof, the Council of Ministers shall have power, by a decision taken in this respect, to issue a Proclamation of Emergency:
>
>> Provided that the President and the Vice-President of the Republic shall separately or conjointly, have a right of veto against any such decision which they shall exercise within forty-eight hours of the date when the decision has been transmitted to their respective offices.
>> Any such Proclamation shall specify the Articles of the Constitution which shall be suspended for the duration of such Emergency.

Several Articles of the Constitution may be suspended by any such Proclamation, which include Article 27, i.e., the right to strike. The state of emergency declared by the President and the Vice-President of the Republic shall, unless, separately or conjointly,

30. Letter from Th. Sidibe, Chief of International Labour standards Dept of ILO, 23 May 1985, referred by C. Christodoulos, *A Study of Labour Law in Cyprus* (Doctoral Dissertation University of Wales), 237-239 (1992).
31. C. Christodoulou, *A Study of Labour Law in Cyprus* (Doctoral Dissertation University of Wales) 240-241 (1992); C. Christodoulou, Εγχειρίδιο Κυπριακού Εργατικού Δικαίου (Nicosia, Epifaniou) 86-88 (2009).
32. C. Christodoulou, Εγχειρίδιο Εργατικού Δικαίου [Handbook of Labour Law] (Nicosia, Epifaniou) 139 (2009); A. Emilianides and C. Ioannou, *Labour Law in Cyprus* (Alphen aan den Rijn, Wolters Kluwer International) 236-237 (2016).

they have exercised their right of veto as provided, promulgate forthwith such Proclamation by publication in the official Gazette of the Republic. Then a Proclamation promulgated must be laid forthwith before the House of Representatives. If the House of Representatives is not sitting, it must be convened as soon as possible for this purpose which has the right to reject or confirm such Proclamation of Emergency. In the case of rejection, the Proclamation of Emergency shall have no legal effect. Also, 'the Proclamation of Emergency shall cease to operate at the expiration of two months from the date of confirmation by the House of Representatives unless the House, at the request of the Council of Ministers, decides to prolong the duration of the state of emergency, whereupon the President and the Vice-President of the Republic, separately or conjointly, shall have a right of veto against such decision of prolongation'.

In late 1963, there was a major crisis which led to inter-communal violence between Greek Cypriots and Turkish Cypriots. However, no state of emergency was declared, despite the de facto suspension of major provisions of the Constitution. The matter reached the Cyprus Supreme Court in 1964, in the case *Ibrahim*,[33] when the Republic was facing a 'crisis government',[34] declared for itself that it is performing the function of reflecting on the social situation of a crisis-ridden society and is obliged to seek legal solutions to continue the very functioning of the state. The crisis began in 1963, when the Cypriot President Archbishop Makarios proposed to amend basic provisions of the Constitution. This amendment of some of the fundamental provisions of the Constitution removed many of the consociational elements which provided for power-sharing and communal rights of the Turkish Cypriots. The Turkish Cypriots withdrew from the state administration in protest. Since then, with the Turkish Cypriots out of governance, the control of the Republic remained in the hands of the Greek Cypriots. In July 1964, a law was enacted to provide that the Supreme Court should continue the jurisdiction of both the Supreme Constitutional Court and the High Court.[35] The court in *Ibrahim* considered that it performs an 'extraordinary social function':[36]

> This court now, in its all-important and responsible function of transforming legal theory into living law, applied to the facts of daily life for the preservation of social order, is faced with the question whether the legal doctrine of necessity discussed earlier in this judgment, should or should not, be read in the provisions of the written Constitution of the (RoC). Our unanimous view, and unhesitating answer to this question, is in the affirmative.

33. The *Attorney-General of the Republic v. Mustafa Ibrahim and others*, Criminal Appeals No. 2729, 6 October 1964, 7, 8, November 102734, 2735 (1964) CLR 195.
34. S. Kyriakides, *Cyprus Constitutionalism and Cyprus Government* (Philadelphia, University of Pennsylvania Press) (1968).
35. Administration of Justice (Miscellaneous Provisions) Law 33 of 1964.
36. The *Attorney-General of the Republic v. Mustafa Ibrahim and others*, Criminal Appeals No. 2729, 6 October 1964, 7, 8, November 102734, 2735 (1964) CLR 195. The matter was considered to be of such significance that it was placed in the summary judgment, p. 97.

The Supreme Court ruled that the functioning of the Government must continue on the basis of the 'doctrine of necessity':[37]

> In the light of the principles of the law of necessity as applied in other countries and having regard to the provisions of the Constitution of the Republic of Cyprus ... I interpret our Constitution to include the doctrine of necessity in exceptional circumstances which is an implied exception to particular provisions of the Constitution and this to ensure the very existence of the State. The following pre-requisites must be satisfied before the doctrine may become applicable:
>
> - An imperative and inevitable necessity of exceptional circumstances;
> - No other remedy can apply;
> - The measure taken must be proportionate to the necessity; and
> - It must be of a temporary character limited to the duration of the exceptional circumstances.

Ever since 1964, most laws start with a proviso referring to the 'abnormal situation'. The crisis was expanded further in 1974: With the Greek junta coup, the Turkish army invasion, and the de facto partition of Cyprus, the use of 'doctrine of necessity' was extended further despite some critical perspectives on the 'doctrine of necessity';[38] the dominant Greek Cypriot paradigm remained essentially as apologetics for the order produced following the collapse of the bicommunal Republic and the running of the Republic by Greek Cypriots.[39] More than half a century later, the doctrine of necessity was invoked for economic reasons in the case of *Alexandros*

---

37. *Attorney General of the Republic v. Mustafa Ibrahim* (1964) Criminal Appeals No. 2729, 6 October 1964, 7, 8, November 102734, 2735, CLR 264-265.
38. C.M. Constantinou, 'On the Cypriot States of Exception'; N. Trimikliniotis, *The Nation-state Dialectic and the State of Exception: Sociological and Constitutional Studies on the Eurocyprian Conjuncture and the National Question* (Athens, Savalas) (2010); N. Trimikliniotis, 'The Proliferation of the Cypriot States of Exception: The Erosion of Fundamental Rights as Collateral Damage of the Cyprus Problem', *Cyprus Review* 30:2, 43-84 (2018); K. Özersay, 'The Excuse of State Necessity and Its Implications on the Cyprus Conflict', *Perceptions* (Winter 2004-2005); Stratilatis, C., 'Η άδοξη καριέρα του στη Κύπρο: Η δημιουργία και τα πρώτα έτη του βίου της Κυπριακής δημοκρατίας από σμιτιανή σκοπιά', in Emilianides, A., Papastylianos, C. & Stratilatis, C. (eds), Η Κυπριακή Δημοκρατία και το δίκαιο της ανάγκης (Athens, Sakkoulas) (2016); Papastylianos, C., 'Το δίκαιο της ανάγκης και τα θεμελιώδη δικαιώματα των Τουρκοκυπρίων: Η εδαφικότητα και η κυριαρχία ως προϋποθέσεις άσκησης των δικαιωμάτων', Emilianides, A.C., Papastylianos, C. & Stratilatis, C. (eds), Η Κυπριακή Δημοκρατία και το δίκαιο της ανάγκης (Athens, Sakkoulas) (2016).
39. C.G. Tornaritis, *Cyprus and Its Constitutional and Other Legal Problems* (2nd ed. Nicosia) (1980); C.G. Tornaritis, Το πολιτειακό δίκαιο της Κυπριακής Δημοκρατίας (Nicosia) (1982); C. Pikis, *Constitutionalism: Human Rights – Separation of Powers, The Cyprus Precedent* (Leiden/Boston, Martinus Niijhoff) (2006); L. Papaphilippou, Το Δίκαιο της Ανάγκης στη Κύπρο (Nicosia) (1995); A.C. Emilianides, Η υπερβαση του Κυπριακού Συντάγματος (Athens, Sakkoulas) (2006); C. Kombos, *The Doctrine of Necessity in Constitutional Law* (Athens: Sakkoulas) (2015); A.C. Emilianides, 'Το δίκαιο της ανάγκης 50 χρόνια μετά: Σκέψεις επί του Κυπριακού "μηδενικού νόμου,"' Emilianides, A.C., Papastylianos, C. & Stratilatis, C. (eds), Η Κυπριακή Δημοκρατία και το δίκαιο της ανάγκης (Athens, Sakkoulas) (2016); P. Polyviou, *The Case of Ibrahim the Doctrine of Necessity and the Republic of Cyprus* (Nicosia, Chrysafinis and Polyviou) (2015).

Phylaktou v. the Republic of Cyprus,[40] in the context of the austerity package deducting salaries of public sector employees.

The 'doctrine of necessity' has not been invoked on matters pertaining to the right to strike. The only situation in which the doctrine may have played some kind of 'background' reason is the case of a threatened strike action in the Electricity Authority referred to above.

3 COMPENSATORY GUARANTEES FOR WORKERS DEPRIVED OF THE RIGHT TO STRIKE

Under the Agreement on the Settlement of Labour Disputes in Essential Services,[41] the parties have agreed to maintain 'minimum service' in essential services, adopting the ILO interpretation to ensure that the basic needs of the population are met during strikes. In case of disagreement over the content of minimum service, the dispute is referred to arbitration to a three-member committee established by the Ministry of Labour whose decision is mandatory for all parties. Mixed committees have been established consisting of equal members from trade unions and employers' associations to monitor and apply the minimum service provided in cases of strikes or lockouts. However, they have not agreed upon the issue of strikes in essential service.[42]

Also relevant is the amendment to the Civil Aviation Law in 2012.[43] The amended law prohibits any person who is required by the terms of his or her employment to provide Air Traffic Flow Management Services to refuse, when requested to do so by the Director of the Civil Aviation Department, to provide such services on the grounds of the right to strike, if the exercise of that right would result in the degradation of those services below the Minimum Air Traffic Flow Management Service Provision Limit or would be likely to adversely affect national security.

The debate about legislation to be enacted to regulate the right to strike of public servants, particularly those in essential services, intensified during the presidency of the right-wing government of Nicos Anastasiades (2013-2023). The federation OEB has repeatedly called for legislation to regulate the right to strike in essential services.[44]

40. Αλέξανδρου Φυλακτού, Επαρχιακό Δικαστήριο Πάφου και Κυπριακής Δημοκρατίας, *μέσω* Γενικού Λογιστή Υπόθ. 397/2012397/2012 και 480/2012. The attorney general unsuccessfully invoked the case of *Ibrahim*, which invented the 'doctrine of necessity', in arguing that the imperative 'economic necessity' for the austerity salary cuts of all public servants, including judges, was part of the doctrine of necessity.
41. 'Συμφωνία για την διαδικασία διευθέτησης εργατικών διαφορών στις ουσιώδεις υπηρεσίες', https://www.mlsi.gov.cy/mlsi/dlr/dlr.nsf/All/5275C97BEF460B4DC22586E90041F30A/$file/%CE%A3%CF%85%CE%BC%CF%86%CF%89%CE%BD%CE%AF%CE%B1.pdf?OpenElement.
42. C. Christodoulou, Εγχειρίδιο Εργατικού Δικαίου [Handbook of Labour Law] (Nicosia, Epifaniou) 139 (2009); A. Emilianides and C. Ioannou, *Labour Law in Cyprus* (Alphen aan den Rijn, Wolters Kluwer International) 236-237 (2016).
43. Section 6 of Chapter II of the Civil Aviation Law, 2.13 (I)/2020 as amended by 12 (I)/2012, Ο Περί Πολιτικής Αεροπορίας Νόμος του 2002, http://www.cylaw.org/nomoi/enop/non-ind/2002_1_213/full.html.
44. 'Time Regulate Essential Services', *Phileleftheros*, 7 October 2018.

There is strong opposition by trade unions and opposition parties ever since as they consider that such a regulation of such kind amounts to penalization of strike action.[45]

Amid the general election of 2023, a general strike (i.e., stoppage of work) was announced in December 2022, and the employers and industrialist organization, the Federation of Employers & Industrialists (OEB), called on trade unions to suspend the announced strikes and apply the provisions of the statutory procedures to resolve any disputes and reiterated its call for new legislation that would regulate the exercise of the right to strike in essential services.[46]

The debate continued when the new government took office in March 2023. Recent labour disputes rekindle disagreement over banning strikes by law in essential services. The debate on regulation of strikes in essential services in the form of limiting or even banning them rekindled in 2024, when public sector doctors scheduled a strike over a pay dispute with the public sector body in charge of health (OKYPI).[47] The dispute with the doctors was eventually resolved,[48] but once more the employers' associations and trade union crossed their swords. This continued the debate, in the ling of other labour disputes, such as the port disputes when dock workers announced strike action; in the end, dock workers returned to work after the Minister of Labour agreed to meet them.[49]

Employers' associations reiterated their position that strikes in essential services are 'unlawful' and bad for the economy and must therefore be banned by law.[50] The opposite view is taken by trade unions which reiterated their position about the importance of protecting labour rights, including their right to strike; they consider such regulation as penalization of their right to unionize.[51] While ministers criticized the scheduled doctors' strike,[52] the Government has not taken a position on whether it will introduce a bill or reactivate the old legislative bill proposed by the right-wing Democratic Rally leader banning strikes in essential services. Since 2016, when the Democratic Rally, then governing party, submitted a proposal for a law to regulate the

45. 'Δεν πρόκειται για ρύθμιση αλλά για ποινικοποίηση της απεργίας', *Dilalogos*, 6 April 2016.
46. The OEB calls on the EAC Trade Unions to suspend the strikes, 13 December 2022, https://www.oeb.org.cy/i-oev-kalei-tis-syntechnies-tis-aik-na-anasteiloyn-tis-apergies-2/.
47. In a post on 'X' on Saturday, the health minister urged all involved to consider the consequences of the strike action on the public, expressing the hope that it would be averted, https://cyprus-mail.com/2024/06/30/minster-calls-on-striking-doctors-to-consider-consequences.
48. I. Damaskinos & J. Shkurko, 'Doctors' Strike Called Off At Last Minute', *Cyprus Mail*, 1 July 2024, https://cyprus-mail.com/2024/07/01/last-ditch-effort-underway-to-call-off-doctors-strike/.
49. 'Τερματίστηκε η απεργία στο λιμάνι Λάρνακας: Βλέπουν αύριο τον Παναγιώτου οι εργαζόμενοι', *Philenews*, 8 May 2024, https://www.philenews.com/oikonomia/kypros/article/1466899/termatistike-i-apergia-sto-limani-larnakas-vlepoun-avrio-ton-panagiotou-i-ergazomeni/.
50. 'ΟΕΒ-ΚΕΒΕ: Παράτυπη η απεργία στο λιμάνι Λάρνακας – Ζητούν νομοθετική ρύθμιση απεργιών στις ουσιώδεις υπηρεσίες', *Politis*, 8 May 2024, https://politis.com.cy/politis-news/koinonia/784264/oev-keve-paratypi-i-apergia-sto-limani-larnakas-zitoyn-nomothetiki-rythmisi-apergion-stis-oysiodeis-ypiresies; Νομοθετική ρύθμιση των απεργιών στις ουσιώδεις υπηρεσίες ζητά το ΚΕΒΕ, *Cyprus New Agency*, 8 May 2024.
51. PEO 'Προσπάθεια ενοχοποίησης των συνδικαλιστικών και κοινωνικών αγώνων', Pancyprian Federation of Labour, 3 August 2021, https://peo.org.cy/apantisi-peo-se-ergodotikes-organoseis/.
52. N. Brakka, 'Finance Ministry Condemns Upcoming Doctors' Strike', *Cyprus Mail*, June 2024, https://cyprus-mail.com/2024/06/29/finance-ministry-condemns-upcoming-doctors-strike/.

right to strike in essential services, the debate comes on and off stage depending on the various labour disputes. The bill proposed to ban strikes or lockouts in essential services at any stage of dispute resolution and until the decision of the Arbitration Committee, which, according to the bill, would be established to examine the issues at stake in the dispute.

When Larnaca Port workers decided to proceed with strike action, the employer's association accused the Government that it 'does not dare to regulate strikes in key services'[53] and brought forward again the proposal that restrictions must apply to the eight essential services via an obligatory procedure before trade unions can go on strike. Both the OEB and the KEBE condemned the decision of the workers at the port of Larnaca to strike, accusing the unions of violating the labour institutions and procedures since there is an agreement in force for years on the Procedure for the Resolution of Labour Disputes in Essential Services. They called on the Government to proceed with its legislation since the absence of a regulatory framework damages the economy.

The unions vehemently oppose any such legislation. The unions argue that strike regulation has already an established and a well-functioning general framework of regulating strikes by law with a procedure for the convening of a general assembly, a secret ballot and in the case of a majority, the union is allowed to take any measures, including strike action. Trade unions consider that this general arrangement may not apply to essential services, and the specific agreement for a different procedure is sufficient.

As in 2016, when the governing party could not obtain the necessary support in public and secure a parliamentary majority to get it through,[54] no such public support and/or parliamentary support seems to exist today.

As the Government has no position and has not revealed its plans, the public debate is set to continue.

4 CONCLUSION

The Constitution of the Republic of Cyprus protects the right to collective bargaining and the right to strike. The right to strike is recognized, and its exercise may be regulated by law for the purposes only of safeguarding the security of the Republic or the constitutional order or the public order or the public safety or the maintenance of supplies and services essential to the life of the inhabitants or the protection of the rights and liberties guaranteed by this Constitution to any person.

There is however an absolute prohibition on the right to strike for the army and the police, which according to the Constitution may be extended by legislation to cover members of the public service. No such legislation has been enacted, despite calls from

53. C. Zakos, 'Δεν τολμά η κυβέρνηση να ρυθμίσει τις απεργίες σε νευραλγικές υπηρεσίες', *InBussiness News*, 10 May 2024, https://www.brief.com.cy/oikonomia/kypros-oikonomia/den-tolma-i-kybernisi-na-rythmisei-tis-apergies-se-neyralgikes-ypiresies.
54. 'Αβέρωφ: Πρόταση για ρύθμιση απεργιών σε ουσιώδεις υπηρεσίες', *Kathimerini*, 31 March 2016.

the employers' associations and threats from governments, as there is strong labour resistance.

According to the ILO Committee of Experts, the definition of essential services in colonial wartime legislation is too widely defined and contrary to the ILO Conventions. It does not also comply with the Social Charter, the EU Charter of Fundamental Rights. However, the Republic has refused to repeal these laws, suggesting that it is unnecessary to repeal such laws as the Constitution and international treaties take precedence over other legislation and as such, any legislation must be interpreted to comply with these.

Cyprus presents a distinctive paradigm in regulating the right to strike, characterized by robust constitutional protections juxtaposed with unresolved tensions and evolving socio-legal dynamics. The Constitution explicitly guarantees the right to strike (Article 27) while permitting regulation only for narrowly defined purposes of public security, order, or essential services. However, it imposes an absolute prohibition on strikes for the armed forces and police (Article 27(2)) – a provision widely contested by legal scholars for its incompatibility with international standards, including ILO Conventions 87 and 98, the European Social Charter (Article 6(4)), and the EU Charter of Fundamental Rights (Article 28). Despite decades of debate, no legislation has been enacted to extend this prohibition to the broader public sector or to define permissible restrictions, reflecting Cyprus' deep-rooted tripartite tradition and persistent lack of political consensus.

Efforts to impose statutory restrictions have consistently faltered. Colonial-era laws (e.g., Cap 175A) remain technically active but are interpreted restrictively to align with constitutional and international norms, following ILO guidance that limitations must be confined to 'essential services in the strict sense of the term'. Governments have periodically *threatened* legislative action, particularly during labour disputes in critical sectors, yet these initiatives invariably collapse due to overwhelming public opposition, trade union resistance, and insufficient parliamentary support. Instead, regulation relies on voluntary frameworks, notably the 2004 tripartite *Agreement on Settlement of Labour Disputes in Essential Services*, which institutionalizes minimum service levels through arbitration – a pragmatic solution preserving industrial peace while avoiding contentious legislation.

Historically, public sector unions wielded significant influence, securing favourable conditions for permanent employees and fostering a climate of collaboration rather than militancy. However, the post-2013 financial crisis – and the austerity measures imposed under the Troika memorandum – catalysed a transformative shift. Segments of the public sector, including essential workers like nurses and doctors facing eroded pay and conditions, have embraced unprecedented militancy, manifesting in disruptive strikes and work stoppages. This new assertiveness has intensified employer demands for legislative bans in essential services, vehemently opposed by unions as a criminalization of fundamental rights.

Ultimately, Cyprus' approach remains defined by voluntarism and negotiated compromise, underpinned by constitutional safeguards but strained by unresolved contradictions. The absolute ban on security forces' strikes remains a legal anomaly, colonial statutes linger symbolically, and employer-union deadlock persists. Yet, the resilience of tripartite dialogue - coupled with societal resistance to restrictive legislation - continues to shield the right to strike from statutory erosion. As labour dynamics evolve amid economic pressures, this equilibrium faces renewed tests, but the absence of viable political pathways for legislative change suggests continuity will prevail. The Cypriot model thus endures as a testament to constitutional prioritization of strike rights, tempered by pragmatic social partnership - even as its fault lines grow more visible.

CHAPTER 10

Restrictions on the Right to Strike in the Czech Republic

Nataša Randlová

1 GENERAL INFORMATION

1.1 Legal Basis of the Right to Strike

The right to strike is one of the basic social rights and is one of the fundamental means available to workers and their organisations (trade unions) to promote their economic and social interests. The Charter of Fundamental Rights and Freedoms of the Czech Republic (the 'Charter'),[1] in its section 27(4), provides that 'the right to strike is guaranteed under the conditions provided for by law'. The only law that further realises this provision is Act No. 2/1991 Coll. on Collective Bargaining effective as of 1 February 1991 (the 'ACB'). However, the rules on how to call a strike specified in ACB apply only to strikes called in connection with collective bargaining.

Unfortunately, there is no other special or general act on strike that would regulate the conditions for realising the right to strike in a complex manner.

1.2 Main Features of the Regulation

For a strike to be legal under the ACB, relatively strict conditions set forth in section 16(1) and section 17 of the ACB must be met, as follows:

1. Resolution No. 2/1993 Coll. of the Presidium of the Czech National Council on the promulgation of the Charter of Fundamental Rights and Freedoms as part of the constitutional order of the Czech Republic. English translation available online: https://www.usoud.cz/fileadmin/user_upload/ustavni_soud_www/Pravni_uprava/AJ/Listina_English_version.pdf.

- the unsuccessful completion of a mediation procedure – the parties are free to choose their own mediator. If they do not agree on a mediator, the Ministry of Labour and Social Affairs shall appoint one at the request of one of the parties. This request to the Ministry may be made no earlier than 60 days after the first written proposal for a collective agreement has been submitted. The mediator's role is to try to bring the parties to an amicable settlement. The mediator must submit the proposal for resolution of the dispute within 15 days of the commencement of the proceedings (unless otherwise agreed with the parties). If the dispute is not resolved within 20 days of the commencement of the mediation proceedings, the mediation proceedings shall be deemed unsuccessful. These rules of the mediation procedure are specified in sections 11 and 12 of the ACB;
- the consent of at least two-thirds of the employees expressed in a ballot in which at least half of the employees affected by the strike must participate;
- the organiser of the strike (i.e., the trade union) is obliged to announce the strike to the employer at least three days in advance. Such announcement must include the reasons and goals of the strike, as well as the number of participating employees and the list of workplaces which will not be operational during the strike.

No one may be prevented from participating in the strike, but no one may be forced to participate.

With respect to working time and remuneration:

- participation in the strike is considered as an excused absence with no compensation of salary, and the employee shall not be penalised for it;
- if the employee decides not to participate and wants to perform the work, the employer is obliged to allow them such work. If due to the strike, the employer has no work for such employee, compensation of salary must be paid to them.

The ACB also provides in section 16(3) for a solidarity strike, i.e., a strike in support of the demands of employees on strike in a dispute over the conclusion of a different collective agreement. The declaration of a solidarity strike does not require participation in a mediation procedure (*see* above). However, a solidarity strike is legal only if the employer of the participants in the solidarity strike, particularly with regard to economic affiliation, can influence the course or outcome of the strike of the workers whose demands are supported by the solidarity strike. This condition, according to the views expressed in the available literature, would be met where there are certain commercial, technological, ownership, or other ties of such intensity that a solidarity strike would create real economic pressure on the employer with whom the collective bargaining dispute is pending. This would include, for example, a major supplier to the undertaking in which such a dispute is taking place and undertakings with the same owner.[2]

---

2. Šubrt, B. *Odbory, zaměstnavatelé a právo. Karviná: Nakladatelství* Paris, p. 165 (1995).

As strikes in connection with collective bargaining are very limited, the Supreme Court in its judgment of 14 November 2002, Case No. 21 Cdo 2104/2001, ruled that the right to call a strike could also be based on the direct realisation of section 27(4) of the Charter. This means that a strike, which is not connected to collective bargaining, is not (at least not necessarily) illegal.

The problem is that the procedure of calling a strike pursuant to section 27(4) of the Charter is not described by law, and the ACB procedure and limits stipulated in the ACB cannot be - according to court rulings - applied in these cases.

The Supreme Court however provided for some guidelines on how a strike would be legal even if called outside the framework of the ACB. The following conditions shall be met:

- the strike would have to pursue a legitimate aim of promoting the economic and social interests of the employees;
- the strike would have to be proportionate to the legitimate aim pursued;
- the strike would be legal only if it would not disproportionately interfere with the rights of others;
- the right to strike must be exercised in a manner that respects both the rights of persons not participating in the strike and the rights of the employer;
- participation in a strike does not entitle the person taking part to restrict the rights of others beyond what is necessary for the exercise of the right to strike.

2 PERMITTED RESTRICTIONS

Czech law restricts the right to strike in relation to certain groups of employees and also in connection with specific situations. These restrictions are first in the Charter itself, specifically in its Article 27(4). Those apply to all types of strikes. Second, restrictions of the right to strike are also contained in section 20 of the ACB. Those, however, only apply to the strikes connected to collective bargaining and cannot be analogically applied to other types of strikes.

2.1 Certain Categories of Public Servants

Section 27(4) of the Charter limits the right to strike when it says that this right 'does not apply to judges, prosecutors, members of the armed and security forces'.

Moreover, section 44 of the Charter states that the law may limit the right referred to in Article 27(4) of the Charter (right to strike) in relation to employees of the state administration and local administration in specified functions and to persons in occupations that are directly necessary for the protection of life and health.

The ACB in section 20(i) and (j) further restricts the right to strike of additional groups of employees who can be considered public servants. The strike of these employees is not always forbidden generally, but only if some other conditions are met, such as endangering life and health of persons and so on. Under the ACB, strikes of below-mentioned employees would be illegal:

- judges, prosecutors, members of the armed forces and employees in the management and security of air traffic;
- members of fire protection units and members of rescue teams established according to special regulations for relevant workplaces and employees ensuring telecommunications operations if the strike would endanger the life or health of a citizen, or property.

Section 82(1) of Act No. 234/2014 Coll. on Civil Service (governing the relationship of civil servants performing state administration in administrative offices) limits strikes only in relation to so-called superiors (superiors cannot go on strike).

We believe that since strikes not connected with collective bargaining are not regulated by law, no specific groups of employees are excluded from this right (except for the groups specified in the Charter – judges, prosecutors, members of armed and security forces).

2.2 Essential Services in the Strict Sense of the Term

The ACB, or any other act, does not contain any general definition of essential services for the purposes of restricting or prohibiting the right to strike.

However, the ACB in section 20(g) and (h) restricts the strike of certain employees, who can be viewed as providing essential services in the strict sense of the term. These are, in particular, employees of medical facilities or social care facilities if the strike would endanger the life or health of citizens, as well as employees operating nuclear power plant equipment, equipment with fissile material and oil or gas pipeline equipment. Those are all forbidden to strike.

Again, it must be reiterated that these restrictions do not apply for the strikes which are not connected to a dispute in collective bargaining.

2.3 Situations of Acute National or Local Crisis

The right to strike is also limited by certain emergency situations. According to section 20(f) of the ACB, a strike is illegal if it takes place during the period of mobilisation or in the case of extraordinary measures under section 23 of Act No. 585/2004 Coll. on Defence Obligation and its Provision (the 'Defence Act').

Further, a strike by employees who work in areas affected by natural disasters in which emergency measures have been declared by the relevant state authorities would also be illegal under section 20(k) of the ACB.

In addition, under section 5(f) of the Act No. 240/2000 Coll. on Crisis Management (the 'Crisis Act'), the government may restrict the right to strike during a state of emergency or state of threat to the state if the strike would lead to disruption or impossibility of rescue and relief work.

3 COMPENSATORY GUARANTEES FOR WORKERS DEPRIVED OF THE RIGHT TO STRIKE

Employees whose right to strike is restricted do not have any special protection to compensate them for this restriction under the Czech law such as specific impartial conciliation and eventually arbitration procedures.

As for impartial mediation and arbitration procedures, these are available in principle to all workers and employers in the context of collective bargaining. That is because, as stated above, the participation in the mediation led by a mediator either chosen by the parties or designated by the Ministry of Work and Social Affairs is a necessary condition to begin a lawful strike during collective bargaining.

4 CONCLUSION

The right to strike is a fundamental right enshrined at the constitutional level in the Charter. Despite the fact that the Charter envisages the adoption of a law that would regulate the strike in more detail, such a general law on strikes has not yet been adopted (and its adoption is not yet on the horizon). Thus, only strikes in the context of a dispute over the conclusion of a collective agreement are regulated in more detail by law, namely the ACB.

This legislative loophole does not mean that a strike other than in a dispute over the conclusion of a collective agreement is not possible. The courts have concluded that employees have the right to strike even when defending other economic and social interests. However, the lack of legislation creates considerable legal uncertainty as to the legality of any strike. This may be one of the reasons why strikes rarely occur in the Czech Republic. In the last 30 years, there were two attempts to adopt an act, which would generally regulate strikes and lockouts. Both of them were unsuccessful, however, because none of the proposals gained support from the trade unions.

The Charter excludes from the right to strike certain groups of employees whose work is crucial to the state (like judges, prosecutors, members of armed and security forces). In accordance with the Charter, the right to strike is further limited for certain other groups of employees by the ACB. Those restrictions seem reasonable and proportionate.

CHAPTER 11

Restrictions on the Right to Strike in Denmark

Mette Søsted Hemme

1 GENERAL INFORMATION

Denmark is a constitutional monarchy, and state powers are divided between the three branches of parliament (legislative), government (executive), and the courts (judiciary). The Danish labour market is characterised by 'the Danish model', which entails that pay and working conditions are primarily determined by negotiating collective agreements with little interference by the legislator.

The Danish model characterises both public and private sector employment. The collective agreement coverage is close to 100% in the public sector, whereas the private sector coverage is estimated to 73%.[1] Denmark has a large public sector that employs close to 900,000 persons, which amounts to almost a third of the active labour force.[2] The majority of public employees are entitled to engage in industrial action. Available statistics show that the public sector experienced nine cases of work stoppages (strikes by employees or lockout by the employer) in 2022 and only eight cases in 2023.[3] In 2021, however, the public sector experienced a major conflict during negotiations of

1. *Analysis by the Confederation of Danish Employers* (DA Analyse, 2020); https://www.da.dk/politik-og-analyser/overenskomst-og-arbejdsret/2018/hoej-overenskomstdaekning-i-danmark/. Denmark has a unionisation rate of 67% and an overall collective agreement coverage of 82%.
2. Covering both full- and part-time employees, the public sector employs 881,226 persons. The total number of employees in Denmark are 3,002,612 persons. Few jobs cannot be divided by sector but are included in the total. The data does not account for the employees' working time. Source: *Statistics Denmark, employees divided by sector*, dataset from May 2023, table LBESK02; https://www.statistikbanken.dk/10312.
3. Source: *Statistics Denmark, strikes and lockout*, https://www.dst.dk/da/Statistik/emner/arbejde-og-indkomst/fravaer-og-arbejdskonflikter/strejker-og-lockout. The numbers cover both legitimate and unlawful industrial action.

collective bargaining agreements for nurses. That year, there were 63 work stoppages in the public sector, involving 12,559 employees and amounting to 238,400 lost working days.[4] The conflict lasted 10 weeks and was the longest-lasting conflict in recent times in Denmark.

In the following, the Danish legal framework on the right to strike and restrictions to the right to strike will be examined in more detail.

1.1 Legal Basis of the Right to Strike

In Denmark, the right to strike is not expressly protected by legislation; i.e., it is not protected in the Constitution, and statutory legislation interferes very little in industrial relations. As an example, the legislation does not define what constitutes a collective agreement, requirements for being recognised as a union, or the right to engage in industrial action, including strike. In Denmark, the right to strike is protected in legislation as part of the freedom of association under the European Convention on Human Rights, Article 11.[5] The right to strike is recognised in statutory legislation, e.g., the Labour Court Act, section 9.[6]

The lack of statutory legislation has to do with the fact that the right to industrial action, including the right to strike, has been developed within the industrial relations system. The right was first recognised as a fundamental principle under the historic September Agreement from 1899 and is now recognised in the main (collective) agreements between social partners. The right to strike is considered a fundamental right under Danish law.[7] It is an unwritten principle of law, which enjoys a wide recognition with only a few limitations. These limitations, or conditions for exercising the right to strike, have been defined in case law by the Danish Labour Court and by the social partners in collective agreements. The social partners enjoy a considerable room of manoeuvre when it comes to determining the conditions/limitations on the right to strike.

1.2 Main Features of the Regulation

Under Danish labour law, disputes between labour market parties can be divided into two categories: 'disputes of rights' and 'disputes of interest'.[8] 'Disputes of rights' concern the interpretation of an existing collective agreement and its prerequisites – or a possible breach hereof. Under Danish labour law, parties are under peace obligations once they have concluded a collective agreement, and as a general rule, neither party

4. Source: *Statistics Denmark, strikes and lockout* (2021), https://www.statistikbanken.dk/statbank5a/selectvarval/saveselections.asp.
5. The European Convention on Human Rights is implemented into Danish law, cf. Act No. 138 of 26 January 2022.
6. The Labour Court Act, No. 1003 of 24 August 2017.
7. Jens Kristiansen, *Den kollektive arbejdsret* 447 (DJØF Forlag 4th ed. 2021).
8. Ole Hasselbalch, *Labour Law in Denmark* § 39 (Wolters Kluwer 5th ed. 2019).

has the right to initiate industrial action in case of 'disputes of rights'.[9] 'Disputes of interest' exist when the parties are not covered by an existing collective agreement, but at least one of the parties wishes to have the working conditions regulated by means of the conclusion of a collective agreement.[10] The Danish model allows for industrial action, including strikes, to be initiated only in this latter category of disputes.[11]

The material requirements for the right to strike have been developed in industrial case law. The right to strike is protected only when the purpose is the pursuit of salary and working conditions ('a legitimate professional purpose').[12] Strikes are – as a general rule – allowed in a trade union's pursuit of negotiating a collective agreement with an employer or an employers' association. Similarly, strike is allowed when the parties to an existing collective agreement cannot reach an agreement for renewal. Formal requirements are few, such as a clear and precise notification, notification of the Public Conciliator, and in the case of renewal of existing agreements, correct notice of termination of existing agreements.[13] Main agreements may contain different prerequisites of a procedural nature, such as conciliation and advance notices.[14] The social partners may also agree on further limitations in the right to strike. Finally, the purpose must be proportionate with the measures used.[15] In this way, the proportionality principle acts as a general limitation on the right to strike.[16] As an example, conflicts that result in a complete restriction of the other party's access to conduct business are deemed illegitimate.[17] Overall, the right to strike in Denmark is wide and well protected, including the right to engage in secondary action.

Another important aspect of the right to strike is the role of the Public Conciliator. The Public Conciliation Institution is an impartial state institution that acts as a mandatory conciliator for social partners during conflicts for the renewal of collective agreements.[18] The Public Conciliator may attempt to reduce the number of industrial conflicts by way of conflict resolution measures. The Public Conciliator may order a postponement of a work stoppage, where notice hereof has been given but not yet effected, cf. the Conciliation Act, section 3(3).[19] A pending strike may – as a general rule – be postponed for up to two weeks by the Public Conciliator when the parties are engaged in a conciliation process. If a pending strike has damaging societal effects, the Public Conciliators (in unison) may order a further postponement of up to two weeks, cf. section 4(5). The Act does not define damaging societal effects. The possibility of

9. *Ibid.*, § 41.
10. *Ibid.*, § 39.
11. Per Jacobsen, *Kollektiv Arbejdsret* 277 (Jurist- og Økonomforbundets Forlag 5th ed. 1994).
12. *See*, Ole Hasselbalch & Natalie Videbæk Munkholm, *Den Danske Arbejdsret*, s. XXI, 2.4 (Karnov, online, 2022); Kristiansen, *supra* n. 7, 486-487, and Jacobsen, 280.
13. *See, e.g.*, Jacobsen, *supra* n. 11, 313-326; Hasselbalch & Videbæk Munkholm, *supra* n. 12, s. XXI, 3; Kristiansen, *supra* n. 7, 481-486.
14. *See* Hasselbalch & Videbæk Munkholm, *supra* n. 12, s. XXI, 3.
15. *See, e.g.*, The Danish Labour Court, ruling of 27 June 2023 (AR 2022.1390).
16. Jacobsen, *supra* n. 11, 291; Hasselbalch & Videbæk Munkholm, *supra* n. 12, s. XXI, 2.5.
17. The Danish Labour Court, ruling of 29 November 2012 (AR 2012.0341). *See also* Hasselbalch & Videbæk Munkholm, *supra* n. 12, s. XXI, 2.5.
18. Kristiansen, *supra* n. 7, 459.
19. *Act on Conciliation in Labour Disputes*, No. 709 of 20 August 2002.

postponing pending strikes is used regularly.[20] The Public Conciliator cannot force the parties to reach a settlement, cannot order a pending or ongoing conflict to end, and cannot cancel a notification of conflict.

As a last resort, the legislators may choose to end an ongoing conflict by enacting statutory legislation (*see* more below).

2 PERMITTED RESTRICTIONS

2.1 Certain Categories of Public Servants

In the Danish public sector, two forms of employment exist: Contractual public employees and statutory civil servants. The main form of employment in the Danish public sector today is employment under collective bargaining agreement (contractual public employees).[21] For contractual public employees, there is no restriction on the right to strike, and their terms and conditions of employment are largely comparable to private sector employees.

The right to strike for statutory civil servants is restricted by law. Historically, most public employees were employed as civil servants under statutory law, the Civil Servants Act,[22] and employment as statutory civil servant is embedded in the Danish Constitution from 1849. Statutory civil servants are restricted from the right to strike.[23] Employment as civil servant was originally seen as a life-long relationship, and a special loyalty to the public employer was presumed from the civil servant. The use of employment as statutory civil servant has over time declined and now account for approximately 5% of all public employees.[24] This form of employment is – according to ministerial degree – reserved for top managerial positions in the state, such as the permanent secretaries in the ministries (*departementchefer*), and certain positions in, e.g., the police, military, prisons, the state church, as well as certain positions in the judiciary.[25] In municipalities and regions, some top managerial positions are also still employed as statutory civil servants.

2.1.1 Personal Scope of Freedom of Association

Under Danish law, there is no restriction to the personal scope of the freedom of association for public employees. All employees in Denmark are covered by the Danish

20. Kristiansen, *supra* n. 7, 529.
21. The use of employment on individual contract is limited but does occur also in public employment relations.
22. *The Civil Servants Act*, No. 511 of 18 May 2017.
23. Hasselbalch & Videbæk Munkholm, *supra* n. 12, s. XXI, 4.1.
24. Karsten Revsbech, Mette Søsted Hemme & Søren Højgaard Mørup, *Forvaltningspersonalet* 11 (DJØF Forlag 5th ed. 2023).
25. *Ministerial Circular on use of employment as statutory civil servant in the state and national church*, No. 210 of 11 December 2000.

statutory Act on Freedom of Association.[26] Public employees are, therefore, irrespective of their type of employment entitled to be a member of a union and exercise their rights in this connection. Particular limitations apply for statutory civil servants with regard to the exercise of the right to strike, *see* further below.

2.1.2 Personal Scope of the Right to Strike

As mentioned above, statutory civil servants are restricted from exercising the right to strike under Danish law. Historically, wages and working conditions for civil servants were traditionally unilaterally determined by statutory law, the Civil Servants Act, without any right to negotiation. Over time, the legal framework for statutory civil servants has however developed, and in many aspects now resemble the general labour law system for contractual employees.[27] Today, wages and working conditions for statutory civil servants are primarily determined by negotiation and set out in an agreement between the Minister for Finance and four specified employee confederations, the 'wage adjustment agreement'.[28] The wage adjustment agreement is renewed every third year in connection with the ordinary collective bargaining rounds in the public sector. These wage agreements are negotiated but without being subject to the ordinary collective dispute resolution system in Denmark, i.e., the Danish Labour Court and the Public Conciliation Institution. If the parties are not able to agree on the financial framework for wages to statutory civil servants, industrial action is not allowed.[29] Instead, the Civil Servants Act, section 46(1), provides that the Minister for Finance is entitled to propose legislation on the matter. Wage setting for statutory civil servants may still - theoretically - be established by law and not by negotiation. There are no recent examples of the parties not being able to agree on terms for wages and working conditions, and there are no examples of extraordinary legislation in this regard.

In conclusion, the restriction on the right to strike for statutory civil servants is derived from the Civil Servants Act, which explicitly gives mandate to legislate on wages and working conditions should the parties not be able to agree when negotiating every third year.[30] For the statutory civil servants, there is no right to engage in industrial action, and participation in industrial action is, regardless of the purpose, considered a breach of the employment contract, more specifically the duty to perform work under the employment relationship.[31] Statutory civil servants, who nonetheless engage in strikes, risk disciplinary sanctions (issued by Civil Servants Tribunals) and/or pay deductions (issued by the employer).[32]

---

26. *Act on Freedom of Association*, No. 424 of 8 May 2006.
27. Recognised by the Danish Supreme Court, judgment of 14 August 2019, U 2019.3552.
28. *The Civil Servants Act*, s. 45.
29. Poul Andersen, *Dansk forvaltningsret* 196 (Gyldendal 5th ed. 1965); Finn Hoffmann, *Den danske model og den offentlige sektor* 83 (*100-året for Septemberforliget*, Ministry of Finance, 1999); Kristiansen, *supra* n. 7, 454-455.
30. *The Civil Servants Act*, ss 45 and 47.
31. Andersen, *supra* n. 29, 196; Hasselbalch & Videbæk Munkholm, *supra* n. 12, s. XXI, 4.1.
32. Mette Søsted Hemme, *The Civil Service in Denmark* (Adam Krzywoń et al. eds, Routledge 2025).

The Danish level of restrictions on the right to strike for statutory civil servants was criticised by the Committee on Freedom of Association of the International Labour Organization (ILO) in case 1950.[33] The complaint concerned a ruling of the Local Civil Servant Disciplinary Tribunal (*den kommunale tjenestemandsret*) ordering a penance of DKK 100,000 to the Central Organisation of Teachers (LC) for letting teachers, employed as statutory civil servants, be included in the boycott.[34] The Tribunal held that it was inconsistent with Danish civil servant law when, in connection with an official strike organised by the LC, that same organisation established a boycott of the teaching positions affected by the strike. The ILO Committee considered that workers in education are not covered by the definition of essential services or of the public service exercising the powers of the public authority (the categories for which the right to strike can be prohibited or restricted).

Therefore, the Committee requested the Danish Government to take the necessary measures to ensure that all teachers, regardless of their classification as public servants, enjoy the right to strike. The criticism was, in part, the reason behind a reform in 1999, where the Danish state reduced the range of positions where a person can be employed as a statutory civil servant.[35] This development of reducing the use of statutory civil servant employment relationships has continued since. The ILO criticism has, however, not led to a change in the civil servants' legislation, and as long as some statutory civil servants, who fall outside the two categories outlined above, are prohibited from exercising the right to strike, the criticism remains.[36]

2.2 Essential Services in the Strict Sense of the Term

Except for statutory civil servants, public employees' right to strike is not limited in Danish legislation. The extent of the strike for contractual public employees is, as outlined above, not subject to restrictions or requirements in any statutory legislation on 'essential services' or similar in Denmark. The scope, content, and extent of the right to strike for contractual public employees are instead, in principle, in the hands of the social partners. This was confirmed in industrial arbitration practice already in 1934.[37] Thus, this section focuses only on 'negotiated minimum service'.

2.2.1 Concept of Essential Services

Not applicable as noted above.

33. Case 1950, *The Danish Union of Teachers (DUT) and the Salaried Employees' and Civil Servants' Confederation (FTF)*, complaint date: 22 January 1998.
34. The Local Civil Servant Disciplinary Tribunal, Cases 918/95 and 919/95, ruling of 8 January 1997.
35. Natalie Videbæk Munkholm & Christian Højer Schjøler, *Collective Bargaining in Labour Law Regimes: Denmark* 234-235 (Ulla Liukkunen ed., Springer 2019).
36. *Ibid.*, 235.
37. Industrial arbitration ruling in Case No. 2027 of 16 October 1934.

2.2.2 *Activities Not Considered Essential Services*

Not applicable as noted above.

2.2.3 *Negotiated Minimum Service*

The Danish social partners have agreed to certain limitations on the right to strike in both main agreements and sector agreements.

It is common that main agreements in the public sector specify that managerial positions, as well as 'members whose participation in the negotiations are necessary for the completion of the negotiations and cease of the conflict', are excluded from strikes. Sometimes specific positions are exempted such as 'military personnel'.[38] Moreover, the main agreements often exempt 'employees that are exempted by agreement between the parties'. Sometimes, it is an express condition that this (framework) agreement must at least ensure a necessary 'emergency service' within affected areas. The exact scope of the restrictions on the right to strike varies in different areas. As an example, the main agreement between the Health Cartel and the Danish Regions, section 5(4), stipulates that strikes cannot include managerial positions as well as 'employees that are exempted by agreement between the parties', and the agreement must at least ensure a necessary emergency service.

It is common to negotiate such 'framework agreements' on an ad hoc basis in the face of pending industrial action. The agreements are often negotiated as an overall framework agreement supplemented by a local agreement at the shop level. The framework agreement for the emergency services is negotiated between the unions and the employer. The framework agreement often more closely defines 'emergency services'. In a framework agreement from 2018, in connection with a pending lockout in the public sector, 'emergency services' were defined as 'life essential and urgent tasks, tasks necessary to avoid health or permanent mobility threatening consequences and tasks connected to the preservation of great values'.[39] The framework agreement also sets out procedures for selecting which employees are exempted from strike as well as applicable salary and working conditions during the strike. The working conditions of the shop steward during the strike may also follow from the framework agreement. Finally, the framework agreement may contain specific provisions concerning 'disasters', e.g., that 'in case of disaster all employees covered by the work stoppage may be called in for work'.[40] Based on a framework agreement, an emergency services agreement and -plan is then negotiated at shop level between the shop steward and the employer. This process may lead to intense negotiations over the precise delimitation of the exempted work tasks at the specific workplace.

38. Under some main agreements, 'vocational trainees' are also exempted from a strike.
39. *Framework agreement on emergency services between KL and FOA concerning employment of the organization's members during pending work stoppages in connection with the renewal of collective agreements in 2018*, s. 1(1).
40. *Ibid.*, s. 4.

Also, in the private sector, it is common that 'life essential' tasks are excluded from industrial action, depending on the specific agreement obtained by the social partners in the situation of a pending strike.[41] As an example, the main agreement for Copenhagen Airport allows for agreements to exempt employees from a strike due to flight security. The parties may agree to other exemptions.[42]

The fact that the delimitation of 'emergency services' is part of the voluntaristic model of collective bargaining and is negotiated in each situation of a pending strike, the limitations on the right to strike vary depending on the area of the strike. The process is in the hands of the social partners involved, and their agreements are binding for affected members of the organisations. As an example, an individual (unionised) employee cannot refuse to be considered 'emergency services' and thus cannot refuse to continue work during a strike. There is a strong incentive for social partners to ensure a necessary emergency service, as the alternative may be a legislative intervention in the parties' conflict. The Danish practice of legislative intervention in industrial relations is briefly outlined in the following.

2.2.4 Legislative Interventions

The far-reaching right to industrial action, including secondary action, may lead to intense conflicts. Against this backdrop, the Danish legislators regularly bring conflicts to an end. Between 1969 and 2013, there were eight conflicts in the public sector, and four of these were settled with legislative intervention.[43] There are no statutory rules on the framework for or conditions for legislative intervention. It is not possible to establish a common practice or preconditions for the situations, where the Danish legislator chooses to intervene, as it also depends on a political assessment.[44] The decisive factors or relevant conditions seem to be: (1) the duration of the conflict, (2) the damaging effect for society, and (3) the outlook for a result between the parties within a reasonable time.[45] The mechanism entails that statutory legislation is passed to replace the parties' own agreement, i.e., a legislated 'collective agreement'. To balance the parties' interests, the intervening legislative act typically either prolongs the existing collective agreement with minor changes or bases itself on a draft proposal of the Public Conciliator.[46] The most recent example of a legislative intervention is from 2021, where a legislative act ended a large nurses' strike that had been going on for 10 weeks.[47] The costs for patients and health services were increasing after the long

41. Hasselbalch & Videbæk Munkholm, *supra* n. 12, s. XXVI, 2.4.
42. Main Agreement (agreement on procedure for concluding and renewal of collective agreement) between Københavns Lufthavne A/S and Academic Organizations, 12 January 2000.
43. Laust Høgedahl, *Den danske model i den offentlige sektor* 166 (Djøf Forlag, 2019).
44. Jacobsen, *supra* n. 11, 207; Høgedahl, *supra* n. 43, 170.
45. Kristiansen, *supra* n. 7, 542; Høgedahl, *supra* n. 43, 170. *See also* Hasselbalch, *supra* n. 8, §§ 1004-1007.
46. Videbæk Munkholm & Højer Schjøler, *supra* n. 35, 240; Nana Wesley Hansen & Åsmund Arup Seip, *Government Employers in Sweden, Denmark and Norway: The Use of Power to Control Wage and Employment Conditions* (European Journal of Industrial Relations, 24:1, 2018) https://doi.org/10.1177/0959680117708371.
47. *Act on renewal of collective agreements and agreements for nurses*, No. 1722 of 27 August 2021.

conflict, and there was no outlook for the parties' reconciliation.[48] In the next round of negotiating public collective agreements, which takes place in 2024, the Act will cease to exist, and the parties will negotiate a new collective agreement for the nurses.

There are examples where the Danish practice of legislative intervention has not been limited to the two categories of recognised restrictions on the right to strike as acknowledged by the Committee on Freedom of Association of ILO. As an example, in the case of 1971, the Committee noted that the impact of the intervention by the Danish Government in 1998 impacted a large number of employees (over 400,000) covered by over 500 collective agreements.[49] The Committee criticised that the Government had not distinguished between those sectors which might have been argued to be genuinely essential (or likely to cause an acute national crisis) and those which could not be considered as such.[50]

2.3 Situations of Acute National or Local Crisis

There is no general statutory legislation restricting the right to strike in cases of acute national or local crisis in Denmark. Such a situation may, however, activate existing rules or collective agreements and thereby impact the right to strike.

First, as described above, the Public Conciliator may postpone a pending strike two times for up to two weeks in case of 'damaging societal effects'. The Public Conciliator cannot restrict the right to strike as such, as it may only order postponement of pending strikes during conciliation.

Second, as described above, public sector collective agreements entail that the social partners are committed to establish emergency services throughout strikes. In some framework agreements (union level), it is also specified that in case of 'disaster', all employees covered by the strike may be called in for work, i.e., a restriction of the right to strike. These restrictions to the right to strike depend solely on the agreement that can be obtained by the social partners.

Finally, as described above, the legislators may intervene in existing conflicts and bring them to an end with a 'legislated' collective agreement. This only takes place if there is no outlook for the parties' own settlement of the conflict within reasonable time. There are no examples that any acute crisis has led to legislative intervention, without prior attempts to reach a settlement first between the parties themselves.

If an acute local (or national) crisis has the effect of establishing risks to safety and health, employees are entitled to refrain from working as a protective measure. Under Danish law, employees are entitled to cease work in case of 'safety or health risks' or 'violations of personal integrity'. The right to work stoppage in these situations follows expressly from the Standard Rules on negotiation and conciliation of conflicts,

48. Ministry of Employment, Press release of 27 August 2021, https://bm.dk/nyheder/pressemeddelelser/2021/08/folketinget-slutter-sygeplejerskekonflikten-ved-lovindgreb/.
49. Case No. 1971 (Denmark), complaint date 7 May 1998.
50. *Ibid.*, para. 58.

section 17.[51] The Standard Rules are collective rights and, thus, only apply to work covered by collective agreement.[52] It must be noted that the right to work stoppage only applies to those particular employees who are exposed to the mentioned risks or violations.[53] It may be regarded as a derogation from the general duty to observe peace for the duration of an applicable collective agreement. For areas without collective agreements, a similar rule is found in the Danish Act on Occupational Health and Safety, section 17a.[54]

3 COMPENSATORY GUARANTEES FOR WORKERS DEPRIVED OF THE RIGHT TO STRIKE

Under Danish law, the two major categories of workers that are restricted from exercising the right to strike are: (1) statutory civil servants and (2) employees covered by a specific agreement (at least covering emergency services) between social partners in case of a pending strike.

As for statutory civil servants, it may be argued that they enjoy certain rights that are not granted to other public employees, thus compensating for the restriction on the right to strike. This was the argument by the Danish Government in the ILO Committee on Freedom of Association case 1950: 'the rules on decorum and the corollary duty not to strike are offset by favourable rules on severance pay, pension due to any other unforeseeable event than age and early retirement'.[55] The special rights include as an example the right to severance pay (or 'availability pay') for three years if the public employer abolishes the civil servant's position due to changes in the authority's organisation or work tasks. If the person cannot be transferred to another position (which he or she is obliged to accept as part of the employment relationship), the abolishment of the position results in a dismissal, where the civil servant – as a general rule – continues to receive ordinary pay for the following three years, cf. Civil Servants Act, section 32(1). Moreover, statutory civil servants enjoy the right to pension (directly) from the public employer, whereas other public employees are covered by labour market pension schemes embedded in the collective agreements. The arguments were dismissed by the ILO Committee that stressed that it is decisive whether the functions of the employees covered by the strike ban show that they are engaged in an essential service or in a public service exercising the powers of the public authority.[56]

It may be added that statutory civil servants have in fact engaged in strikes over the years. As a direct response to an increase in (unlawful) strikes, the Civil Servants

51. *Standard rules on negotiation and conciliation of conflicts of 27 October 2006*. Social partners are obliged to observe the Standard Rules, if they have not themselves agreed on adequate rules, cf. the Labour Court Act, s. 33(2).
52. A similar right to cease work is – as an individual right – also assumed to be applicable to statutory civil servants, cf. Hasselbalch & Videbæk Munkholm, *supra* n. 12, s. XXI, 4.1.
53. Jacobsen, *supra* n. 11, 269.
54. *Act on Occupational Health and Safety*, No. 2062 of 16 November 2021. The provision implements Council Directive 1989/391.
55. *See* s. 2.1.2 above.
56. *Ibid.*

Tribunals were set up in the early 1980s.[57] As noted in a Parliament Committee report, earlier, it was considered unthinkable that statutory civil servants engaged in strikes.[58] The change in attitude rendered one of the preconditions for this type of employment, ensuring continuity in service, less effective.[59] Civil Servants Tribunals handle collective breaches of the duties for statutory civil servants, including unlawful industrial action.[60] The set-up of the tribunals can be viewed as offering statutory civil servants some compensatory guarantee, as the procedure for the assessment of the legality of the work stoppage is now in the hands of a judicial body and no longer an administrative decision by the public employer.[61] The background was that cases concerning unlawful industrial action had not been treated similarly by different employers in the public administration.[62] It may be added that neither statutory civil servants' duties nor possible sanctions were changed with the new tribunals.[63] The relevant sanctions for unlawful industrial action are warnings, reprimands, or fines.[64] In addition to the individual sanctions, the tribunals may sanction unions that have been supportive of or have neglected to try to stop or prevent industrial action.

As for the employees that are exempt from strike due to an agreement between social partners, the compensatory guarantees are limited. The framework agreements on emergency services will typically include provisions on how to solve conflicts regarding 'emergency services', which may be regarded as a guarantee against management decisions at shop level that conflict with the agreed framework at union level. As an example, the framework agreement from 2018 (mentioned above) stipulates that as far as possible it must be agreed in advance which work tasks are covered by the emergency services. If this is not possible, the task must be performed if management deems that the task is covered by the emergency services. In case of such disagreement, the shop steward may (afterwards) require a specialist opinion, e.g., by a doctor.[65] More generally, disputes at shop level concerning: (1) the interpretation of the framework agreement, (2) the practical facilitation of the emergency services, and (3) the delimitation of emergency services can be requested for negotiation between the organisations to the framework agreement as soon as possible.[66]

57. Jens Kristiansen, *Retsgrundlaget for offentlig personaleforvaltning* 184 (Niels Fenger ed., Jurist- og Økonomforbundets Forlag 2018).
58. *Report of Parliamental Committee concerning the 90ies agreements and collective agreements*, No. 1150/1988, 56, https://www.elov.dk/media/betaenkninger/90_ernes_aftaler_og_overensk omster.pdf.
59. *Ibid.*
60. The tribunals are regulated in the Civil Servants Act, Chapter 12. The municipal and regional civil servant tribunals are regulated separately, Act of 23 August 2016, No. 1124.
61. Legislative proposal, L 144 of 29 January 1981, FT 1980-81, Appendix A, column 3515.
62. *Ibid.*, column 3513.
63. *Ibid.*, columns 3514-3518.
64. Civil Servants Act, s. 54(2).
65. *Framework agreement on emergency services between KL and FOA concerning employment of the organization's members during pending work stoppages in connection with the renewal of collective agreements in 2018*, s. 3(2).
66. *Ibid.*, s. 8.

4 CONCLUSION

In Denmark, the right to industrial action is wide and well protected, and the right is exercised with only minimum intervention by the legislator. One particular restriction is embedded in statutory law, as it follows from the Civil Servants Act that statutory civil servants cannot engage in strikes. Traditionally, this type of employment was regarded as linked to a special duty of loyalty to the state, and the restriction on strike, thus, has historical explanations. The number of persons employed as statutory civil servants has been drastically reduced. Instead, the large majority of public employees are employed under collective agreements and enjoy the right to strike without restrictions.

There is no statutory legislation on essential services during conflicts; instead, social partners have in their agreements obliged themselves to reach agreements on 'emergency services' in case of pending conflicts. This restriction on the right to strike is embedded in the collective agreements, and social partners enjoy full autonomy in deciding which work tasks should be regarded as emergency services. The emergency plans vary across different areas and may vary from conflict to conflict.

In practice, the Public Conciliator plays an important role in mandatory conciliation between social partners. Pending conflicts may be postponed up to two times, but the conciliator cannot force conflicts to an end. Ongoing conflicts may, however, be ended with a legislative intervention. Such intervention cannot be described as rare in the public sector but is not used in case there is a realistic outlook for a result between the parties within a reasonable time. The duration and damaging effect for society are taken into consideration. In 2021, a nurses' strike in the public sector went on for 10 weeks before the Government intervened with legislation. When performed, the 'legislated agreement' compromises prior attempts between the parties and is limited to the next rounds of negotiations (every second or third year).

The 'double role' of the public employers as both counterparty to collective negotiations and at the same time the legislator, who can end existing conflicts by law, has been discussed in recent years. Political ambitions to reform the organisation of the Danish model in the public sector have been expressed, but this issue has not yet been resolved.

It is the outspoken standpoint of (any) government in Denmark to respect the Danish model by not interfering in elements of the collective bargaining processes. Overall, the said restrictions or 'interferences' in the right to strike respect the autonomy of the social partners to a very wide extent.

CHAPTER 12

Restrictions on the Right to Strike in Estonia

Gaabriel Tavits

1 GENERAL INFORMATION

1.1 Legal Basis of the Right to Strike

According to paragraph 29(5) of the Constitution of Estonia, the following principles are established. 'Unions and associations of employees and employers may uphold their rights and lawful interests by means, which are not prohibited by the law. The conditions and procedure for the exercise of the right to strike will be provided by a law.'[1]

It follows from this that the Constitution of the Republic of Estonia does not directly provide that employees and employers have the right to strike. At the same time, the Constitution gives the legislator the authority according to which the law specifies the conditions and procedure for organising a strike. A separate legal act, the Collective Labour Dispute Resolution Act, has been adopted to fulfil the mandate arising from the Constitution. The said law provides for different types of strikes, requirements for organising strikes and restrictions. This law also regulates the mandatory conciliation procedure. In general terms, the said legislation also regulates the provision of essential services in the event of a strike.

1. The Constitution of the Republic of Estonia, passed on 28 June 1992, entered into force on 3 July 1992: https://www.riigiteataja.ee/en/eli/530102013003/consolide.

1.2 Main Features of the Regulation

The main legislative act regulating the right to strike in Estonia is the Collective Labour Dispute Resolution Act (CLDRA).[2] It determines the procedure for resolving collective labour disputes and calling and organising strikes and lockouts.

The Trade Unions Act provides for the right of trade unions to organise strikes.[3]

The Civil Service Act, as the main source of regulation in the public sector, prohibits civil servants from striking.[4]

The Emergency Act provides a list of essential services where a minimum level of services must be ensured during a strike.[5]

The CLDRA defines a strike as an interruption of work on the initiative of employees or an association or a federation of employees in order to achieve concessions from an employer, an association, or a federation of employers to lawful demands in labour matters (Article 2 of the CLDRA).

According to Article 13 of the CLDRA, the right to organise a strike belongs to employees or associations or federations of employees. Employees can be represented either by a trade union or by employees' trustees.

Article 18 of the Trade Unions Act provides that, in order to achieve their objectives, trade unions have the right to organise general meetings, political meetings, street parades, pickets, and strikes pursuant to the procedure prescribed by law. The election, obligations, and rights of employees' trustees are specified in the Employees' Trustee Act.[6]

The following types of strike are provided for in the CLDRA:[7]

- regular strike;
- warning strike lasting no longer than one hour (and with a notification of at least three days in advance);
- sympathy (solidarity) strike lasting no longer than three days in support of employees engaging in a strike and with a mandatory five-day notice period.

According to Estonian case law, the purpose of the sympathy strike is to show solidarity to striking workers and to bring greater impact to the striking workers' cause. This implies, for example, that sympathy strikes can also be organised at a time when employees participating in a sympathy strike are obliged to work with their employer. The CLDRA does not prohibit the organisation of a sympathy strike to support workers in one or more other sectors.

---

2. The Collective Labour Dispute Resolution Act (CLDRA), passed on 5 May 1993, entered into force on 7 June 1993: https://www.riigiteataja.ee/en/eli/511112014002/consolide.
3. The Trade Unions Act, passed on 14 June 2000, entered into force on 23 July 2000: https://www.riigiteataja.ee/en/eli/518112013006/consolide.
4. The Civil Service Act, passed on 13 June 2012, entered into force on 1 April 2013: https://www.riigiteataja.ee/en/eli/509072014003/consolide.
5. The Emergency Act, passed on 8 February 2017, entered into force on 1 July 2017: https://www.riigiteataja.ee/en/eli/513062017001/consolide.
6. The Employees' Trustee Act, passed on 13 December 2006, entered into force on 1 February 2007: https://www.riigiteataja.ee/en/eli/510012014001/consolide.
7. Article 18 of the CLDRA.

The Estonia Supreme Court has also highlighted that, in a situation where workers stage a solidarity strike in sympathy with striking workers at other establishments and it turns out that one of the main strikes is illegal, the sympathy strike can still be legal since the CLDRA does not provide otherwise.

The Court has established that the CLDRA does not give the right to submit political or other non-work-related demands as grounds for a collective dispute. Trade unions may submit any demands that are not related to working conditions for discussion at meetings, demonstrations, and pickets in accordance with the Trade Union Act and the Public Meeting Act.[8]

However, the Supreme Court has also established that if the participants of the main strike submit political demands in addition to the demands regarding working conditions, the strike can still be considered lawful. This also applies if the participants of a sympathy strike submit political demands in addition to the demands relating to the working conditions of the main strike.[9]

Procedural requirements are provided for in the CLDRA.

Article 13 of the CLDRA defines several conditions for the right to strike to arise:

- if conciliation procedures have been conducted but no conciliation has been achieved;
- if the agreement reached is not complied with;
- if a court judgment is not executed.

Strikes which are not preceded by negotiations and conciliation proceedings are declared unlawful. In the event of a strike, the parties to the collective labour dispute have an obligation to resume negotiations in order to reach an agreement in the collective labour dispute (Article 13 of the CLDRA).

A decision to organise a strike is taken by the general meeting of employees or an association or a federation of employees. According to Article 5 of the Employees' Trustee Act, the general meeting of employees may be called by:

- a trade union operating at the employer;
- the majority of the members of a trade union who are employed with the employer if the trade union has not been founded at the employer; or
- at least 10% of the employees of the employer.

The person who calls the general meeting must notify the employees of the reason for calling and the time of the general meeting at least two weeks in advance.

The law does not lay down any specific requirements for voting in order to approve a decision to call a strike. The trade union must adhere to its rules regarding the decision-making process. At least half of the company's workforce must participate in the general assembly of the employees (Article 6 of the Employees' Trustee Act). The

8. The Public Meeting Act, passed on 26 March 1997, entered into force on 2 May 1997: https://www.riigiteataja.ee/en/eli/514112013003/consolide.
9. Case No. 3-2-1-159-13 of the Supreme Court, decision of 19 December 2013, *Eesti Energia Narva Elektrijaamad AS-i hagi Narva Energia Ametiühingu vastu streigi korraldamise õiguse puudumise tuvastamiseks*, paras 15-18.

law does not specify whether a simple or a qualified majority of the participants is required for a decision to be adopted.

The advance notice requirement is two weeks in the case of an actual strike, three days in the case of a warning strike and five days in the case of a sympathy strike.

If an actual strike is declared, the organisers of the strike are required to notify the other party, a public conciliator, and the local government of a planned strike in writing at least two weeks in advance. The notice must set out the reasons, exact time of commencement, and possible scope of the strike. An employer has a duty to inform its contracting partners, other interested enterprises or institutions, and, through the media, the general public that a strike is taking place (Article 15 of the CLDRA).

No particular form of strike is prohibited. However, the right to strike is limited depending on the objective of the strike – strikes that are organised for the purpose of influencing the work of the courts are unlawful.[10] Strikes, which are not preceded by negotiations and conciliation proceedings, are also considered unlawful, as are strikes that are called or organised in violation of the procedure established by law.[11] Consequently, political strikes are in principle prohibited.

In Estonia, the lawfulness of a strike is decided by the courts. Before there is no court decision, it can be presumed that the strike is lawful.

There are significant consequences for workers in situations where a strike is either legal or illegal.

In the case of a lawful strike:

- it is prohibited to terminate the employment contracts of participants in lawful strikes on the initiative of the employer;
- employees are not paid wages for the period of a strike;
- participation in a strike is not considered a violation of the relevant employment contract and does not result in the liability of the employee;
- upon the full or partial satisfaction of the demands of employees or an association or a federation of employees, the employer pays compensation in an amount agreed upon by the parties to the employees or the association or federation of employees who called the strike;
- by agreement of the parties to a collective labour dispute, participants in a strike may make up for the time lost by reason of the strike outside working time. The time spent making up for the time lost because of a strike is not deemed to be overtime or work on days off or public holidays (Articles 24, 25 and 28 of the CLDRA).

The CLDRA establishes that an employee who does not participate in a strike but who is unable to perform his or her work by reason of the strike will be remunerated by the employer on the same basis as for the period of work stoppages which are not the fault of the employee or to the extent prescribed by a collective agreement (Article 25(2) of the CLDRA).

10. Article 22 of the CLDRA.
11. Article 22 of the CLDRA.

If a strike is found to be unlawful by a decision of the Court:

- participation in the strike is considered a violation of the relevant employment contract and will result in the liability of the employee if the employee is the organiser of the strike;
- resuming a strike or lock-out that has been declared unlawful or suspended or commencing/resuming a strike that has been postponed before the specified time is punishable by a fine of up to 200 fine units or by detention and by a fine of up to EUR 3,200 if committed by a legal person;
- organisation of the commencement or resumption of a strike or lock-out declared unlawful or suspended or postponed before the specified time is punishable by a fine of up to 300 fine units or by detention and by a fine of up to EUR 3,200 if committed by a legal person (Articles 23, 23 and 24 of the CLDRA).

In addition, Article 26 of the Trade Unions Act states that failure by an elected representative of a trade union to ensure observance of the obligation to refrain from striking during a period prescribed by law or a collective agreement is punishable by a fine of up to 100 fine units (one fine unit is equal to EUR 4).

2 PERMITTED RESTRICTIONS

2.1 Certain Categories of Public Servants

According to Article 20 of the CLDRA, participation in a strike is voluntary. It is prohibited to impede the performance of work by employees who are not participating in the strike.

The right to strike is denied to civil servants working for governmental authorities and other state bodies and local government, as well as for the Defence League (the unified armed forces of the Republic of Estonia), courts, and rescue service agencies. The law further clarifies that the prohibition to strike does not apply to persons who are employed under an employment contract. An exception is provided for rescue workers employed under an employment contract in a rescue service agency and persons employed under an employment contract in the Ministry of Defence, the Defence Resources Agency, the Defence Forces or the Defence League (Article 21 of the CLDRA).

Institutions and other organisations specified in the CLDRA, whose right to strike is denied, must resolve collective labour disputes by means of negotiations, with the help of a public conciliator or in court (Article 21 of the CLDRA). Public conciliator is impartial official who help the parties to labour disputes reach mutually satisfactory resolutions (Article 8 of the CLDRA).

Article 59 of the Civil Service Act establishes that an official is not allowed to strike. An official is not allowed to participate in other collective pressure actions which interfere with the performance of functions of an authority that has recruited the official or of other authority arising from the law. The pressure action is collective if at least half of the officials of the authority participate therein.

The definition of an official is included in Article 7 of the Civil Service Act: An official is a person who is in the public-law service and trust relationship with the State or local government. He or she is appointed to a post in an authority, which involves the exercise of official authority.

The exercise of official authority means the performance of the following functions:

- the directing of an authority;
- the exercise of state and administrative supervision, as well as the conduct of internal audit;
- the ensuring of the security and constitutional order of the State;
- the permanent military defence of the State and preparation thereof;
- the proceeding of offences;
- the diplomatic representation of the Republic of Estonia in foreign relations;
- the taking of decisions necessary for the performance of the principal functions of the Parliament of Estonia (*Riigikogu*), the President of the Republic, the National Audit Office, the Chancellor of Justice and the courts, the substantive preparation or implementation thereof;
- the substantive preparation or implementation of the policy-making decisions within the competence of the Government of the Republic, local government council, municipal or city government, and authority;
- the activities which, in the interests of strengthening and developing the official authority, cannot be given to the competence of a person who is only in the relationship governed by private law with the authority.

An official is distinguished from an employee in public administration. An employee is recruited for a job in an authority that does not involve the exercise of official authority but involves only work in support of the exercise of official authority. Accordingly, the ban on the right to strike does not apply to employees in public administration, except rescue workers employed under an employment contract in a rescue service agency and persons employed under an employment contract in the Ministry of Defence, the Defence Resources Agency, the Defence Forces or the Defence League (Article 21 of the CLDRA). Specific limitations have to be respected, for instance, in the case of the duty to ensure a minimum level of services.

In addition, while permitting sympathy strikes, the CLDRA provides that individuals who are not employed by an enterprise, institution or other organisations where a labour dispute arises or who do not represent the employees pursuant to the procedure prescribed by law are prohibited from instigating a strike (Article 20 of the CLDRA).

Case law clarifies that the existence of a valid collective agreement (in force) does not prohibit sympathy strikes. The legitimacy of a sympathy strike depends on whether the main strike is legal (lawful). If a sympathy strike is held in support of two (different) major strikes, it can be legal even if one of the main strikes is legal and the other is illegal.[12]

2.2 Essential Services in the Strict Sense of the Term

For certain categories of employees, the CLDRA lays down the requirement to provide a minimum level of services. According to Article 21 of the CLDRA, the continuity of indispensable services or production must be ensured in enterprises and institutions which satisfy the primary needs of the population and economy. The minimum level of services or production that must be ensured during a strike is determined by the agreement of the parties. In the case of disagreements, the minimum level of services is determined by the public conciliator whose decision is binding on the parties (Article 21(3) of the CLDRA). The list of enterprises and institutions which satisfy the primary needs of the population and economy is established by the Government of the Republic of Estonia. Based on the provision of the mentioned law, the Government of the Republic has not established a list of companies that must guarantee a minimum level of essential services.

In the event of a national emergency, the provision of essential services is regulated differently. When a state of emergency is declared, different ministries are responsible for providing different services. Although, by analogy, this list could also be used in the case of a strike, so far there is no case law in this regard, and different interpretations do not say that these restrictions are applicable in the case of a strike.

The list of essential services and institutions responsible for the provision thereof is provided in Article 36 of the Emergency Act:

(1) The Ministry of Economic Affairs and Communications shall organise the continuity of the following vital services:
  - phone service;
  - mobile phone service;
  - data transmission service;
  - digital identification and digital signing.

(2) The Ministry for Climate Affairs shall organise the continuity of the following vital services:
  - electricity supply;
  - natural gas supply;
  - liquid fuel supply;
  - ensuring the operability of national roads.

(3) The Ministry of Social Affairs shall organise the continuity of emergency care for the purposes of the Health Services Organisation Act.

(4) The Bank of Estonia shall organise the continuity of the following vital services:

12. Case No. 3-2-1-159-13 of the Supreme Court, *Eesti Energia Narva Elektrijaamad AS-i hagi Narva Energia Ametiühingu vastu streigi korraldamise õiguse puudumise tuvastamiseks* (19 December 2013).

- payment services;
- cash circulation.

(5) Local authorities organise services provided by a provider of a vital service and on the territory of which over 10,000 residents live organise in their administrative territory the continuity of the following vital services:
- district heating;
- ensuring the operability of local roads;
- water supply and sewerage.

Estonian case law has established that the provision of essential (vital) services is not directly dependent on the company's economic situation, and, second, the services of railway undertakings are not essential within the meaning of the CLDRA.[13]

'Essential services' in the strict sense of the term have been defined by the International Labour Organization (ILO) as those services 'the interruption of which would endanger the life, personal safety or health of the whole or part of the population'.

2.3 Situations of Acute National or Local Crisis

The CLDRA does not prescribe the extent to which services are to be provided in case of crises of national or local significance. The aforementioned principles, which are reflected in the Emergency Act, are also applicable to the said crises (as outlined in section 2.2 above). According to the Emergency Act paragraph 2(1), an emergency is an event or a chain of events or an interruption of a vital service that threatens the life or health of many people, causes major property damage, major environmental damage or serious and extensive disruptions in the operation of a vital service, and for the solution of which the rapid coordinated action of several institutions or the persons involved is a necessary activity, implements a different management arrangement than usual and involves significantly more people and resources than usual.

An essential service is a service that has an overwhelming impact on the functioning of society and the interruption of which directly threatens the life or health of people or the functioning of another vital service or service of general interest. A vital service is considered as a whole, together with the building, equipment, personnel, stock, and the like that are unavoidably necessary for its operation.

3 COMPENSATORY GUARANTEES FOR WORKERS DEPRIVED OF THE RIGHT TO STRIKE

There are no compensatory guarantees for workers who are deprived of the right to strike.

13. Case No. 2-12-9463 of the Harju County Court Kentmanni Courthouse (*Harju Maakohus Kentmanni kohtumaja*) (5 December 2012), para. 22.5.

In the institutions where the strike is not allowed (the right to strike is deprived), the collective labour disputes are resolved through negotiations through a public conciliator or in court.

The main task of the public conciliator is to contribute to the resolution of the collective labour dispute in the conciliation procedure. The public conciliator finds out the causes and circumstances of the labour dispute and proposes solutions.

The parties turn to the public conciliator in writing if an agreement is not reached during the negotiations and there is a risk of disruption of the labour peace.

The Government of the Republic appoints the public l conciliator for five years.

4 CONCLUSION

In Estonian law, the regulation of the right to strike is limited. Although the law contains the basic requirements for organising a strike (among other things, a mandatory conciliation procedure), the law does not specify the services that must be guaranteed in any case in the event of a strike. Striking parties specify the services to be provided and their volume. It is also important to let the public know to what extent the provision of services is limited.

Regarding the provision of essential services in the event of a strike, it is necessary to supplement the Estonian law in order to ensure the necessary legal regulation and legal clarity for the provision of essential services.

CHAPTER 13

Restrictions on the Right to Strike in Finland

Ulla Liukkunen

1 GENERAL INFORMATION

1.1 Legal Basis of the Right to Strike

Section 13, paragraph 2 of the Constitution of Finland (*Suomen perustuslaki*, 731/1999) guarantees freedom of association, stating that everyone enjoys freedom of association. Freedom of association entails the right to form an association without a permit, to be a member or not to be a member of an association, and to participate in the activities of an association. The freedom to form trade unions and to organize in order to look after other interests is likewise guaranteed. Section 13 does not explicitly mention the right to collective action. However, according to the Government Bill for the Constitution, securing the right to freedom of association means that the exercise of this right is not to result in adverse consequences. The Government Bill for the Constitution stated, *inter alia*, that participation or non-participation in the activities of an association or legal industrial action is not a ground, for example, to dismissal or differential treatment in working life.[1] The constitutional protection of the right to industrial action can be based on this statement.[2] The Constitutional Law Committee of the Parliament has confirmed that the right to collective action relates to the right to freedom of association set out in section 13, paragraph 2 of the Constitution.[3]

1. *See* Government Bill *Hallituksen esitys eduskunnalle perustuslakien perusoikeussäännösten muuttamisesta* HE 309/1993 vp, p. 61.
2. *See also* Government Bill *Hallituksen esitys eduskunnalle laiksi välttämättömän terveydenhuollon ja kotihoidon turvaamisesta työtaistelun aikana* HE 130/2022 vp.
3. *See* Constitutional Law Committee Statement *Perustuslakivaliokunnan lausunto* PeVL 12/2003, p 3. *See also* Constitutional Law Committee Statement *Perustuslakivaliokunnan lausunto* PeVL 3/1998 vp. *See also* Supreme Court judgment KKO 2010:93.

In addition to the right to industrial action belonging to the sphere of protection concerning the right to organize under section 13, paragraph 2 of the Constitution, this right is also protected by international conventions binding Finland, such as the International Labour Organization (ILO) Convention No. 87, the European Convention on Human Rights and the revised European Social Charter. When restrictions on the right to industrial action are assessed, both international obligations and general restrictions on fundamental rights are taken into account.[4]

Although the right to strike relates to the freedom of association guaranteed by section 13 of the Constitution, the detailed content of the right to industrial action is to be determined substantively by the provisions of ordinary law. According to the Constitutional Law Committee, the legislature also enjoys a relatively wide discretion in regulating the exercise of the right. Restrictions on the right to strike must be evaluated against these starting points and the general conditions for restrictions of fundamental rights.[5]

According to section 22 of the Constitution, the public authorities must guarantee observance of fundamental rights and liberties, and human rights. A ground for restriction of a fundamental right must be acceptable in terms of the entirety of the fundamental rights system. A ground for restriction can, for example, be an attempt to protect another fundamental right than the one being restricted or to achieve an aim which is acceptable from a normative perspective when assessed on objective grounds in terms of the entirety of the fundamental rights system. Restrictions on fundamental rights must, *inter alia*, be based on a law enacted by Parliament and cannot contradict the human rights obligations of Finland.[6]

1.2 Main Features of the Regulation

The legislation contains particular regulation on the right to industrial action by employees, on the one hand, and by civil servants, on the other. According to section 1, Chapter 13 of the Employment Contracts Act (*Työsopimuslaki*, 55/2001), employers and employees have the right to belong to associations and to be active in them. They also have the right to establish lawful associations. Employers and employees are likewise free not to belong to any of the associations referred to above. Prevention or restriction of this right or freedom is prohibited. Any agreement contrary to freedom of association is null and void. The freedom to organize is also taken into account as an illegal ground for dismissal in the Employment Contracts Act and, correspondingly, the Seafarers' Employment Contracts Act (*Merityösopimuslaki*, 756/2011). According to the Government Bill concerning the Employment Contracts Act, participation in industrial action could be a proper and weighty reason for dismissal only when

4. *See* Constitutional Law Committee Statement *Perustuslakivaliokunnan lausunto* PeVL 15/2007 vp; Constitutional Law Committee Statement *Perustuslakivaliokunnan lausunto* PeVL 12/2003 vp, pp. 2-3.
5. *See* Constitutional Law Committee Statement *Perustuslakivaliokunnan lausunto* PeVL 12/2003 vp.
6. *See also* Constitutional Law Committee Statement *Perustuslakivaliokunnan lausunto* PeVM 25/1994 vp, pp. 4-5.

industrial action has been taken within the duration of a collective agreement in order to affect conditions of employment without decision or involvement by the employee organization.[7]

Section 8 of the Collective Agreements Act (*Työehtosopimuslaki*, 436/1946) sets out a labour peace obligation which concerns collective action targeting a collective agreement during the time the agreement is in force.

Improving industrial peace is one of the labour market reforms set out in the current government's Programme. On the basis of the programme, a significant and far-reaching reform of the legislation was carried out in 2024. The legislation was amended to limit disproportionate sympathy actions and to limit the duration of political strikes as well as to increase compensatory fines for breaching industrial peace. According to the new section 8 a of the Collective Agreements Act, disproportionate sympathy industrial action cannot be taken. A sympathy industrial action is considered disproportionate if:

(1) the employer's service or production activities are restricted beyond the scope of the activities that serve or benefit the employer in the main dispute; and
(2) the restriction would have such adverse consequences for the employer whose employees are engaged in the sympathy action, or for the employer's contractor, as cannot be regarded as reasonable in the circumstances.

If the sympathy action is taken to demonstrate support without directly affecting the activities of the employer in the main dispute, the action must not have harmful consequences disproportionate to the main dispute.

Until 2024, there was no separate regulation for political action, but it did not fall within the scope of the peace obligation under section 8 of the Collective Agreements Act. The legislative reform introduced a definition of political industrial action into the legislation. Political industrial action means industrial action aimed at influencing supranational, national, regional or local political decision-making.

The legislative reform included a restriction on the permitted duration of political industrial actions. According to the new section 8b of the Collective Agreements Act, political industrial action in the form of a work stoppage which is subject to the obligation to maintain industrial peace may not continue after 24 hours have elapsed since the start of the work stoppage.[8] In addition, the work stoppage must be organized in such a way that it does not cause any disruption to production before or after the end of the work stoppage, provided that such disruption can reasonably be avoided by the means available to the executive. However, this obligation shall not prevent the implementation of a political work stoppage. Political industrial action other than a work stoppage may not last more than two weeks. Political industrial action may not be taken if, within 12 months, the implementing association actually continues the political industrial action it has previously taken in order to achieve the same objective.

7. *See* Government Bill *Hallituksen esitys eduskunnalle työsopimuslaiksi ja eräiksi siihen liittyviksi laeiksi* 157/2000 vp, p. 99.
8. Similar provisions were adopted to the Act on Mediation in Labour Disputes.

According to the legislation concerning civil servants, a permanent peace obligation governs civil servants even outside the period when a collective agreement is in force.[9] Only certain types of collective action are permitted. Under the Civil Service Collective Agreements Act (*Valtion virkaehtosopimuslaki*, 664/1970), a complete stoppage of work in the form of lockout or strike is permitted, but other types of industrial action are forbidden. This means that other kinds of industrial action or partial industrial action, such as refusing some kind of official duties, are not permitted.

In addition to the requirement that industrial action has to involve a complete stoppage of work, a requirement is set for the objectives of the action by the Civil Service Collective Agreements Act. Industrial action cannot be targeted against the contents, validity or interpretation of a collective agreement in force. Moreover, the objectives of a strike may not influence the list of issues in section 2 of the Civil Service Collective Agreements Act. It is not allowed to agree on:

- eligibility requirements for a position, promotion criteria, a civil servant's duties, supplements, and compensation payments made to foreign mission officials due to local special circumstances;
- pensions, survivor's pensions or other comparable benefits, the amount of rent for official residences or use of other state property, except for workspaces and work tools of someone acting in a co-operative role between the employer and civil servants;
- matters that cannot be agreed upon by collective agreements for employees.

Furthermore, civil servants may participate in a strike only on the basis of a decision by the trade union concerning the action.

Political strikes are forbidden in the public sector. The Municipal and Well-being Services County's Civil Servants Collective Agreements Act (*Laki kunnan ja hyvinvointialueen virkaehtosopimuksista*, 669/1970), the Act on Collective Agreements for Officials of the Evangelical Lutheran Church (*Laki evankelis-luterilaisen kirkon virkaehtosopimuksista*, 968/1974), the Parliamentary Civil Servants' Act (*Laki eduskunnan virkamiehistä*, 1197/2003), the Act on Civil Servants of the Bank of Finland (*Laki Suomen Pankin virkamiehistä*, 1166/1998), and the Law of the Office of the President of the Republic (*Laki tasavallan presidentin kansliasta*, 100/2012) contain provisions similar to section 8 of the Civil Service Collective Agreements Act. All these statutory restrictions on the right to strike are thus similar as regards civil servants in the public sector nor have they been differentiated in terms of different public employee positions. So, the right to strike is quite extensively restricted in the public sector.

No industrial action may be taken in respect of a public collective agreement in force. This is regulated by section 9 of the Civil Service Collective Agreements Act, and the other acts on civil servants mentioned above contain similar provisions. This rule applies to public official and employee organizations which are bound by the agreement, to associations that are members of such organizations or have been members during the term of the agreement, and to public officials and employees. When a

9. *See also* Labour Court judgments TT 2000:55 and TT 2006:107.

collective agreement is in force, employees may take political or sympathy action. However, such public action is prohibited in the case of civil servants.

In 2024, as a part of the legislative reform discussed above, the amount of a compensatory fine for unlawful industrial action was increased to a maximum of EUR 150,000 and a minimum of EUR 10,000. In addition, an employee who continues a strike that has been found unlawful by the Labour Court is subject to a penalty payment of EUR 200 for continuing to take part in unlawful action.[10]

2 PERMITTED RESTRICTIONS

2.1 Certain Categories of Public Servants

The Civil Service Collective Agreements Act does not differentiate between different categories of civil servants. For example, the right to political strikes is forbidden without exception in this Act.

The Labour Court judgment TT 2017:161 dealt with the question of whether a labour market organization had breached the Civil Service Collective Agreements Act and the industrial peace obligation laid down in the Civil Service Collective Agreements Act, and the Collective Agreements Act when its members – who were civil servants from different sectors – took part in a demonstration organized at Helsinki railway station on 18 September 2015. The Finnish trade union confederations announced the demonstration after the government had published planned measures to improve Finland's cost competitiveness on 8 September 2015. The demonstration was therefore a political industrial action against the government's plans. The decision by the court stated that the participation in a political demonstration by members of the trade union who were employed by the government could not be prevented. The claim was dismissed in this regard. The Labour Court also found that civil servants, as a rule, have a permanent obligation to industrial peace, but provisions limiting their right to strike must be interpreted in accordance with the provisions on freedom of assembly and association in international obligations and the under the Civil Service Collective Agreements Act as public servants, who wield public authority, participated in the strike. However, it could not be determined that the industrial action would have been contrary to section 9 of the Civil Service Collective Agreements Act and section 8 of the Collective Agreements Act. As the trade union did not engage in measures to stop the industrial action despite being notified of it, the court found that it had violated section 8 of the Civil Service Collective Agreements Act and the trade union was ordered to pay a compensatory fine.

2.2 Situations of Acute National or Local Crisis

According to section 7 of the Act on Mediation in Labour Disputes (*Laki työriitojen sovittelusta*, 420/1962), it is only permissible for a work stoppage to be extended or

10. The provisions on this penalty payment are contained in the Employment Contracts Act and Seafarers Employment Contracts Act.

commenced in connection with a labour dispute if the office of the National Conciliator and the other party to the dispute have been given notice in writing at least two weeks beforehand, with an indication of the causes of the intended stoppage or the extension of the stoppage, the date of its commencement, and its scope. The party giving notice is not permitted, without the consent of the other party, to postpone the commencement or extension of the intended action until a later date than stated in the notice or to restrict such action to a more limited field.

This section was amended as a part of the 2024 reform. The obligation to notify about industrial action was extended to sympathy action and political industrial action organized in the form of work stoppages. No sympathy industrial action or extension thereof may be taken unless the organizer has notified the employer subject to the sympathy industrial action, i.e., the employer whose employees are taking part in the sympathy industrial action, and, in the case of a peace obligation, the opposing party to the collective agreement, of this information in writing no later than seven days before the date on which the sympathy industrial action or extension thereof is due to begin. A political work stoppage or its extension may not take place unless the organizer has notified the other party to the collective agreement under the obligation of industrial peace of this information in writing at least seven days before the date on which the work stoppage or its extension is to begin. There is no obligation to notify political industrial action outside the obligation of collective peace. Similarly, industrial action against a foreign ship aimed at combating social dumping is not subject to prior notification.

In certain situations, it is possible to postpone the start of a work stoppage under section 8 of the Act on Mediation in Labour Disputes. A labour dispute may be postponed if it is intended to give rise to a work stoppage or its extension is under consideration, in the light of its scope or the nature of the sector involved, to affect the essential functions of society or to prejudice the general interest to a considerable extent. The Ministry of Economic Affairs and Employment may, on a proposal by the conciliator or conciliation board involved, and with the object of reserving sufficient time for mediation, prohibit an intended stoppage or its extension or commencement for a maximum of 14 days from the date announced for its commencement. In the case of a labour dispute over the terms of employment of public officials, the Ministry may extend its prohibition of the work stoppage for an additional 7 days for special reasons on a proposal by the conciliator or conciliation board involved. The parties must be notified of the prohibition at least three days prior to the date on which the action was intended to begin or, in the latter case, before the expiry of the prohibition period. Neither party is permitted, without the consent of the other party, to commence an intended work stoppage or to extend a stoppage after more than three days have elapsed since the end of the prohibition. The date on which action in connection with a labour dispute is to begin must invariably be notified to the conciliator and to the other party at least three days before the prohibition ends.

Public sector employee legislation contains provisions on the Civil Servant Dispute Board (*Virkariitalautakunta*), which can postpone industrial action planned or already under way or an extension thereof when the labour market organization or the main contracting organization considers the action can be capable of seriously disrupting important functions of society. The Board must resolve a matter concerning a danger of industrial action to society within 14 days. The Board can call on the parties to give up, in part or in full, collective action which is considered dangerous to society.[11]

When there is a threat of industrial action, protective work can be resorted to in order to secure critical services and operations. The obligation to perform protective work of civil servants who are outside the industrial action is regulated separately in the Civil Service Collective Agreements Act. Protective work refers to work which is necessary in order to prevent the life or health of citizens from being endangered or to protect property that is particularly at risk due to the industrial action. Officials participating in industrial action and persons with employment relationships are not subject to the statutory protection work obligation. The employer decides on the protective work and the number of persons needed to perform it.

It is noteworthy that a couple of times the government has used temporary legislation to restrict industrial action in order to ensure that industrial action does not endanger the health and lives of individuals. In 2007 and in 2022, the government turned to this exceptional means, but in both cases, an agreement was eventually reached between the parties so that the temporary act was not applied.

On 15 October 2007, the Union of Health and Social Care Professionals *Tehy* issued a strike warning regarding mass resignations in the municipal sector. On 9 November 2007, the government submitted to Parliament a Bill on a Patient Safety Act.[12] The purpose of the Bill was to ensure a minimum level of patient safety in situations where the remaining staff in employment would not be sufficient to ensure the life and health of patients under care. According to the Bill, the State Provincial Offices were empowered to order healthcare professionals to carry out patient safety work in municipal healthcare units in particular situations in which the life or health of patients is seriously endangered due to shortage of staff caused by industrial action. The Patient Safety Act (*Laki potilasturvallisuuden varmistamisesta terveydenhuollon työtaistelun aikana*, 1027/2007) was enacted and was in force from 17 November 2007 until 31 March 2008.

In 2022, a Government Bill for an Act Securing Essential Healthcare and Home Care during Industrial Action was introduced in a situation where industrial action was starting to such an extent in the intensive care and home care that the government deemed it necessary to take legislative measures to prevent endangerment of the life and health of service recipients.[13] The purpose of the Government Bill was to secure healthcare and home care in situations where, due to a labour dispute, the necessary healthcare or home care organized by a municipality or a municipal association would not have enough staff and the life or health of clients or patients would be seriously endangered as a result. The Act on Securing Essential Healthcare and Home Care

11. *See* ss 13-18 of the Civil Service Collective Agreements Act.
12. *See* Government Bill *Hallituksen esitys Eduskunnalle laiksi potilasturvallisuuden varmistamisesta terveydenhuollon työtaistelun aikana* 153/2007 vp.
13. *See* Government Bill *Hallituksen esitys eduskunnalle laiksi välttämättömän terveydenhuollon ja kotihoidon turvaamisesta työtaistelun aikana* 130/2022 vp.

during Industrial Action (*Laki välttämättömän terveydenhuollon ja kotihoidon turvaamisesta työtaistelun aikana*, 826/2022) gave the Regional State Administrative Agency the power to order social or healthcare professionals taking part in industrial action to work in positions corresponding to their skills in order to secure essential healthcare or home care in their employer's social or healthcare operational unit. The Act was in force from 20 September 2022 until 31 January 2023.

3 COMPENSATORY GUARANTEES FOR WORKERS DEPRIVED OF THE RIGHT TO STRIKE

In Finland, the labour dispute mediation system is based on compulsory conciliation. After the National Conciliator has received advance notification under the Act on Mediation in Labour Disputes, the National Conciliator or a conciliator nominated by the National Conciliator must take measures to settle the labour dispute without delay. Compulsory conciliation concerns the time when a collective agreement is not in force. The Act on Mediation in Labour Disputes does not apply to political strikes or sympathy strikes as they do not derive from a labour dispute which could be ended by an agreement between the parties.[14]

A party must attend or send a representative to negotiations ordered by the conciliator and, within a reasonable period set by the conciliator before the negotiations begin, provide the conciliator with a written account of the subject of the dispute, its content, the claims presented in the case, and any other information considered necessary by the conciliator. A party may impose a condition that the information provided may not be disclosed to others without its consent. Before or during the negotiations, the conciliator may request the parties to consider whether the commencement of the intended industrial action should be postponed until the outcome of the conciliation is known. The Act on Mediation in Labour Disputes does not apply to industrial action taking place when a collective agreement and related peace obligation are in force. This kind of industrial action is not governed by the labour dispute conciliation system. In addition, political and sympathy strikes are not in the sphere of the advance notification and conciliation obligation laid down in the Act on Mediation in Labour Disputes.

It can be added that a report on mechanisms for resolving disputes relating to the choice of collective agreements and the functioning of the conciliation system was published in 2021.[15] It deals with disputes over the choice of collective agreements and their resolution mechanisms with the aim of avoiding disturbances to industrial peace. Voluntary dispute resolution mechanisms have not had a significant impact on preventing and resolving disputes, unlike conciliation under the Act on Mediation in Labour Disputes. The report therefore proposed that, in addition to conciliation based on notification of industrial action, a voluntary conciliation procedure should be

14. *See* Jorma Saloheimo, *Työ- ja virkaehtosopimusoikeus* (Alma Talent 2020).
15. *See* Minna Etu-Seppälä & Simo Zitting, *Työehtosopimuksiin liittyvien rajariitojen ratkaisumekanismeja ja sovittelujärjestelmän toimivuutta koskeva selvitys. Loppuraportti. Työ- ja elinkeinoministeriön julkaisuja 2021:50* (Työ- ja elinkeinoministeriö 2021).

established for disputes relating to the choice of collective agreements and other labour disputes, during which the parties could not take industrial action. The parties to the dispute would be required to prepare for the conciliation, which would increase their responsibility for the success of conciliation. The report also proposed that, in case a dispute on the choice of collective agreements arises in Labour Court proceedings, all parties to the dispute should be heard. It was also proposed that preservation of industrial peace based on a so-called normally applicable collective agreement should be improved by clarifying the use of a condition that a collective agreement applies only to the members of an employee union that is a party to the agreement.

In 2023, the Act on Mediation in Labour Disputes was amended to include an opportunity for voluntary conciliation. The aim of the amendment was to include voluntary conciliation in the range of means of the Labour Disputes Act and to regulate its conditions.[16] The Government Bill was largely based on the report published in 2021.[17] Under the new section 9a of the Act, the National Conciliator or a conciliator appointed by the National Conciliator may, at the request of a party or parties to the labour dispute, initiate voluntary conciliation if all parties agree. The parties will be asked to consent to initiation of the conciliation procedure, and they will be given an opportunity to submit a written statement following the request. The conciliator will consider, on the basis of the request and statements by the parties, whether to initiate a conciliation procedure. The conciliator may decide to end voluntary conciliation under section 9a if it becomes evident during the negotiations that the conditions for conciliation cannot be met. Voluntary conciliation ends if a party gives notice of implementation of a work stoppage referred to in section 7.

4 CONCLUSION

Restrictions on the right to strike are weighed against both the Constitution and international human rights conventions to which Finland is party. The Civil Service Collective Agreements Act contains provisions on protective work, which civil servants who do not take part in a strike must perform in order to prevent danger to the life or health of citizens. In addition, protective work may relate to situations where the protection of property is endangered due to the strike. Restrictions on strike action related to endangering health and life have twice been imposed by the government through temporary legislation but have not been applied as the parties have reached an agreement. The 2024 legislative reform introduced new types of restrictions on the right to strike. These restrictions on sympathy industrial action and political industrial action are based on provisions that have no precedent in Finnish legislation

16. *See* Government Bill *Hallituksen esitys eduskunnalle laeiksi työriitojen sovittelusta annetun lain ja oikeudenkäynnistä työtuomioistuimessa annetun lain 32 a §:n muuttamisesta* 214/2022 vp.
17. *See* Government Bill *Hallituksen esitys eduskunnalle laiksi välttämättömän terveydenhuollon ja kotihoidon turvaamisesta työtaistelun aikana* 130/2022 vp.

CHAPTER 14

Restrictions on the Right to Strike in France

Francis Kessler

1 GENERAL INFORMATION

1.1 Categories of Workers

At the end of 2021, the French civil service employed around 5.6[1] million persons. France's civil service is made up of three branches, each with some common rules and some specific rules.[2] The central government civil service employs some 2.49 million employees (both tenured and non-tenured). These employees work in government ministries, devolved government departments and national public establishments. Recruitment is governed by public law. The local government civil service has 1.94 million employees who work for local and regional authorities such as regional councils, *département* councils and municipalities. The hospital civil service comprises 1.18 million employees who work for public healthcare facilities (public hospitals) and medical/social care facilities (retirement homes, etc.).

There are two main forms of employment in the French public service: the *fonctionnaires*, or civil servants, are recruited through a process that involves examinations and training. Although there are three categories of *fonctionnaires*, corresponding to three public functions: state civil servants (*les fonctionnaires de l'État*), territorial

1. *See* Ministère de la transformation publique, DGAFP, *Tansforming the French Civil Service to Meet the Challenges of the 21st Century* (2022).
2. Published on 1 March 2022, a civil service code unifies all the laws (and eventually all the regulations) applicable to public employees. The code covers the four acts establishing the general civil service regulations (the Civil Servants' Rights and Obligations Act of 13 July 1983, known as the 'general regulations', which covers all three branches; the Central Government Civil Service Act of 11 January 1984; the Local Government Civil Service Act of 26 January 1984; and the Hospital Civil Service Act of 9 January 1986). The code also covers more recent amending instruments, such as Order 2021-702 of 2 June 2021 on senior management reform in the central government civil service and the civil service Transformation Act of 6 August 2019.

civil servants (*les fonctionnaires territoriaux*) and hospital workers (*les fonctionnaires hospitaliers*), they benefit from a special status which ensures them lifetime employment in the public service.[3] The specific statutes of the corps have two purposes: they define the posts that corps members may occupy and the arrangements for access to the corps and they establish the minimum career path guaranteed to corps members. The career system is so called because of this minimum career path guaranteed to all public servants. The second category is *agents contractuel*, or 'contract agents', which are one of the categories of non-permanent agents in the civil service, along with auxiliaries, temporary workers, trainees and cabinet jobs. For the most part, these staff are governed by public law. Labour law is only conditionally applicable to these non-civil servants (*non-titulaires*).[4] Although many of their rights and obligations are contractually defined, many of the rules in force for permanent civil servants are also applicable to them, and disputes between them and their employer are decided by the administrative courts. However, they do not belong to specific job corps. Contracts are often for a fixed term, although, expressed in full-time equivalents, there are more permanent than fixed-term contracts. In a few cases, some contract staff in the administrative public services are governed by private law.[5] The Public Service Transformation Act of 2019 initiated a profound transformation by facilitating the use of contract employment (*agents contractuels*), as opposed to lifetime public servants.

Another segment of the public sector is state-owned companies that provide industrial or commercial services (*Service Public Industriel et Commercial*, e.g., La Poste, EDF/electricity, SNCF/railways).[6] Some of these companies have the legal form of an *Etablissement public industriel et* commercial – Public Establishment of Industrial and Commercial Character – EPIC. Although, as a result of privatization, they have been greatly reduced[7] and partly transformed into joint-stock companies and they do not employ their staff in the status of civil servants, but their working conditions are regulated by special laws, the so-called *Statut du personnel*: the employees enjoy

3. Public-servant status is granted to persons appointed to a permanent post and established within a grade. A further condition essential to public-servant status is the public nature of the person appointing and employing the public servant. Appointment is by means of a unilateral administrative order. Public servants are divided into corps. In addition to the General Statute for Public Servants, there are specific statutes. The purpose of these is to establish the specific rules or regulations that apply in particular to each corps of the public service.
4. The Labour Code contains only (relatively few) provisions on the consequences of a strike on labour contract law. The fifth book of Part Two of the Labour Code is devoted to collective disputes. The first chapter, entitled 'General Provisions', has only one Article L 2511-1, according to which 'the exercise of the right to strike cannot justify the termination of the employment contract, except in the case of gross violations by the worker. Its exercise can in no case lead to a discriminatory measure ..., including wages and social benefits. Any dismissal except for gross negligence is unlawful'.
5. Overall, a significant share of contract agents occupy support and assistance functions, such as supervisors, technical assistants, etc.
6. In contrast to the state administration, the core of the French civil service, the reform efforts of various French governments have had significant effects in the industrial sector, i.e., a large part of the state-owned companies have either been restructured or completely privatized such as Air France, France Télécom, Gaz de France or Renault.
7. Franz Beckmann, *The Gutting of the Public Service: Liberalisation, Privatisation and Commercialisation in France, in Bieling, Deckwirth Schmalz, Liberalisation and Privatisation in Europe: The Reorganisation of Public Infrastructure in the European Union* (Westfälisches Dampfboot 2008).

special rules such as a high level of job security, shorter working hours, higher pension payments and various benefits as a result of these laws enacted after the Second World War. However, these privileges are increasingly at odds with the profitability criteria demanded by liberalized markets. Strikes in these companies have usually been linked to attempts to change or reduce these special working conditions. Collective agreements are largely irrelevant in these companies, as they are in the original public service.

Article 4 of Title 1 of the General Statute for Public Servants provides that 'a public servant is in a statutory and regulatory position vis-à-vis the administration': the salary and working conditions for the majority of civil servants (*fonctionnaires titulaires*) are set by law and regulation, so from a purely legal point of view, there is no collective bargaining. Moreover, law passed in 1983 stipulates that trade unions have the right to 'negotiate with the government' before decisions are made to increase pay and that they can 'discuss issues relating to working conditions and work organisation'. For example, there is a national council here, the *Conseil Supérieur de la Fonction Publique* (CSFP), as well as the *Conseil Supérieur de la Fonction Publique territoriale* (CSFPT), which has to take a position on legislative proposals with a potential impact on civil servants working in municipalities.

There are also local committees, *Comité technique paritaire* (CTP), that deal with the organization of work in authorities with at least 50 employees.[8] If this number is not reached, this task is transferred to the *Commissions administratives paritaires* (CAP) working at departmental level, which deals with career planning. In both cases, these are joint committees with elected employee representatives. The unions are allocated seats according to the election results, although at national level, membership of the committees also guarantees seats for nationally representative unions. These committees only represent civil servants, not employees and workers.

The Civil Service Transformation Act of 6 August 2019 authorizes the government to issue orders to help reach negotiated agreements, particularly at local level, while granting some of them legal force. The Order of 17 February 2021 on civil service collective bargaining agreements allows labour and management to work together to find the most suitable solutions to issues considering the specifics of their administrative department and geographic location. The new legal framework has already led to an embryo of 'collective agreements' with a first agreement in July 2021 on work-from-home arrangements in all three branches of the civil service and a second in January 2022 on supplementary health insurance for civil service employees.

2 LEGAL BASIS OF THE RIGHT TO STRIKE

The international framework for the right to strike is the International Covenant on Economic, Social and Cultural Rights (UN Covenant on Social Rights or ICCPR) of 16 December 1966, and in particular Article 8 thereof, which is applicable in France.

8. Local authorities, despite the highly centralized system, the possibility for bonus and additional payments, but only within national limits.

France has also ratified the revised version of the European Social Charter of 1996, known as the 'Revised European Social Charter', Article 6.4 of which grants 'the right of workers and employers to take collective action, including the right to strike, in the event of conflicts of interest, subject to any obligations arising from collective agreements in force', and section 28 of the Charter of Fundamental Rights of the European Union of 2000, which is binding on France.[9] France did not ratify Convention No. 151 concerning Labour Relations (Public Service) and Convention No. 154 concerning the Promotion of Collective Bargaining.

Strike is defined by the courts as 'any collective and concerted stoppage of work in support of occupational demands'.[10] Fundamentally, the right to strike is treated in French law as a right whose bearer is each worker individually. The form commonly used to define the ownership of the right to strike is 'an individual right for workers with a collective exercise': the right to strike is a personal right. In France, the right to strike is proclaimed and protected as a specific right. Formally, on one side, it is distinct from trade union freedom, of which it is not an expression, on the other side of collective bargaining. Collective bargaining has a constitutional basis in the right to participate proclaimed in the 1946 Constitution Preamble, which refers to the current Constitution Preamble. The right to strike is therefore never treated as an auxiliary to the right to collective bargaining. For a long time, the right to strike in the public service has traditionally rested on judicial law that the interaction of the right to strike with the 'continuity of *"services publics"*', which is also protected by the Constitution, is to be reconciled.[11] The Winkell judgment, handed down by the *Conseil d'État* on 7 August 1909 stated: 'By accepting the employment conferred on him, the civil servant has submitted to all the obligations deriving from the very necessities of public services and has renounced all the faculties incompatible with a continuity essential to national life".[12] Paragraph 7 of the Preamble to the French Constitution of 1946, to which the current Constitution of 1958 refers, proclaims that 'the right to strike shall be exercised within the framework of the laws which regulate it'.[13] The Constitutional Council has repeatedly stressed that it is up to the legislature to draw 'the limits of the right to strike' and to ensure 'the necessary mediation between the defence of professional interests, of which a strike is the means, and the protection of the general interest, which a strike may affect'.[14] As early as 1950, the French Council of State held that administrative

9. Francis Kessler, *The Right to Strike: France*, in Waas (ed.), *The Right to Strike. A Comparative View*, 207 (Kluwers 2014).
10. For example, Cour de cassation Labour Law Chamber (hereinafter '*Soc.*') 18 June 1996, Bull. V No. 243; Moreau, *La grève* (Economica 1998); Farouz-Chopin, *Le droit de grève* (L'Harmattan 2003).
11. Crouzatier-Durand & Kada (dir.), *Grève et droit public 70 ans de reconnaissance. Actes de colloques de l'IFR* (Presses de l'Université Toulouse Capitole, LGDJ – Lextenso Editions 2017).
12. One recalls the uncompromising positions of Hauriou, who considered the strike of civil servants with '*acts of war*' (comments under sous Council of State (hereafter CE 7 August 1909, Winkell, S. 1909, 3, 145) or of Duguit, who saw it as a 'crime' when these agents 'commit the most serious of attacks on collective life itself' (*Traité de droit constitutionnel*, T. III, Paris, de Boccard, 1912, 219); Walter C., Der Grundsatz der Kontinuität der 'services publics' und das Streikrecht im öffentlichen Dienst in Frankreich, ZaöRV 55/1 1995, 191.
13. Constitutional Council (*Conseil constitutionnel*), 16 August 2007, No. 2007-556 DC.
14. Constitutional Council, 25 July 1979, No. 79-105 DC.

authorities may not regulate the right to strike but can, so as to ensure the continuity of public services, organize minimum services on a case-by-case basis.[15] Faced with the problem of the legality of strikes in disputes arising in public services managed by legal persons governed by private law, the Court of Cassation has adopted an identical solution with regard to the employees assigned to them.[16]

3 PERMITTED RESTRICTIONS

The fifth book of Part Two of the Labour Code is devoted to collective disputes. The first chapter, entitled 'General Provisions', also applicable to the public sector, has only one Article L 2511-1, according to which 'the exercise of the right to strike cannot justify the termination of the employment contract, except in the case of gross violations by the worker. Its exercise can in no case lead to a discriminatory measure ..., including wages and social benefits. Any dismissal except for gross negligence is unlawful'.

Although the guidelines set out in the Preamble to the 1946 Constitution, which recognizes the right to strike 'within the framework of the laws that regulate it',[17] the legislative interference in the right to strike is very few except .... in the public sector![18]

Since a law of 31 July 1963, the right to strike in the public sector has been explicitly recognized, but the exercise of the right to strike is regulated by Article L. 2512-1 to L.2512-5 of the Labour Code, which restrict strike in the public services whether they are provided by public entities[19] or by private bodies[20] (section 3.1). Some other specific sectoral laws prohibit strike and, moreover, collective actions (section 3.2).

3.1 Restriction of Strikes

In public services, the 'concerted cessation of work' has first of all to be preceded by prior notice; surprise strikes are therefore unlawful. In public services, strikes can only be called by representative trade unions.[21]

---

15. CE, *Dehaene*, No. 01645 of 7 June 1950, hereinafter called 'Dehaene judgment'.
16. Soc, 27 January 1956 in Dalloz 1956, 481, note Gervais A.
17. This wording is repeated in the general statute of in the general status of civil servants (Art. 10 law No. 83-634 of 13 July 1983).
18. For a presentation of the lively discussion before and after the 1963 law Sinay Hélène & Javillier Jean-Claude, *La grève*, in Camerlynck (ed.), *Traité de droit du travail* 389 seq. (Dalloz 1984).
19. Hospitals, social welfare offices, national social security funds, social housing companies, professional associations, the Atomic Energy Commission (Soc. 5 July 1984), the Autonomous Port of Bordeaux (Soc. 16 July 1997), etc. are considered to be invested with the management of a public service.
20. Companies which that have entered into an agreement with the State with a view to carrying an activity, which is the case of private educational establishments under a contract of association, an apprentice training center, managed by an association; enterprises, whatever the terms of their remuneration, entrusted with the management of a public service; bodies directly entrusted with a public service mission, like social security funds.
21. For the constitutional judge, 'given the particular nature of the right to strike, the legislator may, as it has already done, confer on representative trade union organizations special prerogatives

Article L. 2512-3 of the Labour Code provides for an obligation to give at least five days' *notice of the strike action*. This must include an indication of the motives for the strike and the announcement of its place, time and duration. The notice must come from 'a representative trade union organisation at national level, in the professional category or in the company, the organisation or the service concerned': this requirement prohibits 'wildcat strikes'.[22] The notice must specify 'the reasons for the strike' and fix the place, date and time of the beginning as well as the duration, limited or not, of the planned strike.

Since 1982, the norm has been supplemented to the effect that during this waiting period, the parties are obliged to negotiate on the strike demands raised.

Specific provisions exist for land transport and passenger air transport. Law No. 2007-1224 of 21 August 2007, which has now been incorporated, for the most part, into the Transport Code, imposes, in companies responsible for a public service mission of regular passenger transport by land, negotiations prior to the lodging of the notice. This negotiation – which is required even if the planned movement is the result of a national call for action – takes place under the conditions set out in a framework agreement specific to the company in question. In the absence of such an agreement, negotiations prior to the notice period are organized in accordance with the procedures laid down by the branch agreement. In the absence of any agreement, it is governed by a body of provisions laid down by regulation. In public land transport, each employee who intends to join the strike must announce it to his employer two days before stopping work. Once informed of the number of strikers, the company must establish and make public the level of service it will be able to provide. This is determined in accordance with the 'collective agreement on service predictability', which the company must have negotiated with the representative trade unions or, in the absence of an agreement, the 'predictability plan' it has drawn up.

An almost similar model has been introduced by Law No. 2012-375 of 19 March 2012 in Article L. 1114-1 and following the Transportation Code, which is applicable to passenger air transport companies as well as companies providing aerodrome operations, airport security, fire and rescue, animal control and aircraft line maintenance services and ground handling services.[23]

For teachers in the primary education system (kindergarten and elementary), since 2008 and the introduction of the '*Service Minimum d'Accueil*', each teacher is required to declare his or her intention to take part in the strike at least 48 hours,

relating to the calling of a strike; that this role recognized to these organizations for the filing of a strike notice leaves each employee free to decide personally whether or not to participate in it'. Constitutional council 16 August 2007, No. 2007-556 DC.

22. The notice required is addressed to 'the hierarchical authority or ... the management of the establishment, undertaking or body concerned'. When it comes from civil servants, it must therefore be addressed to the minister concerned or his representative. If it relates to a conflict affecting the employees of a company managing a public service, it should be sent to the head of the company or of the establishment or service that will be affected by the cessation of activity.
23. Bernaud, *La loi relative à l'organisation du service et à l'information des passagers dans les entreprises de transport aérien de passagers est conforme à la Constitution*, 70 (Droit social 2012).

including at least one working day, before participating in the strike.[24] For schools of the 1st degree, teachers (personnel 'in front of pupils') must send their declaration of intention two days before the strike, including at least one working day. The modalities of the declaration are therefore specified by the Ministry of Education in a circular of 26 August 2008, which states 'This declaration is made to the academy inspector, or to the national education inspectors when the academy inspector has entrusted them with the mission of collecting the declarations and the personnel concerned by this obligation to declare have been informed. The declaration must be made in writing, by letter or by fax and must reach the competent authority 48 hours before the person concerned goes on strike.'[25]

Following article L. 2512-2 Code du Travail special limitations, in particular the maintenance of an *emergency or minimum service* ('*service minimum*') have to be taken into account. The concept of a service minimum is to be understood broadly; it can go as far as the complete exclusion of the right to strike. However, these restrictions must be necessary, and there is a great deal of uncertainty about what constitutes a service minimum. An attempt by the legislator to define the service minimum by law was overturned by the *Conseil d'État* in a decision of 12 May 1989.[26]

The minimum service resulting from the *Dehaene* case restrictions on the right to strike may be established by the territorial authority, under the authority, under control of the administrative judge, when the necessities of the service require it. Case law has gradually reduced the limits of the so-called designation procedure. According to the case law, restrictions on the right to strike can be imposed in order to avoid an abusive use of this right contrary to public order.[27] They cannot be of a general nature. They must be limited to jobs of the services strictly essential to the continuity of the public service public service. They cannot concern all the employees of a given hierarchical category, for example, even if the judge more easily accepts restrictions on authority.[28]

In kindergarten elementary and 1 degree school, there is '*Service Minimum d'Accueil*': this reception service is normally provided by the State, but when the number of strikers is high (more than 25% of the number of teachers in the school), it is the responsibility of the local administration.[29]

---

24. Unlike teachers, private law employees are not bound by any advance notice and, in the event of a nationwide strike, do not have to inform their head of school of their intention to join the strike.
25. *Official Bulletin of National education* (BOEN) of 4 September 2008.
26. The former law No. 84-1286 of 31 December 1984 contained a far-reaching provision that would have made any strike in the aviation sector impossible (Art. 2.4: '*la mission nécessaire à la sauvegarde des personnes et des biens*' must be maintained). Because there was no general justification for this, it was found to be incompatible with the concept of the service minimum.
27. CE 4 February 1966 Nos 62479, 62494 and 62495.
28. CE 6 December 1966 also CE 1 June 1984 No. 22820.
29. Article L. 133-7 of the Education Code provides for the establishment in each municipality of a list of persons likely to provide the reception service. The identification of these persons is the sole responsibility of the mayor. The municipality may call not only on municipal employees, in accordance with their status, but also on nursery assistants, leaders of associations managing leisure centers, members of family associations, retired teachers, students, parents, etc. The provisions of the Code of Social Action and the Family do not impose any obligation in terms of

Some specific texts provide for the creation of special 'sectoral' minimum services. For example, a law of 26 July 1979[30] on radio and television companies and bodies, which must broadcast one news and one entertainment programme per day, a law of 25 July 1980 on nuclear plants, which aims to ensure the necessary continuity of service for maintenance, repair and operation, a law of 31 December 1984[31] and a decree of 1985, which create a minimum service for the control of air traffic control.[32] Finally, there are a number of laws and regulations concerning public health. For instance, in the hospital sector, Ministry of Social Affairs Circular No. 5 of 22 April 1983 empowers hospital directors to define and organize the functioning of services that may not be interrupted, the physical safety of persons, the upkeep of care and accommodation to patients in hospital the maintenance of premises and equipment. The 'minimum service' in local public transport has taken other forms. In 2008, the UTP negotiated an agreement with the transport unions on minimum service in the event of a strike. This averted a decree by which the State would otherwise have ordered the establishment of minimum services. The transport companies RATP (Paris area, 60% of the French public transport workforce) and SNCF (railway company) have concluded their own agreements.

Article 56 of 2019 on the transformation of the civil service"[33] limits the right to strike in a range of territorial services within the framework of an agreement negotiated with the trade unions. The relevant services include the collection and treatment of household waste; public transport; care for the elderly and disabled; early years education of children under three; after-school care; and collective and school catering. The limitation of the right to strike would be justified by the fact that the interruption of these services, in the event of a strike by public officials directly participating in their execution, would contravene respect for public order, in particular public health or essential needs. Employees at whatever hierarchical level whose presence at their workplace is necessary to ensure the uninterrupted operation of public services within the limits defined above may be summoned[34] or requisitioned.

The *designation* does not concern persons but jobs and consequences only on the agents who carry out the corresponding functions. The jobs giving rise to restrictions on the right to strike must be precisely designated by a decree of administrative

staff qualifications or staffing levels for childcare facilities not exceeding 14 days per year. The law provides that the State will pay the communes financial compensation within a maximum of 35 days.

30. Law No. 74-696 of 7 August 1974 was amended by Law No. 79-634 of 26 July 1979.
31. Law No. 84-1286 of 31 December 1984 was amended by Law No. 87-1014 of 18 December 1987, *see also* the Code of Education, Art. L. 133-2, Art. L. 133-3, Art. L. 133-4.
32. As included in the Transport Code by Ordinance No. 2010-1307 of 28 October 2010, and amended by Law No. 2012-375 of 19 March 2012.
33. Article 56 (Law No. 2019-828 of 6 August 2019, has created an Art. 7-2 in the statutory law 84-53); Taillefait, *L'exercice du droit de grève dans les services publics locaux*, 1020 (Droit social 2019).
34. A summons is a written administrative decision by the director of the organization, under the control of the administrative judge. Its purpose is to ensure continuity of care in case of strike. The summons takes the form of an individual letter from the administration to the agents concerned. Refusal to respond to a summons will result in liability for misconduct of the personnel involved.

authority. This designation must be motivated and notified to the employees concerned. Jobs that are absolutely essential for the proper functioning of the public service (if any) or the proportion of jobs in a service that are essential to its proper functioning could be fixed in advance. The list of the jobs concerned would then be published and the employees would be informed before assignment or transfer. The administrative authority may distinguish, among these jobs, those for which the designation is permanent and those for which the designation will be notified in case of in case of a strike notice. In the latter case, the authority will decide whether or not to designate the agents occupying the posts, depending on the jobs, the duration, the modalities and the extent of the strike of the strike. The resulting list or lists of jobs may be modified at any time according to the same rules when circumstances so require. The judge strictly controls whether the deprivation of the right to strike affects only essential to the functioning of the activities whose maintenance is necessary.

The second tool is the *power of requisition*. In order to organize the continuity of a public service essential to public order or personal safety, the hierarchical authority may limit the right to strike of employees without relying on a legislative text. In this case, the authority has the power of requisition, which means that it can impose on the indispensable agents, even if they wish to strike, to accomplish their mission.

On the level of a département, the Prefect[35] also has this power of requisition. In application of Article L2215-1 4° of the general code of local authorities (Code général des collectivités territoriales CGCT), in the event of a case of emergency, when the foreseeable good order, public health, tranquillity and public safety so requires and when the means available to the Prefect no longer allow them to pursue the objectives for which he has police powers, the Prefect may, by order, for all the *communes* of the *département* or several or one requisition any goods or services, require any person necessary for the operation – of this service or the use of this property and prescribe – measures until the breach of public order has ceased or the conditions public order has ceased or the conditions for its maintenance are ensured A prefectorial order must specify the nature of services required, the duration of the requisition measure and the terms and conditions of its application. These are highly regulated procedures that only apply in times of crisis. More often than not, public officials are 'designated'.

Requisitioning of public health workers by the Prefect is provided for in Articles L.3131-8 et seq. of the French Public Health Code, which states that. 'If the influx of patients or victims or the health situation so warrants, on a proposal from the Director General of the Regional Health Agency, the representative of the Prefect may requisition public health workers of the regional health agency, the representative of the State in the department may make the necessary requisitions of all goods and services, and in particular require the services of any health professional, whatever their mode of practice any health or medico-social establishment.'

35. The Prefect, representing the State at a level of a Département, has the non-titular roles of chief controller of regional, departmental, and communal public accounts, and of chief inspector of good (i.e., law-abiding) governance of the authorities of the respective territorial entities.

In addition to times of war,[36] Law No. 2003-239 of 18 March 2003[37] on internal security allows Prefects to requisition strikers by order in cases of emergency, when required by a real or foreseeable breach of the peace, by public health, by public order or public safety, and when the means at the Prefect's disposal no longer allow him to pursue the objectives for which he has powers of enforcement. The order establishes the type of the requisitioned service, the duration of the requisition and how it will be carried out.[38] The purpose of the requisition must be to guarantee a minimum service, not a full service: only the personnel essential to the minimal functioning of the structure can be requisitioned and it is important that before proceeding, all other organizational solutions have been sought. This power of the Prefect remains under judicial review by administrative courts.[39] Refusal to obey a requisition order is a criminal offence.

3.2 Prohibition of Strikes

By deciding that 'the time of cessation and the time of resumption of work may not be different for the various categories or members of the personnel concerned', rotating strikes or 'rolling strikes' are prohibited by law.[40]

Furthermore, some civil servants are, by law, totally deprived of the right to strike in all circumstances as their presence is considered necessary to maintain an element of service which, if it were to be interrupted,[41] would 'disrupt the essential needs of the country'.[42]

These are:

- Members of the national republican security forces.[43]
- Members of the national police.[44]
- Judges.[45]
- Members of the (air, ground, marine, *gendarmerie*) armed forces.[46]
- Members of the prison administration.[47]

36. Articles L2141-3 and L2211-1 et seq. of the Defence Code.
37. Law No. 2003-239 of 18 March 2003 for internal security.
38. Article L2215-1 of the General Code of Territorial.
39. CE 9 December 2003, No. 262186, CE Réf. 27 October 2010, No. 343966. As an example a prefectural order prescribing a general requisition measure leading to the establishment of a full service and not a minimum service is vitiated by a manifest illegality that seriously infringes the right to strike (CE 9 December 2003 No. 262186).
40. Saramito, *La prohibition des grèves tournantes et des grèves-surprise dans les services publics,* 1795 (JCP G 1963).
41. Constitutional council. No. 79-105 DC 25 July 1979, Rec., p. 33.
42. CE 12 April 2013, *Fédération FO Energie et Mines, Rec.*, p. 94, *RFD adm.* 2013, p. 637.
43. Law No. 47-2384 of 27 December 1947 laying down a new organizational structure for the Republic Security Corps.
44. Law No. 48-1504 of 28 September 1948 on the special status of police personnel.
45. Law No. 58-1270 of December 1958 laying down the organic statute of the magistrature.
46. Law No. 72-662 of 13 July 1972 laying down a General Statute for Military Staff.
47. Law No. 58- of 6 August 1958 on the special status of external services of the prison administration.

- Some categories of staff in air navigation.[48]
- Staff of the national communications network of the Ministry of the Interior.[49]

Sometimes, the law is less explicit and does not directly refer to the prohibition of the right to strike. This is the case, for example, for employees working in establishments where nuclear materials are held, to whom the special provision of Article L. 1333-10 of the Defense Code applies.

4 CONSEQUENCES OF A STRIKE

4.1 Participating in a Lawful Strike

The strike has no effect on the civil servant's statutory status and the employer cannot take discriminatory measures in terms of remuneration and social benefits.[50] Consequently, strike days have no impact on the calculation of annual leave days. However, the exercise of the right to strike has a consequence in the calculation of the days of Reduced Working Time (RTT) as the employee is not at the disposal of the employer; this period cannot be considered actual working time and therefore cannot be taken into account for the RTT (reduced working time).[51] Finally, it is forbidden to sanction an employee who participates in a regular strike. The strike entails a deduction from pay. Indeed, the agent is entitled to remuneration after service. However, there is no service done in case of strike. Therefore, there is no remuneration. The deduction is made on the remuneration according to the dates of authorization and liquidation of the pay. Therefore, it is often made one or even two months after the strike. As far as the amount of the deduction is concerned, a distinction must be made here between the case of agents belonging to the State civil service and those belonging to the two other civil services (territorial or hospital). For State civil servants, the principle is that of the indivisible 30th. Each day of strike results in the withholding of 1/30th of the total remuneration,[52] even if the strike is shorter than one day. Moreover, if an employee goes on strike from Friday to Monday inclusive, he/she will have four days of pay deducted since Saturday and Sunday are taken into account, even though he/she is not

48. Law No. 84-1286 31 December 1984 on the exercise of the right to strike in the air navigation services.
49. Law No. 68-695 31 July 1968.
50. CE 2 November 1990, Req. No. 42875 and CE 1 February 1963.
51. Article 2 of the Decree of 25 August 2000, No. 2000-815.
52. The deduction is calculated on the whole of the remuneration: indexed salary, residence allowance, premiums and allowances. Bonuses paid annually are included in the basis for calculating the deduction. They must be reduced to an average monthly equivalent, on the basis of the amount paid during the previous year, in order to calculate the amount of the 1/30th to be withheld. However, the family salary supplement is maintained in full. Expense reimbursements are not taken into account. The deduction must not exceed the seizable portion of the salary. If the strike lasts several consecutive days, the number of 30 minutes is equal to the number of days from the first day of the strike to the last day. This calculation applies even if, during some of these days, the agent had no service to perform (holidays, weekends). Thus, for example, when an agent goes on strike on a Friday and the following Monday, 4/30th are deducted.

expected to work on the weekend. This financial sanction has been repeatedly criticized by the European Committee of Fundamental Social Rights as a violation of § 6.4 of the revised European Social Charter but is considered proportionate by the French Constitutional Council. For agents from other civil service sectors, the deduction is proportional to the duration of the strike,[53] i.e., 1/30th for a day's absence, 1/60th for half a day's absence, and 1/151.67th for each hour of absence. In the event of a strike replacing a shift, the deduction is proportional to the number of monthly shifts

4.2 Participation in an Illegal Strike or Other Measures

Like in the private sector, political strikes are prohibited. Thus, participation in a strike that is not justified by work-related reasons exposes the employees to a disciplinary sanction but does not deprive them of the disciplinary guarantees.[54] In the same way, the incitement of a political strike by distributing tracts constitutes a breach of the duty of reserve and the duty of reserve and justifies a disciplinary sanction.[55]

The participation, even as a staff representative, in the illegal occupation of premises and in the sequestration of management personnel is unlawful.[56] The public authority may, in the interest of the public service, prohibit the occupation of the premises or order their evacuation.[57] A social movement consisting of abstaining from carrying out a part of its missions does not constitute a legal strike; the fact of participating in it is liable to a sanction.[58] The knowingly participating in a strike which is not regular[59] is unlawful. An action which does not have the character of a strike or unlawful behaviour during a strike[60] justifies the implementation of a disciplinary

53. The decision of the Constitutional Council No. 87-230 of 28 July 1987 rejects the rule of the indivisible thirtieth for strike action in the territorial public service.
54. For example, CE 1 February 1963 Audibert.
55. For example, CE 12 October 1956 Cochand.
56. 'Considering, first of all, that it appears from the documents in the file that during the strike of a part of the staff of the center of help by work Gauthière, in Aubagne, managed by the regional association of aid to cerebral palsy (A.R.A.I.M.C.), five representatives of the staff representatives took part in the occupation of the administrative premises and the closure of the workshops and, on February 24 1982, to the expulsion by force of the director of the establishment and of two of his assistants; that among them Mr. X, a full member of the works council, actively participated in these acts; that it is not established that he played a moderating role; that, even though Mr. X. was not the only protected employee to have behaved in this way, his behaved in this way, his actions characterize an abnormal and seriously wrongful exercise of the mandate with which he of the mandate with which he was entrusted and of such a nature as to justify his dismissal.' CE 22 June 1988, No. 59660.
57. For example, CE 11 February 1966 No. 65509.
58. For example, Administrative Appeal Court Paris, 13 May 2013 No. 11PA01255.
59. CE 20 January 1967, Nos 66321, 66322.
60. The following are subject to sanction in case of strike: civil servants who do not inform their administration of their intention to strike if required; employees who go on strike during their service when the administration asks them to strike for the whole duration of their service; agents who return to work before the end of the strike without informing their administration; employees subject to a minimum service requirement who do not inform their administration in advance of their intention to strike; agents prohibited from striking who ignore the prohibition.

sanction against each participant.[61] Article L. 2512-4 of the French Labor Code specifies that these decisions are taken in accordance with the principle of adversarial proceedings: employees must be given the opportunity to present their observations on the facts of which they are accused and to have access to the file concerning them. Furthermore, dismissal and demotion can only be pronounced in accordance with the disciplinary procedure normally applicable. In these circumstances, dismissal is pronounced without loss of pension rights. However, case law moderates the sanction for non-respect of the provisions governing the right to strike. Indeed, the participation of employees in an irregularly initiated strike does not constitute a fault as long as they have not knowingly disregarded the provisions governing the exercise of the right to strike in the public sector. As an example, the Council of State considered that the participation of employees in a strike irregularly called by a union may not constitute misconduct if the employees participating in the strike were not informed of the illegality of the strike notice. In order to constitute a fault, they would have had to be informed by the union of the need to verify the legality of the strike notice, that they were thus aware of its irregularity and that they nevertheless participated in this illegal strike with full knowledge of the facts.[62] Several criminal sanctions could be applied to a civil servant in case the strike is illegal or disqualified.[63]

A strike may give rise to civil liability claims, particularly against the trade unions that took the initiative for the movement. Thus, a failure to comply with the provisions of Article L. 2512-2 of the Labour Code constitutes a fault on their part that may engage their liability towards the company that is the victim of a strike called under irregular conditions.[64]

5 CURRENT SOCIAL PROTEST MOVEMENTS

Despite the multiplication of tools and the attempts to structure general social dialogue in a strictly regulated system, French trade unions have always used strikes to paralyze public services as a means of exerting pressure. Strikes in the public sector arise from the combination of the multiplicity of competing unions, their relatively weak position and a lack of social dialogue combined with the gradual privatization of certain sectors of the public service. The strike, which is not seen as a sign of failure but as a means

61. CE 20 January 1967, Req. Nos 66321 and 66322.
62. CE decision, 8 January 1992, Nos 90634 & 90635.
63. As far as the agent is concerned, several offences can be committed during a strike: (1) Offenses against the person: Violence Art. 222.7 and following of the Criminal Code, Threats Art. 222.17 and following of the Criminal Code, Sequestration Art. 224.1 of the Criminal Code, Slanderous denunciations Art. 226.10 and following of the Criminal Code, Breach of secrecy, including professional secrecy Art. 226.13 of the Criminal Code. (2) Offences against property: Theft Art. 311.1 and following of the Criminal Code, Destruction, degradation and deterioration of property Art. 322.1 and following of the Criminal Code. (3) Attacks on the authority of the State: Obstacles to the exercise of freedom of expression, work, association, assembly or demonstration Arts 431.1 to 431.2 and following of the Criminal Code. (4) As far as service managers and elected officials are concerned, several criminal offences may occur: Moral harassment Art. 222-33-2 of the Criminal Code, Discrimination Art. 225-1 to 225-4 of the Criminal Code, Slanderous denunciations Art. 226.10 and following of the Criminal Code.
64. Soc, 6 February 1985: Juri-social 1985, F 53.

of struggle, is therefore common.[65] In public transport, they are also very spectacular.[66] Political strikes are frequent as shows the recent social protests against the government's 2023 retirement reform which leaded to protests across the country. Although union density in the French public sector is not significantly higher than in the private sector and is also low by international standards (15% and falling),[67] trade unions have greater mobilization potential here than in the private sector.[68] According to official records, twice the number of working days were lost due to strikes in the public sector as in the private sector. Other forms of social actions appear.: in 2011, for example, there appeared what was called the 'hearings strike' by magistrates, which aimed to circumvent Article 10 of the Ordinance of 22 December 1958, regularly denounced by the magistrates' unions: the practice consisted of the magistrate, while ensuring the hearing, automatically postponing the case presented by the bailiff to a later date, thus ensuring the continuity of public service; urgent hearings (of the type of immediate appearances, assizes trials with detained defendants) were, however, ensured. Another illustration relates to what the media called the 'clerks strike', which took place in April 2014, which consisted of circumventing the proscription of the right to strike by organizing demonstrations in front of courthouses to protest their working conditions and pay. The police movements in October 2016 used the same channels: 'zeal strikes' organized by the unions consisting of only dealing with emergencies in police stations or skipping an inconvenient parking lot but also daily demonstrations organized by non-unionized officers that raise questions since these demonstrations are sometimes organized with departmental vehicles or resources, may offend their duty of reserve, or most are not subject to prior declaration.

65. Strikes in the public sector are completely or partially excluded from the statistics reported to the ILO. This is not without influence on the overall strike record, as there is a comparatively large amount of strike action in this sector, especially in the course of political strikes. Laulom Sylvaine & Leclerc Olivier, *Chapter 6 France*, in Mironi & Schlachter (eds), *Regulating Strikes in Essential Services: A Comparative 'Law in Action' Perspective*, 145 (Kluwer 2019).
66. There is usually no local competition in public transport. People who depend on public transport are massively restricted in their mobility by strikes. Since the big strike movements of the 1990s and 2000, a part of French society has been questioning a system of negotiation based on social conflict, often making users hostage to this conflict.
67. *See Report of the European Foundation for the Improvement of Living and Working Conditions* (2007).
68. On the mythology of the public service strike, *see, e.g.*, Sylvie Chauvet, *Guten Morgen, Frankreich! Der Streik im Öffentlichen Dienst in Frankreich 1995* in Marcks & Seiffert (eds), *Die großen Streiks, Episoden aus dem Klassenkampf*, 123 (Unrast-Verlag 2008). Siwek-Pouydesseau J., *Les grèves de fonctionnaires sous la IVe république*, Revue française d'Administration Publique, 108/4 2003, 533 https://doi.org/10.3917/rfap.108.0533.

CHAPTER 15

Restrictions on the Right to Strike in Germany

Bernd Waas

1 GENERAL INFORMATION

1.1 Legal Basis of the Right to Strike

In Germany, the right to take industrial action is guaranteed by the Constitution. As part of the freedom of association, which is enshrined in Article 9(3) of the Basic Law (*Grundgesetz, GG*), it is a significant component of this fundamental right. It is true that Article 9(3) explicitly mentions industrial action in the context of a situation of national emergency only. However, the right to take industrial action must also be regarded as constitutionally protected independently of this. The decisive factor here is the connection with the right to collective bargaining. To use the words of the Federal Constitutional Court: 'An essential purpose of the coalitions [trade unions and employers' associations] protected by Article 9(3) of the GG is the conclusion of collective agreements. (...). The choice of the means they consider suitable to achieve this purpose is in principle left to the coalitions by Article 9(3) (...). The protected means also include industrial action aimed at concluding collective agreements. They are in any case covered by the freedom of association to the extent that they are generally necessary to ensure a functioning autonomy of collective bargaining.'[1] The Federal Labour Court put it even more succinctly, stating that 'collective bargaining without the right to strike would generally be no more than "collective begging"'.[2] However, the relationship between the right to take industrial action and the right to bargain collectively forms at the same time a limitation of the former. 'A fundamental right to

1. Federal Constitutional Court of 26 June 1991 – 1 BvR 779/85 (C. I. 1a).
2. Federal Labour Court of 10 June 1980 – 1 AZR 822/79 (A. I. 2a).

strike', as the Federal Labour Court once put it, 'detached from its functional reference to collective bargaining autonomy, is not guaranteed by Article 9 (3) of the Basic Law'.[3] The concept of international labour law is broader. For example, the European Committee of Social Rights has repeatedly expressed the view that the German law on industrial action, with its trade union monopoly on strikes and its restriction of the right to strike to objectives that can be regulated by collective agreements, violates Part II, Article 6 No. 4 ESC.[4]

There is no comprehensive legal regulation of the right to industrial action in Germany. Rather, there are only a few provisions, for example, on the question of the use of temporary agency workers as strikebreakers. In legal literature, this area of law is often seen as a prime example of a legal lacuna that both legitimises and obliges the courts to close it through the so-called judicial development of the law.[5] In fact, industrial action law in Germany is almost exclusively judge-made. This applies in particular to the question of the lawfulness of industrial action, which is to be decided on the basis of principles developed by the courts.

1.2 Main Features of the Regulation

According to the concept applicable in Germany, the decisive factor for the legality of industrial action is that industrial action is (only) guaranteed as a means of concluding collective agreements. This means, first of all, that industrial action must be directed towards the enforcement of objectives that can be regulated by collective agreements. Thus, for example, industrial action can only be considered if it is conducted between parties that have collective bargaining capacity (*Tariffähigkeit*), i.e., can effectively conclude collective agreements. It is noteworthy that the requirements for collective bargaining capacity have also been developed by the courts. For example, the courts require a certain degree of assertiveness on the part of trade unions vis-à-vis the employer side in order for collective bargaining capacity to be affirmed and justify this with the need to ensure the 'functioning of the autonomy of collective bargaining'.[6] In the view of the Federal Labour Court, it is 'compatible with the fundamental right of freedom of association to allow only those coalitions to participate in the autonomy of collective bargaining that are able to meaningfully shape the room of working life left free by the state legal system by means of collective agreements, in order to bring social peace to society'.[7] Furthermore, the lawfulness of a strike requires that it does not violate the peace obligation of an applicable collective agreement. In this respect, it is

3. Federal Labour Court of 20 November 2012 – 1 AZR 179/11 (note 111); 20 November 2012 – 1 AZR 611/11 (note 49).
4. *See* only Buchholtz, *Streiken im europäischen Grundrechtsgefüge*, pp. 124 and 125 et seq. (2014); *see also* Peramato, *Streikrecht und Arbeitsvölkerrecht* (2020).
5. Cf. Krois, in: Frieling, Jacobs & Krois, *Arbeitskampfrecht* § 2 note 143 with further references (2021).
6. Federal Labour Court of 14 August 2018 – 1 AZR 287/17 (note 36): 'Under the legal system, neither side is granted such a strong weapon that the opposing party is left with no effective way of responding but the chances of achieving an appropriate negotiation outcome are destroyed.'
7. Federal Labour Court of 22 June 2021 – 1 ABR 28/20 (note 36).

noteworthy that according to the courts, each collective agreement establishes a mutual peace obligation for the parties to the collective agreement that is related to the content of the collective agreement, which does not have to be expressly agreed.[8] In addition, as already mentioned above, the lawfulness of industrial action is also determined by principles developed in case law. The principle of proportionality (*Verhältnismäßigkeitsgrundsatz*)[9] has become the most important of these principles for some time.[10] Moreover, the courts are always concerned with ensuring that the 'parity' between the parties is maintained.[11]

2 PERMITTED RESTRICTIONS

2.1 Certain Categories of Public Servants

The legal status of so-called civil servants (*Beamte*) is essentially regulated by constitutional law. According to Article 33(4) of the GG, 'the exercise of sovereign powers (...) shall as a rule be entrusted as a permanent task to members of the public service who are in a public-law service and loyalty relationship'. The rights and duties of civil servants do not result from contractual agreements[12] but are unilaterally regulated by the legislature. Article 33(5) also provides that 'the law of the civil service (...) is to be regulated and developed taking into account the traditional principles of the civil service'. From the beginning, the Courts assumed that civil servants were prohibited from striking under Article 33 of the Basic Law. This position was only seriously called into question by the decision of the European Court of Human Rights in the case of Enerji Yapi-Yol Sen.[13]

In its judgment of 12 June 2018, the Federal Constitutional Court for the first time gave detailed reasons for the ban on strikes by civil servants. In doing so, the Court also dealt with the case law of the ECtHR. The Court explicitly stated that the personal scope of protection of Article 9(3) of the GG – in addition to public sector employees – also includes civil servants. Furthermore, it reaffirmed that freedom of association also guarantees the freedom to engage in labour disputes. At the same time, however, the Court held that freedom of association is limited by the 'traditional principles of the civil service' laid down in Article 33(5) of the GG. These principles include, among others, the 'duty of loyalty' (*Treuepflicht*) of civil servants, as well as the 'principle of

8. *See* only Federal Labour Court of 12 September 1984 – 1 AZR 342/83 (A. I. 2a): 'For the duration of the collective agreement, each party to the collective agreement shall refrain from industrial action against the collective agreement and from calls by its members for such action.'
9. Cf. Münder, in: Frieling, Jacobs & Krois, *Arbeitskampfrecht* § 4 note 269 with further references (2021).
10. Federal Labour Court of 19 June 2007 – 1 AZR 396/06 (note 22): 'The central and appropriate standard for assessing the various forms of industrial action is the principle of proportionality in the broader sense'; cf. also Münder, in: Frieling, Jacobs & Krois, *Arbeitskampfrecht* § 4 note 269 with further references (2021).
11. *See*, for instance, Federal Labour Court of 19 June 2007 – 1 AZR 396/06 on the lawfulness of solidarity strikes and of 14 August 2018 – 1 AZR 287/17 on bonuses for strike-breakers.
12. Accordingly, the rules of labour law also do not apply to civil servants.
13. ECHR of 21 April 2019, Enerji Yapi-Yol Sen (Application No. 68959/01).

alimentation' (*Alimentationsprinzip*) and the 'corresponding principle that the remuneration of civil servants is to be regulated unilaterally by law'.[14] As far as the duty of loyalty is concerned, the Court held that 'the use of economic means of struggle and pressure to enforce one's own interests, in particular also collective measures of industrial action within the meaning of Article 9 (3) of the Basic Law, such as the right to strike' could not be reconciled with this.[15] The 'principle of alimentation', according to the Federal Constitutional Court, 'obliges the employer to adequately support the civil servant and his family for life and to grant him an adequate living according to his rank, according to the responsibility associated with his office and according to the importance of the civil service for the general public in line with the development of the general economic and financial circumstances and the general standard of living'. Accordingly, 'the salary of the civil servant (...) does not constitute remuneration for specific concrete services', but is 'a "consideration" of the employer for the fact that the civil servant places his entire personality at his disposal'.[16] The Court went on to state that with the direct objective guarantee of an adequate livelihood, Article 33(5) establishes an 'individual right, similar to a fundamental right, of the individual civil servant vis-à-vis the state'. Accordingly, the civil servant 'faces the state as his employer (*Dienstherr*), which in its position as legislator is at the same time solely responsible for the regulation of the legal relationship as well as the distribution of the mutual rights and duties'. The individual civil servant, according to the Court, 'has no means of influencing the detailed formulation of his legal relationship'.[17] In conclusion, the Court stated the following: 'According to the current constitutional conception of the civil service, the ban on strikes is inseparably linked to both the principle of alimentation and the duty of loyalty. A right to strike for civil servants cannot be reconciled with these two essential principles; rather, the prohibition of strikes guarantees and justifies the current structure of the aforementioned principles.'[18]

The Federal Constitutional Court considers this result to be compatible with international law, in particular with the European Convention on Human Rights (as interpreted by the ECtHR). While the Court explicitly recognised that the Basic Law is to be interpreted in a way that is 'friendly to international law',[19] it emphasised that the limits of such an interpretation derive from the Basic Law itself. According to the Court, 'the possibilities of a convention-friendly interpretation end where this no longer appears justifiable according to the recognised methods of statutory interpretation and constitutional interpretation'.[20] Moreover, according to the Court, even in the context of a convention-friendly interpretation of the Basic Law, the case law of the ECHR must

14. Federal Constitutional Court of 12 June 2018 – 2 BvR 1738/12 a. o. (note 120).
15. Federal Constitutional Court of 12 June 2018 – 2 BvR 1738/12 a. o. (note 121).
16. Federal Constitutional Court of 12 June 2018 – 2 BvR 1738/12 a. o. (note 123).
17. Federal Constitutional Court of 12 June 2018 – 2 BvR 1738/12 a. o. (note 124).
18. Federal Constitutional Court of 12 June 2018 – 2 BvR 1738/12 a. o. (note 152). Specifically on the 'principle of alimentation', the Court also stated the following (note 158): 'In this reciprocal system of interrelated rights and duties, extensions or restrictions on one side of the civil servant relationship usually also result in changes on the other side. The civil service relationship does not allow for "cherry-picking" (...)'.
19. Federal Constitutional Court of 12 June 2018 – 2 BvR 1738/12 a. o. (note 126).
20. Federal Constitutional Court of 12 June 2018 – 2 BvR 1738/12 a. o. (note 133).

be 'fitted as gently as possible into the existing, dogmatically differentiated national legal system'.[21] As a result, the Court does not attribute more than an 'orientation and guiding function' to the case law of the ECHR.[22] On 14 December 2023, the ECHR held that the ban on strikes by civil servants' teachers did not take away the core of their freedom of association and did not violate the right of association as guaranteed by Article 11 of the ECHR.[23]

2.2 Essential Services in the Strict Sense of the Term

According to case law, the principle of proportionality – already mentioned above – can also result in an obligation on the part of the workers' side to provide specific services in the case of a strike. In this regard, a distinction is made between emergency work (*Notstandsarbeiten*) and maintenance work (*Erhaltungsarbeiten*). Maintenance work is understood to be work that is necessary 'in order to prevent the material equipment from becoming unusable'.[24] The operating facilities (think of the operation of blast furnaces, for example, which can no longer be used when they cool down) are to be protected from damage. In contrast, emergency work is 'work intended to ensure the supply of essential services and goods to the population during an industrial dispute'.[25] In the legal literature, opinions differ widely as to what specific level of service must be maintained by an emergency service.[26] In any event, the extent of an emergency service is a question of the individual case. In principle, it is upon the parties to the industrial dispute to reach appropriate emergency agreements, although some courts consider it sufficient if an emergency service is established without an agreement[27] or if the company is able to maintain an emergency service with either workers affiliated with another union or civil servants.[28] Whether (the organisation of) emergency services is the joint responsibility of the parties to the labour dispute or the sole responsibility of the employer is a matter of dispute.[29] The Courts sometimes assume that the union must give reasonable notice of a strike in order to allow the employer to

21. Federal Constitutional Court of 12 June 2018 – 2 BvR 1738/12 a. o. (note 135).
22. Federal Constitutional Court of 12 June 2018 – 2 BvR 1738/12 a. o. (notes 129 and 132).
23. ECHR *Humpert and others v. Germany* (14 December 2023) (Applications Nos 59433/18, 59477/18, 59481/18 and 59494/18).
24. Federal Labour Court of 31 January 1995 – AZR 142/94 (II. 1.).
25. Federal Labour Court of 31 January 1995 – AZR 142/94 (II. 1.). The State Labour Court Hesse of 12 March 2024 – 10 GLa 229/24 (note 95) recently adopted a rather narrow interpretation of the term with regard to a rail strike: 'Emergency work can play a particularly serious role in the event of a strike in hospitals, at the blood donation service or in a nuclear power plant. Measured against these principles, it cannot be recognised in the present case that certain emergency work (...) is necessary.'
26. Cf. Münder, in: Frieling, Jacobs & Krois, *Arbeitskampfrecht* § 4 note 268 with further references (2021).
27. State Labour Court Berlin-Brandenburg of 20 October 2021 – 12 Ta 1310/21 (note 20).
28. State Labour Court Hesse of 7 November 2014 – 9 SaGa 1496/14 (note 264).
29. A joint responsibilty is assumed, for instance, by Grimm & Vitt, *Der Notdienst im Arbeitskampf*, in: Der Betrieb (DB), 388 (2023). *See also* State Labour Court Saxony of 10 June 2024 – 4 GLa 10/24 (note 59): 'The fact that both parties bear responsibility in the labour dispute – including for third parties – and are therefore best able to reconcile their mutual interests in an agreement speaks in favour of a joint obligation.'

establish emergency services.[30] Whether the employer can order emergency services unilaterally if necessary is also disputed.[31] In the event of disagreement between the parties to the industrial dispute on the scope of an emergency service, the Court may make an emergency service regulation. In this case, the obligation to establish a specific emergency service is the milder measure compared to a Court order to refrain from a strike.[32] Thus, if there is a risk that a strike is unreasonable and thus unlawful because of its effects on third parties, providing emergency services can establish reasonableness and thus bring about the lawfulness of the strike.[33] In practice, the sword of Damocles of a Court order may regularly influence the parties' willingness to compromise.[34] The question of which specific emergency service is to be established must be 'oriented on the one hand to its purpose, but on the other hand must be reduced to what is indispensable in order to give effect to the freedom of industrial action guaranteed by Article 9 (3) of the Basic Law'.[35] In arriving at their decision, the Courts tend to take a pragmatic approach, while it should also be noted that these are regular decisions on interim relief. The question of the appropriateness of an emergency service is seen as a clash of different fundamental rights positions, which must be balanced as optimally as possible.[36] The main question to be asked is which fundamental right of a third party is affected by a strike and with what intensity.[37] Extraordinarily difficult questions can arise in this context, such as when a strike aims at a hospital and the employer demands emergency services, which may exceed

30. *See* State Labour Court Berlin-Brandenburg of 14 August 2012 – 22 SaGa 1131/12 (2.2.2.3.2.5). The strike concerned the supervision of a nuclear facility.
31. In the affirmative recently, State Labour Court Mecklenburg-Vorpommern of 9 July 2024 – 4 GLa 3/24.

    Cf. Münder, in: Frieling, Jacobs & Krois, *Arbeitskampfrecht* § 4 notes 201 and 269 with further references (2021).
32. *See* only State Labour Court Berlin-Brandenburg of 20 October 2021 – 12 Ta 1310/21 (note 27): 'It follows from the principle of proportionality, which requires the least possible interference with fundamental rights, that the court, instead of issuing an injunction, must impose the obligation to establish a specific emergency service. Such a procedure goes easy on the fundamental right of freedom of association. The strike can be carried out with the improved emergency service without the threat of disproportionate interference with the rights of third parties.'
33. Cf. Münder, in: Frieling, Jacobs & Krois, *Arbeitskampfrecht* § 4 note 270 (2021).
34. *See* State Labour Court Cologne of 16 March 2023 – 8 SaGa 3/23: Amicable and full agreement of the parties on the scope of the emergency service and in particular the staffing for the site fire brigade in the case of an airport strike.
35. State Labour Court Hamm of 13 July 2015 – 12 SaGa 21/15 (note 29). *See also* State Labour Court Baden-Württemberg of 18 July – 4 SaGa 3/23 (note 33) adding the following: 'The emergency service must not be misused to maintain operations as far as possible, but rather a 'minimum supply' orientated towards the respective public service mandate.' *See also*, more recently, State Labour Court Baden-Württemberg of 18 July 2023 (note 35).
36. *See*, for instance, State Labour Court Hanover of 26 March 2023 – 1 Ta 1/23 (note 61): 'Essential services include the maintenance of emergency care for the population in hospitals. In this respect, it is a matter of maintaining a practical concordance between the affected fundamental rights, namely the fundamental rights of persons dependent on such care, in particular the fundamental right to the protection of life and physical integrity under Article 2 (2) of the Basic Law and the fundamental right to freedom of association under Art. 9 (3) of the Basic Law (...)'.
37. Cf. Münder, in: Frieling, Jacobs & Krois, *Arbeitskampfrecht* § 4 note 272 (2021).

normal staffing levels.[38] Some authors have pointed out that German law is in a certain state of tension with international labour law as Article 11(2) ECHR requires that restrictions on the freedom to engage in labour must be 'prescribed by law'.[39] However, the required scope of emergency works can hardly ever be clearly foreseen in advance.

In practice, the problem of emergency services is particularly relevant in the case of strikes in the area of so-called basic public services (*Daseinsvorsorge*).[40] The term goes back to the famous constitutional and administrative lawyer *Ernst Forsthoff* and today generally refers to 'the supply of essential goods and services to be ensured by the community'.[41] A specific term is often used for the area of labour law. According to this concept, services of general interest – following the essential facilities doctrine in competition law – should primarily include those services that are necessary and irreplaceable for the general public.[42] Often, these are privatised sectors where the relevant tasks were previously provided by civil servants who, according to the case law of the Federal Constitutional Court, do not enjoy the right to strike.[43] It is recognised in case law, however, that the privatisation of sovereign tasks does not lead to the loss of the freedom of association of the workers now entrusted with the performance of these tasks and their associations.[44] Since employees are not entitled to the special rights of civil servants, they remain, according to the Federal Labour Court, 'dependent on negotiating their working conditions at the level of collective agreements' and in doing so are 'because of their subordination (...) also dependent on the means of pressure of industrial action'.[45] With regard to ordering emergency services, the first point to be determined is whether such services are necessary to protect the life and limb of third parties and whether they are affected directly or indirectly. Depending on the objective of the emergency service and the extent of the risk of damage without a corresponding emergency service, the right to strike then prevails to a greater or

38. So indeed State Labour Court Berlin-Brandenburg of 12 April 2012 – 5 SaGa 450/12: 'The emergency staffing in a hospital has to be oriented exclusively to compelling medical and other requirements for the sufficient care of patients and therefore does not necessarily have to fall short of the planned normal staffing, which will also not always be available for other reasons, e.g., illness and holidays of the staff. Even if this would render the strike ineffective in individual areas, as the defendant fears, this does not change the fact that the absolutely necessary medical and other care of the patients must be guaranteed in order to avert dangers to life and limb and to safeguard their human dignity.' Very critical on this Tschenker, *Effektiver Streik und Notdienstarbeiten*, in: Neue Zeitschrift für Arbeitsrecht – Rechtsprechungsreport (NZA-RR), p. 337 (340) (2022).
39. *See* Münder, in: Frieling, Jacobs & Krois, *Arbeitskampfrecht* § 4 note 273 (2021). *See also* Thüsing & Musiol, *Gemeinwohlbindung des Streiks*, in: Der Betrieb (DB), p. 52 (2024) indeed demanding a 'statutory framework' for agreements between the parties.
40. Cf. the comprehensive discussion by Rudkowski, *Der Streik in der Daseinsvorsorge* (2010).
41. Schmidt, *Die Liberalisierung der Daseinsvorsorge*, in: Der Staat, p. 225 (2002).
42. Cf. Münder, in: Frieling, Jacobs & Krois, *Arbeitskampfrecht* § 4 note 215 with further references (2021).
43. Münder, in: Frieling, Jacobs & Krois, *Arbeitskampfrecht* § 4 note 209 (2021).
44. Federal Labour Court of 25 August 2015 – 1 AZR 754/13 (note 55) concerning a strike of air traffic controllers.
45. Federal Labour Court of 2 March 1993 – 1 BvR 1213/8 (C. II. 1.).

lesser extent.[46] In legal literature, however, there are repeated calls for establishing restrictions on the right to take industrial action in essential services. These voices have recently become even louder in the face of increasing strike activity (particularly by smallish 'specialist unions'), especially in the transport sector (rail and aviation).[47]

2.3 Situations of Acute National or Local Crisis

With an amendment in the year 1968, another sentence was added to Article 9(3) sentences 1 and 2 of the GG. The amendment concerns the protection of the right to take industrial action against individual measures (conscription for military or alternative service and service obligations on the one hand, and deployments of the Federal Armed Forces, the Federal Border Guard and the police on the other), which are provided for in certain cases of emergency (especially the case of defence, the so-called case of tension preceding it, the case of disaster and the case of danger to the free democratic basic order). However, the provision is of a declaratory nature, as the use of the above-mentioned measures would in any case be unlawful.[48]

3 COMPENSATORY GUARANTEES FOR WORKERS DEPRIVED OF THE RIGHT TO STRIKE

Freedom of association of civil servants is explicitly recognised in ordinary law. According to section 52 sentence 1 of the Civil Servants Status Act (*Beamtenstatusgesetz*), civil servants have 'the right to join trade unions or professional associations'. Moreover, according to section 52 sentence 2, 'they may not be reprimanded or discriminated against in the service for activities on behalf of their trade union or professional association'. However, freedom of association of civil servants does not give them the right to negotiate collective agreements with their employer through their

46. *See* Preedy & Günther, *Notdienste bei Arbeitskämpfen: Eine Systematisierung von Voraussetzungen und Umfang*, in: Neue Zeitschrift für Arbeitsrecht (NZA), p. 167 (174) (2024) with an evaluation of the relevant case law.
47. *See*, for instance, Bayreuther, *'Generalstreik' im öffentlichen Verkehrssektor*, in: Neue Zeitschrift für Arbeitsrecht (NZA), p. 411 (2023). Some time ago, academics presented a draft law to regulate strikes in essential services; *see* Franzen, Thüsing & Waldhoff, *Arbeitskampf in der Daseinsvorsorge. Vorschläge zur gesetzlichen Regelung von Streik und Aussperrung in Unternehmen der Daseinsvorsorge* (2012); cf. on this, for example, Bayreuther, *Gesetzliche Regelungen kollektiver Arbeitskonflikte in der Daseinsvorsorge*, in: Neue Zeitschrift für Arbeitsrecht (NZA), p. 704 (2013); Stegmüller, *Einschränkungen des Streikrechts in Betrieben der Daseinsvorsorge*, in: Neue Zeitschrift für Arbeitsrecht (NZA), p. 723 (2015); Rudkowski, *Eine 'scharfe Waffe' wohl gebrauchen: Der Professorenentwurf zur Regelung des Arbeitskampfs in der Daseinsvorsorge*, in: Zeitschrift für Arbeitsrecht (ZfA), p. 467 (2012). The legislator did not take it up. On current proposals for the codification of (parts of) labour dispute law Ubber & von Grundherr, *Regelungsvorschläge zur gesetzlichen Gestaltung des Arbeitskampfrechts*, in: Neue Zeitschrift für Arbeitsrecht (NZA), p. 1 (2025); on relevant aspects of EU-law Rudkowski, *Der Arbeitskampf in regulierten Infrastrukturen unter dem Einfluss des Unionsrechts?*, in: Zeitschrift für Arbeitsrecht (ZfA), p. 139 (2025).
48. In particular, industrial action will never be able to meet the (very restrictive) requirements of one of the emergency situations mentioned in the provision. *See* Scholz, in: Dürig, Herzog & Scholz (eds); *Grundgesetz-Kommentar*, Art. 9 Grundgesetz note 388 (2024).

trade unions or professional associations, as is the case with other employees, since public service law is exclusively in the hands of the legislature.[49] On the other hand, the law provides for certain powers of participation of the civil servants' representatives in the legislative process. According to section 118 of the Federal Civil Servants Act (*Bundesbeamtengesetz*), the umbrella organisations of the competent trade unions are to be involved 'in the preparation of general regulations on civil servants' legal relationships'. Section 53 sentence 1 of the Civil Servants Status Act (*Beamtenstatusgesetz*) provides for a corresponding right of participation also 'in the preparation of statutory regulations of civil servants' legal relationships by the supreme Land authorities'. According to section 53 sentence 2, the participation may also be arranged by agreement.[50] The Federal Constitutional Court also referred to the statutory law in its decision on the (non-) existence of a civil servant's right to strike.[51] In doing so, the Court stressed that these statutory provisions (as well as the similar civil service laws of the *Länder*), though not granting umbrella organisations of the trade unions a right of co-decision, do grant them rights of participation in the preparation of statutory regulations on civil service conditions. The Court also pointed out that according to the legislator's intention, 'participation is to be seen as compensation for the collective bargaining autonomy under Article 9 (3) of the Basic Law that does not exist for civil servants and the ban on strikes'.[52] In all this, the Court expressly recognised that the procedural right of the associations does not change the fact that the employer has the 'last word'.[53] At the same time, however, in view of the principle of democracy enshrined in Article 20(1) and (2) of the Basic Law, it saw no possibility of strengthening the legal position of the trade unions. As 'representatives of particular interests', the unions, according to the Court, 'should not be granted genuine co-decision rights in the legislative process, since otherwise the sovereignty of the (...) legislator would be violated'. The possibilities of strengthening participation rights to compensate for a comprehensive ban on strikes were therefore 'severely limited' by the Constitution.[54]

4 CONCLUSION

Civil servants' strikes are prohibited in Germany. Case law has addressed numerous questions that arise in connection with 'essential services'. The specific decisions are based on a consideration of the fundamental rights of those affected and always depend on the circumstances of the individual case.

49. *See* Reich, *Beamtenstatusgesetz* § 52 note 2 (4th ed. 2025).
50. In practice, in addition to the umbrella organisations, individual trade unions that do not belong to an umbrella organisation are also involved. Furthermore, it should be noted that the legislative process is becoming increasingly transparent due to the publication of draft bills and the possibility of submitting comments. *See* Leppek & Grandjot, in: Brinktrine & Schollendorf (eds), *BeckOK Beamtenrecht Bund* § 118 BBG note 9 (37tht ed. 2025).
51. Federal Constitutional Court of 12 June 2018 – 2 BvR 1738/12 a. o. (note 158).
52. Bundestag/Printing Matter 16/4027 of 12 January 2007, p. 35.
53. Federal Constitutional Court of 12 June 2018 – 2 BvR 1738/12 a. o. (note 162).
54. Federal Constitutional Court of 12 June 2018 – 2 BvR 1738/12 a. o. (note 162).

CHAPTER 16

Restrictions on the Right to Strike in Greece*

Costas Papadimitriou & Ioannis Skandalis

1 GENERAL INFORMATION

1.1 Legal Basis of the Right to Strike

The right to strike is safeguarded by the Greek Constitution not only as an expression of the freedom of association but also as an autonomous individual right. In particular, Article 23(1) of the Greek Constitution stipulates that: '*The State shall adopt due measures safeguarding the freedom to unionise and the unhindered exercise of related rights against any infringement thereon within the limits of the law*', whilst Article 23(2) of the Greek Constitution provides that '*Strike constitutes a right to be exercised by lawfully established trade unions in order to protect and promote the financial and the general labour interests of working people.*'[1]

1.2 Main Features of the Regulation

The more specific aspects of the right to strike (e.g., typical requirements for its lawful exercise) are regulated in implementation of Article 23(1) of the Constitution by

* Sections 1, 2, 2.1 and 3 have been prepared by Costas Papadimitriou and ss 2.2, 2.3 and 4 have been prepared by Ioannis Skandalis. It is clarified that the whole chapter expresses the views of both authors.

1. For the meaning and the nature of strikes under Greek law, *see* Dimitrios Zerdelis, *Collective Labour Law*, 317 et seq. (Sakkoulas2021) (in Greek); Georgios Leventis, *Collective Labour Law*, 659 et seq. (Sakkoulas2023) (in Greek); Ioannis Koukiadis, *Labour Law: Collective Labour Relations*, 797 et seq. (Sakkoulas 2021) (in Greek); Costas Papadimitriou, *Collective Labour Law*, 213 et seq. (Nomiki Vivliothiki 3rd ed. 2022) (in Greek); Effrosyni Bakirtzi, *The Right to Strike: Greece*, in Bernd Waas (ed.), *The Right to Strike*, 259 seq. (Wolters Kluwer 2014).

Articles 19 to 22, 30 and 30a of Law 1264/1984, as well as by Article 2 of Law 2224/1994 designating the essential services staff that shall be provided during strikes in entities, enterprises or utilities referred to in Article 19(2) of Law 1264/1982 offering services and goods being vital for the public.[2] The above provisions constitute a detailed regulatory framework for the exercise of the right to take collective action.

Greek law provides for two reasons for strikes (industrial action). In particular, according to Article 19 paragraph 1 of Law 1264/1982, a strike is recognized: (a) for the protection or promotion of employees' interests; (b) as a declaration of solidarity for other employees who are also on strike, under the condition that their strike has direct consequences for the former employees.

Thus, under Greek law, strike is the collective temporary abstention of employees from work, decided by a trade union, with the aim of exercising pressure on the employers' side, mainly or on the state, in order that employees may safeguard or promote their common collective interests of any kind, e.g., financial, labour, trade union and insurance interests.[3]

The legislation (Law 1264/1982) regulates in detail the conditions for the lawful exercise of the right to strike. In brief, according to the applicable legal regime, a strike is legal when the following conditions are met:[4]

(a) the strike decision is adopted by a legally established trade union and the competent body of said union;
(b) the demands of the strike should be lawful;
(c) the strike decision should be duly and timely notified to the employer;
(d) security staff should made available;
(e) in the event of strikes in the public sector or in the field of essential services, public dialogue should precede the strike and the provision of staff covering the basic needs of the society should also be made available.

As far as the competent body for the declaration of the strike is concerned, according to Article 20 of Law 1264/1982, the General Assembly is the competent body for first-level employees' trade unions,[5] whilst, for second (federations) or third-level trade unions (confederations), the strike might be decided by the management board of the trade union.[6] Especially for work stoppages of brief duration, even if such work stoppages are declared by first-level trade unions, the competent body for the adoption

2. Evdokia Maria Liakopoulou, *The Right to Strike in the Public Services Greece*, 4 (2021) (updated by Diana Balanescu and reviewed by EPSU/ETUI) available at https://www.epsu.org/sites/default/files/article/files/Greece%20-Right%20to%20strike%20in%20public%20sector.pdf (accessed June 2025).
3. Viktoria Sp. Douka, Vasilis Koniaris & Konstantinos I. Dimarellis, *Labour Law in Greece*, 346 (Kluwer Law International B.V. 2022).
4. Viktoria Sp. Douka, Vasilis Koniaris & Konstantinos I. Dimarellis, *Labour Law in Greece*, 356 (Kluwer Law International B.V., 2022). Effrosyni Bakirtzi, *The Right to Strike: Greece*, in Bernd Waas (ed.), *The Right to Strike*, 268 seq. (Wolters Kluwer 2014).
5. Dimitrios Zerdelis, *Collective Labour Law*, 350 (Sakkoulas 2021) (in Greek).
6. Athanasios Tsimikalis, *The Right to Strike: Terms and Conditions for Exercising the Right*, 2019, Greek Law Digest, available at: http://www.greeklawdigest.gr (accessed June 2025).

of the relevant decision is the management board, as an exception to the rule that in the first-level trade unions, the strike decision should be adopted by the General Assembly. The rationale of the above provisions applying to employees of the private sector is to facilitate the adoption of the strike decision and this is the reason why for second (federations) and third-level trade unions (confederations), the competent body is the management board and not the General Assembly, which is more difficult to convene.

Notwithstanding the above, specific rules apply regarding the competent body for the adoption of the strike decision in the event of civil servants. More specifically, according to Article 30 paragraph 8 of Law 1264/1982, for any strike declared by civil servants, the relevant decision should be adopted exclusively by second (federations) or third-level trade unions (confederations) and the competent body for the adoption of the strike decision is exclusively the General Assembly of the above trade unions. The requirement for the adoption of the strike decision exclusively by the General Assembly of the second (federations) or the third-level trade unions (confederations) in the case of civil servants safeguards, on the one hand, the lawfulness and the mature character of the relevant decision; however, on the other hand, objections have been raised in Greek legal theory as to the compatibility of this requirement with the constitutional provisions, given that it renders the adoption of the strike decision extremely difficult.[7]

2 PERMITTED RESTRICTIONS

The second paragraph of Article 23 of the Greek Constitution provides that: ‘Strikes of any nature whatsoever are prohibited in the case of judicial functionaries and those serving in the security corps. The right to strike shall be subject to the specific limitations of the law regulating this right in the case of public servants and employees of local government agencies and of public law legal persons, as well as in the case of the employees of all types of enterprises of a public nature or of public benefit, the operation of which is of vital importance in serving the basic needs of the society as a whole. These limitations may not be carried to the point of abolishing the right to strike or hindering the lawful exercise thereof.’

2.1 Certain Categories of Public Servants

On the basis of the above, it emerges that, under Greek law, according to Article 23 paragraph 2 of the Greek Constitution, strikes of any nature and form are prohibited to judicial functionaries and those serving in the security corps. It should also be noted that quite paradoxically, the drafting of the above provision does not cover those serving in the armed forces; however, it is accepted that, according to the teleological interpretation of the above provision, the right to strike of those serving in the armed forces should also be prohibited.[8]

7. Georgios Leventis, *Collective Labour Law*, 692 (Sakkoulas 2023) (in Greek).
8. Costas Papadimitriou, *Collective Labour Law*, 217-218 (Nomiki Vivliothiki 3rd ed. 2022) (in Greek).

Additionally, according to the above provision, the right to strike is subject to specific limitations provided by law in the case of public servants, employees of local government agencies and public legal persons, as well as in the case of employees of all types of enterprises of a public nature or of public benefit, the operation of which is of vital importance for the society.[9] However, these limitations may not be of such intensity and extent as to abolish the right to strike or hinder the legal exercise of this right.

2.2 Essential Services in the Strict Sense of the Term

In Greece, the law provides that in the public sector, in local government organizations and, in a wider context, in undertakings providing essential services for the public, irrespective of their legal form (as such undertakings are defined by Law 1264/1982), the exercise of the right to strike is subject to additional conditions/limitations, compared to the ones applying to the strikes in the private sector.

Article 19 paragraph 2 of Law 1264/1982 specifies exclusively the undertakings and organizations offering essential services as those engaging in: (a) the provision of health, services by any kind of institution; (b) the purification and distribution of water; (c) the generation and distribution of electricity and gas; (d) the production or refining of crude oil; (e) the transport of persons and goods by land, sea or air; (f) telecommunications and postal services; (g) the drainage and disposal of sewage water and solid refuse; (h) the loading and unloading and storage of merchandise in ports; as well as (i) the Bank of Greece, Civil Aviation and any type of services or service departments that are engaged in the settlement and payment of the salaries of their staff according to Article 14 of Law 4270/2014 (A' 143) of the public sector.

In the event of a strike in 'essential services', the law provides that, prior to any strike action, the trade union calling the strike is obliged to notify and invite the employer to discuss the strike's demands (public dialogue). The invitation must be made in writing and be notified to the employer, the Ministry of Labour and the supervising Ministry. The above notification shall be served to the above recipients at least four days prior to the initiation of the strike, and no new demands may be introduced once this notification has been made;[10] otherwise, the strike is considered illegal. This constitutes a basic difference compared to strikes outside the field of 'essential services', which are subject only to a 24-hour notification to the employer, whilst the performance of public dialogue is not necessary but remains voluntary.

Thus, on the basis of the above, in the event of strikes in the field of essential services, following the announcement of the strike demands or the strike decision, the

9. Evdokia Maria Liakopoulou, *The Right to Strike in the Public Services Greece*, 4 (2021) (updated by Diana Balanescu and reviewed by EPSU/ETUI) available at https://www.epsu.org/sites/default/files/article/files/Greece%20-Right%20to%20strike%20in%20public%20sector.pdf (accessed June 2025).
10. Viktoria Sp. Douka, Vasilis Koniaris & Konstantinos I. Dimarellis, *Labour Law in Greece*, 354 (Kluwer Law International B.V. 2022); Effrosyni Bakirtzi, *The Right to Strike: Greece*, in Bernd Waas (ed.), *The Right to Strike* 274 seq. (Wolters Kluwer 2014).

public dialogue should take place between the employer and the employees' representatives, which is a condition for the legality of the strike. Public dialogue is the last resort for the avoidance of the strike through discussion among the concerned social partners, which takes place before a mediator of the Mediation and Arbitration Organization (OMED).[11] OMED is an independent body founded by the Greek State, but managed jointly by employers and employees and provides services of conciliation, mediation and arbitration. In the majority of cases, the invitation for public dialogue is served by the employees to the employer in order to avoid the risk of the strike being declared illegal,[12] whilst it is a rather rare scenario for the procedure of public dialogue to result in the avoidance of the strike.[13]

Moreover, in every strike declared either in the private or in the public sector, employees' trade union must ensure that a number of employees remain available in sufficient numbers to guarantee the safety of the employer's premises and equipment, as well as to prevent disasters or accidents during the strike ('security staff'). Especially for strikes that are declared in the public sector or in the field of 'essential services', sufficient staff must also be made available to ensure a minimum level of service, i.e., the staff covering the basic needs of society.

With regard to the ways through which the essential services staff is determined, according to Greek law, this determination is effected through collective agreements. Otherwise, these issues are regulated by a specific agreement concluded between the most representative employees' trade union at the enterprise and the employer, which should be reached each year by 25 November and applies for any strikes that may be called in the enterprise during the following year and it might also be valid for subsequent years, unless terminated.[14] Said agreement must be submitted to the Ministry of Labour within five days from its conclusion. The agreement shall refer at least to the contracting parties, the enterprise to which it applies, the services and departments of the enterprise which will operate during the strike, the number of employees per specialty required, procedural issues of appointment of the security staff and the essential services staff, as well as its duration, which should be at least one year.[15]

In the event that the negotiations for the determination of the essential services staff might fail, a mediation procedure before OMED follows. If mediation does not offer any results, the number of the staff is defined by an award of an Arbitration Committee on the basis of 'the nature and social significance of the goods and services provided by the company and the need to ensure the exercise of the right to strike'. In particular, Article 16 of Law 1876/1990 provides that arbitration shall be conducted by a three-member arbitration committee. The three arbitrators are appointed through an

11. For the procedure of public dialogue, *see* analytically in Costas Papadimitriou, *Collective Labour Law*, 244-247 (Nomiki Vivliothiki 3rd ed. 2022) (in Greek).
12. Dimitrios Zerdelis, *Collective Labour Law*, 363 (Sakkoulas 2021) (in Greek).
13. Costas Papadimitriou, *Collective Labour Law*, 247 (Nomiki Vivliothiki 3rd ed. 2022) (in Greek).
14. Ioannis Koukiadis, *Labour Law: Collective Labour Relations*, 816-817 (Sakkoulas 2021) (in Greek).
15. Viktoria Sp. Douka, Vasilis Koniaris & Konstantinos I. Dimarellis, *Labour Law in Greece*, 353 (Kluwer Law International B.V. 2022).

agreement between the parties among the persons in an official list of arbitrators of the Mediation and Arbitration Organization, whilst if no relevant agreement is reached, the persons of arbitrators are determined through ballot.

Following a recent amendment of Article 21 of Law 1264/1982 through Article 95 of Law 4808/2021, it is now provided that the essential services staff should safeguard that the minimum service provided during the strike shall correspond at least to the one-third of the regularly provided services, regardless of the specificities of each case. Thus, the parties are not, in principle, allowed to agree that the provided personnel during the strike will offer services to a lesser extent than one-third of the regular service. However, the law provides that each party or both parties might jointly request the appointment of personnel offering services to a lesser extent than one-third of the regular service, which however remains subject to the discretion of the government, since it requires the issuance of a relevant joint decision by the Minister of Labour and the competent Minister (e.g., the Minister of Health, if the strike is declared to a hospital).

In light of the above, the social partners enjoy limited discretion as to the determination of the minimum staff for the coverage of the basic needs of society during a strike declared in the field of 'essential services'.[16] In this regard, the parties do not have the possibility to evaluate the various factors so as to determine the appropriate level of essential staff, given that in any case, the essential services should, in principle, correspond to at least one-third of the regularly provided services. Just to offer an illustrative example, in the case of strike that is declared by an airline company, under the previous regime, the parties could take into consideration other forms of transportation (e.g., through trains or vessels or other providers of air transport) that would be available for the public so as to determine the essential staff that should remain available in the context of this strike. On the contrary, under the currently applicable regime, the discretion of the parties to consider the overall circumstances is severely restricted, since, in any case, the essential services should, in principle, correspond to at least one-third of the regular service and this poses issues of compatibility with the constitutional status of the right to strike under Greek law.[17]

As already mentioned, either the employer's side or the employees' side or the parties jointly may apply before the Minister of Labour and the competent Minister in order for the essential staff to be exceptionally determined to a percentage less than one-third. However, the competence of the Ministries in this regard poses issues of compatibility with Conventions Nos 87 and 98 of the International Labour Organization (ILO),[18] which, according to Article 28 of the Greek Constitution, constitute supranational sources of law. In particular, according to the Committee on Freedom of Association of ILO, the above Conventions impose the obligation on the States to provide for the resolution of any disputes regarding the determination of the essential

16. Costas Papadimitriou, *Collective Labour Law*, 251 (Nomiki Vivliothiki 3rd ed. 2022) (in Greek).
17. Costas Papadimitriou, *The Provisions of Law 4808/2021 Concerning Collective Agreements and the Settlement of Labour Disputes*, 7 (DEE 2023) (in Greek).
18. Essential services for the purposes of restricting or prohibiting the right to strike, according to the ILO Conventions, are only those the interruption of which would endanger the life, personal safety or health of the whole or part of the population.

services staff by independent bodies, including the judiciary, and not by administrative authorities, such as the Ministry of labour.[19]

2.3 Situations of Acute National or Local Crisis

Article 48 of the Greek Constitution lays down that the Parliament or the President of the Republic, at the suggestion of the Government, may suspend, throughout the State or in part of it, the application of Article 23 (right to strike), in case of war or mobilization owing to external dangers, in the case of serious disturbances or in the case of evident threat to public order and the security of the state.[20]

Moreover, Article 22 paragraph 4 of the Greek Constitution lays down that 'special laws shall determine the requisition (conscription) of personal services in case of war or mobilisation or in order to face urgent social emergencies'. Additionally, according to Law 4325/2015, the so-called political conscription of strikers (the obligation to end the strike and provide compulsory work or services) is prohibited in general and it is permitted only and strictly in the case of war for the purposes of national defence, as well as in the case of physical disasters or when public health is threatened.[21] The Greek case law has adopted a very broad interpretation of the above law, which has been criticized by Greek legal theory as being in violation of the Greek constitutional provisions safeguarding the right to strike. For example, quite paradoxically the Greek Council of State has ruled that the psychological pressure felt by the students and their parents, during the panhellenic competition for the admission to the University constituted a public health threatening reason, which justified the conscription of the school professors, who were on strike.[22]

3 COMPENSATORY GUARANTEES FOR WORKERS DEPRIVED OF THE RIGHT TO STRIKE

Under Greek law, there are no compensatory guarantees for workers deprived of the right to strike. However, it should be clarified that for the persons for which the right to strike is prohibited, i.e., members of the judiciary and persons serving in the security corps, it is still possible to establish trade unions in order to safeguard and promote their interests.

19. Costas Papadimitriou, *Collective Labour Law,* 251 (Nomiki Vivliothiki 3rd ed. 2022) (in Greek).
20. Viktoria Sp. Douka, Vasilis Koniaris & Konstantinos I. Dimarellis, *Labour Law in Greece,* 347 (Kluwer Law International B.V. 2022).
21. Evdokia Maria Liakopoulou, *The Right to Strike in the Public Services Greece,* 10 (2021) (updated by Diana Balanescu and reviewed by EPSU/ETUI) available at https://www.epsu.org/sites/default/files/article/files/Greece%20-Right%20to%20strike%20in%20public%20sector.pdf (accessed June 2025).
22. *See* analytically in Costas Papadimitriou, *Collective Labour Law,* 232-233 (Nomiki Vivliothiki 3rd ed. 2022) (in Greek).

4 CONCLUSION

In light of the above, it emanates that the right to strike in the public sector and within the sector of essential services more generally is subject to a number of conditions under Greek law. According to a relevant comparative study conducted by Papadimitriou, it is proven that Greek law on strikes was in 2014 within the European average level regarding its regulation.[23]

Especially with regard to the recent legal amendment, according to which, in the event of strikes in essential services, the basic level of services that should be offered during the strike shall correspond to at least one-third of the normally provided services; said requirement has been approached with some cautiousness by Greek legal theory regarding its compatibility with the Greek Constitution and the ILO Conventions Nos 87 and 98. The above should also be considered alongside the implications arising from the non-provision of sufficient staff for the coverage of basic needs of society, which is the illegality of the concerned strike action. Thus, in the event of absence of agreement between the social partners on this issue, it is the employees' trade union that faces the risk of its strike being declared illegal.

23. Costas Papadimitriou, *The Conditions for Declaring a Strike and Counter-Strike in the European Union in the Private and Public Sector*, 465 et seq. (Labour Law Bulletin 2015).

CHAPTER 17

Restrictions on the Right to Strike in Hungary

Tamás Gyulavári

1 GENERAL INFORMATION

Hungary is not the land of strikes.[1] If there is any strike at all, it will most probably happen in public services,[2] where employees are well organised in sectors like transport, education or healthcare, and they have the real possibility to put pressure on the employer.[3] Therefore, restrictions on the right to strike are crucial, in particular that of essential services. There has been an apparent hostility in the Government against strikes in the last decade, which is elucidated by several legislative waves to weaken the right to strike. The most important and effective attempt concerned the statutory rules on essential services.

In this context, the chapter starts with the outline of Hungarian strike law and restrictions on the personal scope. This is followed by the analysis of recent legislative attempts to weaken the right to strike through new procedural rules regarding essential services. Finally, the recent teacher strike will be used as an example to show what the new rules brought about in strikers' lives.

1. The author is grateful to Erzsébet Berki, Gábor Kártyás and Attila Kun for their comments on the drafts. The usual disclaimers apply.
2. Berki, Erzsébet: Illúziók és kiábrándulások. Sztrájkok és más direkt akciók 2008-ban. In: *Érdekképviselet felsőfokon. Szakszervezeti tisztségviselők gyakorlati kézikönyve.* Raabe Kiadó, Budapest (2009).
3. Ajtay-Horváth, Viola: Quo vadis sztrájkjog? Gondolatok a még elégséges szolgáltatásról. *De Iurisprudentia Et Iure Publico* (2013/2), p. 1.

1.1 Legal Basis of the Right to Strike

In socialist labour law before 1989, the right to strike did not exist, since, as a matter of principle, communist workers could not strike against the state they 'owned and controlled'. So it was a remarkable achievement of the political negotiations at the system change that the right to strike was announced by the amended 1989 Constitution: '*the right to strike may be practiced in the framework of the regulating Acts*'.[4] Act 7 of 1989 on the right to strike (Strike Act),[5] passed with qualified majority, contains this legal framework referred to by the constitutional provision.

The constitutional basis of strikes was changed by the new Fundamental law from 2011: '*employees, employers and their organisations shall have the right … to take collective action to defend their interests, including the right of workers to discontinue work*'.[6] The substance was not changed; thus, the regulation of the right to strike still has two levels: a constitutional provision and the detailed regulation in statutory law. The Strike Act is a short law consisting of seven articles; however, it fully covers all regulatory issues from the meaning of strike to the conditions of and limitations on practicing this right and also the rights of workers on strike. And this legal framework is supplemented by profuse case law of the Supreme Court and lower courts interpreting constitutional and statutory concepts.[7]

2 PERMITTED RESTRICTIONS

2.1 Certain Categories of Public Servants

2.1.1 Personal Scope of Freedom of Association

Trade union means 'all organizations of workers whose primary function is theenhancement and protection of employees' interests related to their employmentrelationship',[8] which definition complies with ILO Convention No. 87. Trade unions are associations (civil organisations) with this special objective.[9] Any material person may be a member of an association, so any worker may be a trade union member, irrespective of her employment status (except civil secret service).[10] However, the preconditions of membership are defined by the founding document. Trade union membership of workers in the public sector is not limited in any way, but trade union

4. Article 70/C(2), in Hungarian: https://www.alkotmanybirosag.hu/alkotmany-1989 (accessed 6 May 2025).
5. In Hungarian: https://net.jogtar.hu/jogszabaly?docid=98900007.tv (accessed 6 May 2025).
6. Article XVII.(2), in English: https://www.parlament.hu/documents/125505/138409/Fundamental+law/73811993-c377-428d-9808-ee03d6fb8178 (accessed 6 May 2025).
7. Case law in Hungarian: https://birosag.hu/birosagi-hatarozatok-gyujtemenye (accessed 6 May 2025).
8. Article 270(2)(a) of Act 1 of 2012 on The Labour Code (Labour Code). In English: https://mta-pte.ajk.pte.hu/downloads/12-01.tv-en.pdf (accessed 6 May 2025).
9. Under the scope of Act 5 of 2013 on the Civil Code and Act 175 of 2011 on the right to association.
10. Article 3333(1) of Act 42 of 2015: members of civil secret service cannot make a trade union and/or cannot be a member of a trade union.

rights are restricted for some workers in the public sector (e.g., members of the armed forces) in several aspects, which may question compliance with ILO Convention No. 87.[11]

2.1.2 *Personal Scope of the Right to Strike: Prohibitions*

The Strike Act restricts and prohibits the personal scope of the right to strike in the case of some public servants. Strike is fully prohibited in the following public organisations: judiciary bodies, armed forces, armed bodies, law enforcement agencies, civil security services, and the National Tax and Customs Authority.[12] Therefore, the workers of these public organisations are absolutely excluded from strikes.

2.1.3 *Personal Scope of the Right to Strike: Restrictions*

There are also some restrictions in the Strike Act, since in public administration authorities, '*the right to strike may be exercised according to the special regulations fixed in the agreement between the Government and the trade unions concerned*'.[13] This agreement was concluded in 1994 and it is still in force.[14] This statutory authorisation is vague, as it does not clarify the potential parties ('the trade unions concerned') and contents of the agreement, but it fundamentally restricts the exercise of a constitutional right. A generally binding rule of conduct may be established only by legislation and only by a body with legislative powers specified in the Fundamental Law.[15] However, no agreement between unions and the Government can in any way be considered legislation, as unions do not have legislative powers.[16] In addition, the agreement of 1994 declares that only a trade union can organise a strike, which signed the 1994 agreement. This is a fundamental restriction compared to the constitutional provision and the Strike Act.

The same (problematic) legal technique was utilised by the law on health service relationship in 2021. Accordingly, the right to strike may be practised in public health institutions in accordance with the special provisions in the agreement of the Government and 'the trade unions concerned'.[17] According to the Government, the new law is intended to determine the conditions for the exercise of the right to strike with the involvement of stakeholders. However, five Hungarian trade union confederations submitted a complaint to the ILO Freedom of Association Committee (*the Committee*)

11. Szakszervezeti jogok, http://www.fbvszosz.hu/wp-content/uploads/2015/04/ILO_Szakszervjogok.pdf (accessed 6 May 2025).
12. Strike Act, Art. 3(2).
13. Strike Act, Art. 3(2).
14. Official Journal (Magyar Közlöny) 1994/8.
15. Article T of the Fundamental Law of Hungary.
16. Kártyás, Gábor: Severe Restrictions on Hungarian Public Health-Care Workers' Collective Rights Violate ILO Principles. *International Labor Rights Case Law* 8 (2022), pp. 126-127.
17. Act 100 of 2020 on health service relationship, Art. 15 (11).

alleging that the new regulations on the status of public healthcare workers violate collective bargaining rights and the right to strike.[18]

The Committee recalled its previous practice that the right to strike may be restricted or prohibited only in essential services in the strict sense of the term (endanger life, personal safety, health). The Committee also observed that healthcare workers not considered essential will not be able to exercise the right as long as such an agreement is not concluded. Therefore, the Committee requested the Government to review the law to ensure that, for those who are not considered to be essential services in the strict sense of the term, an independent body shall determine the minimum service, in case there is no agreement on this between the parties.[19] I must remark that an agreement on the right to strike has not been reached yet in the health sector, so the right to strike cannot be practised at all during its absence.

2.1.4 Personal Scope of the Right to Strike: Covid Restriction in Air Traffic Control

The strike was planned to start in civil air traffic control service in August 2021 for an unlimited period. The Supreme Court allowed the strike as lawful, and defined the appropriate level of services in July 2021.[20] As a response, Government Decree No. 446/2021[21] prohibited strike in air traffic control service during the Covid State of Danger.[22] The Decree simply stated this prohibition without any explanation, so the reasons remain unclear. There is a serious doubt about the potential violation of the Strike Act and the Constitutional strike provision. It is rather questionable if this prohibition is in connection with the Pandemic or its effects and whether it is in a sector where such a prohibition is allowed by the ILO Convention.

However, 'the Constitutional Court rejected the constitutional complaint aimed at establishing the lack of conformity with the Fundamental Law ... According to the contested provision, in addition to the organisations defined in section 3 (2) of Act VII of 1989 on Strike, in the interests of national defence and national security, no strike may be called by the organisation responsible for the provision of air traffic control services operating a system element designated by the sectoral designating authority for national defence systems and installations as a national critical system element in the interests of national defence ... In the petitioners' view, the contested provision completely excludes them from exercising the right to strike, as enshrined in the Fundamental Law, and is therefore contrary to the Fundamental Law'.

18. ILO, Committee on Freedom of Association, Case No. 3399 (Hungary), Complaint date: 13 January 2021. https://www.ilo.org/dyn/normlex/en/f?p=NORMLEXPUB:50002:0::NO::P50002_COMPLAINT_TEXT_ID:4121007 (accessed 6 May 2025).
19. Kártyás, Gábor: Severe Restrictions on Hungarian Public Health-Care Workers' Collective Rights Violate ILO Principles. *International Labor Rights Case Law* 8 (2022), pp. 125-126.
20. Metropolitan Court of Budapest decision: 13.Mpk.75.206/2021/20.
21. In Hungarian: https://net.jogtar.hu/jogszabaly?docid=a2100446.kor (accessed 6 May 2025).
22. Based on Act 1 of 2021 on the State of Danger; https://helsinki.hu/en/wp-content/uploads/sites/2/2021/05/HHC_Hungary_emergency_measures_overview_25052021.pdf (accessed 6 May 2025).

The Constitutional Court found in its decision that the regulation concerns an essential service of general interest. As regards the scope of subjects, it applies to persons with a special status, i.e., employees working for an organisation designated as a national critical control element in the interest of national defence, operating an element responsible for the provision of air traffic control services. It could not be established, on the basis of the content of the petition, that the contested provision was not capable of contributing to the fight against the state of danger during the period of the special legal order. As also indicated in the submission of the competent minister, the purpose of the regulation is to ensure the full and uninterrupted operation of the air traffic service during the state of danger, in order to contribute to the full implementation of the measures necessary to manage the epidemic and to mitigate and combat its consequences. The absence of this, the 'provision of still sufficient services' under the Strike Act, may entail a risk which does not make it unnecessary to prohibit the exercise of the right to strike during the state of danger as provided for in the Decree. The panel of the Constitutional Court, therefore, rejected the constitutional complaint.[23]

2.2 Essential Services in the Strict Sense of the Term

The requirement to provide a minimum level of essential services has been part of strike law since 1989. The relevant provision was amended in 2010, which provided a stricter approach by restricting employees' freedom. The teachers' strike elucidated the weaknesses of this new Article 4(2) from the employees' prospect and led to further statutory limitations of strike law in 2022. This section will summarise the basic provisions and case law on essential services in a historic context with special emphasis on the outcome.

2.2.1 Original Rules on Essential Services (1989-2010)

The obligation to ensure essential services has been constantly present in the Strike Act.[24] According to the original rule (in force up to 2010): '*In the case of employers who perform activities of fundamental public concern – such as, in particular, in the field of mass transportation on public roads and telecommunications, as well as at suppliers of electricity, water, gas and other energy – the right to strike may be exercised in a way so as not to impede the performance of services maintained at a level deemed sufficient. Its level and conditions are the subject of negotiations prior to the strike.*'

Article 4(2) states the obligation to provide a basic level of services in sectors providing public services of fundamental importance, and this rule is still in force (unchanged). The list of these sectors was left open by the Strike Act with a flexible list

23. No. 3065/2022. (II. 25.) http://public.mkab.hu/dev/dontesek.nsf/0/9066D8584B891CA0C125877C005AA8F9?OpenDocument&english (accessed 6 May 2025); http://public.mkab.hu/dev/dontesek.nsf/0/9066d8584b891ca0c125877c005aa8f9/$FILE/3065_2022%20AB%20hat%C3%A1rozat.pdf (accessed 6 May 2025).
24. *See* Art. 4(2).

of examples (open taxation). The potential list of affected sectors is quite obscure and seems to be wide. It looks to be at the discretion of the disputing parties (and also legislation after 2010) to decide which sectors fall into this category. However, this question is finally decided by the court in case of a legal dispute or the Constitutional Court based on complaints.

So the courts must decide on who (which employees) must comply with this condition; thus, they must behave like a lawmaker, whose task is complied with elaborating the following judicial test. According to the Supreme Court, on the assessment of which services are considered of fundamental public concern, only direct and serious aspects affecting the population shall be taken into account, but these must go beyond the economic and security interests of the employer. If the employer cannot be defined, the Government shall be the other (employer) party.[25] For example, education is not specifically mentioned in the above list, but the Government introduced requirements on essential services (*see* below). In case of the teachers' strike in 2022 (*see* below), the Supreme Court stated that teachers fall under the category of 'activities of fundamental public concern' in the meaning of Article 4(2) of the Strike Act.

In addition, there was an obligation of the parties to negotiate about the level of minimum services to be provided. In former practice, 60% of strikes required an agreement on sufficient level of services.[26] However, there was no obligation to make an agreement on essential services prior to the strike, and the strike was not considered illegal in the lack of such an agreement.[27] Therefore, trade unions were obliged to negotiate, but they could go on a strike without an agreement on essential services. Certainly, this solution raised serious practical problems of the lack of a conclusion and enforceability of an agreement prior to the strike.[28]

2.3 Amended Rules on Essential Services (from 2010)

The Parliament amended Article 4(2) of the Strike Act on essential services in 2010.[29] The new provision maintained the 'old' obligation that in the case of employers performing activities of fundamental public concern, the right to strike may be exercised in a way so as not to impede the performance of services maintained at a level deemed sufficient.

25. Supreme Court Opinion No. 1/2013.(IV.8.) KMK. In Hungarian: https://kuria-birosag.hu/hu/kollvel/12013iv8-kmk-velemeny-sztrajkjog-gyakorlasanak-egyes-kerdeseirol (accessed 6 May 2025).
26. Berki, Erzsébet: *Sztrájk! Sztrájkok és más direkt akciók Magyarországon a rendszerváltás után.* Munkaügyi Kutatások Szakmai Műhelye, Budapest, p. 80 (2000).
27. *See* Art. 3 of the Strike Act ont he closed list of unlawful strikes, which did not include Art. 4(2) on the obligation to maintain a sufficient level of services. *See also* the case law: Supreme Court BH 1991. 255 (1991).
28. Ajtay-Horváth, Viola: Quo vadis sztrájkjog? Gondolatok a még elégséges szolgáltatásról. *De Iurisprudentia Et Iure Publico* (2013/2), p. 13. In public transport, there was an agreement on sufficient level of services in only 42% of strikes (Berki Erzsébet: Az elégséges szolgáltatás problémája. *Pécsi Munkajogi Közlemények* (2009/1), p. 114).
29. Act 178 of 2010 on amendment of Act 7 of 1989 on the right to strike.

The change was about the way this minimum level of services is defined: '*The level of service deemed sufficient and the related requirements may be defined by an act of Parliament. If not governed by an act of Parliament, the level of service deemed sufficient and the related requirements shall be agreed upon previously, during the pre-strike negotiations; in this case the strike may be carried out if the parties concluded the agreement, or failing this, if the level of service deemed sufficient and the related requirements had been determined by final decision of the court hearing labor disputes, acting on the request of either of the parties.*'[30]

So, there is a sequence to define the sufficient level of services:

- If there is a provision in an act, it must be followed.
- If there is no such legal provision, there must be a pre-strike agreement (with a minimum of seven days of negotiation).[31]
- If there is no law and agreement, the trade union must wait until the final decision of the court.

In the new system, the minimum service is determined by law; in its absence, either the parties agree to it, or the court determines it.[32] Presently, only the following sectors have legal provisions on the level of sufficient services: public transport (2012),[33] postal services (2012),[34] and public education (in 2022, *see* 2.4 on the teachers' strike). It is an apparent question: why is there no law in all relevant sectors? In principle, it could be regulated in all relevant laws in accordance with the ILO Convention and guidance, but there are some sectors where such a regulation would be extremely difficult (e.g., electricity supply). This would help to avoid insecurity (former problem) and time-consuming litigation (present obstacle).

However, the main danger of this solution is if the required level is not sufficient but remarkably high, as is the case with the above-mentioned provisions on public transport, postal services and education.[35] For example, in public transport, the Government determined the mandatory minimum services at 66% of regular services for local and suburban mass transport and 50% for countrywide and regional public transport.[36] The case is even worse in education, as it is described in the next section.

As for the agreement, the Government has elaborated a practice of blocking it in the public sector, thereby pushing the trade unions to time-consuming litigation.[37] At the same time, the parties may have access to voluntary mediation and arbitration.[38]

30. Article 4(3) of the Strike Act.
31. Article 2(1) of the Strike Act.
32. Act 7 of 1989 on Strikes Art. 4(2), (3).
33. Article 39 of Act 41 of 2012 on Public Transport Services.
34. Article 34(3) of Act 159 of 2012 on Postal Services.
35. Berki, Erzsébet: Sztrájk 2.0. A munkaharc eszközeinek alkalmazása Magyarországon. *Dura Kiadó,* Budapest (2016), p. 328; Ajtay-Horváth, Viola: Quo vadis sztrájkjog? Gondolatok a még elégséges szolgáltatásról. *De Iurisprudentia Et Iure Publico* (2013/2), p. 16; Metropolitan Court of Budapest, Labour Division Decision No. 12.Mpk.75.018/2022/10.
36. Kajtár, Edit & Kun, Attila: Right to Strike in a Changing Regulatory Environment. *Pázmány Law Working Papers* (2013/3), p. 8, https://plwp.eu/docs/wp/2013/2013-03-Kajtar-Kun.pdf (accessed 6 May 2025).
37. Supreme Court Decisions: Mpk.X.10.116/2020/6; Mpk.VIII.10.051/2022/4.
38. Articles 291-293 of the Labour Code.

In the lack of a law and an agreement, the court shall decide on the rate and conditions of the sufficient level of services. According to case law, the court decision is based on the consideration of both parties' proposals and by accepting one of the parties' final proposal.[39] If there is no clear, serious professional proposal, the court may refuse the claim. The decision must comply with the requirement to provide a basic level of services for the population; however, it may not endanger the objective of the strike, namely the success of placing effective pressure on the employer.[40] The lawfulness of the strike must be evaluated and assessed by the court only if there is a request for it by one of the parties.[41] Finally, the sufficient level of services shall be assessed on the basis of laws in force at the time of the request to the court, so it cannot be refused on the basis of laws passed and conditions changed after this date.[42]

The court shall adopt a decision within five working days, in non-contentious proceedings, upon hearing the parties where this is necessary. The decision of the court may be appealed within five days from the date of delivery of the decision. The court of the second instance shall adopt a decision within five working days.[43] So, the court procedure has short deadlines, which guarantees a quite rapid process; however, it takes rather long, taking into account the special lifecycle of strikes. And the courts often have problems of making such a decision without the necessary knowledge of the sector in such a short time. So this amendment has the effect of creating a quite effective obstacle to rapid, immediate strikes, as it may take weeks to be able to commence the strike, if the decision supports them. So workers decide to strike on 1 March and they can start it only around the end of the month, when the situation and atmosphere may be totally different. It also often happens that litigation ends up in a long process of interpreting procedural issues, and the trade union finally gives up the strike. In my view, this amendment created a procedural system which seriously impedes strikes in the effected sectors. However, the new system guarantees, unlike the former provisions, that the level of sufficient services is somehow defined, since the strike is unlawful, if it violates Article 4(2) of the Strike Act.[44]

2.4 Litmus Test: Teachers' Strike 2022

2.4.1 Debates and New Laws on Essential Services

The preconditions of a successful strike were all present in public education in 2022. Teachers (over 100,000 public employees) are relatively well organised: the Teachers'

39. Supreme Court Opinion No. 1/2013.(IV.8.) KMK. In Hungarian: https://kuria-birosag.hu/hu/kollvel/12013iv8-kmk-velemeny-sztrajkjog-gyakorlasanak-egyes-kerdeseirol (accessed 6 May 2025); EBH2013. M.10. II.
40. Supreme Court Decisions: Mpk.50.096/2011/7; Mpkfv.636.580/2011/5; Mpk.X.10.116/2020/6.
41. Supreme Court Opinion No. 1/2013.(IV.8.) KMK. In Hungarian: https://kuria-birosag.hu/hu/kollvel/12013iv8-kmk-velemeny-sztrajkjog-gyakorlasanak-egyes-kerdeseirol (accessed 6 May 2025).
42. Supreme Court Decision No. Mpk.X.10116/2020. In Hungarian: https://kuria-birosag.hu/hu/sajto/meg-elegseges-szolgaltatas-targyaban-hozott-hatarozatot-kuria (accessed 6 May 2025).
43. Article 5 of the Strike Act.
44. Article 3(1)(a) of the Strike Act, in force from the 2010 Amendment.

Trade Union is the largest sector-level union in the country itself, with a membership of over 25,000 teachers,[45] but the second trade union also has 22,000 members.[46] In addition, teachers are absolutely underpaid even in a Hungarian comparison, as their monthly net wage varies between EUR 500 and 1000,[47] which is only 60% of the average pay of diploma-holder employees.[48]

Against this background, the trade unions of public school teachers announced a strike on 31 January 2022 to raise wages and also reform the centralised and overburdened school system. The Ministry did not agree on sufficient services, so the trade unions should have waited for the final decision of the court. But after the decision of the first instance court, stating the lawfulness of their strike and ruling on sufficient services, the trade unions ran out of their announced strike timeline and did not wait for the final decision (there were four more days for the first instance decision to become final, if the Ministry did not appeal against it). The strike was finally organised on 31 January 2022, without the final decision of the court, as the first instance decision was not final at that time.

After the two-hour warning strike on 31 January 2022 (20% of teachers joined), the first instance court stated the unlawfulness of the strike due to the lack of a final court decision. However, the Supreme Court changed this judgment by stating the lawfulness of the warning strike.[49] The Supreme Court clarified that the main issue at stake is whether the lack of a final decision of the court makes the strike automatically unlawful or not. Article 4(2) of the Strike Act clearly requires that the level of service deemed sufficient and the related requirements be determined by final decision of the court. Therefore, the trade unions and the employees undertook a great risk when they went on strike without it. However, the Supreme Court put the emphasis on the substantial instead of the formal criteria of lawfulness of a strike. Stated that the strike may be lawful, in the lack of a formal final decision, if:

- the sufficient level of service, as ruled by Court of First Instance, was maintained during the strike;
- this was not debated by the other party (the Ministry), or the court of second instance also accepted the sufficient level of service as stated by the first instance court.

If all these conditions are met, the strike will not be unlawful on the sole ground that the court decision did not become final. With this sophisticated interpretation, the Supreme Court impedes employers from stopping strikes with a clearly obstructive behaviour, namely using all legal deadlines to cool down the strike atmosphere. A further argument was that the decision of the first instance court affected a certain date,

45. https://pedagogusok.hu/ (accessed 6 May 2025).
46. http://www.pdsz.hu/ (accessed 6 May 2025).
47. *See* net teacher pay in 2022: https://www.hrportal.hu/hr/pedagogus-bertabla-2022-20220109.html (accessed 6 May 2025).
48. https://telex.hu/belfold/2022/10/05/oktatas-tanarok-fizetes-pedagogusok-berek-tiltakozasok (accessed 6 May 2025).
49. Mpk.VIII.10.051/2022/4, Tájékoztató a Kúria Mpk.VIII.10.051/2022/4. számú végzésről a 2022. január 31-én megtartott pedagógus sztrájk tárgyban | Kúria (kuria-birosag.hu).

so the missing of this date would have required the setting of a new date and launching a new procedure, which would have meant an unreasonable burden. If the date of the desired strike is not defined in advance, the court will not assess the request at all. It was also emphasised that legal provisions must not be construed in a way that makes strikes impossible. This is an important argument, which is totally missing from the recent decisions of the Constitutional Court (*see* 2.4.3 below).

After the warning strike on 31 January 2022 and the related litigation described above, the trade unions announced a normal (not warning) strike for an unlimited period from 16 March 2022. So, this time, the trade unions left a long period to acquire the final decision of the court, as it was clear that the Government (relevant Ministry) did not want to agree on sufficient services.

After all, the Government suddenly issued Government Decree No. 36/2022 on sufficient services in public schools.[50] It obliged teachers to provide care for children in their original groups (merging groups is prohibited) between 7 am and 4-6 pm (depending on the school level) during the COVID-19 State of Danger. This made a strike practically impossible but at least invisible.

Several schools (a part of teachers, mostly in Budapest) started 'civil disobedience': they stopped working and demonstrated against the Government Decree. After a week, several schools and teachers joined this civil disobedience movement. The trade unions also filed a complaint against the Decree at the Constitutional Court.

On 16 March 2022, the trade unions announced an undefined term strike; however, it happened at a limited scale. It ended on 1 April due to the upcoming Parliamentary elections. In the meantime, the Parliament passed Act 5 of 2022 on regulatory issues concerning the cessation of the COVID State of Danger.[51] This includes Article 14, which enacts the provisions of Government Decree No. 36/2022, obliging teachers to provide care for children in their original groups, making a strike practically impossible.

2.4.2 Disciplinary Measures

As a consequence of the limitations on strike law, many teachers started civil disobedience, which means the refusal to work (in practice, a strike) in certain short periods (hours or days). As a retaliation, several teachers' public servant employment relationship was terminated with immediate effect with reasoning on the basis of violating employee obligations to perform work. However, Article 33/A(3) of Act 33 of 1992 on the Legal Status of Public Servants[52] and Article 78(2) of Act 1 of 2012 on the Labour Code[53] requires the employer to hand over the termination letter within 15 days of acquiring information by the employer on the violation of employee rights.

50. In Hungarian: https://net.jogtar.hu/jogszabaly?docid=A2200036.KOR&celpara=&searchUrl=/jogszabaly-kereso%3Fevszam%3D%26sorszam%3D%26para%3D%26tipus%3Dnincs%26kif%3D%26searchfor%3Don%26pagenum%3D11 (accessed 6 May 2025).
51. In Hungarian: https://magyarkozlony.hu/dokumentumok/0342bbf4d2fc62d04bc14e7a241aab91cffe9530/megtekintes (accessed 6 May 2025).
52. In Hungarian: https://net.jogtar.hu/jogszabaly?docid=99200033.tv (accessed 6 May 2025).
53. In Hungarian: https://net.jogtar.hu/jogszabaly?docid=a1200001.tv (accessed 6 May 2025).

On 12 January 2023, the Government issued Government Decree No. 4/2023 on altering the above-mentioned provisions. The State of Danger as a response to the war in Ukraine is the legal basis of the Decree, which is quite problematic, as the teachers' strike is not connected in any way to the war. The substance of the legal change: the employer may terminate public servant employment or employment relationship of employees in public education with an immediate effect with reasoning until 1 August of the given education year; in case of a later violation (practically in August), then the end of the next academic year is the deadline, irrespective of the (normal, former) 15-day deadline. Furthermore, the Decree has a retrospective effect, as the new deadline shall be applied, if the 15-day deadline has not been passed on 12 January 2023.

This practically means that the teacher's employment may be terminated with an immediate effect many (even 10) months after the breach of the contract. The aim of this measure is to keep teachers on civil disobedience and also on strike in a constant fear of retaliation. It may happen that the teacher refuses to work for a day in September and she can teach the whole school year, but her employment is terminated with an immediate effect in the next year at the end of the school year in July. In my view, this measure violates fundamental labour law values and principles.

2.4.3 Constitutional Court Decision on Teachers' Right To Strike

The Constitutional Court passed a decision on 29 November 2022, stating the constitutionality of the above-mentioned limitations on essential services in strike of teachers.[54] According to the reasoning of the decision, the right to education of children is the legitimate aim of the strike restriction. Since the restriction has a legitimate aim (protection of students' right to education), it was considered automatically necessary and proportionate. The Constitutional Court, strikingly, did not investigate at all the necessity and proportionality of the measure.

In my opinion, this is a mistaken decision, since the legitimate aim cannot make the strike restriction automatically necessary and proportionate. This is indeed a strike restriction, which violates ILO laws and principles on the right to strike, and it is also clearly disproportionate, as it makes the strikes invisible. It obliges teachers to provide care for children in their original groups between 7 am and 4-6 pm. This makes a strike practically impossible in public education. Frankly speaking, this Constitutional Court decision allowed the Government and the Parliament to block strikes freely by regulating an extremely high level of essential services. I am afraid the same may also happen in other strike sensitive sectors in the future.

54. Constitutional Court Decision No. 1/2023. In Hungarian: http://public.mkab.hu/dev/dontesek.nsf/0/16ca2ae08696d9c6c1258885005b23f2/$FILE/1_2023%20AB%20hat%C3%A1rozat.pdf (accessed 6 May 2025).

3 CONCLUSION

The Strike Act was born in the moment of political change in 1989 and had the objective of ensuring a liberal regulation of the right to strike. In terms of the fundamental services, it left the regulation of sufficient level of services to the parties. The main problem with this system was the lack of an obligation to regulate and the missing enforceability of minimum services.

From the 2010 Amendment of the Strike Act (Article 4), there is an obligation to regulate the level of sufficient services; otherwise, the strike is unlawful. The first option for such a regulation is to apply the relevant Act. However, such provisions were passed only for postal services, public transport and education. It could be a good solution in some sectors, if the set level complies with the ILO principles of ensuring fundamental services for the population while guaranteeing the objective of the strike by allowing pressure on the employer. The Government provided bad examples by the laws on postal, transport services and education by making the strike invisible. Teachers must be at the disposal of the employer and provide care for children in the full working time without teaching. So, regulation of essential services by law could be a feasible method, but definitely not this way by putting the minimum extremely high.

Agreement of the parties has been practically blocked by the Government in the public sector. The lack of the will of the employer to agree on minimum services pushes trade unions to the obligation to litigate. The court procedure takes long; it is complicated and full of dangers of losing the right to start the strike as a consequence of procedural debates. All of the problems above lead to serious difficulties in launching a strike.[55] This new system is the main reason why the number of strikes significantly decreased after the modified Strike Act came into force.[56]

55. Berki, Erzsébet: Sztrájk 2.0. A munkaharc eszközeinek alkalmazása Magyarországon. *Dura Kiadó*, Budapest (2016), p. 328.
56. Kajtár, Edit & Kun, Attila: Right to Strike in a Changing Regulatory Environment. *Pázmány Law Working Papers* (2013/3), https://plwp.eu/docs/wp/2013/2013-03-Kajtar-Kun.pdf (accessed 6 May 2025), p. 8.

CHAPTER 18

Restrictions on the Right to Strike in Ireland

Anthony Kerr

1 GENERAL INFORMATION

1.1 Legal Basis of the Right to Strike

A right to strike is not expressly guaranteed by the Constitution of Ireland 1937, Article 40.6.1(iii) of which merely guarantees 'the right to form associations and unions'. The Supreme Court, however, has recently indicated that 'this right implies at least some – perhaps as yet undefined – zone of freedom for [trade] unions to organise and campaign' and must be understood 'to recognise the legitimacy of trade union activity'.[1]

The ability of workers and trade unions of which they are members to take lawful strike or industrial action such as picketing is regulated by the provision of statutory immunities that protect workers and trade unions from certain criminal and civil liabilities associated with strikes and other forms of industrial action.[2] These immunities are contained in Part II of the Industrial Relations Act 1990 (the 1990 Act) and are dependent on workers and trade unions acting 'in contemplation or furtherance of a trade dispute'.[3] If that condition is not satisfied, the workers involved and their trade

1. *Per* Hogan J. and O'Donnell C.J. in *HA O'Neil Ltd v. Unite the Union* [2024] IESC 8; [2024] E.L.R. 121 at 155 and 144 respectively. *See also* Murray J. at 175 who said that the defendants' right to engage in collective industrial action was 'necessarily acknowledged by their constitutional right to form trade unions'.
2. *See* A. Kerr, *The Right to Strike: Ireland* in B. Waas ed., *The Right to Strike: A Comparative View*, 303-315 (Kluwer 2014).
3. Part II of the Industrial Relations Act 1990 repealed and re-enacted, with some significant amendments, the provisions of the Trade Disputes Act 1906: *see* A. Kerr, *Irish Industrial Relations Legislation: Consensus not Compulsion* 20 I.L.J. 240 (1991) https://doi.org/10.1093/ilj/20.4.240;

union are exposed to potential fines, injunctions and awards of damages, together with the legal costs associated with defending claims by the employer or third parties affected by the strike or other industrial action.[4]

1.2 Main Features of the Regulation

The term 'trade dispute' is defined in section 8 of the 1990 Act as meaning 'any dispute between employers and workers which is connected with the employment or non-employment, or the terms and conditions of or affecting the employment, of any person'.

The word 'worker' is defined in section 8 of the 1990 Act as meaning 'any person who is or was employed whether or not in the employment of the employer with whom a trade dispute arises, but does not include a member of the Defence Forces or of the Garda Síochána [the Irish police force]'.

Sections 11 (peaceful picketing), 12 (removal of liability for certain acts such as inducement of breach of contract) and 13 (restriction of actions in tort against trade unions) of the 1990 Act apply only to 'authorised trade unions which for the time being are holders of negotiation licences under the Trade Union Act 1941, and the members and officials of such trade unions, and not otherwise'.[5] It follows that workers who are not members of such trade unions cannot rely on those statutory immunities in the event that they engage in a strike or some other form of industrial action. The immunities in respect of civil and criminal conspiracy provided by section 10 of the 1990 Act, however, do apply to non-unionised workers.[6]

One of the most significant restrictions on the ability of workers to engage in a strike or other industrial action is contained in section 14 of the 1990 Act. This section requires the rules of a trade union to contain a provision that the union 'shall not organise, participate in, sanction or support a strike or other industrial action without a secret ballot' against the wishes of a majority of those voting in the ballot. The rights conferred by this section are conferred 'on the members of the trade union concerned

A. Kerr ed., *The Industrial Relations Act 1990: 20 Years On* (Round Hall 2010); and A. Kerr, *The Trade Union and Industrial Relations Acts*, 209-262 (6th ed., Round Hall 2022).

4. So, in *Nolan Transport (Oaklands) Ltd v. Halligan* [1999] 1 I.R. 128, the High Court (Barron J.) had awarded the plaintiff company IRP 601,000 in damages, and the costs of a 27-day hearing, against the worker defendants' trade union, following a strike at, and picketing of, the company's premises. On appeal, the decision was overturned, some 42 months later, by the Supreme Court because the defendants were found to have been acting in furtherance of a 'trade dispute' and, consequently, the statutory immunities applied.
5. *See* s. 9(1) of the Industrial Relations Act 1990. A negotiation licence is granted by the Minister for Enterprise, Tourism and Employment where the trade union satisfies the various conditions set out in the Trade Union Act 1941, as amended by the Trade Union Act 1971 and the 1990 Act. A trade union requires such a licence before it can lawfully engage in collective bargaining: *see* s. 6 of the Trade Union Act 1941.
6. Section 10 re-enacts s. 3 of the Conspiracy, and Protection of Property Act 1875 and s. 1 of the Trade Disputes Act 1906. Section 17(1) of the Industrial Relations Act 1990 provides, however, that s. 10, as well as ss 11 and 12, shall not apply in respect of proceedings arising out of or relating to a strike or other industrial action by a group of workers in disregard of or contrary to the outcome of a secret ballot relating to the issue or issues involved in the dispute.

and on no other person'. Consequently, an employer cannot seek an injunction to restrain a strike or other industrial action merely because the trade union did not conduct a ballot. If a ballot is conducted, the result of which is in favour of a strike or other industrial action, and at least one week's notice is given to the employer, section 19 of the 1990 Act severely restricts the ability of employers and others to obtain an injunction to restrain a strike or other industrial action.[7]

The Supreme Court has confirmed that the availability of the statutory immunities is dependent on whether the strike or other industrial action is 'in contemplation or furtherance of a trade dispute' not on there being a ballot.[8] The only consequence of not holding a ballot is that the benefits of section 19 are not available to the trade union and its members and the normal rules relating to the granting of injunctions will apply.

The *right* to strike, in the sense that the workers who go on strike, or their trade union, should not be exposed to civil or criminal sanction, is also confirmed by the Supreme Court decision in *Becton, Dickinson & Co Ltd v. Lee*[9] that there is 'to be read into every contract of employment an implied term that the service of a strike notice of a length not shorter than would be required for notice to terminate the contract would not in itself amount to notice to terminate the contract and would not in itself constitute a breach of the contract and that to take action on foot of the strike notice would likewise not be a breach of the contract'. In such a case, the contract of employment is neither broken nor terminated but is suspended.[10]

2 PERMITTED RESTRICTIONS

2.1 Certain Categories of Public Servants

There are no statutory restrictions on the ability of civil or public servants (such as teachers, nurses, ambulance/fire service staff, prison officers, etc.) to engage in a strike or other industrial action other than in the case of members of An Garda Síochána (the Irish police force) or members of the Defence Forces. Both are expressly excluded from the definition of 'worker' in section 8 of the 1990 Act and, consequently, a dispute over their 'terms and conditions of employment' would not constitute a 'trade dispute' and would not attract any of the statutory immunities provided by the 1990 Act. The legality of their actions would fall to be decided by common law principles, which regard strikes and other forms of industrial action, such as picketing, to be unlawful if not illegal.[11]

7. *See Dublin City Council v. Technical, Engineering and Electrical Union (No. 1)* [2010] E.L.R. 221 and, most recently, *HA O'Neil Ltd v. Unite the Union* [2024] IESC 8; [2024] E.L.R. 121.
8. *See Nolan Transport (Oaklands) Ltd v. Halligan* [1999] 1 I.R. 128 at 135 (*per* O'Flaherty J.) and 156 (*per* Murphy J.).
9. [1973] I.R. 1, 24-25, *per* Walsh J. *See also Bates v. Model Bakery Ltd* [1993] 1 I.R. 359.
10. Such an implied term would not be read into a contract of employment where there is an express 'no-strike' clause; nor would it apply where no, or inadequate, notice is given of the strike; or where the industrial action does not consist of a 'cessation of work' amounting to a 'strike' within the meaning of that word in s. 8 of the Industrial Relations Act 1990.
11. *See* the comments of Laffoy J. on the legality of peaceful picketing at common law in *Dublin City Council v. Technical, Engineering & Electrical Union (No. 2)* [2010] 4 I.R. 667 at 698 and those

The inability of Garda and Defence Force members to engage in strike action was part of separate complaints against Ireland brought by the European Confederation of Police (EuroCOP)[12] and the European Organisation of Military Associations (EUROMIL),[13] alleging various breaches of Article 6 of the revised European Social Charter ('the Charter'). In both cases, Ireland submitted that the prohibition on the right to strike pursued the legitimate aim of ensuring the maintenance of public order, national security and the rights and freedom of others by having such members 'fully operational at all times' and was 'strictly necessary' in the circumstances. In addition, Ireland submitted, in the case of Defence Force members, that the taking of industrial action would conflict with 'military discipline'.

In both cases, the members of the European Committee of Social Rights ('the Committee') were satisfied that the prohibition pursued a legitimate aim but they then had to consider whether the prohibition was 'necessary in a democratic society'. The Committee arrived at different conclusions on this issue in the two complaints, albeit in both cases by a majority.

In *EuroCOP*, the Committee, by a majority of 6 to 5,[14] found that the reasons put forward by Ireland 'did not demonstrate the existence of a concrete pressing social need' for an 'absolute prohibition' on the ability of gardaí to take strike action. Ireland, in the view of the majority, had not 'justified' that the legitimate purpose of maintaining public order and national security might not be achieved by establishing 'restrictions' on the exercise of the right to strike, such as requirements relating to the 'mode and form' of industrial action.

In its subsequent observations to the Committee of Ministers, Ireland reiterated that the gardaí provided security and intelligence services, as well as policing and that it was 'critically important' that these services were fully operational at all times. Giving gardaí the right to strike would raise the most serious issues in respect of the capacity of the State to ensure the maintenance of law and order.[15] Nevertheless, Ireland said it took 'careful note' of the Committee's findings and would keep the matter 'under review'.

Following the Committee's decision, a Private Member's Bill was introduced in Dáil Éireann seeking to give legislative effect to the decision. Section 5 of the Industrial Relations (Members of the Garda Síochána and the Defence Forces) Bill 2015[16] proposed that the definition of 'worker' in section 8 of the 1990 Act should be amended by the deletion of the words 'or of the Garda Síochána'. This would have brought gardaí within the scope of the definition of 'trade dispute' but, as was not pointed out, they would still have been precluded from availing of the statutory immunities in

of O'Donnell C.J. in *HA O'Neil Ltd v. Unite the Union* [2024] IESC 8; [2024] E.L.R. 121 at 131-133 on the common law's treatment of trade union activity.

12. Complaint No. 83/2012.
13. Complaint No. 112/2014.
14. With Monika Schlachter being one of the dissentients.
15. *See* paras 17-23 of the address of the Ireland representative on 19 June 2014, attached as an Appendix to Resolution CM/ResChS (2014) 12 (adopted on 8 October 2014).
16. No. 9 of 2015.

sections 11 and 12 of the 1990 Act as gardaí are precluded from being members of a trade union, let alone one holding a negotiation licence.[17]

The Bill was opposed by the Government and it was eventually defeated by a vote of 69 against and only 24 in favour.[18] During the debate, the Minister of State at the Department of Justice and Equality, in response to the introducer of the Bill (Michael McNamara TD), accepted that, although 'there is no single specific prohibition on striking by members of the Garda Síochána, a combination of provisions in law, including the Industrial Relations Act 1990, as well as Garda Discipline regulations, effectively preclude strikes'.[19]

The Policing, Security and Community Safety Act 2024 (Standards of Professional Behaviour) Regulations 2025[20] do not expressly prohibit gardaí going on strike, but they do provide that neglect of duty and dishonestly absenting oneself from duty on grounds of illness or injury are potential disciplinary matters. Furthermore, section 98(1) of the Policing, Security and Community Safety Act 2024 provides that a person is guilty of an offence[21] if he or she 'induces, or does any act calculated to induce, any member of An Garda Síochána to withhold his or her services or to commit a breach of the standards of professional behaviour'.[22]

---

17. Gardaí are only entitled to join a 'representative association': *see* s. 59(1) of the Policing, Security and Community Safety Act 2024, subs. (3) of which provides that a member of An Garda Síochána 'shall not be or become a member of a trade union or association ... any object of which is to control or influence the pay, pension or conditions of service of An Garda Síochána'. Subsection (2) provides that a representative association 'shall be independent of, and not associated with, any person or body outside An Garda Síochána' but subs. (5) permits the Minister to authorise an association to be associated with any person or body outside An Garda Síochána. Similar membership restrictions apply to the Defence Forces: *see* s. 2 of the Defence (Amendment) Act 1990. This section was subsequently amended by s. 24 of the Defence (Amendment) Act 2024 by substituting a new subs. (3) and inserting subs. (3A). The former provides that an association 'shall be independent of, and not associated with, any trade union or any other body outside of the Defence Forces' but the latter permits the Minister, notwithstanding subs. (3), to authorise an association to be associated with a trade union or any other body outside of the Defence Forces, subject to such conditions or restrictions as may be specified. The predecessor to s. 59 of the 2024 Act (s. 18 of the Garda Síochána Act 2005) and s. 2 of the 1990 Act (before it was amended) were central to both the *EuroCOP* and *EUROMIL* complaints. The amendments to the 1990 Act will allow the agreement reached in the High Court in May 2022 with the Defence Forces representative associations to be formalised and will facilitate their attendance at future national pay talks. This agreement permitted the associations to become 'temporary associate members' of the Irish Congress of Trade Unions. In return, the associations agreed that they would not ask their members to take part in any form of trade dispute or industrial action and that their members would not call for or support industrial action in the Defence Forces or any other sector.
18. 876 *Dáil Debates* 55-57 (30 April 2015).
19. 875 *Dáil Debates* 175 (24 April 2015).
20. S.I. No. 116 of 2025.
21. Section 98(2) provides that the maximum penalty, in the event of a summary conviction in the District Court, is a fine of EUR 4,000, or twelve-months' imprisonment, or both. The maximum penalty, in the event of a conviction on indictment in the Circuit Court, is a fine of EUR 50,000, or five-years' imprisonment, or both.
22. *See also* s. 9(2) of the Offences Against the State Act 1939 which provides that '[e]very person who shall incite or encourage any person employed in any capacity by the State to refuse, neglect, or omit (in a manner or to an extent calculated to dislocate the public service or a branch thereof) to perform his [or her] duty' is guilty of a criminal offence punishable by imprisonment 'for a term not exceeding two years'.

In *EUROMIL*, however, the Committee, by a majority of 9 to 4, held that a State's 'margin of appreciation' is greater in the case of the military and, consequently, that there was no violation of Article 6(4) in the case of Defence Force members. An absolute prohibition on strike action in this case, unlike that in the case of members of An Garda Síochána, was considered to be proportionate to the legitimate aim pursued.[23]

Following this decision, which found against Ireland in other respects under Article 6 of the Charter, another Private Member's Bill was introduced seeking to give legislative effect to the Committee's decision. Section 3 of the Industrial Relations (Defence Forces) (Amendment) Bill 2017[24] proposed that the definition of 'worker' in section 8 of the 1990 Act should be amended by the deletion of the words 'the Defence Forces or of'. The Bill lapsed following the dissolution of the Dáil and Seanad in January 2020 and has not been reintroduced.

Section 254 of the Defence Act 1954 provides that any person who 'by any means whatsoever' incites, or attempts to incite, any person subject to military law to, *inter alia*, refuse, neglect or perform any of his or her duties is guilty of a criminal offence punishable by imprisonment for a term not exceeding two years.

Section 2A(1) of the Defence (Amendment) Act 1990[25] now provides that a representative association shall not:

(a) call for or support industrial action in the Defence Forces or in any other body or sector;
(b) encourage members to go on strike or engage in any strike action or any form of trade dispute or industrial action;
(c) encourage, directly or indirectly, members to go on strike or engage in strike action or any other trade dispute or any industrial action by another organisation, trade union or person;
(d) encourage members to refuse to follow a lawful order to pass a picket line;
(e) encourage members to contravene their obligations under military law;
(f) endorse or support any official position taken, endorsed or supported by the Irish Congress of Trade Unions or other organisations in support of any industrial action taken by any party.

2.2 Essential Services in the Strict Sense of the Term

Disputes in 'essential services' are not addressed by the 1990 Act other than indirectly in the context of 'secondary picketing'. Section 11(2) of the 1990 Act provides that the picketing of the premises of an employer who is not a party to the dispute is only

23. Only five of the Committee's members had been involved in the *EuroCOP* proceedings, including two of the reported dissentients – Monika Schlachter and Birgitta Nyström. The Committee's decision was adopted by the Committee of Ministers on 10 April 2018: *see* Resolution CM/ResChS (2018) 2.
24. No. 79 of 2017.
25. As inserted by s. 24 of the Defence (Amendment) Act 2024.

permitted where it is reasonable for the picketers at all relevant times to believe that that employer has 'directly assisted' the employer in dispute 'for the purpose of frustrating the strike or other industrial action'. Section 11(3) of the 1990 Act provides that, for the avoidance of doubt, 'any action taken by an employer in the health services to maintain life-preserving services during a strike or other industrial action shall not constitute assistance for the purposes of subsection (2)'.

Instead, a *Code of Practice on Disputes Procedures* (including procedures in essential services) was prepared and adopted pursuant to section 42 of the 1990 Act.[26] Section 42(4) of the 1990 Act provides that, in any proceedings before a court, the Labour Court, the Workplace Relations Commission or one of its adjudication officers, a Code of Practice 'shall be admissible in evidence' and any provision of the Code which appears to be relevant to any question arising in the proceedings 'shall be taken into account in determining that question'. Section 42(5) of the 1990 Act provides, however, that a failure on the part of any person to observe any provision of a Code of Practice 'shall not of itself render him [or her] liable to any proceedings'.

Section V of the Code deals with agreements on special procedures in essential services. Paragraph 30 references such services as including those 'whose cessation or interruption could endanger life, or cause major damage to the national economy, or widespread hardship to the Community' citing health services; energy supplies (including gas and electricity); water and sewage services; fire, ambulance and rescue services; and certain elements of public transport. Telephone and postal services, refuse disposal, customs and excise, air traffic control, teaching and banking were not specifically mentioned.

In cases involving the referenced services, the Code stipulates that 'additional procedures and safeguards' should be introduced 'through consultation and agreement' with the parties recognising their 'joint responsibility' to resolve disputes in the referenced services and employments 'without resorting to strikes or other forms of industrial action'.[27] Paragraph 33 of the Code provides that, except where other procedures and safeguards have been introduced which ensure the continuity of essential supplies and services, collective agreements should include one of the following provisions 'in order to eliminate or reduce any risk to essential supplies and services arising from industrial disputes', namely:

(a) acceptance by the parties of awards, decisions and recommendations which result from the final stage of the dispute settlement procedure, where these include investigation by an independent expert body such as the Labour Court, an agreed arbitration board or tribunal or an independent person appointed by the parties; or
(b) a specific undertaking in agreements that, in the event of any one of the parties deciding that an award, decision or recommendation emerging from the final stage of the dispute settlement procedure is unsatisfactory, they will

26. Industrial Relations Act 1990, Code of Practice on Dispute Procedures (Declaration) Order 1992 (S.I. No. 1 of 1992).
27. Paragraph 31 of the Code.

agree on the means of resolving the issue without resort to strike or to other forms of industrial action, such agreements to include a provision for a review of the case by an agreed recognised body after twelve months, such review to represent a final determination of the issue; or

(c) provision that the parties to an agreement would accept awards, decisions or recommendations resulting from the operation of the final stage of the dispute procedure on the basis that an independent review would take place at five-yearly intervals to examine whether the employees covered by the agreement had been placed at any disadvantage as a result of entering into such agreement and if so to advise, having regard to all aspects of the situation, including economic and financial considerations, on the changes necessary to redress the position.

Paragraph 34 of the Code, under the heading 'Essential Services – Maintenance of Industrial Peace', provides:

> Where the parties have not concluded an agreement incorporating the procedures referred to in paragraph 33 (a) (b) or (c) and otherwise where for any reason a serious threat to the continuity of essential supplies and services exists, or is perceived to exist, as a result of the failure of the parties to resolve an industrial dispute and where the [Workplace] Relations Commission is satisfied that all available dispute procedures have been used to try to effect a settlement, the [Workplace] Relations Commission should consult with the Irish Congress of Trade Unions and [Ibec] about the situation. The objective of such consultation should be to secure their assistance and co-operation with whatever measures may be necessary to resolve the dispute, including, where appropriate, arrangements which would provide a basis for a continuation of normal working for a period not exceeding six months while further efforts by the parties themselves or the dispute settlement agencies were being made to secure a full and final settlement of the issues in dispute.

Persons 'employed by or under the State' do not have access to the dispute resolution machinery provided by the Workplace Relations Commission and the Labour Court.[28] Instead, various non-statutory Conciliation and Arbitration (C&A) Schemes have been established for such workers.[29] Paragraph 89(2) of the C&A Scheme for the Civil Service provides that where industrial action could have 'serious and adverse consequences for the community or for sections of the community', the staff side and the official side, prior to the commencement of any such action, shall 'make arrangements to ensure minimum cover or service'.[30]

28. *See* s. 23(1) of the Industrial Relations Act 1990. Since the enactment of the Industrial Relations (Amendment) Act 2019, members of An Garda Síochána have access to this machinery.
29. *See* M. McGinley, *Industrial Relations in the Public Sector* in T. Murphy & W. Roche eds, *Irish Industrial Relations in Practice*, 227-275 (2nd ed., Oak Tree Press 1997), discussing the C&A schemes for civil servants, teachers and members of the Defence Forces.
30. Paragraph 89(3) of the Scheme further provides that persons in certain designated posts 'shall not participate in any industrial action'. These posts include, amongst many others, senior civil servants dealing with 'general industrial relations matters'.

2.3 Situations of Acute National or Local Crisis

There have been many and varied situations where members of the Defence Forces have been called upon, in aid of the Civil Authority, to alleviate hardship caused by strikes or other industrial action in certain sectors. Ireland's submissions on the merits, in response to the EUROMIL complaint, listed an extensive range of military deployments between 1967 and 2015 involving, *inter alia*, manning sewage pumping stations,[31] operating fire tenders, repairing burst water mains, distributing oil and petrol, providing public transport, disposing of refuse, and repairing lifts.[32] More recently, in 2019, there was a deployment of 88 Defence Force personnel following requests for support from the Health Authorities due to industrial action by ambulance personnel.[33]

3 COMPENSATORY GUARANTEES FOR WORKERS DEPRIVED OF THE RIGHT TO STRIKE

There are no compensatory guarantees to safeguard the position of members of An Garda Síochána and the Defence Forces in the collective bargaining process, as their representative associations are not permitted to engage in 'collective bargaining' as that term is understood in either an industrial relations or a legal context.[34] It is the case, however, that gardaí were given access to the industrial relations machinery provided by the Workplace Relations Commission and the Labour Court through the amendment of section 23 of the 1990 Act by the Industrial Relations (Amendment) Act 2019.[35]

Ireland did attempt, in the *EUROMIL* proceedings, to put forward various compensatory measures to justify the prohibition, all of which were strongly contested,[36] but the Committee did not consider this matter in its majority decision.

---

31. The involvement of Defence Force personnel in this dispute was particularly controversial: *see* 367 *Dáil Debates* Cols. 1428-1436 (5 June 1986).
32. The full list is set out at pp. 29-34 of the submissions. The involvement of six Defence Force personnel in the repairing of the lifts in Ballymun involved their passing an official trade union picket: *see Dublin City Council v. Technical, Engineering & Electrical Union* [2010] 4 I.R. 667 at 677-678, where Laffoy J. noted that the Council's inspector gave evidence that he had been instructed by the trade union of which he was a member not to assist those personnel; an instruction with which he complied.
33. *See* Department of Defence, *Annual Report 2019*, p. 47.
34. *See Services Industrial Professional Technical Union v. Ashford Castle Ltd* [2004] E.L.R. 214, 217. The term is now defined in s. 1A of the Industrial Relations (Amendment) Act 2001 (inserted by s. 27 of the Industrial Relations (Amendment) Act 2015) as comprising 'voluntary engagements or negotiations between any employer or employers' association on the one hand and a trade union of workers or excepted body to which this Act applies on the other, with the object of reaching agreement regarding working conditions or terms of employment, or non-employment, of workers'.
35. Section 23(1C)(b) makes it clear, however, that nothing in the amendments 'shall operate to apply the Trade Union Acts 1871 to 1990 [which includes Part II of the Industrial Relations Act 1990] to the Garda Síochána'.
36. *See* para. 111 of Ireland's submissions on the merits and para. 9.5 of EUROMIL's Response thereto.

4 CONCLUSION

The last time that the issue of strikes in essential services featured prominently in the national media was in 1991.[37] The then main employers' association – the Federation of Irish Employers (now Ibec) – had called for changes to the 1990 Act to allow aggrieved parties to sue trade unions which sanctioned strikes in essential services and proposals which were rejected by the Irish Congress of Trade Unions ('Congress'). Congress favoured the use of a Code of Practice, an approach eventually adopted by the Minister.[38]

The approach taken by those involved in the drafting of the Code of Practice[39] was that the most effective way of dealing with the issue of strikes in essential services was not through the removal of the statutory immunities nor by the creation of statutory wrongs, but through voluntary 'no strike' agreements in return for specific pay determination procedures. Collective agreements in those services considered essential should specify the activities which should be maintained and the financial terms on which this should be done. In the event of disagreement, an independent ruling could be sought. Restricting industrial action by means of the civil and/or criminal law – something unlikely to achieve its object – did not then feature, and has not subsequently featured, on successive governments' agendas.

Paragraph 35 of the Code of Practice provides that the Workplace Relations Commission will review the Code and its operation 'at regular intervals' and advise the Minister of any changes that may be 'necessary or desirable'. No such changes have been advised to date.

It might be noted that the number of workdays lost through strikes in 2023 and 2024 were 4,203 and 3,656 respectively.[40]

---

37. *See Irish Times*, 2 May 1991. The issue had previously arisen in 1940 following strikes by municipal employees in Dublin and carpenters in Limerick: *see* F. D'Arcy & K. Hannigan eds, *Workers in Union: Documents and Commentaries on the History of Irish Labour*, 200-206 (National Archives 1988). The 'sweeping nature' of the legislation, proposed by the Minister for Industry and Commerce to outlaw strikes in public utilities and other essential undertakings, caused alarm in Government circles, with the Attorney General expressing the fear that sections of the proposed legislation would not survive a challenge in the courts. Eventually, the Minister abandoned his attempt to legislate in this area.
38. Industrial Relations Act 1990, Code of Practice on Dispute Procedures (Declaration) Order 1992 (S.I. No. 1 of 1992).
39. These included not just the social partners and government Departments (Finance and Labour) but also representatives from the International Labour Organisation.
40. *See* Central Statistics Office, *Labour Market Statistics Industrial Disputes*, Quarters 1-4 (2023 and 2024). The 2022 figure was 5,256. In the five-year period (1987-1991) straddling the introduction, and enactment, of the Industrial Relations Act 1990, the number of work-days lost was 766,519: *see* T. Brannick, L. Doyle & A. Kelly, *Industrial Conflict* in T. Murphy & W. Roche eds, *Irish Industrial Relations in Practice*, 309 (2nd ed., Oak Tree Press 1997).

CHAPTER 19

Restrictions on the Right to Strike in Italy*

Edoardo Ales

1 GENERAL INFORMATION

In order to have a good and complete understanding of the complex subject matter dealt with in this paper, some preliminary remarks seem to be necessary. They refer to the juridical nature of the employment relationship, which links who is going to strike to the relevant employer and to the consequences this nature will produce as far as the applicable legislation is concerned. Such remarks will also explain the reason why, at present, in Italy, it is not correct to talk about a specific regulation of strike in *public* services, but one has to refer to strike in *essential services*. As a matter of fact, for many years, from the different juridical nature, public or private, of the employment relationship, part of scholars have tried to derive a different treatment of the abstention from work due to the fact that someone who depended on a public employer (Public Administration) was theoretically and, most of the time, practically speaking involved in and consequently responsible for the delivery of a service of 'public interest', so that his/her abstention from work was able to provoke a damage to the community.

For this reason, it is important to highlight a first distinction between *employee* as someone who is employed by a private employer under a work contract ruled by Labour L and *civil servant* as someone who works for a public administration in a juridical relationship ruled by Administrative Law, i.e., submitted to unilateral decision of the employer, without any chance for the employee to bargain working conditions, under the jurisdiction of administrative tribunals. This distinction has excluded for a long time a relevant part of workers from the application of Labour Law, creating what has been called *'Pubblico impiego'*, an independent system of employment relationship

* This chapter has been published as E. Ales, *Strike in Public-Essential Services in Italy*, in M. Rigaux & F. Dorssemont (eds), *Vitale Behoeften, essentiële diensten, minimumprestaties en strakingrecht*, Antwerp: Intersentia, 159 (2003).

with Public Administrations. Furthermore, it has contributed to affirming the idea of the existence of a Public Sector characterised by a peculiar mission aimed at realising public interest, which justifies a regulation of employment relationship different from private sector. Since 1993, this distinction has fallen for the great majority of civil servants whose employment relationship is now ruled by Labour Law, so that now, by *employee,* we understand someone who is employed by a private employer or by a public administration under a work contract.

Nevertheless, also before 1993, a perfect coincidence between dependency from a public administration and worker's involvement in the delivery of services of public interest has never been affirmed as such, since, as we will *see* above, another distinction was introduced, this time based on the nature of tasks performed by the worker, that one between *public officer* and *person charged of a public service*. The first is defined as someone who works by a public administration and who is charged with duties connected to the exercise of legislative, judiciary or administrative powers (so-named *public offices*); the second one as someone, employee or civil servant, who is responsible for the delivery of a service aimed at guaranteeing basic needs of the population (*public service*). Until 1990, this distinction has to be considered relevant in order to evaluate the consequences of the abstention from work of the above-mentioned persons.

1.1 Historical Background

Bearing in mind the above-drawn definitions, it is easier to follow the evolution of the historical background of strike in general, which is strictly linked to the development of a specific regulation of strike in public-essential services. As a matter of fact, during the period in which the Italian national State was built and shaped according to strict liberal political and economic doctrine (1853-1892), workers' coalition aimed at putting pressure on the employer to obtain better working conditions and was considered a criminal offence for both *employees* and *civil servants*. Consequently, it is clear that in this period, it is impossible, from a legal point of view, even to talk about strike since the same decision of creating a coalition will be considered illegal, and the organisers, as well as participants, will be prosecuted under Criminal Law.

The situation started to change after 1892, when a new Penal Code came into force, withdrawing workers' coalition as a criminal offence. Also, from the point of view of Private Law, trade union is tolerated in the sense that no civil liability is recognised against it in case of damages provoked to the employer by a strike called by it. However, as far as the single worker is concerned, strike is considered a mere freedom so that strikers are liable for damages caused to the employer and the abstention from work is considered a breach of contract for both *employees* and *civil servants* and can lead to the dismissal of the striker.

At the same time, however, interruption and abandonment of public office by a *public officer* was considered a criminal offence giving, in this way, the opportunity to the highly conservative jurisprudence of that time to restore, de facto, penal sanctions for striking *civil servants* by extending the definition of *public officer* much further than the extent to which it was originally provided. Consequences of this aptitude were even more relevant because, in the same period, direct state intervention was increasing in many branches of the economy, as, for instance, it happened in railways sector, with a consequent growth of the number of civil servants.

Notwithstanding this difficult situation from a legal point of view, the rate of strikes, also carried out by civil servants, increased significantly after the First World War and the lack of a clear-cut political solution to the problem of industrial conflict was one of the reasons which favoured the coming of the fascist regime. During that period (1926-1944), a peculiar corporative model was imposed by the dictatorship, in which no freedom of association was recognised since all employers and employees belonging to one branch were aggregated within a corporation composed of one compulsorily joined association for each party. The aim of corporation was to control the economic development of the country by enacting directives coming from the Fascist Party and to develop peaceful industrial relations; peaceful meant that controversies could not derive a conflict, so that strike (and lock out) were considered criminal offences for both employees and civil servants. Collective controversies if arisen were solved at judicial level by a special court.

Within this legal framework which drastically excluded any form of industrial action, not surprisingly the new penal code of 1942 at Articles 330 and 333 considered interruption and abandonment of public office by *public officers* or of a *public service* by *employees* or *civil servants* as a criminal offence.

2 THE RIGHT TO STRIKE, THE ABSTENTION OF LAW AND STRIKE IN ESSENTIAL SERVICES (1948-1990)

Withdrawn in 1944, the corporative system, in 1948 Italian Constitution, came into force. It gives great relevance to workers' rights both on individual and collective levels: from this point of view, we have to stress that trade union freedom of association is affirmed as a constitutional right by Article 39, as well as strike by Article 40. This latter, inspired by Article 7 of the Preamble of the French Constitution, does not give any definition of strike, entrusting the legislator with the task of providing a legal framework within which the right must be exerted. Until 1990, no such legal provision had been issued, partly because of the strong opposition of trade unions and partly because of the lack of political agreement on the way strike had to be regulated. This has led to a massive intervention of the jurisprudence, highly influenced by the dominant doctrine of the time, which has, de facto, taken the place of the reluctant legislator giving a strict definition of lawful strike, very close to the German one.

However, the fascist Penal Code was kept in force and, within it, the abovementioned Articles 330 and 333. That would have been in evident contrast with Article 40 if those articles had been applied in case the interruption or the abandonment of a public office by *public officers* or of a public service by *employees* or *civil servants* were due to the participation to a strike. Also, in this case, the lack of intervention by the legislator in order to abolish or amend Articles 330 and 333 emphasised the role of judges who, doubting the constitutionality of such provisions after the coming into force of Article 40, suspended decisions concerning the above-mentioned controversies and asked the Constitutional Court to rule about the question.

Consequently, during almost 30 years (1958-1977), the Constitutional Court undertook the task of defining conditions within Articles 330 and 333 of the Penal Code that could be considered not contrasting with Article 40. In doing this, the Court took the opportunity to single out, on new and sound theoretical basis, the distinction between strike in general and strike in *essential services*, starting from the notion of *public office* and *public service* laid down by the above-mentioned provisions of the Penal Code. Even though in a concise way, this case law is worth summing up because of the role it has played in funding the basics of the present legislation. First of all, according to the Constitutional Court, no penal sanction can be applied in case of abandonment or interruption motivated by the participation in a *lawful strike*, i.e., a strike which does not endanger the exercise of constitutional rights of the human being.

This consideration led the Court to define as *essential services* those ones which are aimed at guaranteeing the exercise of such rights, apart from the fact that services are managed by a private or by a public body. This does not mean that strike in essential services must be prohibited at all, but that it has to be exercised taking into account the peculiar area in which it is taking place. For this purpose, the Constitutional Court laid down the principle of the *reconciliation* of the constitutional right to strike and constitutional rights of the human being. In order to allow the exercise of all the above-mentioned constitutional rights involved in industrial action, reconciliation has to be reached through the guarantee of the very core of each one of them. As a matter of fact, according to the Constitutional Court, within each essential service, it is possible to find some indispensable performances that must be in any case guaranteed in order to protect the very core of all constitutional rights involved.

Notwithstanding the clearness of principles laid down by the Constitutional Court, it was evident, and the Court itself underlined this fact in its last judgment in 1977, that a legislative intervention was needed in order to make them applicable in concrete, above all as far as the way of definition of indispensable performances was concerned. But even in presence of this authoritative 'call to order', the legislator did not provide any regulation of the matter, also because trade unions as far as strike in essential services were concerned, did not limit themselves to a mere opposition to the enforcement of an act but decided to intervene directly on the subject in order to avoid legal intervention. This happened through the spontaneous development of a self-restraint aptitude enforced through Code of Practice issued, at first, in transport service sector by major Trade Unions Confederation (CGIL - CISL - UIL) and after being adopted in many other essential services (healthcare, education, etc.) (1967-1982).

In this case too, it may be of some interest to sum up the most relevant and common contents of Code of Practices since they have influenced the present legislation and the practical definition of indispensable performances. First of all, a strike notice of 10 days had to be given to the provider of the service; second, strike will not be carried out during certain periods of the year (Christmas, Easter and summer holidays); third, part of the services has to be anyhow guaranteed, even though under different forms, for instance, trains in rush hours, first aid or final exams at school. In this way, a set of rules, indispensable performances included, begin to be established even though on voluntary basis.

The effort done by major Confederation to regulate the exercise of the right to strike through self-restraint seemed to be highly appreciated by the legislator: As a matter of fact, when in 1983, Act No. 93 introduced a peculiar form of collective bargaining for civil servants, the adoption of a Code of Practice was provided as requirement trade unions has to fulfil in order to take part in negotiations. Nevertheless, this experience did not produce hoped results due to problems deriving from the limited internal and external binding effect of the Codes. From the first point of view, difficulties have to be referred to the scarce discouraging effect of sanctions that could be imposed on members who violate provisions laid down by the Code. As a matter of fact, being union shop clauses unlawful within the Italian system, even the exclusion of a member from the association will not provoke him/her relevant consequences. From the second point of view, obviously, no effect was produced by Code of Practices on other trade unions which, most of the time, represent more or less large groups of highly skilled workers employed in key roles within the delivery of essential services (e.g., engine-drivers, medical doctors etc.), so that, the principle of reconciliation was not respected and Confederation faced a loss of members due to the self-restraint politics.

The failure of what has been called the season of self-restraint in a moment in which (1980-1990) the number of strikes in essential services rapidly increased gave the chance to right-wing parties to ask for a radical legal intervention aimed at prohibiting industrial action within this sector. For this reason, the same Confederations appointed a committee of experts in order to elaborate a proposal based on the principle of reconciliation of constitutional rights, also taking into account results reached within the Codes. Supported by the Government and merged with another two proposals coming from the Socialist and the Communist Party, it became in a few months Act No. 146 of 1990.

3 THE END OF THE ABSTENTION OF LAW AS FAR AS STRIKE IN ESSENTIAL SERVICES IS CONCERNED: ACT NO. 146 OF 1990

Constitutional Court's jurisprudence and results acquired during the season of self-restraint represent the sound theoretical basis of Act No. 146, which has no equivalent, at the moment, in Europe. Its aim is to reconcile the exercise of the constitutional right to strike with the exercise of constitutional rights of the human being by defining rules and procedures in order to guarantee the very core of such rights consisting in some indispensable performances. Reconciliation in this perspective can be considered, at the same time, a goal and a method to guarantee the above-mentioned constitutional rights in case of strike. As a matter of fact, essential services are defined as those ones aimed at guaranteeing the exercise of constitutional rights of the human being apart from the legal status of the provider and of the employment relationship (Article 1, paragraph 1). In this view, Articles 330 and 333 of the Penal Code - still referring, although within the mentioned conditions laid down by the Court, to the interruption and abandonment of public office or a public service as a criminal offence – have been eventually repealed.

3.1 Definition of Essential Services

Constitutional rights of the human being are listed exhaustively in the law (the right to life, healthcare, freedom and security, freedom of movement, social security, justice, education, freedom of communication) (Article 1, paragraph 1) while, the same Act No. 146 provides a non-exhaustive list of services which must be considered essential (Article 1, paragraph 2). In this way, the chance is left open for any sort of technical evolution which can, in the future, provide new means (and, consequently, new services) to exercise the above-mentioned rights. One can say that the legislator has opted for the technique of a dynamic definition of essential services in relation to their aptitude to guarantee the exercise of constitutional rights of the human being.

3.2 Requirements of Lawful Strike in Essential Services

So defined the objective scope of application of the law, also the requirements of lawful strike in essential services laid down by Act No. 146 of 1990 (Article 2, paragraphs 1 and 2) have also to be seen within the view of reconciliation. The first procedural requirement is a written strike notice of at least 10 days addressed to the provider by the relevant trade union in order to make it able to reorganise the service, taking into account the fact that some workers will join the strike. The second one is the indication of the duration of the strike that has to be indicated within the notice, i.e., the day of beginning and the end of industrial action, in order to allow the provider to communicate to users the duration of the inconveniences: This means that the so-named all-out strike cannot be considered lawful according to Act No. 146. The third one is the indication of the way the strike will be organised that has to be contained within the same notice. Fourth, most important and also most difficult requirement to be realised in concrete is the guarantee of indispensable performances during the strike.

3.2.1 Indispensable Performances

As a matter of fact, one of the crucial aspects of an effective reconciliation between the right to strike and constitutional rights of the human being is represented by the fact that, in one way or another, a lawful strike cannot lead to the complete stop of the service. So, the question is: How and by whom shall *indispensable performances* be defined? Coherently to the above-described principle of open and dynamic definition of essential services, *indispensable performances,* too, are not directly and statically defined once and for all by the law, but their individuation is entrusted to collective bargaining carried out among service providers and trade unions representing workers involved in the delivery of the service. This means a peculiar application of the principle of vertical subsidiarity, according to which the legislator lets parties daily involved in the organisation of the service or the task to define performances that have to be considered indispensable because they are able to realise the very core of the constitutional right concerned. This also means that the content of *indispensable performances* may vary from service to service according to the nature of the right that has to be guaranteed. For instance, in the railway sector, it has been decided that not only a train that leaves its station of departure has to arrive at the final destination but also that trains scheduled at certain periods of the day have to be always guaranteed and that within the same day, at least a certain number of trains has to connect major towns of the Country. However, a similar quantitative interpretation of indispensable performances may not fit into other services and rights. Let us take the example of healthcare sector in which first aid has to be always guaranteed without any restriction on time and number of practitioners and nursing staff.

This choice which has the big advantage of a direct involvement of knowledge and competence acquired by the parties during the structuring and the managing of the service in the definition of indispensable performances also presents some relevant problematic aspects. First of all, if it is possible to derive from Act No. 146 a duty to fairly bargain imposed on the parties, this does not mean that an agreement will be certainly reached. And even in case an agreement is reached, how is it possible to be sure that performances singled out as indispensable really reach the aim of reconciliation? Second, due to the fact that Italian trade union movement, above all in essential services, is highly fragmented, an agreement, although signed by the most important trade unions, will hardly cover all workers involved in the delivery of the service. If we add that in Italy, collective agreements apply only to the signing parties and to their members, an evident problem of effectiveness of indispensable performances may arise.

3.3 The Commissioner

In order to solve at least some of these problems, Act No. 146 provides the institution of an independent Commissioner composed of nine experts in Labour Law, Constitutional Law and Industrial Relations appointed every three years by the Presidents of the Chambers of Parliament which, in case of agreement, has the task to evaluate the suitability of *indispensable performances* to reach the aim of reconciliation. If the agreement is considered not suitable or if the parties do not succeed in reaching it, the Commissioner issues a provisional proposal, which is considered binding until a suitable agreement is reached. Such a solution, which was not directly contained in the law, has been elaborated by the same Commissioner, supported by case law, and eventually accepted by Act No. 83 of 2000 (and called *provisional regulation*) which, as we will *see* below, has substantially modified Act No. 146. Starting in 1991, the Commissioner has made a tremendous effort in order to stimulate the conclusion of suitable agreements in all sectors in which essential services are delivered, so that only a few of the provisional regulations issued by the Commissioner are still in force.

3.4 Sanctions

In order to give effectiveness to the above-described system, a complex system of sanctions has been provided by Act No. 146. It concerns all the subjects involved in the delivery of essential services because of the spreading of responsibility among individual workers, trade unions and providers. The provision of sanctions by the law has to be considered very important and innovative, since until 1990 in Italy, it was almost impossible to affirm the existence of an unlawful strike, as has now to be considered that one carried out in violation of the above-mentioned sanction. Due to the fact that the involvement of the above-mentioned subject is realised on the ground of highly differentiated juridical situations, sanctions obviously differ in contents and in nature.

Individual workers who do not respect the duty to perform indispensable performances are subjected to disciplinary sanctions, according to disciplinary code, usually provided by enterprise regulations or collective agreements, except for dismissal, which is considered inapplicable.

Trade unions that strike violating the above-mentioned requirements are submitted to monetary sanctions through the withdrawal of pay leaves due according to legal provisions to their officers or to the exclusion from collective bargaining for a certain period of time. The application of sanctions to trade unions has raised many problems as Act No. 146 entrusted the relevant employer with this task, giving him or her the relevant power to evaluate trade unions' behaviour. This has led legislator to modify the provision by Act No. 83 of 2000 in the sense that before sanctions are imposed by the employer, trade unions' behaviour has to be evaluated by the Commissioner.

Last but not least, providers which do not cooperate in guaranteeing the respect of the above-mentioned requirements or in reactivating the service immediately after the strike are subjected to administrative pecuniary sanctions.

3.5 Summoning

Apart from this sanctioning system, Act No. 146 (Article 8) recognises to the Government, relevant ministers, majors and prefects the power of summoning workers. It has to be said that well before the enforcement of Act No. 146, summoning was widely used by the executive in order to avoid inconveniences deriving for users by the unregulated exercise of the right to strike in essential services. For many years, it was the only instrument of intervention on it due to the above reminded abstention of law. Within the preliminary debate on the drafting of Act No. 146, it was proposed to abolish summoning as a way of intervention in case of strike, but, at the end it was decided to confirm it only in case of an impending and serious danger for the very core of constitutional rights of the human being. In issuing the summoning order, competent authorities have to take into account, if possible, Commissioner's proposals and regulations. Summoning has also been modified by Act No. 83 of 2002 in order to limit its use in emergency situations.

4 A CHANGE OF PERSPECTIVE: CONFLICT IN ESSENTIAL SERVICES

Under the Light of Act No. 83 of 2000

In 2000, 10 years after its coming into force, Act No. 146 was deeply modified by Act No. 83, above all for two reasons. First, as clearly comes up by the analysis of lawful strike requirements, Act No. 146 intervened only *ex post*, when the dispute degenerated into conflict and the conflict led to a strike. This means that Act No. 146 did not prevent strikes in essential services but only regulated them according to the principle of *reconciliation*. Second, more and more, the delivery of essential services is endangered by the abstention of self-employed (for instance, barristers) or of small entrepreneurs (for instance, chemists); meanwhile, Act No. 146 only applied to strikes, i.e., to *employees*. So, even though it was possible to affirm that Act No. 146 was reaching its aim, from a general point of view, users of essential services claimed a more effective legal intervention in order to face, on the one hand, the increasing number of lawful strikes, carried out according to the requirements laid down by Act No. 146, and, on the other, interruptions of the service deriving from the abstention from their activity of non-employees.

Following these considerations, Act No. 83 of 2000 has intervened above all on two points, besides the still mentioned modifications: First of all, it has introduced preventive measures in order to reduce to the minimum the risk that disputes degenerate into conflicts and strikes; second, it has coped with the problem of abstention of non-employees.

From the first point of view, Act No. 83 has established rules and procedures in order to look for a solution to the dispute or the conflict instead of strike; it has imposed obligation on the parties to go through conciliation procedures, either established by collective agreement or provided by the Labour Office; it has imposed a duty of trade union to declare within the written notice motivations of the strike; finally it has given powers to the Commissioner to intervene within the dispute or within the conflict as conciliator.

From the second point of view, Act No. 83 of 2000 has extended provisions laid down in case of strike to all abstentions which endanger the very core of essential services. In this case too, the system of indispensable performances has been provided, obviously not through collective agreements but through unilateral code of practice issued by self-employed and entrepreneurs associations, submitted to the suitability evaluation of the Commissioner.

CHAPTER 20

Restrictions on the Right to Strike in Latvia

Annija Kārkliņa

1 GENERAL INFORMATION

1.1 Legal Basis of the Right to Strike

The right to strike is one of the fundamental rights incorporated in the Constitution of the Republic of Latvia - *Satversme* (hereinafter 'Constitution').[1] Article 108 of the Constitution states: 'Employed persons have the right to a collective labour agreement, and the right to strike.' The Constitution of Latvia was adopted in 1922, but the regulation of the right to strike has been included in it only since 1998, when the Constitution was supplemented with Chapter VIII, 'Fundamental Human Rights', including an expanded and modern catalogue of fundamental rights.

The legal definition of a strike is given in section 1 paragraph 3 of the Strike Law, which defines a strike as a means of resolving a collective interest dispute that manifests itself in such a way that employees or a group of employees of a branch of an undertaking voluntarily, completely or in part, discontinue work in order to attain the fulfilment of demands.[2] The case law of the Constitutional Court of Latvia explains that the right to strike as one of the most important means that employees can use to promote and protect their economic and professional interests.[3]

1. The Constitution of the Republic of Latvia (15 February 1922), https://likumi.lv/ta/id/57980-latvijas-republikas-satversme.
2. Strike Law of the Republic of Latvia (23 April 1998), https://likumi.lv/ta/id/48074-streiku-likums.
3. Judgment of the Constitutional Court of the Republic of Latvia Case No. 2006-42-01, 16 May 2007, para. 7.2, chrome-extension://efaidnbmnnnibpcajpcglclefindmkaj/https://www.satv.tiesa.gov.lv/wp-content/uploads/2006/12/2006-42-01_Spriedums_ENG.pdf, with a reference to *Freedom of Association: Digest of Decisions and Principles of the Freedom of Association Committee of the*

In the context of the right to strike, reference should also be made to the content of Article 89 of the Constitution, which states that: 'The State shall recognize and protect fundamental human rights in accordance with this Constitution, laws and international agreements binding upon Latvia.' International norms of human rights and the practice of their application at the level of Constitutional Law are a means of interpretation in order to determine the content and scope of fundamental rights and other general principles of law, insofar as this does not lead to a reduction or restriction of the fundamental rights enshrined in the Constitution. The Constitutional Court of Latvia has recognized that in disclosing the rights specified in the Constitution, it is necessary to be guided by international human rights documents, i.e., that the legislator's goal to achieve harmony of the human rights norms enshrined in the Constitution with the norms of international law follows from Article 89 of the Constitution.[4] Taking into account that Latvia is bound by the documents of the universal, European, and European Union human rights systems, it is also bound by the obligations specified in these sources of law in the context of the right to strike.

1.2 Main Features of the Regulation

To fully understand the content of the right to strike, it is necessary to identify the group of subjects who enjoy the right to strike. Article 3 of the Strike Law stipulates that 'the employees of a branch of an undertaking' are entitled to declare a strike, later denoting this group of persons with the common term, i.e., *employees*. However, this umbrella term identifies a group of people entitled to strike incompletely and requires a more comprehensive explanation.

The term *employee* is commonly used to designate a person who works for another person on the basis of a legal relationship established through an employment contract signed between the employer and employee. Thus, the term *employee* does not include all persons working in the public service.

Notwithstanding the aforesaid, the civil servants also are entitled to strike. The legal doctrine explains that a complete prohibition for civil servants to strike constitutes a violation of the right to strike.[5] People working in the public service must also have a right to discontinue their work and it is not sufficient if civil servants are allowed to declare a strike only symbolically while continuing working, i.e., without interrupting work.[6] However, the right to strike of people working in the public service is limited to

Governing Body of the ILO (Geneva: International Labour Office, 5th ed. 2006), p. 109, https://www.ilo.org/sites/default/files/wcmsp5/groups/public/%40ed_norm/%40normes/documents/publication/wcms_090632.pdf.

4. Judgment of the Constitutional Court of the Republic of Latvia Case No. 01/05/2021, 4 November 2021, para. 10.1, https://www.satv.tiesa.gov.lv/wp-content/uploads/2021/01/2021-05-01_Spriedums.pdf.
5. A. Kovaļevska, *Komentars Satversmes 108.pantam* [*Commentary on Art. 108*], in *Latvijas Republikas Satversmes komentari. VIII nodaļa. Cilveka pamattiesības* [*Commentary on Constitution of the Republic of Latvia. Chapter VIII. Fundamental Human Rights*] Autoru kolektīvs prof. Baloža R. zinatniska vadība. Rīga: Latvijas Vestnesis (2011), p. 544.
6. *Ibid.*

cases laid down in the Strike Law (for more information about limitations of the right to strike *see* section 2).

Once a group of people who enjoy the right to strike is identified, it is necessary to briefly outline the procedure according to which these subjects are entitled to exercise their right to strike. There are two models of exercising the right to strike in the countries of the European Union:

(1) a trade union of employees has the right to declare a strike based on the decision taken at the general meeting of members; and
(2) a strike can be declared by employees themselves, adopting a resolution on declaring a strike in the general meeting of employees.

The European Court of Human Rights (ECHR) has pointed out that Article 11 of the Convention protects only the rights of a trade union to declare a strike of its employees (members), which is considered to be the minimum protection guaranteed by the right to strike.[7] However, the Latvian legislator has provided a higher level of protection to the right to strike. Article 11 paragraph 1 of the Strike Law establishes a procedure for declaring the strike by the trade union, i.e., 'A trade union shall take a decision regarding the declaration of a strike in accordance with the procedures prescribed by the articles of association at a general meeting of the members thereof and in which more than half of the number of members of such trade union participate. A decision shall be taken in a simple majority of the members of the relevant trade union ... .'

Besides that, paragraph 1 of Article 12 of the Law entitles the employees to make a decision on declaring the strike themselves: 'Employees shall take a decision regarding the declaration of a strike at a general meeting of employees of the relevant undertaking in which at least half of the number of the employees of this undertaking participate. The decision shall be taken when a simple majority of the employees of the relevant undertaking who are present have voted for it by secret ballot ... .'

Thus, the aforementioned legal norms not only reveal the commitment of the Latvian legislator to comply with higher measures for the protection of the right to strike but also indicate that there is a certain procedure for declaring strikes. Observance of the prescribed procedure should be seen not as a formal whim of the legislator but as an essential prerequisite for the validity of a strike application.

The State has the right to determine the procedure for the declaration of a strike. However, the procedural requirements to apply for a strike should not be so complex that it is almost impossible to declare a strike.[8]

Pursuant to paragraph 1 of Article 23 of the Strike Law, a strike or a declaration of strike shall be regarded as unlawful (illegal) if this law has been violated or the strike

7. Judgment of the European Court of Human Rights (ECHR) *Selçuk BARIŞ v. Turkey*, No. 66828/16, 14 December 2021, para. 45.
8. A. Kovaļevska, *Komentars Satversmes 108.pantam* [*Commentary on Art. 108*], in *Latvijas Republikas Satversmes komentari. VIII nodaļa. Cilveka pamattiesības* [*Commentary on Constitution of the Republic of Latvia. Chapter VIII. Fundamental Human Rights*] Latvijas Vestnesis (2011), p. 544.

was initiated in order to express political requirements, political support or political protest. A strike is considered to be unlawful also if it pertains to the issues upon which the parties have already agreed during strike negotiations.[9]

Only the court has the authority to declare a strike or a declaration of strike unlawful.[10] It must be stated in this regard that in Latvia, the court quite rarely exerts its control over declaration of strikes. Between 2008 and 2021, three court judgments of general jurisdiction have been adopted and enforced whereby declarations of strike have been acknowledged as unlawful.[11] In all those cases, it was concluded that a declaration of strike does not comply with the requirements laid down in Article 3 paragraph 2 of the Strike Law, i.e., the right to strike was not exercised as the last resort for solving the dispute.

Paragraph 2 of Article 3 of the Strike Law stipulates that the right to strike is exercised as a measure of last resort if no agreement and reconciliation has been reached in the collective interest dispute. The Constitutional Court of Latvia also has explained that the strike is the ultimate mechanism for the protection of interests of employees, which nevertheless may not be put forth as a goal in itself. The exercise of the right to strike is related to a set of certain circumstances and conditions that demonstrate the impossibility of solving a collective labour dispute. The possibility to exercise this right only exists when no agreement and no reconciliation have been achieved in a dispute over collective interests.[12] It is a principle of *ultima ratio* which has been determined, taking into account the potential impact of the strike not only on the economic interests of the employer but also on public interest of society and the State.[13]

The relevant trade union or group of employees who have accepted the decision to strike has the obligation to prove that negotiations with the employer have been conducted before the implementation of the strike, but the employer has not responded to the requirements put forward by the employees. Furthermore, a vital role in the question of the legality of the strike declaration must be attached to whether the employer has been made aware of all the disputed circumstances of which the strike is actually taking place.[14] For example, a strike prior to which an employer has been notified of the employees' objections to circumstance *A*; however, a declaration of strike lists objections to both circumstance *A* and a new circumstance *B* that was not known to the employer is not lawful.

---

9. *See* Art. 23(2).
10. *See* Art. 24(1).
11. *See* judgment of Kurzeme Regional Court of the Republic of Latvia Case No. C69265119, 17 June 2019; judgment of Riga City Vidzeme District Court of the Republic of Latvia Case No. C30714521, 29 October 2021; judgment of Riga City Northern District Court of the Republic of Latvia Case No. C32244117, 5 October 2017.
12. Judgment of the Constitutional Court of the Republic of Latvia Case No. 2006-42-01, 16 May 2007, para. 7.1.
13. A. Repšs & M. Badovskis, *Par Streiku likumu: ar konkretam piebildem* [*About the Law on Strikes: With specific comments*] Jurista Vards, No. 10 (117) (18 May1999).
14. *See* judgment of Kurzeme Regional Court of the Republic of Latvia Case No. C69265119, 17 June 2019; judgment of Riga City Vidzeme District Court of the Republic of Latvia Case No. C30714521, 29 October 2021; judgment of Riga City Northern District Court of the Republic of Latvia Case No. C32244117, 5 October 2017.

The initiation and declaration of strike as well as the participation in a strike leads to consequences arising out of the Strike Law. Pursuant to paragraph 1 of Article 26 of the Strike Law, the initiation and declaration of a strike and participation in a strike shall not be considered to be a violation of the employment contract or labour rights and, therefore, shall not constitute grounds for the dismissal of employees. During the strike, the employees keep their jobs and may not be subject to disciplinary sanctions.[15] Imposing sanctions on trade unions or members of the trade unions for organizing a lawful strike is a gross violation of the freedom of trade unions. No one can be punished for a lawful strike or an attempt thereof. Employees who are not members of the trade union which declared the strike but who participate in the strike must receive the same level of protection as the members of the trade union.[16]

In addition to the aforesaid, it must be stressed that not in each case of a strike declared by a group of employees or a trade union, all employees of an employer will actually exercise their rights to strike granted by the Constitution and the Strike Law. Given that employees usually do not receive remuneration (Article 28 paragraph 1 of the Strike Law) during the strike, some employees may not be interested in striking and rather continue their jobs. In such situations, special attention must be paid to paragraph 2 of Article 30 of the Strike Law, which stipulates that 'employees who do not participate in a strike and continue to work may not be forced to assume the work of the striking employees'. This legal framework of the Strike Law corresponds to provisions of Article 56 of the Labour Law, which in essence prohibits the employer from unilaterally instructing an employee to take on additional duties not stated in their employment contract.[17]

According to statistical data, the right to strike is actively used not only in Europe but also in other countries.[18]

Strikes in Latvia occur rather seldom. In fact, since the restoration of independence of Latvia in 1990, there has not been a single strike in the private sector of Latvia. The largest strikes have taken place in the healthcare and education sectors, where they were related to issues of salary of teachers and medical staff and demanded to increase budget for these sectors in general.[19]

---

15. Articles 26 (2) and 26 (3) of the Strike Law.
16. A. Kovaļevska, *Komentars Satversmes 108.pantam* [*Commentary on Art. 108*], in *Latvijas Republikas Satversmes komentari. VIII nodaļa.* Cilveka pamattiesības [*Commentary on Constitution of the Republic of Latvia. Chapter VIII. Fundamental Human Rights*] Latvijas Vestnesis (2011), p. 545. With a reference to *Freedom of Association: Digest of Decisions and Principles of the Freedom of Association Committee of the Governing Body of the ILO* (Geneva: International Labour Office, 5th ed. 2006), p. 129.
17. *Latvijas Brīvo arodbiedrību savienība. Darba likums ar komentariem,* [*Commentary on the Labour Law*] (2020), p. 158, https://arodbiedribas.lv/wp-content/uploads/2020/02/new_dl_ar_kom.pdf.
18. S. Yanatma, *Which Countries Have the Most Strikes in Europe and What Impact Does It Have on the Economy?* (7 March 2023), https://www.euronews.com/next/2023/03/07/industrial-action-in-france-and-the-uk-which-countries-have-the-most-strikes-in-europe. With a reference to: *Strike Map of Europe*, https://www.etui.org/strikes-map.
19. European Trade Union Institute, *Strikes in Latvia: Background Summary* (23 January 2017) https://www.etui.org/covid-social-impact/latvia/strikes-in-latvia-background-summary; A. Katlaps, *Streiku kustība Latvija* [*Strike Movement in Latvia*], https://providus.lv/raksti/streiku-kustiba-latvija/.

Although strikes are organized relatively rare in Latvia, in cases where healthcare and education workers have exercised these rights, the strike has proven to be an effective means of legal protection - as a result of these strikes, the demands of employees of the relevant sectors have not only been heard but also fulfilled in most cases.

Legislation of Latvia also determines administrative liability in the field of strike; for example, a fine is provided for the employer for forcing an employee who does not participate in a strike to take on the work of striking employees, as well as for hiring employees instead of striking employees in order to prevent or stop a strike or to hinder the fulfilment of the requirements of striking employees.[20] However, a person authorized by a trade union may be held liable for invitation to an illegal strike or for continuation of an illegal strike.[21]

2 PERMITTED RESTRICTIONS

2.1 Certain Categories of Public Servants

The right of employees to strike is not absolute. Article 116 of the Constitution also stipulates *expressis verbis* that the individual's right to strike under Article 108 of the Constitution may be restricted in cases laid down in law to ensure one of five legitimate goals mentioned in the Constitution, i.e., rights of other people, democratic structure of the State, public safety, welfare, and morality.[22] Similarly, the ECHR has stated that the right to strike may be restricted, but in individual cases regarding certain professions which are vital for society, such restriction may be absolute. In this aspect, it should be mentioned that a complete prohibition of exercise of these rights must have a solid ground that justifies such limitation.[23] The Latvian legislator, just like legislators of other countries,[24] has listed several professions in Articles 16 and 17 of the Strike Law which either are completely prohibited from striking or their possibility to exercise the right to strike under the Constitution is limited to an extent stated in the law.

Article 16 of the Strike Law states: 'Judges, prosecutors, police officers, employees of fire safety, firefighting and rescue services, border guards, employees of the State security institutions, warders and persons who serve in the National Armed Forces are prohibited from striking.' This legal norm contains a list of working individuals mentioned before to whom the prohibition to strike is absolute. Without the work of those persons, there is a general threat mostly to persons' rights and freedoms as well

20. Article 34.
21. *See* Arts 35 and 36.
22. Judgment of the Constitutional Court of the Republic of Latvia Case No. 2006-42-01, 16 May 2007, para. 8.
23. Judgment of the ECHR *Ognevenko v. Russia*, No. 44873/09, 20 November 2018, paras 72-73.
24. N. Mickeviča, Project of the European Social Fund 'Strengthening of the administrative capacity of Free Trade Union Confederation of Latvia'. Report of 30 December 2010. *Streiku regulejums Eiropas Savienības dalībvalstīs* [*Regulation of Strikes in the Member States of the European Union*] (2010), p. 16, https://arodbiedribas.lv/wp-content/uploads/2019/11/streiku_tiesiskais_regulejums_30122010.pdf.

as interests of the State.[25] A limitation of the right to strike under Article 16 of the Strike Law corresponds to the notion of 'absolute prohibition' defined in its practice by the Constitutional Court. Namely, in the practice of the Constitutional Court, an absolute prohibition is a prohibition that applies to all persons in a certain group without evaluating certain cases individually, and it is determined for life.[26] When evaluating the constitutionality of an absolute prohibition, the Constitutional Court has elaborated and so far consequently applied a methodology for evaluating the constitutionality of the absolute prohibition, according to which the court makes sure if the legislator has:

(1) substantiated a need for absolute prohibition;
(2) evaluated the essence of absolute prohibition and consequences of application;
(3) substantiated that by including exceptions in this absolute prohibition, its goal would not be achieved at the same quality.[27]

Recently – in the year 2022 – a draft law prepared by the Cabinet of Ministers on amending section 16 of the Strike Law was submitted for consideration to the Latvian Parliament. The draft law provided for extension of the strike restriction also to officials (employees) of the tax and customs police of the State Revenue Service. The annotation of the draft law explained that the legitimate aim of this absolute restriction would be 'to find appropriate balance between the rights and legitimate interests of employees and the protection of the rights of other people'.[28] However, the previous convocation of parliament did not accept this draft law and the newly elected convocation decided not to proceed with the bill.[29]

2.2 Essential Services in the Strict Sense of the Term

Article 17 of the Strike Law determines professions which, although not completely denied, nevertheless have a limited right to strike. Namely, paragraph 1 of Article 17 states: 'The employer and the strike committee shall ensure that during a strike the minimum amount of work is continued in the services, undertakings necessary to public (hereinafter 'the services necessary to public') the discontinuation of which would cause a threat to national security or the safety, health or life of the entire population, certain groups of inhabitants or particular individuals.'

25. A. Repšs & M. Badovskis, *Par Streiku likumu: ar konkretam piebildem* [*About the Law on Strikes: With Specific Comments*] Jurista Vards No. 11 (118) (18 May 1999).
26. A. Kučs & I. Šņepste, *Absoluti cilvektiesību ierobežojumi Satversmes tiesas judikatura* [*Absolute Restrictions of Human Rights in the Jurisprudence of the Constitutional Court*] Jurista Vards, No. 49 (1211) (7 December 2021), pp. 51-55.
27. *See* for example: Judgment of the Constitutional Court Case No. 2020-18-01, 17 December 2020, para. 21.
28. *Assessment report on the initial impact of the draft law 'Amendment to the Strike Law'* (annotation), https://tapportals.mk.gov.lv/annotation/ea597be3-4b66-4703-bc9c-6c8d20cac339.
29. *Ibid.*

Meanwhile, paragraph 2 of Article 17 defines what is understood under a term 'services necessary to public'. Namely, during the strike, the persons working in the following services must continue to work at the minimum scope:

- medical treatment and first aid services;
- public transport services;
- drinking water supply services;
- electricity and gas production and supplies services;
- communication services;
- air traffic control services and the services which provide air traffic control services with meteorological information;
- services related to the safety of movement of all forms of transport;
- waste and wastewater collection and treatment services;
- radioactive substances and waste storage, utilization, and control services;
- civil defence services.

It has been concluded in the legal literature that the previous list can only be considered a general list of services which are necessary to public.[30] This approach is justified by the fact that it is actually not possible and not even desirable to provide an exact list of such services in the law: 'If the list of such services was too broad, the principle of restricting the right to strike in the services important for public would lose its meaning. The Strike Law outlines the main criteria to be consulted in order to determine if the relevant service is important for public. In order to determine it, one must conclude to what extent the public life depends on the service in question.'[31]

The employer and the strike committee reached an agreement on continuing the minimum level of work according to provisions of paragraph 3 of Article 17 of the Strike Law. But in case the parties to the labour dispute from the collective do not ensure that these needs are met, the State Labour Inspectorate provides them with binding guidelines to continue the work in the service necessary for public at minimum scope by specifying the number of employees who must perform the said task.[32] Employees working in the essential services are bound by:

- the scope of practical work determined by the employer and decrees aiming at providing the work of the service necessary for public;
- the minimum scope of work stated in the employment contract or collective agreement during the strike.[33]

Article 18 of the Law states that, if needed, the strike committee and the employer may agree on the measures to be taken during the strike in the following three cases:

30. A. Repšs & M. Badovskis, *Par Streiku likumu: ar konkretam piebildem* [*About the Law on Strikes: With Specific Comments*] Jurista Vards, No. 12 (119) (27 March 1999).
31. *Ibid.*
32. *See* Art. 21.
33. A. Repšs & M. Badovskis, *Par Streiku likumu: ar konkretam piebildem* [*About the Law on Strikes: With Specific Comments*] Jurista Vards, No. 12 (119) (27 March 1999).

(1) maintain the undertaking, machinery, and equipment or devices thereof in such condition which would allow the recommencement of work immediately after the termination of the strike;
(2) ensure the guarding of raw materials, finished and unfinished products of an undertaking;
(3) assume the guarding of the machinery and premises of an undertaking.

It must however be emphasized that such an agreement applies only to the minimum level of the tasks mentioned in Article 18. If other circumstances different from those laid down in this law are determined in a collective employment agreement or an employment contract with an employee who does not work at the services necessary for public, a refusal of the employee to perform a certain task cannot be considered a violation of the working rules and he or she may not be held liable.[34]

2.3 Situations of Acute National or Local Crisis

The right to strike may also be restricted during a state of exception declared in the State. Such situations are regulated in Latvia in the *Law On Emergency Situation and State of Exception*. Clause 4 of paragraph 1 of Article 17 of this Law states that depending on the type, intensity, and nature of threat to national security, the Cabinet of Ministers may determine restrictions for organizing strikes or a prohibition to organize them.[35]

A matter of admissibility of strikes during emergency situations was brought to attention in 2020 when, during the COVID-19 pandemic in Latvia, just like in other countries, an emergency situation was declared and significant restrictions were imposed, including mandatory staying at home and prohibition of various forms of gathering. Back then, labour law experts reflected on a hypothetical possibility of whether such an emergency situation implies a restriction to exercise the right to strike. Special laws and regulations that governed restrictions during the pandemic did not elaborate on strikes. Labour law specialists concluded that although a strike in its common meaning usually brings associations with gathering of the working people, processions, and pickets of workers, at the same time, a strike, pursuant to Article 1 of the Strike Law, is a way of resolving a collective interest dispute that manifests itself in such a way that employees or a group of employees of a branch of an undertaking voluntarily, completely or in part, discontinue work in order to attain the fulfilment of demands. Therefore, strike as such means a discontinuation of work and public pickets or processions within the framework of the strike are not mandatory.[36]

34. *Ibid.*
35. *On the Emergency Situation and State of Exception* (7 March 2013), https://likumi.lv/ta/en/en/id/255713-on-emergency-situation-and-state-of-exception.
36. K. Racenajs & N. Preisa, *Arodbiedrību tiesības un to īstenošana arkartejas situacijas laika* [*Trade Union Rights and Its Implementation During an Emergency Situation*] (LBAS 23 April 2020), https://arodbiedribas.lv/news/arodbiedribu-tiesibas-un-to-istenosana-arkartejas-situacijas-laika/.

3 COMPENSATORY GUARANTEES FOR WORKERS DEPRIVED OF THE RIGHT TO STRIKE

With a view to the fact that the representatives of several previously mentioned professions are prohibited from striking, the State provides various compensatory mechanisms to the representatives of these professions. The compensatory guarantees are mainly linked to payment of salary, organization of working hours, benefits, and legal framework of pensions.

Matters of employment for the representatives of professions listed in Article 16 of the Strike Law are mainly governed by:

- Law On Remuneration of Officials and Employees of State and Local Government Authorities (hereinafter 'Remuneration Law').[37]
- Law on the Course of Service of Officials with Special Service Ranks Working in Institutions of the System of the Ministry of the Interior and the Prison Administration (hereinafter 'Course of Service Law').[38]

The Remuneration Law governs the salary of judges, prosecutors, and soldiers while the Course of Service Law and Remuneration Law governs that of police employees, fire safety, firefighting, and rescue service employees, customs guards, employees of state security bodies, and prison guards. Further, only some compensatory mechanisms for the previously mentioned representatives of professions will be indicated, since the range of these mechanisms is rather wide.

Hence, according to Clause 4 of paragraph 3 of Article 3 of the Remuneration Law, judges are entitled to several additional holidays (e.g., a paid day off on the first school day when the child starts attending school, holidays when getting married, a paid day off on the graduation day, when the official (employee) or his/her child graduates from an educational establishment, etc.). Article 15 also determines special supplements. For example, if a judge has received a positive statement in the regular assessment of the professional activity of a judge, a service supplement to the monthly salary shall be determined for the judge in the following amount: 5% (after 6 years worked in the office), and 10% of the monthly salary (after 10 years worked in the office).

In addition to general and special supplements as well as bonuses, the Remuneration Law determines a compensation of various expenses. For example, paragraph 1 of Article 26 of the Remuneration Law states that tuition expenditures may be compensated for officials (employees), if they, upon initiative of the authority or upon mutual agreement, successfully study in higher education in order to acquire the special knowledge necessary for the performance of the office duties.

37. *Law on Remuneration of Officials and Employees of State and Local Government Authorities of Republic of Latvia* (1 December 2009), https://likumi.lv/ta/en/en/id/202273-law-on-remuneration-of-officials-and-employees-of-state-and-local-government-authorities.
38. *The Law on the Course of Service of Officials with Special Service Ranks Working in Institutions of the System of the Ministry of the Interior and the Prison Administration* (15 June 2006), https://likumi.lv/ta/id/138750-iekslietu-ministrijas-sistemas-iestazu-un-ieslodzijuma-vietu-parvaldes-amatpersonu-ar-specialajam-dienesta-pakapem-dienesta-gai.

The law specifically discerns compensations intended for soldiers. For example, covering expenditures for the rental of living quarters and public utilities. The Remuneration Law also provides for various compensatory mechanisms in connection with healthcare of the officials (employees).

The regulation of term of service and service pensions for persons who have served in the system of the Ministry of the Interior, the Prison Administration or military services can also be considered compensatory mechanisms.[39]

4 CONCLUSION

- The right to strike is one of the fundamental rights enshrined in the Constitution of the Republic of Latvia. Considering the principle of harmonization, international European Union law and the case law of those courts also play an important role in the development and disclosure of the content of this fundamental right.
- Strike is a collective interest dispute that manifests itself in such a way that employees or a group of employees of a branch of an undertaking voluntarily, completely or in part, discontinue work in order to attain the fulfilment of demands.
  It is one of the key measures the employees can use to promote and protect their economic and professional interests. The right to strike is enjoyed also by all persons working in public service with some exceptions laid down in Articles 16 and 17 of the Strike Law.
- The State is entitled to put forth a procedure to follow when declaring a strike. However, the procedural requirements for declaring the strike must not have the complexity that almost prevents the strike from being declared. A failure to comply with the procedure laid down for declaration of the strike constitutes solid grounds to announce the strike declaration invalid.
- Since a strike may affect not only the economic interests of an employer but also interests of the entire public and the State, it must be used only as an ultimate means (last resort) for solving collective labour disputes. A trade union or a group of employees in question that has adopted a declaration of a strike must prove that negotiations with the employer took place before the strike; however, the employer did not respond to the requirements put forth by the employees.
- The right of employees to strike is not absolute. The Latvian legislator has listed several professions which either are completely prohibited from striking or limited to exercising this right to the extent stated in the law. Laws provide several compensatory mechanisms regarding these professions' salaries, their right to rest, their right to retire, and other social guarantees.

39. *On the Service Pensions of Employees with Special Service Ranks Working in the System of the Ministry of the Interior* (2 April 1998), https://likumi.lv/ta/id/47744-par-izdienas-pensijam-iekslietu-ministrijas-sistemas-darbiniekiem-ar-specialajam-dienesta-pakapem.

CHAPTER 21

Restrictions on the Right to Strike in Lithuania

Tomas Davulis

The present article examines the limitations and restrictions of the right to strike in Lithuania. Analysis of the general legal framework of the settlement of collective disputes over rights in Lithuania provides the foundation for more specific research on the limitations of the right to strike. They are related to the worker's status, specific sectors of the employer's activities, or certain extraordinary situations, which may be used to justify the deprivation of employees of this necessary instrument to demand higher pay or improvement of other working conditions. Against the broader background of international and European standards, this article highlights problematic points of the Lithuanian legal provisions regulating the right to strike.

1 GENERAL INFORMATION

1.1 Legal Foundation of the Right to Strike

The first industrial actions in the territory of Lithuania were registered relatively late (49 stone masons working on the railway construction went on strike in 1861) and they were not frequent or large in terms of the number of striking workers. The stoppage of work by workers was mostly perceived as a last resort measure to resisting the brutal violation of rights (non-payment of wages, unilateral reductions of pay, mass dismissals)[1] and not as the regular outcome of the ongoing collective bargaining process. This is true for the late industrialization period until 1940, when Lithuania lost its independence after the soviet annexation. Naturally, in the Soviet Union, strikes were a 'taboo issue' under the state socialist regime like other Eastern European countries of the

1. P. Stukas, *Streikai Lietuvoje* (Strikes in Lithuania), *Lietuvos darbininkas*, No. 17, p. 8 (1998).

socialist block, in spite of the fact that the countries concerned had ratified a number of international treaties, including International Labour Organisation (ILO) Conventions, which included the right to strike.[2]

The lack of traditions and the long history of the strong role of the repressing state as a regulator of social life can basically explain why, after the restoration of independence in 1990, there was a poor perception of the phenomenon of the strike in modern society. The legislator's attitude towards strikes was rather cautious and even distrustful. The right to strike was formally recognized and declared in the new Constitution of the Republic of Lithuania and in new laws but was surrounded by restrictive clauses and preconditions.[3] This, in turn, has had an invisible but felt impact on the process of reinforcement of trade-unionist ideas in the society in general and in the practical exercise of the right to strike in particular. The first sceptical political and public perceptions in the society also had an influence on the courts' decisions and case law. At first, when dealing with the new phenomenon of strikes, the courts assessed the lawfulness of the strikes reservedly and formalistically. Only in recent years, they began to assess the preconditions to strike more adequately and in a more global context of industrial relations and international labour standards.[4] Against this background, the right to strike in the Lithuanian labour law context has evolved from an instrument of resistance and protestation to an instrument of social dialogue and collective bargaining, from public scepticism and disapproval to public support and empathy.

The data indicators show that Lithuanian workers are still not inclined to strike,[5] as the culture of social dialogue and industrial action is in the stage of development.[6]

2. A. Tóth & L. Neumann, *Labour Dispute Settlement in four Central and Eastern European Countries, EIRO-Observer,* No. 6, pp. i-viii (2003).
3. Article 51 of the Constitution of 1992 states that 'workers have the right to strike for protection of their economic and social interests. The restriction of this right, and the conditions and procedures for its exercise shall be established by law'.
4. Lithuania has ratified the ILO conventions No. 87 and No. 98 in 1994, and European Social Charter (revised) in 2001.
5. The State Data Agency of the Republic of Lithuania, which is obliged by law to collect data on strikes, informs that during the 2015-2020 period, 737 strikes in total were held in the country (including 346 warning strikes) and 26,934 workers participated in strikes (including 17,000 in warning strikes), but no strikes were organized in 2020. The numbers are very low for the country with 1.5 million active workforces. There are huge discrepancies in the number of strikes and employees participating in strikes. E.g., in 2017, there was only one strike (2,205 employees on strike), whilst in 2018, already 196 strikes (4,498 employees on strike). In contrast, in 2019, there were only two strikes but 6,810 employees involved. These numbers can be explained by the fact that the industry-level strikes are organized at the level of companies and institutions as single strikes separately (e.g., the sectoral strike of teachers in 2019 was performed in more than 100 schools simultaneously which is reflected in statistics as 100 strikes). The great majority of strikes were organized in the public sectors (health services and education). *See* State Data Agency (2021), https://osp.stat.gov.lt/darbo-rinka-lietuvoje-2021/darbo-uzmokestis-darbo-sanaudos-ir-streikai/streikai (accessed 6 May 2025).
6. E.g., M. Kalanta provides four groups of political and historical explanations which are behind the Lithuanian reluctance to strike – historical (soviet) institutional legacies, the modern need of liberal and radical economic reforms in the period of transition, the deficiencies in the adoption of EU acquis and low labour mobilization. *See* M. Kalanta, *The Weakness of Social Dialogue in the Baltic Countries: An Employer-Centric Political Economy Perspective,* European Journal of Industrial Relations (Vol. 26, Issue 3, 2020) https://doi.org/10.1177/0959680119838933 (accessed 6

The coverage of collective bargaining in Lithuania is one of the lowest in the EU, with only 7.9% of workforce covered by collective agreements and only 7.4% by trade unions in 2019.[7] It is suggested that the current legal framework in general corresponds to both international and European legal standards.[8] However, trade unions' activists advocate for a more liberal approach to the example of Nordic countries.[9]

1.2 Main Features of the Regulation

The Soviet legal doctrine of industrial relations had been based on the theoretical assumption that the holder of jointly exercised employees' rights at the level of workplace is the so-called 'collective' of workers within given enterprise and the local trade union organization is a mere legal representative of that 'collective'.[10] This declaration had no impact whatsoever on the practical implementation of collective rights, as the representation was possible only through a local unit (committee) of the one and only soviet trade union organization.[11] This historical snapshot can explain some indetermination at the early stage of the labour law reform in 1992: The *newborn* right to strike was vested both in the 'collective' of workers and, alternatively, in the trade union organization (Article 2 of the Law on Settlement of Collective Disputes).[12] The provision of Article 51 of the Lithuanian Constitution which declares the right to strike for *workers* (and not trade unions) has contributed to the prediction that the right to strike will be possibly exercised not only by trade unions (organic theory)[13] but also without the trade unions – by jointly or even individually acting employees (individual doctrine). However, in 1994, the legislator had chosen to recognize the exclusivity of the right to collective bargaining (and the right to strike) to trade unions only but made it dependent on the consent of the majority of all employees within a given company or institution.[14] In spite of proclaimed trade unions' pluralism but in the absence of

May 2025). *See also* earlier critical analysis by Ch. Woolfson & M. Beck, *The Right to Strike, Labor Market Liberalization and New Labor Code in Pre-accession Lithuania,* Review of Central and East European Law, pp. 77-102 (Vol. 28, Issue 1, 2002-2003) https://doi.org/10.1163/157303502124667701 (accessed 6 May 2025).

7. OECD, *Collective Bargaining Coverage. Trade Union Density* (2020) https://stats.oecd.org/index.aspx?DataSetCode=CBC (accessed 6 May 2025).
8. T. Davulis, *Lithuanian Labour Law in the Context of EU Charter of Fundamental Rights,* Studia z zakresu prawa pracy i polityki społecznej, pp. 301-302 (Vol. 23, 2016).
9. J. Bakaite, *Legal Obstacles or Cultural Attitudes: Why Lithuanians Don't Strike?* (2023), https://www.lrt.lt/en/news-in-english/19/1855182/legal-obstacles-or-cultural-attitudes-why-lithuanians-don-t-strike (accessed 6 May 2025).
10. The formal rights to collective bargaining or participation in the production management under soviet model of industrial relations.
11. *See also* M. Weiss, *Arbeitsrechtliche Regelungsprobleme in Mittel- und Osteuropa,* pp. 211-212 (ROW 1994).
12. State Gazette, 1992, No. 12-307.
13. For classical doctrinal division between the different theories *see* R. Ben-Israel, *Strikes, Lockouts and Other Kinds of Hostile Actions,* International Encyclopaedia of Comparative Law, p. 38 (Vol. XV 'Labour Law', Chapter 15, A.B. Hepple ed.,1994).
14. The constitutional conformity of this solution has never been questioned in the Constitutional Court. In 1999, Constitutional Court has confirmed the right of trade union to strike but under previous regime, the trade unions were deemed not to act independently but were seen as a

nationwide and sectoral agreements, this solution was in reality indirectly pushing the practice to the previous 'one company – one collective bargaining agreement – one trade union' model.

The erosion of the trade union movement, the lack of collective bargaining, and the lack of industrial disputes have caused steady experimentation with the national model of industrial relations until the new Labour Code of 2016 strengthened the exclusivity and independency of trade unions – the collective bargaining and industrial action became the matter of the union only.[15] Hence, the strike can be called by the trade union independently in accordance with the procedure established by its statutes. For an institution-level strike, the consent of at least a quarter of the trade union members is needed,[16] whilst for nation- or industry-level strikes or any warning strikes, no requirement of ballot or consent of the members or employees is required.

The union's right to strike is subject to procedural requirements. In Lithuania, the strike is understood as an *ultima ratio* measure as the ad hoc Conciliation Commission (composed of the representatives of the two parties to the dispute) is a mandatory stage of the dispute. Labour arbitration and mediation are two possible alternative non-obligatory procedures to settle the dispute after Conciliation Commission, but they are very rarely used in practice because the trade unions are of the opinion that they are simply 'time delay' that benefits employers.[17] The law prohibits sympathy strikes.

In order to call a strike, the trade union must give an employer (employers' organization) a written notice. The general strike notice is 5 working days (in case of a warning strike, it is 3 working days), but in companies or branches that provide urgent (vital) services to the public it is 10 working days (in case of a warning strike it is again ten working days). In accordance with Article 247 paragraph 4 of the Labour Code, the following are considered 'urgent (vital) services' for the public: healthcare services, electricity supply services, water supply services, heat and gas supply services, sewerage and waste removal services, civil aviation services, including flight control, telecommunication services, railway, and city public transport services.

An important feature of the Lithuanian collective bargaining system (introduced by the new Labour Code in 2017) is related to the possibility for an employer to employ external workers during an ongoing strike. As a general rule, the employer is prohibited from interfering in strike action and also explicitly prohibited from recruiting new employees to the positions of striking workers (Article 250 of the Labour Code).

'representative' of all employees within the enterprise ('collective of employees' doctrine) because the possibility to exercise the right to is strike was dependent on the consent of majority of all employees in an enterprise. *See* Constitutional Court of the Republic of Lithuania, No. 8/98, 14 January 1999.

15. In 2004, the voluntary works councils were introduced in the Lithuanian system of industrial relations and from 2005-2017, works councils enjoyed the right to collective bargaining and the right strike in non-unionized workplaces. There is no exact data, but in quite number of companies, there existed collective bargaining agreements concluded by works councils. However, no strikes were initiated by works councils in that period.
16. To be established in accordance with the procedure provided by the statutes of the trade union.
17. G1PS (Trade Union of the 1 May), *Nedrįstame ar negalime? Streiko įstatymo istorija Lietuvoje* (Don't We Dare or Can't We? History of the Strike Law in Lithuania) (2020), https://g1ps.lt/streiko-istatymo-istorija-lietuvoje (accessed 6 May 2025).

However, there are two essential exceptions. One of them is related to lock-out,[18] and another is established especially for the strikes in sectors of urgent (vital) services: the recruitment ban is not effective if 'it is necessary to ensure the provision of minimum services, but it is not possible to do so in accordance with the procedure and conditions established by this Code'. The exception is formulated ambiguously, as the 'impossibility to provide services' may have a very broad interpretation. The lack of case law does not allow to firmly conclude how far this exception may go – is it the fixed-term employment or employment for an indefinite period of time allowed, what level of production shall be re-established by use of new employees, what is the status of those employees after the end of the strike, etc.

There are several options open to employers to oppose the strike. The employer (employers' organization) has the right to seek court's ruling to postpone or temporarily suspend the strike or to declare illegality of the strike (warning strike). Article 252 of the Labour Code allows the employer to apply to the court, which has the right to postpone a strike that has not yet started (or to suspend the strike that has already started) for 15 days, if there is a direct threat that minimum urgent (vital) services for the public services will not be provided (are not provided) during the strike, and this may endanger people's lives, health, and safety. The current provision has had a history of development since the first rigid regulation of the Law on the Settlement of Collective Disputes of 1992,[19] which allowed the court to postpone or suspend any strike in any sector for 30 days for 'very important reasons'. In the Labour Code of 2002, the discretion of the court has been narrowed to 'urgent (vital) services' only.

The dispute over the level of minimum urgent (vital) services has been very often in the middle of debates about major strikes in Lithuania. Initially, neither the Government authorities nor courts were willing to ensure the effectiveness of collective action by echoing employers' requests for a higher threshold of minimum services. For example, the 70% threshold was considered by the courts in 1999 as necessary minimum in the city public transport. Later (in 2022), the threshold of 50% was already recognized by the courts as appropriate in the same city public transport sector.[20]

As far as the declaration of illegality of the strike (warning strike) is concerned, the legislator has always emphasized the need to observe the procedural requirements when exercising the right to strike.[21] In accordance with Article 251 paragraph 3 of the Labour Code, the court recognizes a strike as illegal if:

(1) Its objectives contradict the Constitution of the Republic of Lithuania, the Labour Code, or other laws.

18. The prohibition to recruit new workers is lifted, when the employer declares the lock-out (Art. 250 para. 8 of the Labour Code).
19. State Gazette, No. 12-307 (1992).
20. Vilnius regional court, No. e-2A-1327-643/2022, 24 May 2022.
21. Article 51 of the Constitution has also a strong emphasis on the procedural requirements: The restriction of this right (right to strike) and the conditions and procedures for its exercise shall be established by law.

(2) It is declared due to demands not raised in the prescribed manner, political or other demands unrelated to the work of the striking workers and their related interests.
(3) It is declared without complying with the procedure and requirements established in the Labour Code or is called in cases where the Labour Code or other laws prohibit strikes.

If, due to various intricacies of announcing a strike, the strike is declared illegal by the court, the employer will obtain the right to demand compensation for the damage suffered by the trade union (Article 254 of the Labour Code). If the funds of the trade union are not sufficient to compensate for the losses, the employer may use the funds allocated under the collective agreement for employee extraordinary remuneration (salary bonuses, other additional, non-statutory benefits, and compensations), but the employer does not have the right to demand compensation from individual employees.

As far as the declaration of illegality of strike is concerned, the provisions of legislation have not changed much since 1992,[22] but the case law indicates the dynamic approach of the courts with respect to the execution of all formal requirements to call the strike. Restrictions on the right to strike are an exception to the basic principle and must be interpreted and applied in such a way as not to unreasonably restrict the workers' right to strike.[23] If the employer challenges the legality of the strike on the ground that the minimum services were not provided, he bears the burden of proof.[24] In addition, the court is also ready to examine the action of the employer in guaranteeing the minimum services, as the 'employer himself (the plaintiff) realized his duty to ensure the minimum conditions (services) necessary to meet the urgent (vital) needs of society'.[25]

Disputes related to the legality of the strike or postponement and suspension of the strike (these disputes are recognized as collective disputes over rights)[26] are assigned to the courts of general jurisdiction but not the Labour Disputes Commissions or obligatory tripartite bodies of pre-trial dispute resolution in employment cases, which are also competent to hear collective labour law-related cases. The Labour Dispute Commission is in charge, however, to decide first upon the level of minimal services, if the parties cannot reach an agreement (Article 247 paragraph 2 of the Labour Code).

22. Article 10 of the 1992 Law on the Settlement of Collective Disputes, Art. 81 para. 2 of the Labour Code 2002.
23. Lithuanian Supreme Court, No. 3K-3-141/2008, 3 March 2008.
24. Lithuanian Supreme Court, No. 3K-3-212/2001, 6 March 2001.
25. *Ibid.*
26. T. Davulis, *Lietuvos Respublikos darbo kodekso komentaras* (The Commentary of the Labour Code of the Republic of Lithuania), Art. 213 (Vilnius 2018).

2 PERMITTED RESTRICTIONS

2.1 Certain Categories of Public Servants

Persons falling under the scope of the prohibition of the exercise of the right to strike may be classified on several grounds. The first classification can be based on a formal criterion of a legal act that provides for these restrictions.[27] That would allow to differentiate between prohibitions established by the Labour Code and prohibitions consolidated in other laws, regulating specific areas of public activities or the legal status of certain groups of professionals. As the Labour Code is considered an act *primus inter pares,*[28] this classification would make sense in the case of the not clarified relationship between the restrictions in the Labour Code and the restrictions in other laws. This shall not be the case because Article 248 paragraph 2 of the Labour Code explicitly prohibits the strike of 'workers whose right to strike is restricted by law'. This means that the special laws may provide for restrictions for other types of workers,[29] and their conformity with the Labour Code may not be questioned.[30]

More meaningful could be the classification of restrictions based on the legal status of the persons concerned: employees, on the one side, and public servants, on the other. In Lithuania, the notions of *employee* and *public servant* are clearly separated. The *employee* (in Lithuanian *darbuotojas*) is a natural person who works under the subordination and for remuneration under the contract of employment (Article 32 of the Labour Code), whereas the *public servant* (in Lithuanian *valstybės tarnautojas*) is a person who is directly engaged in exercise of public administration. The legal status of the first group is regulated by the Labour Code and other employment laws, whereas the second is regulated by the Law on Public Service[31] and separate laws (some of them are called *statutes*) governing separate branches or institutions of public administration.[32] Moreover, the notion of *statute* allows to draw another division within the second group, namely the division between *public servants*

27. In accordance with established case law of the Constitutional Court, the restrictions of human rights shall be provided only in the special legal act (in Lithuanian *įstatymas*) adopted under regulated procedure by the Parliament. *See, e.g.*, ruling of 6 May 1997 of the Constitutional Court of the Republic of Lithuania.
28. Pursuant to Art. 3 para. 2 of the Labour Code, in case of a contradiction between a provision of the Labour Code and provisions of another law or a regulatory act, the provision of the Labour Code shall apply, except for cases where Labour Code provides for priority to the norms of other laws.
29. In this case, the meaning of the term of *worker* shall not only exceed the usual scope of application of the provisions of Labour Code but also extends to the public servants due to special provision of Art. 234 para. 2 of the Labour Code which states that 'the provisions of this chapter apply to employees and other persons working on the basis of legal relations equivalent to the employment relations specified in the Employment Law of the Republic of Lithuania'.
30. This passage does not, however, provide for immunity of assessment of constitutionality of the said provision or the examination of their compliance with international and European labour and human rights standards.
31. Registry of Legal Acts, No. 12037 (2018).
32. The employment laws and Labour Code is applied to public servants in the way of analogy of law (Art. 6 of the Law on Public Service).

and *statutory public servants*, because the statutory public servants are subject to more severe personal restrictions.

As far as employees are concerned, the prohibition of the right to strike is foreseen only for employees of emergency medical services (Article 248 paragraph 2 of the Labour Code) and employees working in nuclear energy facilities (Article 51 of the Law on Nuclear Energy).[33] Other groups of employees only theoretically can be subject to the prohibition to strike if they are registered in the civil reserve of mobilization personnel and must perform the functions assigned to them in cases of declared mobilization and partial mobilization (Article 22 paragraph 3 of the Law on Mobilization and Preparation of the Mobilization Reserve of the Republic of Lithuania).[34]

As far as public servants are concerned, it should be noticed, that the right to organize is granted to all public servants, except those under contractual professional military service.[35] The basic legal framework for collective bargaining in public service (national, sectoral, and institution-level collective agreements) is defined by Article 6 paragraph 2 of the Law on Public Service sets, but the detailed rules and procedures for collective bargaining and the conclusion of collective bargaining agreements for public servants are stipulated by the Labour Code.

Article 17 paragraph 1 number 4 of the Law on Public service explicitly guarantees the right to strike to public servants but imposes one general restriction based on hierarchical rank. The head of the institution (in Lithuanian *įstaiga*) and the head of the branch of an institution (in Lithuanian *įstaigos padalinys*) are prohibited to strike.

Other branch-specific restrictions are separately foreseen for different groups of public servants (in most cases, statutory public servants) by specific pieces of legislation dealing with the legal status of those servants. The following heterogeneous groups of public servants are deprived of the right to strike by specific legislation:

- Professional military servicemen (Article 36 paragraph 7 of the Law on the Organization of the National Defence System and Military Service of the Republic of Lithuania).[36]
- Diplomats, i.e., a statutory civil servant with a diplomatic rank, working under a diplomatic service contract or a fixed-term diplomatic service contract (Article 33 paragraph 3 of the Law on the Diplomatic Service).[37]
- State Prosecutors (Article 21 paragraph 3 of the Law on State Prosecutors).[38]

33. State Gazette, No. 119-2771 (1996), No. 91-4314 (2011).
34. State Gazette, No. 72-3464 (2011).
35. *See, e.g.*, D. Petrylaite, *Asociacijų laisve valstybes tarnyboje: norai ir galimybes (*Freedom of Association in Public Service: wishes and possibilities*)*, No. 1, pp. 50-58 (Justitia, 2007); N. Kasiliauskas, *Asociacijų laisves įgyvendinimo valstybes tarnyboje, policijoje, kariuomeneje ypatumai (*Peculiarities of the Implementation of Freedom of Association in the Civil Service, Police, and Army*)*, No. 55, pp. 18-26 (Teise, 2008); *Darbo teises principai ir jų taikymas Lietuvos teismų praktikoje* (Principles of Labour Law and Their Application in Lithuanian Court Practice), pp. 96-103 (Vilnius, MRU 2016).
36. State Gazette, No. 49-1325 (1998).
37. Registry of Legal Acts, No. 12064 (2018).
38. State Gazette, No. 42-1919 (2003).

- Officers of internal service, i.e., police officers (Article 24 paragraph 7 of the Statute of Internal Service).[39]
- Officers of the State Security Department (Article 11 paragraph 1 of the Statute of State Security Department).[40]
- Officers of the Office of Investigation of Financial Crimes (Article 13 paragraph 1 number 6 of the Law of Office of Investigation of Financial Crimes).[41]
- State secret intelligence Officers (Article 40 number 11 of the Law on Intelligence).[42]
- Officers of the Office of Special Investigations (Article 23 paragraph 1 number 6 of the Law on the Office of Special Investigations).[43]
- Officers of the Office of the Protection of the Heads of the State (Article 31 paragraph 1 number 6 of the Law on Protection of the Heads of the State).[44]
- Officers in the Department of Prisons (Article 28 paragraph 2 of the Statute of the Department of Prisons).[45]
- Offices of the Office of State Border Control (Article 19 paragraph 1 number 3 of the Law on State Border Control).[46]
- Officers of the Department of Customs (Article 24 paragraph 1 number 7 of the Statute of the Department of Customs).[47]
- Intelligence Ombudsperson, appointed by the Parliament (Article 9 paragraph 1 number 7 of the Law on Intelligence Ombudsperson).[48]

In the course of the creation of the public service, constitutional principles governing public service were formulated:[49] the unity of the public service, the loyalty of public servants to the State of Lithuania and its constitutional order, impartiality, openness, publicity, obeying only the Constitution and law, the principles of separation of powers and limiting the powers of the authorities, high qualification and professional requirements for public servants, the primacy of statutory regulation, differences from the contractual employment relationship, stability of remuneration.[50] The Constitutional Court itself has stated on a number of occasions that[51] no matter the similarity, the legal relationship of the civil service is not identical to the employment

39. Registry of Legal Acts, No. 12049 (2018).
40. State Gazette, No. 73-3101 (2002).
41. State Gazette, No. 33-1250 (2002).
42. State Gazette, No. 72-3019 (2002).
43. Registry of Legal Acts, No. 21647 (2017).
44. Registry of Legal Acts, No. 10898 (2020).
45. State Gazette, No. 39-1088 (2000).
46. State Gazette, No. 92-2848 (2000).
47. Registry of Legal Acts, No. 12049 (2018).
48. Registry of Legal Acts, No. 26905 (2021).
49. *See* rulings of the Constitutional Court of the Republic of Lithuania of 18 December 2001, 13 December 2004, 20 March 2007.
50. N. Glebove, *Valstybes tarnybos samprata ir valstybes tarnautojo teisinio statuso ypatumai,* (Concept of the Public Service and Particularities of the Legal Status of Public Servant), No. 76, p. 141 (Teise, 2020).
51. *See* rulings of the Constitutional Court of the Republic of Lithuania of 13 December 2004, 20 March 2007, 11 December 2009.

relationship between the employee and the employer.[52] In accordance with the jurisprudence of the Constitutional Court, a public servant is not an employee and due to the exceptional public importance of the function he or she performs (defence of public interest), certain greater restrictions may apply compared to employees working under an employment contract (e.g., requirement of no conflict of public and private interests, etc.). The court *weights* the necessity, reasonableness, and proportionality of all restrictions very carefully also in the context of fundamental human rights and, as V.A. Vaičaitis concludes, sought to defend disproportionate restrictions on those involved in the public service (e.g., restrictions of the property rights).[53] However, this does not explain to what extent a public servant can be (or cannot be) subject to the single elements of the legal regime provided for by the Labour Code for an employee. The court itself tends to solve such problems casuistically. For example, stating, on the one hand, that each person's right to fair remuneration provided for in paragraph 1 of Article 48 of the Constitution must be guaranteed to a civil servant *at the extent not less* than to other workers, then it immediately makes this statement relative: 'Due to the character of the civil service, as a specific working activity, certain *peculiarities* in its implementation are possible',[54] in the application of which 'rules and principles of the Constitution must be respected.'[55]

As one can observe, the constitutional doctrine creates a strong basis for the differentiation between employees' rights (for employees) and the rights of public servants (for public servants) in Lithuania. The denial of some employees' specific rights to public servants' rests on the abstract idea of the necessity of protection of public interest. The validity of this general justification of the restrictions of the right to strike has never been challenged on their conformity with the Constitution or international labour standards.

2.2 Essential Services in the Strict Sense of the Term

The restrictions of the right to strike may be imposed not only by reason of one's legal status or the relations *vis-à-vis* the state (e.g., public servants) but also by reason of particular activities of the employer, especially where the interruption of which may endanger the life, personal safety of the part or of the whole of population.[56]

In Lithuania, the path of evolution went from an approach of strict restraints to gradual permission and removal of restrictions in some sectors. Despite the fact that the

52. However, in the doctrine of the Constitutional Court, we can find many examples where the status of employee and civil servant are compared though there is no valid reason for this (e.g., removal of a civil servant from work and removal of an employee from work have different purposes). *See* the ruling of the Constitutional Court of the Republic of Lithuania of 22 December 2021.
53. V.A. Vaičaitis, *Konstitucine valstybes tarnybos samprata ir valstybes tarnybos tobulinimo koncepcija* (Constitutional Concept of Public Service and the Amelioration of the Conception of Public Service), No. 78, p. 128 (Teise, 2011).
54. Rulings of the Constitutional Court of the Republic of Lithuania of 13 December 2004, 11 December 2009, 29 May 2019.
55. Ruling of the Constitutional Court of the Republic of Lithuania of 11 December 2009.
56. Freedom of Association and Collective Bargaining. ILO. General Survey, p. 70 (1994).

notion of essential services was not initially used by the legislator, the sectors where the strikes were prohibited due to their societal importance were enumerated already at the very beginning of the creation of the system of industrial relations (1992). The sectors where employees are deprived of the right to strike can be defined as 'essential services' in *stricto sensu.*[57] On the contrary, the sectors where the right to strike was in principle allowed but aggravated by procedural requirements, such as longer notice periods and, most importantly, the necessity to provide a minimum level of services, can be defined as minimum services.[58] Lithuanian national legal framework, however, partially reflects these considerations (e.g., minimum services are called 'urgent (vital) services for the public') and in substance allows for similar categorization. If the provisions do not contain the general ban on strikes and stipulate procedural requirements as well as determination of minimum services, they basically refer to *minimum services* and not to *essential services* in the meaning of case law of the Committee on Freedom of Association of the ILO.

The list of public activities, which shall be understood as *essential services* and *minimum services*, have a history of legislative development. Initially, the Law on Settlement of Collective Disputes of 1992 has forbidden to announce a strike not only in the internal affairs, national defence, and national security systems[59] but also in sectors of electricity, centralized heat and gas supply, as well as in emergency medical services. The demands of the employees of these services and companies had to be decided by the Government of the Republic of Lithuania (Article 10 of the 1992 Law on Settlement of Collective Disputes). Hence, the law imposed a general ban on strikes in electricity, centralized heat and gas supply companies, whereas in other areas of sensitive public services (railway and urban public transport, civil aviation, communications, energy, health services, and production of pharmaceuticals, food, water, sewage and waste removal, oil refining, continuous production) and 'other companies, the suspension of which is associated with severe and dangerous consequences for society or to human life or health', strikes were allowed, but the notice period was considerably higher than in other sectors: 21 (instead of 7) calendar days for an ordinary strike and again 21 calendar days (instead of 24 hours) for warning strike.

Perhaps as a result of criticism expressed by the ILO Committee on Freedom of Association in the Lithuanian cases related to the transport sector,[60] a different perception of essential service companies was formed in 2005. Legislative amendments abolished the prohibition to strike in electricity and centralized heat and gas supply companies, and those activities were transformed from the group of essential services

57. Essential services are only those, the interruption of which would endanger the life, personal safety, or health of the whole or part of the population. For definition and distinction of terms *see* Freedom of Association and Collective Bargaining. ILO. General Survey, p. 71 (1994).
58. Minimum services should meet at least two criteria: It should be limited to operations which are strictly necessary to meet basic needs of the population or the minimum requirements of the service, and the workers organizations shall be able to participate in defining such a service, alongside with employers and the public authorities. *See* Freedom of Association and Collective Bargaining. ILO. General Survey, p. 71 (1994).
59. Currently, these restrictions are transposed in the legislation on public servants (*see* above).
60. Freedom of Association case No. 2078, Report No. 324.

to the group of *minimum services*.[61] In 2008, the unexhausted list of minimum services ceased to exist, as the legislator stroked out a very widely formulated prescription of 'other companies, the suspension of which is associated with severe and dangerous consequences for society or to human life or health' from the list.[62] The list of minimum services was again updated to include only railway and urban public transport, civil aviation, medical services, water, electricity, heat and gas supply, sewerage and waste removal companies,[63] and the strike notice period was decreased to 14 days in areas for those services. The new Labour Code of 2016 introduced the special Article 247 dealing with strikes 'in companies and branches providing urgent (vital) services' and again updated the list of such services by including flight control and telecommunication (!) companies.

Today, essential services *stricto sensu* in Lithuania remain regulated by Article 248 paragraph 2 of the Labour Code, which only contains prohibition of strikes for employees of emergency medical services and employees whose right to strike is limited by law (e.g., specific groups of public servants – as outlined in section 2.1 above). Nuclear power industry workers, who are banned from strike by a special law provision of 1996 (Article 51 of the Law on Nuclear Energy), are employed only by one specific enterprise – Ignalina nuclear power station. Ignalina nuclear power plant has not been operating since 2009, and the closure process is scheduled until 2038. Approximately 1,600 employees still work there and they are deprived of the right to strike. The critical change in the nature of services provided by the enterprise is not reflected in the change of the existing ban on strike.

2.3 Situations of Acute National or Local Crisis

In accordance with Article 248 paragraph 2 of the Labour Code, strikes are prohibited (nationally or in separate areas or regions), where the state institutions declare:

- the state of natural disaster;
- mobilization;
- the state of war;[64]
- the state of emergency.

The ban holds until the effects of the natural disaster are liquidated, demobilization is declared, or the state of war, or state of emergency is revoked. This means that the ban is effective for a limited period of time.

---

61. Law No. X-188 (State Gazette, No. 67-2400 (2005)).
62. Law No. X-1534 (State Gazette, No. 63-2375 (2008)).
63. In 2014 the continuous service of elevators was added to the list.
64. In addition, Art. 16 of the Law on State of War (State Gazette, No. 52-1482 (2000)) public servants and employees working under contracts of employment are prohibited from striking in territories where the status of war (martial law) has been imposed.

The separate laws provide for procedural rules for the declaration of a state of natural disaster, mobilization, the state of war or a state of emergency.[65] In all cases, after establishing objective circumstances justifying the declaration of a relevant exceptional situation, a formal decision to be taken by authorized institutions (i.e., Parliament, President, Government) is prescribed by law.

From the standpoint of the Constitution and the laws, there are significant differences between different types of crisis situations. Pursuant to Article 141 of the Constitution, the *Seimas* (Parliament) shall impose the state of war, announce mobilization or demobilization, adopt a decision to use the armed forces when a need arises to defend the homeland or to fulfil the international obligations of the State of Lithuania. Article 144 of the Constitution states that in the event of a threat to the constitutional order or public order in the state, a state of emergency may be introduced in the entire territory of the state or part of it. These two different situations are then addressed in Article 145, according to which, following the introduction of a state of war or state of emergency, the rights and freedoms are specified in Articles 22, 24, 25, 32, 35, and 36 of the Constitution. In contrast, neither the Constitution nor the special laws on mobilization or declaration of the state of natural disaster contain special provisions on the restriction of human rights and liberties.

The analysis of the current legal framework allows us to draw the first conclusion that:

- There are different legal regimes for emergency situations which imply different sets of preconditions and legal consequences for human rights (e.g., state of natural disaster and the fact of mobilization does not allow the restriction of civil rights and liberties under the Constitution), but in the Labour Code, they are treated alike for the purpose of banning of strikes.
- The right to organize (Article 48 of the Constitution) and the right to strike (Article 51 of the Constitution) are not mentioned in Article 145 of the Constitution among possible restrictions of human rights (Article 145 of the Constitution), but nevertheless, they are restricted by ordinary statutory law (Article 248 paragraph 2 of the Labour Code) and this creates the problem of conformity of the Labour Code provision with the Constitutional framework of exceptional situations.
- The limitation to the right to strike is limited in time, but no time frames are provided by law. The duration of the limitation of the right to strike is closely connected with the duration of a declared exceptional state and is effective in the territory where the state is declared.

The preconditions for declaring these crisis situations differ and these differences are obvious for quite natural reasons – the state of war differs from the natural disaster situation and should have a different impact on social life and personal limitations.

65. Respectively, the Law on the Crisis Management and Civil Protection Law (State Gazette, No. 115-3230 (1998)), the Law on mobilization and host country support (State Gazette, No. 116-2695 (1996)), the Law on the State of War (State Gazette, No. 52-1482 (2000)), the Law on the State of Emergency (State Gazette, No. 64-2575 (2002)).

However, examples of effective judicial control over the decision on the declaration of the state of war, state of emergency, mobilization or the state of natural disaster are still lacking.

It is important to observe that when evaluating the specific statutory provisions of the Law on the Legal Status of Foreigners,[66] which were adopted in relation to the influx of foreign asylum seekers from Belarus territory, the Constitutional Court had the chance to clarify the preconditions for the declaration of a state of emergency situation and what restrictions of human rights are permissible during the declared state of emergency. However, it failed to do so, taking on the examination of the possible restrictions in relation to Article 20 (protection of the freedom of the person) only and simply shortly mentioning (but not analysing) Article 145 (restrictions of human rights in case of a declared state of emergency) of the Constitution. This can be explained by the more centric role of Article 20 and the broader scope of the applied restrictions,[67] but it provides little help in understanding the limits for the legislators to impose restrictions on other human rights under the declared regime of emergency. Therefore, the guidelines for the possible direction of the Constitutional Court in appreciation of the seriousness of the circumstances and the evaluation of the potential impact on the normal functioning of the society are still missing in a constitutional doctrine.

Observers may refer to the possible link to the constant formula applied by the Lithuanian Constitutional Court on possible limitations to the exercise of constitutional human rights and freedoms. According to the Court, the following conditions shall be satisfied:

- It is imposed by law by a special act of the Parliament.
- Restrictions are necessary in a democratic society in order to protect the rights and freedoms of other persons and the values enshrined in the Constitution, as well as constitutionally important goals.
- Limitations do not negate the nature and essence of rights and freedoms.
- The constitutional principle of proportionality is observed.
- The legal regulation that restricts the rights and freedoms of a person must be such that it provides the prerequisites for assessing the individual situation of each person as much as possible and, taking into account all important circumstances, the specific measures that limit the rights of that person to be applied accordingly.

These universal conditions served as a basis for the evaluation of the constitutionality of human rights restrictions and the restrictions of labour or social rights in the context of the financial crisis back in 2008 and 2009[68] and the health crisis.[69]

66. Registry of Legal Acts, No. 16266 (2021).
67. The restrictions were imposed not only in the period of the state of emergency but also before – in the state of an extreme situation – another type of status for extraordinary situations under the Law on Crisis Management and Civil Protection Law, which formally does not entail the restriction of the human rights and liberties.
68. In words of D. Petrylaite, lack of strikes during the crisis (zero strikes in 2009-2011) demonstrated that 'Lithuanian employees endured the unpopular decisions of the crisis in silence'. *See* D. Petrylaite. Social Rights, in E. Kuris ed. *Crisis, the Rule of Law and Human Rights in Lithuania*, 2015(pp. 209-210).

The history of past declarations of exceptional situations and their impact on the right to strike is rather fragmental. Back in 1992, the Parliament of the Republic declared the territory of Lithuania 'devastated by natural disaster' based on the difficult climate conditions due to the drought.[70] The decision of the Parliament was adopted solemnly with the view to ensure the provision of significant financial support for the sector of agriculture, but, nevertheless, it served as a main legal argument to recognize the strike in the Kaunas city bus transport company illegal and to oblige seven strike committee members - employees - to individually compensate the damages for the company.[71]

In the new history of industrial relations, this sort of legal misunderstanding can hardly emerge, but it seems that the current legal framework in force still contains significant problematic aspects: There is a general ban to strike regardless of the type of emergency, there is a lack of practice of judicial control over the declaration of the state of the exceptional situation and there are serious doubts of compatibility of Article 248 paragraph 2 of the Labour Code with the Constitution of the Republic of Lithuania.

The problematic nature of the situation became evident in recent years when the Government needed to react when faced with a turbulent situation related to dangerous external factors.

The orchestrated influx of foreign asylum seekers was the first time that the state of the extremal situation was declared by the Government, and later, the state of emergency was declared by the Parliament on 9 November 2021.[72] In the case of an explicitly mentioned ban on assembly, the right to move freely and the right to correspondence was imposed in bordering territories (5 km) of the country.

Later, the Russian military aggression in Ukraine produced another cause for the declaration of a state of emergency in the whole territory of the Republic of Lithuania on 24 February 2022 by the decree of the President. The state of emergency has been prolonged ever since for several times (and is effective at a time when this publication is being prepared). On 20 March 2022, the state of emergency was declared already by the Parliament and the resolution of the Parliament contained certain explicit prohibitions to collect and disseminate certain information as well as to gather for support of Russian aggression (Articles 25 and 36 of the Constitution).[73] The restriction of other human rights, including labour rights, was not mentioned here. Since 16 September 2022, the territorial scope of the emergency situation has been limited to the border territories only.

These decisions on emergency situations in 2021 and 2022 were declared in a time of ongoing industrial disputes in the public transport sector and the sector of

69. In this context, the recent jurisprudence of the Constitutional Court in quarantine-related cases may be of particular relevance, ruling of 24 January 2023 on the restriction of freedom of economic activity following the declaration of quarantine (17 July 2023) https://lrkt.lt/en/court-acts/search/170/ta2816/content (accessed 6 May 2025), and the ruling of 31 May 2023 on the restrictions of the number of close contacts of persons in closed spaces after the declaration of quarantine, https://lrkt.lt/en/court-acts/search/170/ta2816/content (accessed 6 May 2025).
70. State Gazette, No. 21-621 (1992).
71. Lithuanian Supreme Court, No. 3K-107/1996, 19 March 1996.
72. Registry of Legal Acts, No. 23202 (2021).
73. Registry of Legal Acts, No. 04618 (2022).

production of mineral traces. As a result, several different legislative initiatives were recently put on the table to deal with industrial disputes in emergency or similar situations:

- The initiative to amend Article 248 paragraph 2 of the Labour Code and to allow the strikes which 'are not or could be directly related' to the circumstances which *cause* the declaration of the state of war, state of emergency, mobilization or the state of natural disaster.[74]
- The initiative to amend the Law on State of Emergency,[75] and the Law on Crisis Management and Civil Protection[76] to allow the responsible Minister (Member of the Government) to postpone the strike after consulting the Tripartite Council of Lithuania in order 'to eliminate the consequences of the emergency situation' or 'to control the extremal situation' respectively.

It became obvious that the general ban on the right to strike cannot hold the criticism from trade unions and some employers but the delicate solution to create the legal framework for the exercise has not been adopted yet.[77] In the discussions of the social partners and in the legislative proposals, strong emphasis is put on the procedural requirements of the exercise of the right to strike but not on the definitions or establishment of the substantive material preconditions for strike in situations of acute crisis.

3 COMPENSATORY GUARANTEES FOR WORKERS DEPRIVED OF THE RIGHT TO STRIKE

It is generally acknowledged that in the system of industrial relations, the restrictions or the exclusion of the right to strike or the freedom to strike will be only accepted as suitable, if conflicts are solved by compulsory conciliation, arbitration or automatic salary increase.[78] In the view of the Freedom of Association Committee, if the workers are deprived of essential means of defending their socio-economic and occupational interests, they should be afforded compensatory guarantees, for example, conciliation and mediation procedures in the event of deadlock – to arbitration machinery where arbitration awards should be binding on both parties and once issued should be implemented rapidly and completely.

The legal and social analysis of the industrial relations in Lithuania does not allow us to firmly state that these standards are well-known and practically implemented. For a very long period of time, employees and trade unions, which were

74. Draft Law No. XIVP-1607.
75. Draft Law No. XIVP-2792.
76. Draft Law No. XIVP-2793.
77. Most probably, the laws will be adopted in the autumn of 2023 session of the Parliament, but the legislator will have to scrutinize procedural issues around the declaration of the strike in emergency and extremal situations.
78. R. Birk, *The Law of Strikes and Lock-outs, in Comparative Labour Law and Industrial Relations*, p. 286 (Vol. I, R. Blanpain ed., Kluwer, 1990).

deprived of the right to strike, had no say in the resolution of their demands (if any).[79] The Law on Settlement of Collective Disputes of 1992 had the rather opposite perception when it had the provision (Article 10) that the strikes in the system of internal affairs, national defence and national security systems, as well as in electricity, centralized heat and gas supply companies, emergency medical services are prohibited and the demands of the employees of these services and companies are decided by the Government, i.e., the actual addressee of the demands and direct or indirect party of the collective dispute itself.[80]

The Labour Code of 2002 has abolished this acrimonious solution and established the rule that the demands of those workers shall be settled by the labour arbitration, i.e., ad hoc institution, composed of a district judge (president of the arbitration) and arbitrators, proposed by the parties, which can issue a binding judgment by voting. The Labour Code of 2016 has not changed much in this respect, stating that the demands of those workers shall be examined and settled by institutions for settlement of collective disputes over interests, i.e., an internal Conciliation Commission of the parties of the Dispute or the external mediator or the labour arbitrage (Article 248 paragraph 1 of the Labour Code).

This legislative solution can only at first glance appear appropriate. In fact, Labour arbitration similar to mediation services is almost non-existent in the Lithuanian system of industrial relations.[81] The number of cases where the parties referred the dispute to the Labour arbitration or mediation could be less than 10 in more than 30 years of the history of collective labour law in Lithuania. The experience of arbitration in collective disputes is non-existent and therefore it is practically hard to imagine how the *demands* of *employees'* representatives can be *met* or *solved* by the external non-judicial body.

Second, the demands of workers, deprived of the right to strike, have rarely been a specific concern for politicians, Government, or public authorities. Throughout the years, statutory public servants, who compose basically the major part of this group, have very rarely been put in a position where their remuneration conditions were worse than wages of other public sector employees. The softly formulated appeals to increase the salaries or other type of compensation are presented publicly by the heads of institutions but not by trade unions.[82] Other types of demands, especially in heavily

79. There was no single case registered, when the employees deprived from the right to strike went public demanding changes or collective bargaining rights.
80. G. Dambrauskiene, *Lietuvos Respublikos darbo kodekso komentaras: I dalis* (The Commentary of the Labour Code of the Republic of Lithuania: Part I) Art. 78 (Vilnius, Justitia 2004).
81. Criticism already by D. Petrylaite, *Kolektyviniai darbo ginčai* (Collective Labour Disputes), pp. 167-169 (Vilnius, Justitia 2005).
82. Y. Koleva, *Teisejai niršta del jau dešimtmetį nekeliamų algų: '1800 eurų į rankas'* (Judges Are Concerned About Salaries That Have Not Been Raised for a Decade: 'EUR 1800 Euros Netto') (2023), https://www.tv3.lt/naujiena/video/teisejai-nirsta-del-jau-desimtmeti-nekeliamu-algu-1800-euru-i-rankas-n1226504 (accessed 6 May 2025); Prosecutor General: lack of funds for provision, salaries – uncompetitive (corrected), https://www.bns.lt/topic/1912/news/672056 15/print/true/ (accessed 6 May 2025).

organized sectors,[83] are usually presented in pickets of public statements. In all cases, unilateral decisions to meet the demands taken by the authorities or direct negotiations with trade unions were organized to prevent the escalation of the industrial dispute. In other words, the procedure prescribed by law to compensate for the exclusion of the right to strike does not work in practice.

In the public sector, for decades, the wage system was based on a statutory remuneration scheme unilaterally set by the legislator and the Government. The Labour Code of 2016 slightly improved the mechanism of collective bargaining in the public sector and the national sectoral and inter-sectoral collective bargaining for the whole public sector, including public servants, have been concluded. The progress, which was triggered by the willingness to avoid criticism over the low coverage of collective bargaining, has led to an increase in the number of sectoral collective bargaining agreements in branches of education, social services, and health services. But for public servants, the emergence of inter-sectoral collective agreements, concluded by the Government and ministries, became an important part of the social dialogue because the agreement formally fixed the base, needed for the calculation of the salary for every public servant. The exact coefficient for all public wages is already regulated by the law and there is no intention yet to change that system.

4 CONCLUSION

It should be no surprise that the country, which found itself in transition from plan economy to market economy and was tasked with the creation of a new system of industrial relations, had been more than cautious in recognizing the liberty to strike. The lack of understanding of the rationale and modus operandi of settlement of industrial disputes in western countries as well as the lack of knowledge of international labour standards – all these factors contributed both to the late evolution of the national legal framework and slowly changing case law. The law consolidates the right to strike both at the constitutional level and the level of legislation but contains significant safeguards and procedural restrictions for the sake of public interest. It prohibits emergency medical service workers and nuclear energy sector workers from the right to strike, although some restrictions have become obsolete. Law enforcement officials and the country's security-related personnel are deprived of the right to strike explicitly, and therefore, no real collective bargaining can take place in relation to these workers. Alternative procedures for the impartial and rapid settlement of claims for these workers deprived of the right to strike simply do not work and, consequently, working conditions are determined by the Government and authorities on a case-by-case basis. The law also contains a general ban to call a strike if the state institutions declare the state of natural disaster, mobilization, the state of war, or the state of emergency. The general ban on the right to strike cannot hold the criticism as it

83. In 2021, the dissatisfaction of the unions with the Government's decision to refuse to vaccinate officials according to the priority order was heard. In 2023, the police officers threatened stoppage of work because lack of agreement with authorities on conditions of rehabilitation for officers.

prevents the settlement of already ongoing industrial disputes, which are not in relation to the reasons for declaring the state of emergency. The delicate solution to create the legal framework for the exercise of the right to strike in crisis situations will have to be adopted soon.

CHAPTER 22

Restrictions on the Right to Strike in Luxembourg

Jean-Luc Putz

1 GENERAL INFORMATION

In general, the right to strike is strictly regulated in Luxembourg, both in the private and public sectors.

There are only two levels in the Luxembourg public sector, namely the state level and the municipal level. For civil servants (*fonctionnaire public)* and assimilated personnel, the exercise of the right to strike is governed by the laws of 1979 and 1985, which have not been substantially amended since. Employees hired by public actors under private law contracts follow the general regime of the Labour Code.

There is no extensive doctrine on strike action in the public sector.[1] Similarly, we were unable to identify any relevant case law. Generally speaking – the private sector included – the exercise of the right to strike remains an exceptional phenomenon in the Grand Duchy, and very few cases are brought before the courts. The legislation sets up conciliation and mediation procedures, which often bear fruit. This can be explained by a willingness on the part of both the unions and the public authorities to favour dialogue in order to avoid open conflict. The trade union power in the public sector is in the hands of two major trade union confederations, one at state level (CGFP)[2] and the other at municipal level (FGFC).[3] Although they defend the interests of their members, these actors are mostly aware of the general interest of the country and are willing to make concessions, especially in times of crisis.

1. The few contributions that can be found are mostly limited to reproducing the text of the law. We admit that to a large extent we are forced to do the same.
2. Confédération générale de la fonction publique.
3. Fédération générale de la fonction communale.

While in the private sector, the coverage rate of collective agreements is around 50%, in the public sector, there is also a tradition of collective bargaining. For civil servants, there are no collective agreements as such, as their status is not contractual. Nevertheless, political agreements are negotiated and then transposed through legislation and regulations. Innovations are often negotiated at the level of the state civil service and then taken up at the municipal level.

The social peace observed in Luxembourg can also be explained by the fact that civil service salaries are high when compared internationally (average monthly amount of EUR 8,688 and average accessories of EUR 9,384 per year for civil servants).[4] Similarly, civil servants were the first to benefit from the automatic adaptation of salaries to the evolution of the cost of living, a mechanism from which all employees in Luxembourg currently benefit. The preservation of purchasing power is therefore automatically guaranteed.

It should be noted from the outset that, in addition to the trade unions, which are freely constituted associations, the Luxembourg system also has a system of professional chambers (*chambres professionnelles*),[5] which are public institutions (*établissements publics*) and whose role is also to defend the socio-professional interests of their members. All civil servants and assimilated staff are automatically members of the *Chambre des fonctionnaires et employés publics* (hereinafter 'CHFEP'); the chambers intervene in an advisory capacity in the legislative procedure.

1.1 Legal Basis of the Right to Strike

1.1.1 The Constitutional Recognition of the Right to Strike

Until 1879, striking was a criminal offence. Indeed, the French Criminal Code of 1810 was applicable, Article 415, which provided for the offence of coalition (*délit de coalition*). In 1879, Luxembourg's criminal law was reformed by an almost verbatim adoption of the Belgian Criminal Code,[6] whose Article 310 punished the use of physical and moral coercion during a strike. Although today, such a prohibition seems obvious, at that time, it was considered an obstacle to the effective exercise of the right to strike. The turning point came in 1936 when the law recognised the freedom of association[7] and repealed Article 310 of the Criminal Code.[8] A conciliation body, the *National Labour Council*, was created,[9] and the approach adopted at the time still marks the current legislation. However, it was not until 1948 that trade union freedoms were

4. 'Les accessoires de la rémunération dans la Fonction publique', Study published by the Ministry of the Civil Service in 2022.
5. In 1924, five professional chambers were established: two for workers (private employees and blue-collar workers) and three for employers (trade, crafts, agriculture). It was not until 1964 that their circle was completed by a professional chamber for the civil service. With the constitutional reform that comes into force on 1 July 2023, the chambers are anchored in the Constitution.
6. Loi du 18 juin 1879 portant révision du Code pénal (introduisant le Code pénal belge révisé).
7. Loi du 11 mai 1936 garantissant la liberté d'association.
8. Loi du 11 mai 1936, portant abrogation de l'art. 310 du Code pénal.
9. Arrêté grand-ducal du 23 janvier 1936, ayant pour objet l'institution d'un Conseil National du Travail pour la conciliation des conflits collectifs de travail; Arrêté du 13 février 1936 ayant pour

incorporated into our Constitution. At the time, it was discussed whether the right to strike should be explicitly mentioned; however, it was considered too recent to be formally anchored in the Constitution.[10] The Chamber of Deputies thus limited itself to an interpretative motion in the following terms: 'The Constituent declares that the guarantee of freedoms enshrined in the Luxembourg Constitution includes the right to strike to safeguard the legitimate social claims of those who work.' As early as 1952, the Court of Cassation confirmed that participation in a strike 'constitutes for the worker a right implicitly proclaimed by Article 11 of the Constitution'.[11]

In 2007, the right to strike was explicitly mentioned in the Constitution,[12] whose Article 11 paragraph 4 reads as follows: 'The law guarantees trade union freedoms and organises the right to strike.' A major constitutional revision was adopted in January 2023 and will enter into force in July 2023.[13] The rules on the right to strike have not led to discussions and have not been subject to substantive changes. Article 21 will now states: 'Trade union freedoms are guaranteed. The law shall organise the exercise of the right to strike.'

1.1.2 The Legal Framework of the Right to Strike in the Public Sector

The first law on the civil service, dating back to 1872,[14] did not mention the right to strike in any of its successive amendments. The statute, which was introduced in 1979, on the other hand, recalls that 'Civil servants shall enjoy freedom of association and trade union freedom' while adding that 'However, they may only resort to strike action within the limits and under the conditions of the law regulating the exercise thereof.'[15] Indeed, a bill was tabled in parallel to regulate this aspect.[16] At the time of the drafting of the general statute, the CHFEP considered that the statute itself should regulate the right to strike and proposed a text while recognising that 'the principle of the continuity of public services and the safeguarding of the general interest require special measures with regard to the exercise of the right to strike and even the exclusion of certain categories of civil servants from this right'.[17] It proposed to exclude magistrates and civil servants of the courts and tribunals, officers, and civil servants of the Prosecution

objet les mesures d'exécution de l'arrêté grand-ducal du 23 janvier 1936, concernant l'institution d'un Conseil National du Travail pour la conciliation des conflits collectifs du travail.

10. The Council of State was opposed to explicitly mentioning the right to strike; while recognising that the right to strike is likely to support workers' claims, it was of the opinion that, in order to become a constitutional right, the right must have stood the test of time and become sufficiently stable. Projet de révision de la Constitution n° 158, Avis du Conseil d'État, p. 215.
11. Cass. 24 Jul. 1952, Pas. 15, 355.
12. Loi du 29 mars 2007 portant - 1. révision des paras1, 3, 4, 5 et 6, alinéa 1er de l'article 11 de la Constitution; - 2. création d'un article 11bis nouveau de la Constitution.
13. Loi du 17 janvier 2023 portant révision du chapitre II de la Constitution.
14. Loi du 8 mai 1872, concernant les droits et les devoirs des fonctionnaires de l'État.
15. Projet de loi n° 1907 fixant le statut général des fonctionnaires de l'État.
16. *Ibid.*
17. Projet de loi n° 1907, Avis de la Chambre des fonctionnaires et employés publics sur l'avant-projet de loi fixant le statut des fonctionnaires de l'État et le régime applicable aux employés de l'État, p. 1713.

service, and members of the armed forces. In the end, however, the 1979 statute only mentions the right to strike and refers to another law for its exercise.

This specific law on the right to strike was passed the same year and still regulates the right to strike in the state civil service today.[18] The drafting of this law was not easy, as the bill had already been submitted in 1973. The legislator had analysed the situation in Switzerland, the Netherlands, Belgium, Germany, Italy, and France. French law was chosen as the main source of inspiration.[19]

The authors of the bill also reviewed the various historical arguments for and against the right to strike in the public sector. The aim of the bill was to regulate 'the exercise of the right to strike in the public sector with restrictions that are intended to reconcile the principle of continuity of public services with the freedom of the right to strike'.[20] The purpose of the restrictions is to make the exercise of the right to strike 'as little harmful as possible for all citizens who are entitled to the proper functioning of vital public services'.[21]

The 1979 law has only been subject to two minor amendments;[22] the main principles have not been put up for discussion. Nevertheless, on the occasion of one of these amendments in 2014, the Council of State considered that this law 'must undergo a fundamental revision'.[23] This has not yet taken place.

In 1985, a law was passed to regulate strikes at the municipal level, closely following the 1979 law.

1.2 Main Features of the Regulation

For the purposes of regulating the right to strike in the public sector, a distinction must be made between three categories of workers:

18. Law of 16 April 1979 regulating strikes in the services of the State and public establishments under the direct control of the State; *Loi du 16 avril 1979 portant réglementation de la grève dans les services de l'État et des établissements publics placés sous le contrôle direct de l'État.*
19. Projet de loi n° 1726 portant réglementation de la grève dans les services publics, Commentaire des articles, p. 18: 'The text of the draft takes up certain articles of the French law of 31 July 1963 relating to certain modalities of strikes in the public services, supplementing them, if necessary, with rules of principle which have been developed by French case law and which have not been taken up in the aforementioned law, because the French legislator only considered this law as a supplement to existing laws and regulations and to case law already established.'
20. Projet de loi n° 1726, Avis du Conseil d'État n° 26640, p. 2.
21. Projet de loi n° 1726, Avis du Procureur général d'État, 16 October 1973, p. 210.
22. Loi du 25 mars 2015 modifiant: (1) la loi modifiée du 16 avril 1979 fixant le statut général des fonctionnaires de l'État; (2) la loi modifiée du 9 décembre 2005 déterminant les conditions et modalités de nomination de certains fonctionnaires occupant des fonctions dirigeantes dans les administrations et services de l'État; (3) la loi du 16 avril 1979 portant réglementation de la grève dans les services de l'Etat et des établissements publics placés sous le contrôle direct de l'État (...); Loi du 27 mars 2018 portant organisation de la sécurité civile et création d'un Corps grand-ducal d'incendie et de secours.
23. Projet de loi n° 6457, Avis du Conseil d'État, 21 January 2014, p. 30: 'Les difficultés d'application qui se sont fiat jour, avec de plus en plus d'acuité, au fil des trente-quatre années d'existence de cette loi, demandent une réflexion approfondie sur la grève dans la fonction publique et sur les moyens à mettre en œuvre afin de la canaliser dans des voies qui ne mettent pas en danger la survie de l'État ni le fonctionnement ordonné des services garantissant les fonctions vitales de l'État'.

- State civil servants and assimilated persons, i.e., trainee civil servants, state employees, and auxiliaries working for the state or public establishments under the direct control of the state.
- Municipal civil servants (permanently or temporarily appointed), contractual municipal employees, and auxiliary staff working for the municipalities, municipal associations (*syndicats communaux*) and public establishments under the supervision of the municipalities.
- Persons under private law contracts.[24]

1.2.1 State Civil Servants and Assimilated Persons

The right to strike is regulated by the above-mentioned law of 1979. Collective disputes must be subject to a conciliation procedure before a *conciliation commission* (*commission de conciliation*). This commission is chaired by a magistrate of the judiciary and consists of five representatives of the public authority and five representatives of the trade unions. If the dispute is widespread (*litige généralisé*), only the most nationally representative trade union organisations for the public sectors (in fact, there is only one, the CGFP) appoint the members. If the collective dispute is not generalised but limited to one or another administration or to a sub-group of workers or functions, the nationally representative trade union organisation will appoint three representatives, while the trade union organisations representing more specifically the staff members in dispute will appoint the other two (Article 2 paragraph 2).

In case of non-conciliation, the dispute is submitted to the President of the Superior Court of Justice (*Cour Supérieure de Justice*) sitting as mediator (Article 2 paragraph 3).

The conciliation and mediation procedures are detailed in a Grand-Ducal regulation.[25]

If the conciliation procedure and, where appropriate, mediation fail and the staff decide to strike, the strike must be preceded by written notice, the aim being to avoid a *surprise strike* (*grève surprise*).[26] The strike must take place within six months following the failure of the conciliation procedure or, where appropriate, mediation

24. The draft law envisaged a uniform regulation of the right to strike for staff in the entire public sector and in the public services. In the end, the personnel concerned (civil servants, trainees, employees and auxiliaries) were listed in the law because of difficulties that would otherwise have arisen regarding the composition of the conciliation commission and the procedure to be followed. Projet de loi n° 1726, Avis du Conseil d'État n° 26640, p. 4. 'Private employees employed in the service of the State, employees of public establishments working under a contract of service, State workers'; *Ibid.*, p. 5.
25. Règlement grand-ducal du 30 septembre 2015 fixant la procédure de conciliation et de médiation.
26. Projet de loi n° 1726 portant réglementation de la grève dans les services publics, Commentaire des articles, p. 18: 'The "surprise strike" is prohibited. It is incompatible with the very notion of public service because it undermines the functioning of the services, it does not allow the authorities responsible to ensure, in any case, safety, nor to take the necessary measures to maintain the essential services in working order.'

(Article 3). This notice must be issued by the above-mentioned trade union organisations and must indicate the reasons, the place, the date, the time of the beginning, and the duration of the planned strike.

Article 4 of the 1979 Law prohibits certain forms of exercising the right to strike that are considered abusive. The aim was to outlaw, among other things, concerted stoppages that constitute 'political strikes (including government support strikes), warning strikes, solidarity strikes, work-to-rule strikes and pearl strikes'.[27]

Similarly, acts of violence against people or property and obstructions to freedom of work that accompany the strike make the strike illegal and strike as such becomes illegal for them.

Absence due to strike action results in a loss of pay at the rate of 30% of the monthly pay per day. Parts of a day are considered a full day.[28]

1.2.2 Municipal Civil Service

In the same way as for state civil servants, Article 43 paragraph 1 of the statute of municipal civil servants recognises trade union freedoms while referring to a legal framework for the exercise of the right to strike.[29] This framework in the municipal sector is provided by a 1985 law,[30] largely inspired by the 1979 law. The aim was to 'give civil servants in the municipal sector the possibility to strike under the same conditions and in the same forms as State civil servants'[31] while taking into account the specificities of the municipal sector.

There is also a conciliation commission chaired by a magistrate, the functioning of which is regulated by Grand-Ducal regulation.[32] The commission is composed differently depending on whether the conflict is limited to a single municipality or not. The President of the Superior Court of Justice acts as mediator. The rules on notice of strike, abusive forms of strike, and loss of pay are the same.

At both state and municipal levels, failure to comply with most of the rules governing the exercise of the right to strike results in a criminal fine between EUR 251 and 5,000 for staff members and trade union representatives.[33] This is the case, for example, if a strike is called without prior conciliation, without notice or in an abusive manner. Staff members may also face disciplinary consequences.

---

27. Projet de loi n° 1726 portant réglementation de la grève dans les services publics, Commentaire des articles, p. 21. The legal text was supposed to be a summary of the general principles applied by French judges to condemn certain abuses of the strike.
28. Projet de loi n° 1726 portant réglementation de la grève dans les services publics, Commentaire des articles, p. 21: 'The proportional deprivation of pay for failure to perform a service as a result of a concerted cessation of work is neither a sanction nor another disciplinary measure. It is a simple measure of good administration which is applicable whether or not the strike is lawful.'
29. Loi du 24 décembre 1985 fixant le statut général des fonctionnaires communaux.
30. Loi du 24 décembre 1985 réglementant le droit de grève dans les services du secteur communal.
31. Projet de loi n° 2658, Exposé des motifs, p. 1.
32. Règlement grand-ducal du 29 août 1988 portant fixation de la procédure à suivre devant la commission de conciliation et devant le médiateur en matière de droit de grève dans les services du secteur commun.
33. Article 6 of the 1979 Act, Art. 8 of the 1985 Act.

1.2.3 Staff under Private Law Contracts

Public actors have the possibility to recruit using private law contracts. In this case, the employment contract will be subject to the rules of the Labour Code, and the right to strike will be identical to that of employees in the private sector.

There are significant differences between the two regimes. The conciliation procedure works differently. There are three cases that can give rise to conciliation and the exercise of the right to strike: (a) disagreement in the case of negotiation of a collective agreement, (b) disagreement in the case of negotiation of a social plan (collective redundancies), and (c) more generally, collective labour disputes.

If conciliation fails, there is no mediation procedure but an optional arbitration procedure. The specificity of this procedure is that the arbitrator's decision is binding on the parties to the dispute, a solution that was considered unacceptable for public actors.[34]

Similarly, if conciliation has failed, strike action can be taken without the need to give notice. There is no requirement that it has to be one or more unions deciding to call a strike, although, in practice, this will usually be the case.

The law does not regulate the conditions for exercising the right to strike in any other way. According to the case law, the employment contract is not terminated but suspended. This leads to a proportional loss of pay. It is not clear whether the exercise of violence makes the strike as such unlawful for the person exercising it. Even in the absence of a text, it can be accepted that certain forms of strike, such as a slowdown, are prohibited. Since the object of a strike can only be professional claims against the employer, both political and solidarity strikes are in principle excluded. The requirement of prior conciliation prevents surprise and warning strikes. However, there are voices questioning these strong restrictions.

2 PERMITTED RESTRICTIONS

2.1 Certain Categories of Public Servants

2.1.1 State Level

At the state level, section 1 paragraph 2 of the 1979 law excludes a number of persons from exercising the right to strike. The original bill did not contain such exclusions and

34. Projet de loi n° 1726 portant réglementation de la grève dans les services publics, Commentaire des articles, p. 189: 'The State, in its relations with its employees, cannot be placed on the same footing as a private employer. Unlike the latter, it may be obliged to refuse to satisfy certain professional demands for reasons which engage the general responsibility of the Government. This is the case, in particular, when the satisfaction of these demands would compromise the budget balance. The intervention of an irresponsible arbitrator would, in this case, be both inconceivable and useless. Parliament itself could not play this role, both because it would encroach on the executive's own powers, and because it cannot bring the Government's political responsibility into play if ... It follows from these considerations that a real arbitration procedure is not conceivable in the public sector ...'; Projet de loi n° 1726, Avis du Procureur général d'État, 16 October 1973, p. 211: 'Non conciliation cannot, for obvious reasons, give rise to a real arbitration but only to a subsequent phase called "mediation"'.

was based solely on the right of requisition, discussed below. It would therefore have been up to the authority to decide who is deprived of the right to strike. In the end, the system adopted is twofold: Certain categories of people are automatically excluded from the right to strike, while others can be requisitioned.

The balance sought between the freedom to strike and the continuity of public services implied, according to the Council of State, that 'the use of strike action is purely and simply forbidden to certain categories of public employees'.[35] The CHFEP agreed with such restrictions: 'The Chamber ... considers that categories of civil servants whose task it is to ensure the maintenance of public order, i.e., magistrates and staff of the judicial administration and the prison administration and members of the public force not seconded to other services, must be positively forbidden to strike.'[36]

In the original bill, it was intended that an implementing regulation (decree-law) would define the public services whose operation is considered essential. The CHFEP objected to this, arguing that it was up to the legislator to decide on this list.[37] The State Attorney General had also objected to the reference to a simple implementing regulation. He feared that the great freedom given to the government would allow it to empty the law of some of its substance. He therefore advised listing the indispensable sectors in the text; 'these would be functions that involve the immediate exercise of sovereignty, power or public force, which excludes strikes by members of the Government, the judiciary, the gendarmerie and the police, as well as functions such as the medical service, education and civil protection'. With the exception of education, the legislator will essentially follow this enumeration.

Thus, in the new text proposed by the government in 1975, the reference to an implementing regulation was deleted in favour of a list of persons excluded from the right to strike. The CHFEP agreed with this new text; it 'agrees in principle that the civil servants mentioned cannot refuse service without seriously compromising the functioning of the State, public order or the safety of citizens'.[38]

The list of persons deprived of the right to strike, which – except for firemen – has not changed since 1979, is as follows:

(1) Members of the government, more precisely 'officials whose functions were created on the basis of Article 76 of the Constitution'. Since the constitutional revision of 2023, the reference to Article 76 is no longer accurate.[39]
(2) The diplomatic corps, specifically 'Envoys Extraordinary and Ministers Plenipotentiary, Legation Counsellors, and other diplomatic agents, if they exercise

35. Projet de loi n° 1726, Avis du Conseil d'État n° 26640, p. 3.
36. Projet de loi n° 1726, Avis de la Chambre des fonctionnaires et employés publics, 19 July 1974, p. 216.
37. *Ibid.*, p. 221.
38. Projet de loi n° 1726, Avis de la Chambre des fonctionnaires et employés publics, 25 November 1975, p. 160.
39. It would probably be appropriate to refer to Art. 88 of the Constitution. The question arises whether the Secretaries of State (*Secrétaire d'État*), who are now mentioned in the Constitution, would also be deprived of the right to strike.

the functions of Head of Mission abroad on a permanent or ad interim basis.' The diplomatic corps was not included in the original bill due to an *oversight*.[40]

(3) Magistrates of the judicial order. The authors of the law were inspired by French law concerning the exclusion of strikes for the judiciary.[41] This addition was made on the proposal of the Council of State.[42] It should be noted that at that time, the Council of State was also the only administrative court. In the meantime, the Administrative Tribunal and the Administrative Court have come into being. One may wonder why the right to strike is open to them when they seem to be just as indispensable.

(4) Heads of administration and their deputies.

(5) The directors of educational institutions and their deputies.

(6) Staff of the judicial and prison administrations.

(7) Members of the *force publique*. This includes the Luxembourg army,[43] as well as the police force. While in 1979 there was a gendarmerie and a national police force, these two bodies were merged on 1 January 2000 into a single grand-ducal police force.[44]

(8) The professional firefighters of the Grand-Ducal Fire and Rescue Service (CGDIS, *Corps grand-ducal d'incendie et de secours*). Firemen were added in 2015 by the law that professionalised and reorganised rescue in Luxembourg.[45] In this addition, which comes 36 years after the 1979 law, the authors of the bill do not ask themselves many questions about the justification of this restriction. They were inspired by the philosophy of the 1979 law admitting 'restrictions on the right to strike in the public services, in particular when it is a question of guaranteeing the continuity of the services necessary for the good functioning of the State'. The inclusion of professional firefighters in the list 'is justified by the fact that the functioning of the emergency services must be guaranteed at all times, in order to safeguard the general interests of the State and the municipalities and, in particular, to guarantee their safety in the event of vital distress, accidents, calamitous events, disasters and fires'.[46]

(9) Medical and paramedical staff on duty (*personnel medical et paramedical des services de garde*), security agents (*agents de sécurité*), and staff responsible for security (*personel chargé de la sécurité dans les services*). The exact scope of this restriction is subject to interpretation. The CHFEP had raised the fact

40. Projet de loi n° 1726, Avis du Conseil d'État n° 26640, p. 6.
41. Article 10 of French Ordinance No. 58-1270 of 22 December 1958 on the organic law relating to the status of the judiciary lays down rules that have a dual basis in the historical tradition of ruling out the risk of obstruction of the judiciary and in the need to allow citizens to seek justice at any time.
42. Projet de loi n° 1726, Avis du Conseil d'État n° 26640, p. 13.
43. In its initial version, Bill 1726 only referred to *civil* personnel.
44. Loi du 31 mai 1999 portant création d'un corps de police grand-ducale et d'une inspection générale de la police.
45. Loi du 27 mars 2018 portant organisation de la sécurité civile et création d'un Corps grand-ducal d'incendie et de secours.
46. Projet de loi n° 6861, Commentaire des articles, p. 59.

that the notions of *service de garde* and *agents de sécurité* are not defined.[47] The State Council also considered that the Government should provide a justification and clarify these notions.[48] The CHFEP furthermore questioned the scope of *medical personnel.*[49]

2.1.2 Municipal Level

At the municipal level, the exclusion list set out in Article 1 paragraph 2 of the 1985 law is much shorter. It refers only to 'medical and paramedical personnel in the on-call services, security agents and personnel responsible for security'.

It is noted that this formula was taken over from the 1979 law. The Council of State has reiterated its criticism that these concepts are not clearly defined.[50] The parliamentary commission has provided some clarification,[51] which is not reflected in the legal text. The objective here was 'to ensure at all times the proper functioning of the services of the communal sector and in particular the medical and security services. The right to strike will therefore only be exercised within the limits compatible with the safeguarding of the responsibilities involved'.[52]

The original text of the bill still referred to 'administration and their deputies'. This text was taken from the 1979 law. However, the CHFEP opposed it, pointing out that the situation is not comparable at the municipal level;[53] the Council of State was

47. Projet de loi n° 1726, Avis de la Chambre des fonctionnaires et employés publics, 25 November 1975, p. 161: 'As for the *security agents*, unless the Chamber is mistaken, and apart from the forces of law and order which are already mentioned in the text, the State has only one service which could be described as such. ... The notion is open to extension at will, which proves the need to specify it if, in the event of a conflict, one wishes to avoid unpleasant surprises on both sides.'
48. Projet de loi n°1726, Avis du Conseil d'État n° 26640, p. 7: 'The Council of State shares the view that there is currently no text defining these concepts and finds neither in the body of the explanatory memorandum nor in the commentary on the articles a definition, or even a precise qualitative indication, that would enable it to form an idea of the scope of the prohibition rule. The Council of State is in no way opposed to medical or paramedical staff of *station services* and *security agents* falling within the scope of this rule, but it considers that the Government should provide a justification for this restrictive measure, while specifying its field of application.'
49. Projet de loi n° 1726, Avis de la Chambre des fonctionnaires et employés publics, 25 November 1975, p. 161: 'In the medical field, does it refer to all the staff of the clinic who, in a city, are on call or does it refer, in each clinic, to the members of the team who are on call in accordance with the internal regulations?'.
50. Projet de loi n° 2658, avis du Conseil d'État, 22 March 1984, p. 2.
51. Projet de loi n° 2658, Rapport de la Commission des affaires communales et de l'aménagement du territoire, p. 23: 'It is understood that among the personnel deprived of the right to strike, the terms *medical and paramedical personnel of the services on duty* refer to doctors and nurses on duty, that the terms *security agents* refer in particular to the professional fire brigade and that the terms *personnel responsible for security in the services* refer only to personnel specially appointed for this task.'
52. Projet de loi n° 2658, Commentaire des articles, p. 2.
53. Projet de loi n° 2658, Avis de la Chambre des fonctionnaires et employés publics, 25 March 1983: Heads of administration and their deputies 'are not the counterparts in the communal sector of the heads of administration and their deputies, referred to in the law of 16 April 1979. The latter excludes from the strike the directors and deputy directors of the large State administrations, but not the heads of department. The heads of administration in the communal sector are rather the

in favour of maintaining this exception.[54] The parliamentary commission finally decided not to deprive them of the right to strike,[55] while recalling that they can be requisitioned.

At the time, the Association of Luxembourg Cities and Municipalities also questioned whether this list was exhaustive; it felt that the fire and civil protection services should be explicitly listed.[56]

It should also be noted that Luxembourg has no municipal police, so there is no need to mention the public forces at municipal level. Only a municipal police pilot project has recently been launched as a temporary test phase in two cities; the officers involved remain members of the national police force.

2.2 Essential Services in the Strict Sense of the Term

For services deemed essential, a general right of requisition (*droit de réquisition*) is provided in the public sector. However, this only applies to civil servants and similar persons and not to employees under private law contracts.

According to Article 5 of the 1979 law, by decision of the Government in Council, ministers may be authorised to requisition or cause to be requisitioned all or some of the civil servants and similar persons 'necessary to the functioning of the services essential to meet the needs of the country' (*indispensables au fonctionnement des services essentiels pour assurer les besoins du pays*).

At the municipal level, the original bill only gave the right of requisition to the Minister for the Interior. However, the CHFEP considered that this right should be given to the local authority.[57] Following a proposal by the Council of State,[58] both the Minister for the Interior and the mayor can now make requisitions.[59]

Requisition orders may be individual or collective. They are brought to the attention of the people concerned by appropriate means such as individual notification, posting, publication in the Mémorial (official journal), and in the daily written and spoken press. Refusal to comply with such a requisition is punishable by a criminal fine

elected representatives and not salaried employees, even managers, who are only executors of the directives given by the elected local authorities'.

54. Projet de loi n° 2658, avis du Conseil d'État, 22 March 1984, p. 1: 'The Council of State considers, however, that the presence of the heads of the services is required in the event of a strike, firstly to advise the communal authorities called upon to take decisions, and secondly to organise the implementation of these decisions.'
55. Projet de loi n° 2658, Rapport de la Commission des affaires communales et de l'aménagement du territoire, p. 2.
56. Projet de loi n° 2658, Avis de l'association des villes et communes luxembourgeoises, p. 1.
57. Projet de loi n° 2658, Commentaire des articles, p. 3: 'As regards any requisitions that may be necessary to ensure the functioning of essential services, the Chamber is of the opinion that the authority best placed to judge this is the local authority, but not the Minister of the Interior.'
58. Projet de loi n° 2658, avis du Conseil d'État, 22 March 1984, p. 3: 'The professional chamber considers that the local authority would be best placed to do this. The Council of State shares this opinion. However, it fears that in certain cases the mayor, for reasons of local politics, may not hesitate to resort to requisitions. For this reason, the Minister of the Interior should also be allowed to act.'
59. Respectively the President of a communal association (*Président d'un syndicat communal*).

of EUR 251 to 5,000 (Article 6), which may be increased to twice the maximum in the event of a repeat offence within two years. It is also a disciplinary offence.

At the state level, this right of requisition was justified on the grounds that 'the government, which is responsible for the proper functioning of public services, must have the right to requisition personnel to guarantee the functioning of services that it deems essential to meet the needs of the country'.[60] The assessment of the essential character is thus subject to the government's appreciation: 'The government will use this means according to the conception it has of the general interest. If this conception is not approved, the executive is always liable to be politically sanctioned'.[61]

At the time, the CHFEP considered that this right of requisition was too broad and therefore unconstitutional.[62] It even proposed that the union should decide, at the time of the strike notice, which services were essential to meet the country's needs and that it should, as it were, *requisition* the necessary staff who could not strike.[63] However, the law was kept as it was and the solutions at state level were taken up in 1985 at the municipal level.

If the authors of the bill were thus of the opinion in the 1970s that there is no recourse against requisition, it must be admitted today that the civil servant should have the possibility of challenging the qualification of *essential service*. They could probably do so by appealing to the administrative court against the requisition order or by challenging a criminal or disciplinary sanction imposed on them. In this case, the judges will have to balance the interest of service continuity against the free exercise of the right to strike. In this context, account may be taken of the ILO Convention No. 87 and its interpretation by the competent committees. The right to strike as guaranteed by the Constitution may also play a role. Since the 2023 reform, Article 37 of the Constitution states: 'Any limitation of the exercise of public freedoms must be provided for by law and respect their essential content. In accordance with the principle of proportionality, limitations may only be made if they are necessary in a democratic society and effectively meet objectives of general interest or the need to protect the rights and freedoms of others.'

60. Projet de loi n° 1726 portant réglementation de la grève dans les services publics, Commentaire des articles, p. 21.
61. *Ibid.*
62. Projet de loi n° 1726, Avis de la Chambre des fonctionnaires et employés publics, 19 July 1974, p. 219: 'This text, which is too broad, confers on the Government a general right of requisition which may render the right of public employees to strike illusory. As the Constitution requires that the law guarantees this right, the proposed text is unconstitutional and therefore unacceptable. The Chamber agrees that certain essential services must be provided at all times. For this reason, it has already proposed in Art. 1 that certain categories of civil servants should not be allowed to go on strike at all. Of course, there are other essential services besides justice and law enforcement, but it is difficult to list them in advance, as needs may change. But then, could we not, as a first step, trust the public agents themselves? They are the ones who have always been able to ensure, without constraint, that the machinery of the state functions properly; they will certainly not be the ones who, in order to support a legitimate demand, would start to demolish the "engine room" that they have built and which supports them.'
63. Projet de loi n° 1726, Avis de la Chambre des fonctionnaires et employés publics, 19 July 1974, p. 22.

More generally, there is also the question of whether international and constitutional law allow for a text that grants such a broad discretion to the public authority in deciding what is considered to be an *essential service*.

2.3 Situations of Acute National or Local Crisis

There are no specific rules when it comes to an acute national or local crisis situation. However, according to Article 48 of the Constitution, the government may declare a state of urgent crisis 'in the event of an international crisis, real threats to the vital interests of all or part of the population, or imminent peril resulting from serious breaches of public security'. In such cases, the government may issue temporary emergency regulations *(règlements d'urgence temporaires)*, which may derogate from existing laws. It would therefore be possible to derogate from the 1979 and 1985 laws to further restrict the exercise of the right to strike. The state of emergency has so far been used only once, namely in the context of the COVID-19 pandemic.

3 COMPENSATORY GUARANTEES FOR WORKERS DEPRIVED OF THE RIGHT TO STRIKE

Luxembourg legislation does not explicitly provide for compensation rules for categories of civil servants deprived of their right to strike.

In 1975, the CHFEP demanded that groups of civil servants who are prohibited from striking should nevertheless be able to use the conciliation procedure if their normal negotiations do not lead to a satisfactory result. It considered that the text did not preclude this but proposed to mention it explicitly.[64]

It is true that the 1979 and 1985 laws are limited to prohibiting the above-mentioned people *from going on strike*. Conciliation and mediation procedures should therefore be available to them.

Luxembourg thus seems to satisfy the requirement that 'when the right to strike is restricted or prohibited in certain enterprises or services considered essential, or for certain public servants exercising authority in the name of the State, the workers should be afforded adequate protection so as to compensate for the restrictions imposed on their freedom of action'.

4 CONCLUSION

In conclusion, it should be noted that Luxembourg law largely excludes categories of public personnel from exercising the right to strike. In addition, the right to requisition is very broad with little legal framework.

It is questionable whether these restrictions are in line with the ILO Convention No. 87 on Freedom of Association and Protection of the Right to Organise. In particular,

64. Projet de loi n° 1726, Avis de la Chambre des fonctionnaires et employés publics, 25 November 1975, p. 161.

the interpretation given by the *Committee of Experts on the Application of* Conventions *and Recommendations* (CEACR) and the *Committee on Freedom of Association* (CFA) should be considered.

Luxembourg legislation is still based on the spirit of 1979. The Convention No. 87, which dates from 1948 and came into force in Luxembourg in 1958, was certainly applicable at the time but the question of compliance with international law does not appear in the parliamentary proceedings and discussions. On the contrary, the parliamentary work shows that the very question of the legitimacy of the strike in the public sector was still under discussion. Nobody questioned the fact that essential state services must be guaranteed, and apart from a few details, everyone agreed on the list of people deprived of their right to strike.

It should be noted in particular that, in contrast to the international interpretation of the ILO Convention, prison staff is excluded from the right to strike in Luxembourg. Teaching staff is not listed except for the directors of the institutions and their deputies. The exclusion of all medical and rescue services seems highly questionable.

No effort has been made to limit exclusions to what is strictly necessary.

Thus, it is highly likely that, as it stands, Luxembourg legislation is not in line with international law. The same questions arise with regard to the conformity of these laws with the Constitution; thereby, a referral to the Constitutional Court (*Cour constitutionnelle*) seems conceivable. This being said, given the very limited number of decisions on the right to strike, the likelihood that a court will be seized of these issues in the near future seems low. It is to be hoped that the legislator will take the lead and reform the right to strike, both in the private and public sector, in a way which is less restrictive and more respectful of fundamental freedoms. However, the past experience of a great social peace that did not require recourse to strike action creates reticence as to whether it is appropriate to loosen the conditions for exercising the right to strike. Nevertheless, especially in the private sector, the tide is turning and the trade unions are demanding a liberalisation of the right to strike.

CHAPTER 23

Restrictions on the Right to Strike in Malta

Lorna Mifsud Cachia

1 GENERAL INFORMATION

1.1 Legal Basis of the Right to Strike

There is no written provision in the Constitution of Malta on the right to strike. There is indeed no provision in Maltese Law giving workers the right to strike. This was confirmed by the Constitutional Court in 1977 in the landmark judgment *Dr Walter Cuschieri and Dr Carmel Vella v. Hon. Prime Minister on Behalf of the Government of Malta.*[1] This was a landmark judgment because of a number of reasons. It also came in a period of turmoil in Maltese history, which was seeing the extent of the effects of widespread industrial action. The facts were, initially, quite run-of-the-mill. In May 1977, the Medical Association of Malta (MAM) ordered a partial industrial action in the form of a partial strike in government hospitals. This order was not of course issued in a vacuum but was the culmination of a number of political and social events, which then culminated in this industrial action order. As a reaction, the Government of Malta, led at the time by Hon. Dominic Mintoff, passed Act number XX of 1977 through Parliament in June 1977 that, in essence, prohibited any private hospital or clinic from engaging any striking government doctor. Act XX of 1997 radically changed the medical landscape of Malta and, specifically, seriously reduced the field of practice of all those government doctors who had participated in the strike action.

One of the effects of said Act of 1977 was that even if such striking government doctors were dismissed from their government employment, they would still be precluded from being employed by private hospitals or clinics unless they were renounced in writing to any strike action in the future. It must be said that most

1. 30 November 1977; Appeal No. 70/77.

government doctors had private engagements because it was the nature of the medical profession at the time and hence, Act XX affected a significant number of government doctors. Succinctly put, Act XX not only curtailed the right to associate themselves with any union's action but, furthermore, significantly reduced the doctors' earning potential if, essentially, they did not renounce their freedom of association.

It must be stated again that the freedom of association argument was used in this case because there is no constitutionally protected the right to strike. Hence, some doctors filed an action alleging that Act XX of 1977 was a *retribution* for their having taken part in a legitimate act in furtherance of a trade dispute and, therefore, contravened Article 42 of the Constitution of Malta and, specifically, their freedom of association to belong to a trade union for the protection of one's interests.

The case was lost both at first instance and at appeal by the applicants.

The reasoning of the Court was that Act XX did not deprive any doctor of joining any trade union. Indeed, the doctors were members of MAM and were engaged in negotiations which protracted for months on end and which, regretfully, at that stage had given no solution. However, the mere fact that the doctors had joined the trade union showed that Act XX of 1977 was not violating any freedom of association of the doctors. The Court stated that the act of striking in those circumstances (i.e., for a period of six months) could only be taken as meaning that the other party (i.e., the Government) was being *invited* to retaliate and retaliate they did by enacting Act XX of 1977. Indeed, the Court went even to the lengths of describing a strike as not *a legal procedure* but *a trial of strength* between two opposing forces.

Hence, the Court, after quoting from various sources, stated that Act XX of 1977 was only a countermeasure to a previous one (i.e., the strike) in this *trial of strength* but the right protected under Article 42 paragraph 1 of the Constitution of Malta was not breached in any manner because the doctors could be and, effectively, were associated with MAM.

The reasoning in the judgment was, at best, the thin end of the wedge. There can be no real use of freedom of association if one's association can only be expressed on paper. What is the use of joining a trade union or any other association of persons without being able to actively participate in its acts to bring about a purpose? It is indeed a very superficial way of looking at the protection of freedom of association and, really, any fundamental right. It is also dangerous to call *strikes* as a trial of strength. Indeed, even though strikes can be abused, it has been through strikes that current worker protection throughout the European Union (but also in Malta) has evolved over the decades. Strikes – and all industrial action in general – may be the only tool in the hands of the worker to shape his own future and destiny. Hence, the arguments brought by the Court in the judgment were quite superficial and, it is submitted, the Court refused to look at the real reason behind the protection of freedom of association – that of furthering one's legitimate interests.

However, it highlighted one important factor: That the Court at the time did not consider that there was a right to strike.

It must be stated that in that same year, another momentous strike was taking place. In the first quarter of 1977, 200 bakers went on a strike. This had been unprecedented. At the time, Malta was, in fact, transitioning, economically and politically, though not legally, from its status as a colony of Great Britain, from which it had gained independence on the 21 September 1964, to a full-fledged and economically independent nation.[2] However, the 1970s brought along political and social unrest, which culminated in the late 1970s being overshadowed by widespread and wide-ranging strikes. Monochromatic pictures of long queues of housewives waiting in line outside bakers for their bread rations became imprinted in national memories, and even the court members' opinions were, no doubt, redolent of those pictures, which are still found on the internet till this very day.[3] Hence, this particular case had a particular social and political context, which could have, inadvertently perhaps, shaped the two judgments (at first instance and at appeal). However, it must be said that whatever the historic context, the judgment left much to be desired by way of protection of the (unwritten and indirect) right to strike.

The effects of this judgment were effectively reversed by another judgment, *Charles Spiteri v. Minister for Public Buildings and Works and Director of Public Works.*[4] In this case, decided a full 11 years after the *Cuschieri* judgment,[5] the applicant was President of the United Union for Gozitan Workers and Students and employee with the Public Works Department in Gozo, which is one of the islands making up the archipelago of Malta. In his capacity as President of the aforementioned Union, Mister Spiteri had ordered union strike action by means of a Directive issued for the purpose. A short time later, the applicant (and all striking employees) was denied a specific concession open to all Gozitan employees to leave work earlier on Friday afternoons. Ironically, after the strike was over, the concession was reinstated for all striking employees except for the applicant.

It was patently and manifestly clear that the concession had been withdrawn for the President of the Union and not reinstated precisely because the applicant, in his capacity as President of the Union, had ordered industrial action, and hence, the Government (his employer) wanted to *punish* him for ordering industrial action.

The arguments raised in this case were in relation to the applicant's freedom of association, freedom of expression, and freedom from discriminatory treatment. With respect to the applicant's freedom of association, the Court stated that, in withdrawing and not reinstating the applicant's concession to leave his workplace early on Friday (and returning later on Monday),[6] the Government was effectively *hindering* the applicant from enjoying his freedom of association and all that came with it, including of course, his activities as a member of the said trade union to protect his own interests. The Court also found that, as a result, the applicant was also subjected to discriminatory treatment since he was the only one whose concession had not been reinstated.[7]

2. Malta had obtained its independence in 1964.
3. https://www.bbc.co.uk/programmes/w3ct3c6m (accessed 30 July 2024, 12:24hrs).
4. Kollezzjoni Decizjoniji Vol. LXXIII.1.71.
5. Vide No. 1.
6. The concession was open to Gozitans working in Malta and Maltese working in Gozo to enable the workers sufficient time to travel to their islands and being able to have sufficient free time to enjoy the weekend with their families.
7. There were other arguments arising out of the applicant's public participation in general elections with a party which was different to the one in government.

This was a refreshing stance from the one adopted eleven years earlier. The Court here made it clear that one cannot divorce the freedom of association from the acts which one performs through the associations to protect his own interests, as the Constitution of Malta puts it. Furthermore, the Court made it clear that the wording of the Constitution is such as to ensure that even just a *hindrance* would amount to a breach of the Constitution – not just outright exclusion or prohibition. The wording of the Constitution is the following: 'No person shall be hindered in the enjoyment of his freedom of peaceful assembly and association, that is to say, his right peacefully to assemble freely and associate with other persons and in particular to form or belong to trade or other unions or associations for the protection of his interests.'

The Court therefore concluded that, with the non-renewal of the concession, the applicant's freedom of association was being hindered, and hence, the Court found for the applicant.[8]

It is arguably clear that the Court sought to push back the damage done to the freedom of association inflicted by the Court 11 years earlier and make it clear that any act which hindered the freedom of association was unconstitutional. Undoubtedly, the government doctors who had been precluded by means of Act XX of 1977 from practising in private hospitals and clinics were very much *hindered* in the exercise of their right of association. So, a full circle was made in these two cases, which confirm that: (1) there is no right to strike written (as it were) in Maltese Law but (2) it is a by-product and a legal inescapable consequence of the protection of the freedom of association of individuals.

Another important judgment in this sphere of employment law is the fact that the Court ruled that the freedom of association included the freedom of not associating. In the case *Philip Spiteri v. Sammy Meilaq as Chairman for and on behalf of the Drydocks Corporation*, the applicant was an employee of the state-owned Malta Drydocks.[9] The applicant was denied overtime for the very simple reason that he was not a member of a particular trade union. The applicant sued the Corporation, claiming that denial amounted to a breach of his freedom of association, which he argued included the right NOT to associate with any union. The Court confirmed indeed that the right not to associate oneself is a fundamental part of the exercise of one's freedom of association and, as a consequence, upheld the applicant's pleas.[10]

1.2 Main Features of the Regulation

No Article of Maltese Law stipulates that an employee has the right to strike. The Employment and Industrial Relations Act, 2002 (Chapter 452 of the Revised Edition of the Laws of Malta) (hereinafter 'the Act'), which is the parent Act and regulates

8. Not all the pleas of the applicant were upheld because the applicant had brought also other grievances. However, the Court upheld the applicant's pleas with respect to his right of association.
9. Kollezzjoni Vol. LXXIX.I.33, 8 March 1995.
10. The Court also found that the denial of overtime was also an infringement of applicant's right to freedom of expression and protection from discrimination.

industrial action in Malta, defines what trade unions and trade disputes are and the consequences of acts which are done in furtherance of a trade dispute.

The Act defines *trade dispute* as a dispute between employers and workers or between workers and workers, which is connected with any one or more of working conditions, termination and engagement, allocation of work or duties, discipline, facilities, negotiations, and any other matter related to employment:[11]

- terms and conditions of employment, or the physical conditions in which any workers are required to work;
- engagement or non-engagement, or termination or suspension of employment or the duties of employment of one or more workers;
- allocation of work or the duties of employment between workers or groups of workers;
- matters of discipline;
- facilities for officials of trade unions;
- machinery for negotiation or consultation, and other procedures relating to any of the foregoing matters, including the recognition by employers or employers' associations of the right of a trade union to represent workers in any such negotiation or consultation or in the carrying out of such procedures;
- membership or non-membership of a worker in a particular trade union.[12]

The Act also defines *trade union* as 'an organisation consisting wholly or mainly of workers and of which the principal purpose is by its rules the regulation of relations between workers and employers or employers' associations'.[13]

The Act makes it clear that there shall be no legal consequences arising out of trade disputes and the Act restricts legal liability in case of any act in furtherance of any trade dispute.[14] It is in this manner that Maltese Law makes it legal (as it were) to perform acts in furtherance of a trade dispute. The Act further stipulates what renders a trade dispute legal and what procedures and proceedings need to be followed with respect to trade dispute.

2 PERMITTED RESTRICTIONS

2.1 Certain Categories of Public Servants

2.1.1 Personal Scope of Freedom of Association

There are no specific exceptions to the freedom of association in the Maltese Constitution. In other words, there is no provision in the Constitution of Malta restricting the right to industrial action to any specific category of workers, such as police officers or air traffic controllers.

11. Article 2 of the Act.
12. *Ibid.*
13. *Ibid.*
14. Title II, Part I, Sub-Part II of the Act.

However, in and of itself, the Constitution of Malta makes it clear that there may be exceptions to the freedom of association for public officers.

The Constitution of Malta makes it clear that no law is to be deemed to be inconsistent with the Constitution of Malta if the law in question makes provision that is reasonably required in the interests of defence, public safety, public order, public morality or decency or public health; for the purpose of protecting the rights or freedoms of other persons;[15] or that imposes restrictions upon public officers.[16]

The *Cuschieri* case could have arguably fallen within the category of the doctors having no freedom of association when medical services had been suspended for six months due to the strike which was underway at the time.[17] However, it did not do so and, instead, ruled that the right to strike is *divorced* from the freedom of association. That case remains the only case which has tested the exceptions to the freedom of association against the background of (potentially) public health.

The *Cuschieri* case has found reverberations through history in the form of a decision taken by the Government of Malta in October 2011 that, through an amendment to the Police Act, Chapter 138 of the Revised Edition of the Laws of Malta, police officers could (and still can) join a trade union but not strike. Hence, it is interesting to note that the ramifications of the *Cuschieri* case, overturned in 1988 with the *Spiteri* judgment, still find scope as recently as 2011 with the decision with respect to police officers. Whether this was done unwittingly or otherwise is moot. However, the political decision to afford police officers the right to join a union was not courageous enough to allow them the right to strike. Subsequently, all members of the disciplined forces have the right to join a union but not strike.[18] In 2022, the Malta Police Union filed a constitutional action against the State, claiming that the prohibition against strikes is a constitutional breach. The action was rejected by the Constitutional Court and it upheld the first plea, which was based on the European Social Charter, which, the law held, is not part of Maltese Law on which a constitutional case can be based and unenforceable before the Maltese Constitutional Law in terms of Maltese Procedural Law.[19]

However, the Act precludes that holders of an office in the public service, declared by the Prime Minister to be an office, shall not become, and if he is shall cease to be, a member of that trade union in respect of which he may be required to represent or advise the Government in industrial relations with the union or unions representing its employees. In other words, there are holders of public offices who are precluded by reason of their employment from becoming members of a trade union when they are members of that same trade union and they may be required, as part of their employment regulations, to advise the Government about affairs with that particular

15. Article 42 para. 2 lit. a of the Constitution of Malta.
16. Article 24 para. 2 lit. 2 of the Constitution of Malta.
17. *See supra* s. 1.1 hereabove.
18. Article 67A.
19. Kawza 201/2022 – Malta Police Union (MPU) – *RTU 302 v. L-Avukat ta' l-Istat et.*

trade union in relation to its employee.[20] The Law describes such obligation as an implied term of his terms of service with the Government.[21]

The same restriction applies to any person employed in a managerial or executive post in any body corporate (public or private) having a distinct legal personality or any other person who, as part of his position, has to represent or advise the corporation (being his employer) in its relations with the union or union representing its other employees or a part thereof.[22] However, this prohibition applies only to a limited number of posts as defined in the Act. Whilst this is not a prohibition which is aimed at ensuring continuity of essential services, it is clearly aimed at ensuring that such individuals do not find themselves in a position of conflict of interest. To this end, it must be said that the fact that the numbers of these positions are limited shows that the real aim behind these provisions is the preservation of the integrity of the advice and consultation given to the employer by the relative worker and not the continuation of the provision of an essential service.[23]

2.1.2 Personal Scope of the Right to Strike

Maltese Law regulating industrial action, including strikes, bestows unto individuals following a strike directive issued immunity from tort and dismissal which would otherwise result from industrial action.[24] Furthermore, an employment agreement is suspended during a strike.[25] Article 64 paragraph 4 states clearly that: 'An act done by a person in contemplation or furtherance of a trade dispute and in pursuance of a directive issued by a trade union, whether he belongs to it or not, shall not be actionable in damages on the ground only that it consists in a breach of a contract of employment; and any act done as aforesaid, not being an act in breach of a collective agreement, or of a settlement, decision or agreement which is still binding in accordance with the provisions of article 70 or 72, or of a decision or award of the Tribunal, shall not by itself entitle the employer to terminate the contract of employment of, or discriminate against, any person doing any such act as aforesaid, and shall not constitute a break in the service of such person.'

However, there are categories of workers who do not benefit from the application of this Article and the Act lists the categories of workers to whom the provisions of Article 64 paragraph 4 do not apply:[26]

---

20. Article 67 para. 1.
21. *Ibid.*
22. Article 67 para. 2.
23. The actual number of posts subject to this prohibition is limited. Art. 67 para. 3 states that: *'Sub-article (2) shall apply only to such posts, being:(a) not more than three in the case of a corporate employer employing not more than two hundred persons;(b) not more than seven in the case of a corporate employer employing more than two hundred employees, as such employer shall have indicated in writing to the trade union of which the holder of the said posts may not be a member.'*
24. Article 63 paras 1-3.
25. Article 64 para. 4.
26. Article 64 para. 6.

- persons employed as Air Traffic Controllers at the Malta International Airport and in the Airport Fire Fighting Section of the said airport;[27]
- members of the Civil Protection Corps established by virtue of the Civil Protection Act;[28]
- persons employed to provide pilotage and mooring, tug services, firefighting, medical health services, and pollution combating services as may be required in cases of port emergency.[29]

The three categories listed above are identifiable from the services they perform. Their numbers seem to be immaterial – the Act does not distinguish there being one hundred or one thousand Air Traffic Controllers, by way of example. As long as one is an Air Traffic Controller, one cannot strike.

However, the list continues by depriving the protection of Article 64 paragraph 4 by virtue of the number of workers actually carrying out a specific service. The list in Article 64 paragraph 6, goes on to read as follows:

(1) Such minimum number of persons needed to guarantee that life is not endangered through the non-import or discharge into Malta of wheat, grain, domestic gas, aviation fuel, diesel, and petrol and oil fuel for the operation of air transport facilities and power generation and water facilities, as agreed upon by their respective employer and the recognized trade union or in default of such agreement, as shall be decided by the appropriate controlling body or in the absence of such body, the Industrial Tribunal.[30]

(2) Such minimum number of persons as may be required to guarantee the combined production, provision, and distribution of water and electricity, as agreed upon by their respective employer and the recognized trade union or in default of such agreement, as shall be decided by the Industrial Tribunal.[31]

(3) Such number of persons in such posts as the Minister may by notice in the Malta Government Gazette prescribe, as being necessary to provide service at the level of one-half of the public passenger transport services in Malta and Gozo and one-half of the scheduled public ferry services between Malta and Gozo and it shall be deemed to be an implied condition of the contract of employment of any employee employed in the public passenger transport services and scheduled ferry transport services that the said employee shall be obliged to perform duties as directed by the employer thereof in order to constitute the number designated as aforesaid and any employee failing to perform such duties without justification shall be liable to dismissal.[32]

27. Article 64 para. 6 lit. a.
28. Article 64 para. 6 lit. b.
29. Article 64 para. 6 lit. c.
30. Article 64 para. 6 lit. d.
31. Article 64 para. 6 lit. e.
32. Article 64 para. 6 lit. g.

It is clear that the Law has as its aim the continuation and non-interruption of the services provided, even though there is a difference between the first three categories of workers and these three categories of workers. This second set of three categories of workers depends on the actual agreed number of workers to apply, whilst the first set depends entirely on whether an employee is employed in that particular designation or otherwise.

An even broader category of workers is included in sub-article 64 paragraph 6 letter f, which states that the application of Article 64 paragraph 4 is precluded for such number of persons as may be required to maintain the continued and uninterrupted services listed in the Schedule to the Act and required to be manned at all times for the continued provision by the Government of essential services to the community. The Schedule to the Act goes on to list many different designations within the healthcare sector including the administration, consultants, paramedics and such like. The Act states that, in the case of these workers, however, where the number of public officers holding or employed in any of the offices listed in the Schedule is greater than the number indicated in the said Schedule as essentially required, only the more seniors of those officers who, together, make up that number. Seniority is to be reckoned either by means of whoever is more senior in the office or by the length of service or by age (in case of equality of seniority and length of service).

Finally, the Act also states that a trade union representing members of a disciplined force shall not be entitled to take any action in contemplation or furtherance of a trade dispute. Hence, whilst a member of a disciplined force may join a trade union, they cannot strike. The Malta Armed Forces Act, Chapter 220 of the Revised Edition of the Laws of Malta, makes it even clearer that any member of the Force who takes industrial action or who participates in any industrial action taken in the Force in contemplation or furtherance of a dispute may be guilty of a military offence against good order and military discipline.[33]

2.2 Essential Services in the Strict Sense of the Term

There is no definition of what constitutes an *essential service* in Maltese Law for the purpose of strikes and industrial action. However, it is implied from the Articles listed above that the Law deems all the services provided by the officials as being essential services. It is only with respect to the officers listed in the Schedule which the law lists as *essential* but it is undoubted that all the services provided by the workers and listed in Article 64 paragraph 6 are deemed to be essential.

The *essential* characteristic in the services listed in Article 64 paragraph 6 is self-evident and becomes even more self-evident when one considers the nature and the size of Malta. Air Traffic Controllers, for example, are considered to be providing an essential service. The same applies to all the other workers and sectors stipulated in Article 64 paragraph 6.

33. Armed Forces Act, Chapter 220 of the Revised Edition of the Laws of Malta, Art. 185.

The prohibition on the disciplined forces to strike is another implied recognition that public order prevails over any individual freedom to engage in act in furtherance of a trade dispute.

Indeed, even though Maltese Law does not define *essential services* and does not list any one service as being essential, it is clear that in not affording sectors of employees the possibility of striking without being in breach of their employment agreements/obligations, it is showing that the Law considers the services provided by those categories of workers as being *essential*.

2.3 Situations of Acute National or Local Crisis

The Constitution of Malta defines a period of public emergency as (*inter alia*) when there is a proclamation by the President in force declaring that a state of public emergency exists.[34] It is notable, however, that the Constitution of Malta does not define what amounts to a *public emergency* warranting a Presidential Proclamation. It had been extensively argued, in the early months of 2020, when the COVID-19 pandemic reached the Maltese shores and essentially ground it to a hold, that the President could and should have issued a Proclamation declaring there to be a situation of public emergency. Notwithstanding, given the unprecedented nature of the public health emergency, however, no Presidential Proclamation was issued, possibly because, if one were to apply the *eiusdem generis* rule to Article 47, COVID-19 and any other pandemic would seem to be excluded, given that *public emergency* seems to be equated to situations which threaten the integrity of the nation and/or democracy.[35] Instead, a Declaration of a Public Health Emergency was issued.[36] Essentially, this was enacted under the Public Health Act,[37] under which Law, the Superintendent of Public Health has wide-ranging powers including 'order such other action be taken as he may consider appropriate'.[38] What is worthy of note, however, is that three fundamental rights protected by the Constitution of Malta may be derogated from on the basis of there being a *period of public emergency* but not under a period of public health emergency in terms of the Public Health Act. So, one question which has arisen during the COVID-19 pandemic was whether even fundamental human rights can be suspended during such action and whether, therefore, the right to strike (as a ramification of the right to freedom of association) could be suspended. As a matter of fact, one such right which can be suspended as a consequence of Presidential Proclamation during a

34. Article 47 of the Constitution of Malta.
35. Article 47para. 2 reads as follows: ' – (2) In this Chapter 'period of public emergency' means any period during which – (a) Malta is engaged in any war; or (b) there is in force a proclamation by the President declaring that a state of public emergency exists; or (c) there is in force a resolution of the House of Representatives supported by the votes of not less than two-thirds of all the Members of the House declaring that democratic institutions in Malta are threatened by subversion.'.
36. Declaration of Public Health Emergency Order, 2020 repealed by Legal Notice 243 of 2020.
37. Chapter 465 of the Revised Edition of the Laws of Malta.
38. Article 15 lit. g of the Revised Edition of the Laws of Malta.

period of public emergency is precisely the right to protection from forced labour,[39] as a result of which the Constitution states that there shall not be deemed to be any forced labour in case of 'labour required during a period of public emergency or in the event of any other emergency or calamity that threatens the life or well-being of the community'.[40]

What is also of relevance is that Malta did not invoke Article 15 of the European Convention on Human Rights during the COVID-19 pandemic which notably deals with the situation of public emergency. Article 15 reads: 'In time of war or other public emergency threatening the life of the nation any High Contracting Party may take measures derogating from its obligations under this Convention to the extent strictly required by the exigencies of the situation, provided that such measures are not inconsistent with its other obligations under international law.'

Had Malta done so, the situation would have been far more clear cut but, for some reason, it did not.

So, the question arises: Could there be the right to strike during a situation of public emergency or national crisis? The Constitution of Malta makes it clear that forcing somebody to work during such a period (if so proclaimed) - and hence prohibiting them from striking - would not be tantamount to forced labour and the European Convention of Human Rights concurs in its own way.

Another situation of public emergency arose during the 1977 Doctors' Strike, which led to the judgments in *Cuschieri.*[41] The State had argued then that the doctors had brought about a national emergency because of their strike, but the doctors argued that it was not their protracted strike which had brought the situation of emergency but the fact that the Government had locked out the doctors of their workplaces just because they decided to strike. This situation did not in any manner throw light on whether strikes would be lawful in terms of public emergency, but it would appear that, only if the President proclaims it to be so, a period of derogation from (*inter alia*) protection against forced labour is lawful. Whether the Superintendent of Public Health has such wide-ranging powers, including that of (essentially) allowing for derogation from fundamental rights, is still quite unclear.

Medical doctors tested the matter during the COVID-19 pandemic in the Summer of 2020 when they went on strike in Malta when the Government decided to lift the ban on mass events, thus endangering public health and risking a second deadly COVID-19 wave without having any evidence supporting that lifting such a ban would be in the interest of public health at the time. The strike, unsurprisingly, was widely followed and declared to be an overwhelming success,[42] but the point that many made was whether doctors could go on strike given that Malta was going through a public health emergency with the doctors quickly pointing out that the declaration of public health emergency had been repealed.

39. Article 35 para. 2 lit. d.
40. *Ibid.*
41. *See supra* n. 1.
42. https://timesofmalta.com/articles/view/doctors-strike-is-overwhelming-success-mam.809775 (accessed 30 July 2025, 12:34 hrs).

It must be said that, at the time of the strike, the COVID-19 pandemic in Malta was held to be under control so much so that the Government reinstated all public mass events – a move which brought an explosion in COVID-19 infections in the space of a few weeks. The strike was a test of sorts in that particular climate and it further solidified the need to clearly distinguish what was and what was not permissible during a period of (undeclared) national emergency. Many were holding that we were not in a period of national emergency. The doctors begged to differ. Be that as it may, the issue was resolved eventually and the medical services returned to their normal pace.

It would appear, therefore, that in times of public emergency threatening to subvert the State, the nation or democracy duly proclaimed by the President, the (informal) right to strike is suspended whilst, under the European Convention on Human Rights, the right to strike is also suspended. If, however, there is no such proclamation and no invocation of Article 15 of the European Convention on Human Rights, but there is a declaration of public health emergency, the situation is not clear cut at all given that the Superintendent of Public Health may order any action as he may consider appropriate. Whether this action would be lawful if it is in violation of the protection from forced labour is unclear.[43]

3 COMPENSATORY GUARANTEES FOR WORKERS DEPRIVED OF THE RIGHT TO STRIKE

In order to compensate the workers who are deprived of their right to strike, the Act establishes a Joint Negotiating Council as a special negotiating machinery to address and deal with trade disputes concerning the conditions of work of persons providing the services listed in Article 46 paragraph 4 of the Act.[44] If no agreement is reached on the conditions of the workers providing such services, then the matter would have to be referred to the Industrial Tribunal.[45]

In a way, the Joint Negotiating Council is a representative body of sorts which seeks to address the issues arising out of the fact that, Article 46 paragraph 6, workers cannot participate lawfully in a strike.

4 CONCLUSION

Malta's restriction of the right to strike attempts is clearly aimed at the continuity of those services which the State considers to be essential for the proper functioning of the country. Even though unwritten, there undoubtedly is a right to strike as an expression of the freedom of association and the restrictions written in Maltese Law to the right to strike are a clear expression of what the country deems to be essential for its proper functioning.

43. It must also be stated.
44. Article 72 para. 1.
45. Article 72 para. 4.

CHAPTER 24

Restrictions on the Right to Strike in Montenegro

Vesna Simović-Zvicer

1 GENERAL INFORMATION

1.1 Legal Basis of the Right to Strike

The right to strike in Montenegro has a level of constitutionally guaranteed rights. Thus, the Constitution of Montenegro, in Article 66, provides that employees have the right to strike and that this right can be exercised limited to employees of the Army, police, state bodies, and public service in order to protect the public interest, in accordance with the law.

The strike as a method of resolving labour disputes was regulated by the Law on Strike of 2003, which envisaged a rather restrictive condition for the exercise of this right. This restrictiveness was reflected both in terms of exclusion of certain categories of employees from exercising the right to strike and in terms of conditions for the organization.[1] This is particularly the case for public interest activities, a move

1. The Law on Strike from 2003 provided for an absolute limit on strikes for government employees and professional police officers, whose employment was terminated when it was determined that they had organized or participated in a strike. As this provision was contrary to international standards, in which the right to strike is treated as a 'modern fundamental social right', which has the same rank as the right to work, property rights, and freedom of entrepreneurship, the Law on Amendments to the Law on Strike ('Official Gazette of Montenegro', No. 49/08), a more flexible solution was envisaged. Thus, employees of the Army of Montenegro, police and state bodies could not organize a strike if in that way the general interests of citizens, national security, security of persons and property, as well as the functioning of government bodies would be endangered. If it was determined that the mentioned categories of employees organized a strike contrary to the provisions of the Law, their employment relationship would be terminated. However, the mentioned provision did not substantially change the statement on exclusion of some categories of employees from exercising the constitutionally guaranteed right to strike,

indicating that trade union representatives as well as experts from relevant international organizations in the field of work – especially the International Labour Organisation and the European Union.

The current Law on Strike was adopted in 2015 and the solutions contained in it will be presented in the continuation of this paper.

1.2 Main Features of the Regulation

The Law on Strike contains a comprehensive definition of a strike.[2] A strike is defined as a work stoppage organized by employees to protect their professional, economic and social interests based on work. In doing so, work stoppage means an organized and continuous refusal of employees to perform their work tasks. According to the level at which it is organized, a strike can be organized as: a strike with the employer; in a particular branch, group, subgroup or activity; and as a general strike organized for the territory of Montenegro. If the method of organization is taken as a criterion, in addition to the warning strike, the following types of strike are also envisaged:

(1) *Rotating strike*, which is organized in such a way that only a part of the employees interrupt their work in a certain period, so that another group of employees comes in their place. This type of strike is in theory also known as a *circular strike*, since the stoppage of work refers to a part of the employees in one organizational unit, then in another and so on in a circle.

(2) *Selective strike*, which is organized in certain organizational units or business units of the employer. This type of strike means that only a part of the employees of the employer interrupt their work. This is especially important if it is a strike in activities of public interest, given that special conditions for organizing a strike, e.g., the number of employees covered by the minimum work process, refers only to that organizational unit with the employer.

(3) *Solidarity strike*, which is organized to support employees or trade unions that are already on strike with the same employer, in the same branch, group, subgroup or activity or at the state level, and can last up to one day. This solution in the Law is widely criticized by employers. One of the main objections to this solution is that the solidarity strike conflicts with the definition of strike in the Law. Namely, a strike is, according to the definition contained in Article 2 of the Law, a stoppage of work organized by employees in order to protect their professional, economic, and social interests arising on the basis of work. Thus, in the event of a solidarity strike, employees do not protect their interests but provide support to employees who are already on

because the legislator did not specify what is meant by the formulations: 'general interest of citizens', 'national security', 'security of persons and property', 'functioning of government bodies', which in practice left the possibility for broad interpretations, and thus left employees in state bodies and the police without the possibility to exercise this right. So, it is about the application of an international standard that was not sufficiently precise in our country and left doubts about the basic law – which is the right to strike.

2. 'Official Gazette of Montenegro', No. 11/15.

> strike, whether it is a strike on the part of the employer or a strike in the same branch, group, subgroup or activity or at the state level. A solidarity strike is also problematic in the case of providing support to employees who are on strike organized at the state level, which is defined in the Law as a general strike, given that by logic, the general strike should include all Montenegrin employees. One of the questions that arises in connection with the solidarity strike is the issue of determining the legality of the strike, from the aspect of material conditions for the strike or proving its subject, which is another argument in favour of criticism of this legal solution.[3]

The Law on Strike regulates the conditions and procedure for organizing a legal strike. Regarding the initiator of the strike at the employer level, the decision to go on strike within the employer shall be made by a competent body of the representative trade union[4] or more than half of the employees of the employer or its division. The decision to go on strike within a branch, or the decision to go on general strike, shall be made by a competent body of the representative trade union organized on a branch level or a state level.

When it comes to the procedural conditions for organizing a strike, it is envisaged that in case a strike is organized at the employer, the strike committee is obliged to announce the strike in writing to the employer no later than five days before the day set for the strike, or 24 hours before the warning strike. In the case of a strike at the branch level, the decision is delivered to the competent representative association of employers, the founder, and the state administration body in the area where the strike is organized, where the deadline is no later than 10 days before the day set for the start of the strike. The decision to go on strike contains the following information: type of strike, demands of strike participants, strike start time, the venue and manner in which the strike is conducted, the composition of the strike committee that represents the interests of employees and leads the strike on their behalf, and the list of employees who are on strike. In addition, the obligation of the strike committee is to submit

3. Cf. V. Simović-Zvicer, *Labour Law and Industrial Relations in Montenegro*, p. 229 (Kluwer Law International 2022).
4. The conditions for acquiring the status of a representative trade union (general and special), as well as the procedure for determining the representativeness of a trade union are defined by the Law on the Representativeness of Trade Unions. The general conditions are: to be registered in the Register of Trade Unions, which is kept by the Ministry of Labour and Social Welfare; to be independent of state bodies, employers, and political parties; and to be financed from membership fees and other sources, while special conditions depend on the level at which representativeness is determined.

   Special conditions for determining representativeness refer to the percentage of employees who are members of a trade union and it is determined differently, depending on the level of trade union organization. Thus, in order to determine the representativeness of the trade union, it is required that the trade union gathers at least 20% of the employees at the employer. At the level of branch of activity, group or subgroup – that percentage is 15% of the total number of employees in that branch, group, or subgroup. To determine a representative trade union at the state level, the percentage of employees who are members of that union is 10%, but with this condition, it is also required that at least five representative branch-level trade unions are members of that union. *See* more: V. Simović-Zvicer, *Labour Law and Industrial Relations in Montenegro*, p. 199 (Kluwer Law International 2022).

possible changes to the list of employees who are on strike within 24 hours. Such a solution can be criticized for the possible consequences that employees whose names are on the list may suffer from the employer after the end of the strike (e.g., mobbing). However, such a solution is fully justified, if the other provisions contained in the Law are considered. Namely, the strike can be expressed by the absence of employees from work. In that case, the employer, if there is no list of employees who are on strike, and some of them are not at work, may, in accordance with the Labour Law and the collective agreement, take appropriate measures (disciplinary liability, termination of employment contract) to sanction their absence from work. In case their names are on the list of employees who are on strike, there will be no danger of the mentioned consequences. In addition, employees who are on strike do not have the right to earnings. However, a number of employees may give up on further work interruptions during a strike. For this reason, the strike committee is obliged to submit changes to the list within 24 hours of their occurrence. Such a solution is in the interest of employees who have decided to continue working because as long as their name is on the list of employees, they will not have the right to earnings.

A strike can be expressed by a peaceful gathering of employees within the employer's workspace or in the vicinity of the employer's workplace. Therefore, there is no possibility for the strike to be expressed also in the workplaces of employees who are on strike. Such a solution is in accordance with the principles of protection of property and means for the work performance of the employer, as well as the obligations of participants during the strike. Namely, members of the strike committee and participants in the strike must not prevent and obstruct employees who are not on strike in the performance of their work duties, nor must they prevent or obstruct the employer from using and disposing of the means for performance of activities. In addition, the strike committee and employees participating in the strike may not use the means for the work of the employer during the strike. This solution has been criticized by trade union representatives with the argument that it can only limit their right to strike. However, such an argument is not adequate, nor is it in line with the principles of protection of property and means for work of the employer.

A logical question arises: If employees are on strike – which by definition implies an interruption of work – why would they use the means for work of the employer?

In addition, this provision should be brought into context with the solutions contained in the Labour Law, which imply the obligation of the employer to provide conditions for the work of the trade union (which includes both space and its equipment).

2 PERMITTED RESTRICTIONS

2.1 Certain Categories of Public Servants

The Law on Strike provides some restrictions regarding the exercise of the right to strike. According to the solutions contained in the Law on Strike, employees of the Army of Montenegro, police and state bodies, and businesses of public interest can organize a strike in a way that will not endanger national security, security of persons and property, general interest of citizens, and the functioning of government bodies, in accordance with the Law. The assessment of whether the organization of a strike in the Army of Montenegro, police and state bodies endangers national security, security of persons and property, general interest of citizens, as well as the functioning of government bodies is given by the state administration body in charge of national security, within 24 hours from the day of the announcement of the strike, about which it adopts an act in writing.

However, the Law on Strike does not differentiate between employees in state bodies who are holders of public authority and those employees who do not have that authority. Having in mind the fact that the purpose of restricting the right to strike in a specific case is *public interest*, that restriction of the right to strike for employees in state bodies who are not holders of public authority has no justification.

2.2 Essential Services in the Strict Sense of the Term

The restrictions on the exercise of right to strike refer to four categories of employees, as follows:

- employees in the army, police, and state bodies;
- employees in activities of public interest;
- employees in the field of secondary and higher education;
- employees in activities with special technological requirements.

One of the conditions for organizing a strike in these activities is to ensure a minimum work process. The Law on Strike provides two ways to determine the minimum work process. Specifically, it is envisaged that the act on the minimum work process is determined by an agreement between the competent state administration body, the representative association of employers, and the representative trade union no later than 90 days from the day the Law enters into force. If an agreement is not reached within this deadline, it is envisaged that the procedure for determining the minimum work process will be conducted before the Agency for the Peaceful Settlement of Labour Disputes. In contrast to the first three categories of employees, in which the minimum work process is introduced to protect the public interest, in the fourth category of employees, the reason for the minimum work process is special technological processes, such as chemical industry, ferrous and nonferrous metallurgy. Explicitly, these activities are about specific technological processes whose interruption of work, due to the nature of work, could lead to damage to work equipment, i.e., cause immediate danger to life and health of employees or create unfavourable conditions for work and environment. For these reasons, one of the conditions for organizing a strike in these activities is to ensure the technological minimum of the work process.

Another question concerning the minimum work process deserves special attention, and that is: Who should determine the employees who will work during the strike – the employer or the strike committee? The Law on Strike stipulates that employees who are obliged to work during a strike in order to ensure the minimum work process are determined by the management body of the employer at the proposal of the strike committee. In doing so, the strike committee is obliged to submit a proposal no later than 24 hours before the start of the strike, and the governing body of the employer has the right to determine the employees who are obliged to work to ensure the minimum work process. In addition, there is an obligation for the strike committee to cooperate with the employer during the strike in order to ensure a minimum work process. The strike committee has the right to propose the rotation of employees who are obliged to work during the strike at certain time intervals. This solution is especially important due to the fact that employees who are hired to ensure the minimum work process are entitled to earnings, in proportion to the time spent at work.

2.3 Situations of Acute National or Local Crisis

When it comes to strikes in activities of public interest, the Law on Strike distinguishes between *vital services*, in which more restrictive conditions for organizing a strike are necessary, and *public services*, in which these restrictions do not necessarily exist.[5] However, services that are not considered vital can become so (which justifies a ban on extending the strike), if the strike is long-lasting or when it takes on such proportions that it directly endangers the life, health or personal safety of (part or all) the population. This differentiation of vital and public services is necessary not only because of the flexibility of conditions for the exercise of basic social rights, such as the right to strike but also because of the need to establish a balance between general and professional interests. Therefore, activities of public interest, in the sense of the Law on Strike, are as follows:

- production and distribution of basic food products (flour, milk, oil, sugar, and baby food);
- production, transmission, distribution, and supply of electricity;
- transport of passengers in traffic (road, rail, and air traffic);
- postal traffic (universal postal services);
- public electronic communications in accordance with the law;
- information programmes of the public broadcasting service;
- public utility services/activities (production and water supply, garbage collection, production, distribution and heat supply, funeral services, etc.);
- production, distribution and supply of oil, coal, and gas;
- fire protection;
- health and veterinary protection;
- pre-school and primary education;

5. The term *vital service* must be understood in a much narrower sense than the term *public service*. Not all public services are considered vital. In other words, it does not mean that all public services are – just because they are public – vital, essential importance to the community, public safety, security, well-being, and health.

- social and child protection;
- fulfilment of obligations from confirmed international agreements.

Thus, the Law on Strike distinguishes between two types of activities of public interest. The first, which are listed above, are activities whose interruption of work due to the nature of the work could endanger the life and health of people or the general interest of citizens. In these activities, employees are obliged to adhere to the minimum work process from the first day of organizing the strike. From these types of activities, the Law distinguishes activities in the field of secondary and higher education, which in terms of legal solutions are considered activities of public interest, if the strike due to the duration and scope could take such proportions to jeopardize the implementation of the educational programme for the current school year. The decision that the implementation of the educational programme for the current school year is endangered due to the duration and scope of the strike in these activities is made by the Arbitration Council established at the Agency for Peaceful Settlement of Labour Disputes at the request of the state administration body responsible for education.

Positive legal solutions in Montenegro envisage the possibility of resolving disputes arising during the strike through arbitration in two cases, that is: On the occasion of deciding on the minimum work process and on determining whether the public interest is endangered due to the strike in the field of secondary and higher education.

In the first case, dispute resolution before the Agency for Peaceful Settlement of Labour Disputes is in the spirit of the idea that a strike, although a forced method of resolving collective labour disputes, should contribute to the development of social dialogue, so that the decision on determining the minimum work process should be the result of compromise of the parties to the dispute. This means that when deciding on the minimum work process, one of the basic principles in labour law must be respected - the principle of tripartism. Exactly such a solution is contained in the Law on Strike. Namely, if it is not possible to determine the minimum work process at the level of a certain branch, a procedure is initiated before the Agency for Peaceful Settlement of Labour Disputes. The procedure is initiated based on a notification by the competent state administration body, after which the director of Agency for Peaceful Settlement of Labour Disputes is obliged to establish an Arbitration Council within fifteen days to determine the minimum work process. The Arbitration Council shall consist of one representative of the parties to the dispute and one member from among the experts in the field for which the minimum work process is determined. The parties to the dispute shall appoint their representatives as members of the Arbitration Council, and a member from among the experts shall be nominated by the competent state administration body in the field for which the minimum work process is determined. It is important to note that although the decision on the establishment of the Arbitration Council is made by the Director of the Agency, that decision is made based on a proposal from the Agency's Management Board (consisting of representatives of employees, employers, and the government), so the principle of tripartism is respected. The Arbitration Council shall decide on the minimum work process within 30 days of the date of establishment.

In the other case, on the occasion of organizing a strike in the field of secondary and higher education, an Arbitration Council with a tripartite composition is established by the Director of the Agency for Peaceful Settlement of Labour Disputes within five days from the day of submitting the request. The Arbitration Council is obliged to make a decision on whether the realization of the educational programme for the current school year is endangered due to the strike within 10 days from the day of its establishment. It is important to note that employees in the field of secondary and higher education are obliged to adhere to the minimum work process only after it has been determined in the decision of the Arbitration Council that the public interest is endangered due to the strike in these activities.

3 COMPENSATORY GUARANTEES FOR WORKERS DEPRIVED OF THE RIGHT TO STRIKE

The right to strike in Montenegro belongs to all employees. The employment status of employees who participated in the strike is protected in such a way that the organization of the strike, i.e., participation in the strike under the conditions determined by the Law, does not constitute a violation of work obligations and therefore cannot be the basis for initiating proceedings to determine disciplinary and material responsibility of the employee, for lock-out of an employee from work and cannot result in termination of employment of the employee. In addition, the employer may not employ new persons during the strike to replace the participants in the strike, unless the following are compromised: Maintaining a minimum work process that ensures the safety of property and persons and fulfilling obligations arising from ratified international agreements. In order to prevent misuse, it is envisaged that the employer may not, during the strike, provide higher salaries or other more favourable working conditions for employees who do not participate in the strike.

In addition to the strike, the Law provides another mechanism for forcibly resolving disputes on the part of employees, and that is strike guards. They can be organized in places in front of the entrance to the business premises of the employer in order to inform the employees and the public about the dispute that has arisen and about the justification of the striker's request. This is one of the methods of resolving collective labour disputes, which is also known in comparative law and in the theory as *picketing*. This method of resolving disputes aims to put additional pressure on the employer to accept the demands of the strikers by informing the public and employees who did not support them and presenting the justification of the request to influence their support, as well as the public support. The media plays an extremely important role here which, by providing significant support to the participants in the strike, may improve their negotiating position in relations with the employer, which should ultimately result in the acceptance of their demands stated in the decision to go on strike. At the same time, this *pressure* that the participants in the strike exert on the employer does not imply the use of force. Namely, members of the strike guard cannot apply physical coercion, set up physical obstacles or blockades of access to business premises, i.e., the workplace, threaten or insult employees, nor prevent the employer from performing its activity. It is important to note that the strike guard must be established on the basis of a decision, which must be reasoned and contain the names of the members of the strike guard, and which is delivered to the employer within the deadline for submitting the decision to go on strike, as an integral part thereof or as a special act during a strike.

The Law on Strike provides for sanctions in case of non-compliance with the rules for organizing a strike, which concern both the obligation to compensate the employer and the employment status of employees. In this way, the difference is made between the responsibilities of the members of the strike committee and the participants in the strike. Namely, members of the strike committee who organized a strike contrary to this Law may have their employment terminated by termination of the employment contract by the employer, based on the final decision of the competent court that the strike is illegal. However, participants in a strike will be disciplined for a serious breach of duty, if, during the strike, they endanger the safety of persons and property or human health or prevent employees who do not participate in the strike from working or prevent the continuation of work after the strike or prevent the employer uses and dispose of the means with which the employer performs the activity. Also, a serious violation of the work obligation is committed by the employee who refuses to execute the order of the employer issued with the aim of ensuring the minimum work process. The Law also provides for a procedure for establishing the illegality of a strike or illegal lock-out from work, which can be initiated by the employer or the representative association of employers, the representative trade union, or the strike committee. The competent court shall decide on the request for determining the illegality of the strike or illegal lock-out from work within five days from the day of submitting the request.

As it begins with a decision, a strike ends with a decision to end the strike and may end with an agreement between the parties to the dispute. After that, for each new strike, a new decision must be made about going on strike. Such a solution is justified in the need to prevent the so-called *restarting of strikes*,[6] which was present in practice. Employees who took part in the strike are not entitled to salaries, unless they have been engaged to ensure a minimum work process – in which case they are entitled to salaries in proportion to the time spent at work. However, the Law on Strike provides a basis for the payment of salaries to employees who were out of work during the strike. This possibility means that the employer and the employees in the strike agree on it.

4 CONCLUSION

The right to strike is treated as a *modern fundamental social right*, which has the same rank as the right to work, property rights and freedom of entrepreneurship. The right to strike in Montenegro has a level of constitutionally guaranteed right.

Restrictions on the right to strike refer to four categories of employees, namely: employees in the Army, police, and state bodies; employees in activities of public

6. These are situations in which employees make a decision to go on strike and during negotiations with the employer they manage to resolve the dispute peacefully, only to suspend work again later, referring to the decision on strike they organized in the previous period.

interest; employees in the field of secondary and higher education; employees in activities with special technological requirements. Restrictions on the right to strike include the obligation to respect the minimum work process, longer deadlines for announcing a strike, as well as the possibility of cancelling a strike in the event that endanger national security, security of persons and property, general interest of citizens, and the functioning of government bodies.

Employees cannot suffer negative consequences for participating in the legal period, except that the employer is not obliged to pay them wages for that period. In the case of an illegal strike, consequences in the form of termination of employment are foreseen for members of the strike committee.

CHAPTER 25

Restrictions on the Right to Strike in the Netherlands

Miriam Kullmann & Suzanne Kali

1 GENERAL INFORMATION

1.1 Legal Basis of the Right to Strike

For as long as labour relations exist, collective labour disputes exist. Collective labour disputes were, especially in the early days and in the heyday of industrialisation, widespread.[1] Taking collective action can force a breakthrough in a collective labour dispute. Three types of collective actions can be distinguished in the Netherlands.[2] The first is the 'normal type of collective action' (*normaaltype collectieve actie*), referring to the traditional work strike. This type of collective action is characterised by the common refusal by a group of employees, or all employees, to perform the stipulated work in order to compel the (group of) employer(s) to a certain concession and with the intention of resuming work as soon as the goal is achieved.[3] Second, the collective action 'equivalent to the normal type', which is characterised by the circumstance that workers lay down their work to a greater or lesser extent but which differs in form, duration, content or purpose of the action. This would cover punctuality actions, slow-to-work actions, relay strikes, protests, sit-ins,[4] shorter and repeated work stoppages, offering services for free, or working Sunday shifts on a weekday (especially

1. Antoine TJM Jacobs, *Collectief arbeidsrecht* 205 (Wolters Kluwer 4th ed. 2017).
2. The three types of collective actions can, in general, be derived from Dutch Supreme Court ECLI:NL:HR:1986:AC9402, *NJ* 1986/688, 30 May 1986, *Nederlandse Spoorwegen*, point 3.3.
3. Kim van Belle, *De reikwijdte van art. 6 lid 4 ESH*, 5 Tijdschrift Recht en Arbeid 12, 13 (2015).
4. *See* on this Dutch Supreme Court ECLI:NL:HR:2015:1687, 19 June 2015, *FNV/Amsta*.

in the healthcare sector).[5] Such actions are often less radical and have less far-reaching consequences than classic work strikes.[6] And third, 'derogatory collective action', which is generally characterised by the fact that the emphasis is not (primarily) on refusing to work but on otherwise 'inconveniencing' the employer.[7] Covered are actions such as gate blockades, boycotts,[8] or blockades aimed at cutting off the targeted party, mostly the employer, from economic links, affecting the delivery of products and/or services; it may also result in employees working for the employer's business relationships to take collective action out of solidarity (*besmetverklaring*).[9] Given the variety of forms of collective action, this contribution will not be limited to work strikes in the traditional sense.

Strikes and other forms of collective action are not pleasant phenomena, not for those involved, not for third parties, and not for the government. Therefore, the Dutch legislator tried to regulate the (exercise of the) right to collective action. Initiatives for the private sector were taken in the 1960s and the 1970s and for civil servants in the 1980s and 1990s, yet without success.[10] Consequently, for collective actions, there is no legal basis in Dutch (labour) law. Instead, the right to take collective action has been acknowledged by the Dutch courts, who derive this right from Article 6(4) European Social Charter (ESC). This directly applicable provision allows the national courts to directly rely on this provision for the purpose of assessing the legality of collective actions.[11]

1.2 Main Features of the Regulation

With no national legislation in place regarding the right to take collective action, its 'regulation' in terms of interpretation and application mainly takes place by means of case law. However, it is useful to mention that many cases in which a collective action is planned are never brought before and thus tested in court. If a trade union is supporting or threatening with a collective action, usually negotiations will take place. Yet if negotiations do not lead to an agreement, legal action can be instituted by employers against that union via summary proceedings. In such proceedings, the preliminary injunction judge will usually be asked to uphold an injunction against the action with the imposition of a penalty payment in case the trade union, against the injunction, will take collective action. Judges quite often show the necessary understanding of the positions of both parties and then resourcefully make intermediate judgments, e.g., a temporary injunction against the collective action, possibly with an order to renegotiate and come back to court a week later, or a ban on certain aspects of

5. Buby den Heeten & Stefan Kleijer, *De (on)mogelijkheden van collectieve acties in de zorg*, 12 Tijdschrift Recht en Arbeid 4, 5 (2021).
6. Kim van Belle, *De reikwijdte van art. 6 lid 4 ESH*, 5 Tijdschrift Recht en Arbeid 12-13 (2015).
7. *Ibid.*, 14.
8. Antoine TJM Jacobs, *Collectief arbeidsrecht* 206 (Wolters Kluwer 4th ed. 2017).
9. *See* on this Dutch Supreme Court ECLI:NL:HR:2014:3077, 31 October 2014, *Enerco*.
10. Antoine TJM Jacobs, *Collectief arbeidsrecht* 210 (Wolters Kluwer 4th ed. 2017).
11. Dutch Supreme Court ECLI:NL:HR:1986:AC9402, *NJ* 1986/688, 30 May 1986, *Nederlandse Spoorwegen*. The Netherlands ratified the ESC in 1980.

the collective action. Where a collective action is banned, trade unions immediately call off the action and employees resort to work. If the collective action is allowed to continue, however, employers often quickly choose to renegotiate and, usually within a short period, the collective action will end, frequently resulting in an agreement.[12]

For a long time, the Supreme Court ruling in the *Nederlandse Spoorwegen* case contained the leading principles regarding the right to collective action.[13] It was in this court ruling that the Supreme Court confirmed the right to take collective action in the light of collective bargaining. Moreover, according to the Supreme Court, it is not necessary for the collective action to be directed at the employer: a collective action aimed at stopping government plans changing applicable employment law protection may equally fall within the protective scope of Article 6(4) ESC. Apart from interpreting the right to take collective action quite broadly, the Supreme Court identified a strict set of rules to be complied with in order for collective actions to be considered lawful: the so-called rule of the game test (spelregeltoets). According to the Supreme Court, the collective action had to be announced in a timely manner and used only as a means of last resort (*ultimum remedium*). This strict test opened up more possibilities to limit the right to collective action than Article G ESC appears to allow. In the more recent Supreme Court cases *FNV/Amsta*[14] and *Enerco*,[15] this view has been altered. The (previously) strict rules have since 2014 become viewpoints to take into consideration by national judges, together with other viewpoints such as public order and the rights and interests of third parties. This will be explained further in section 2.2 below.

2 PERMITTED RESTRICTIONS

2.1 Permitted Restrictions According to Dutch Case Law

The current test to decide whether or not the right to collective action may be restricted stems from the *Enerco*[16] and *FNV/Amsta*[17] cases. In *Enerco*, the rule of the game test from the Nederlandse Spoorwegen case[18] was not applied (anymore). Instead, this reflects a change and shift in long-standing jurisprudence; the Supreme Court ruled that the right to collective action can be restricted on the basis of Article G ESC, if the action infringes the rights of third parties to such an extent that restrictions are urgently necessary from a social point of view. Whether and, if so, to what extent restrictions can be placed on the (exercise of the) collective action depends, according to the Supreme Court, on weighing the fundamental right to collective action against the

12. Antoine TJM Jacobs, *Collectief arbeidsrecht* 201-211 (Wolters Kluwer 4th ed. 2017).
13. Dutch Supreme Court ECLI:NL:HR:1986:AC9402, *NJ* 1986/688, 30 May 1986, *Nederlandse Spoorwegen*.
14. Dutch Supreme Court ECLI:NL:HR:2015:1687, 19 June 2015, *FNV/Amsta*.
15. Dutch Supreme Court ECLI:NL:HR:2014:3077, 31 October 2014, *Enerco*.
16. Dutch Supreme Court ECLI:NL:HR:2014:3077, 31 October 2014, *Enerco*.
17. Dutch Supreme Court ECLI:NL:HR:2015:1687, 19 June 2015, *FNV/Amsta*.
18. Dutch Supreme Court ECLI:NL:HR:1986:AC9402, *NJ* 1986/688, 30 May 1986, *Nederlandse Spoorwegen*.

rights which will be infringed by exercising that fundamental right.[19] National judges have to take all the relevant circumstances of the case into account when weighing the relevant interests at stake. This line of reasoning has been further refined in *FNV/Amsta*,[20] which is currently the leading case for assessing the lawfulness of collective actions.

The Supreme Court's *FNV/Amsta* ruling concerned collective actions organised by the trade union FNV at healthcare provider Amsta. During these actions, the business was occupied by staff members, denying directors and executives access to the premises. This action had not been announced beforehand, and in court, Amsta set out to prevent such an action from happening again. Basically, the parties disagreed about whether or not this collective action falls within the scope of Article 6(4) ESC. The Court of Appeal in this case conformed to the rule of the game test from the Nederlandse Spoorwegen case,[21] deciding that FNV could not invoke the protection of Article 6(4) ESC since the collective action had not been announced in a timely manner and had not been used as an *ultimum remedium*. The Supreme Court, however, ruled differently. With reference to *Enerco*, the Supreme Court noted that the considerations of that ruling imply that (compliance with) the rules of the game – i.e., whether the collective action is used as an ultimum remedium and whether the collective action has been announced in a timely fashion, are no longer considered an independent standard for assessing whether a collective action is lawful.[22] This does, however, not alter the fact that those rules are still important in answering the question of whether the exercise of the right to collective action can be restricted in the light of Article G ESC. Consequently, the rule of game test is still a point of view in assessing whether the action should be restricted or prohibited. Interestingly, the Supreme Court added that the importance of the rules of the game from a point of view is not always the same; their weight will depend on the type of collective action. Thus, in case of a general strike, the rules of the game will have great weight, but this is less the case for a small collective action of limited duration not causing major damage.

According to the Supreme Court, a restriction of the right to collective action is only justified on the basis of Article G ESC if this restriction is urgently necessary from a social point of view.[23] In order to assess whether a restriction is urgently necessary, all circumstances must be weighed.[24] These circumstances may include: (a) the nature and duration of the action, (b) the relationship between the action and its intended purpose, (c) the damage caused by the action to the interests of the employer and/or third parties, and (d) the nature of the interests and the damage involved. In this context, it may also be considered whether the rules of the game have been taken into account. Without further specifying, according to the Supreme Court, under certain

19. Dutch Supreme Court ECLI:NL:HR:2014:3077, 31 October 2014, *Enerco*, para. 3.8.1.
20. Dutch Supreme Court ECLI:NL:HR:2015:1687, 19 June 2015, *FNV/Amsta*.
21. Dutch Supreme Court ECLI:NL:HR:1986:AC9402, *NJ* 1986/688, 30 May 1986, *Nederlandse Spoorwegen*.
22. Dutch Supreme Court ECLI:NL:HR:2015:1687, 19 June 2015, *FNV/Amsta*, para. 3.3.3.
23. Dutch Supreme Court ECLI:NL:HR:1997:ZC2309, 21 March 1997, *Vervoersbond FNV/VSN*.
24. Dutch Supreme Court ECLI:NL:HR: 1986:AC9402, 30 May 1986, *Nederlandse Spoorwegen*; Dutch Supreme Court ECLI:NL:HR:1997:ZC2309, 21 March 1997, *Vervoersbond FNV/VSN*.

circumstances, these rules of the game may even be decisive.[25] The criteria formulated in *FNV/Amsta* are valid for both civil servants and other workers, although it is apparent that a collective action by civil servants may have a higher risk of disrupting public order and being restricted as a result thereof.[26] An example can be found in a case where a planned collective action by special investigating officers (BOAs) on King's Day was prohibited due to considerations of safety (as outlined in section 2.2 below).[27] Correspondingly, the Supreme Court considers in *FNV/Amsta* that if a collective action also affects persons with a special vulnerability and affects the possibility of their care, as a result of which those persons are exposed to the danger of their mental or physical health being harmed, the action can be regarded as unlawful under Article G ESC.[28] The principles set out in *FNV/Amsta* have been applied in later case law and are still applicable.

In addition to the restrictions based on the case law described above, it is good to note that the right to collective action may also be restricted as a result of a peace clause in a collective agreement.

2.2 Compatibility of the Permitted Restrictions with Article G ESC

With its rulings in FNV/Amsta and Enerco, as said earlier, the Supreme Court set out a new direction for assessing the legality of collective actions in the Netherlands. On 12 July 2021, the European Committee of Social Rights (ECSR) received a complaint submitted by the European Trade Union Confederation (ETUC) and the Dutch trade unions FNV and CNV, alleging that the way in which Dutch higher and lower courts impose restrictions on collective actions would not be too restrictive and therefore not in conformity with Articles 6(4) and G ESC.[29]

The complaint raises four issues. First, the fact that in summary proceedings, courts use a legal standard (Article 6:162 Dutch Civil Code), namely proper social conduct, to assess whether an imminent or unlawful act has taken place. While this standard is usually applied after an act has taken place, in the context of the right to collective action, the standard is used in a prior assessment in which the court will judge the lawfulness of the collective action (paragraph 50).

Second, courts may impose restrictions on the (exercise of the) right to collective action, which may result in trade unions being limited or even prohibited in their right to collective action (paragraph 56). This results in an unstable and unforeseeable

25. Dutch Supreme Court ECLI:NL:HR:2015:1687, 19 June 2015, *FNV/Amsta*, para. 3.3.5.
26. Civil servants are usually employees due to the *Wet normalisering rechtspositie ambtenaren*.
27. Court of Amsterdam ECLI:NL:RBAMS:2019:3024, 26 April 2019, *Gemeente Amsterdam/FNV Veiligheid*.
28. Dutch Supreme Court ECLI:NL:HR:2015:1687, 19 June 2015, *FNV/Amsta*, para. 3.3.6; *see also* Dutch Supreme Court ECLI:NL:HR:1991:ZC0424, *NJ* 1992/508, 22 November 1991, *ABVA/KABO*.
29. Complaint No. 201/2021, *European Trade Union Confederation (ETUC), Netherlands Trade Union Confederation (FNV) and National Federation of Christian Trade Unions (CNV) v. the Netherlands*, Case Document No. 1.

framework of standards, affecting the (effectiveness of the) right to collective action (paragraph 57).

Third, while there is theoretically a possibility for trade unions to appeal an interim judgment, appeal may be rejected because the trade union may have no or an insufficient interest in an appeal because the collective action already has been terminated, a collective agreement has been concluded in the meantime, or other obligations have been fulfilled (paragraph 58). It is thus difficult for trade unions to submit the interim judgment to a proper assessment as to the correct application of Article 6(4) and G ESC.

And, fourth, the fact that the losing party may be ordered to pay the costs made by the other party for the appeals procedure may deter trade unions from taking collective action.

As said, with the FNV/Amsta and Enerco rulings, the rule of the game test takes place in the context of an assessment under Article G ESC. Therefore, based on these cases, the judge must weigh all circumstances to assess whether a restriction or limitation on the right to collective action is justified. These circumstances may, following FNV/Amsta, include: (a) the nature and duration of the action, (b) the relationship between the action and its intended purpose, (c) the damage caused by the action to the interests of the employer and/or third parties, and (d) the nature of the interests and the damage involved. In this context, it may also be considered whether the rules of the game – whether the collective action is used as an ultimum remedium and whether the collective action has been announced in a timely fashion – have been taken into account.

With this shift in case law, the complainants argue: 'the Supreme Court has created an overly broad framework for the Article G test'.[30] To recall, Article G ESC determines that rights shall not be subject to any restrictions or limitations not specified, except where they are:

- prescribed by law: which may be statutory or case law, provided that the text is sufficiently clear, meaning the text must be precise and foreseeable;
- pursue a legitimate purpose, such as the protection of rights and freedoms of others or for the protection of public interest, national security, public health, or morals: the state may, in principle, legitimise and define the public interest by striking a fair balance between the needs of all members of society. There is, thus, a margin of appreciation in doing so, limited by the need to offer appropriate guarantees of a level of protection to adequately meet basic social needs. This excludes, however, resorting to external institutions to fill in this second condition; and
- necessary in a democratic society for the pursuance of these purposes: this implies a reasonable relationship of proportionality between the restriction on the right and the legitimate aim(s) pursued.[31]

30. Complaint No. 201/2021, Response by ETUC, FNV and CNV to the submissions by the Government on the merits, Case Document No. 4, p. 2.
31. Digest of the Case Law of the European Committee of Social Rights, December 2018, 234-235.

The complainants, comparing the criteria under Article G ESC with those developed by the Supreme Court, argue that:

- restrictions are allowed on the ground of social urgency: this criterion is not included in the exhaustive list of Article G ESC and therefore goes beyond what is allowed under Article G ESC;
- all circumstances of the case can be taken into consideration to conclude that restrictions can be imposed: which would also go beyond what Article G ESC allows; and
- the rules of the game still are used as a criterion on which a restriction can be based: this concerns an open-ended standard, subject to change, leaving much unclear to the trade unions.

In its Conclusions 2018, the ECSR found the Netherlands to be in conformity with the ESC since the changes being made in the assessment. The assessment now takes place under Article G ESC. However, the complainants argue that the ECSR was unable to actually assess whether case law in general is in conformity with Article G ESC. Basically, the framework to assess the legality of a collective action, the complainants put forward, is much broader than would be allowed under a stricter reading of Article G ESC.[32] In its decision on the case, the ECSR concluded that although the framework as set out by the Dutch Supreme Court does not constitute a violation of Article 6(4) ESC,[33] it does need to be developed further to guarantee a uniform interpretation by lower courts.[34]

2.3 Essential Services in the Strict Sense of the Term

The general starting point is that collective actions are, in principle, allowed. This includes collective actions in sectors in which the rights of third parties could be (seriously) impacted by the collective action, following which the nature of the sector in which the collective action is planned to take place might restrict the possibilities for collective actions. This is especially the case if the collective action affects persons with a special vulnerability and affects ensuring their care, as a result of which those persons are exposed to the danger of their mental or physical health being harmed.[35] Healthcare is a prominent example of a sector in which such a risk is present.[36] Where collective actions in sectors like healthcare could endanger public safety or potential victims like

32. Complaint No. 201/2021, Response by ETUC, FNV and CNV to the submissions by the Government on the merits, Case Document No. 4, p. 7.
33. European Committee of Social Rights 24 January 2024, Decision on the merits, *European Trade Union Confederation (ETUC), Netherlands Trade Union Confederation (FNV) and National Federation of Christian Trade Unions (CNV) v. the Netherlands*, Complaint No. 201/2021.
34. *See* on this paras 127-131 of the Decision, as well as Pauline Burger et al., *Nederlands stakingsrecht getoetst: Niet systemisch in strijd met ESH*, Nederlands Juristenblad, 29 (2024).
35. Dutch Supreme Court ECLI:NL:HR:2015:1687, 19 June 2015, *FNV/Amsta*, para. 3.3.6; *see also* Dutch Supreme Court ECLI:NL:HR:1991:ZC0424, *NJ* 1992/508, 22 November 1991, *ABVA/KABO*.
36. An example of such a restriction can be found in Court of Midden-Nederland ECLI:NL:RB-MNE:2015:4232, 10 June 2015, regarding ambulance staff.

vulnerable patients, the action seems more likely to be restricted or even prohibited.[37] However, as the Supreme Court in its *FNV/Amsta* ruling makes clear, there is no general prohibition for collective action, not even in sectors where persons with (special) vulnerabilities may be affected.[38]

Other circumstances, however, can also lead a court to restrict or prohibit a planned collective action. A recent example is a case from 2022 in which a planned collective action by special investigating officers (BOAs) on King's Day in Amsterdam, consisting of, *inter alia*, a work stoppage from 18.00-21.00 pm, was prohibited due to considerations of safety.[39] The Court considered that the exercise of the BOA's right to collective action can only be limited on the basis of Article G ESC. Given the crowds on King's Day, a collective action during the exact time in which many people start to move disorganisedly through the city on their way home, while possibly under the influence of alcohol, takes away an essential link in the security chain. The Court feared that this could lead to disorder, destruction, and violence. On these grounds, the Court held that the intended action does serve a reasonable purpose but is disproportionate in the given circumstances. Therefore, the Court concluded that the prohibition of the right to collective action is urgently necessary from a social point of view and necessary in a democratic society for the protection of the rights and freedoms of others and for the protection of public order. Notably, there is no general prohibition on collective actions in essential sectors. The possible restriction of the right to collective action is judged on a case-to-case basis. For example, police officers are allowed to collective action if the conditions set by Article G ESC are being met.[40]

If the collective action does not necessarily cause danger to third parties' safety or health but does impact a sector that is of great importance to the country, limitations may apply as well. Examples can be found in the sectors of public transport and postal services.

In November 2022, the Court of The Hague ruled that collective actions at PostNL (postal services) were only allowed if certain conditions were met, namely guaranteeing the timely delivery of funeral mail, medical mail, and parcels.[41] Acknowledging the right to collective action being a fundamental right, with a view to the conditions set out in *FNV/Amsta*, the Court concludes that this limitation is urgently necessary from a social point of view.[42]

37. Buby den Heeten & Stefan Kleijer, *De (on)mogelijkheden van collectieve acties in de zorg*, 12 Tijdschrift Recht en Arbeid 4, 5 (2021) 6.
38. Leonard G Verburg, *Het stakingsrecht na Enerco en Amsta: terugblikken en vooruitzien*, 12 Tijdschrift Recht en Arbeid 3, 6 (2017).
39. Court of Amsterdam ECLI:NL:RBAMS:2019:3024, 26 April 2019, *Gemeente Amsterdam/FNV Vervoer*.
40. Nataschja Hummel, *Het 'genormaliseerde' collectief actierecht van de politie*, 6/7 Tijdschrift Recht en Arbeid 9, 10 (2016). *See*, for example, Court of The Hague 3 September 2015, Court of Utrecht ECLI:NL:RBUTR:2012:BW5227, 3 May 2012, *Politieregio Haaglanden c.s./Algemeen Christelijke Politiebond c.s.*
41. Court of The Hague ECLI:NL:RBDHA:2022:13241, 22 November 2022, *PostNL/FNV*.
42. Court of The Hague ECLI:NL:RBDHA:2022:13241, 22 November 2022, *PostNL/FNV*, paras 4.3 and 4.13.

A similar consideration was made in a case from 2019 concerning a planned collective action in public transportation, which would have had the effect that no regional and train transportation to and from Schiphol Airport would be possible for a whole day.[43] The disruptive consequences for third parties were weighed against the rights of trade unions and employees in order to determine that restrictions on the right to collective action are urgently necessary from a social point of view. The Court ruled that during the collective action, the staff of the Dutch National Railways (*Nederlandse Spoorwegen*) had to run an emergency shuttle to Schiphol Airport four times an hour. Interestingly, more comprehensive collective actions have occurred since this case, including the large-scale collective actions at *Nederlandse Spoorwegen* during multiple days in the summer of 2022, where no train transportation was possible in an entire region or even the entire country. These collective actions have not led to a court ruling. However, based on the aforementioned case law, it is very much possible that the right to collective action in 2022 at *Nederlandse Spoorwegen* would have been limited, given the consequences for train travellers nationwide. This appears to be even more likely considering a case from 2024 regarding *Nederlandse Spoorwegen* and Schiphol Airport, in which the Court gave a similar ruling as in 2019.[44]

3 COMPENSATORY GUARANTEES FOR WORKERS IN THE EVENT OF A STRIKE

3.1 Compensation for Workers During Strikes

The main rule formulated in Article 7:628 Dutch Civil Code entails that employees continue to receive their wages even if they do not work. An exception to this rule applies if the full or partial non-performance of the (contractually) agreed work should reasonably be borne by the employee. In the event of a collective action where the work is (partially) not performed, two factors are important to determine whether it is the employer or the employee who should bear the risk of not working: first, whether or not the collective action has been organised by a trade union and, second, whether or not the employee is a willing participant in the collective action, or is unable to work due to the actions of the participants.

If the employee does not work due to a collective action organised by a trade union, he will not be entitled to continue receiving wages. Instead, if he is a member of the trade union that organised the collective action, he will usually be able to claim a so-called strike benefit from the trade union. While the benefit may cover some of the financial loss suffered by trade union members in a collective action, overall, it can be said that not receiving some form of financial compensation while participating in a collective action may seriously inhibit employees from joining a collective action. Non-members may join the collective action but are neither entitled to their wages nor

43. Court of North-Holland ECLI:NL:RBNHO:2019:5857, 26 May 2019, *Royal Schiphol Group c.s./FNV*.
44. Court of North-Holland ECLI:NL:RBNHO:2024:9760, 20 September 2024, *Royal Schiphol Group c.s./FNV*.

to the trade union's strike benefit. Also, if an employee is willing to work but is unable to do so as a result of the collective action undertaken by other employees, he will not be entitled to his wages either. The underlying reasoning, according to the Supreme Court, is that an organised collective action may also lead to favourable consequences for employees who are willing to work even if not taking part in a collective action. It is for that reason that the Supreme Court ruled that the consequences of not receiving an income while a collective action is taking place should reasonably be borne by all affected employees.[45]

Compensation is organised differently in the event of an unorganised collective action. Most importantly, in case a collective action is not organised by a trade union and the employee decides to join that action, he will neither be entitled to wages nor to a strike benefit even if the employee would be a trade union member. An unorganised collective action (a so-called wild strike) may, however, turn out more favourable for employees who are willing to work but are prevented from doing so. These employees can claim their salary from the employer based on Article 7:628 Dutch Civil Code. A crucial aspect leading the Supreme Court to this conclusion in a case concerning a wild strike is the fact that it is not the fault of either party that the work could not be performed and this circumstance therefore lies more in the sphere of risk of the employer or his business than in that of the employee.[46]

3.2 Compensation for Workers Deprived of the Right to Strike

The Netherlands does not have any legislation on compensation in situations where employees are not allowed to take collective action. The starting point, as confirmed in the Enerco and FNV/Amsta judgments, is that employees are allowed to take collective action. If an employer aims to prevent or limit a planned collective action, the case must be brought before the court. It is then up to the court to assess, in line with the test set out earlier (as outlined in section 2.2 above), whether or not, and under which conditions, the right to collective action may be restricted.

As mentioned before, the right to collective action can also be limited, i.e., by making it subject to certain conditions upfront by means of a collective agreement. However, this derogation from the right to collective action does not automatically imply that employees are deprived of their rights and are thus in need of compensation. As collective agreements are concluded between trade unions and employers or employer's organisations, the employees' rights are represented in the process that leads to the limitation or even prohibition of a collective action. As these agreements are established in a bargaining process, it is likely that employees have gained more advantageous employment conditions in exchange for the agreement not to take collective action.

45. Dutch Supreme Court ECLI:NL:HR:1976:AB9771, 7 May 1976, *Wielemaker/De Schelde*.
46. Dutch Supreme Court ECLI:NL:HR:1972:AC1656, 10 November 1972, *De Schelde*.

4 CONCLUSION

The right to take collective action is acknowledged in the Netherlands and its protection has a wide scope. Not only traditional strikes but also collective actions where workers lay down their work in a different manner or in which the employer is inconvenienced are protected. There is no national legislation on the right to collective action; instead, this right is regulated by means of case law. However, there are two noteworthy points of attention regarding this form of 'regulation'.

The first is that many (planned) collective actions are never tested in court. When a collective action is being prepared or announced, the parties will usually negotiate in order to prevent the collective action from happening. If this does not lead to an agreement, the employer might decide to bring the case to court; however, the employer may also decide against legal action. This means that we do not know whether or not the collective actions in question are legally permissible, as no ruling is given.

The second point of attention is that if summary proceedings are indeed brought before the court, the criteria applied by Dutch courts may not fully comply with Article G ESC. As argued by the ETUC, FNV, and CNV in a complaint submitted to the ECSR, the framework to assess the legality of a collective action appears to be broader than would be allowed under a stricter reading of Article G ESC. Although the ECSR did not find a violation of Article 6(4) ESC, it did conclude that the framework provided by the Dutch Supreme Court needs to be developed further to guarantee a uniform interpretation by lower courts. This means that, regardless of the right to collective action's wide scope, this right may in practice be insufficiently safeguarded.

CHAPTER 26

Restrictions on the Right to Strike in North Macedonia

Todor Kalamatiev & Aleksandar Ristovski

1 GENERAL INFORMATION

1.1 Legal Basis of the Right to Strike

The legal framework regulating the right to strike, in the period from the independence of the Republic of North Macedonia (then the Republic of Macedonia) from the former SFR Yugoslavia in 1991 to the present day, is characterized by a "combined" constitutional-legislative approach. In that sense, the most significant legal sources are the Constitution and the statutory regulations. The 1991 Macedonian Constitution[1] in Article 38 not only lays down that "the right to strike is guaranteed" but also states that "the law may restrict the conditions for the exercise of the right to strike in the armed forces, the police and administration bodies."

There are two stages of development in the regulation of the right to strike by means of *statutory regulations*. During the first stage, strike was regulated by the special (*lex specialis*) Law on Strike.[2] The Law on Strike was applied until the adoption of the Law on Labour Relations in 2005,[3] the entry into force of which marked the second and still ongoing stage of regulating the right to strike in North Macedonia. The Law on Labour Relations (hereinafter: "LLR") as a general law (*lex generalis*) has established the general regime of strikes, applicable to all workers in an employment relationship, regardless of whether they are employed in the private or in the public sector. In addition to the LLR, certain aspects (primarily restrictions) of the right to

1. *See* the Constitution of the Republic of Macedonia (*Official Gazette of the Republic of Macedonia*, No. 52/1991).
2. Law on Strike (*Official Gazette of the SFRY*, No. 23/91).
3. Law on Labour Relations (*Official Gazette of the Republic of Macedonia*, No. 62/05).

strike are also subject matter to regulation by several special (*lex specialis*) laws, which apply to certain categories of public sector employees or refer to certain specific activities of general interest and essential services (the armed forces, police, prison police, public enterprises, institutions, health care, primary education, secondary education, children protection services, utility services, postal services, judicial service, public prosecutor's service, firefighting, etc.) and which constitute the so-called special regime for exercising the right to strike. Statutory regulations represent essential and dominant, but not exclusive, sources regulating the right to strike.

Certain issues related to the exercise of the right to strike can also be regulated by *collective agreement*. The limits in relation to the material scope of collective agreements as legal sources for regulating the right to strike can be indirectly derived from the practice of the Constitutional Court of North Macedonia. Here, the following general principles are relevant: (1) workers exercise the right to strike in accordance with the law and collective agreement but not in accordance with the Strike Rules (as internal acts of the trade union); (2) the provisions of collective agreements regarding the exercise of the right to strike must not contradict the Constitution and the laws governing the exercise of this right; and (3) the collective agreements are of secondary importance to laws, which means that they may and should regulate certain issues beyond the minimum standards established by law and cannot set out lesser rights and less favorable working conditions than those laid down by law.[4]

As an ILO and Council of Europe Member State, North Macedonia has ratified the most significant human rights instruments of these organizations that implicitly or explicitly guarantee the right to strike. It includes the Freedom of Association and Protection of the Right to Organise Convention No. 87 and the Right to Organise and Collective Bargaining Convention No. 98 (as ILO instruments) and the European Convention for the Protection of Human Rights and Fundamental Freedoms and the European Social Charter (revised) as instruments of the Council of Europe. These instruments are an integral part of the country's internal legal order and cannot be changed by law, while employers and employees are obliged to comply with their provisions.[5] The dialogue between the State Government and the ILO supervisory bodies also has a certain significance in shaping the right to strike in North Macedonia. An example of a successful dialogue that resulted in a corresponding amendment to the LLR in 2008[6] is the abolishment of the obligation of workers' organizations to specify the duration of strike.[7]

4. *See* Decision of the Constitutional Court of the Republic of Macedonia, No. 125/1998-0-0 of November 18, 1998 and Decision of the Constitutional Court of the Republic of Macedonia, No. 182/2000-0-0 of February 21, 2001.
5. *See* Law on Labour Relations, Art. 12, para. 1.
6. *See* Law on amending and supplementing the Law on Labour Relations of 2008 (*Official Gazette of the Republic of Macedonia*, No. 106/2008).
7. *See* Direct Request (CEACR)—adopted 2006, published 96th ILC session (2007).

1.2 Main Features of the Regulation

The existing Macedonian labour legislation does not contain a definition of the term "strike," but it determines the basic requirements (essential elements) for organizing a legal strike. Such requirements principally stem from the deductive interpretation of Article 236, paragraph 1 of the LLR, according to which "the trade union and its associations at a higher level shall be entitled to call a strike and to start it in order to protect the economic and social rights of its members from employment, in accordance with the law." Therefore, the legality of strikes in North Macedonia depends on defining the holder and the permitted aim, i.e., objective of the strike, as main elements in exercising the right to strike. In addition to these elements, according to the "common" understanding of a strike, another essential element is the cessation of work.[8] A special type of strike, which is explicitly recognized by the LLR, is *the solidarity strike.*[9] Practice also recognizes the so-called *warning strike*. It usually takes place over a short period of time (one or two days), is organized during rest breaks at work, outside of working hours or in a short interval during working hours (e.g., up to two hours) and is undertaken while collective bargaining is ongoing in order to exert pressure on the employers and draw their attention to certain contentious issues.[10] Given that it is not provided for by the labor legislation, it is unclear whether and to what extent warning strike is subject to the procedural requirements to which the "classic" and the solidarity strike are subjected. What is also unclear is the status and legality of strikes whose accompanying activity are certain types of collective actions of the workers such as "plant occupation," "picketing," etc. According to Article 236, paragraph 6 of the LLR, "the strike shall be organized in such manner as not to disable or hinder the organization and performance of the working process of workers who do not participate in the strike, nor to prohibit the entry of workers and responsible persons in the premises of the employer." In our view, in case of assessing the permissibility of the "disablements, hindering or prohibitions" provided for in the mentioned legal provision (Article 236, paragraph 6), the courts should take into account the relevant views of the ILO supervisory bodies indicating the unlawfulness of picketing and occupation of workplace, but only in the event of disturbing public order, violence or coercion of non-strikers or in general, in the event of absence of a peaceful way of expressing dissatisfaction.[11]

The existing labor legislation in North Macedonia determines the trade union, that is, its associations at a higher level, as the sole *holder* of the right to strike. The strike, which is initiated by a group of workers who are not organized in a trade union, including the so-called *wildcat strike* as a cessation of work by employees without

8. *See* Todor Kalamatiev & Aleksandar Ristovski, *International and National Dimensions of the Right to Strike*, ***Четврти Скопско-Загрепски правен колоквиум, Скопје***, 83 (2013).
9. Law on Labour Relations, Art. 236, para. 4.
10. *See* Todor Kalamatiev & Aleksandar Ristovski, *National Dimensions of the Right to Strike*, ***Годишник на Правниот Факултет "Јустинијан Први" во Скопје во чест на Љиљана Спировиќ-Трпеновска***, 498 (2013).
11. *See, e.g.*, Jean-Michel Servais, *ILO Law and the Right to Strike*, Canadian Labour and Employment Law Journal, Vol. 15, 147, 151 (2009-2010).

consent of the trade union, shall be considered illegal.[12] However, a distinction should be made between who is entitled to exercise the right to strike and who is capable of calling a strike.[13] Hence, in a Macedonian context, the legal nature of the strike can be described as a mixture between the "individualist" and the "organic" (collective) doctrine.[14] It means that the exercise of the right to strike is an individual right of workers from an employment relationship that is due to them as members of the trade union that organized the strike, members of another trade union or non-unionized employees, but at the same time, the right to organize and call a strike belongs exclusively to the trade union, i.e., the trade union at a higher level. Macedonian labour legislation does not set out clear rules on the manner and levels of organizing trade unions. Even more problematic are the amendments to the LLR from 2012, which formally abolished the previously existing possibility of registering and acquiring legal personality of the trade unions at an employer level.[15] From then on, it is considered that the registration and functioning, and thus the very existence of the trade unions at the level of an employer, depend on their association in a newly formed or accession to an already existing trade union at a higher level (e.g., a trade union at level of a branch—federation or at a national level—confederation). Such a situation significantly limits the freedom of association and the right to organize and join a trade union, guaranteed by the Constitution of the Republic of North Macedonia (Article 37) and the relevant international instruments ratified in accordance with the Constitution, of employees who wish to exercise their freedom of trade union association and organization independently of the association and organization in a higher-level trade union. In our view, this situation in North Macedonia deviates from the practice of the European Committee of Social Rights of the Council of Europe, which, in its opinions on various cases, in addition to ascribing the right to strike as the right of all workers (including any ordinary group of workers without any legal status), has on several occasions also legitimized the possibility of reserving the right to call a strike exclusively to a trade union, but only if workers may "easily, and without excessive requirements form a trade union for the purpose of a strike,"[16] i.e., under the condition of existence of "complete freedom to form trade unions ... in a ... process that is not subject to excessive formalities,"[17] which is not the case in North Macedonia.

---

12. That also includes the Judgment of the Appellate Court of Skopje (РОЖ-1465/19) of May 21, 2020, which confirms the first-instance court's decision referring to decision on termination of an employee's employment contract (dismissal) due to participation in an illegitimate strike that was arbitrarily started by a group of employees on its own initiative without prior announcement and organizing by a trade union.
13. *See, e.g.*, Stein Evju, *The Right to Collective Action under the European Social Charter*, European Labour Law Journal, Vol. 2 No. 3, 213 (2011) https://doi.org/10.1177/201395251100200303 (accessed May 6, 2025).
14. *See, e.g.*, Erika Kovacs, *The Right to Strike in the European Social Charter*, Comparative Labour Law and Policy Journal, Vol. 26, 457 (2005).
15. *See* Law on amending and supplementing the Law on Labour Relations (*Official Gazette of the Republic of Macedonia*, No. 11/2012).
16. *See* Rolf Birk, *European Social Charter 355* (Wolters Kluwer 2007), Addendum to Conclusions XV-1, pp. 28-29 (Germany).
17. *See* Rolf Birk, *European Social Charter 355* (Wolters Kluwer 2007), Conclusions 2004, Vol. 2, p. 565 (Sweden).

The Macedonian approach in determining the lawful aims for calling a strike is largely different or contrary to the usual approach taken by the ILO supervisory bodies, as well as to Article 6, point 4 of the European Social Charter (revised). According to Article 236, paragraph 1 of the LLR, the aim of the strike is the protection of the *economic and social rights* of the members of the trade union from an employment relationship. We believe that such a legal provision according to which the legitimate aim of the strike is only to protect the economic and social "rights," but not the "interests" of the workers, contains an "innate anomaly." Fortunately, practice gives legitimacy to both strikes that are initiated due to a conflict of interests (e.g., failure of collective negotiations for concluding, amending, supplementing or extending a collective agreement, requests for wage increases, etc.) or similar reasons (e.g., declaring "surplus" workers in the event of collective redundancies, etc.) and due to a conflict of rights (e.g., due to unpaid salaries, health and pension insurance contributions, reimbursements of allowances for food and travel expenses, etc.).[18] In parallel with the LLR, the scope of legitimate aims for calling a strike is also indirectly set forth by the Law on Amicable Settlement of Labour Disputes, which defines a collective labor dispute as a dispute on the conclusion, amendment, supplementation or application of a collective agreement, exercising the right to trade union organization and the right to strike.[19]

The legality of the strike in North Macedonia, despite the fulfilment of the basic requirements, i.e., the essential elements (cessation of work, initiation by a trade union or its associations at a higher level and existence of a legitimate aim), also depends on the fulfilment of certain procedural requirements preceding the strike such as: the obligation for a compulsory written notice of the strike and the obligation to conduct a conciliation procedure before the commencement of the strike. The *obligation for a compulsory written notice* refers to both the classic and the solidarity strike. The former shall be announced to the employer, i.e., to the employers' association against which the strike is directed, while the latter to the employer where the strike is organized.[20] It is usually considered that the solidarity strike should be noticed both to the employer where the initial (primary) strike takes place, and the immediate employer with whom the workers concluded an employment contract. Mandatory elements to be contained in any strike notice letter (regardless of whether it is a classic or a solidarity strike) are: the reasons for the strike, the location where it will take place and the day and time of its start.[21] The LLR, however, does not set out the earliest period in which the strike can begin, i.e., the time (expressed in days or weeks) that should elapse from the moment of announcement to the moment of the actual start of the strike (i.e., cooling off period), nor does it explicitly determine whether or not within this time, the period

18. *See, e.g.,* Todor Kalamatiev & Aleksandar Ristovski, *Industrial Relations in North Macedonia 30 Years After the Fall of the Berlin Wall: Key Challenges Faced by Industrial Actors,* Iustinianus Primus Law Review, Law Review Special Issue – Conference Proceedings, 15 (2019), https://pf.ukim.edu.mk/law-review/ (accessed May 6, 2025).
19. Law on Amicable Settlement of Labour Disputes (*Official Gazette of the Republic of Macedonia,* No. 87/2007), Art. 2, para. 1.
20. Law on Labour Relations, Art. 236, para. 2.
21. *See* Law on Labour Relations, Art. 236, para. 5.

intended for conciliation is included.[22] The second procedural requirement preceding the commencement of the strike provides for the *prohibition of starting the strike before the completion of the conciliation procedure*.[23] However, in the same provision regulating this requirement, the LLR stipulates that the obligation to conciliate shall not limit the right to strike. Such a contradictory legal formulation poses several dilemmas regarding the meaning and application of the obligation to conduct a conciliation procedure before the commencement of the strike. This was also ascertained by the European Court of Human Rights (ECHR) in the case "Trade union in the factory '4th November' against the former Yugoslav Republic of Macedonia,"[24] in which the ECHR declared the trade union's application inadmissible, citing the interpretation of the Macedonian Constitutional Court according to which "the strike is a last resort to protect the economic and social rights of the workers [...] which cannot be started without prior exhaustion of the conciliation procedure."[25] Therefore, it becomes evident that for a strike to be lawful, it should be used as a last resort (ultima ratio) after previously conducting a conciliation procedure in accordance with the Law or other procedure agreed upon by the parties to the dispute[26] which is usually subject to regulation in a collective agreement. The only exception to this rule provided for by the LLR concerns the solidarity strike, which may begin even without conducting a conciliation procedure but not prior to the expiry of two days from the date of the start of the strike for which support is organized.[27]

2 PERMITTED RESTRICTIONS

2.1 Certain Categories of Public Servants

The possibility of introducing restrictions on the exercise of the right to strike for certain categories of public sector employees primarily derives from the Constitution of the Republic of North Macedonia, which in Article 38 states that "the law may restrict the conditions for the exercise of the right to strike in the armed forces, the police and administration bodies." The constitutional provision refers to several significant elements regarding the restriction on the right to strike. First, the restriction on the conditions for the exercise of the right to strike may only be regulated by law.[28] This indicates that such a restriction cannot be laid down in an Act of a Minister (especially when such an Act prescribes a conciliation procedure) or a collective agreement. Second, the possibility of restricting the conditions for the exercise of the right to strike

22. *See* Law on Labour Relations, Art. 236, para. 3.
23. *See* Law on Labour Relations, Art. 236, para. 3.
24. *See* European Court of Human Rights, Appication No. 15557/10.
25. *See* Decision of the Constitutional Court of the Republic of Macedonia, U.No.187/2005-1 of 10 May 2006.
26. *See* Law on Labour Relations, Art. 236, para. 3.
27. *See* Law on Labour Relations, Art. 236, para. 4.
28. *See* Decision of the Constitutional Court of the Republic of Macedonia, No. 125/1998-0-0 of November 18, 1998 and Decision of the Constitutional Court of the Republic of Macedonia, No. 182/2000-0-0 of February 21, 2001.

refers to: the armed forces, the police and the administration bodies. According to the Law on Defense,[29] the term *armed forces* primarily means the Army of the Republic of North Macedonia. Strike in the armed forces is allowed, but only if it does not endanger the combat readiness of the Army and the life and health of the Army members.[30] Therefore, during a strike, the Minister of Defense and the Chief of the General Staff of the Army are obliged to ensure realization of the vital functions of the Army, and the participants in the strike are obliged to remain at their positions and carry out the activities necessary for the realization of the vital functions of the Army.[31] Additional procedural restrictions exist in relation to the period of notice of the strike (at least 10 days before its commencement), the maximum number of participants (no more than 10% of the Army employees) and the duration of the strike (no longer than 3 days).[32] The conditions restricting the right to strike in *the police* are provided for by the Law on Police.[33] Much like the armed forces, a strike by police officers is in principle permitted, provided that it does not significantly disrupt the regular performance of police work. Restrictions on the exercise of the right to strike, as applied to police officers, also exist for *members of the prison police*. However, it is worth noting that in the regulation of these restrictions, in addition to the provisions of the Law on Sanctions Enforcement, the provisions of the Rulebook on work during a strike, which is adopted by the Minister of Justice after a previously obtained opinion from the trade union, are also applied.[34] Taking into account the aforementioned case law of the Constitutional Court, according to which the restriction on the conditions for the exercise of the right to strike may be stipulated only in law, the question that arises is whether their restriction by an Act of the Minister will be considered permissible. Despite the "*ratione personae*" restrictions in relation to certain categories of persons (the armed forces and the police), the Constitution provides for the possibility of restricting the conditions for the exercise of the right to strike in the *administration bodies* as well. According to the Law on Organization and Work of State Administration Bodies, the state administration bodies may be established as: ministries, other state administration bodies and administrative organizations.[35] Hence, the possibility of restricting the right to strike in the administration bodies is set out very extensively. The Constitution in Article 37 similarly provides for the possibility of restricting the conditions for the exercise of the right to trade union organization, which, in addition to the armed forces and the police, also applies to the administration bodies. This provision is subject to supervision of the ILO Committee of Experts on the Application of Conventions and Recommendations (CEACR). Referring to Convention No. 87, under which only the armed forces and the police may be subject to limitations of the freedom of association and the right to trade

29. Law on Defense (*Official Gazette of the Republic of Macedonia,* No. 42/2001).
30. Law on Defense, Art. 48, para. 2.
31. Law on Defense, Art. 48, para. 3 and para. 4.
32. Law on Defense, Art. 48, para. 5.
33. Law on Police (*Official Gazette of the Republic of Macedonia,* No. 114/06).
34. Law on Sanctions Enforcement (*Official Gazette of the Republic of North Macedonia,* No. 99/2019), Art. 84, para. 8.
35. Law on Organization and Work of State Administration Bodies (*Official Gazette of the Republic of Macedonia,* No. 58/00).

union organization, and highlighting the need to harmonize the constitutional provisions with the provisions of the Convention, the Committee of Experts in the last observation of 2021 requested the Government of the Republic of North Macedonia to eliminate the possibility for the law to restrict the conditions for the exercise of the right to trade union organization in administration bodies.[36] Despite the possibility of limiting the conditions for exercising the right to strike in the administration bodies provided by the Constitution, neither the aforementioned Law on Organization and Work of the State Administration Bodies, which primarily regulates the organization, powers and activities of the state administration, nor the Law on Administrative Servants regulating the employment relationship of civil and public servants does not prescribe any specific restrictions on the exercise of the right to strike in the administration bodies.[37]

2.2 Essential Services in the Strict Sense of the Term

In addition to *ratione personae* restrictions on the exercise of the right to strike, which include certain categories of public sector employees, Macedonian legislation also provides for material restrictions (*ratione materiae*) that refer to certain activities of general interest and activities in which the cessation of work could endanger the life or health of people or inflict major damage (essential activities in the strict sense of the term). The only Law that systematically enumerates these activities is the Law on Amicable Settlement of Labour Disputes, which includes: electricity supply, water supply, traffic, radio and television founded by the Republic of Macedonia or the local self-government units, postal services, utility services, production of basic nutritional products, health and veterinary care, education, children protection services, social protection, the police and the defense.[38] The Law on Amicable Settlement of Labour Disputes (hereinafter: "LASLD") does not distinguish activities of general interest from essential activities in the strict sense, but it limits the right to strike with the obligation for a compulsory amicable settlement before the commencement of the strike, regardless of in which of the listed activities the dispute arose. Limitations that seem to exceed the permitted restrictions for the exercise of the right to strike can be found in certain activities. Thus, the special laws regulating primary and secondary education, healthcare and the activity of care and education of children of preschool age provide for the possibility of replacing striking employees during a strike. The restriction in the context of primary and secondary education is subject to supervision of the ILO Committee of Experts (CEACR), which, in its direct request to the Government of the Republic of Macedonia dating from 2016, states that "teachers and public education services may not be considered an essential service in the strict sense of the term and that the provisions allowing for the replacement of striking workers are a serious impediment

36. *See* Direct Request (CEACR), adopted 2018, published 108th ILC session (2019).
37. Law on Administrative Servants (*Official Gazette of the Republic of Macedonia*, No. 27/14).
38. Law on Amicable Settlement of Labour Disputes, Art. 18, para. 3.

to the legitimate exercise of the right to strike."[39] So far, the Macedonian Government has not yet taken appropriate measures to act on the request of the CEACR.

Exercising the right to strike in activities of general interest and in essential activities in the strict sense of the term is usually conditional upon the establishment of a minimum uninterrupted performance of the institution's functions and a necessary level of realization of the rights and interests of citizens and legal entities (so-called *minimum services*). The manner, procedure and conditions for maintaining minimum services when exercising the right to strike are primarily regulated by the Law on Employees in the Public Sector.[40] This Law provides for an obligation to establish minimum services in the broadest sense, which concerns all the public sector employees. An additional problem is caused by the way the establishment of minimum services itself is regulated because they are determined by an act of the head of the institution. The head of the institution sets out the manner of performing the responsibilities, that is, the institutional activities of public interest, the number of employees who will perform them, as well as the way of ensuring the conditions for the exercise of the right to strike.[41] Similar provisions by which the founder of the public enterprise or public institution unilaterally determines the persons who cannot participate in a strike, the job positions where the activity of public interest is carried out and the way of performing the activities and tasks of those job positions are stipulated both in the Law on the Public Enterprises[42] and the Law on the Institutions.[43] Such approaches in determining the minimum services are again subject to supervision of the CEACR. In the direct request addressed to the Macedonian Government (initially from 2016), the CEACR stated that the minimum service introduced should meet at least the following requirements: (1) it must genuinely and exclusively be a minimum service, that is one which is limited to the operations which are strictly necessary to meet the basic needs of the population or the minimum requirements of the service while maintaining the effectiveness of the pressure brought to bear; and (2) since this system restricts one of the essential means of pressure available to workers to defend their interests, their organizations should be able, if they so wish, to participate in defining such a service, along with employers and the public authorities.[44] So far, the Macedonian Government has not yet taken appropriate measures to act on the request of the CEACR. In addition to the obligation to establish a minimum service which is primarily intended for public sector employees, a similar obligation for activities that must not be interrupted during the period of a strike (so-called production maintenance and indispensable activities) is also provided for by the general Law on Labour Relations. Production maintenance activities are those activities which must be carried out by workers during a strike for the purpose of enabling continuation of the working process after the termination of the strike. Indispensable activities are those activities that are absolutely necessary for

39. *See* Direct Request (CEACR), adopted 2016, published 106th ILC session (2017).
40. Law on Employees in the Public Sector (*Official Gazette of the Republic of Macedonia*, No. 27/2014).
41. *See* Law on Employees in the Public Sector, Art. 32, para. 4.
42. Law on Public Enterprises (*Official Gazette of the Republic of Macedonia*, No. 38/96), Art. 35.
43. Law on Institutions (*Official Gazette of the Republic of Macedonia*, No. 32/2005), Art. 86.
44. *See* Direct Request (CEACR), adopted 2016, published 106th ILC session (2017).

the purpose of preventing threats to the life, personal safety or health of the citizens.[45] Compared to the Law on Employees in the Public Sector, which, in the event of a strike, provides for the establishment of minimum services by a unilateral act of the head of the institution, the LLR takes a completely opposite and, in our view, right approach. According to the LLR, the activities that must not be interrupted during a strike (production maintenance and indispensable activities) and the number of workers who must perform them during a strike are determined by Rules that are adopted on employer's proposal but *in agreement* with the trade union.[46] If the trade union and the employer do not reach an agreement within 15 days after submitting the employer's proposal to the trade union, the employer or the trade union may, within the following 15 days, ask for arbitration to decide on those matters.[47] The determination of such activities by means of arbitration is provided as an option, not as an obligation for the parties to the dispute. Hence, a dilemma arises whether a strike that started without a previous agreement between the employer and the trade union or without an arbitration award on the activities that must not be interrupted during a strike will be considered a legal strike. It is also unclear whether and to what extent the competent court, which, otherwise in accordance with Article 243, paragraph 1 of the LLR, is authorized at the request of the employer, i.e., the employers' association to exercise *ex ante* judicial control over the legality of the strike, can prohibit organizing and initiating a strike if the parties to the dispute have not agreed on determining the activities that must not be interrupted during the strike.[48]

2.3 Situations of Acute National or Local Crisis

The right to strike in North Macedonia may not only be restricted but also completely prohibited during martial law, state of emergency, state of crisis, etc. The terms martial law and state of emergency and the manner of their proclamation are defined in the Macedonian Constitution, while the state of crisis is regulated by the Law on Crisis Management and can be declared at the level of the entire Republic or part of it, but

45. *See* Law on Labour Relations, Art. 238, para. 2.
46. Law on Labour Relations, Art. 238, para. 1.
47. Law on Labour Relations, Art. 238, para. 4.
48. For example, such was the case of the strike organized by the Independent Union of Clinical Centers and other Health Organizations from 2012. Before it was organized, the Ministry of Health of the Republic of Macedonia filed a lawsuit for annulment of an illegal decision on a strike to the Basic Court Skopje 2 Skopje, with a request to ban the organizing and conducting of a strike contrary to the provisions of the LLR and a proposal for an interim measure to ban the conducting and organizing the strike until the final conclusion of the dispute. The Court accepted the proposal from the plaintiff (the Ministry of Health) with reasoning that the defendant (the Union) in conducting the procedure for organizing a strike *did not adopt specific rules for the activities that must not be interrupted during a strike* in accordance with the LLR and the Law on Health Care. *See* Todor Kalamatiev & Aleksandar Ristovski, *Collective Bargaining in the Public Sector of the Republic of Macedonia with a Particular Review of the Collective Bargaining in the Health Care (Tertiary Healthcare)*, Business Law, Year XIV, No. 28, Skopje, 273-277 (2013).

only when there are no conditions for declaring a state of emergency.[49] The possibility of restricting the right to strike in conditions of martial law or state of emergency arises indirectly from the general constitutional provision, according to which the freedoms and rights of the individual and citizen can be restricted during martial law or state of emergency.[50] During the pandemic caused by COVID-19, with several subsequent Decisions of the President of the Republic, a state of emergency was declared in North Macedonia on the entire territory of the country for a little more than three months (from March 18, 2020 to June 23, 2020). However, it is worth noting that for the entire duration of the state of emergency, the country's Government did not adopt any Ordinance with force of law prohibiting or restricting the right to strike. The complete ban on the exercise of the right to strike is explicitly regulated in relation to the *armed forces* (in crisis, state of emergency and martial law, as well as in the case of the execution of international agreements relating to exercise activities, training, peace-keeping or humanitarian operations in or outside the Republic), *police officers* (in martial law or state of emergency) and *members of the prison police* (in martial law, state of emergency or crisis). The Law on Police makes a distinction between restrictions regarding the exercise of the right to strike by police officers in cases of martial law or state of emergency, on the one hand, and in cases of complex security situation, disruption of public order and peace on a larger scale, natural disasters and other disasters or endangering life and health of people and property on a larger scale, on the other hand. In the second case, police officers are not prohibited from exercising the right to strike but are subject to additional restrictions of a procedural character in relation to the maximum number of employees who can simultaneously participate in the strike (no more than 10% of the total number of police officers) and the duration of the strike (no longer than three days).[51] Almost identical additional restrictions of a procedural character in similar situations to police officers also exist in relation to the exercise of the right to strike by members of the prison police.

3 COMPENSATORY GUARANTEES FOR WORKERS DEPRIVED OF THE RIGHT TO STRIKE

Workers whose right to strike is restricted because they perform activities of general interest or essential activities in the strict sense of the term have the right to adequate protection of their rights and interests, which is exercised through *conciliation* in accordance with the Law on Amicable Settlement of Labour Disputes. In principle, the conciliation procedure is voluntary and the parties to the dispute are free to decide whether to accede to a peaceful resolution of the dispute. However, in the event of a strike or dispute in activities of general interest or essential interest in the strict sense of the term, the conciliation procedure is compulsory for the parties to the dispute, who are obliged to submit a joint proposal for conciliation on the following day from the day

49. Law on Crisis Management (*Official Gazette of the Republic of Macedonia*, No. 29/2005), Art. 1, para. 2.
50. *See* Constitution of the Republic of North Macedonia, Art. 54, para. 2.
51. Law on Police, Art. 108, para. 2.

the dispute arose.[52] The procedure is conducted before a Conciliation Board, in which, despite a conciliator, an equal number of representatives from the parties to the dispute participate.[53] In cases of strike or dispute in activities of general interest or essential activities in the strict sense of the term, the procedure should end within 10 days from the day of submission of the proposal for a peaceful resolution of the dispute,[54] with a conclusion or non-conclusion of an Agreement. If the procedure ends with a conclusion of an agreement and the subject matter of the dispute is a collective agreement, the agreement becomes an integral part of the collective agreement. If the subject matter of the dispute is not a collective agreement, the agreement shall have a force of a court settlement.[55] The LASLD does not provide for the possibility of resolving a collective labor dispute, including a strike in the activities of general interest or essential activities in the strict sense of the term, through *arbitration*. According to LASLD, only an individual labor dispute may be settled by arbitration.[56] Arbitration as a way of voluntary settlement of a collective labor dispute is usually provided for in collective agreements. Collective agreements determine that arbitration can be applied either as an alternative to conciliation or as a procedure for amicable settlement of the collective dispute after an unsuccessful conciliation, which is a more common case. Considering the compulsory nature of conciliation in the event of strikes in activities of general interest or essential activities in the strict sense of the term regulated by the LASLD, we believe that the resolution of the dispute in the mentioned activities by way of arbitration could only be acceded in the event of unsuccessful conciliation. Collective agreements lay down the manner in which the procedure before arbitration, i.e., the arbitration board shall be initiated and conducted and the term in which it shall be completed. The arbitrator's decision shall be final, enforcing and binding on the parties to the dispute.[57]

4 CONCLUSION

Throughout the past several years, industrial relations in North Macedonia have been characterized by a rise in strike activities, most of them organized in the public sector. Reasons for the frequent strikes are usually the demands of the trade unions to increase workers' salaries set by collective agreements. This is primarily due to the fact that the national minimum net wage has more than doubled in the last eight years (increasing from EUR 195 in September 2017 to EUR 396 as of March 2025). **However, in most cases, this increase did not trigger a corresponding spiral of upward adjustments in the salaries of workers employed in more complex job positions covered by collective agreements.** In such circumstances, the question of the right to strike, the

52. Law on Amicable Settlement of Labour Disputes, Art. 19, para. 1.
53. Law on Amicable Settlement of Labour Disputes, Art. 20, para. 1 and para. 2.
54. Law on Amicable Settlement of Labour Disputes, Art. 18, para. 2.
55. Law on Amicable Settlement of Labour Disputes, Art. 25, para. 3 and para. 4.
56. Law on Amicable Settlement of Labour Disputes, Art. 4, para. 2.
57. *See* General Collective Agreement for the Private Sector in the field of Economy (*Offical Gazette of the Republic of Macedonia*, No. 88/2009), Art. 51, para. 6; General Collective Agreement for the Public Sector (*Offical Gazette of the Republic of Macedonia*, No. 10/2008), Art. 32, para. 5.

legal framework in which it is exercised and the permitted restrictions in its application are becoming more and more topical issues in the context of Macedonian industrial relations.

The right to strike in North Macedonia is regulated by the Constitution, by the Law on Labour Relations (as *lex generalis* in the field of labor relations), by the Law on Employees in the Public Sector (as *lex fundamentalis* for public sector employees) and by several special laws (*lex specialis*) that primarily regulate certain restrictions on the exercise of the right to strike relating to certain categories of public sector employees or certain specific activities of general interest or essential activities in the strict sense of the term. Certain aspects of the right to strike in North Macedonia, whose minimum conditions are determined by the Law on Labour Relations, are subject to more favorable regulation by collective agreements. However, there are dilemmas in practice about the scope of issues related to the right to strike and the extent to which they can be regulated by a collective agreement, especially when it comes to certain restrictions on the exercise of the right to strike, the regulation of which is primarily stipulated in law. *De lege ferenda*, the Macedonian labour legislation should reconsider the regulatory approach on several significant issues related to the basic material and procedural requirements that precondition the legality of a strike. Such are the issues regarding: the *holder of the right to strike* (because in North Macedonia, only the trade union is entitled to organize and call a strike, and not a group of workers, but at the same time, the legal framework contains significant obstacles and restrictions on trade union organization at the level of an employer), the *legitimate aims, i.e., reasons* for organizing a strike (because the Macedonian labour legislation formally provides for only the protection of the economic and social "rights," but not the "interests" of workers) and clarification of the legal status, i.e., the compulsoriness of the *conciliation procedure* before the commencement of the strike, the manner, i.e., the legal mechanisms through which such a procedure may or should be conducted (e.g., the mechanisms provided for by the Law on Amicable Settlement of Labour Disputes or collective agreements) and its relationship with the obligation for a compulsory written notice of the strike.

Regarding the restrictions in the exercise of the right to strike, subject of supervision and criticism of the ILO supervisory bodies are certain regulations that determine the minimum services during a strike in the public sector. Such regulations apply to all public sector employees, that is, to a very broad scope of persons, and they completely ignore the involvement of workers' organizations in determining the minimum services. The Government of the Republic of North Macedonia has not yet acted on the recurring requests and observations of CEACR to abolish the possibility of replacing striking employees in primary and secondary education as activities that cannot be considered essential activities in the strict sense of the term.

The system of amicable settlement of labor disputes in North Macedonia, which includes compulsory conciliation in the event of a collective labor dispute or strike in activities of general interest or essential activities in the strict sense of the term, has been built for more than a decade now. The insufficiently clear provisions in the Law on Amicable Settlement of Labour Disputes and the parallel existence of separate "channels" for peaceful resolution of collective labor disputes through conciliation and arbitration with collective agreements lead to a state of incoherence and uneven application of the obligation to conciliate in strike conditions. It is also unclear how and in what procedure public sector employees may seek protection of their rights in case of restriction on the right to strike, which stems from the unilateral dictation of minimum services by the employer. Similar dilemmas exist in the context of the general Law on Labour Relations, which, despite the fact that it provides for a consensual determination of the activities that must not be interrupted during a strike by the employer and the trade union, in the event of a dispute concerning the determination of these activities, refers to voluntary and not to compulsory arbitration or other impartial and objective dispute resolution mechanism, whose decision will be binding on the parties.

CHAPTER 27

Restrictions on the Right to Strike in Norway

Alexander Sønderland Skjønberg

1 GENERAL INFORMATION

1.1 Legal Basis of the Right to Strike

The social partners play a key role in the Norwegian industrial relations system. Trade union density is about 50% and the collective agreement coverage is even higher: approximately 70% of all employees are covered by a collective agreement. A characteristic element of the industrial relations system is the wage coordination model ('Frontfagsmodellen'). This model implies that certain key industries that are more vulnerable to international competition negotiate first and set a framework for the rest of the labour market. The model aims to maintain wage stability by avoiding large wage differentials between industries and ensuring wage growth in line with productivity, and to prioritize wage growth for low-wage workers to reduce income inequality. It is considered an overall economic success.[1] Nevertheless, strikes occur relatively often in connection with collective bargaining, and in the private sector, even lockout is used sometimes.[2]

1. *See* further, for example, NOU 2013: 13 *Lønnsdannelsen og utfordringer for norsk økonomi* og NOU 2021: 9 *Den norske modellen og fremtidens arbeidsliv*, pp. 33-34.
2. According to numbers from the ETUI, an average of 55 working days were lost each year in Norway in industrial disputes per 1,000 employees from 2010 to 2019. https://sciencenorway.no/labour-market-wages-work/these-are-the-european-countries-with-the-most-labour-strikes/2185665 (accessed 6 May 2025).

Historically, the right to use industrial action was derived from the freedom of action and the freedom of contract.[3] Hence, the right to strike and to lockout were merely *freedoms*, which could be limited by legal norms. Neither the freedom to organize nor the right to strike were stated explicitly in statutory law. However, the first legislation on industrial disputes and collective agreements, the Labour Dispute Act of 6 August 1915 No. 2, recognized indirectly the right to take industrial action by introducing a framework for and restrictions on the use of it. The freedom of association has, for many years, been an important *unwritten* legal principle,[4] and recourse to industrial action has, notwithstanding the absence of a constitutional guarantee, been considered a fundamental right.[5] In connection with the 200th anniversary of the Norwegian Constitution in 2014, a constitutional reform was carried out, giving the freedom of association a positive basis in Article 101(1), stating, '[e]veryone has the right to form, join and leave associations, including trade unions and political parties'.

Norway has also, for a long time, been bound by international conventions protecting the right to strike. The European Convention on Human Rights (ECHR) was ratified in 1952, and the UN Covenant on Economic, Social and Cultural Rights (ICESCR) in 1972. However, the dualistic principle applies, meaning, simply said, that international law needs to be transformed into national legislation.[6] Both the ECHR and the ICESCR are incorporated through the Human Rights Act of 21 May 1999 No. 30. These conventions even have precedence over other legislation that conflicts with them, cf. section 3. Therefore, ECHR Article 11 is directly applicable and relevant when determining the content of the right to strike under Norwegian law. However, Norway has explicitly reserved the right not to be subject to Article 8(d) of the ICESCR.[7] The background for the reservation was a concern that the practice of government intervention in industrial conflicts in the form of compulsory arbitration could violate the right to strike following this provision, as outlined in section 2.2.2 below.

The ILO Convention No. 87 on Freedom of Association and Protection of the Right to Organise (1948), ILO Convention No. 98 on the Right to Organise and Collective Bargaining (1949), and the European Social Charter (ESC) are considered important when it comes to the protection of the right to strike. These conventions are all ratified, but have not been incorporated in Norwegian law. Nevertheless, the principle of presumption in Norwegian law implies that Norwegian law to the extent possible must be interpreted in conformity with the ratified conventions.[8]

Both the content of the right to strike and its recognition in Norwegian law may therefore vary depending on the relevant international instrument and its status in

3. *See* further Alexander N. Skjønberg, *Retten til lockout,* in Hvor din skatt er, vil også ditt hjerte være. Festskrift til Ole Gjems-Onstad 70 år, 629-635 (Tore Bråthen et al. eds, 2020).
4. *See, e.g.*, Rt. 2001 p. 1413 and Rt. 2008 p. 1601.
5. *See* Stein Evju, *The Right to Strike in Norwegian Labour Law,* in Arbeidsrett. Utvalgte artikler 2001-2010, 171-186 (172) (2010).
6. *See, e.g.*, HR-2010-2057-P (133).
7. *See* St.prp. (1970-71) pp. 4 and 11. The reservation has not been withdrawn, *see* NOU 2001: 14 p. 37 and Ot.prp. nr. 46 (2001-2002).
8. *See, e.g.*, HR-2010-2057-P (133).

Norwegian law. In HR-2016-2554 *Holship*, the Supreme Court ruled that when determining the scope of the right to form or join a trade union according to Article 101(1) of the Constitution, it is natural to take as a starting point the right to freedom of assembly and association pursuant to Article 11 of the ECHR.[9] This means that a right to strike also has constitutional protection.[10] This raises several questions. One is whether this constitutional protection of the right to strike goes beyond the protection provided by the ECHR Article 11. Another question is whether lockout, which in Norwegian law in many ways has equal legal status as strike, also is protected by Article 101 of the Constitution. These questions have so far not been clarified in case law.

1.2 Main Features of the Regulation

The main regulation on industrial action can be found in the Labour Disputes Act of 27 January 2012 No. 9 (the LDA), which replaced the similar act of 1927 (which succeeded the first act of 1915). The current act largely represents a continuation of the previous acts. A separate law, the Public Service Dispute Act of 18 July 1958 No. 2, covers employees engaged in civil service (PSDA). Both acts are based on the principle of freedom to collective bargaining and freedom to use industrial action.

Norwegian labour law is based on a fundamental distinction, a dichotomy, between *interest disputes* and *rights disputes*. The point of departure is that strike (and lockout) is legitimate in interest disputes, while it is forbidden in rights disputes. The general ban on rights disputes applies to all disputes concerning the existence, validity, interpretation or application of a collective agreement and disputes pertaining to claims based on the agreement, cf. LDA section 8 paragraph 1, cf. section 1, and PSDA section 20 paragraph 1. This peace obligation also covers disputes on managerial decisions.[11]

In interest disputes, the point of departure is that strike and lockout is legitimate. An interest dispute is a dispute between a trade union and an employer or employers' association concerning the organization of future employment and wage terms or other working conditions, cf. LDA section 1. Such disputes concern either an initial establishment of a collective agreement or revision of an existing collective agreement. The restrictions on the right to strike (and lockout) are governed by two sets of peace obligation rules.

First, *procedural rules* apply in *all* interest disputes, cf. LDA section 8 paragraph 2. A party calling a strike or lockout is required to give *notice of collective work stoppage* in writing to the opposite party, cf. LDA section 18 and section 15. This rule is based on the historical conception, deriving from contract law, that the employment agreement needs to be terminated if the work stoppage shall not be contrary to the contractual duty to work. Originally, when notice of collective work stoppage was given, this resulted in termination of the employment contract, meaning that the employees, in principle, had no right to return to their work after the strike was over. Today, the legal

9. *See also* the ruling of the Labour Court, ARD 2017 p. 249 paras 96-98.
10. Skjønberg, *supra* n. 3, at 650.
11. *See, e.g.*, ARD 2014 p. 25.

effect is only a *suspension* of the employment agreements.[12] However, the obligation to give notice of collective work stoppage still applies, and a contractual approach is decisive when determining the content of this requirement.[13] If a strike (or lockout) is initiated without proper notice in accordance with the law, the strike will be illegal, and the individual employee (or employer) will be in breach of the employment agreement.

If there is a collective agreement, notice of collective work stoppage is necessary for the collective agreement and thus its peace obligation to cease. The collective agreement does not lapse on the expiry of its ordinary period of validity but continues to have effect under a special rule (LDA section 8 paragraph 3). Notice of collective work stoppage is necessary for this continued effect to cease, and in case law, it has been established that a work stoppage cannot be limited in time or scope unless agreed upon.[14] Hence, the requirement of notice of collective work stoppage is an obstacle to use other forms of industrial action than strike and lockout, for example, go-slow actions, work-to-rule, partial work refusal, etc.

The notice period is 14 days unless otherwise stipulated in a collective agreement or other written agreement, cf. LDA section 15 paragraph 1, meaning that the ordinary dismissal notice periods do not apply, cf. the Working Environment Act of 17 June 2005 No. 61 sections 15-17. For some peculiar reason, the preparatory works of the LDA states that this provision shall not apply to employees on board ships, although they are covered by the act. No explanation is given, and it is difficult to see what justifies an unequal treatment.[15] Without a common and shorter notice period, it may be more difficult for employees on board ships who do not have a collective agreement with an agreed shorter notice period to go on strike, which could unduly restrict their right to strike.

At the same time as a notice of collective work stoppage is given, a notification must be given to the National Mediator, cf. LDA section 18. Further rules on the content of this notice are given, cf. LDA section 16. The strike cannot lawfully be implemented until four (business) days after such notice was given. The National Mediator *shall* then impose a temporary ban on industrial action and summon the parties to compulsory mediation if the strike *may* harm the public interest, cf. LDA section 19 paragraph 1.[16] To be binding, the temporary ban must be sent within two (business) days after the notice was received. This cooling-off period lasts for at least 14 days, cf. LDA section 25, and the aim is to conduct mediation with a view to having the parties reach a reasonable voluntary compromise without resorting to implementing industrial action.

Furthermore, if the interest dispute concerns the revision of a collective agreement, the validity of the agreement must have expired, cf. LDA section 8 paragraph 2.

The procedural rules pursuant to the PSDA are largely similar, although there are some differences. The main differences are that the PSDA establish a legal right and

12. *See, e.g.*, AR-2020-23.
13. *See* further Alexander N. Skjønberg, *Fredsplikten i tarifforhold* 411-418 (2019).
14. *Ibid.*, at 414-415.
15. *Ibid.*, at 413-414.
16. *See* further Alexander N. Skjønberg, *Riksmeglers inngrepskompetanse i arbeidskonflikter: et forsøk på å beskrive det prinsipielle*, in Sui Generis. Festskrift til Stein Evju 601-612 (Bernhard J. Mulder et al. eds, 2016).

duty to bargain collectively, and that the capability to conclude collective agreements with the state is reserved to trade unions fulfilling certain requirements of size and representativeness, cf. section 3 of the act. Another difference is that compulsory mediation is always required, and industrial action is expressly forbidden during this period; an issue of a temporary is not needed. The minimum cooling-off period is 21 days opposed to 14 days under the LDA.

Second, a peace obligation exists during the tenure of the collective agreement. This peace obligation rests on a dual basis, from the collective agreement itself as a contractual obligation and by statute law (LDA section 8 and PSDA section 20). This peace obligation is *relative*.[17] As a point of departure, this means that the peace obligation only comprises industrial action whose purpose is to force the resolution of a question regulated in the collective agreement; if the purpose of the collective action is detached from this, the action is not in contravention of the peace obligation. What is considered regulated in the collective agreement in this context has been stretched far; *the principle of negative regulation*, developed in case law, implies that the peace obligation also prohibits industrial action over regulation that is not directly regulated in the collective agreement. This relatively implies, however, that the peace obligation does not comprise collective action where the purpose is to express or impose an opinion on political issues (*political strike*) or collective actions where the purpose is to support a party in another (lawful) dispute of interest (*sympathy action*). There are no specific statutory restrictions on the use of sympathy action; a sympathy strike or sympathy lockout will however be covered by the LDA / PSDA, and the abovementioned procedural rules apply. A political strike is, however,not a strike in the sense of this legislation, and no statutory rules apply. It is still a precondition to not contravene the contractual peace obligation, that the political strike is of short duration, or that there is a reasonable degree of proportionality between the duration of the political strike and its consequences.[18] In general, it is also considered a precondition to give notice of the political strike in advance.

There is no other statutory law restricting the right to strike. There is no legislation on compulsory arbitration or limitations on how extensive or how long a strike (or lockout) can be. In principle, it is up to the parties in the industrial conflict to decide this. A permanent arbitration body exists at the disposal of the parties, the National Wage Board, but voluntary arbitration is rarely used. In a large number of interest disputes, the parties themselves, often through mediation, reach an agreement. If not, the state may, if it deems necessary for the protection of life or health, etc., intervene in the conflict ad hoc by deciding that the dispute shall be solved by compulsory arbitration and that industrial action is forbidden. If the Parliament (Stortinget) is not sitting, the government may, pursuant to the Constitution, adopt such legislation itself. Such intervention occurs relatively often and has drawn criticism from the supervisory bodies of ILO and the European Social Charter. The significant number of interventions is, among other things, related to the lack of legal obligations for the parties in the conflict to have minimum service to ensure that life and health are

17. *See* further Skjønberg, *supra* n. 13, at 1-442.
18. *See* ARD 2001 p. 99; *See also* ARD 2016 p. 1.

not endangered and for compulsory arbitration to be avoided, as outlined in section 2.2.2 below.

2 PERMITTED RESTRICTIONS

2.1 Certain Categories of Public Servants

There is in general no restrictions on the freedom of association for certain categories of public servants. However, there are restrictions on the right to strike applicable to some groups.

A certain group of civil servants, *embetsmenn*, which are appointed by the government, do not have the right to strike, cf. the PSDA section 22 implicitly. This is due to the regulation on termination of their employment pursuant to Article 22 of the Constitution and not necessarily their functions. The government determines which group of civil servants shall be appointed as this type of civil servants.[19] The category has become increasingly smaller over the years, and today, judges make up the majority. Furthermore, civil servants in the *military forces* are presupposed to not have the right to strike due to the nature of their work.[20] These groups have the right to negotiate collective agreements, but there is a special arrangement for compulsory arbitration according to the PSDA section 26a. Previously, there was also a strike prohibition for members of the *police force*.[21] The statutory prohibition was introduced in 1959 after a strike involving, among others, police officers at the Oslo Police Department[22] but was abolished in 1995.[23]

The Public Service Dispute Act is based on a special arrangement where only unions of a certain size and with a certain representativeness have the right to negotiate and enter into collective agreements with the state. The right to strike corresponds to this right to negotiate, and during the period when civil servants who are members of a union with the right of negotiation have a peace obligation, other civil servants employed in the same agency, service branch or group also have a peace obligation, cf. PSDA section 20 No. 4. Hence, civil servants who are a member of a union without the right to negotiate or who are unorganized do not have the right to strike. The justification for the prohibition is not related to the civil servants' function but to the system of PSDA, which is designed to ensure a centralized and concentrated bargaining system in the state sector.[24] In 2000, the European Committee of Social Rights (ECSR) expressed that the extended peace obligation pursuant to PSDA section 20 No. 4 'is too general and goes beyond the restrictions on the right to strike permitted under Article

19. *See* further Skjønberg, *supra* n. 13, at 37.
20. *See* further e.g., Ot.prp. No. 20 (1958) pp. 22-23, NOU 1996: 14 p. 18, NOU 2001: 14 p. 34; *See also* Stein Evju, *Organisasjonsfrihet, tariffavtaler og streik* 135 (1982) and Skjønberg, *supra* n. 13, at 37.
21. *See* Act 13 March 1936 No. 3 concerning the police s. 20.
22. *See* Ot.prp. No. 14 (1959).
23. *See* further Doc. No. 89 (1993-1994) and Innst. O. No. 12 (1994-1995).
24. *See* further Skjønberg, *supra* n. 13, at 153-155, *see also* 126-127.

6 paragraph 4 of the Charter'.[25] Nevertheless, this has not led to any changes in the PSDA when the act was revised in 2002, and the violation of the ESC must be considered as accepted by the legislator.[26]

Strike prohibition for certain groups of public servants may also be included in collective agreements. The collective agreements for the public sector contain a prohibition against strike for chief executives. The Basic Agreement for the Civil Service section 47 No. 1, for example, states that '[t]he chief executive of an agency and head of the personnel function shall not be involved in a strike'. Similar provisions can be found in the agreements for the municipal sector.[27] According to the Basic Agreement for the Civil Service section 3, an agency shall be defined as 'any government body or state institution', and it follows from the provision that ministries, agencies, and universities are all regarded as agencies. Hence, a department manager will not be covered by the prohibition. Similar agreements for the municipal sector do not have a definition of agency. It is therefore unclear whether the concept of agency according to these provisions on strike prohibition should be interpreted as being each municipally, which is in accordance with the general understanding in Norwegian law,[28] or whether a unit *within* a municipality can be considered an agency according to these provisions. All these agreed strike prohibitions are linked to the function of the positions, meaning that also any deputies will be covered.

Furthermore, these agreements also have provisions which imply that, after a notice of work stoppage is given, negotiations *shall* take place concerning exemptions (dispensations) for additional groups. The Basic Agreement for the Civil Service section 48 No. 2 states, for example, that 'discussions shall be initiated immediately to establish which other officers shall be exempted [from the strike]', and it is stated that '[t]his may apply to the chief executive in an operational unit or other necessary coverage of management and personnel functions' or 'employees who must be present to avert danger to life and health or prevent loss of damage to property, materials, equipment etc.'. Nevertheless, these provisions do not imply any obligation to enter into an agreement on exceptions. The provisions are linked to the system of agreement on restrictions for essential services, cf. section 2.2.1 below.

2.2 Essential Services in the Strict Sense of the Term

2.2.1 An Autonomous Regulation System

As mentioned above in section 2.1, there are few exceptions in the legislation from the right to strike for specific groups of public servants, etc. There is no general statutory regulation on essential services or minimum services in the case of an industrial action

25. ECSR (2000:432).
26. Skjønberg, *supra* n. 13, at 155, cf. 127.
27. The Basic Agreement for the Norwegian Association of Local and Regional Authorities (KS) 2024-2025 Part A s. 5-1-2 and Document No. 24 The Basic Agreement and other collective agreements entered into between the Municipality of Oslo and union 2002 s. 22. The wordings of the provisions are not identical.
28. *See, e.g.*, Rt. 1998 p. 1357.

either. The autonomy of the social partners is strong in the Norwegian system, and the main way of regulating industrial actions in essential services is by an autonomous regulation, either *ex ante* or ad hoc. However, if the industrial action endangers the life, personal safety or health of the population, the government will, as mentioned, intervene in the industrial conflict ad hoc with a decision on compulsory arbitration and prohibition of industrial action, cf. section 2.2.2 below.[29] The social partners' system of regulating essential services and minimum services consists of two main concepts: *pre-agreements* and *dispensations*.

In both the private and the public sector, the basic agreements contain provisions stipulating that agreements necessary to avert danger to life and health or substantial material damage, etc., must be negotiated in advance, cf., i.e., The Basic Agreement between LO (The Norwegian Confederation of Trade Unions) and NHO (The Confederation of Norwegian Enterprises) 2022-2025 section 3-3. Such pre-agreements may be entered into on different levels in the collective agreement system, also locally. The provisions in the basic agreements normally do not imply an obligation to reach an agreement, but the main organizations may require the parties on the local level to enter into such agreement.[30]

Pre-agreements can also regulate conditions, i.e., minimum service, for the sound closing down and restarting of operations. Within, for example, the metallurgical industry, a central pre-agreement imposes an obligation on local parties to enter into agreements. For smelting plants, a gradual shutdown has been agreed upon, reducing capacity by 20% in the first month, etc., which means that the shutdown can take a long time. This became significant in the major strike in the private sector in April 2023, where the second round of strike action included large aluminium plants, which pressured the employer to return to the negotiation table and find a solution to the industrial conflict to avoid the long shutdown process.

An alternative way to limit the consequences of industrial disputes is for the trade union to *unilaterally* restrict who shall participate in the strike, so that essential services are not affected. The trade union will, however, once a notice of collective termination of the employment is given, be bound by this.[31] Hence, the union is, after this point, depended on acceptance from the employer's side to limit the strike action. This is typically part of the trade union's considerations in relation to a strike. Nevertheless, it can sometimes be difficult for the union to anticipate the consequences of a strike action. An example is the laundry workers' strike in 2014. The government intervened in the conflict after the strike had lasted for only five days by issuing a decision for compulsory arbitration because the strike resulted in hospitals and other healthcare institutions not receiving clean laundry, and the shortage of workwear and

29. In Moti Mironi's different sources of regulation of essential services, this will be a hybrid of mixed mode regulation, *see* further Moti M. Mironi, *Introduction: Theory, Conceptualization and Methodology in Regulating Strikes in Essential Services* 13-14 (Mironi and Schlachter 2019).
30. *See* further Aira Din, *Forhåndsavtaler om arbeid ved konflikt*, 116-133 (Arbeidsrett 2019).
31. *See* Skjønberg, *supra* n. 13, at 417-418.

patient garments required the institutions to implement measures that limited their operations.[32]

Dispensations is the other main concept for the social partners to regulate minimum services. The dispensation scheme involves making exceptions for specific individuals who are initially included in the strike. According to, e.g., The Basic Agreement for the Civil Service section 48 No. 2, negotiations on dispensation shall, as mentioned above in section 2.1, 'be initiated immediately' after a notice of collective work stoppage is given. It is, however, the employer who must seek dispensation from the trade union, and it is up to the union whether dispensation shall be given. Thus, the scheme relies on an agreement between the parties. Whether dispensation negotiations take place between the organizations centrally or locally varies according to different collective agreements.

Some have argued that the dispensation scheme is undesirable because it practically means that the responsibility for determining what constitutes necessary or adequate operations lies with the workers in a strike committee.[33] In practice, it often happens that employers refrain from applying for dispensation, thereby endangering life or health, which results in the intervention through compulsory arbitration. It has been argued that this is tactically used by the employer's side to prompt government intervention and thus force a resolution to the conflict.[34] In the abovementioned strike among laundry workers in 2014, for example, the union was willing to grant applications for exemption from the strike to avoid government intervention.[35] Nevertheless, the employer's side refused to apply for dispensation.

Although regulation on essential services is agreement-based, there is some legislation imposing duties on the parties in the case of an industrial conflict. There are two sets of relevant rules. Pursuant to the Regulation of 12 February 2010 No. 158 on health, safety, and environment in the petroleum activities and at certain onshore facilities (the Framework Regulations) section 50, the employer and employees in each company, which is comprised by the regulations, are obliged to enter into an agreement on safety work during an industrial dispute *ex ante*. The agreement must comprise both regulations on shutdown and minimum safety service. The Regulations of 1 April 1996 No. 319 on staffing of mobile offshore units sets general requirements for staffing onboard mobile offshore units but does not explicitly require any obligation to enter into a pre-agreement on the matter.

In contrast, there is no legislation regarding minimum staff, etc., in the case of industrial action at hospitals and other healthcare institutions. It is difficult to derive specific obligations on this matter based on the general health legislation. Pre-agreements are depended on consensus. However, The Norwegian Board of Health Supervision monitors any strike (or lockout) action in this sector and reports to the

32. PRE-2014-09-19-1205 *Provisorisk anordning om lønnsnemndbehandling av arbeidstvisten mellom Industri Energi og Norsk Industri i forbindelse med tariffoppgjøret for vaskerier og renserier i 2014*.
33. *See* further Tor O. Carlsen, *Arbeidskampen maktmidler*, 80 (Arbeidsrett 2019).
34. *See* further Kristin Alsos & Kristine Nergaard, *Lockout som kampmiddel i moderne arbeidskonflikter*, 191 (Arbeidsrett 2019).
35. *Supra* n. 32; *See also* CFA Case No. 3147 Norway (2016) para. 542.

ministry when there is a risk of failure to meet the necessary requirements for adequate healthcare services, which often results in the use of compulsory arbitration.

2.2.2 The Practice of Interventions in the Form of Compulsory Arbitration

The major point of contention when the first legislation on industrial disputes was established in the early 1900s was whether there should be a system of compulsory arbitration.[36] There was a significant disagreement on this issue, but a proposal for such a scheme gained majority in the parliament. According to the proposal, the government would have the authority to decide that a dispute that, due to its nature or extent, poses a significant risk to societal interests should be resolved through compulsory arbitration.[37] However, due to the threat of a general strike, 'when a world war rages outside our door', as the prime minister expressed, the proposal was not enacted.[38] Subsequently, there have been several temporary acts on compulsory arbitration, particularly in the 1920s and from 1945 until the early 1950s. Later, the current practice emerged where the government intervenes in industrial disputes on an ad hoc basis.

As mentioned, such intervention occurs relatively often. From 1990 to 2022, intervention has happened 53 times. The law, as enacted in each individual case, will grant the National Wage Board (Rikslønnsnemnda) the authority to resolve the dispute, and a decision by the National Wage Board has the same legal effects as a collective agreement.[39] The decision on compulsory arbitration will normally not provide any further guidelines regarding the resolution of the dispute, and it is up to the National Wage Board to determine any new conditions in the collective agreement. In practice, the National Wage Board is unlikely to arrive at any other conclusion than that provided for in the collective agreements applicable to the relevant sector, and anyone who wants something outside this framework or something new will normally not gain anything on compulsory arbitration.[40]

In an industrial dispute, as mentioned, the unions often try to structure the strike in a way to minimize the risk of government intervention. At the same time, the employer side has its tactical means in the dispute and can use lockout to make a conflict more extensive, thereby increasing the likelihood of intervention. An example is the conflict in the oil and gas industry in 2012, where the unions announced strike by 700 workers and the employers announced lockout affecting 6,500 workers, which resulted in the government's immediate intervention. As mentioned, Norway has been criticized by international supervisory bodies for the use of compulsory arbitration, among others, in the oil and gas industry. From 1994 to 2010, the ECSR dealt with 19 cases of arbitration intervention, and 7 of them were considered violations of the

36. *See* further Skjønberg, *supra* n. 13, 117-119.
37. *See* Ot.prp. No. 23 (1913) p. 31.
38. Oth.forh. 1915 p. 603.
39. *See* Act 27 January 2012 No. 10 on wage committees in industrial disputes s. 2 para. 2.
40. *See* Skjønberg, *supra* n. 3, at 642; *See also* Alsos & Nergaard, *supra* n. 34, at 184.

conventions.[41] The International Labour Organization's Committee on Freedom of Association (CFA) has also voiced criticism against Norway in several cases.[42] The CFA has urged Norwegian authorities to engage in discussions with social partners to find ways of ensuring a minimum staffing level to protect life and health and to avoid compulsory arbitration.[43]

The Norwegian government has argued that there is no obligation to establish 'a general legal basis for minimum services connected to industrial actions'[44] and stressed that any amendments to the existing framework 'must be handled with understanding and in close cooperation with the social partner'. In the latest case for the CFA, from 2020, the government assured that it would continue discussing the issue with the social partners and the committee 'welcome [d] this engagement'.[45] The criticism from the supervisory bodies has not resulted in any legislative changes.

Furthermore, in legislative proposals regarding compulsory arbitration, it is often expressed that the government considers the intervention to be in accordance with Norway's international legal obligations. The proposal will also include a provision stating something like that: 'If, however, a contradiction between international conventions and Norway's use of compulsory arbitration were to be identified, the Ministry of Labour and Social Affairs, in line with established practice in such cases, believes that the consideration for life and health necessitates intervention in the conflict under any circumstances.'[46] Such an expression of the legislator's intent will generally hinder the possibility of a violation of the ILO conventions and the ESP, resulting in the decision on intervention being set aside by the courts, as these conventions are not implemented into Norwegian law, cf. section 1.1 above.

2.3 Situations of Acute National or Local Crisis

There is no legislation prohibiting industrial action, including strike, in the event of an acute national or local crisis, as this term is understood under the ILO instruments. However, the Act No. 7 of 15 December 1950 relating to special measures in time of war, threat of war, and similar circumstances gives the King (the government) competence to issue provisions of legislative nature to ensure the security of the realm, public order, public health, etc., and if necessary, the provisions may derogate from applicable statutory law. In any way, in the event of an acute national or local crisis, it can be expected that the government, if necessary, would intervene in the industrial conflict ad hoc with a decision on compulsory arbitration and prohibition of industrial action in line with general practice, cf. section 2 above.

41. *See* Kristin Alsos, *Tvungen lønnsnemnd: finnes det alternativer?*, 136 (Arbeidsrett og arbeidsliv 2010).
42. *See, e.g.*, CFA Case No. 1576 Norway (1991), CFA Case No. 1763 Norway (1994), CFA Case No. 2545 Norway (2008), CFA Case No. 3038 Norway (2014).
43. *See* CFA Case No. 3038 Norway (2014), CFA Case No. 3147 Norway (2016).
44. *See* CFA Case No. 3147 Norway (2016) para. 548.
45. *See* CFA Case No. 3372 Norway (2020) para. 858.
46. *See, e.g.*, Prop. 217 L (2020-2021); *See* differently Prop. 3. L (2022-2023) and Prop. 69 L (2022-2023).

3 COMPENSATORY GUARANTEES FOR WORKERS DEPRIVED OF THE RIGHT TO STRIKE

As described in section 2 above, only a few categories of civil servants are deprived of the right to strike, but these groups have the right to organize and bargain collectively. Judges constitute, as mentioned, a large group of such civil servants. The collective agreements that are applicable to civil servants in the state sector do not apply to them unless otherwise stated in the agreement, and the ministry (or the Parliament for the Supreme Court judges) determines their salary administratively. Compared to other public servants, they have a high salary level. This arrangement has its basis in an agreement between the government and the relevant unions from 1999. However, a legislative committee has recommended evaluating this arrangement to find a system that better ensures the independence of the judiciary.[47]

4 CONCLUSION

The Norwegian system of industrial relations grants a high degree of autonomy to the social partners, with broad rights to strike and impose lockouts. There is a strong expectation that these powers will be exercised responsibly, and most industrial disputes are resolved without resorting to industrial action. However, the lack of restriction means that once initiated, strikes or lockouts can have substantial societal impacts. This raises the question of whether the current framework of autonomous regulation is sufficient to mitigate the risk of essential services being disrupted, thus preventing government intervention through compulsory arbitration. This is a complex issue. The frequency of such interventions, combined with criticism from international supervisory bodies, highlights a potential weakness in the model of industrial relations. One concern is the absence of binding regulations concerning essential services. Another is that compulsory arbitration has sometimes been used not just to resolve disputes but also to enforce wage coordination, raising further concerns about the system's impartiality.[48] In response, the Ministry of Labour and Social Inclusion appointed a working group in March 2023 to explore ways of reducing the need for compulsory arbitration. Composed primarily of representatives from unions and employer associations, the group delivered its report in March 2024.[49] However, the working group does not propose any significant changes, concluding that while there are challenges, the system generally functions well. It emphasized the need for caution in making major reforms that could disrupt the delicate balance of power between the social partners.

47. *See* NOU 2020: 11 *Den tredje statsmakt – Domstolene i endring*, 211.
48. *See* Torgeir Aarvaag Stokke, Stein Evju and Hans Otto Frøland, *Det kollektive arbeidslivet: Organisasjoner, tariffavtaler, lønnsoppgjør og inntektspolitikk* 173 (2003); *See also* Alsos, *supra* n. 41, 154.
49. Arbeidskonflikter og tvungen lønnsnemnd. Rapport fra arbeidsgruppe nedsatt av Arbeids- og inkluderingsdepartementet.

CHAPTER 28

Restrictions on the Right to Strike in Poland

Leszek Mitrus

1 GENERAL INFORMATION

In Poland, there are express constitutional guarantees of trade union rights. Article 12 of the Constitution of 2 April 1997 states that the Republic of Poland shall ensure freedom for the creation and functioning of trade unions, socio-occupational organizations of farmers, societies, citizens' movements, other voluntary associations, and foundations. According to Article 59 of the Constitution, the freedom of association in trade unions, socio-occupational organizations of farmers, and employers' organizations shall be ensured (item 1).[1] Trade unions and employers and their organizations shall have the right to bargain, particularly for the purpose of resolving collective labour disputes and to conclude collective labour agreements and other arrangements (item 2). Trade unions shall have the right to organize workers' strikes or other forms of protest subject to limitations specified by statute. For the protection of the public interest, statutes may limit or forbid the conduct of strikes by specified categories of employees or in specific fields (item 3). The scope of freedom of association in trade unions and in employers' organizations may only be subject to such statutory limitations as are permissible in accordance with international agreements to which the Republic of Poland is a party (item 4). Thus, the Supreme Law expressly refers to the right to strike and indicates that this right might be subject to statutory limitations.

1. Journal of Laws 1997, No. 78, item 483 with further amendments, English version of the Constitution is also available at www.sejm.gov.pl/prawo/konst/angielski/kon1.htm (last accessed on 27 July 2024).

Moreover, within certain limits, it provides the option to lay down statutory ban on the right to strike in order to protect 'public interest' (pol. *dobro publiczne*).

Polish labour law is mainly statutory law, and collective bargaining plays a secondary role. The industrial relations pattern was determined during the transformation from a centrally planned to market economy in the 1990s.[2] The current system of collective labour law is not a result of a spontaneous process but constitutes the outcome of the legislator's actions undertaken after the political and economic breakthrough in 1989. Therefore, the Polish system of collective labour relations is – to a large extent – a political subject.[3]

1.1 Legal Basis of the Right to Strike and Main Features of the Regulation

Article 1 item 1 of the Law of 23 May 1991 on trade unions provides that a trade union is a voluntary and self-governing organization of working people founded to represent and defend their rights, as well as occupational and social interests.[4] In Poland, trade unions are powerful in large enterprises but practically do not exist in small workplaces. This fact affects the Polish system of industrial relations to a large extent because only trade unions are competent to conclude a collective labour agreement or declare a strike. Under Article 7 of the Law on trade unions, concerning collective rights and interests, trade unions represent all workers regardless of their trade union membership (item 1). Concerning individual matters connected to paid work performance, trade unions represent the rights and interests of their members (item 2). At the request of a worker who is not a trade union member, a trade union may undertake to protect his rights and interests before the employer (item 3).[5]

For the sake of the present analysis, it should be emphasized that under Polish law, the legal strike action can be organized only by a trade union organization. Strikes

2. J.-M. Servais, *The Trade Unions' Movement in Central and Eastern Europe: The Great Transformation, in Trade unions in Central and Eastern Europe Within Thirty Years of Systemic Transformation* pp. 23 and following (M. Zbucka-Gargas ed., Gdańsk University Press 2021).
3. For further analysis *see* E. Kovacs, N. Lyutov & L. Mitrus, *Labor Law in Transition: From a Centrally Planned to Free Market Economy in Central and Eastern Europe, in Comparative Labor Law* pp. 429 and following (M.W. Finkin & G. Mundlak eds, Edward Elgar Publishing, Cheltenham, UK; Northampton, MA, USA 2015).
4. Consolidated text: Journal of Laws 2025, item 440; For English texts of the statutes referred to in the present elaboration *see*: N. Faulkner, B. Glogier – Osińska & J. Sikora, *A Collection of Labour Law Acts and Ordinances. Prawo pracy: zbiór ustaw i rozporządzeń* pp. 1 and following (Warsaw 2013); L. Florek, *The Notion and Scope of Trade Union Freedom, in Studia Iuridica tom 60. Collective Labour Law* pp. 41 et seq. (J. Stelina & Ł. Pisarczyk eds, Warszawa 2015).
5. *See, e.g.*, L. Mitrus, *European Trade Unions in Age of Flexicurity and Segmented Labor Markets: The Case of Poland*, 38 Comparative Labor Law & Policy Journal pp. 59 and following (Fall 2016); Z. Hajn, in Z. Hajn & L. Mitrus, *Labour Law in Poland* pp. 254 and following, 3rd ed., Wolters Kluwer 2024); M. Zbucka-Gargas, *Trade Unions in Poland: Regulations, Successes, Missed Opportunities, Challenges, in Trade Unions in Central and Eastern Europe Within Thirty Years of Systemic Transformation* pp. 145 and following (M. Zbucka-Gargas ed., Gdańsk University Press 2021).

and other collective actions are regulated by the Law of 23 May 1991 on the collective labour disputes settlement (consolidated text Journal of Laws 2020, item 123, hereinafter 'the Law'). According to Article 1 of the Law, a collective dispute between employees and an employer or employers may concern the conditions of work, wages or social benefits, as well as the liberties and freedom of association rights of employees and other groups entitled to associate in trade unions. Article 2 of the Law provides that the collective rights and interests of employees are represented by trade unions. The rights and interests of employers in collective disputes may be represented by the relevant employers' organizations. Under Article 3 of the Law, where there is more than one trade union organization in a work establishment, in the event of a collective dispute, each such organization may represent the interests that are the subject of the dispute. If the trade union organizations operating in a work establishment so decide, joint trade union representation may act in a collective dispute.

The system of collective labour dispute settlement has been subject to numerous elaborations.[6] Here let us only briefly outline the legal regulations on that matter. Under Article 7 item 1 of the Law, a collective dispute exists as of the day on which the entity representing the employees' interests makes demands to the employer in cases referred to in Article 1, where the employer fails to satisfy all the demands within the specified deadline, which cannot be shorter than three days. There are several stages to collective dispute settlement. The obligatory elements are negotiations, covered in Articles 7-9 of the Law, and mediation, covered in Articles 10-15 of the Law. Under Article 15 of the Law, a failure to reach an agreement after mediation proceedings authorizes a trade union to initiate strike action. As an alternative, a trade union may also attempt to resolve the dispute by submitting it for resolution by a board of social arbitration, which is composed of a judge of a regional labour court and six other members (three members appointed by each party). The decision of a board is adopted by majority of votes. According to Article 16 of the Law, the board's decision is binding on the parties, unless either of the parties reserved otherwise before submitting the dispute for resolution by the board.

Article 17 item 1 of the Law defines strike as employees' collective refusal to work in order to settle a dispute concerning the interests referred to in Article 1. Under Article 17 item 2 of the Law, a strike is a measure of last resort and cannot be announced without having previously exhausted all possibilities to resolve the dispute in accordance with the principles set out in Articles 7-14 of the Law (i.e., after conducting negotiations and mediations). A strike may be organized without respecting these

6. *See, e.g.*, K.W. Baran, *Collective Labour Disputes*, in *Outline of Polish Labour Law System* pp. 425 and following (K.W. Baran ed., Wolters Kluwer, Warszawa 2016); B. Cudowski, *Employee Representation in Collective Labour Disputes: de lege lata and de lege ferenda, in Studia Iuridica tom 60. Collective Labour Law* pp. 27 and following (J. Stelina & Ł. Pisarczyk eds, Warszawa 2015); Z. Hajn, in Z. Hajn & L. Mitrus, *Labour Law in Poland*, pp. 283 and following, 3rd ed., Wolters Kluwer 2024); A.M. Świątkowski & M. Wujczyk, *Polish Regulations Concerning Settlement of Collective Disputes in the Light of European Standards, exemplified by the Right to Strike, in Studia Iuridica tom 60. Collective Labour Law* pp. 237 and following (J. Stelina & Ł. Pisarczyk eds, Warszawa 2015).

principles if the unlawful actions of the employer prevented negotiations and mediation or when an employer terminated the employment relationship with the trade union officer conducting the dispute procedure. According to Article 17 item 3 of the Law, when taking a decision on announcing a strike, the trade union should consider whether the demands are commensurate with the losses associated with the strike.[7] Article 18 of the Law expressly determines that participation in a strike is voluntary, while Article 19 of the Law introduces the prohibitions to conduct strikes (as outlined in section 2 *infra*).

Article 20 of the Law provides that both single-establishment and multi-establishment strikes can be announced by a trade union after receiving the consent of the majority of voting employees, provided that at least 50% of employees participated in the vote. Article 20 of the Law stipulates that strikes should be announced at least five days in advance. According to Article 21 of the Law, during a strike, the manager of an establishment cannot be limited in performing his duties with respect to employees who are not participating in a strike or, to the extent necessary, in ensuring protection of the establishment and restoring the regular operation of the undertaking. The strike organizers are obliged to cooperate with the manager in order to achieve the above-mentioned tasks. Article 22 of the Law provides that in order to protect the rights and interests of employees who do not have the right to strike, a trade union operating in another work establishment may organize a solidarity strike for no longer than half of a working day. In such a situation, Articles 17-21 of the Law apply accordingly. Article 23 of the Law states that participation in a strike organized, according to the Law on Collective Dispute Settlement, is not an infringement of an employee's duties and that an employee retains his rights under the social insurance system and employment relationship, except for the right of remuneration. The period of a break in performing work is included in the period of employment at a work establishment. According to Article 24 of the Law, trade unions may decide about the creation and use of strike funds. These funds are not subject to enforcement.

Finally, Article 25 of the Law pertains to non-strike protest actions. Thus, besides strikes, other protest actions can be organized in order to protect rights and interests referred to in Article 1 of the Law. Such collective actions can be conducted if they do not pose any threat to human life or health and if they do not cause work disruption once the negotiations and mediation procedure has been exhausted and subject to respecting the applicable legal order. The right to organize non-strike protest actions may also be exercised by employees who do not have the right to strike. Such industrial actions can include, e.g., obstructionism (zeal strike), picketing and displaying flags for protests, occupations of buildings or public facilities, and demonstrations.

7. For example, the Supreme Court is of the opinion that hunger strike poses the threat to life and health of participants. Such a threat is in principle non-commensurable with the financial benefits from a potential winnings of a hunger strike. *See* the judgment of 27 November 1997, I PKN 393/97, OSNP [Orzecznictwo Sądu Najwyzszego, Izba Pracy, Ubezpieczeń Społecznych I Spraw Publicznych – *Judicial Decisions of Supreme Court, Chamber for Labour, Social Security and Public Affairs*], No. 17/1998, item 511.

2 PERMITTED RESTRICTIONS

2.1 General Remarks

Article 31 item 3 of the Constitution provides that any limitation upon the exercise of constitutional freedoms and rights may be imposed only by statute and only when necessary in a democratic state for the protection of its security or public order or to protect the natural environment, health or public morals, or the freedoms and rights of other persons. Such limitations shall not violate the essence of freedoms and rights. As already mentioned, Article 59 item 3 of the Constitution expressly determines that for the protection of the public interest, statutes may limit or forbid the conduct of strikes by specified categories of employees or in specific fields. Under Article 59 item 4 of the Constitution, the scope of freedom of association in trade unions and in employers' organizations may only be subject to such statutory limitations as are permissible in accordance with international agreements to which the Republic of Poland is a party. Moreover, under Article 233 item 1 of the Constitution, the statute specifying the scope of limitations of the freedoms and rights of persons and citizens during states of natural disasters may limit certain constitutional freedoms and rights, including, i.e., the right to strike.

Poland is bound by the International Labour Organization (hereinafter 'ILO') Convention No. 87 concerning the Freedom of Association and Protection of the Right to Organize, as well as the ILO Convention No. 151 concerning protection of the Right to Organize and Procedures for Determining Conditions of Employment in the Public Service.[8] Poland has also ratified the European Social Charter (hereinafter 'the Charter') adopted by the Council of Europe.[9] However, Poland has not included Article 6 item 4 of the Charter in the list of regulations it is bound with. This provision stipulates that signatory parties should recognize the right of workers and employers to collective action in cases of conflicts of interest, including the right to strike, subject to obligations that might arise out of collective agreements previously entered into.

The express statutory prohibitions on the right to strike have been introduced by Article 19 of the Law on collective labour dispute settlement. Article 19 item 1 of the Law stipulates that it is not permitted to cease work as a result of strike action on work posts, equipment and installations where the cessation of work threatens human life or health or the security of the state. Under Article 19 item 2 of the Law, it is not permitted to organize a strike at the Internal Security Agency, the Intelligence Agency, the Military Counterintelligence Service, the Military Intelligence Service, the Central Anti-Corruption Bureau, the State Protection Service, in units of the Police and the Polish Armed Forces, the Prison Service, the Border Guard, the Marshall's Guard, the National Tax Administration, where the Customs-Tax Service officers serve, and the organizational units of the fire service. According to Article 19 item 3 of the Law, the employees employed in state authorities, state administration, local governments, courts, and prosecutor's offices do not have the right to strike.

8. Journal of Laws 1958, No. 29, item 125; Journal of Laws 1994, No. 22, item 78.
9. Journal of Laws 1999, No. 8, item 67.

The Law on collective labour dispute settlement does not introduce the notion 'essential services'. Instead, the above-mentioned Article 59 item 3 of the Constitution allows the legislator to limit or deny the right to strike in order to protect 'public interest' (pol. *dobro publiczne*). Article 19 of the Law prohibits the strike in three situations. First, on workstations where the work stoppage may pose a threat to human life or health or state security. Second, in the expressly indicated law enforcement agencies. Third, with regard to employees employed in broadly understood public service.

2.2 Workstations Where a Strike Threatens Human Life or Health or the State Security

Article 19 item 1 of the Law pertains to the situation where the work stoppage would pose a risk to human life or health or would jeopardize the security of the state.[10] It applies only to those employees who, during a strike appear to be necessary for the operations of the establishment in such sense that their absence from work caused by participation in a strike would threaten fundamental values protected by the legislature, that is, human life, health, and state security.[11] The provision at stake applies both to the public and private sectors. It does not prohibit the strike action in the entire establishment, but only on particular work posts. In other words, Polish legislation introduces the division of employees into those who can refrain from work and those who do not have such a right. Even in case of strike at certain workstations, the Law obliges strike organizers to secure the continuation of those activities that are indispensable to maintain essential services or resume operations at the particular establishment.

Article 19 item 1 of the Law introduces quite a general description, which leaves a broad room for interpretation. Under Polish law, the prohibition of strike action may pertain to the healthcare sector, social assistance facilities, power engineering sector (e.g., power plant or combined heat and power station), some aspects of transport activities (e.g., air traffic control), city cleaning units, water supply installation, and different types of rescue teams.[12] Moreover, the ban on strike provided in Article 19 item 1 of the Law covers strike action in the workplace such as oil refinery, which is often defined as sensitive. The prohibition of a strike in the oil refinery should be justified by the great complexity of the refinery's installations and special risks connected with breaking work stability.[13] In my opinion, the latter example pertains to

10. For an analysis of the discussion on that provision during the legislative process *see* P. Grzebyk, *Od rządów siły do rządów prawa. Polski model prawa do strajku na tle standardów unijnego i mie̜dzynarodowego prawa pracy* pp. 187 and following (Wydawnictwo Scholar, Warszawa 2019).
11. A.M. Świątkowski, *Strike Restrictions in Contemporary Polish Labour Law*, 1 Hungarian Labour Law E-Journal pp. 65-66 (2018).
12. K.W. Baran, *Ustawa z dnia 23 maja 1991 r. o rozwiązywaniu sporów zbiorowych, in Zbiorowe prawo pracy. Komentarz* p. 441 (K.W. Baran ed., Wolters Kluwer, Warsaw 2016).
13. P. Pettke, *Ograniczenie prawa do strajku w zakładach generujących powazne zagrozenia dla państwa*, 9 Praca i Zabezpieczenie Społeczne pp. 22 and following (2013).

the security of the state, since energy and fuel safety undoubtedly constitutes one of its major components.

The essential services include the healthcare sector, since even during the strike, every sick person should be able to have recourse to medical assistance. The legislator, however, does not clearly specify which medical professionals are covered by the prohibition of strike action. The medical staff employed in a hospital consists of doctors, nurses, lab technicians, and other auxiliary health care workers.[14] The major question is whether, under Article 19 item 1 of the Law, there is a general ban to strike in the healthcare sector or whether and potentially under what circumstances the strike action would be admissible.[15]

M. Kurzynoga points out that Article 19 item 1 of the Law does not introduce the general prohibition of strike that would pertain to certain professional categories or employees employed in specific establishments. This provision prohibits work stoppage for those employees whose duties are connected to protection of human life or health or state security.[16] The denial of the right to strike to all employees of the healthcare sector would constitute an unacceptable restriction on this right. In urgent cases, however, medical doctors are always obliged to provide medical assistance. The strike based on treatment of those who have been already admitted to the hospital, while no new patients would be taken care of by medical staff, should be regarded as illegal.[17]

A.M. Świątkowski emphasizes that in order to assess the legality of strike organized in a hospital, the number of medical staff people is significant. Certainly, the general participation in the strike of all employees belonging to the hospital medical staff would pose a threat to the health or life of patients because there would not be a single employee in the hospital who would be able to take and carry out the necessary medical activities in the case of an emergency situation. The common practice used by trade unions organizing strikes of medical staff in hospitals is to refrain from performing the work of medical personnel except those who perform 'emergency duty' – they are on standby to take the necessary rescue procedures in sudden and unexpected situations. The strike organizer is under the obligation to decide how many employees who belong to the substantive medical staff (doctors, nurses, lab technicians) must be excluded from the planned strike, so there would be no danger to the health and life of those treated.[18]

We should submit that the Polish legislature attempts to balance the right to strike in the healthcare sector on the one hand and the protection of human life and

14. A.M. Świątkowski, *The Right to Strike in Health Service*, 2 Roczniki Administracji I Prawa p. 303 (2017).
15. For an extensive analysis *see* M. Kurzynoga, *Kwestia prawa do strajku lekarzy*, 5 Praca I Zabezpieczenie Społeczne pp. 18 and following (2012).
16. M. Kurzynoga, *Warunki legalności strajku, in Wolters Kluwer Business* p. 91 (Warszawa 2011).
17. M. Kurzynoga, *Warunki legalności strajku, in Wolters Kluwer Business* pp. 95-96 (Warszawa 2011).
18. A.M. Świątkowski, *The Right to Strike in Health Service*, 2 Roczniki Administracji I Prawa p. 305 (2017).

health on the other hand.[19] There is no ground to conclude that under Polish law, there is a general ban on strike action in the healthcare sector. We cannot say that a *priori* any strike action of medical staff would violate the law. The strike would be admissible, provided that human life and health would be adequately protected. In other words, the hospital covered by strike must be in a position to provide medical assistance for those who are treated.

The Law on collective labour dispute settlement does not provide any mechanism or protocol to determine and verify whether a work stoppage would in practice imply a hazard to human life or health or state security. There is no legal procedure to resolve the dispute between the employer and strike organizer on the question of whether the strike is legal or not. *De lege lata,* there is no competence given to judicial authority or social partners to determine the legal nature of a strike action. Therefore, in practice, the burden lies on the strike organizer, who is obliged to assess *ad casum* the legality of the work stoppage, both before the commencement and during the strike action. In the Supreme Court's opinion, doubts concerning the interpretation of legal regulations concerning strike should – in accordance with the *in dubio pro libertate* principle – be resolved for the sake of, and not against, the freedom of strike.[20]

2.3 Uniformed Services

Article 19 item 2 of the Law introduces an exhaustive list of law enforcement agencies where the strike action is prohibited. Consequently, it provides for a strike ban according to the scope of activity. It should be emphasized that according to Article 8 item 2 of the UN International Covenant on Economic, Social and Cultural Rights, the right of everyone to form trade unions and join the trade union of his choice shall not prevent the imposition of lawful restrictions on the exercise of these rights by members of the armed forces or of the police or of the administration of the State.[21]

The military institutions, as well as other agencies listed in the above-mentioned provision, employ not only public officers, including professional soldiers, but also individuals under an employment contract. The prohibition of strike action introduced by Article 19 item 2 of the Law pertains to the entire units and organizational structures of law enforcement agencies. Consequently, under Polish law, both public officers and civil staff performing work under contracts of employment are deprived of the legal guarantees of the right to strike. Article 19 item 2 of the Law should be interpreted pursuant to the principle of literal interpretation. This provision exhaustively enumerates uniformed services in which strike actions are prohibited. It should not apply to the employees in establishments conducting auxiliary and service operations for listed

19. Article 38 of the Constitution provides that the Republic of Poland shall ensure the legal protection of the life of every human being; Art. 68 of the Constitution stipulates that everyone shall have the right to have his health protected.
20. Jugdment of 7 February 2007, I PK 209/06, OSNP No. 5-6/2008, item 65.
21. Ratified by Poland, Journal of Laws 1977, No. 38, item 169.

law enforcement agencies. Therefore, it seems that the ban on strike action in military or police units does not violate international standards.[22]

2.4 Employees in State Authorities, State Administration, Local Governments, and Administration of Justice

Under Article 1 item 2 of the ILO Convention No. 151 on labour relations in public sector, the extent to which the guarantees provided for in this Convention shall apply to high-level employees whose functions are normally considered policy-making or managerial or to employees whose duties are of a highly confidential nature shall be determined by national laws or regulations. In other words, international standards allow for the limitation of the right to strike with regard to those employees who exercise public power in the name of the state. Under Polish law, Article 19 item 3 of the Law denies the right to strike to employees employed in state governing bodies and local government, courts, and prosecutors' offices.[23]

There is no doubt that the prohibition to strike refers to members of civil service corps. Civil service corps is formed by officials employed in organizational units with a great importance for the performance of state activities. Some persons employed in the civil service carry out services relevant to society, the continuity of which has to be ensured. Moreover, Article 78 item 3 of the Law of 21 November 2008 on Civil Service provides that members of the civil service corps are not allowed to participate in strikes or in actions of protest that would interfere with the regular functioning of an office.[24] The scope of Article 19 item 1 of the Law on Collective Labour Disputes Settlement is, however, much broader. In practice, the prohibition at stake pertains to a wide range of individuals with the status of employee, including those holding civil servant positions and also those hired under contracts of employment for auxiliary and servicing activities in state governing bodies and local government. It is not possible to make an exhaustive list of employees denied the right to strike under the above-mentioned provision.[25] With regard to administration of justice, the public interest was clearly given priority over the interests of employees, since many cases dealt with by courts are such that the lack of, or delay in taking, a decision could cause considerable perturbations in the functioning of the State, local government units, and legal and natural persons. The prohibition of strikes concerns both the judges or officers of justice and other court employees.

To sum up: the prohibition of strike as regulated by Article 19 item 3 of the Law applies to a civil service *sensu largo* and introduces an excessive exclusion from the

22. P. Grzebyk, *Od rządów siły do rządów prawa. Polski model prawa do strajku na tle standardów unijnego i międzynarodowego prawa pracy* p. 171 (Wydawnictwo Scholar, Warszawa 2019).
23. A. Reda-Ciszewska, *Prawo do strajku pracowników słuzby publicznej w Polsce w świetle prawa Międzynarodowej Organizacji Pracy*, 2 Prawo i Więź pp. 54 and following (2014).
24. Consolidated text: Journal of Laws 2024, item 1505.
25. *See also* A.M. Świątkowski, *Strike Restrictions in Contemporary Polish Labour Law*, 1 Hungarian Labour Law E-Journal pp. 68 and following (2018).

right to strike of some civil service employees. It seems that the provision at stake does not meet the international standards.[26]

2.5 Situations of Acute National or Local Crisis

There are further statutes that make it possible to suspend the right to strike in acute crisis situations. Article 19 item 1 of the Law of 29 August 2002 on martial law and on competences of the Commander in Chief of the Armed Forces and the principles of his subordination to the constitutional authorities of the Republic of Poland provides that according to the martial law, it is admissible to suspend the right to employee strikes and other forms of collective protests by specified categories of employees or in specific fields.[27] The basis of such a decision would be ordinance of the President of Poland issued under Article 3 item 1 of the above-mentioned Law. Moreover, Article 16 item 1 section 3 of the Law of 21 June 2002 on the state of emergency provides a legal basis to suspend the right to strike and other protest actions.[28] Article 21 item 1 section 17 of the Law of 18 April 2002 on the state of a natural disaster allows to introduce the prohibition to strike for specified categories of employees or in specific fields.[29]

3 CONCLUSION

It has been observed that in the Polish traditional culture, there exists a firmly grounded truth reflected by the saying 'while some must sleep, some must watch'. The legislature rightly considered the human life and health, state security, and a material substance of the work establishment employing the workers on strike a 'common good'.[30] It goes without saying that the right to strike should have a broad scope of application and limitations should be only exceptional. Moreover, the Constitution expressly determines that any limitation of the right to strike must be compatible with the international agreements to which the Republic of Poland is a party. It seems that Polish law introduces the prohibition of the right to strike in essential services, even if this notion has not been expressly used, and the essential services have been indicated in a rather vague and descriptive manner.

From the perspective of ILO standards, there are no problems concerning the admissibility of the prohibition of the right to strike in armed forces and other uniformed services listed in Article 19 item 2 of the Law. However, doubts arise with regard to the ban on strike actions at workstations where a strike threatens human life or health or state security (Article 19 item 1 of the Law), as well as employees in state authorities, state administration, local governments, and administration of justice

26. *See also* P. Grzebyk, *Od rządów siły do rządów prawa. Polski model prawa do strajku na tle standardów unijnego i międzynarodowego prawa pracy* p. 181 with further references (Wydawnictwo Scholar, Warszawa 2019).
27. Consolidated text: Journal of Laws 2022, item 2091.
28. Consolidated text: Journal of Laws 2017, item 1928.
29. Consolidated text: Journal of Laws 2017, item 1897.
30. A.M. Świątkowski, *Poland, in Regulating Strike in Essential Services* p. 320 (M. Mironi & M. Schlachter eds, Wolters Kluwer 2019).

(Article 19 item 3 of the Law). The strike restrictions under Polish law have been subject of assessment by the ILO's Committee on Freedom of Association in case No. 3111 (Poland).[31]

The complainant (the Independent Self-Governing Trade Union 'Solidarność') denounced, i.e., the violation of Convention No. 151 by depriving some of the employees in the state governing bodies and local government, courts, and prosecutor's offices of the right to strike. With regard to Article 19 item 1 and Article 19 item 3 of the Law, the complainant underlined that Polish legislation did not specify a particular position or even a procedure that would be helpful in determining the list of positions on which the interruption of work would be a threat to life, health or security of the state. The complainant also questioned the compliance with ILO standards of the restrictions on the right to strike in relation to certain employees in public administration, since national law denied this right to a wide range of people with the status of employee.

The Committee on Freedom of Association observed that Article 19 item 3 of the Law on Collective Labour Disputes Settlement denied the right to strike to the members of the civil service corps, to employees in courts, and prosecutors' offices and that Article 19 item 1 of the Law prohibited any work stoppage due to a strike that affects positions, equipment, and machinery, where interruption of work would constitute a danger to human lives or health or to the security of the state.

The Committee recalled that the right to strike may be restricted or prohibited:

- in the public service only for public servants exercising authority in the name of the State; or
- in essential services in the strict sense of the term (that is, services the interruption of which would endanger the life, personal safety or health of the whole or part of the population).

The Committee further emphasized that too broad a definition of the concept of 'public servant' is likely to result in a very wide restriction or even a prohibition of the right to strike for these workers and that the prohibition of the right to strike in the public service should be limited to public servants exercising authority in the name of the state. Against this background, the Committee invited the Government of Poland to consider establishing a procedure for determining which public servants enumerated in section 19 item 3 of the Law on Collective Labour Disputes Settlement and in section 2 of the Law on Civil Service are exercising authority in the name of the state and for whom the right to strike could therefore be restricted, as well as for defining minimum services where appropriate. Such a procedure could also be used with respect to section 19 item 1 of the Law on Collective Labour Law Dispute Settlement in order to determine the cases where an interruption of work would be deemed a hazard under section 19 item 1 of the Law on Collective Labour Law Dispute Settlement and where

31. Definitive Report – Report No. 378, June 2016.

the right to strike would thus be prohibited or restricted, as well as to define minimum services where appropriate.[32]

Thus, with respect to the restrictions of the right to strike, the Committee on Freedom of Association formulated three recommendations for Polish Government.

First, to establish a procedure to determine which public servants are exercising authority in the name of the State and for whom the right to strike could be restricted.

Second, to establish a procedure for determining the cases where an interruption of work would be deemed a hazard for human life or health or the state security.

Third, to establish a procedure for defining minimum services where appropriate.

Therefore, we should conclude that the prohibition of the right to strike under Polish law is too excessive. In order to meet international standards and also to balance the right to strike with the protection of public interest, there is a need to define the scope of minimum services, as well as to introduce the list or procedure for determining which posts involve activities aimed at protecting human life or health or state security, as well as which posts involve exercising authority in the name of the state.[33]

32. Definitive Report – Report No. 378, June 2016, paras 715 and 718.
33. *See also* M. Kurzynoga, *Zapewnienie usług minimalnych w czasie strajku: uwagi de lege ferenda*, *in Przyszłość prawa pracy. Liber Amicorum. W pięćdziesięciolecie pracy naukowej Profesora Michała Seweryńskiego* p. 554 (Z. Hajn & D. Skupień eds, Wydawnictwo Uniwersytetu Łódzkiego, Łódź 2015).

CHAPTER 29

Restrictions on the Right to Strike in Portugal

José João Abrantes & Isabel Valente Dias

1 GENERAL INFORMATION

1.1 Legal Basis of the Right to Strike

The Portuguese Constitution expressly recognizes the right to strike as a fundamental right of employees (Article 57(1) of the Constitution). The right to strike is 'a fundamental instrument for rebalancing the positions of strength and power in labour relations and, therefore, as an instrument for the realisation of the constitutional promise of material equality between all citizens'.[1]

The strike integrates the set of *rights, freedoms, and guarantees* enshrined in the Portuguese Constitution. From this qualification arises certain effects foreseen in Article 18 of the Fundamental Law, namely:

- the provision which enshrines the right to strike is directly applicable and binds public and private entities;
- such right can only be restricted by law in the cases expressly foreseen in the Constitution and such restrictions should be limited to the strictly necessary to safeguard other constitutional rights and interests;
- the law establishing restrictions to this right must have a general and abstract nature and safeguard the essential content of the constitutional provision.

1. José João Abrantes, *Sobre os limites da greve, in Revista de Direito Comercial* 512 (2021), available at https://www.revistadedireitocomercial.com/sobre-os-limites-da-greve (accessed 8 June 2023).

The strike is an individual right of employees, regardless of whether they are unionized or not, which, however, has an undeniable collective dimension, considering that the (individual) right to join a strike depends on a prior declaration of strike by trade unions or an assembly of employees.[2]

The Constitution prohibits the legislator from limiting the 'scope of interests to be defended through strike action' (Article 57(2) of the Portuguese Constitution). This means that the law cannot restrict the scope of the interests that may ground the collective stoppage of work. Under Article 530(2) of the Portuguese Labour Code (hereinafter 'PLC'), employees have the power to 'define the scope of interests to be defended through the strike', thus pointing to a broad concept of strike.[3] Therefore, the aim of the right to strike goes beyond the scope of the conditions of work and may comprise the defence of other lawful interests that are related to the condition as an employee and citizen.

Portuguese law does not define the concept of strike. However, the definition of such concept is essential to delimit the content of the right and the respective limits. According to the doctrinaire and jurisprudential construction, the concept of strike requires a collective and concerted abstention from the provision of work, potentially carried out by multiple employees, with a view to the satisfaction of common goals.[4] Such abstention should be total, in the sense that no work is provided by employees when on strike, which means that partial abstention, whereby employees are not absent from providing work but fulfil only part of their role, would be excluded from the concept of strike.[5]

Some Portuguese scholars refer to *improper strikes*, indicating that they do not fit the concept of strike and, therefore, are not a legitimate form of labour fight. These include cases, for instance, of partial strikes, in which employees only perform part of their functions, or the so-called *greve de zelo* ('go-slow' strike), which is characterized by a slowdown in productive activity that does not result from employees stopping work but from performing their roles with such a meticulous and excessively rigorous application of the procedures that constraints are caused on the normal operation of the company. The right to strike does not legitimate partial or defective compliance of employees' labour obligations. Some court decisions state that the conduct of employees that does not represent a total abstention from the provision of work should be qualified as non-compliance with the labour activity, with potential disciplinary and civil effects.[6]

2. Thus, 'although the right to strike is by nature a right to be exercised collectively, it is held by each and every employee' (Ruling of the Constitutional Court No. 306/2003, of 25 June 2003, available at https://www.tribunalconstitucional.pt).
3. Approved by Law No. 7/2009, of 12 February, as subsequently amended.
4. Please *see*, for instance, the Opinion No. 1/2023, of 9 February 2023 and the Opinion No. 6/2023, of 22 March 2023, issued by the Portuguese Attorney General's Office, available at https://www.ministeriopublico.pt.
5. José João Abrantes, *Direito do Trabalho II: Direito da Greve* 75-76 (Almedina, Coimbra 2012).
6. Please *see* the Ruling of Oporto Court of Appeal, dated 19 December 2012 (Proc. No. 123/12.3TTVFR-A.P1), available at https://www.dgsi.pt. Please *see also* the Opinion No. 6/2023, of 22 March 2023, issued by the Portuguese Attorney General's Office, available at https://www.ministeriopublico.pt.

Whilst collective abstention from the provision of work by employees, a strike aims to disrupt the company's activity and organization and, therefore, to cause damages to the employer.[7] A strike is a means of pressure on the employer to accept the claims voiced by employees for declaring the strike. The strike concept implies a collision of rights, in which, in principle, the right to strike will prevail over employers' economic rights, namely their right to private economic initiative. Therefore, the mere fact that the strike causes, or may potentially cause, damage to the company is not sufficient to consider it illegal.

However, the Portuguese Constitution accepts the imposition of certain restrictions to the exercise of the right to strike, establishing, in Article 57(3), that 'the law shall define the conditions for the provision, during the strike, of services that are needed to ensure the safety and maintenance of equipment and facilities, as well as minimum services that are indispensable to the fulfilment of unavoidable social needs'.[8] Therefore, the constitutional legislator leaves the definition of the conditions for the provision of minimum services to the law, understood in a broad sense (i.e., the services that aim to satisfy unavoidable social needs and those that are necessary to ensure the safety and maintenance of equipment and facilities). We will expand on this below.

1.2 Main Features of the Regulation

In general terms, the right to strike is recognized in relation to all subordinated employees, including employees of private companies and civil servants.

The right to strike is regulated in Articles 530 to 543 of the PLC, applicable to employees subject to a private employment relationship, as well as in Articles 394 to 399 of the Legal Framework applicable to Civil Servants ('Lei Geral do Trabalho em Funções Públicas', hereinafter 'LGTFP'), applicable to employees subject to a public employment relationship.[9] The rules governing the exercise of the right to strike, namely concerning the legitimation to declare the strike, the mandatory prior notice,

7. In this sense, please *see* the Ruling of Coimbra Court of Appeal, dated 16 December 2015 (Proc. No. 2509/15.2T8VIS.C1), available at https://www.dgsi.pt. As referred to in the Ruling of Lisbon Court of Appeal, dated 3 December 2014 (Proc. No. 2028/11.6TTLSB.L1-4), available at https://www.dgsi.pt, from the concept, nature, and exercise of the right to strike arise that the strike may cause damages of different nature to employers. Such damages may occur even in the sectors of activity covered by the obligation of providing minimum services.
8. This provision was inserted in the constitutional text in 1997. Until then, the right to strike was not subject to an express restriction foreseen in the Constitution, although it was understood that the strike was not an absolute right, in particular when its exercise came into conflict with other legal assets. With the Constitutional Revision of 1997, it was foreseen that the legislator has the obligation to regulate the provision of essential services during a strike and it was established that the criteria for the definition of such essential services and the type of interests must be protected.
9. Approved by Law No. 35/2014, of 20 June, as subsequently amended. It should be noted that, according to Arts 4 (1)(m) and 394(3) of the LGTFP, the provisions of the PLC on strike are applicable to public employment relationships, without prejudice of the specificities set out in that law and the necessary adaptations.

the obligation to provide services during the strike, the definition of minimum services, and the effects of the strike are foreseen in the referred legal acts.

Under Portuguese law, trade unions are the only entities empowered to declare strikes, with one exception: an assembly of employees may declare the strike provided that: (a) the majority of employees are not represented by trade unions, (b) the assembly is called by 20% or 200 employees, (c) the majority of employees participate in the voting, and (d) the decision is approved by secret vote of the majority of the participants (Article 531 of the PLC).[10]

The entity that decides to resort to a strike shall serve the employer or the employers' association and the Ministry responsible for the labour area a strike notice at least 5 working days in advance or, if there is an obligation to provide minimum services, at least 10 working days in advance (Article 534(1) of the PLC).[11] The strike notice must contain a proposal of the definition of services needed for safety and maintenance of equipment and premises, and if the strike is carried out in a company or establishment that aims to fulfil unavoidable social needs, it must include a proposal of the definition of minimum services (Article 534(3) of the PLC).[12]

Pursuant to Portuguese law, the strike suspends the employment contract of the striking employees, including the right to remuneration and the duties of subordination and attendance, during the period the employee is on strike (Article 536(1) of the PLC).[13] As a result, the employer does not have to pay the remuneration of striking employees corresponding to the respective period of the strike. Apart from the rights, duties, and guarantees of the parties that do not require the effective provision of work, the rights foreseen in the social security legislation and the benefits arising from occupational accidents and professional disease are maintained during the strike (Article 536(2) of the PLC). The period of suspension counts for seniority purposes and does not prejudice any effects arising from the latter (Article 536(3) of the PLC).

Strikes pursuing unlawful objectives, those undertaken in breach of mandatory rules relating to being legitimately declared, their processing, and the ancillary obligations which must be complied with during the strike (e.g., the case of a strike without the required prior notice) and, in general terms, those that violate the respective constitutional and legal limits, shall be considered illicit. Portuguese labour law sets out two types of consequences that may be applied in case of an illegal strike: (a) the absence of an employee by reason of adhesion to a strike declared or executed in a way contrary to the law is considered an unjustified absence and may constitute a disciplinary offence, and (b) if the strike is declared or executed in a way contrary to the law, the general principles of the civil liability apply (Article 541 of the PLC).

10. Similar rule applies in the case of civil servants (Art. 395 of the LGTFP).
11. Similar prior notice applies in the case of civil servants (Art. 396(1) of the LGTFP).
12. Similar rule applies in the case of civil servants (Art. 396(2) of the LGTFP).
13. This regime also applies to the civil servants (Arts 4(1)(m) and 394(3) of the LGTFP).

2 PERMITTED RESTRICTIONS

2.1 General Overview

Although the right to strike is guaranteed in particularly broad terms under Portuguese law, it is indisputable that it is not an absolute and unlimited right.[14] On the contrary, the right to strike is subject to certain internal and external limits.

Internal limits derive from the concept of strike and the nature, legitimacy, procedure, content, accessory duties, and modalities of the respective exercise. The right to strike should be exercised under the conditions defined by law.

External limits result from the collision between the right to strike and other fundamental rights of equal constitutional value, as well as other relevant constitutional public interests. The right to strike cannot be exercised by jeopardizing other constitutional rights and interests and may have to be restricted to allow harmonization between the different rights and interests at stake.[15] The limits to the exercise of the right to strike reside in a question of practical concordance with other constitutional rights and values.[16]

One of the most significant limits on the exercise of the right to strike consists of the obligation to provide minimum services, which reflects the need for compatibilization of the right to strike with other fundamental rights, as foreseen in Article 57(3) of the Portuguese Constitution. In the event of a strike, the law establishes obligations that fall upon trade unions and employees regarding the continuity of essential services (Articles 537 of the PLC and 397 of the LGTFP). The obligation to provide these services is justified by the need to protect the general interest of the community and the fundamental rights of citizens (e.g., life, health, safety or the minimum conditions of existence and wellbeing) and aims to establish a point of balance between the exercise of the strike and the sacrifice of collective interests.[17] Thus, 'the right to strike should only be sacrificed to the minimum extent essential to guarantee other constitutionally protected interests which conflict with it, and this guarantee may not, moreover, be used in such a way as to affect its essential content'.[18]

The obligation to provide minimum services applies to both public-sector and private-sector employees. Indeed, 'regardless of the sector of activity, the core of the limitation to the strike consists of a commitment between conflicting fundamental rights and, in the specific case of essential services, in the determination of the minimum services which are necessary to ensure the satisfaction of unavoidable needs

14. Please *see* Opinion No. 1/2023, of 9 February 2023, issued by the Portuguese Attorney General's Office, available at https://www.ministeriopublico.pt.
15. Rulings of the Lisbon Court of Appeal of 25 May 2011 (Proc. No. 88/11.7YRLSB.L1-4) and of 24 February 2021 (Proc. No. 1566/18.4T8FNC.L1-4), available at https://www.dgsi.pt.
16. José João Abrantes, *Direito do Trabalho II: Direito da Greve* 100 (Almedina, Coimbra 2012).
17. José João Abrantes, *Sobre os limites da greve, in Revista de Direito Comercial* 533 (2021), available at https://www.revistadedireitocomercial.com/sobre-os-limites-da-greve (accessed 8 June 2023).
18. *Ibid.*, 534.

of the community, which ... constitutes a problem of conflict between rights and interests constitutionally protected'.[19]

The concept of public service cannot be considered to have the same meaning as essential services for the purpose of Article 57(3) of the Portuguese Constitution.[20] According to this constitutional provision, the delimitation of the obligation to minimum services is not based on the legal status of the workers but on the nature of the interests affected by the strike. It means that this provision applies to public servants in the same terms as it applies to other employees. The limits to the exercise of the right to strike by public servants depend on the nature of the activity they perform and the effects of its paralyzation.

In fact, public services refer to activities that satisfy general interests needed for life in society, but not all these services guarantee unavoidable social needs. In the same terms, there are several companies and establishments in the private sector that pursue unavoidable social needs. Therefore, the scope of the obligation to provide minimum services is not connected with the public or private nature of the organization or of the employment relationship maintained with the respective employees.

2.2 Certain Categories of Public Servants

The Portuguese legal framework recognizes the right to strike to public servants, regardless of their professional status. As a rule, there is no connection between the quality of public servants and the application of a specific restrictive regime of strike.

However, in relation to certain categories of agents, such as militaries, magistrates, security forces, and Public Prosecutor's officers, the exercise of the right to strike is prohibited.

Article 270 of the Portuguese Constitution states that 'the law may establish, to the strict extent of the requirements of the respective functions, restrictions on the exercise of the rights of expression, assembly, demonstration, association and collective petition, and on the right to stand for election by military personnel and military officers of the permanent staff on active service, as well as by officers of the security services and forces and, in the case of the latter, the non-acceptance of the right to strike, even where the right of trade union association is recognised.'

Considering the nature and mission of the Public Security Police, the law establishes that these employees are prohibited from exercising the right to strike, although a right to join trade unions is recognized.[21] In addition, the exercise of certain fundamental rights is restricted to military personnel in full service. In their case, besides the right to strike, they are forbidden the freedom of association and the right to create and join a works council. In all these cases, the prohibition of strike is related to the inherent requirements for the performance of their functions.

---

19. Francisco Liberal Fernandes, *A obrigação de Serviços Mínimos como técnica de regulação da Greve nos serviços essenciais* 230 (Coimbra Editora, Coimbra 2010).
20. *Ibid.*, 229-230.
21. Article 3(1)(d) of Law No. 14/2002, of 19 February, amended by Law No. 49/2019, of 18 July.

Regarding the magistrates and Public Prosecutor's officers, according to the respective Statute, they are entitled to trade union freedom, although they cannot exercise the right to strike due to the absence of an express legal provision.[22] They perform an activity inserted within the jurisdictional function, according to Articles 215 and 219(1) of the Portuguese Constitution, and they are not subordinated to any public entity regarding the exercise of their functions. Apart from the absence of an express recognition of the right to strike of judges and public prosecutors, the prohibition on these agents collectively suspending their professional activity is reinforced by the fact that the administration of justice constitutes a sovereign function characterized by an intrinsic requirement of continuity, the protection of which excludes the possibility of being object of paralyzation or concerted interruption by those who ensure such function.[23]

2.3 Essential Services in the Strict Sense of the Term

Article 537(1) of the PLC states that minimum services shall be ensured during the strike in companies or establishments that aim to fulfil unavoidable social needs ('necessidades sociais impreteríveis').[24]

Under Portuguese law, the needs to be ensured through the provision of minimum services are social, i.e., they relate to the common wellbeing of the population. In other words, minimum services do not seek to ensure the company's or the undertaking's normal day-to-day business, and not even the company's or the undertaking's essential needs. The ultimate recipient of the minimum services is the population in general. In addition, the relevant needs must be unavoidable, i.e., imperative, essential, and vital. It is not a question of convenience, commodity, or comfort, even for the population. It is a question of ensuring that the strike does not jeopardize fundamental social needs that cannot be sacrificed or postponed.

Article 537(2) of the PLC contains an indicative list of sectors of activity in which may be determined minimum services:

- post and telecommunications;
- medical, hospital, and medication services;
- public health, including the performance of funerals;
- energy and mining services, including fuel supplies;
- water supply;
- firefighters;
- public-attendance services that ensure the satisfaction of essential needs whose performance is the State's responsibility;

22. Francisco Liberal Fernandes, *A obrigação de Serviços Mínimos como técnica de regulação da Greve nos serviços essenciais* 236 (Coimbra Editora, Coimbra 2010).
23. *Ibid.*, 251.
24. Similar rule applies in the case of civil servants (Art. 397 of the LGTFP).

- transport, including ports, airports, railways, and trucking stations, relating to passengers, animals, and deteriorating foodstuffs as well as goods essential to the national economy, including loading and unloading;
- transport and security of monetary values.

Apart from the sectors of activity referred to above, Article 397(2) of the LGTFP also states that minimum services may be determined in the following sectors: (a) public safety and (b) education, with regard to the carrying out of final assessments, examinations or tests of a national character that have to be held on the same date throughout the national territory.

The fact that a company, establishment or service belongs to one of the sectors of activity included in the referred list is not sufficient to conclude that the provision of minimum services during a strike will be mandatory. This obligation should be assessed on a case-by-case basis, considering the type, duration, and effective dimension of the strike, in order to determine if minimum services are required to safeguard the referred unavoidable social needs. Only if there are no other means to satisfy the referred needs of public interest, the obligation to provide minimum services applies. For instance, the obligation to provide minimum services only rises if such needs cannot be ensured by non-striking workers.

The measure of the minimum services indispensable for satisfying unavoidable social needs is not determined by any strict and absolute criteria but depends on a case-by-case analysis which may lead to different results in relation to strikes of the same sector or even in the same company. The minimum services will be those that are necessary and adequate for providing people with the satisfaction of unavoidable social needs. The fundamental character of the right to strike in the Portuguese legal framework determines the need to preserve as much as possible the essential core of this right.

Apart from the minimum services mentioned above, trade unions and adherent employees must ensure, during the strike, the provision of necessary services to guarantee safety and maintenance of equipment and premises (Article 537(3) of the PLC and Article 397(3) of the LGTFP). This obligation applies to any company, undertaking or service (and not only to those related to sectors in which the provision of minimum services may be justifiable).[25]

This duty aims to ensure the safety and integrity of the equipment and premises during the strike, thus intending to safeguard the freedom of economic initiative and private property as enshrined in Articles 61(1) and 62(1) of the Portuguese Constitution, as well as the maintenance of the employment and of the company's production capacity. For purposes of determining if adherent employees are obliged to provide these services, an assessment is required on whether there is, or not, a need for permanent supervision of equipment and premises due to their specific characteristics and if non-adherent employees may ensure in terms deemed sufficient the safety and maintenance of those equipment and premises.

25. António Monteiro Fernandes, *A lei e as greves* 119 (Almedina 2013).

The solution of the Portuguese law is to establish a legal (and not a contractual) obligation of the trade unions and employees to ensure the continuity of the essential services (exclusively to the extent of the minimum indispensable to satisfy unavoidable needs or the safety and maintenance of the premises and equipment).[26] In that case, the strike is in force, the employment contracts are suspended and, therefore, the contractual obligations of the employees are not applicable. The activities that some striking employees are called to execute may not coincide with those they normally perform. According to Portuguese law, employees allocated to the provision of essential services shall remain, to the extent that is strictly required for such service, under the authority and direction of the employer and are entitled to remuneration (Article 537(4) of the PLC and Article 397(4) of the LGTFP).

The definition of the services to be provided during the strike shall be made in the collective bargaining agreement or by agreement between the employees' representatives and the employers covered by the strike notice or the respective employers' association (Article 538(1) of the PLC and Article 397 of the LGTFP). In the absence of those agreements, the competent service of the Ministry responsible for labour matters, advised whenever necessary by the competent service of the Ministry responsible for the relevant sector of activity, shall call upon the parties to negotiate an agreement on minimum services and the means necessary to ensure them (Article 538(2) of the PLC).[27] In the negotiation of minimum strike-related services substantially identical to at least two previous strikes for which the definition of minimum services by arbitration has been defined, with equivalent content, the competent service of the Ministry responsible for labour matters proposes that parties accept that definition; such proposal should be included in the minutes of the negotiation, in case of rejection (Article 538(3) of the PLC).

In case of absence of agreement within three days upon the strike notice having been served, minimum services as well as the means necessary to ensure them are defined by: (a) a grounded joint order of the Minister responsible for the labour area and the Minister responsible for the sector of activity at stake or (b) in case of a company of the State business sector, by arbitral court, established under the terms of a specific law on compulsory arbitration (Article 538(4) of the PLC).[28] The definition of minimum services shall respect the principles of necessity, adequation, and proportionality (Article 538(5) of the PLC and Article 398(7) of the LGTFP).

The representatives of striking employees shall designate the employees who are assigned to the provision of the minimum defined services and inform the employer

26. *Ibid.*, 107.
27. In the case of public employment relationships, if there is no collective bargaining agreement nor an agreement on the definition of minimum services, the member of the Government responsible for the Public Administration shall convene the representatives of the employees and the representatives of the public employers concerned, with a view to negotiating an agreement on the minimum services and the means necessary to ensure them (Art. 398(2) of the LGTFP).
28. Please *see also* Art. 398(3) of the LGTFP.

thereof at least 24 hours before the start of the strike period.[29] If that is not done, the employer will proceed with such designation (Article 538(7) of the PLC).[30]

In the event of non-compliance with the obligation to provide the defined minimum services, the Government may determine requisition or mobilization (Article 541(3) of the PLC). The civil requisition is foreseen in Article 62(2) of the Portuguese Constitution and is grounded by 'urgent needs of national public interest, of exceptional and abnormality nature'.[31] This power of the Government is not automatic and requires a case-by-case analysis, being also disputable whether a preventive civil requisition may be ordered.[32]

3 CONCLUSION

In Portugal, the right to strike is regulated broadly. However, this right is subject to certain limits, considering that, in specific cases, the law requires that the striking employees provide work and ensure minimum services.

Under Portuguese law, such restrictions may be imposed to pursue two objectives: (a) to ensure the safety and maintenance of equipment and facilities and (b) to ensure the minimum services necessary to satisfy unavoidable social needs. To determine whether the provision of work by striking employees is necessary for any of these purposes, a case-by-case analysis should be made. The legislator uses indeterminate concepts for regulating the minimum services, which need to be fleshed out in the light of a specific situation in order to determine the essentiality (or not) of the minimum services as well as the respective *quantum*.

The imposition of minimum services intends to solve a potential issue of collision between the right to strike and other fundamental rights, ensuring the coexistence of all these rights. In other words, this restriction is 'a mere concretization of the principle of practical concordance which operates in the system of restrictions on rights, freedoms and guarantees' and 'is based on the need to safeguard other fundamental rights, with constitutional dignity, as are, in general, the freedom of economic initiative and the

---

29. The selection of the employees should be based on objective criteria and considering the functional suitability for the job positions that should be maintained in activity during the strike (please *see* Luís Gonçalves da Silva, *Direito do Trabalho. Greve e Lock-out* 623-624 (AAFDL Editora, Lisboa 2023)).
30. Similar rule arises from Art. 398(6) of the LGTFP.
31. The civil requisition is ruled in Decree-law No. 637/74, of 20 November.
32. Although some scholars admit the preventive civil requisition, there are some court decisions that refuse it (for further details on this issue, please *see* Luís Gonçalves da Silva, *Direito do Trabalho. Greve e Lock-out* 632-635 (AAFDL Editora, Lisboa 2023)). For instance, in a decision of the Administrative Supreme Court of 26 June 2008 (Proc. No. 078/06, available at https://www.dgsi.pt), it was ruled that 'the Government may only resort to civil requisition after a strike has taken place and after it has been established that the minimum services are not being ensured' and 'civil requisition may only be ordered when the true scale of the effects of the strike is known and this knowledge results in the ascertainment that the minimum services are not being ensured and, therefore, when it is already possible to identify the means necessary for their compliance'.

right to private property …, the right to life …, the right to travel and the freedom of movement within the national territory …, the right to work …, to health …, among many others'.[33]

33. Luís Gonçalves da Silva, *Direito do Trabalho. Greve e Lock-out* 616-617 (AAFDL Editora, Lisboa 2023).

CHAPTER 30

Restrictions on the Right to Strike in Romanian Law

Raluca Dimitriu & Luminiţa Dima

1 GENERAL INFORMATION

1.1 Legal Basis of the Right to Strike

In Romanian law, the right to strike [*dreptul la grevă*] is explicitly recognised by Article 43 of the Constitution, which states that 'Employees have the right to strike in defence of their professional, economic, and social interests. The law lays down the conditions and limits for exercising this right, as well as the guarantees necessary to ensure the provision of essential services to society.' Notably, the right to strike is regulated independently of the right to trade union association enshrined in Article 40(1).

In application of the constitutional rules, the strike is regulated in general terms in the Labour Code and in detail by the Law on Social Dialogue.

The current Law on Social Dialogue No. 367/2022[1] and Article 234(1) of the Labour Code define the strike as the voluntary and collective cessation of work by workers. Strikes are regarded as a last resort, which employees may use in the event of a collective labour dispute after the possibilities of resolving the collective labour dispute through the compulsory procedures laid down by law have been exhausted. In essence, legislation regulates the strike thoroughly, with the entire development, from procedural to substantive aspects, being subject mainly to legal rules and only marginally to rules negotiated between the social partners.

1. Romanian Official Journal (ROJ) No. 1238 of 22 December 2022.

1.2 Main Features of the Regulation

The right to strike has been regulated by successive laws adopted in 1991, 1999, 2011, and 2022. In general terms, the Labour Code provides that employees have the right to strike in defence of their professional, economic, and social interests. Taking part in a strike as well as organising it in accordance with the law does not constitute a breach of employees' obligations and cannot result in disciplinary action against striking employees or strike organisers. However, strikes are regulated in accordance with the *ultima ratio* principle, i.e., only if amicable methods of settling collective disputes (in particular conciliation) have failed.

The freedom to strike is reiterated and detailed in the Law on Social Dialogue No. 367/2022, with the right to strike being protected in both its dimensions:

- as the right to stop work (to strike);
- as the right not to stop work (not to join employees who have gone on strike).

Thus, no one can be forced to take part or not to take part in a strike, and violation of this prohibition is punishable by criminal penalties of imprisonment of one month to one year or a fine. If the coercion to participate or, conversely, not to participate in a strike is carried out by threats or violence, the penalty is up to two years' imprisonment.

The right to strike is recognised for all employees, regardless of the type of employment contract concluded (open-ended or fixed-term) or the special period in which they may be working (probationary period or notice period).

Although the current Law on Social Dialogue has somewhat relaxed the conditions to be met for a strike to be launched, it is still subject to substantial procedural restrictions. The way in which a strike is carried out is still regulated in detail by law; it imposes time limits, conditions, and obligations to notify the employer and public authorities of the intention to strike. The whole system of strike regulation can be seen as highly bureaucratic.

In contrast, Romanian law has never regulated the right to lock-out.

The new law on social dialogue has broadly maintained the configuration of the strike as it had been outlined in previous laws.[2] However, there are some novelties, for example, the regulation of the Strike Committee and its role in the conduct of the strike. One of the notable changes introduced by the new law on social dialogue concerns the possibility of strikes against the Government's social and economic policy, subject to special procedures. Such strikes can be launched when the Government adopts public policies that lead to a reduction of employees' rights provided by collective labour agreements.

In case of failure to meet all the conditions imposed by law, the employer may apply to the court for a decision to end the strike. If, however, the conditions not complied with by the strikers are purely procedural and can easily be complied with,

2. Law No. 168/1999 on the settlement of labour disputes and, subsequently, the Social Dialogue Law No. 62/2011.

the strike is not considered unlawful but non-compliant [*grevă neconformă*], and the employer can only obtain in court compliance with the legal provisions.

2 PERMITTED RESTRICTIONS

Limitations of the exercise of the right to strike must be regulated with great care, so as not to open a Pandora's box, which would lead to the prohibition of the right to strike whenever the employer is not the only one affected by the work stoppage. In other words, it is natural that society as a whole should sometimes bear the cost of exercising the right to strike, a price paid, after all, for the freedom to bargain collectively. The Romanian legislator has paid particular attention to the subject by regulating in detail the cases of restriction. As has been ruled, the law establishes 'the limits within which this right may be exercised so as not to upset the balance which must exist between the parties and so as not to extend, in an unreasonable manner, the effects of such a protest to third parties'.[3]

2.1 Certain Categories of Public Servants

In Romania, civil servants [*funcţionari publici*] can take strike action and the rules applicable to them are the same as for employees (Article 174 of the Social Dialogue Law and Article 416 of the Administrative Code).

However, since Romanian law ties the possibility of taking strike action to the timing and subjects of collective bargaining, any limitation on the right to collective bargaining has repercussions on the right to strike. And collective bargaining for civil servants and for all public sector staff is subject to an important limitation: it cannot concern salary as long as it is laid down by the legislation in force. Consequently, in public sector, no strike could be launched on the basis of pay claims.

As an exception to the rule of the right to strike of civil servants, Article 170 of the Social Dialogue Law lays down a list of civil servants exercising authority in the name of the State who may not strike: prosecutors, judges,[4] military personnel and personnel with special status within the Ministry of National Defence, the Ministry of Internal Affairs, the Ministry of Justice and the institutions and structures subordinated or coordinated by them, including the National Administration of Penitentiaries, the Romanian Intelligence Service, the Foreign Intelligence Service, the Special Telecommunications Service, personnel employed by foreign armed forces stationed on Romanian territory.

For some of these categories of personnel, the prohibition of exercising the right to strike is repeated and completed in the special legislation. Thus, for example, the Administrative Code provides that prefects and sub-prefects do not have the right to

3. Bucharest Court of Appeal, Decision No. 1080 of 2 March 2010.
4. This category of staff also includes judges of the Constitutional Court or assistant judges of the Constitutional Court and the High Court of Cassation and Justice. *See*, A. Uluitu, *The Strike* [*Greva*] 187 (Lumina Lex 2008).

strike (Article 273(2) of Government Emergency Ordinance No. 57/2019),[5] the Statute of the police officer provides for the prohibition of strike action for police officers (Article 45(1) lit. (e) of Law No. 360/2002),[6] the Statutes of the military personnel prohibit them from striking (Article 28(c) of Law No. 80/1995),[7] the Statutes of the Diplomatic and Consular Corps of Romania stipulate that members of this Corps are prohibited from striking (Article 50(1) lit. f) of Law No. 269/2003).[8]

In addition, air, sea, and land transport staff of any kind may not take part in a strike from the time of departure on a mission/travel until the end of the mission/travel (Article 171 of the Social Dialogue Law). Outside this period, Article 172 stipulates that the personnel embarked on merchant navy ships under the Romanian flag may strike only in compliance with the rules laid down in international conventions ratified by the Romanian State.

Notably, the scope of the right to collective bargaining, which underlies the right to initiate a collective dispute, is wider than the scope of the right to strike. In other words, certain categories of civil servants have the right to negotiate and conclude collective labour agreements and even have the right to initiate collective disputes, though without the right to strike.[9] This category includes, for example, police officers. They are civil servants with special status who are expressly prohibited from striking by Law No. 360/2002 on the status of police officers. However, they do have the right to collective bargaining.

2.2 Essential Services in the Strict Sense of the Term

With reference to the right to strike, Article 43(2) of the Romanian Constitution states that 'the law establishes the conditions and limits for the exercise of this right, as well as the guarantees necessary to ensure the provision of essential services to society'. However, Romanian law does not contain rules completely prohibiting strikes in any sector, not even in essential services in the strict sense of the term (services whose interruption would endanger the life, personal safety or health of the whole or part of the population).

In application of the constitutional rules, the Law on Social Dialogue No. 367/2022 expressly lists the areas in which the right to strike may be restricted, but unlike the constitutional text, the ordinary law no longer refers to these services as essential.[10] It does not define them but expressly lists them. In these areas, a legal strike

5. ROJ No. 555 of 5 July 2019.
6. ROJ No. 440 of 24 June 2002. In the legal literature, it has been proposed that the right to strike be exercised by police officers, subject to certain conditions. *See*, O. Macovei, *Aspects of Police Officers' Right to Strike [Aspecte privind dreptul la grevă al poliţiştilor]*, Romanian Journal of Labour Law No. 2, 91 (2008).
7. ROJ No. 155 of 20 July 1995.
8. ROJ No. 441 of 23 June 2003.
9. L. Dima, *Labour Law [Dreptul muncii]* 372 (CH Beck 2017).
10. However, the Constitutional Court, when asked to examine the constitutionality of the provision in the previous social dialogue law restricting the right to strike in a somewhat similar way to the current law, used the term 'essential services' in its reasoning. The Court pointed out that the text of the law 'ensures the functioning of essential and strictly necessary services in order to

can be called, but only on condition that at least one-third of the work continues. This restriction has been present in successive laws governing the right to strike over time.[11]

On the one hand, some types of services in which strike action may be partially restricted are not among those which, in the view of the Committee on Freedom of Association, would constitute essential services in the strict sense of the term, i.e., public radio and television, rail transport and public transport, as well as refuse collection services. On the other hand, in none of the services is the prohibition of strike action absolute; the only condition imposed by law is that the strike must not affect more than two-thirds of activity.

2.2.1 *Services Where Strike Action Is Partially Restricted*

2.2.1.1 *Categories*

Article 173 of the Law on Social Dialogue stipulates that in health and social assistance facilities, telecommunications, public radio and television, the national energy system, operational establishments of the nuclear sectors, railway transport, facilities providing public transport and sanitation of localities, as well as the supply of gas, electricity, water, and heat to the population, strikes are permitted provided that at least one-third of normal activity is ensured, distributed over the whole day, without endangering the life and health of the population and/or the safe operation of installations.

In addition, Article 106 of the Law No. 145/2019 on the status of prison officers[12] enshrines the right to strike of the personnel of the penitentiary administration system, provided that at least one-third of the activity is ensured and the rights of prisoners and the safety of places of detention are guaranteed.[13] Exceptions are the military personnel and the personnel with special status in the penitentiary system, who are prohibited from striking.

With regard to vital public utilities - water supply, sewerage, wastewater treatment, sanitation, heat supply, natural gas supply, public lighting, and public transport - Article 51(2) of the Law on Community Public Utilities No. 51/2006[14] provides for the obligation to ensure the safe operation and functioning of the systems and to avoid accidents with impact on the environment or on the health of the population.

---

protect the rule of law, fundamental rights and freedoms and national interests' (Decision No. 540/2011, ROJ No. 368 of 26 May 2011). There is clearly a terminological inconsistency in the use of the concept of essential services.

11. Law No. 15/1991 on the settlement of collective labour disputes, Law No. 168/1999 on the settlement of labour disputes, Law No. 62/1011 on social dialogue, and the current Law No. 367/2022 on social dialogue.
12. ROJ No. 631 of 30 July 2019.
13. However, the staff of the National Administration of Penitentiaries are part of the categories of employees who, according to Art. 170 of the Social Dialogue Law, cannot declare a strike at all. The inconsistency between the two legal texts led the People's Advocate to address the Constitutional Court. The Court has not yet ruled on this subject.
14. ROJ No. 121 of 5 March 2013.

The restrictions are applicable to all types of strikes, including the recently regulated strikes against the Government's social and economic policy. Sympathy strikes, which are allowed under Romanian law, are subject to the same restrictions.

Beyond the sectors expressly listed by law, the strike cannot be restricted. In other sectors, which are not listed, even if the strike is prolonged, the court is not empowered to assess its impact on people's lives and health and order its termination. The court may order the cessation of a strike only if it finds non-compliance with a legal requirement.

2.2.1.2 The Issue of 'Continuous Fire' (24/7 Services)

It should be noted that the services where strike action is restricted include 'continuous fire' services [*servicii cu foc continuu*]. The Constitutional Court has been consulted on this restriction,[15] stating that:

> it cannot be argued that, a priori, the category of continuous-fire establishments provides essential services to society. For example, a chemical plant, although it calls itself a continuous-fire plant, does not provide this type of service. Therefore, the legal conditions to be fulfilled for the exercise of the right to strike must be reasonable, so as not to limit considerably the means of action, and the establishment of minimum services can only be possible in the case of services essential to society, i.e., those of fundamental public utility.

The claim of unconstitutionality was, at the time, rejected as inadmissible,[16] but the problem remains. The fact that the employer chooses to organise its activity round the clock, in three shifts, cannot imply that the services thereby provided are essential; the way in which the activity is organised could not be the decisive criterion in limiting the right to strike of the employees of the establishment concerned. On the contrary (although it does not expressly provide for it), the legislator has taken account of the assumption that the continuous activity is not carried out in that way simply as a result of the employer's choice but because the need of the public beneficiary requires it. As has been held, in the absence of a legal definition, the classification of an establishment as a 'continuous fire' service is a factual circumstance which may be established by the court on the basis of evidence. In determining the scope of the concept of a continuous-fire establishment, account must be taken primarily of the specific nature of its activity:

> In other words, it is not the work schedule in the establishment in question that is essential, in particular the shift work schedule, which covers the whole twenty-four hours of a day, but whether the establishment is equipped with plant, machinery, and equipment for continuous operation, which also involves the

15. Decision No. 516 of 11 October 2005, ROJ No. 991 of 9 November 2005.
16. In the viewpoint submitted on that occasion, the Government considered that 'it is permissible to lay down by law such restrictions as are necessary in a democratic society in order to ensure respect for the rights and freedoms of others or to protect public order, national security, public health or morals. The legal provisions at issue do not prevent the exercise of the right to strike, but establish certain limitations arising precisely from the need to avoid consequences for the life and health of individuals, as well as for production processes, which must be carried out uninterruptedly in conditions of complete safety'.

provision of service staff, as well as the category of services which the establishment in question provides and which must be essential services for the community and not only for the employer.[17]

2.2.2 *Minimum Service*

In the services specified above, at least one-third of the activity must be maintained. The social partners could only negotiate to maintain the activity in a higher proportion, never in a lower proportion, irrespective of the particularities of the sector concerned. Notably, the one-third proportion relates to activity, not to the number of employees on strike, so the condition can be met even if less than one-third of employees continue to work.

The previous law provided different conditions depending on the type of service:

- in health and social care, telecommunications, public radio and television, rail transport, public transport and sanitation facilities and establishments supplying gas, electricity, heat, and water to the population – the only condition was that at least one-third of the work continued;
- in the national energy system, operational establishments of the nuclear sectors, establishments operating 24/7, in addition to the condition of maintaining one-third of the activity, it was also provided that the strike should not endanger the life and health of the people and ensure the safe operation of the installations.

The current law no longer makes this distinction; in the case of all these categories of activities, a double condition is imposed: that of the proportion of the activity maintained and that of not affecting human life and health or the functioning of the installations. Thus, the proportion of the activity which must continue and which cannot be affected by the strike may be greater than one-third, if otherwise the life and health of the public or the safe operation of installations would be endangered.

As regards the method of determining a third of the activity to be continued, the Constitutional Court[18] ruled that it concerned the services which are the very object of activity of those establishments, not other additional activities which they might carry out (e.g., administrative activities).

The continuing activity should be distributed throughout the day. Therefore, the work cannot be stopped altogether and then be resumed periodically.

This newly introduced provision is useful. Under previous successive laws, the courts have sometimes held that in sectors where the law imposes the minimum service rule, a total interruption of working hours for a certain period of time would be

17. Constanţa Court of Appeal, Decision No. 384 of 22 May 2012. In the same way, Constanţa Court of Appeal, Decision No. 286 of 17 September 2007. The courts ruled that a decision issued unilaterally by the general manager of the company establishing a different list of jobs, concerning the continuous activity, without consulting and negotiating it with the representative trade union, would not produce legal effects (Alba-Iulia Court of Appeal, Decision No. 65 of 14 January 2010).
18. Decision No. 574/2011, ROJ No. 368 of 26 May 2011.

permissible,[19] and at other times, it would not.[20] Under the current rules, this inconsistency will no longer arise.

Failure to comply with the minimum requirement of one-third of the activity has always rendered the strike illegal.[21] As mentioned above, the new law on social dialogue defines an intermediate concept, 'non-compliant strike', when procedural aspects have been omitted and can be compensated. However, the law does not specify which conditions are procedural and which are substantive, so that some discussions may arise in practice. We consider that the maintenance of the one-third minimum activity is a substantive condition, which could only pertain to the legality, not the compliance of the strike. By contrast, the fact that the Strike Committee did not communicate to the employer the way in which the reduced activity was to be carried out could be considered a formal condition. However, the regulation is too recent for any practice to have already emerged.

Moreover, if strike called in violation of these prohibitions has led to the imminent threat to life or health of the whole or part of the population, the act constitutes a criminal offence.

2.2.3 *Procedure*

From a procedural point of view, the strike in sectors where the law imposes the minimum service rule has a number of particularities.

Under Romanian law, all spontaneous strikes are prohibited. But the time limits for notifying the intention to strike are longer in the case of strikes in services where strike action is partially restricted than in the case of other strikes. Thus:

- the employer must be notified of the strike at least five working days before it is due to start (unlike in non-essential sectors, where the period is only two days);
- the actual strike must be preceded by a short warning strike, at least five days before the actual strike is initiated (again, a longer period than the general two-day period);
- at least 24 hours before the strike begins, the organisers of the strike must notify both the employer or, where appropriate, the employers' organisation

19. For example, Bucharest Court of Appeal, Decision No. 4162 of 6 September 2017. The case regarded a strike in an air transport company. The employer argued that the choice of the period for stopping work during the holidays, when the impact of the strike is greatest, likely to cause particular damage to the transport company, could take the legal form of abuse of rights. The court rejected this argument.
20. For example, a strike on the Bucharest metro was declared illegal because, although the strikers had maintained a third of their activity, 'the timetable chosen for the strike, 4:00 a.m. to 4:00 p.m., was such as to seriously affect the life of the entire local community' (Bucharest Court of Appeal, Decision No. 1080 of 2 March 2010).
21. For example, the court declared a strike in the public transport sector to be unlawful, rejecting the union's defence that ensuring a third of the work 'employees cannot be conditioned on whether or not to participate in the strike', which would have made it impossible to designate employees obliged to continue working (Iasi Court of Appeal, Decision No. 33 of 2 February 2021).

and the territorial labour inspectorate or, where appropriate, the ministry responsible for social dialogue of the arrangements for meeting the obligations to continue at least one-third of the activity.

2.3 Situations of Acute National or Local Crisis

The Labour Code and the Law on Social Dialogue do not include express provisions for situations of national crisis and rules governing strikes during such periods.

However, over time, different regulations with temporary applicability have included a number of restrictions. This is the case of the COVID crisis, during which Law No. 55/2020 on some measures to prevent and combat the effects of the COVID-19 pandemic[22] extended the validity of collective labour agreements – putting any collective bargaining on standby – and completely banned collective disputes (consequently, strikes) in the national energy system, in the operating establishments of the nuclear sectors, in establishments operating continuously 24/7, in health and social care, telecommunications, public radio and television, in rail transport, in public transport and sanitation facilities and in the supply of gas, electricity, heat, and water.

In reality, collective disputes could not be triggered in the other sectors of activity either, since collective bargaining was not possible and the law applicable at the time necessarily linked the possibility of starting a collective dispute to the time of collective bargaining.

On the basis of these provisions, the courts have consistently found that strikes during the COVID-19 crisis were unlawful.[23]

3 COMPENSATORY GUARANTEES FOR WORKERS DEPRIVED OF THE RIGHT TO STRIKE

The Committee on Freedom of Association has stated that the workers who thus lose an essential means of defending their interests should be afforded appropriate guarantees to compensate for this restriction.[24] And indeed, in Romania, the parties (who have already resorted to conciliation because otherwise the strike could not have been legally triggered) can continue negotiations and can submit the conflict to mediation or arbitration. During the time that the employees'/workers' demands are subject to mediation or arbitration, they cannot stop the work, or if they do, the strike is suspended.

However, these possibilities are available for any type of strike. They can hardly be counted as ways of compensating for the restrictions imposed by law, since they are not particular to strikes in essential services.

22. ROJ No. 396 of 15 May 2020.
23. For example, Hunedoara Court, Decision No. 1422 of 15 September 2020; Alba-Iulia Court of Appeal, Decision No. 548 of 8 April 2021.
24. ILO, *Freedom of Association: Compilation of Decisions of the Committee on Freedom of Association*, paras 856, 857, 860 (6th ed. Geneve 2018).

In Romanian industrial labour relations, arbitration is always optional, including in sectors where strikes are restricted or in the case of categories of staff who cannot strike at all. Indeed, on several occasions, the Committee on Freedom of Association has considered compulsory arbitration to be appropriate for essential services or for categories of staff who are prohibited from exercising the right to strike, considering compulsory arbitration to be a compensatory solution, an appropriate guarantee for the protection of the interests of employees without the right to strike.

On the contrary, the Romanian law limits itself to restricting the right to strike in certain areas or for certain professional categories without really answering the question: how will collective conflicts arising in essential services or involving categories of persons who are prohibited from striking be resolved?

When asked about the unconstitutionality of Article 46(1)(e) of Law No. 360/2002 on the status of police officers, the Constitutional Court ruled[25] that the restriction was constitutional. It added that:

> the prohibition on exercising the right to strike does not make it impossible for this socio-professional category to defend its professional and social interests, as well as its legitimate rights. Thus, police officers have the possibility, through the National Corps of Police Officers, to have recourse to amicable means of settling labour disputes in relations with the central administration, consisting of conciliation, mediation, and arbitration, without, however, resorting to strike action.

This is true, but the possibility of having recourse to amicable means of settling disputes is recognised for all employees, including those who may strike. So, while alternative means of dispute settlement are available, they are not specifically dedicated to compensating for the restrictions on the exercise of the right to strike.[26]

4 CONCLUSIONS

There is no provision of the Romanian legislation banning strikes altogether in essential services, in the strict sense of the term. In some services, strikes are partially banned, and the minimum service is not left to the negotiation of the social partners but is established by legal provisions at one-third of the activity. If a category of services is not on the list of those where activity may be restricted, strike action will never be prohibited, regardless of its duration. However, in the services expressly listed in the law, the proportion of activity that must continue and cannot be affected by the strike may be more than one-third, if otherwise the life and health of the population or the safe operation of installations would be endangered.

The exercise of the right to strike in general and restrictions on it are regulated in great detail by law. Hence, one of the consequences is the very narrow margin of freedom left to the social partners to negotiate the conditions under which the strike will take place. Moreover, the qualification of a service as essential is left neither to the

25. Decision No. 1225/2007, ROJ No. 100 of 8 February 2008.
26. For developments, R. Dimitriu, *The Law for the Settlement of Labour Disputes [Legea pentru soluţionarea conflictelor de muncă]*, 200 (CH Beck 2007).

competence of the courts nor to the possibility of negotiation by the social partners. What Romanian law does provide is an exhaustive list of sectors in which strike action is restricted. However, the restriction is never absolute; there are no sectors in which strike action is completely prohibited; what the law requires for certain sectors is the maintenance of a minimum level of activity.

The law also lists categories of personnel who cannot strike; notably, these do not include employees but only civil servants exercising one or other of the powers of the State. All employees in the private and public sector, as well as civil servants, except those expressly excluded by law, may strike.

CHAPTER 31

Restrictions on the Right to Strike: The Russian Federation

Nikita Lyutov

1 GENERAL INFORMATION

Historically, the Russian regulation of strikes, including strikes in essential services, has been very restrictive. There were a few short periods in history when the whole country was almost paralyzed by the strike activity. This happened during the first Russian Revolution of 1905-1907, during the revolutionary events of 1917, and in the course of the Soviet system decay in the early 1990s. Each time, the explosion of a wide protesting movement was preceded by the highly restrictive anti-strike state policy and legal regulation. From the late XIX century up to the fall of the USSR, the strike activity was taken by government as a threat to state security and social stability. Current regulation is based on the early 2000s social consensus between the society and the state when the majority of workers tolerated the low level of industrial and political democracy in exchange for the constant growth of economy and their living standards.

However, this consensus has not operated smoothly since the interruption of economic and income growth and political trend of rising authoritarianism. There is a clear trend of rise of labour protests with the majority of them happening outside the scope of legal framework. Essential services are not the exception in this trend. More than that, taking into account that the chances of performing the strike legally for quite a significant group of employees are close to zero, they do not even try to recourse to the official collective labour dispute resolution procedure.

1.1 Legal Foundation of the Right to Strike

Article 37(4) of the Constitution of the Russian Federation[1] (Constitution) provides for "the right to individual and collective labour disputes with the use of methods of their resolution provided by the federal law including the right to strike." This means that:

- The constitutional right to strike is not absolute but may only be realized in the manner established by the separate federal law. Such federal law regulation is mainly contained in Chapter 61 of the Labour Code of the Russian Federation (Labour Code, LC).[2]
- Other limitations of the right to strike such as bans on strikes in essential services may be and are established by the federal legislation (*see* further).

Article 409 of the Labour Code mentions the right to strike as the method of collective labour disputes' resolution with reference to Article 37 of the Constitution. The definition of strike is set forth in Article 398 of the Labour Code. "Strike is a temporary voluntary refusal of employees to perform their labour duties (in whole or in part) with a goal to resolve the collective labour dispute." The same Article 409 of the Labour Code provides for the voluntary character of strikes and prohibition of any coercion in respect of strike performance, i.e., both positive and negative right to strike.

As long as the strike is understood only as a means of resolving a "collective labour dispute," its legal definition is also essential for the proper understanding of the meaning of the term "strike." The definition of a *collective labour dispute* is given in the same Article of the Labour Code. It is defined as:

> non-resolved disagreements between employees (their representatives) and employers (their representatives) concerning the establishment and alteration of conditions of work (including wages), conclusion, alteration and execution of collective agreements and accords and also concerning the refusal of the employer to take into account the opinion of the employees' elected representative body during the process of adoption of local normative acts [of the employer—N.L.].

The Russian Federation is a party to the *International Covenant on Social, Economic and Cultural Rights,* establishing the right to strike in its Article 8(1)(d). Before its expulsion from the Council of Europe in 2022 and subsequent denunciation of the European Social Charter, Russia was also bound by its Article 6(4), which establishes the right to strike.

Russia is a party to the ILO fundamental Conventions on freedom of association Nos. 87 and 98. These Conventions have no direct statements concerning the right to strike, but the ILO controlling bodies—the Committee of Experts on Application of Conventions and Recommendation (CEACR) and the Committee on Freedom of Association (CFA)—consider that the right to strike is an integral part of freedom of association established by these Conventions. Decisions of the CEACR and the CFA are

1. *Sobraniye Zakonodatelstva Rossiyskoy Federazii* [SZ RF] [Russian Federation Collection of Legislation] January 26, 2009, No. 4, Item 445.
2. *Sobraniye Zakonodatelstva Rossiyskoy Federazii* [SZ RF] [Russian Federation Collection of Legislation] January 7, 2002, No. 1, Item 3.

not themselves sources of law that may be directly applied by Russian courts. Still, they may be used as a secondary source of interpretation of applicable norms.

Political strikes or strikes to announce certain concerns to the public would not be legal because demands of employees would not be addressed to the employer or its representative. For the same reason, all *political* or *quasi-political* strikes or *sympathy actions* would be considered illegal as long as they are not directly addressed at resolution of the dispute with the employer or the dispute between the trade union organization and employers' association, if collective dispute is resolved at a higher level than the level of single enterprise. The latter situation is purely theoretical: although it is envisaged by the Labour Code, in practice, all strikes are performed at a plant level.

Employees or their representatives have the right to call a strike if peaceful procedures have not led to the resolution of the collective labour dispute, or the employer or its representative is evading to take part in peaceful procedures, or he does not execute the decision of labour arbitration which is binding to the parties (Article 409(2) LC), except for cases of prohibition of strikes established by the law (Article 413 LC). Article 410(2) of the Labour Code sets up an exception to this rule: If the strike has been announced by the trade union or trade unions' confederation, it may be performed upon the decision of workers of specific employer without exercising peaceful procedures.

The requirements for the approval of the strike by the workers are set in Article 410 of the Labour Code. The decision to call a strike is taken by a meeting or a conference of employees of the employer. The meeting quorum is no less than half of this employer's employees; the conference quorum is no less than two-thirds of delegates.

Conciliation is the only mandatory procedure among three peaceful collective labour dispute resolution procedures (conciliation, mediation and arbitration). The Conciliation Commission is to be set up within two calendar days from the day of beginning of the collective labour dispute or three days in hypothetical cases of disputes at a level higher than the enterprise level (Article 402 LC). The day of the beginning of collective labour dispute is the day when the employer informs about the declining of all or part of the employees' or their representatives' demands or the failure of the employer to inform about its decision (Article 398 LC). The employer is obliged to provide such information within two days after receiving the demands or within three weeks—for disputes at a level higher than the enterprise level (Article 400 LC). The Conciliation Commission has three calendar days to examine the collective labour disputes (five days—for higher-level disputes).

According to Article 403 of the Labour Code, if collective labour dispute is not resolved by the Conciliation Commission, the parties to the dispute must sign the protocol on disagreement and start negotiations about the resolution of the dispute with the assistance of a *mediator*. Such negotiations must start the next day after signing the protocol. If the parties do not agree on the invitation of the mediator, they are under an obligation to negotiate the issue of resolution of the dispute through *labour arbitration*. The mediator may only make recommendations to the parties concerning dispute resolution, while the condition for holding arbitration is the agreement of the parties to abide by its decision (Article 404 LC). In both cases, the parties to the dispute are only obliged to discuss the possibility of using these two procedures (mediation and arbitration) but not to implement them. Exception to this rule is the case of compulsory arbitration in cases when the strikes are not permitted (Article 404(2) LC).

The strike rules are applied equally in *private and public* sectors. The condition of the applicability of the strike rules established by the Labour Code is the employee status of worker. Civil law contractors, public servants, and other non-employee categories of workers do not have the right to strike (*see* further).

2 PERMITTED RESTRICTIONS

2.1 Certain Categories of Public Servants

Article 413(1) of the Labour Code provides (among other restrictions) that the strikes shall be declared illegal and shall not be allowed in structures of the Military Forces, other military, paramilitary bodies or organizations (or structural subdivisions) that are directly responsible for the issues of the country defense, security of the state, emergency rescuing, searching-rescuing, fire-fighting works, prevention or liquidation of natural disasters or emergency situations and in law-enforcement bodies.

As for the regime of collective bargaining rights' limitations, there may be four legal situations:

(1) Employee's work is not considered an essential service—no limitations of freedom of association and collective bargaining rights, including the right to strike.
(2) The work is in the list of work where the strikes are prohibited—the right to form and join trade unions and to take part in collective bargaining is guaranteed except for the right to strike. Such a regime covers both essential services employees and other categories of workers to whom the Labour Code is applied on the leftover principle, i.e., only for the matters that are not regulated by special norms (the norms regulating state or municipal service, including the police, procurators' office, security services etc.).
(3) The worker is not an employee (army service, civil contractors, etc.). The right to organize and join trade unions is still guaranteed by the Federal Law "On Trade Unions, their Rights and the Guarantees of their Activities," 1996, which states that "a trade union is a voluntary association of *citizens*[3] [*italicized by the author—NL*] that are joined by their production and professional interests which relate to their activity ..."[4] Such trade unions exist.[5]

3. The notion of "citizens" is interpreted by the courts expansively as related to anyone who has legal residence in the territory of Russia.
4. Federalnyi Zakon RF "O professionalnykh soyuzah, ikh pravah i garantiyah deyatelnosti" [The RF Federal Law "On Trade Unions, Their Rights and the Guarantees of Their Activities"] Art. 26, 1996.

However, as such categories of workers are expressly excluded from the scope of the Labour Code (Article 11(8) LC), unlike the second category, these workers are not entitled to collective bargaining and social dialogue rights that are established by Part II of the Labour Code.

For the sake of clarity this variety of regimes may be shown as follows.

Table 31.1 Variety of Regimes

	"Non-essential employees"	*Essential Employees and Civil Servants*	*Military Servicemen and Others Excluded from the LC*
Right to strike	Yes	No	No
Right to collective bargaining	Yes	Yes	No
Right to form and join the union	Yes	Yes	Yes

2.2 Essential Services in the Strict Sense of the Term

Besides the limitations regarding army, police and other law-enforcement bodies (*see* above), Article 413(1) of the Labour Code prohibits strikes in organizations (or structural divisions) that are directly servicing highly dangerous manufacturing and facilities at ambulance stations; in the organizations (or structural subdivisions) that are directly associated with securing life-sustaining of the population (energy provision, heating, water-supply, gas-supply, aviation, railroad and water transport, communications, hospitals); and in cases if the performance of strikes endangers the interests of state defense, security of the state, life and security of the people. Based on the above provisions of the Labour Code, quite a substantial list of occupations and sectors where strikes are prohibited has been set up by the legislation.

The *Constitutional Court of the Russian Federation* (the Constitutional Court) seems to widen the Labour Code approach towards the reasons for possible limitation of the right to strike. In the case where the Federation of Aviation Dispatchers of Russia has made a claim concerning non-constitutionality of the prohibition of strikes of the civil aviation personnel responsible for servicing and management of the air traffic,[6] the Constitutional Court dismissed the claim motivating its decision not only by Article 55 of the Constitution that is mentioned in this respect in the Labour Code but also by

5. *See*, for example, the site of All-Russian Trade Union of Military Servicemen at: http://www.npsv.ru/index.html (accessed May 6, 2025).
6. Opredelenie Konstitutsionnogo Suda Rossiskoi Federatsii [The RF Constitutional Court Ruling] October 16, 2003, No. 318-O // ConsultantPlus Database. Available at: http://www.consultant.ru/cons/cgi/online.cgi?req=doc&base=LAW&n=45141&fld=134&dst=1000000001,0&rnd=0.14454863099112092#0 (accessed May 6, 2025).

Article 17(3) of the Constitution. This Article of the Constitution provides for *inadmissibility to infringe rights and freedoms* of other people in the process of exercising one's own rights.[7] In the case of strikes of the aviation personnel this clearly means the rights of passengers and (probably) the rights of the aviation personnel employers.

In another Constitutional Court case[8] that dealt with railroad transport, the Constitutional Court made a very broad and vague interpretation of justification of limitation of the right to strike. It follows from the motivation part of this Ruling that the Constitutional Court thinks that "any interests of the human and the state that may be affected" can be considered a sufficient justification for limiting the right to strike. Such an interpretation contradicts the approach of the CFA towards the ground for possible limitation of the right to strike being a "a clear and imminent threat to the life, personal safety or health of the whole or part of the population."[9]

The *Supreme Court* usually makes decisions concerning the illegality of strikes in essential services, interpreting Article 55 of the Constitution and Article 413(1) of the Labour Code very expansively. Among the sectors where the stoppage of work was interpreted as dangerous and, therefore, illegal were the following: railroad service,[10] communal heating,[11] air traffic control,[12] aviation personnel in general (the strike was declared illegal in general because it involved the stoppage of work of both workers who have no right to strike as well as the ordinary employees that were entitled to strike),[13] servicing departure flights in the airport,[14] river ports.[15] It seems that among the listed cases, only air traffic control falls within the notion of essential services in the

7. Konstitutsiya Rossiiskoi Federatsii [The Constitution of the Russian Federation] Art. 17, para. 3.
8. Opredelenie Konstitutsionnogo Suda Rossiiskoi Federatsii [The RF Constitutional Court Ruling] February 8, 2007, No. 275-O-P // ConsultantPlus Database. Available at: http://www.consultant.ru/cons/cgi/online.cgi?req=doc&base=LAW&n=68822&fld=134&dst=1000000001,0&rnd=0.007377757137777344#0 (accessed May 6, 2025).
9. The ILO. Freedom of Association: Compilation of decisions of the Committee on Freedom of Association. Geneva, International Labour Office, 6th (revised) ed., 2018, para. 836, p. 156.
10. Opredelenie Verkhovnogo Suda RF [The RF Supreme Court Ruling] July 29, 2002, No. 3-268/02 // SudAct Legal Database. Available at: http://sudact.ru/vsrf/doc/FH0rV9FRj4Yt/ (accessed May 6, 2025).
11. Opredelenie Verkhovnogo Suda RF [The RF Supreme Court Ruling] February 17, 2006, No. 3-25/05// SudAct Legal Database. Available at: http://sudact.ru/vsrf/doc/I3iCBsnF9nLj/ (accessed May 6, 2025).
12. Opredelenie Verkhovnogo Suda RF [The RF Supreme Court Ruling] November 19, 2002, No. 3-183/02 // SudAct Legal Database. Available at: http://sudact.ru/vsrf/doc/hFLvADA2Q5N5/ (accessed May 6, 2025).
13. Opredelenie Verkhovnogo Suda RF [The RF Supreme Court Ruling] February 14, 2003, No. 3-200/02// SudAct Legal Database. Available at: http://sudact.ru/vsrf/doc/6wYMoH6tDeZp/ (accessed May 6, 2025).
14. Opredelenie Verkhovnogo Suda RF [The RF Supreme Court Ruling] February 26, 2009, No. 3-47/08 // SudAct Legal Database. Available at: http://sudact.ru/vsrf/doc/qtleEvUSTSg0/ (accessed May 6, 2025).
15. Opredelenie Verkhovnogo Suda RF [The RF Supreme Court Ruling] October 14, 2005, No. 3P-1-56/05// SudAct Legal Database. Available at: http://sudact.ru/vsrf/doc/MTRzq5MrjwUn/ (accessed May 6, 2025).

strict sense according to the CFA approach;[16] others are specifically mentioned as not being essential services in the strict sense.[17]

The norms on prohibition of strikes are included in the legislation concerning "*state civil service*"[18] and "*municipal service.*"[19] Regulations of law on state civil service and municipal service cover only government and municipal officials. Any employees performing secondary functions in the government institutions are covered by the provisions of the Labour Code and have the right to strike. These two laws also do not cover employees of state-owned companies and institutions. Policemen, procurator's office servants, military servants and people serving an alternative civil service, state messengers, and state security services officials have no right to strike according to separate legislation establishing their status.

The *Federal Law on the "Use of Nuclear Energy"* prohibits strikes, meetings, demonstrations and picketing, transport blocking, and other social actions near nuclear industry enterprises and strikes that may endanger the work of such enterprises.[20]

Article 52 of the *Air Code of Russia*[21] prohibits strikes for the aviation personnel of civil aviation responsible for servicing and directing air transport. Because of these restrictions, flight dispatchers are known to perform hunger strikes. Without the official declaration of the strike in such situations they are taken away from their work by doctors for medical reasons and have the possibility to put pressure on their employer at the cost of their own health. Strikes are prohibited[22] for the employees of *railroad transport* whose work is connected with trains' operations, maneuvering operations, passengers, senders and recipients of cargo shipment service according to the list established by the Federal Law. This list is so wide that almost any railroad employee has no right to participate in strikes.

The norms concerning aviation and railroads were challenged as unconstitutional. In 2007, the Constitutional Court refused to consider that right to strike was

16. The ILO. Freedom of Association: Compilation of decisions of the Committee on Freedom of Association, *supra* n. 9, para. 841, p. 157.
17. *Ibid.*, para. 842, pp. 157-160.
18. Federalnyi zakon "O gosudarsvennoi grazhdanskoi sluzhbe" [Federal Law "On State Civil Service"] Art. 17, para. 15, July 27, 2004. *Sobraniye Zakonodatelstva Rossiyskoy Federazii [FZ RF] [Russian Federation Collection of Legislation]* August 2, 2004, No. 31, Item 3215.
19. Fedearlnyi zakon "O munitsipalnoi sluzhbe" [Federal Law "On Municipal Service"] Art. 14, para. 14, March 2, 2007. *Sobraniye Zakonodatelstva Rossiyskoy Federazii* [SZ RF] [Russian Federation Collection of Legislation] March 5, 2007, No. 10, Item 1152.
20. Federalnyi zakon "Ob ispolzovanii yadernoi energii" [Federal Law "On the Use of Nuclear Energy"*]* November 21, 1995, No. 180-FZ, *Sobraniye Zakonodatelstva Rossiyskoy Federazii* [SZ RG] [Russian Federation Collection of Legislation] January 27, 1995, No. 48, Item 4552.
21. Vozdushnyi Kodeks Rossiiskoy Federatsii [The Air Code of Russian Federation], Federalnyi Zakon [Federal Law] March 19, 1997, No. 60-FZ. *Sobraniye Zakonodatelstva Rossiyskoy Federatsii* [SZ RF] [Russian Federation Collection of Legislation] March 24, 1997, No. 12, Item 1383.
22. Federalnyi zakon "O zheleznodorozhnom transporte" [Federal Law "On Railroad Transport"] January 10, 2003, No. 17-FZ. *Sobraniye Zakonodatelstva Rossiyskoy Federazii* [SZ RF] [Russian Federation Collection of Legislation] January 13, 2003, No. 2, Item 169.

excessively limited in respect of railroad workers.[23] Therefore, the law has been left unchanged.

In a slightly more radical situation concerning civil aviation, the Constitutional Court considered[24] the law unconstitutional in 1995. The then existing law on "Collective Labour Disputes"[25] prohibited strikes in civil aviation enterprises *in whole*. Such prohibition being based only on the fact that an enterprise belonging to a certain economic sector was found unconstitutional and was abrogated by the Constitutional Court.

The obligation of employees to perform the *minimum works (services)* to be performed during any strike is directly associated with the issue of essential services. The employer, the state bodies of executive power, municipal authorities, as well as an employees' body that is in charge of the strike performance are under an obligation to take measures for "keeping the social order, ensuring the preservation of employer's and employees' property, as well as functioning of machinery and facilities, if their stoppage may constitute a direct danger to life and health of people" (Article 412(2)).

The sector-level lists of minimum services have to be adopted by the federal executive power body responsible for the governance in the respective sector of economy according to the methodology approved by the government.[26] One of the most problematic sectors from the point of view of essential services strikes sectors, i.e., the railroads, had its list of minimum works successfully challenged in court. One of two all-Russian railroad unions, being more militant and the only one taking part in strikes in this sector, has appealed the fact of adoption of the list by the Ministry of Transportation without involving this union in the process of coordination of its contents.[27]

The specific list of minimum works (services) to be performed during a particular strike has to be defined by the agreement between the parties to the collective labour dispute together with a local government authority within three days of the announcement of the strike (Article 412(4) LC). It is not permitted to include in such a list the works (services) which are not included in the lists of minimum works (services) adopted in respect of the sector of the economy or territory.

In case of disagreement between the parties concerning the list, it has to be approved by the government authority of the constituent entity of the Russian Federation. The latter issue has been a matter of examination of the ILO monitoring

23. Opredelenie Konstitutsionnogo Suda RF [The RF Constitutional Court Ruling] February 8, 2007 No. 275-O-P. *Sobraniye Zakonodatelstva Rossiyskoy Federazii* [SZ RF] [Russian Federation Collection of Legislation] May 22, 1995, No. 21, Art. 1976.
24. Postanovlenie Konstitutsionnogo Suda RF [Resolution of the Constitutional Court of the RF] May 17, 1995, No. 5-P. *Sobraniye Zakonodatelstva Rossiyskoy Federazii* [SZ RF] [Russian Federation Collection of Legislation] May 22, 1995, No. 21, Art. 1976.
25. Zakon SSSR "O rassmotrenii kollektivnykh trudovykh sporov" [Law of the USSR "On Resolution of Collective Labour Disputes (conflicts)"] May 20, 1991, No. 2179-1. *Vedomosti SND and VS of USSR [Bulletin of the CPD of the RF and SC of the RF]* June 1991, No. 23, Art. 654.
26. Postanovlenie Pravitelstva Rossiiskoi Federatsii [The Resolution of the Government of the Russian Federation] December 17, 2002, No. 901. Garant Database. Available at: http://base.garant.ru/185339/ (accessed May 6, 2025).
27. Opredelenie Verkhovnogo Suda Rossiiskoi Federatsii [The Supreme Court Ruling] July 6, 2006, No. KAC06-221. Consultantplus Database.

bodies. The CFA has noted that any disagreement concerning specific contents of minimum services must be resolved by an independent body that has the credibility of all the parties. The government authority in charge of resolution of such disputes is the *State Service on Labour and Employment* (*Rostrud*) which is subordinated to the Ministry of Labour and Social Protection. It is clear that in many cases, especially when the dispute relates to the state-owned employer, a governmental agency cannot be considered neutral. The CFA addressed the Government of Russia in 2003 with the request to amend Article 412 of the Labour Code in order to meet this requirement.[28] Later (in 2012), the request was repeated by the CEACR,[29] but the legislation has not been changed.

2.3 Situations of Acute National or Local Crisis

Article 413 of the Labour Code provides that:

> the strikes shall be declared illegal and shall not be allowed ... during the period of military alert or the state of emergency, or specific measures taken in accordance with the legislation on the state of emergency; in structures of the Military Forces of the Russian Federation, other military, paramilitary bodies or organizations (or structural subdivisions) that are directly responsible for the issues of the country defense, security of the state, emergency rescuing, searching-rescuing, fire-fighting works, prevention or liquidation of natural disasters or emergency situations; in law-enforcement bodies; in organizations (or structural divisions) that are directly servicing highly dangerous manufacturing and facilities, at ambulance stations.

Apart from general mentioning in Article 413 of the Labour Code, there is a special legislation concerning the prohibition of strikes during a state of military alert,[30] state of emergency[31] or special measures taken in accordance with the legislation on state of emergency; the military forces of the Russian Federation, other military, paramilitary and other organizations or their divisions that are directly involved into the issues of state defense, state security, emergency and rescue services, fire-fighting services, services of prevention and liquidation of consequences of natural disasters

---

28. Committee on Freedom of Association cases. Case No. 2199 (Russian Federation)—Complaint date: April 18, 2002.
    The Russian Labour Confederation (KTR). Paragraphs 991, 995. The ILO Normlex Database: http://www.ilo.org/dyn/normlex/en/f?p=1000:50001:0::NO:50001:P50001_COMPLAINT_FILE_ID:2897348 (accessed May 6, 2025).
29. Direct Request (CEACR)—adopted 2012, published 102nd ILC session (2013) Freedom of Association and Protection of the Right to Organise Convention, 1948 (No. 87)—Russian Federation https://normlex.ilo.org/dyn/nrmlx_en/f?p=1000:13100:0::NO:13100:P13100_COMMENT_ID,P13100_COUNTRY_ID:3086188,102884 (accessed May 6, 2025).
30. The state of military alert is being announced according to the Federal Constitutional Law "On the State of Military Alert" of January 30, 2002, No. 1-FKZ. *Sobraniye Zakonodatelstva Rossiyskoy Federazii* [SZ RF] [Russian Federation Collection of Legislation] Art. 375, February 4, 2002, No. 5.
31. The state of emergency is announced according to the Federal Constitutional Law "On the State of Emergency" of May 30, 2001, No. 3-FKZ. *Sobraniye Zakonodatelstva Rossiyskoy Federazii* [SZ RF] [Russian Federation Collection of Legislation] June 4, 2001, No. 23, Item 2277.

and emergency situations; the police and other state security services; organizations (or their divisions) directly servicing dangerous production or equipment at ambulance stations.

3 COMPENSATORY GUARANTEES FOR WORKERS DEPRIVED OF THE RIGHT TO STRIKE

Compulsory arbitration is a substitution mechanism for the ban of the right to strike provided by law (Article 404(8) LC). According to this norm, if the parties of the collective labour dispute, in which employees are not entitled to the right to strike, cannot agree on creation of ad-hoc voluntary labour arbitration or referral of their dispute to the permanent labour arbitration, the governmental body responsible for the settlement of collective labour disputes shall establish compulsory arbitration to resolve such a dispute, being Rostrud.[32] As it was already said, Rostrud is a governmental structure. Therefore, it cannot be considered fully neutral and independent from the state and employer as it is required by the CFA, especially when it comes to disputes with the state-owned employers that constitute the majority of the cases in essential services.

There is not much open information about the practical outcome of compulsory labour arbitration as it is considered to be confidential information. However, there is case law[33] concerning illegality of strikes when essential services employees were trying to organize the strike without taking part in compulsory arbitration. This may be considered a sign of not enough trust in this institution.

4 CONCLUSION

The general assessment of legal regulation of the right to strike in essential services in Russia is that it is greatly unbalanced in favor of the state and employers. The aim of the legal limitation of the right to strike in essential services is theoretically grounded mainly with regard to the issues of safety of people and state security. Nevertheless, the practical interpretation of these limitations is so expansive that in practice the right to strike as it is regulated now presents no serious obstacle to the proper level of functioning of the employers.

However, such regulation obviously cannot serve as an example of effective collective bargaining. The level of strikes in general, not just in essential services, is negligibly low; in great majority of cases the strikes are declared illegal when contested in courts by employers.

---

32. The power to settle a collective labour dispute is established in para. 5.5.10 of the Rostrud Statute approved by the Decree of the Government of the Russian Federation of June 30, 2004 No. 324. *Sobraniye Zakonodatelstva Rossiyskoy Federazii* of July 17, 2004, No. 28, Item 2901.
33. Opredelenie Verkhovnogo Suda RF [Supreme Court Ruling] February 10, 2006, No. 74-G06-4, Opredelenie Verkhovnogo Suda RF [Supreme Court Ruling] October 14, 2005, No. 11-G05-21 // SudAct Legal Database.

In quite significant number of issues (quorum concerning calling the strike in general, the determination of what is understood by essential services, insufficient impartiality of a state institution that has the power to resolve disputes over the minimum services and compulsory arbitration, etc.), Russian legislation that regulates strikes in essential services cannot be considered complying with the international labour standards imposed by the ILO.

The experience of discussions of personal preferences in collective bargaining and strikes with active trade unionists that are practically involved in strike activities shows that they prefer actions that fall outside of the legal framework. Usually, it is the choice for them either to follow official procedures established in the Labour Code or to be actually involved in the industrial action. From employers' standpoint, the preference for autonomous and informal or official legal regulation in the situations of disputes is not that clear and depends on personal preferences and policy of the management.

It may be stated that the current Russian regulative policy in the area of strikes in essential services is quite consistent in its generally restrictive approach towards the possibility of legally organizing the strikes. This consistency, however, cannot be considered optimal and acceptable because the protests of highly discontented workers happen despite formal legal prohibition, and the legislation on strikes does not serve its goal as a safety valve for the society.

CHAPTER 32

Restrictions on the Right to Strike in Serbia

Senad Jašarević

1 GENERAL INFORMATION

1.1 Legal Basis of the Right to Strike

The Republic of Serbia has undertaken to ensure the right to strike by signing international documents directly or indirectly guaranteeing this right.[1] As a state party to the International Covenant on Economic, Social and Cultural Rights (Article 8)[2] and the Amended European Social Charter (Article 6 paragraph 4),[3] Serbia is committed to guaranteeing the right to strike, i.e., the exercise of the right to collective action of employees and employers.[4] The Covenant, namely, in Article 8, paragraph 1, item d, guarantees the right to strike,[5] and the revised European Social Charter (ESC) - the right to collective action.[6]

1. This right is indirectly guaranteed by the Freedom of Association and Protection of the Right to Organize Convention, 1948, No. 87, of the International Labour Organization (ILO). *See* Bernard Gernigon, Alberto Odero & Horacio Guido, *ILO Principles Concerning the Right to Strike* 8, 9 (International Labour Office 1998), https://www.ilo.org/wcmsp5/groups/public/---ed_norm/---normes/documents/publication/wcms_087987.pdf.
2. This document was ratified in Serbia (i.e., ex. Yugoslavia, which included Serbia at the time) in: Appendix to the Official Gazette of the SFRY - International Treaties, No. 7/1971.
3. The revised European Social Charter was ratified in Serbia in 2009. *See* Official Herald - International Treaties, No. 42/2009. When ratifying the Charter, Serbia exempted the effect of this Article only for members of the Serbian Armed Forces.
4. Serbia has ratified International Labour Organization (ILO) Convention No. 87 (Freedom of Association and Protection of the Right to Organise Convention, 1948 (No. 87)) in: Official Herald of the FNRJ - International Treaties, No. 8/1958.
5. That Article of the Covenant reads: 'The States Parties to the present Covenant undertake to ensure: ... 4) d) The right to strike, provided that it is exercised in conformity with the laws of the particular country.'
6. Article 6 of the European Social Charter (Revised), in the framework - The right to bargain collectively, foresees: 'With a view to ensuring the effective exercise of the right to bargain

Accordingly, the right to strike is guaranteed by the Constitution of Serbia of 2006,[7] in the section regulating 'Human Rights and Freedom'. Article 61 of the Constitution provides for the free exercise of the right to strike (Right to strike). The specific conditions for the legal and legitimate organization of strikes are laid down in the Strike Law (SL) 1996.[8]

The constitutional guarantees of the right to strike in Serbia are very broad. First, it is the right of all employees, almost without restrictions.[9] Second, the Constitution only allows a 'reasonable restriction' on the right to strike - only to the extent necessary, according to the nature or type of activity, and only by law.[10] This approach has been confirmed several times by decisions of the Constitutional Court of the Republic of Serbia and the Supreme Court of Cassation of the Republic of Serbia, which have even caused corrections to the Strike Law[11] and the introduction of a number of new legal solutions in special laws (e.g., on police).[12]

However, if the constitutional basis of the right to strike is considered in relation to Article 6 ESC, this right is somewhat narrower in the Constitution. Namely, the Charter provides for the 'right to collective action' of employees, not just the right to strike.[13] Serbian legislation does not mention other forms of collective action that employees use in comparative practice (picketing, boycott, solidarity strike). Since Serbia ratified the Charter without serious reservations regarding the right to collective action, it should have allowed and regulated other forms of collective action of employees.[14]

As for the provisions in the Strike Law, they are partially outdated, and it can be said that some provisions are controversial in the context of international standards (as outlined below). Experts from the ILO and the EU who have analysed Serbia's law consider the issue of regulating strikes to be one of the most acute in Serbian labour

collectively, the Parties undertake: and recognise: ... (4) the right of workers and employers to collective action in cases of conflicts of interest, including the right to strike, subject to obligations that might arise out of collective agreements previously entered into.'

7. By the way, the right to strike did not exist in socialist Yugoslavia, of which Serbia was a part. It was introduced only in 1988, by amendments to the 1974 Constitution. *See Amendments to the Constitution of the Socialist Federal Republic of Yugoslavia,* Official Gazette of the Socialist Federal Republic of Yugoslavia, year XLIV, No. 70 (Belgrade, Saturday, 26 November 1988), https://sr.wikisource.org/sr-el/Amandmani_na_Ustav_Socijalističke_Federativne_Republike_Jugoslavije_(1988).
8. Official Herald of the FRJ, No. 29/96, Official Herald of the RS, Nos 101/2005, 103/2012.
9. Except for the military and service in state security service.
10. According to Art. 61(2) of the Constitution.
11. For example, by the decision of the Constitutional Court IUz No. 1442/2010 published on 30 October 2012 (Official Gazette of RS, No. 103/2012), part of Art. 18 of the Law, which limited the right to strike to social workers and members of the police, was declared unconstitutional and deleted.
12. *See* Bojan Urdarević, *The Changing Nature of the Right to Strike in the Republic of Serbia* 565-579 (Law in the process of globalisation, Kragujevac 2018).
13. On the right to collective action *see* more: Branko A. Lubarda, *Labour Law, Debate on Dignity at Work and Social Dialogue (Radno pravo, Rasprava o dostojanstvu na radu i socijalnom dijalogu)* 976 (Pravni fakultet, Beograd 2012).
14. More precisely, Serbia is in the Law on Confirmation of the Revised European Social Charter, in Art. 3. during the ratification of the Charter, excluded the effect of Art. 6 para. 4 (on the right to collective action) only towards members of the Serbian Armed Forces.

legislation.[15] Work has been carried out on revisions to the Strike Law for more than a decade. During this time, several drafts of the revised Strike Law have been published, but no text has been adopted so far. The last draft is from 2018[16] but received widespread criticism from the public and from ILO experts.[17]

A separate document of the ILO is devoted to the analysis of this draft Strike Law (*Memorandum of Technical Comments on the Draft Strike Law*).[18] In this document, 10 basic recommendations related to the arrangement of strikes in Serbia were given. These were explained in detail, with a series of concrete proposals for the improvement of strike legislation. In short, the ILO advocates that strike decisions do not undermine the position of representative trade unions, that strikes are defined in such a way that this right is guaranteed to all workers (and for all collective disputes), that procedural demands should not be an obstacle strikes, that dialogue with the social partners regarding the arrangement of strikes should be strengthened, that the provisions on the place and manner of strikes should be laid down more clearly and flexibly, that arbitration where necessary should be completed as soon as possible, that the responsibility of trade unions and employees for illegal strikes is arranged in such a way that they cannot be punished for minor violations.[19]

1.2 Main Features of the Regulation

According to Article 61 of the Constitution: '(1) The employed shall have the right to strike in accordance with the law and collective agreement. (2) The right to strike may be restricted only by law in accordance with the nature or type of business activity.'

On this basis, the following can be concluded: (1) to strike is the right of all employees, (2) the right to strike can be exercised in accordance with the law and collective agreement,[20] (3) restrictions on the right to strike for certain categories of employees may be enforced only by law, and not by a bylaw, collective agreement or

15. *See* ILO, *Memorandum of Technical Comments on Draft Strike Law* (International Labour Office, Geneva, November 2018); *Analytical Report Accompanying the Commission Communication to the European Parliament and to the Council: Opinion of the Commission on Serbia's Application for Membership of the European Union (Analitički izveštaj koji prati Saopštenje Komisije upućeno Evropskom parlamentu i Savetu: Mišljenje Komisije o zahtevu Srbije za članstvo u Evropskoj uniji)* 36, 117, 131 {COM(2011) 668} (Evropska komisija, 3.19), https://www.mei.gov.rs/upload/documents/eu_dokumenta/misljenje_kandidatura/misljenje_ek_2011.pdf.
16. The last draft of the Strike Law (2018), can be seen at: https://www.paragraf.rs/dnevne-vesti/250418/250418-vest16.html.
17. For the EU's position on this issue, *see*, for example: *Mišljenje Komisije o zahtevu Srbije za članstvo u Evropskoj uniji, supra* n. 15, 116.
18. *See supra* n. 15.
19. *See Ibid.*
20. For example, abstaining from a strike during the validity of a collective bargaining agreement. Recently, more and more collective agreements in Serbia contain a clause on preserving social peace, which obliges trade unions participating in the negotiations to refrain from striking during the validity of the collective agreement. *See* Bojan Urdarević, *Clause on Preserving Social Peace as an Integral Part of the Collective Labor Agreement (Klauzula o čuvanju socijalnog mira kao sastavni deo kolektivnog ugovora o radu)* 23-36 (Radno i socijalno pravo, Beograd, XXI 2017, No. 2).

an act/regulation of the employer,[21] (4) when limiting the strike, the nature and significance of the activity must be taken into account.

The specific conditions for the legal and legitimate organization of the strike are laid down in the Strike Law.

According to the Law: 'A strike is a cessation of work organized by employees to protect their professional and economic interests at work.'[22] Therefore, a strike can be organized solely to protect professional and economic interests. A political strike is prohibited.[23] While strikes with direct political demands in Serbia are rare, politically instructed strikes, where the collective action of workers is influenced by political motives and interests, are quite common.[24]

According to the SL, employees are free to decide on their participation in the strike but not always on the organization of the strike itself.[25] Specifically, according to the law, a strike at the workplace can be organized by trade unions or the majority of the employees, while other types of strikes can only be organized by trade unions (so-called wild cat or spontaneous strikes at the branch or national level are prohibited).[26]

A strike in Serbia can be organized as: (1) a workplace strike, (2) a branch strike or a strike in the activity, or (3) a general strike.[27] A 'warning strike' can also be organized – lasting up to one hour.[28] Solidarity strikes (sympathy) are not recognized as a legal form of collective action.[29]

Employees are obliged to announce a strike in a timely manner – within 5 days or 10 days in services of general interest.[30] The strike is announced by the 'Decision on entering into a strike', which determines: the demands of employees; the time of the start of the strike; the place of gathering of participants in the strike (if the strike is manifested by the gathering of employees); and the strike committee that represents the interests of employees and leads the strike on their behalf.[31]

The law stipulates that if the strike is carried out by a gathering of employees, the meeting place of the participants in the strike cannot be off the business premises, i.e.,

21. This is confirmed by the decisions of the Constitutional Court. *See*, for example, the duty of the Constitutional Court which, for this reason, annulled the Decree on strike of police officers. Decision of the Constitutional Court – IU No. 85/2007.
22. Article 1(1) of the Strike Law (SL).
23. About the political strike and other types of strikes, in Serbia and in general, *see* more: Lubarda, *supra* n. 13, 976-1053.
24. *See* Radoje Brković, Ratomir Antonović & Dragan Milovanović, *Zloupotreba prava na štrajk (Zloupotreba prava na štrajk)* 13 (Radno i socijalno pravo, Beograd, XXI, 2017, No. 2).
25. Article 1(2) SL.
26. Article 3 SL. 'According to the established facts, plaintifs went on strike, which was not led by an authorized trade union organization, and the notice of suspension was signed by ten of the twenty-two employees, and no strike committee was formed.' *See* Supreme Court of Serbia, Rev. 2 1575/06, 21 November 2006. *See* Brković, Antonović & Milovanović, *supra* n. 24, 11.
27. Article 2(1) SL.
28. Article 2, paras 2 and 3 SL.
29. *See* Bojić Filip, *Right to Strike in European and Domestic Legislation (Pravo na štrajk u evropskom i domaćem zakonodavstvu)* 524 (Pravo i privreda 2010, Vol. 47, Nos 7-9).
30. And twenty-four hours before the warning strike. Art. 5(1) SL.
31. Article 2 SL.

outside the business premises of the employees who are entering the strike.[32] Thus, picketing is not allowed. Actions of employees by gathering in public places (which are, by the way, very common in Serbia) do not represent a strike but a protest, which, as we have said, is allowed by the Constitution (Article 54)[33] and is regulated by a special law – the Law on Public Assembly, from 2016.[34]

The law stipulates a mandatory attempt to resolve the dispute peacefully – through negotiations before and during the strike. According to Article 6 of the SL, the strike board and representatives of the bodies to which the strike was announced are obliged, from the day of the strike announcement and during the strike, to try to resolve the dispute amicably. At the invitation of the parties to the dispute, representatives of trade unions, if the trade union is not the organizer of the strike, the corresponding employers' associations, and representatives of the competent state authorities, i.e., local self-government bodies (municipal), may be involved in negotiations. This kind of informal 'political mediation' is very common in Serbia. Workers, especially in the case of major strikes, often turn to the Government or the competent ministry for informal mediation. It is probably one of the relics of socialism, when the state unilaterally regulated labour relations, and now the state is expected to settle the disputed issues if this is not possible by an agreement of social partners.

A strike, as a democratic means of pressure, must not be violent or restrictive for employers or employees, except for legal strike activities. The law stipulates that the strike committee and employees participating in the strike are obliged to organize and conduct the strike in a manner that does not endanger the safety of persons and property and human health, prevents the infliction of direct material damage, and enables the continuation of work after the end of the strike. The strike committee and the employees participating in the strike cannot prevent the employer from using and disposing of the funds with which it performs its activities. Also, the strike committee and employees participating in the strike must not prevent employees who do not participate in the strike from working.[35]

It is also envisaged to limit the strike to activities of public interest, i.e., dangerous activities, while ensuring a minimum of work – minimum service levels (as outlined below).

Strikers and organizers of a legal strike are protected from punishment and retaliation and all forms of coercion against them, provided that the strike is organized and carried out in accordance with the law. According to the Strike Law, organizing or participating in a strike under the conditions established by this law does not constitute

32. Article 5(3) SL.
33. The Constitution in Art. 54 envisages 'Freedom of assembly' of citizens, which could include the freedom of assembly of employees in order to organize protests outside the company, i.e., without organizing a strike. According to this Art. of the Constitution (Freedom of Assembly): '(1) Citizens may assemble freely. (2) Assembly held indoors shall not be subjected to permission or registering. (3) Gathering, demonstrating and other forms of assembly held outdoors will be reported to the state body, in accordance with the law. (4) Freedom of assembly may be restricted by the law only if necessary to protect public health, morals, rights of others or the security of the Republic of Serbia.'
34. Official Herald of the RS, No. 6/2016. *See* Filip, *supra* n. 29, 524.
35. Article 5(3) SL.

a violation of work obligation, cannot be a basis for initiating proceedings for determining the disciplinary and material responsibility of an employee and cannot result in the termination of employment of an employee. An employee who participates in a strike is entitled to all basic rights from employment relationship, except the right to wage and the rights from social insurance – in accordance with the regulations on social insurance.[36] Organizers and participants in a strike that is not organized in accordance with this law will not enjoy the provided legal protection.[37]

The Criminal Code of Serbia, from 2005, provides for criminal punishment for serious violations of the right to strike by employees.[38] According to Article 167 of the Code (criminal offence: Abuse of the Right to Strike): 'Whoever organizes or leads the strike in a way contrary to law or other regulations and thereby endangers human life and health or property to a considerable extent, or if grave consequences result therefore, unless elements of some other criminal offence entail, shall be punished with imprisonment up to three years.'

The Strike Law does not allow the engagement of so-called strikebreakers in order to suppress the strike. According to the Law, during a strike organized under the conditions established by this law, the employer may not hire new persons to replace the participants in the strike, unless the safety of persons and property are endangered and it is necessary to maintain minimum work processes to ensure the safety of property and persons, as well as the fulfilment of international obligations. The employer must not prevent an employee from participating in the strike or use coercive measures to end the strike, nor provide for more favourable wages or other favourable working conditions for employees who do not participate in the strike on the basis of non-participation in the strike.[39]

The rights of strikers are also protected in the Criminal Code.[40] Article 166 provides for a criminal offence – Violation of the Right to Strike, which reads as follows: '(1) Whoever by force, threat or otherwise, unlawfully prevents or obstructs employees to, in accordance with law, organize a strike, participate in a strike or otherwise exercise their right to strike, shall be punished with a fine or imprisonment up to two years. The penalty specified in paragraph 1 of this Article shall be imposed on an employer or responsible person – manager.'

36. 'The collective agreement cannot provide for the right to wage compensation for employees participating in the strike.' *See* Decision of the Constitutional Court of the Republic of Serbia U. No. 115/2004 of 22 September 2005 (Bulletin of the District Court in Belgrade, Intermex, Belgrade 2006, No. 70).
37. Article 14 SL. *See* the decisions of the courts that confirm this: Decision of the Supreme Cassation Court, Rev2 921/06, 4 October 2006, Belgrade; Decision of the Supreme Cassation Court, Rev2 690/2014, 26 December 2014, Belgrade; Judgment of the Court of Appeals in Belgrade, Gž. 2911/15, 5 April 2017. *See also* Brković, Antonović & Milovanović, *supra* n. 24, 7; Nikola Kitarović, *Rules for the Legal Organization and Conduct of Strikes (Pravila za zakonito organizovanje i vođenje štrajka)* 611-617 (Radno i socijalno pravo, Udruženje za radno i socijalno pravo Srbije, broj 1/2006).
38. Official Herald of the RS, Nos 85/2005, 88/2005, 107/, 72/2009, 111/2009, 121/2012, 104/2013, 108/2014, 94/2016, 35/2019.
39. Article 14 SL.
40. Official Herald of the RS, Nos 85/2005, 88/2005, 107/, 72/2009, 111/2009, 121/2012, 104/2013, 108/2014, 94/2016, 35/2019.

2 PERMITTED RESTRICTIONS

2.1 Certain Categories of Public Servants

In the original version of the Strike Law, from 1996, in Article 18(1), strikes for employees of state bodies, the police, and professional members of the Serbian Armed Forces were proscribed. According to this provision, the following was stipulated: 'An employee of a state body, a professional member of the Army and a member of the police ceases employment when it is determined that he organized a strike or participated in a strike.' In 2012, the Constitutional Court found the decision unconstitutional – that is, it was not in accordance with the new 2006 Constitution. The strike ban for police members and civil servants – who since then enjoy the right to strike like other employees (possibly with minimum work) – was abolished.[41] Only the ban on strikes by professional members of the Serbian Armed Forces remains valid.[42]

Members of the police have the right to strike with minimum service level limits. According to the provisions of the Law on Police (LP),[43] police officers and other employees have the right to form trade unions and other professional organizations and organize and participate in activities in a manner prescribed by law.[44] They have the right to strike in accordance with the law and collective bargaining agreement and to freely decide on their participation in the strike. They will not be entitled to strike in the following cases: (1) a state of war, a state of emergency, an emergency or a state of increased risk; (2) violent threat to the constitutional order of the Republic of Serbia; (3) declaration of a natural disaster or an imminent danger of its occurrence in the territory of two or more police departments of the ministry or throughout the territory of the Republic of Serbia; (4) other disasters and accidents that interfere with the normal course of life and endanger the safety of people and property; (5) in the event that they are employed in workplaces where there are no conditions for ensuring a minimum of work process (minimum service level).[45] Workplaces where the minimum service level is not provided are regulated by a special act of the Minister. Employees of the Ministry, except for police officers who provide the minimum service level, can

41. *See* the previously mentioned decision of the Constitutional Court from 2012, and in this regard *see* more: *Constitutional Court Ruled: All Employees Have the Right to Strike (Ustavni sud presudio: pravo na štrajk imaju svi zaposleni)*, Zakon.co.rs (9 March 2023), http://www.zakon.co.rs/ustavni-sud-presudio-pravo-na-strajk-imaju-svi-zaposleni.html; *The Constitutional Court Ruled about the Strike Law! (Ustavni sud presudio Zakonu o štrajku!)*, Sindikat poreske uprave Srbije (9 March 2023), http://www.sind-pu.rs/index.php/205-ustavni-sud-presudio-zakonu-o-trajku.
42. A special law envisages a ban on strikes for members of the state security service – Security and Information Agency (BIA). They do not have this right under the Law on Security information agency, Art. 20(2). They also have no right to join a trade union. (Art. 20, para. 2 provides: 'Members of the Agency do not have the right to organize a trade union or the right to strike.') The Law is published in: Official Herald of the RS, Nos 42/2002, 111/2009, 65/2014, 66/2014, 36/2018.
43. Official Herald of the RS, Nos 6/2016, 24/2018, 87/2018.
44. Article 169 LP.
45. Police officers participating in the strike cannot carry weapons and other means of coercion during the strike. Art. 170(10) LP.

start a strike if the minimum service level that ensures the safety of people and property or is an irreplaceable condition of life and work of citizens is ensured.[46]

According to Article 14 of the Law on the Serbian Armed Forces, professional members of the Serbian Armed Forces are not allowed the right to strike. Striking or participating in illegal trade union organizing, i.e., in illegal trade union activities, is a disciplinary offence for which one can be dismissed.[47]

2.2 Essential Services in the Strict Sense of the Term

The Strike Law also limits strikes in essential activities and services. Essential services, according to Article 9 of the Strike Law, are: '(1) An activity of public interest or an activity whose interruption of work due to the nature of the work could endanger the life and health of people or cause large-scale damage; (2) Activities in the fields of: electricity industry, water industry, traffic, information (radio and television), PTT services, communal activities, production of basic food products, health and veterinary care, education, social community, childcare and social protection. (3) Activities of special importance for the defense and security of the Republic of Serbia, which are determined by the competent authority in accordance with the state law, as well as tasks necessary for the fulfillment of the international obligations of the Republic of Serbia. (4) Activities whose interruption of work due to the nature of work, in the sense of this law, could endanger the life and health of people or cause damage on a large scale (chemical industry, steel industry and ferrous and non-ferrous metallurgy).'

Employees who perform the activities referred to in Article 9 of this law may start a strike if the minimum service level is ensured.[48] The minimum work process (minimum service level) for public services and public companies is determined by the founder (factual state – competent state authority) and by another employer – director. Determining the 'minimum service level' starts with the nature of the activity, the degree of endangerment of life and health of people, and other circumstances important for the realization of the needs of citizens, companies, and other entities (season,

46. The head of the organizational unit, no later than 10 days before the start of the strike, determines the employees who are obliged to work during the strike in order to ensure a minimum of the work process, which may not be less than 60% of employees. For more details about the police strike, *see* Art. 170 LP.
47. Article 149 of the Serbian Armed Forces Act. Published in: Official Herald of the RS, Nos 116/2007, 88/2009, 101/2010, 10/2015, 88/2015, 36/2018, 94/2019, 74/2021. *See The Court Stripped the President of the Military Union of His Rank (Sud predsedniku Vojnog sindikata oduzeo čin)* (Epicentar press, 2 November 2018), https://www.epicentarpress.rs/vest/3693/Sud-predsedniku-Vojnog-sindikata-oduzeo-čin/; V.J, *Novica Antic Expelled from the Army (Novica Antic izbačen iz Vojske)* (Danas, 1 November 2018), https://www.danas.rs/vesti/politika/novica-antic-izbacen-iz-vojske/komentari/.
48. The strike must be announced at least 10 days in advance. The strike committee, the employer and the representatives of the competent state body, i.e., the local self-government body, are obliged to offer a proposal for resolving the dispute in the period from the announcement of the strike to the day set for the start of the strike, and to introduce the proposal to the employees who announced the strike and the public. The strike committee is obliged to cooperate with the employer during the strike in order to ensure the minimum of service. Employees who perform tasks in order to ensure minimum of service are obliged to carry out the employer's orders during the strike. Arts 11-14 LS.

tourist season, school year, etc.). The founder or director is obliged to take into account the opinions, objections, and proposals of the union.

The method of ensuring the minimum service level is determined by the act of the employer (employers' regulations) in accordance with the collective agreement. Employees who are obliged to work during the strike in order to ensure a minimum of the work process, according to the opinion obtained by the strike committee, shall be determined by the director no later than five days before the start of the strike. If, five days before the start of the strike, the conditions for minimum work are not provided, the competent state authority (or local self-government body), by the date set for the beginning of the strike, will determine the measures and manner for fulfilling these conditions.[49] If they do not respect the minimum service levels, employees can be dismissed.[50]

This way of regulating the minimum service levels is considered problematic - because they are determined unilaterally by the founder (the state) or the employer (in the case of the private sector). The problem is also that minimum service levels can be determined during a strike or immediately before a strike (which the unions object to). Often, this minimum is set in such a way as to make a strike pointless, which is why there were proceedings before the Constitutional Court in which the minimum service level was deemed unconstitutional.[51]

According to the Law on Peaceful Settlement of Labour Disputes,[52] parties to a collective labour dispute in activities in which there is an obligation to ensure minimum service levels are obliged to proceed to the peaceful resolution of the collective dispute - mediation, in accordance with that law. They are obliged to submit the proposal for mediation within three working days from the date of the announcement of the dispute.[53] Also, in the same procedure, disputes arising over determining the minimum service levels can be resolved.[54]

2.3 Situations of Acute National or Local Crisis

The strike law does not directly regulate the issue of strike in the event of an acute national or local crisis. However, Article 16 of the Strike Law stipulates that the competent state authority is obliged to take the necessary measures provided for by law

49. *See* Art. 10 SL.
50. Article 14(3). *See, e.g.*, 'Workers who are on strike can terminate their employment if they have not ensured the minimum of the work process.' From the Decision of the District Court in Novi Sad, *Gž.1594/06 od 13 Apr. 2006: Bilten sudske prakse Okružnog suda u Novom Sadu, br. 9/2006*, Intermex, Beograd.
51. *See, e.g.*, Decision of the Constitutional Court - No. IU-212/2006 - Determination of non-compliance of the provisions of the Decision on determining the minimum of service during the strike in companies and institutions founded by the Assembly of the Municipality of Ljubovija; Decision of the Constitutional Court - No. IUO-261/2011 - Determination of inconsistency with the Constitution and law of the Decision on determining the minimum work process during the strike - The company 'Dnevnik - Štamparija', Novi Sad.
52. Official Herald of the RS, Nos 125/2004, 204/2009, 50/2018.
53. Articles 18-19 of the Law.
54. Article 2 of the Law.

if it assesses that a violation of the provisions of Article 7, paragraph 1 of the Law (endangering safety or health, causing damage) and Articles 9 and 10 (ensuring minimum work) of the Law, could lead to immediate danger or extremely serious consequences to the life and health of people or their safety and security of property or other irreversible harmful consequences. It does not specify what these measures might be, and in practice, the State has refrained from undertaking any forms of coercion in similar situations. Efforts are made to solve the problem through negotiations between the authorities and the strikers.

The possibility to limit the right to strike in situations of acute national or local crisis exists on the basis of the Constitution. Article 202, which regulates 'Derogation form human and minority rights in the state of emergency and war', provides: '(1) Upon proclamation of the state of emergency or war, derogations from human and minority rights guaranteed by the Constitution shall be permitted only to the extent deemed necessary. (2) Measures providing for derogation shall not bring about differences based on race, sex, language, religion, national affiliation or social origin. (3) Measures providing for derogation from human and minority rights shall cease to be effective upon ending of the state of emergency or war. (4) Measures providing for derogation shall by no means be permitted in terms of the rights guaranteed pursuant to Articles 23, 24, 25, 26, 28, 32, 34, 37, 38, 43, 45, 47, 49, 62, 63, 64 and 78 of the Constitution.' The right to strike is promulgated by Article 61 of the Constitution, so it does not belong to a group of rights that cannot be restricted.

3 COMPENSATORY GUARANTEES FOR WORKERS DEPRIVED OF THE RIGHT TO STRIKE

In Serbian law, only members of the military and security services are denied the right to strike. Members of the Armed Forces have the right to organize trade unions, but it is stipulated that the participation of professional members of the Serbian Armed Forces in groups of a trade union character must be in accordance with the rules of military service.[55] Members of the Security and Information Agency do not have the right to organize nor any compensation for the lack of the right to strike. It is unfortunate that the legislator did not foresee the possibility of mediation (or mediation) under the Law on Peaceful Settlement of Labor Disputes for these categories. Thus, they remain completely unable to express and collectively protect their economic and social interests.

4 CONCLUSION

The conditions for organizing a strike set by the Constitution of Serbia and the Strike Law largely correspond to international standards. However, excessive strike restrictions are imposed on some groups of employees, which challenge their other human rights (the right to organize, the right to express opinions, the right to fair working

55. Article 14(3) Law on the Serbian Armed Forces.

conditions, and dignity). The unjustified restrictions of the strike in Serbian legislation include, for example, that the activities of particular social importance - essential services in which the strike is limited are set too broadly (consequence is that the strike is limited in activities that are not basically essential); the undemocratic way of regulating the minimum work for public services and enterprises (unilaterally determined by the founder or director of the company, i.e., the subject against whom the strike is being organized).[56] This indicates the need to invoke or pass a new Strike Law in Serbia. After all, this was also pointed out by the aforementioned expert opinions of EU and ILO representatives.

56. The above-mentioned objections regarding the Strike Law were pointed out by, for example, Council of Europe experts. *See* Branko A. Lubarda, and others, *Harmonization of the Rights and Practices of Serbia and Montenegro with the Amended European Social Charter (Usklađenost prava i prakse Srbije i Crne Gare sa Izmenjenom evropskom socijalnom poveljom)* 724-726 (Council of Europe, Podgorica 2005).

CHAPTER 33

Restrictions on the Right to Strike in Slovakia

Robert Schronk

1 GENERAL INFORMATION

1.1 Legal Basis of the Right to Strike

In Slovakia, the right to strike is already guaranteed by the Constitution of the Slovak Republic (Act No. 460/1992 Collection of Laws – 'Coll.'). According to Article 37 paragraph 4 of the Constitution, 'The right to strike shall be guaranteed. A law shall lay down the terms thereof.' Claiming the right to strike (Article 37 paragraph 4) is possible only within the limits of the laws implementing this provision (Article 51 paragraph 1 of the Constitution).

It should be noted that the special law as stated in the second sentence of Article 37 paragraph 4 of the Constitution was never adopted. The only law regulating strikes is the Act No. 2/1991 Coll. on collective bargaining, as amended (Articles 16-26).

A strike that is usually implemented and also known to the public is a strike declared and ongoing in connection with the conclusion of a collective agreement. The conditions for its implementation are regulated by Act No. 2/1991 Coll. on collective bargaining, as amended (Articles 16-26). So it comes into consideration a strike on the basis of the Constitution and on the basis of Act No. 2/1991 Coll.

The most famous and practically the only judgment in the matter of strikes is the judgment of the Supreme Court of the Slovak Republic No. 1 Co 10/98, in which it was stated that the absence of a law regulating the right to strike according to the Constitution cannot lead to the questioning of the constitutional right to strike and the right to exercise it. This right can only be limited, as in Article 37 paragraph 4 of the Constitution or according to Article 54 of the Constitution (*see* below). According to this judgment of the Supreme Court – 'In the legal order of the Slovak Republic, there is no law that would the right to strike limited or prohibited, with the exception of Act No. 2/1991 Coll. on collective bargaining, It does not follow from any legal regulation and it cannot be inferred from the interpretation of Article 37 paragraph 4 of the Constitution of the Slovak Republic, that any strikes other than those regulated by the implementing regulation (Act No. 2/1991 Coll.) are prohibited.'

According to the Supreme Court of the Slovak Republic, Article 51 of the Constitution of the Slovak Republic only assumes that a special law will be adopted; it does not exclude the application of the right to strike without its existence. The permission in this case is not expressed by an explicit wording but is based on the possibility (retention) of the realization of the subjective right without specifying a specific method of realization. The Supreme Court further points out that the consequence of the absence of a special legal framework is, at most, the fact that strikers do not have the opportunity to enjoy the benefits and protection that, unlike the Constitution of the Slovak Republic, provides them with the Act on Collective Bargaining.

So, in the current Slovak legal framework, the realization of the right to strike according to the Constitution of the Slovak Republic is not exclusively linked to the existence of a trade union but is granted to every natural person - citizen. The decision to end participation and the strike itself carried out on the basis of the Constitution of the Slovak Republic belongs exclusively to the initiators of the strike, i.e., to persons who used and in practice implemented their right to strike. In this case, the strike is declared by the so-called strike committee, which, however, cannot be unequivocally identified with a trade union organization. In this case, the strike committee is the body that not only announces the strike but also organizes its course.

So it comes into consideration a strike on the basis of the Constitution and on the basis of Act No. 2/1991 Coll. Currently, there is no closer legal regulation of the conditions for the implementation of a strike according to the Constitution, if it is not a case of a strike in connection with the conclusion of a collective agreement.

In our opinion, in the case of assessing the legality of such a strike, the constitutional principle 'what is not prohibited is permitted' would probably be applied. According to Article 2 paragraph 3 of the Constitution of the Slovak Republic, 'everyone can do what is not prohibited by law and no one can be forced to do something that is not required by law'. This rule should also be applied when assessing the right to strike, which will not be implemented on the basis of Act No. 2/1991 Coll. on collective bargaining.

The legal order in the Slovak Republic thus recognizes two types of legal basis for the right to strike - Article 37 paragraph 4 of the Constitution of the Slovak Republic and Article 16 of Act No. 2/1991 Coll. on collective bargaining. The Constitution of the Slovak Republic does not contain a definition of the right to strike and does not specify the range of authorized subjects. Article 16 paragraph 2 of the Act No. 2/1991 Coll. on collective bargaining subsumes under the concept of a strike 'partial or complete interruption of work by employees', which foreshadows not only its content definition but also the range of entities authorized to use it.

Considering the above, three types of strikes come into consideration:

- a strike related to a dispute over the conclusion of a collective agreement;
- solidarity strike (in Act No. 2/1991 Coll. on collective bargaining);
- constitutional strike or 'wild strike'.

In addition to the right to strike, the constitution also mentions the possibility of restricting the activities of unions, for example, in a situation where measures are necessary to protect state security, public order, or the rights and freedoms of others (see below).

1.2 Main Features of the Regulation

The right to strike is regulated in:

- the Constitution of the Slovak Republic (Act No. 460/1992 Collection of Laws - 'Coll.');
- the Constitutional Act No. 23/1991 Coll., which introduces the Charter of Fundamental Rights and Freedoms as a constitutional Act of the Federal Assembly of the Czech and Slovak Federative Republic (still valid) and Constitutional Act No. 227/2002 Coll. on the security of the state in time of war, state of war, exceptional state and state of emergency;
- the Act No. 2/1991 Coll. on collective bargaining, as amended;
- the Labour Code (Act No. 311/2001 Coll., as amended).

1.2.1 The Constitution of the Slovak Republic (Act No. 460/1992 Coll.)

According to Article 37 paragraph 4 of the Constitution of the Slovak Republic, 'The right to strike shall be guaranteed. A law shall lay down the terms thereof. Judges, prosecutors, members of the armed forces and armed corps, and members and employees of Fire and Rescue Squads shall not have this right.' As already mentioned, claiming the right to strike (Article 37 paragraph 4) is possible only within the limits of the laws implementing this provision (Article 51 paragraph 1 of the Constitution).

According to Article 54 of the Constitution, the law may restrict the right to strike to employees of the state administration and territorial self-government in the functions it determines. The law may limit the right to strike for persons in occupations that are immediately necessary for the protection of life and health.

The Constitution of the Slovak Republic does not contain a definition of the right to strike and does not specify the range of authorized subjects. Article 16 paragraph 2 of the Act No. 2/1991 Coll. on collective bargaining subsumes under the concept of a strike 'partial or complete interruption of work by employees', which foreshadows not only its content definition but also the range of entities authorized to use it.

1.2.2 Constitutional Act No. 23/1991 Coll.

Constitutional Act No. 23/1991 Coll. which introduces the Charter of Fundamental Rights and Freedoms as a constitutional Act of the Federal Assembly of the Czech and Slovak Federative Republic (still valid) and Constitutional Act No. 227/2002 Coll. on the security of the state in time of war, state of war, exceptional state and state of emergency.

In connection with the right to strike, also these two constitutional acts should be mentioned.

1.2.2.1 Constitutional Act No. 23/1991 Coll.

The right to strike is also regulated in Constitutional Act No. 23/1991 Coll., which introduces the Charter of Fundamental Rights and Freedoms as a constitutional Act of the Federal Assembly of the Czech and Slovak Federative Republic.

According to Article 27 paragraph 4 of the Charter of Fundamental Rights and Freedoms, the right to strike is guaranteed under the conditions established by law; this right does not belong to judges, prosecutors, members of the armed forces and members of the security forces.

1.2.2.2 Constitutional Act No. 227/2002 Coll.

Constitutional Act No. 227/2002 Coll. on the security of the state in time of war, state of war, exceptional state and state of emergency regulates cases where the right to strike may be restricted or prohibited (*see* below).

1.3 The Act No. 2/1991 Coll. on Collective Bargaining, as Amended

The legal order in the Slovak Republic thus recognizes two types of legal basis for the right to strike – Article 37 paragraph 4 of the Constitution of the Slovak Republic and Article 16 of the Act No. 2/1991 Coll. on collective bargaining. The Constitution of the Slovak Republic does not contain a definition of the right to strike and does not specify the range of authorized subjects. Article 16 paragraph 2 of the Act No. 2/1991 Coll. on collective bargaining subsumes under the concept of a strike 'partial or complete interruption of work by employees', which foreshadows not only its content definition but also the range of entities authorized to use it.

So, the only law regulating strikes is Act No. 2/1991 Coll. on collective bargaining, as amended (Articles 16-26). Although the law grants the employee the right to strike, it does not belong to him to declare or organize it; on the contrary, organizing and declaring a strike belongs exclusively to the trade union body/union organization. According to Article 230 paragraph 1 of the Labour Code, a trade union is a civil association according to a special regulation (Act No. 83/1990 Coll. on the association of citizens, as amended).

According to Article 16 paragraph 1 of the Act, if a collective agreement is not concluded even after proceedings before a mediator and the parties to the contract do not request an arbitrator to resolve the dispute, a strike may be declared as a last resort in a dispute over the conclusion of a collective agreement. A strike shall be defined as a partial or complete interruption of work by the employees (Article 16 paragraph 2).

The Act also allows a solidarity strike to be declared. A solidarity strike shall be defined as a strike in support of requirements of employees on strike in a dispute on conclusion of another collective agreement (Article 16 paragraph 3).

An employee who agreed to the strike is considered a participant in the strike for the entire duration of the strike; an employee who joined the strike is considered a participant from the day of joining the strike (Article 16 paragraph 4).

There are two types of collective agreements. A strike in a dispute on the conclusion of a company collective agreement is declared and the relevant trade union body decides on its initiation if the majority of the employer's employees participating in the vote on the strike, who are to be affected by this collective agreement, agree to it, provided that at least a majority of the employees participate in the vote employees calculated from all employees (Article 17 paragraph 1).

A strike in a dispute on the conclusion of a collective agreement of a higher degree is declared by the relevant higher union body. The relevant trade union body decides on the initiation of a strike if a majority of the employer's employees participating in the vote on the strike, who are to be covered by the higher-degree collective agreement, agree with it, provided that at least a majority of the employees counted from all employees participate in the vote (Article 17 paragraph 2).

The relevant trade union body shall elaborate records of the results of the vote (Article 17 paragraph 3) and collect and store documentation on the results of the strike vote for a period of three years (Article 17 paragraph 4). Details on the preparation and process of strike vote may be regulated in a strike order by the respective trade union body. A strike order may not be in contradiction with this Act and international treaties on economic rights and social rights binding for the Slovak Republic (Article 17 paragraph 5).

There are also some employees excluded from voting. According to Article 17 paragraph 6 of the Act, employees stated in Article 20 paragraph 1 letters h), i) and k) (*see* below) and employees performing works for the employer on the basis of agreements on works performed outside employment relationship shall not be included in the total number of employees according to Article 17 paragraphs 1 and 2 and shall not participate in voting on a strike.

It should also be noted that the provisions of the cited paragraphs 1 to 6 shall also be applied appropriately when declaring and starting a solidarity strike (Article 17 paragraph 7).

The Act also regulates a number of obligations of the trade union body, which it must fulfil towards the employer. According to Article 17 paragraph 8, the relevant trade union body shall notify the employer in writing at least three working days before the start of the strike:

(a) the day of the start of the strike;
(b) reasons and objectives of the strike;
(c) a list of names of representatives of the relevant trade union body who are authorized to represent the participants in the strike.

The relevant trade union body notifies an employer in writing about the changes in the list pursuant to letter c).

The relevant trade union body shall provide the employer in writing at least two working days before the start of the strike with information related to the strike that is known to it and which will help the employer to establish work schedules to ensure necessary activities and necessary services during the strike; essential activities and essential services are those activities and services, the interruption or cessation of which endangers the life and health of employees or other persons and causes damage to those machines, equipment and devices whose nature and purpose do not allow their operation to be interrupted or stopped during strike (Article 17 paragraph 9).

Naturally, the law also protects employees in connection with a strike. According to Article 18 paragraph 1 of the Act, an employee may not be prevented from participating in a strike or forced to participate in a strike. Representatives of the relevant trade union body, who are authorized to represent participants in the strike, must allow adequate and safe access to the employer's workplace and must not prevent employees who want to work from accessing and leaving this workplace or threaten them with any harm; they can only negotiate with them about the interruption of work (Article 18 paragraph 2).

According to Article 19 paragraph 1 of the Act, the relevant trade union body, which decided to start a strike, is obliged to provide the employer with the necessary cooperation for the entire duration of the strike in ensuring the protection of equipment against damage, loss, destruction or misuse and in ensuring the necessary activity and operation of the equipment, where this is required by their nature or purpose with regard to safety and health protection or the possibility of damage to these devices. Employees who perform work in the provision of the activities listed in paragraph 1 are governed by the employer's instructions (Article 19 paragraph 2).

Of particular importance is the provision of the Act on when a strike is illegal. According to Article 20 paragraph 1 of the Act, a strike is illegal according to this Act:

(a) which was not preceded by proceedings before an intermediary (Articles 11 and 12); this does not apply in the case of a solidarity strike (Article 16 paragraph 3);
(b) which was declared or continues after the initiation of proceedings before an arbitrator (Articles 13 and 14) or after the conclusion of a collective agreement;
(c) which has not been declared or has not started under the conditions established in Article 17;
(d) announced or initiated for reasons other than those listed in Article 16;
(e) solidarity, as long as the employer of the participants of this strike, especially with regard to economic continuity, cannot influence the course or outcome

of the strike of the employees, in support of whose demands the solidarity strike is declared;

(f) in the case of state military alert and at the time of extraordinary measures (Articles 2 to 5 of Constitutional Act No. 227/2002 Coll. on security of the state in time of war, state of war, exceptional state and state of emergency, as amended);

(g) employees of medical facilities or social service facilities, if their participation in the strike would endanger the life or health of citizens;

(h) employees operating nuclear power plant equipment, equipment with fissile material, and oil or gas pipeline equipment;

(i) judges, prosecutors, members of the armed forces and armed forces, members and employees of fire brigades and rescue teams and employees in the management and provision of air traffic;

(j) employees providing telecommunications operations and employees servicing and operating public water supply systems, if their participation in the strike would endanger the lives or health of citizens;

(k) employees who work in areas affected by natural disasters, in which special measures have been declared by the relevant state authorities.

According to this Act, a strike by civil servants appointed as supervisors and civil servants who perform official duties directly to protect life and health is also illegal, if their participation in the strike would endanger the life or health of the population (Article 20 paragraph 2).

The employer, employers' organizations, or the prosecutor may submit a proposal to determine the illegality of the strike to the court in whose district the relevant trade union body against which this proposal is directed is based; the proposal does not have a suspensive effect. The court proceeds to make a decision according to the provisions of the Code of Civil Procedure governing proceedings in the first instance (Act No. 160/2015 Coll. Civil dispute procedure, as amended).

The Act also specifically regulates labour-law claims. During the period of participation in the strike, the participant in the strike is not entitled to wages or compensation (Article 22 paragraph 1). Participation in a strike before the legality of the court's decision on the illegality of the strike is considered an excused absence from work (Article 22 paragraph 2). Participation in a strike after the legality of a court's decision on the illegality of a strike is considered an unexcused absence from work (Article 22 paragraph 3).

According to Article 22 paragraph 4 of the Act, the employer will allow employees who are not participants in the strike to perform their work. If, as a result of a strike, these employees cannot perform work or perform activities according to Article 19 (see above), special regulations apply to their wage claims. These separate regulations are Article 54 of the Labour Code, regulating the agreement on the change of the employment contract and Article 142 of the Labour Code, according to which in this case the employer will provide the employee with wage compensation in the amount of his average earning.

The Act also specifically regulates liability for damage. For damage caused by an event that occurred during the strike, the participant in the strike is liable to the employer or the employer to the participant in the strike according to the Civil Code (Articles 420 et seq. of the Civil Code – Act No. 40/1964 Coll.). However, if it is damage that occurred during the provision of activities according to Article 19, they are responsible according to the Labour Code (Articles 177-219).

The participant in strike shall not be liable to the employer and the employer shall not be liable to the participant in strike for damage caused exclusively by an interruption of work due to strike (Article 23 paragraph 2).

According to Article 23 paragraph 3 of the Act, the trade union organization whose body decided to start a strike is liable according to special regulations (Articles 373 et seq. of the Commercial Code – Act No. 513/1991 Coll.) to the employer for the damage that occurred due to the failure to provide the necessary cooperation according to Article 19 paragraph 1 (see above).

If the court decided that the strike is illegal, the trade union organization whose body declared the strike is liable, according to special regulations (Articles 373 et seq. of the Commercial Code. Articles 420 et seq. of the Civil Code), to the employer for the damage caused to him by such a strike (Article 23 paragraph 4).

During the strike, the employer may not hire other citizens to replace the participants in the strike (Article 25).

The strike is ended if the trade union body that declared the strike or decided to start it decided to do so. The competent trade union body must notify the employer in writing of the termination of the strike without undue delay (Article 26).

Last but not least, we must also state that according to Article 32 paragraph 2 of the Act, an employee for the purposes of this Act is also a civil servant who performs civil service in a civil servant relationship.

1.4 The Labour Code (Act No. 311/2001 Coll., as Amended)

The Labour Code primarily contains these two provisions regulating the connection with the right to strike.

According to the fundamental principle No. 10 of the Labour Code, employees and employers have the right to collective bargaining; in case of conflict of their interests, employees have the right to strike and employers have the right to lock out.

According Article 141 paragraph 8 of the Labour Code, the employer is obliged to justify the employee's absence from work during his participation in the strike in connection with the exercise of his economic and social rights; neither the wage nor the wage compensation belongs to the employee. Participation in a strike after the legality of a court decision on the illegality of a strike is considered an employee's unjustified absence from work.

In the context of the current legal situation, it can be stated that the Labour Code in the Article 141 paragraph 8 assumes the assessment of the presence of a natural person (employee) on strike, regardless of the legal basis for its application (the Constitution of the Slovak Republic or the Act on Collective Bargaining), as an obstacle to work on the part of the employee, subject to the fulfilment of the condition consisting in the objective reason for exercising the right to strike due to the protection of economic and social interests of natural persons (employees). The supporting legal argument for such a differentiation between constitutional and labour-law strike is mainly the cited decision of the Supreme Court of the Slovak Republic (No. 1 Co 10/98).

We can also mention the provision of Article 229 paragraph 6, according to which employees have the right to collective bargaining only through the relevant trade union body. According to Article 231 paragraph 4, the procedure for concluding collective agreements is established by a special regulation.

2 PERMITTED RESTRICTIONS

2.1 Certain Categories of Public Servants

As already mentioned above, according to Article 37 paragraph 4 of the Constitution, 'The right to strike shall be guaranteed. A law shall lay down the terms thereof. Judges, prosecutors, members of the armed forces and armed corps, and members and employees of Fire and Rescue Squads shall not have this right.' Claiming the right to strike (Article 37 paragraph 4) is possible only within the limits of the laws implementing this provision (Article 51 paragraph 1 of the Constitution).

According to Article 54 of the Constitution, the law may restrict the right to strike to employees of the state administration and territorial self-government in the functions it determines. The law may limit the right to strike for persons in occupations that are immediately necessary for the protection of life and health.

The Labour Code regulates employment relations in the private sphere and in the public service. Employment relations in the public service are currently regulated by Act No. 552/2003 Coll. on the performance of work in the public interest.

As regards the employees in the civil service, legislation is differentiated. Employment relations in civil service is currently regulated by six Acts:

- the Act No. 73/1998 Coll. on civil service of members of the Police Force, of the Slovak Intelligence Service, of the Prison Wardens and Judiciary Guards Corps of the Slovak Republic and of the Railway Police, as amended;
- the Act No. 154/2001 Coll. on prosecutors and legal trainees of the prosecution, as amended;
- the Act No. 315/2001 Coll. on the Fire Fighting and Rescuing Corps, as amended;
- the Act No. 281/2015 Coll. on civil service of professional soldiers, as amended;
- the Act No. 35/2019 Coll. on financial administration and on amendments to certain acts, as amended;
- the Act No. 55/2017 Coll. on civil service and on amendments to certain acts, as amended.

Some of these employees are prohibited from striking by the above-mentioned provisions of the Constitution of the Slovak Republic:

(a) As regards the civil service and public service, it is necessary to mention above all two Acts:
   (i) Act No. 55/2017 Coll. on Civil Service, as amended.
   (ii) Act No. 552/2003 Coll. on the performance of work in the public interest, as amended.

The Act No. 55/2017 Coll. he Civil Service regulates civil service relations in connection with the performance of civil service by civil servants (Article 1 paragraph 1).

According to Article 1 paragraph 7, this Act does not apply to civil service of:

- members of the Police Force;
- members of the Slovak Intelligence Service;
- members of the National Security Office;
- members of the Corps of Prison and Judicial Guards;
- members of the financial administration;
- professional soldiers;
- members of the Fire Fighting and Rescuing Corps;
- members of the Mountain Rescue Service.

The Act No. 55/2017 Coll. on Civil Service does not regulate strike. According to Article 1 paragraph 3 of this Act, the Labour Code applies to civil service relations, if this Act provides for it.

According to Article 171 paragraph 1 of this Act (Applicability of the Labour Code), the provisions of Article 141 of the Labour Code, among others, shall be applied appropriately to civil servant relations. So also the cited provision of Article 141 paragraph 8 of the Labour Code.

Also, the Act No. 552/2003 Coll. on the performance of work in the public interest, as amended, does not regulate strike. According to Article 1 paragraph 4 of this Act, the Labour Code applies to labour-law relations of employees when performing work in the public interest, if this Act or special regulation does not stipulate otherwise. This Act also does not contain any provisions on strike.

In both cases, it is possible to negotiate the conclusion of a collective agreement and, if there is disagreement, strike. According to Article 4 paragraph 3 of the Act No. 55/2017 Coll. on Civil Service, discrimination against a civil servant is prohibited in civil service relations, among other things, also because of membership in a trade union or activity in a trade union.

Employees covered by the Act No. 55/2017 Coll. on Civil Service and the Act No. 552/2003 Coll. on the performance of work in the public interest, which have the right to organize in accordance with Act

No. 83/1990 Coll. on the association of citizens, can negotiate collectively in accordance with Act No. 2/1991 Coll. on collective bargaining.

(b) According to Article 229 of the Act No. 73/1998 Coll. on civil service of members of the Police Force, of the Slovak Intelligence Service, of the Prison Wardens and Judiciary Guards Corps of the Slovak Republic and of the Railway Police, collective bargaining is carried out in accordance with the Act No. 2/1991 Coll. on Collective Bargaining.

(c) According to Article 34 paragraph 5 of Act No. 385/2000 Coll. on judges and associate judges, judges have the right to associate in accordance with Act No. 83/1990 Coll. on the association of citizens. A judge may hold a position in the status organization of judges and in a trade union (Article 23 paragraph 3 of the Act No. 385/2000 Coll.). A judge does not have the right to strike and may not act in such a way as to impede the activity of the judiciary in any way (Article 30 paragraph 8 of the Act. No. 385/2000 Coll.).

(d) According to Article 252 paragraph 2 of Act No. 154/2001 Coll. on prosecutors and legal trainees of the prosecution, as amended, the Labour Code and the Collective Bargaining Act apply to the activities of trade union bodies and to the collective bargaining of prosecutors and legal assistants of the prosecutor's office.

(e) Collective bargaining in the state service and collective agreements are also regulated by Act No. 315/2001 Coll. on the Fire Fighting and Rescuing Corps (Articles 189-191). Negotiations are carried out in accordance with Act No. 2/1991 Coll. on collective bargaining.

(f) According to Article 277 paragraph 1 of Act No. 35/2019 Coll. on financial administration and on amendments to certain acts in order to ensure the legitimate interests and needs of members of the financial administration, to improve the conditions of service, health, social and cultural conditions, including the conditions for the use of free time, the relevant union bodies and the service office conclude collective agreements on behalf of the members of the financial administration. Negotiations are carried out in accordance with Act No. 2/1991 Coll. on collective bargaining.

We remind the already quoted Article 37 paragraph 4 of the Constitution of the Slovak Republic, according to which judges, prosecutors, members of the armed forces and armed corps, and members and employees of Fire and Rescue Squads shall not have the right to strike.

Public sector teachers are not included in the category of public servants 'exercising authority in the name of the State' (see, for example, the Act No. 131/2002 Coll. on Higher Education, as amended.)

2.2 Essential Services in the Strict Sense of the Term

No act defines the term Essential Services in the Strict Sense of the Term. Particularly important in this context is the provision of Act No. 2/1991 Coll. on collective bargaining when a strike is illegal. According to Article 20 paragraph 1 of the Act, illegal is a strike:

(a) which was not preceded by proceedings before an intermediary (Articles 11 and 12); this does not apply in the case of a solidarity strike (Article 16 paragraph 3);
(b) which was declared or continues after the initiation of proceedings before an arbitrator (Articles 13 and 14) or after the conclusion of a collective agreement;
(c) which has not been declared or has not started under the conditions established in Article 17;
(d) announced or initiated for reasons other than those listed in Article 16;
(e) solidarity, as long as the employer of the participants of this strike, especially with regard to economic continuity, cannot influence the course or outcome of the strike of the employees, in support of whose demands the solidarity strike is declared;
(f) in the case of state military alert and at the time of extraordinary measures (Articles 2 to 5 of Constitutional Act No. 227/2002 Coll. on the security of the state in time of war, state of war, exceptional state and state of emergency, as amended);
(g) employees of medical facilities or social service facilities, if their participation in the strike would endanger the life or health of citizens;
(h) employees operating nuclear power plant equipment, equipment with fissile material, and oil or gas pipeline equipment;
(i) judges, prosecutors, members of the armed forces and armed forces, members and employees of fire brigades and rescue teams and employees in the management and provision of air traffic;
(j) employees providing telecommunications operations and employees servicing and operating public water supply systems, if their participation in the strike would endanger the lives or health of citizens;
(k) employees who work in areas affected by natural disasters, in which special measures have been declared by the relevant state authorities.

In addition to the reasons defined in Article 20 paragraph 1 of the Act, illegal under this Act is also the strike of civil servants appointed as supervisors and civil servants who fulfil official tasks immediately to protect life and health, if their participation in the strike would endanger the life or health of the population Article 20 paragraph 2 Act No. 2/1991 Coll. on collective bargaining).

According to already mentioned Article 54 of the Constitution, the law may restrict the right to strike to employees of the state administration and territorial self-government in the functions it determines. The law may limit the right to strike for persons in occupations that are immediately necessary for the protection of life and health.

2.3 Situations of Acute National or Local Crisis

According to Article 37 paragraph 3 of the Constitution of the Slovak Republic, the activities of trade unions and forming and activities of other associations aimed to protect economic and social interests may be restricted by a law only if it is regarding a measure necessary in a democratic society for the protection of the national security, public order, or for the protection of the rights and freedoms of others.

In this context is very important the Constitutional Act No. 227/2002 Coll. on the security of the state in time of war, state of war, exceptional state and state of emergency.

2.3.1 War

According to Article 2 paragraph 3 of the Act No. 227/2002 Coll., in time of war, basic rights and freedoms may be restricted to the necessary extent and for the necessary time, depending on the course of events, and obligations may be imposed on the entire territory of the Slovak Republic or a part of it, at most to the following extent:

- letter k) prohibit the application of the right to petition and the right to strike;
- letter m) restrict the right to freely associate and limit or prohibit the activity of societies and other civil associations, political parties and political movements and trade unions.

2.3.2 State of War

According to Article 3 paragraph 3 of the Act, in time of state of war, it is possible to limit basic rights and freedoms to the necessary extent and for the necessary time and to impose obligations depending on the course of events on the entire territory of the Slovak Republic or a part of it, and at most to the following extent:

- letter k) prohibit the exercise of the right to strike;
- letter m) restrict the right to freely associate and restrict the activity of societies and other civil associations;
- letter r) limit the right to collective bargaining, to remuneration for work performed, to paid vacation for recovery and to adequate rest after work and allow exceeding the maximum permissible length of working time.

2.3.3 Exceptional State

According to Article 4 paragraph 3 of the Act, exceptional state cannot be declared to suppress a strike decided by the *relevant* trade union body. According to paragraph 4, during exceptional state, basic rights and freedoms may be restricted to the necessary extent and for the necessary time depending on the severity of the threat, and obligations may be imposed on the affected or immediately threatened territory, which may also be the entire territory of the Slovak Republic, at most to the following extent:

- letter l) prohibit the exercise of the right to strike.

2.3.4 *State of Emergency*

According to Article 5 paragraph 3 of the Act, during a state of emergency, except for a state of emergency declared due to a threat to the life and health of persons in causal connection with the emergence of a pandemic, it is possible to limit basic rights and freedoms to the necessary extent and for the necessary time, depending on the severity of the threat, and impose obligations on the affected or immediately threatened territory, which can also be the entire territory of the Slovak Republic, and at most to the following extent:

- letter k) prohibit the exercise of the right to strike.

As we have already stated, according to Article 20 paragraph 1, letters g), j), k) of the Act No. 2/1991 Coll. on collective bargaining illegal is a strike of:

(g) employees of medical facilities or social service facilities, if their participation in the strike would endanger the life or health of citizens;
(h) employees operating nuclear power plant equipment, equipment with fissile material, and oil or gas pipeline equipment;
(j) employees providing telecommunications operations and employees servicing and operating public water supply systems, if their participation in the strike would endanger the lives or health of citizens;
(k) employees who work in areas affected by natural disasters, in which special measures have been declared by the relevant state authorities.

3 COMPENSATORY GUARANTEES FOR WORKERS DEPRIVED OF THE RIGHT TO STRIKE

Compensatory guarantees for workers deprived of the right to strike are not expressly regulated by law. Perhaps we can see them in the dispute proceedings regulated in the Labour Code and in Act No. 2/1991 Coll. on collective bargaining.

According to the fundamental principle No. 9 of the Labour Code, employees and employers who sustain damage due to breach of obligations arising out of labour-law relations may exercise their rights in court. Employers may neither disadvantage nor damage employees for reason of employees exercising their rights arising out of labour-law relations.

Disputes between an employee and employer over claims deriving from labour-law relations shall be heard and decided by courts (Article 14 of the Labour Code).

According to Article 10 of the Act No. 2/1991 Coll. on collective bargaining, collective disputes, as defined by this Act, are disputes regarding conclusion of the collective agreement and disputes regarding fulfilment of obligations of the collective agreement, not giving rise to claims to individual employees.

The contractual parties may agree on an intermediary to resolve the collective dispute in accordance with Article 10. Proceedings before an intermediary shall begin on the day of receipt of the request for resolving dispute by an intermediary (Article 11 paragraph 1 of the Act). When the contractual parties fail to agree on an intermediary, the intermediary shall, by request of any of the contractual parties, be appointed by the Ministry of Labour, Social Affairs and the Family of the Slovak Republic from the list of intermediaries maintained by the Ministry. Proceedings before an intermediary began upon delivery of the decision appointing an intermediary. Such request may, in a dispute regarding the conclusion of a collective agreement, not be submitted before lapse of at least 60 days from submission of the written proposal to conclude the agreement (Article 11 paragraph 2 of the Act). The contracting parties and intermediary are obliged to provide mutual cooperation (Article 11 paragraph 4 of the Act).

If proceedings before an intermediary have failed, the contractual parties may agree to request an arbitrator to make a decision in the dispute. The proceedings before the arbitrator shall be deemed commenced on the date of acceptance of the request by the arbitrator. The arbitrator shall draw up a protocol of acceptance with the contractual parties of their request to resolve the dispute (Article 13 paragraph 1 of the Act). If the contractual parties have failed to agree according to paragraph 1 and if the dispute concerning conclusion of the collective agreement arose at a workplace where strike is forbidden, or a dispute concerning fulfilment of obligations arising from the collective agreement is involved, the arbitrator shall be appointed at the request of any of the contractual parties by the Ministry; proceedings before the arbitrator shall be deemed commenced by delivery of the decision to the arbitrator. The Ministry shall not appoint an arbitrator belonging to one of the contractual parties in the dispute (Article 13 paragraph 2 of the Act).

According to Article 13 paragraph 6 of the Act, the agreement shall be considered concluded once the arbitrator's decision has been delivered to the parties in the dispute concerning conclusion of a collective agreement.

An employee may not be prevented from participating in the strike, nor may he/she be forced to participate in it (Article 18 paragraph 1 of the Act). Representatives of the relevant trade union body, who are authorized to represent participants in the strike, must allow adequate and safe access to the employer's workplace and must not prevent employees who want to work from accessing and leaving this workplace or threaten them with any harm; they can only negotiate with them about the interruption of work (Article 18 paragraph 2 of the Act).

According to Article 22 paragraph 4 of the the Act No. 2/1991 Coll. on collective bargaining, employees not participating in the strike shall be enabled by the employer to perform work. The wage claims of employees who are unable, as the consequence of a strike, to perform their work or exercise activities pursuant to Article 19, shall be regulated by separate regulations (these regulations are Article 54 and 142 of the Labour Code).

4 CONCLUSION

It is possible to state that there is currently no closer legal regulation of the conditions for the implementation of a strike according to the Constitution, if it is not a case of a strike in connection with the conclusion of a collective agreement. The legal regulation of the constitutional right to strike is very marginal and refers to the law that is supposed to regulate the details of this strike.

In the Slovak Republic, only minimal attention is devoted to the analysis of the theoretical foundations or the practical implementation of a strike as one of the legal forms of enforcing the economic and social interests of citizens - employees, despite the fact that it is one of the most important and constitutionally guaranteed rights of employees. There are practically no relevant data available on the number and details of even the few strikes that were carried out in the Slovak Republic.

There is no unified opinion on whether, in addition to legally less problematic labour strikes after unsuccessful collective bargaining, other types of strikes should also be regulated by a special law in Slovakia. Such a decision is probably more political than legal. However, the fact that the right is exercised in a narrow scope is not a constitutional problem.

CHAPTER 34

Restrictions on the Right to Strike in Spain

Joaquín García Murcia, Iván Antonio Rodríguez Cardo & Diego Álvarez Alonso

1 GENERAL INFORMATION

1.1 Legal Basis of the Right to Strike

Article 28(2) of the Spanish Constitution of 1978 enshrines 'the right of workers to strike in defence of their interests' and states that 'the law regulating the exercise of this right shall establish the guarantees necessary to ensure the maintenance of essential community services'. This Article is included in the section of the Constitution dedicated to fundamental rights and public freedoms. This means the right to strike is considered a fundamental right in the Spanish legal system.

This is in line with the relevant international conventions that have elevated the right to strike to the category of human right (by itself or as a part of the freedom of association), as the European Convention of Human Rights (Article 11), the European Social Charter (revised) (Article 6), the International Covenant on Economic, Social and Cultural Rights (Article 22) or the Charter of Fundamental Rights of the European Union (Article 28).

It is worth noting that the right to 'adopt collective labour dispute measures' is recognized to employers by Article 37(2) of the Constitution, which is not included in the section dedicated to fundamental rights. Therefore, the guarantees provided for the right to lockout are not comparable to those provided for the right to strike. A lockout is not allowed as a pure labour dispute measure. However, a lockout can only be declared as a defensive action, that is, in response to a strike or other industrial action taken by workers that is unlawful or causes significant harm to the employer.

1.2 Main Features of the Regulation

The Spanish Constitution does not provide further details on the regulation of the right to strike, so the law theoretically enjoys a wide room for manoeuvre. However, the nature of the right to strike as a fundamental right significantly reduces the scope of action for the law because a fundamental right cannot be restricted without strong reasons. The law regulating the exercise of the right to strike is Royal Decree-Law 17/1977, 4 March 1977, which was adopted more than a year before the Constitution was passed. Therefore, the Constitutional Court had to assess its conformity with that Supreme Law. A very relevant ruling (11/1981) of 8 April 1981 clarified how that law should be interpreted to keep it in conformity with the Constitution. As the Parliament has not adopted a new Law, that ancient Royal Decree-Law 17/1977 could be considered the Strike Law. At all events, case law, both of the Constitutional Court and the Supreme Court, plays a significant role. The Constitution, the Strike Law, and the case law comprise the legal framework of the right to strike nowadays.[1]

2 PERMITTED RESTRICTIONS

2.1 General Remarks

As a preliminary observation, the right to strike is not intended to cause the employer excessive damage, as the principle of proportionality is involved. The strikers lose their wages (and the contributions to Social Security) and the employer loses the production due to the stoppage, but there are certain rules that act as a counterbalance.

The right to strike is a fundamental right, so the permitted restrictions are very few (it is an inalienable right). Apart from the general obligation to negotiate during the strike to end the protest as quickly as possible (the strikers are required to appoint a strike committee for that purpose), there are restrictions based on the personal scope of the right to strike, as well as others based on the particular type of action chosen by the workers to protest.

Indeed, the right to strike does not cover all forms of industrial action, as evidenced by the distinction in the Strike Law between 'illegal' strikes and 'abusive' strikes. Illegal strikes are not allowed due to their aims. They are always unlawful, and all the strikers could be subjected to penalties for their involvement. In contrast, abusive strikes are not unlawful in themselves. They have a valid motive, but the way the action is organized is intended to cause additional harm to the employer. Thus,

1. For more detailed information, vid. Argüelles Blanco, A.R., *Derecho de huelga y determinación de los servicios mínimos* (Tirant lo Blanch 2022), Baylos Grau, A., *Servicios esenciales, servicios mínimos y derecho de huelga* (Bomarzo 2018); García Murcia, J., et al., *Huelga y conflicto colectivo de trabajo en la jurisprudencia del Tribunal Supremo* (KRK 2021); García Murcia, J., *Huelga en servicios esenciales*, Revista Española de Derecho del Trabajo, No. 39 (1989); García Murcia, J., 'El derecho de huelga en España: nuevas piezas para un sistema inacabado', in Jaime Cabeza Pereiro & Jesús Martínez Girón (coord.), *El conflicto colectivo y la huelga* (Laborum 2009); Moreno Vida, M.N., *La huelga en servicios esenciales* (Aranzadi 2007); Vivero Serrano, J.B., *La huelga en los servicios esenciales* (Lex Nova 2002).

there is a presumption that abusive strikes are unlawful, because they might cause a disproportionate damage in an unjustified manner, but the unions can rebut that presumption and prove that there is a legitimate reason to organize the action in such a way. If they successfully prove that, the strike is deemed lawful.

Article 11 of the Strike Law contains the list of illegal strikes. First, political strikes are not allowed, but this limitation is not very strict because the Constitutional Court reminded that the Spanish Constitution does not constrain the right to strike to the circumstances attached to the employment contract. This is a right with a wider scope that allows workers to demand not only improved working conditions but also improved living conditions, so the strike could be directed not only against the employer but also against the government or the parliament, if the claims somehow connect with the interests of the working class.[2]

Second, strikes are not allowed if their only aim is to show solidarity or support for some organizations or people. The goal of a strike has to be somehow related, even indirectly, to the interests of the workers. Third, a strike is also forbidden during the term of a collective agreement if its purpose consists in the amendment of that agreement which is currently in force. Finally, strikes are also illegal when they do not respect the statutory requirements (advance notice, entitlement for that call, etc.). All the same, a lawful strike does not become illegal due to the behaviour of the strikers.

Concerning abusive strikes, Article 7(2) of the Strike Law requires a careful analysis when the strikers organize the protests in a certain way. 'Rotating' strikes or strikes affecting 'strategic workers' are examples of modalities of collective action which might be considered abusive. In both cases, the call for a strike does not affect all the workers potentially affected by the conflict simultaneously but just a part of them. These modalities of strike might seek to significantly decrease the activity, even a total stoppage, with the involvement of not all the concerned workers at the same time, but only some reduced groups of strikers in key positions or moments, consequently forcing the employer to pay the wage of the non-strikers even if there is no production, and so causing a damage equivalent to that of the strike of all workers on the basis of a minor strike involvement and effort by the employees. That does not mean that these kinds of strikes are necessarily not allowed. They are presumed to be abusive, but they are not always unlawful. They are lawful if the unions provide a valid justification for such way of collective action. For example, the so-called 'strategic' or 'neuralgic' strikes, where there is a call for strike involving only some workers in key positions capable of totally stopping or significantly hampering production by themselves would be presumed abusive, but this presumption is rebuttable. Indeed, this kind of strike would be deemed unlawful just when the conflict affects all the workers of the company or sector, but only those employees in strategic positions become strikers to increase the damage with an artificially reduced number of striking workers. Conversely, the strike would be a lawful if the claims and the scope of the conflict were adequately corresponding to the interests of the concrete group of actually striking workers. It is to be outlined that case law has interpreted the notion of 'abusive strike'

2. Constitutional Court 11/1981, 8 April 1981.

very strictly, in favour of a wider understanding of the modalities and possibilities of exercising the right to strike, and narrowing the room for their consideration as unlawful.[3]

Therefore, the legal framework of the right to strike has a twin objective. On one side, it guarantees the exercise of the right to strike. On the other, it seeks to reconcile the rights and interests of both parties and to prevent excessive or disproportionate damage to the undertaking. This is the goal of the security and maintenance services, which are not related to public services or essential services, and they are not considered minimum services.

According to Article 6(7) of the Strike Law, some activity must remain operational during a strike for the common interests of workers and employers. First, the tasks necessary for the safety of persons and goods. Second, the activity indispensable for the maintenance of premises, machinery, installations, raw materials, and other care to ensure the resumption of the activity of the undertaking after the strike. The employer and the strike committee have to collaborate in the designation of the workers who will carry out these tasks. These security and maintenance services may be required both in public and private undertakings and they are only justified if there is a real risk of serious damage that the undertaking would otherwise suffer. They must not be confused with essential or minimum services, even if they are sometimes connected. For example, there is a particular provision regulating the activity of security guards when they perform their duties in entities that provide essential services, even if they have not been directly hired by those entities and they are not public employees.[4]

2.2 Workers under an Employment Contract

Article 28(2) of the Spanish Constitution grants the right to strike to the 'workers' without further clarification. According to a well-established case law (e.g., the aforementioned ruling of the Constitutional Court of 8 April 1981), that word does not include all the people that perform a professional or commercial activity but only the workers under an employment contract. Therefore, self-employed workers do not enjoy the right to strike. They can protest and even stop the activity, but their claims have to be channelled through different legal paths.

Within the strict category of 'workers', this right has even been recognized for foreigners whose status is irregular,[5] so the personal scope of the right to strike is wide. However, there are some exclusions:

3. Constitutional Court 11/1981, 8 April 1981.
4. Vid. Royal Decree 524/2002, 14 June 2002, its Art. 2 establishes a list of activities affected, such as nuclear plants, oil refineries, banks, firearms factories or water, gas and electricity supply and distribution services, among others.
5. Article 11(2) of the Law 4/2000, 11 January 2000, interpreted by Constitutional Court ruling 259/2007, 19 December 2007.

- Inmates working in prison: They are workers under a special employment relationship,[6] but they do not enjoy freedom of association nor the right to strike.[7]
- Civilian staff that work in military establishments enjoy the right to strike, but it could be limited for security reasons.[8]

2.3 Certain Categories of Public Servants

Article 28(2) of the Spanish Constitution does not mention civil servants, so there were initial doubts about the precise coverage of the right to strike. Those doubts were soon overcome because the freedom of trade union association, also a fundamental right according to Article 28(1) of the Constitution, includes the right to strike, and public servants are entitled to freedom of association. Besides, the law has specifically recognized the right to strike to public servants. At this moment, Article 15(c) of the Basic Statute of Public Employees provides that all public employees (both civil servants and workers under an employment contract) enjoy the right to strike, but they have the obligation to ensure the operation of essential community services.[9]

However, military personnel are excluded from the exercise of freedom of trade union association and of the right to strike.[10] The different police bodies, both at a state and a regional (and even at a local) level, enjoy freedom of association but the members of National Police are excluded from the exercise of the right to strike.[11] That exclusion is in conformity with Article 11 of the European Convention on Human Rights.[12]

The right to strike of judges has been a matter in dispute for decades. There is no explicit exclusion, but they are excluded from the exercise of freedom of trade union association,[13] which has been used as an indirect evidence. The lack of freedom of trade union association would imply the lack of the right to strike. This was consistent with the consideration of Judiciary as one of the three branches of the State because none of them might stop functioning. However, after consistent protests from judges in 2017 and 2018, the Ministry of Justice did not sanction the judges that refused to work and acted as if the strike had been called for regular public servants. Therefore, judges do not enjoy an explicit legal entitlement to the right to strike, but it has been implicitly recognized.

There are no other exclusions, so fire service personnel or prison staff, for example, may exercise the right to strike, and they have indeed done so in practice.

6. Royal Decree 782/2001, 6 July 2001.
7. Article 38 of the Prisons Act, Organic Law 1/1979, 26 September 1979.
8. First Additional Provision of Royal Decree 2205/1980, 13 June 1980.
9. Royal Decree-Law 5/2015, 30 October 2015.
10. Article 7(2) of the Organic Law 9/2011, 27 July 2011.
11. Article 6(8) of the Organic Law 2/1986, 13 March 1986.
12. ECHR of 21 March 2015.
13. Article 127(1) of the Constitution.

2.4 Essential Services in the Strict Sense of the Term

Apart from the specific cases commented in the previous section, workers employed in any kind of public services and essential services enjoy the right to strike. There is no prohibition, except in the case of law enforcement bodies. However, according to the second paragraph of Article 10 of the Strike Law, the government can take the appropriate measures to ensure the provision of any kind of public services and of the services of recognized and urgent need. Therefore, 'essential services' refer to public services that cannot be stopped for the community's best interest, but there is no proper definition provided by Law.

In fact, the Strike Law does not provide a list of essential services either, but other laws and the case law of both the Constitutional Court and the Supreme Court have identified such services. The Constitutional Court has warned that the law enjoys a narrow margin to qualify public services as essential. The right to strike is a fundamental right and its limitations must be properly justified. Thus, not every public service meets the requirements to be considered 'essential'. This is a stricter concept. Furthermore, a service could be essential even if it is provided by a private entity.

Within these limits, the following have been qualified as essential services:

- Transport (by air,[14] by road,[15] and by rail),[16] including air traffic control[17] and ground services at airports.[18]
- Stevedoring services.[19]
- Public health care services[20] and residential care.[21]
- Water, gas and electricity supply, and distribution services.[22]
- Garbage collection.[23]
- Education (particularly exams).[24]
- Postal service.[25]
- Phone services (emergency calls in any case and the connection between the public network and the networks of the service providers).[26]

14. Law 9/2010, 14 April 2010, and Constitutional Court 51/1986, 24 April 1986 and 43/1990, 15 March 1990.
15. Constitutional Court 123/1990, 2 July 1990.
16. Law 38/2015, 29 September 2015, and Constitutional Court 26/1981, 17 July 1981.
17. Supreme Court of 16 January 2018, STS 78/2018.
18. Constitutional Court 124/2013, 23 May 2013.
19. Constitutional Court 233/1997, 18 December 1997.
20. Constitutional Court 27/1989, 3 February 1989.
21. Constitutional Court 122/1990, 2 July 1990.
22. Constitutional Court 8/1992, 16 January 1992 and 148/1993, 29 April 1993. *See also*, Art. 2 of the Law 54/1997, 27 November 1997, concerning electricity supply and distribution.
23. Constitutional Court 148/1993, 29 April 1993.
24. Supreme Court of 18 January 2021, STS 533/2021.
25. Law 43/2010, 30 December 2010.
26. Royal Decree 530/2002, 14 June 2002.

- Private security in several activities, such as nuclear power plants, petrochemical plants, refineries, and fuel depots; custody, transport and distribution of money and valuable or dangerous objects; public transport; or firearms and explosives factories.[27]
- Maritime safety.[28]
- Transport, storage and distribution of fuels.[29]
- Public service broadcasting and,[30] to some extent (e.g., the news),[31] private broadcasting.[32]

That list is consistent with the definition of essential services that the Constitutional Court provided at first. In its landmark ruling of 1981, the Court qualified as essential services those intended to satisfy constitutional rights (health, freedom of movement, information, public security, etc.), but its doctrine has evolved and a case-by-case analysis is needed nowadays. Furthermore, the Court has affirmed that there are no public services that are essential by themselves, that is, and from an approach based on the right to strike, there are no public services that require a limitation on the right to strike at all events. The restrictions will depend on the particular circumstances, such as the scope of the strike, both personal and territorial, the duration or even the specific dates decided for the work stoppage.

Therefore, strikes are allowed in the essential services. There are no prohibitions but only special rules or restrictions in certain cases. Concerning the special rules, advance notice of the strike must always be given. There is a 5-day advance notice in general, but the strikes affecting undertakings responsible for public services, essential or not, require a 10-day advance notice (Article 4 of the Strike Law).

The restrictions are more significant than the special rules. Article 10 of the Strike Law allows the competent government authority to take the 'appropriate measures' to guarantee essential services during a strike. There is not a list of these 'appropriate measures', so the replacement of the strikers or the temporary militarization of the workers affected would be among the range of valid choices, even if the case law of the Constitutional Court imposes a very strict interpretation on the matter, avoiding excessive restrictions or hampering to the right to strike. The Strike Law explicitly mentions two different tools for dealing with these situations.

The first one refers to the end of the strike. Usually, strikers decide when to terminate the protest. The right to strike is a fundamental one, so the workers cannot be forced to return to work and they are free to decide the length of the strike. However, Article 10 of the Strike Law contains limitations to that freedom. More specifically, the first paragraph of Article 10 allows the government authority, 'taking into account the duration or consequences of the strike, the positions of the parties and the serious damage to the national economy', to require the temporary resumption of the activity

27. Royal Decree 524/2002, 14 June 2002.
28. Royal Decree 508/2002, 10 June 2002.
29. Law 34/1998, 7 October 1998, and Royal Decree 425/1993, 26 March 1993.
30. Article 50 of Law 13/2022, 7 July 2022.
31. Constitutional Court 183/2006, 19 June 2006 and 191/2006, 19 June 2006.
32. Royal Decree 529/2002, and 531/2002, 14 June 2002.

(while the parties continuous to negotiate) or even a compulsory arbitration, putting the strike to an end. This first paragraph does not mention essential services, so these measures have a broader scope of application.

Additionally, the second paragraph of Article 10 of the Strike Law refers to strikes affecting 'any kind of public services' or 'services of recognized and urgent need', equivalent terms to essential services. In those cases, and providing that there are 'particularly serious circumstances', the government authority can take the 'necessary measures to ensure the functioning of the services' and 'may also adopt appropriate intervention measures for such purpose'. Even if compulsory arbitration is not mentioned, the courts deem that the measures contained in the first paragraph of Article 10 are also available when the requisites of the second paragraph are met. Compulsory arbitration could be a 'necessary' and 'appropriate' measure to deal with strikes affecting essential services when there are 'particularly serious circumstances'. In fact, this possibility has often been used in practice for strikes in essential services when the negotiations between the parties were not close to an agreement (petrol stations in 1981, aeroplane pilots in 1984, 2001, 2011, and 2012, the construction sector in 1988, hotel/catering in 1990, cleaning in 1992, 1996, and 2002, or road transportation in 1994 and 2002).

The second restriction for the strikes that impact essential services is the requirement to maintain minimum services. These minimum services are different from the security and maintenance services already mentioned, which are only justified to guarantee that the activity could be restarted after the end of the strike. However, minimum services are intended to guarantee essential services during the strike.

There is no statutory definition of minimum services, but the Supreme Court states that minimum services are those that are 'rationally necessary' for the community.[33] Therefore, the minimum services consist of the fraction of the activity that cannot be interrupted in an essential service during a strike to prevent an irremediable damage to the fundamental rights enshrined by the Constitution. As a result, minimum services were not allowed in a strike called by the unions representing resident trainee doctors because these doctors are instrumental (or supplemental) and the regular medical staff should be enough to provide an adequate service.[34] However, more recently, the Supreme Court has considered that resident trainee doctors may be taken into account in the setting of minimum services when the strike affects all the medical staff because they are also workers under an employment contract.[35] The doctrine is somehow evolving.

The setting of minimum services in each particular case corresponds to the competent government authority, that is, the central government, a regional government or even a local government, depending on the scope of the strike. The employer/undertaking cannot define the minimum services by itself, so a decision of

33. Supreme Court of 12 May 1988, STS 533/2021.
34. Supreme Court of 27 January 2005, STS 533/2021.
35. Supreme Court of 17 December 2021, STS 533/2021.

the competent government authority is required to ensure impartiality.[36] This public authority has to be a governmental body in the strict sense. Therefore, it would not respect the right to strike if a law assigned this task of defining minimum services to the person or the body that directly manages the relevant service, as such decision should be taken at an upper level by the responsible government authority.[37] Anyhow, the workers do not participate directly in defining such a service and the negotiation between the government authority and the strikers to set minimum services is not mandatory, only recommended.[38]

Of course, the government authority should take a restrictive approach to prevent an improper limitation of the right to strike. The Constitutional Court requires proportionality between the protection of the community interest and the limitation of the right to strike,[39] so the setting of the minimum services cannot be done in an abstract and general way (e.g., for an indefinite term) but must be carried out for each specific strike and according to the particular circumstances.[40] Consequently, the minimum services defined for one strike could be inappropriate for a future strike because each strike is different and has its own features.

There are no strict guidelines to set minimum services, but they have to be duly justified.[41] Sometimes, the competent authority has decided that minimum services should reach 100% and no workers could join the strike. Such a limitation of the right to strike requires particular and very strong reasons and a very significant potential damage to the community interests, so, as a general rule, such a high percentage of minimum services is not allowed.[42] In practice, it has been reasonably common to define minimum services by reference to the number of workers required to work on public holidays.

Once the minimum services are set, the particular workers to perform the activities have to be designated. This designation has to be made by the person/body decided by the competent government authority, so different options are available. The political authority often entrusts the task to the relevant management body of the service affected, but theoretically, the unions or even collective bargaining could take care of that mission.[43] The workers affected must be informed. From the right-to-strike approach, it is recommended to designate workers who are not members of the strike committee. Non-strikers would be an appropriate option to carry out minimum services, but such planning is not easy because workers are not obliged to communicate in advance whether they will join the strike.[44]

The decision of the government authority defining minimum services can be challenged before a court, which is usual in practice because unions usually do not

36. Supreme Court of 17 May 2021, STS 1028/2021.
37. Constitutional Court 58/2013, 11 March 2013 and 296/2006, 11 October 2006.
38. Constitutional Court 51/1986, 24 April 1986 and 193/2006, 19 June 2006.
39. Constitutional Court 123/1990, 2 July 1990.
40. Constitutional Court 26/1981, 17 July 1981.
41. Supreme Court 17 January 2018, STS 4081/2021.
42. Constitutional Court 2/2022, 24 January 2022.
43. Constitutional Court 53/1986, 5 May 1986.
44. Constitutional Court 123/1990, 2 July 1990 and 45/2016, 14 March 2016.

agree with the minimum services decided, which are often considered excessive. The answer from the courts always comes months or years after the strike, so there are no jurisdictional or administrative procedures previous to the strike to assess if the minimum services have been properly defined.

The designated workers are not strikers and they have the obligation to perform their duties because they have to comply with minimum services. According to Article 16(2) of the Strike Law,[45] the refusal could lead to disciplinary action, and it would allow the employer to replace the non-compliant workers.[46] This is an exception to the general rule because, under Spanish Law, the strikers cannot be replaced, neither temporarily nor permanently.[47] Both the Constitutional and the Supreme Court state that this prohibition of replacing strikers means that the employer cannot substitute the strikers for technology or machines, and unusual changes of functions of non-strikers are not permitted either.[48] Those limitations do not apply when the designated workers fail to comply with minimum services.

2.5 Situations of Acute National or Local Crisis

According to the Spanish Constitution (Article 116), the situations of acute crisis could lead to one of these alert states: alarm, emergency, and siege. All of them are regulated by Organic Law 4/1981, 1 June 1981.

The government may declare a state of alarm in the event of:

(1) Catastrophes such as earthquakes, floods, urban and forest fires or major accidents.
(2) Health crises, such as epidemics.
(3) Stoppage of essential services to the community.
(4) Situations of shortages of basic commodities.

Once the state of alarm is declared, the government can take appropriate measures to deal with the situation. In the case of the stoppage of essential services, the right to strike may be affected, as it happened in 2010 after a strike called by the air traffic controllers.[49] The government could replace the strikers with military staff[50] but could also militarize the workers, depriving them of the right to strike. That was the decision made in 2010 because the air traffic controllers had to continue to provide services under the direct organization and supervision of the Air Force.

In addition, the government could also classify several services as essential during a state of alarm. That happened during the COVID-19 pandemic (the state of alarm began on 14 March 2020 and ended on 21 June of that year). The catalogue of

45. For civil servants, *see* Art. 95(2)(m) of the Basic Statute of Public Employees.
46. Article 6(7) of the Strike Law.
47. Constitutional Court 33/2011, 28 March 2011.
48. Supreme Court of 27 January 2021, STS 4081/2021.
49. Royal Decree 1673/2010, 4 December 2010.
50. Article 16(e) of the Law 5/2005, 17 November 2005.

services qualified as essential during the pandemic was partially different from the traditional list of essential services.[51] Even some tourist accommodations were qualified as essential to provide housing for those workers who had to carry out maintenance, healthcare and repair services, and other tasks of general interest during that time.[52] These situations of acute national crisis and the protection of public health require deeper and more ambitious measures than those adopted to deal with the consequences of a strike.

The states of emergency and siege relate to political crisis or even warlike confrontations and their declaration has to be authorized by the Congress. If the Congress allows it, the government could forbid strikes during those periods, not only in essential services but in general (Article 23 of Organic Law 4/1981). That has not happened yet in Spain.

3 COMPENSATORY GUARANTEES FOR WORKERS DEPRIVED OF THE RIGHT TO STRIKE

There are no compensatory guarantees for workers deprived of the right to strike. As we said, the setting of minimum services could be challenged in court and ADR is theoretically possible, but it is not commonly used in Spain for these compensatory purposes. The competent government authority could call for a compulsory arbitration to terminate a strike affecting an essential service if there are 'particularly serious circumstances', but this arbitration is not designed as a compensatory guarantee for workers deprived of the right to strike, but as the best way to satisfy the community's best interest. In fact, this compulsory arbitration is a restraint on the right to strike in essential services because it limits the ability of workers to negotiate for better working conditions and benefits.

4 CONCLUSION

According to the Spanish Constitution, essential services are an explicit limitation on the right to strike. There is no prohibition to call a strike that affects an essential service, but the competent government authority enjoys certain powers that could significantly reduce the impact of that industrial action. Compulsory arbitration and minimum services are the two main tools available for that purpose, although they have different objectives. Compulsory arbitration seeks the termination of a strike that is considered harmful for the community's best interest. In contrast, minimum services are not intended to reduce the length of the strike but to guarantee that essential service continues to be provided during the protest.

The Spanish legal framework, heavily shaped by case law, has been applied with success for decades. However, some issues have arisen. In particular, the determination of minimum services is problematic. The government authority has the power to

51. *See* Annex of the Royal Decree-Law 10/2020, 29 March 2020.
52. Order TMA/277/2020, 23 March 2020.

make that decision on its own and the workers do not enjoy any participation or influence. There are no effective remedies to prevent abusive practices from occurring in advance. Of course, the government decision could be challenged in court, but even if the workers win the case, the compensation (financial compensation) always comes months or years later. Overall, the system relies excessively on governmental intervention, and leaves scarce room for concerted solutions and arrangements on the basis of the autonomy of the parties of labour relations, social dialogue and collective bargaining.

In addition, there are some procedural issues because the claims related to the setting of minimum services fall under the jurisdiction of the Administrative Courts, while claims concerning the designation of the concrete workers in charge of such services fall under the jurisdiction of the Labour Courts.[53] Moreover, the claims against the allegedly abusive minimum services are filed by a union, but the union is not the one directly aggrieved. A financial compensation received by the union does not benefit a worker unlawfully deprived of the right to strike. Those workers should bring an action themselves claiming a compensation, but this is not common in practice, and, eventually, the time limit for court action may have expired. Even the Supreme Court has warned that the regulations on the right to strike, adopted before the Constitution, should be updated to prevent these undesirable effects.[54] However, the right to strike is a sensitive issue and its reform seems highly unlikely in the short term.

53. Supreme Court of 4 November 2021, STS 4081/2021.
54. Supreme Court of 13 October 2021, STS 4081/2021.

CHAPTER 35

Restrictions on the Right to Strike in Sweden

Andreas Inghammar & Erik Sinander

1 GENERAL INFORMATION

1.1 Legal Basis of the Right to Strike

Strikes and other forms of industrial action are central features of the modern labour market, including in Sweden. While most industrialised countries have seen a general decline in the number of days lost to industrial action per year, this development is even more significant in Sweden, where some years, no or almost no days have been lost to industrial action.[1] Still, the right to strike and take industrial action in general is a cornerstone of Swedish labour law. There are no legal possibilities to make collective agreements generally applicable, for example, and no statutory minimum wage. Instead, the model relies entirely on the presumption that employees will organise collectively and, using the threat of industrial actions, demand adequate employment conditions to be set out in collective agreements. In this context, the right to take industrial action is crucial. Consequently, it is protected in the Swedish Constitution. As regards the threat that such industrial actions may entail for essential services, the most striking trait of Swedish labour law is the lack of legislation addressing such strikes.

1. Approximately 4.5-4.6 million people are active on the Swedish labour market. In 2018, only 52 days were lost to industrial action. In 2020, during the pandemic, the figure was zero, and in other years in the past decade, only a few thousand work days were lost per annum, *see*, https://www.mi.se/medling-konflikt/konfliktstatistik/ (accessed 9 June 2025).

1.2 Main Features of the Regulation

Instead of prohibiting strikes in essential services by law, the Swedish legislator has restricted the right to strike for public employees exercising public authority. However, for strikes in essential services carried out by private employees, the responsibility is placed entirely on the industrial parties. The only possibility for the Swedish legislator to intervene in a strike is through ad hoc legislation. Ad hoc legislation is also what the legislator relies on in situations of crisis caused by war. Hitherto, this *laissez-faire* method of regulating strikes in essential services has worked well. Still, there are weaknesses, as the legislation reflects historical circumstances. In the following, we will present the legislation in brief, in light of its historical context.

When the Swedish constitutional Instrument of Government (*Regeringsformen*) was updated in the 1970s, the right to take industrial action was included without much ado, without any special restrictions for civil servants, and with no explicit mention of essential services.[2] Compared with other constitutional rights, the right to take industrial action is particularly weak, as it may be limited not only by law but also by collective agreements.[3] Importantly, the right to industrial action is a collective right (on the employees' side), applied by trade unions and employers or employer federations – not by individuals.

In addition to the seemingly weak direct protection of the right to take industrial action in the Instrument of Government, the right is also indirectly protected by the same Constitutional Act. Since 2010, the Instrument of Government explicitly prescribes that Swedish law must be compatible with the European Convention on Human Rights (ECHR). This clarification is of some importance in Sweden as conventions must normally be implemented to be enforceable in courts.[4] However, the 2010 provision means that limitations of the right to take industrial action that are not compatible with the ECHR are not lawful.

In practice, the constitutional protection of industrial actions does not play a more prominent role for civil servants than for any other employees. As a basic rule, the constitutional right can be described as setting a presumption that industrial actions are allowed. Even if that basic rule comes with notable exceptions, it should be stated that there is no general proportionality requirement nor any general requirement that an industrial action shall be taken to achieve a collective agreement.

The situation has developed over time. Unlike all other employees in Sweden, civil servants were excluded from collective bargaining until the 1960s. The change came with the 1965 Act on Civil Servants (*statstjänstemannalagen [1965:264]*). In the preparatory works to this Act, it was explained that the model of collective bargaining, including the use of industrial actions, could be used not only in the private sector but also in the public sector.[5] The former general restriction for civil servants to take

2. KU 1973:26 p. 51.
3. *See* Chapter 2 s. 14 of the Instrument of Government (*Regeringsformen*).
4. *See, e.g.*, AD 1972 No. 5.
5. Prop. 1965:60 p. 25.

industrial action had been justified by the special loyalty to the government that service for the state presupposed.[6]

Though the private labour market served as a model for the liberalisation of the public labour market, civil servants were not granted an equally extensive right to take industrial actions in the 1965 Act on Civil Servants. For situations of acute crises, a reservation enabling the state powers to cancel industrial action was underlined.[7]

General exceptions to the right to strike are found in the Co-Determination in the Workplace Act (*lag [1976:580] om medbestämmande i arbetslivet*). The general exceptions are worded negatively, stating when industrial actions may not be taken. Many of the general restrictions are also of relevance for public employees. It follows from these restrictions that a consequence of a collective agreement is a mutual peace obligation for employees and employers bound by the collective agreement (section 41 of the Co-Determination Act). Additionally, industrial action may never be initiated to settle legal matters (section 41 letter f), as those should be referred to litigation.

2 PERMITTED RESTRICTIONS

2.1 Certain Categories of Public Servants

All categories of public servants are able to join trade unions and engage in legal industrial actions initiated by the unions. It is noteworthy that this applies also to traditional civil servants such as judges, professors, and directors of public bodies. Still, as a measure to prevent strikes in essential services, the Act on Public Employment (*lag [1994:260] om offentlig anställning*) imposes some special restrictions on public sector employees.

According to section 23 of this Act, employees involved in the exercise of public authority may only perform industrial actions in the form of lockout, strike, refusal of working overtime, or recruitment blockade. The most important implication of this limitation in practice is that partial industrial actions are not allowed (except refusal of working overtime). Also, the purpose of the industrial action must not relate to anything other than the relations between the industrial parties. Consequently, sympathy actions are significantly restricted for employees in the public sector. In addition to being dependent on whether the primary industrial action was allowed, sympathy actions are only allowed for employees in the public sector if they concern similar public employment situations. Regardless of whether an employee is involved in the exercise of public authority, political strikes are prohibited for all public sector employees (section 23, last paragraph). If a dispute on the compatibility of a strike with the restrictions described above arises, section 24 prohibits the performance of the strike until that dispute has been resolved.

Even if the statutory restrictions for public employees exercising public authority do not necessarily apply to essential services only, it is apparent that the restrictions

6. Sven-Hugo Ryman, *Förhandlings- och strejkrätt inom den offentliga sektorn: en historisk återblick*, p. 259 (Arbetsmarknad & Arbetsliv, 1999).
7. Prop. 1965:60 p. 105.

have been applied to mitigate the consequences or potential consequences of strikes in essential services. Compared with when the restrictions on the right to strike in public employment were enacted, more services are currently performed in the private sector – in fact, many, many more services.

A striking example is public transportation, which has undergone significant privatisation since the 1980s. In 1986, the Labour Court made an interesting judgment on the right to strike for public transportation employees, taking a partial industrial action in the form of refusing to sell and check train tickets.[8] The main issue in the 1986 case was whether the publicly employed train crew members were exercising 'public authority' in the sense of the restriction rule for public employees when they were selling and checking train tickets. The court reasoned that train crew services are not typically seen as exercise of public authority but made a *ratio legis* interpretation of the rule, concluding that the intention of the legislator had been to impose restrictions for essential services. The court stated that the public employer had 'good cause for its apprehension of problems in upholding public order and security in train traffic if the conductors' refusal to control tickets would be allowed and known by the general public. In such a situation, one must expect that it would be hard or impossible to uphold order in a normal way.

It is clear that the reasoning of the court in the 1986 train crew strike case quoted above focused on the necessity of restricting strikes in essential services. Even if train services are probably just as essential in contemporary society, the Labour Court would not be able to apply the case law from 1986 if train service employees worked in the private sector. As already mentioned, there are no statutory restrictions on the right to strike for private employees, even if they perform essential services.

This is a potential problem not only for public transportation. Other essential infrastructure services, such as telecommunication, energy production and distribution, and postal services, are entirely or partly performed by private companies nowadays. Some hospitals and other forms of health care services have also been privatised during the past decades. Further examples of private services that may be crucial in the case of a national crisis are farming, harbour work, and distribution of food and other necessities. For those services, which may in fact be essential, there are no statutory restrictions on the right to strike if they are performed by private employees, and there is no explicit definition of what could constitute essential services.

A practical example of when the old statutory restrictions have faced new realities is the Swedish trade union IF Metall's strike against Tesla that was initiated in 2023 and is still ongoing. The conflict has successively been extended by sympathy actions directed against Tesla. One such sympathy action was the Swedish trade union gathering postal workers, SEKO's, sympathy action not to deliver post to Tesla. As the postal workers are not publicly employed, the restrictions mentioned above do not

8. AD 1986 No. 111.

apply. When this is written, the sympathy actions are subject to different court cases where Tesla seeks to stop the actions.[9]

Though the aforementioned limitation of the right to strike in public employment deviates from an otherwise generous legal situation in relation to industrial action, the limitation should be viewed in context and can then be considered to be relatively minor. The right to strike is broadly applicable for all levels of civil servants in public employment.

2.2 Essential Services in the Strict Sense of the Term

As there are no statutory restrictions on the right to strike related explicitly to essential services, no such legal concept is defined. It is, as pointed out in both the preparatory works and the legal literature, very difficult to make an exact definition of what constitutes essential services.[10] Many different services might prove to be essential to uphold public order in society, depending on the scenario at hand. Swedish law does not reflect that. Instead, statutory restrictions on the right to strike are applicable in the public sector and to public employees only, as a consequence of the fact that the statutory restrictions on the right to strike in essential services are enshrined solely in the Act on Public Employment. It is clearly the case that most essential services in the strict sense of the term were historically performed in the public sector. An assumption for regulating restrictions in essential services by limiting employees in the public sector from taking industrial actions is that most essential services are performed in the public sector. In modern society, it is not certain that all essential services are actually performed in the public sector. Many of the essential services previously performed in the public sector have been subject to privatisation in recent decades.

In addition to the general legislative restrictions for public employees to take industrial actions in some situations, Swedish labour law relies heavily on the industrial parties' self-regulation of the matter. Since the constitutional right to industrial action can be limited not only by law but also by (collective) agreements, the industrial parties in both the public and private sectors have regulated such conflicts separately in their collective agreements. The industrial parties have collectively concluded agreements to limit the impact of industrial actions on services essential to core aspects of society. Various general collective agreements with such contents are applicable in both public and private sectors, leaving the very definition of essential

9. *See* particularly Solna District Court's judgment of 11 October 2024 in case T 10724-23 where Tesla urged the court to stop the sympathy actions in the postal services. The district court's judgment has been appealed to the Svea Court of Appeals, where it has case number T 14647-24. As per 9 June 2025, it has yet not been adjudicated. For a comment of the case when it was still undecided by the court of first instance, *see* Michael Hansson, *Rätten till stridsåtgärder på arbetsmarknaden: från orättsligt grundad frihet till rättsligt grundad ofrihet, in De Lege, Regeringsformen 50 år 1974-2024*, pp. 121-140, pp. 136-138 (Anna Jonsson Cornell, Mikael Ruotsi, Caroline Taube, Olof Wilske eds, Uppsala University Publications 2024).

10. Prop. 1965:60 p. 265, SOU 1984:18 p. 35; *see also* Birgitta Nyström, *Samhällsfarliga konflikter i svensk arbetsrätt, in Festskrift till Örjan Edström*, pp. 372-386, pp. 380-381 (Ruth Mannelqvist, Staffan Ingmanson, Carin Ulander-Wänman eds, Umeå University 2019).

services in the hands of the industrial parties.[11] This is an important restriction in practice, but it must be emphasised that the restrictions in collective agreements apply only to employees who are members of the contracting trade unions. Employees who are not members of the trade unions are not bound by such limitations.

In the public sector, there are central collective agreements covering conflicts in essential services (*samhällsfarliga konflikter*).[12] The agreement covering state employment (encompassing the military, the police, judges, university teachers, and those employed in central authorities and similar bodies) includes some special arrangements for essential services and makes general exceptions from the right to strike for public employees included in a detailed list. The list contains not only heads of public authorities, military leaders, central and local leadership in the police force but also, more generally, all employees working with certain tasks, such as icebreaking (at sea), and employees primarily engaged in foreign countries.[13]

Swedish regions and municipalities (through the organisation *Sveriges Kommuner och Regioner, SKR*) are covered by other collective agreements, which limit industrial actions in essential services in a general way. If an industrial party considers an industrial conflict to inappropriately and adversely affect essential services or put human life or the health of others at risk, the organisation must call for negotiation with the other party in order to avoid, limit, or discontinue the industrial action. If the other party refuses to comply with such measures, the first party has the option to refer the conflict, which is considered to endanger essential services, to a special board. Industrial actions are not allowed until the board has reached a conclusion.[14] It is explicitly stated that healthcare workplaces (hospitals, nursing homes) are not, per se, excluded from the ordinary rights to take industrial action, even though the sector as such involves issues of life and death, but industrial action in this particular sector must be performed with special precautions taken.

There has been limited use of these boards for the assessment of public essential services. Before 2024, the last time any of them convened was in a dispute on telecommunication in 2016.[15] However, in the spring of 2024, a nationwide nurse strike caused the activation of several such boards. Without the boards having to

11. The famous General Agreement *Saltsjöbadsavtalet 1938* in the private sector contained provisions on essential services, and agreements have later been concluded in other sectors of the labour market.
12. The topic has been thoroughly examined by Birgitta Nyström, *Sweden, in Regulating Strikes in Essential Services* pp. 409-439 (Moti Mironi, Monika Schlachter eds, Wolters Kluwer 2019); Birgitta Nyström, *Samhällsfarliga konflikter i svensk arbetsrätt, in Festskrift till Örjan Edström,* pp. 372-386 (Ruth Mannelqvist, Staffan Ingmanson, Carin Ulander-Wänman eds, Umeå University 2019).
13. The Collective Agreement *Huvudavtal 2000-06-13* is available (in Swedish) at https://editorial.st.org/sites/default/files/2023-01/huvudavtalet.pdf (accessed 9 June 2025).
14. KHA 94 *Kommunalt Huvudavtal* is available at https://skr.se/download/18.40c889381840e60521a9edeb/1667987883060/KHA-94-i-lydelse-2022-10-01.pdf (accessed 9 June 2025).
15. Birgitta Nyström, *Samhällsfarliga konflikter i svensk arbetsrätt, in Festskrift till Örjan Edström,* pp. 372-386, p. 379 (Ruth Mannelqvist, Staffan Ingmanson, Carin Ulander-Wänman eds, Umeå University 2019); for a broader description of the case *see also Avtalsrörelsen och lönebildningen 2016,* Medlingsinstitutets årsrapport, Swedish National Mediation Office, p. 72 (2016).

formally assess the strike's risk for essential services, the trade union recalled strike actions that the employer reported to the board for assessment.[16]

The private labour market has, as indicated in the introduction, been subject to a comparatively high union density and coverage of collective agreements, which has shaped the status of industrial action in essential services. The aforementioned General Agreement (*Saltsjöbadsavtalet*) from 1938 between the employer federation and the blue-collar workers' union federation (*Landsorganisationen*, LO) created the core of negotiations and industrial action that largely remains in place to this day. The 1938 General Agreement, Chapter 5, regulates how to minimise the impact of industrial actions on essential services. Any conflicting party or public bodies representing the interests of the essential services might call for an assessment of the situation, meaning that the conflict can (or rather could – this has not been done in decades) be referred to a central body.[17]

The overarching impression is of a labour market highly dependent on collective bargaining and industrial relations, also for the assessment of conflicts posing threats to essential services. The situation is largely similar in private employment relations and different forms of public employment relations. It is also strikingly clear that conflicts in essential services are very rarely subject to assessment in the special boards. The extraordinarily low number of days lost to any industrial conflict over the past decades might be part of the reason for this.

2.3 Situations of Acute National or Local Crisis

There is a dormant Act on Labour Law for Crisis Situations (Arbetsrättslig beredskapslag *[1987:1262]*). If activated, section 7 of the Act gives the government an extensive mandate to limit the right to strike in any service.

The dormant Act is automatically activated if Sweden 'is at war', pursuant to section 1. If there is a risk of war or if there are extraordinary circumstances caused by war in other countries, the government may activate the Act (section 2). Such an activation will enter into force immediately but must be approved by the Parliament within one month.

The Act on Labour Law for Crisis Situations contains several automatic changes of rules on, e.g., co-determination, working time, employment protection, and parental leave (section 5). As regards industrial actions, the Act contains no automatic changes.

16. *See, e.g.*, the information published by Region Skåne, which is the public employer responsible for hospitals in the southernmost Swedish region Scania (Skåne), available at: https://press.newsmachine.com/pressrelease/view/strejk-vid-vardcentraler-bedoms-vara-samhallsfarlig-48579 (accessed 9 June 2025).

17. Interestingly, a new general agreement body has been established after a recent update of the Employment Protection Act. These recent changes are not related to essential services and strikes but emphasise the long-standing efforts to also regulate difficult issues between the industrial partners collectively, with limited interference by politics, *see* Collective Agreement on Special Main Agreement Council (Kollektivavtal rörande Huvudavtalsnämnd) https://www.ptk.se/wp-content/uploads/2022/06/Svenskt-Naringsliv-PTK-2022-06-22-Forhandlingsprotokoll-huvudavtal-trygghet-omstallning-anstallningsskydd.pdf (accessed 9 June 2025).

Instead, an excessive mandate is given to the government to impose prohibitions on industrial actions that may cause harm to the military defence of the country (section 7).

For crisis situations caused by anything other than war, there are no specific restrictions on the right to strike. Parliamentary *in casu* legislation is the only statutory measure there is to prohibit ongoing strikes in essential services. The only occasion when the Parliament passed such a law was in 1971 to end a massive strike on the part of the Swedish Confederation of Professional Associations, which organises white-collar workers.[18] The controversial act obliged all employees to go back to work and extended the collective agreements that had expired.

Though the situation in 1971 is the only occasion when the legislator has actually passed an ad hoc restriction, there are a few examples of when this tool has been suggested for use. An example of a proposed draconian ad hoc legislation followed a deep financial crisis with dramatic inflation in 1989-1990. In February 1990, the Social Democrat government presented a proposal aimed at halting wage increases by prohibiting all industrial actions for nearly two years. An unusual aspect of this proposal was that it carried the sanction of imprisonment. The proposal was driven by a spiralling cost and wage crisis, but it was dismissed by the Parliament after massive criticism, ultimately leading to the fall of that Government.[19]

The Swedish labour law professor Birgitta Nyström has also pointed out a more recent general restriction to the right to strike being implemented based on the need to restrict strikes in essential services.[20] The background to the situation was the industrial relations in the harbour of Gothenburg. Gothenburg's harbour is the largest in Scandinavia and is important for the economies of both Sweden and Norway. The labour relations in the harbour have long deviated from what is normal in Sweden.

Unlike in most workplaces in Sweden, the majority of the workers in the harbour are members of an unaffiliated trade union. For decades, the employer signed collective agreements with the minority trade union only. Though the trade union that signed the collective agreement was in a minority in the harbour, it belonged to the *national trade union* confederation, which gathers most employees nationally. However, the fact that most of the employees belonged to a trade union that did not have a collective agreement had the effect that the employer did not secure a peace obligation.

As harbour services are especially vulnerable to sudden industrial actions, the relatively common industrial actions in the harbour had spill-over effects for the entire Swedish economy and labour market. In 2019, legislation was adopted to strengthen the peace obligation for employers with collective agreements.[21] This was done in part

18. Prop. 1971:50.
19. Prop. 1989/90:95, *see also* the protocol from the Swedish Parliament 1989/90:68, 15 February.
20. *See* Birgitta Nyström, *Samhällsfarliga konflikter i svensk arbetsrätt in Festskrift till Örjan Edström*, pp. 372-386, p. 379 (Ruth Mannelqvist, Staffan Ingmanson & Carin Ulander-Wänman eds, Umeå universitet 2019); For a broader description of the case, *see also Avtalsrörelsen och lönebildningen 2016*, Medlingsinstitutets årsrapport, Swedish National Mediation Office, p. 73 (2016).
21. SOU 2018:40 *Vissa fredspliktsfrågor*, Prop. 2018/19:105 *Utökad fredsplikt på arbetsplatser där det finns kollektivavtal och vid rättstvister*, SFS 2019:503.

not only by codifying existing case law principles on prohibiting strikes, which aimed to supplant existing collective agreements, but also by restricting the right to strike so that any trade union not bound by a collective agreement could not take industrial actions for anything other than to achieve a collective agreement. Though the restrictions were general, it was clear that they aimed to restrict the right to strike in the essential services performed in the harbour.

3 COMPENSATORY GUARANTEES FOR WORKERS DEPRIVED OF THE RIGHT TO STRIKE

There are no compensatory guarantees for workers deprived of the right to strike, neither in statutory law (of which there is none in the area) nor explicitly in the collective agreements restricting the right to strike.

4 CONCLUSION

As has been shown in this contribution, the statutory restrictions on the right to strike that are intended to prevent strikes in essential services apply only to employees in the public sector who exercise public authority. Such a statutory restriction rests on the assumption that essential services are performed primarily in the public sector. Compared with when the rules were instated, the Swedish economy of today is to a much higher degree dependent on essential services being performed by employees in the private sector.

In addition, the responsibility to manage strikes in essential services has been delegated to the industrial parties, which have regulated the issue in collective agreements. This may be seen as an example of a laissez-faire legislative approach that encourages collective self-regulation. However, the mandate of the industrial parties can never stretch outside the reach of their collective agreements. Consequently, the industrial parties cannot control strikes by unaffiliated trade unions. Traditionally, trade union organisation in Sweden has been highly concentrated on the unions that are part of the national trade union confederations, which have been bound to the collective agreements regulating strikes in essential services. As the level of trade union organisation has decreased and new types of competition between trade unions have become a reality in Sweden, there is a potential vulnerability in relying on collective agreements to regulate strikes in essential services.

If neither the statutory restrictions nor the collective self-regulation can restrict a strike that affects what is considered to be an essential service, the last resort in Swedish labour law is for the legislator to intervene with ad hoc and *in casu* legislation. Today, this possibility is considered an ultima ratio option. A worst-case scenario would be that the legislator devalues the ultima ratio option by using it more frequently. Though the implicit threat by the legislator may be the reason why the system has worked relatively well, one can just as well question whether it is actually a sophisticated way of managing strikes in essential services.

In conclusion, it seems that Swedish legislation is unprepared for detrimental strikes in essential services. Valuing the right to strike in relation to a situation ad hoc instead of generally in advance risks leading to fast solutions that are not thought through from the beginning. The obvious alternative to the Swedish way of handling restrictions to strikes in essential services is to think things through first and value what is at stake with restrictions to the right to strike in essential services. Not doing anything is not necessarily a good way of handling things, even if it has worked well thus far.

CHAPTER 36

Restrictions on the Right to Strike in Switzerland

Christoph Reusser & Wolfgang Portmann

1 GENERAL INFORMATION

1.1 Legal Basis of the Right to Strike

1.1.1 Constitution and Acts

In Switzerland, the right to strike is derived primarily from Article 28(3) and (4) of the Federal Constitution of the Swiss Confederation.[1] According to this, strikes and lockouts are permitted if they relate to employment relations and if they do not contravene any requirements to preserve peaceful employment relations or to conduct conciliation proceedings (paragraph 3), although the law may prohibit certain categories of person from taking strike action (paragraph 4). However, there is no Strike Act in Switzerland that concretizes the right to strike. Rather, the criteria for the existence of a lawful strike have been developed by doctrine and case law,[2] the latter being relatively limited due to the fact that strikes are quite rare in everyday working life in Switzerland.

1. Bundesverfassung der Schweizerischen Eidgenossenschaft vom 18 April 1999 (BV), Systematische Rechtssammlung: SR 101.
2. Cf. Federal Supreme Court, 28 June 1999, BGE 125 III 277 [3.b], and 13 May 2005, BGE 132 III 122 [4.4.2].

1.1.2 Public International Law

At the level of international law, Switzerland has signed various international treaties that also affect the right to strike.

The European Convention for the Protection of Human Rights and Fundamental Freedoms (ECHR),[3] ratified by Switzerland, lacks an explicit right to strike, but the European Court of Human Rights recognizes a right to strike based on Article 11 of the Convention. The Court justifies this, among other things, with the recognition of the right to strike by the supervisory bodies of the ILO and the anchoring of a right to strike in the European Social Charter.[4]

Article 22 of the International Covenant on Civil and Political Rights,[5] which has been ratified by Switzerland, also contains no explicit provision on the right to strike. But it is disputed whether it nevertheless guarantees the right to strike.[6]

Furthermore, Article 8(1)(d) of the International Covenant on Economic, Social and Cultural Rights,[7] which provides for an explicit right to strike, is also binding on Switzerland, but - in contrast to Article 11 of the European Convention for the Protection of Human Rights and Fundamental Freedoms and Article 22 of the International Covenant on Civil and Political Rights - it lacks the self-executing character at least with regard to the holder of the right, which is why it is not directly applicable, at least with regard to the permissibility of wildcat strikes.[8]

While the European Social Charter was signed by Switzerland but never ratified, Switzerland has signed and ratified ILO Convention No. 87 concerning Freedom of Association and Protection of the Right to Organise,[9] Convention No. 98 concerning Right to Organise and Collective Bargaining,[10] Convention No. 151 concerning Labour Relations (Public Service),[11] and Convention No. 154 concerning Collective Bargaining.[12]

---

3. SR 0.101.
4. *Enerji Yapi-Yol Sen v. Turkey*, No. 68959/01, § 24, Eur. Cr. H.R. 2009. Cf. Federal Supreme Court, 9 October 2018, BGE 144 I 306 [4.2.1].
5. SR 0.103.2.
6. Federal Supreme Court, 28 June 1999, BGE 125 III 277 [2.e].
7. SR 0.103.1.
8. Wolfgang Portmann, *Das Streikrecht: Recht des Individuums oder des Verbands? Eine Betrachtung des wilden Streiks nach schweizerischem Recht im Lichte des Uno-Pakts über wirtschaftliche, soziale und kulturelle Rechte*, in Aktuelle Juristische Praxis (AJP) 2007, pp. 352-362, at pp. 358 et seq. (Dike Verlag AG, Zurich/St. Gallen); Wolfgang Portmann & Roger Rudolph, *Basler Kommentar, Obligationenrecht I, Art. 319-362 OR*, at Art. 357a para. 11 (Corinne Widmer Lüchinger & David Oser eds, 7th ed., Helbing & Lichtenhahn, Basel 2020); Jean-Fritz Stöckli, *Berner Kommentar, Vol. VI/2/2/3, Art. 356-360 OR*, at Art. 357a para. 21 (Stämpfli Verlag AG, Berne 1999). Cf. Federal Supreme Court, 11 February 1994, BGE 120 Ia 1 [5c]. Different opinion: Arthur Andermatt et al., *Handbuch zum kollektiven Arbeitsrecht* at Chapter A para. 70 (Helbing & Lichtenhahn, Basel 2009).
9. SR 0.822.719.7.
10. SR 0.822.719.9.
11. SR 0.822.725.1.
12. SR 0.822.725.4.

This is important in the present context because, among others, the Committee on Freedom of Association of the ILO derives an implicit right to strike from Conventions No. 87 and No. 98.[13] However, the Federal Supreme Court is reluctant to assume that the ILO Conventions are directly applicable and denied the self-executing character of Conventions No. 98 and No. 154.[14] With regard to Convention No. 87, the Federal Supreme Court left the question open,[15] but it can be concluded from BGE 125 III 277 that even if the self-executing character is assumed, the right to strike does not belong to the individual but can only be legally exercised at the collective level, i.e., by employee organizations.[16]

1.2 Main Features of the Regulation

In Switzerland, the right to strike is subject to five conditions, all of which must be met for a strike to be legal.

According to the Federal Supreme Court, the right to strike is only granted to bodies of collective labour law, i.e., employee organizations. Only these organizations have the right to call a strike.[17] Thus, the legal capacity to conclude collective labour agreements is a prerequisite *(Tariffähigkeit)*.[18] Trade unions can represent the interests of their members in both the private and public sectors.

In addition, it must be possible to regulate the objective pursued by the strike in a collective labour agreement,[19] and it must be possible for the counterparty, i.e., employers' associations or individual employers, to fulfil this objective.[20] Legitimate objectives are, in principle, new regulations of working conditions, which means that they must be newly created and do not result from existing contracts or law.[21]

Another criterion stated is compliance with the obligation to maintain peace *(Friedenspflicht)*, which already follows from Article 28(3) of the Constitution.[22] Peace obligations can arise from the law (e.g., from Article 357a(2) of the Code of Obligations,[23] or Article 6 of the Act on the Federal Conciliation Board for the Settlement of

13. Janice R. Bellace, *The ILO and the Right to Strike*, 153 International Labour Review (2014), No. 1, pp. 29 et seq., at pp. 42 and 47 https://doi.org/10.1111/j.1564-913x.2014.00196.x (accessed 7 June 2025).
14. Federal Supreme Court, 13 September 2005, 4C.422/2004, [3.2] (partially published in BGE 132 III 122) and 24 Sep. 2012, 6B_758/2011 [1.3.3].
15. Federal Supreme Court, 28 June 1999, BGE 125 III 277 [2.e], and 6 September 2017, BGE 144 I 50 [5.3.3.1].
16. Federal Supreme Court, 28 June 1999, BGE 125 III 277 [3.a]; cf. Christine Kaufmann & Christoph Good, *Die Anwendbarkeit von ILO-Recht vor Schweizer Gerichten: Potenzial und Grenzen, Rechtsgutachten im Auftrag des Schweizerischen Gewerkschaftsbundes (SGB)*, in Aktuelle Juristische Praxis (AJP) 2016, pp. 647-664, at p. 654 (Dike Verlag AG, Zurich/St. Gallen).
17. Federal Supreme Court, 28 June 1999, BGE 125 III 277 [3.a].
18. Wolfgang Portmann, Isabelle Wildhaber & Roger Rudolph, *Schweizerisches Arbeitsrecht* at para. 1043 (5th ed., DIKE Verlag AG, Zurich/St. Gallen 2024).
19. Federal Supreme Court, 28 June 1999, BGE 125 III 277 [3.b].
20. Stöckli, *supra* n. 8, at Art. 357a paras 39 et seq.
21. Stöckli, *supra* n. 8, at Art. 357a para. 41.
22. Federal Supreme Court, 28 June 1999, BGE 125 III 277 [3.b].
23. Bundesgesetz vom 30 March 1911 betreffend die Ergänzung des Schweizerischen Zivilgesetzbuches (Fünfter Teil: Obligationenrecht) (OR), SR 220.

Collective Labour Disputes),[24] may be based on a collective labour agreement or can arise from ongoing arbitration proceedings (e.g., Article 335j of the Code of Obligations).[25] On the one hand, the peace obligation requires the collective parties to refrain from labour disputes that violate the law or the agreement. On the other hand, the associations involved must influence their members to refrain from labour disputes.[26] In Switzerland, the relative peace obligation *(relative Friedenspflicht)*, which is enshrined in Article 357a(2) of the Code of Obligations, is distinguished from the absolute peace obligation *(absolute Friedenspflicht)*, which must be agreed in the collective labour agreement in order to be valid. In the first variant, the parties must refrain from labour disputes insofar as matters are concerned that are regulated in the collective labour agreement.[27] In the second variant, any kind of labour disputes during the period of validity of the collective labour agreement are prohibited.[28]

Furthermore, there must be no legal exclusion of the right to strike (cf. Article 28(4) of the Constitution).[29] Such a ban on strikes for selected categories of personnel is laid down in Article 24(1) of the Federal Personnel Act,[30] in conjunction with Article 96 of the Federal Personnel Ordinance.[31] Comparable exclusions are also provided for in certain cantons, whereby they must comply with federal law and in particular Article 28 of the Constitution.[32]

As a final condition, the principle of proportionality must be respected.[33] The *ultima ratio* principle is enshrined in Article 28(2) of the Constitution as the most significant application of the principle of proportionality, according to which disputes are to be settled by negotiation or mediation if possible.[34] A strike may be initiated only as a last resort. Other aspects of proportionality are, for example, that the goals pursued must be in reasonable proportion to the consequences of the strike. Furthermore, necessary services in vital areas must be maintained, and violence, criminal acts, or the goal of wiping out the counterpart must be refrained from.[35]

2 PERMITTED RESTRICTIONS

2.1 Certain Categories of Public Servants

In the context of the revision of the Constitution, it was stated that not all public servants perform indispensable functions, which is why they should not be prohibited

24. Bundesgesetz vom 12 February 1949 über die eidgenössische Einigungsstelle zur Beilegung von kollektiven Arbeitsstreitigkeiten, SR 821.42.
25. Portmann, Wildhaber & Rudolph, *supra* n. 18, at para. 1045.
26. Stöckli, *supra* n. 8, at Art. 357a para. 28.
27. Article 357a(2) of the Code of Obligations.
28. Stöckli, *supra* n. 8, at Art. 357a para. 32.
29. Portmann, Wildhaber & Rudolph, *supra* n. 18, at para. 1047; cf. s. 2 *infra*.
30. Bundespersonalgesetz vom 24 March 2000 (BPG), SR 172.220.1.
31. Bundespersonalverordnung vom 3 July 2001 (BPV), SR 172.220.111.3.
32. Cf. s. 2 *infra*.
33. Federal Supreme Court, 28 June 1999, BGE 125 III 277 [3.b].
34. Portmann, Wildhaber & Rudolph, *supra* n. 18, at para. 1046.
35. Portmann, Wildhaber & Rudolph, *supra* n. 18, at para. 1046. Cf. s. 2 *infra*.

from striking in principle. Conversely, it must be possible to restrict or prohibit strikes for persons who perform an indispensable service, regardless of whether they are in the public service or not.[36] Prohibitions or restrictions on the right to strike may be established, on the one hand, by legal regulations pursuant to Article 28(4) of the Constitution. On the other hand, they can result from the principle of proportionality, in the context of which a prevailing public interest must be taken into account. These cases will be dealt with in the following.

2.1.1 Public Servants Named in the Law

At the federal level, a legal basis has been created to abolish or restrict the right to strike for certain categories of employees. According to Article 24(1) of the Federal Personnel Act in conjunction with Article 96 of the Federal Personnel Ordinance, the exercise of the right to strike is prohibited for members of the following categories of personnel who perform essential duties for the protection of state security, for the safeguarding of important interests in foreign affairs, or for ensuring the national supply of essential goods and services:

- the members of the civilian and military command staffs of the departments;
- the federal law enforcement agencies;
- the employees of the FDFA (Federal Department of Foreign Affairs) who are subject to mandatory transfer and are working abroad;
- the Border Guard Corps and customs personnel;
- the members of the surveillance squadron, military air traffic control personnel and the professional formation of military security.

Furthermore, certain cantons have also enacted legal provisions for the restriction of the right to strike for public-law employment relationships with cantonal employees, which must, however, comply with Article 28 of the Federal Constitution as superior law. Various cantons therefore provide that the right to strike may be restricted or abolished for certain categories of employees. Thus, according to the Personnel Act of the Canton of Berne, the cantonal government may, by ordinance or in individual cases, restrict the right to strike for individual administrative functions and professional groups to the extent that this is absolutely necessary to ensure public safety, order, health, the operation of schools, and basic parish services.

In the Canton of Lucerne, too, the Law on Public Employment Relations provides that the highest administrative authority may restrict or abolish the right to strike for certain groups of employees to the extent that higher-ranking public interests outweigh the employees' interest in pursuing collective claims by means of strike action. Higher-ranking public interests include, in particular, the maintenance of public peace and safety as well as the protection of the health and property of the population.[37]

36. Botschaft über eine neue Bundesverfassung vom 20 November 1996, BBl 1996 I pp. 1 et seq., at p. 181.
37. E.g., *Berne:* Art. 12(2) Personalgesetz des Kantons Bern vom 16 September 2004, Systematische Sammlung des Kantons Bern (BSG) 153.01; *Jura:* Art. 59(5) Loi sur le personnel de l'État du

According to Article 46 of the Public Employment Relations Act,[38] the Canton of Nidwalden is the only canton in Switzerland that provides for an absolute ban on strikes for employees subject to the corresponding Act.[39] However, this is hardly compatible with Article 28 of the Federal Constitution.[40]

Apart from this specific case, it can be stated that most cantonal regulations only provide for a restriction or cancellation of the right to strike if its exercise jeopardizes services necessary for the population. As a rule, areas related to public safety, order, or the protection of health and property are mentioned. For example, the Canton of Fribourg provides for an explicit ban on strikes for policemen and policewomen as well as for specialists in the area of law enforcement.[41]

2.1.2 Further Public Servants

Even if there is no explicit legal restriction on the right to strike, which is the rule in Switzerland, it has long been recognized that employees may nevertheless be subject to a prohibition or restriction on the right to strike.[42] In this case, the requirement that a strike can only be lawful if proportionality is maintained is of great importance.[43] In principle, employees in sensitive areas have the right to strike. However, the unrestricted exercise of this right would be disproportionate because the public interests of the population outweigh the private interests in exercising the right to strike.[44] Therefore, in the event of a strike, it must always be examined whether milder measures exist, such as the provision of emergency services. This is the result of a predominant public interest, which must be assessed within the framework of the principle of proportionality. It applies to both public-law and private-law sectors.[45] This restriction is due to the fact that in Switzerland labour disputes are considered the ultimate means of bringing about industrial peace, the strike being considered ultima ratio.[46]

Canton du Jura du 22 September 2010, Recueil systèmatique du droit jurassien (RSJU) 173.11; *Lucerne:* § 46 Personalgesetz des Kantons Luzern vom 26 June 2001, Systematische Sammlung des Kantons Luzern (SRL) No. 51. For an overview of all existing cantonal regulations, *see* Federal Supreme Court, 9 October 2018, BGE 144 I 306 [4.3.4].

38. Article 46 Personalgesetz des Kantons Nidwalden vom 3 June 1998, Systematische Sammlung des Kantons Nidwalden (NG) 165.1.
39. Cf. Federal Supreme Court, 9 October 2018, BGE 144 I 306 [4.3.4].
40. Cf. Botschaft BV (*supra* n. 36), BBl 1996 I 1 et seq., at p. 181; Béatrice Aubert-Piguet, *L'exercice du droit de grève,* in Aktuelle Juristische Praxis (AJP) 1996, pp. 1497-1506, at p. 1502 (Dike Verlag AG, Zurich/St. Gallen).
41. Article 68(7) Gesetz über das Staatspersonal des Kantons Freiburg vom 17 October 2001, Systematische Sammlung des Kantons Freiburg (SGF) 122.70.1.
42. Cf. Federal Supreme Court, 23 March 1995, in La Semaine judicaire (SJ) 1995, p. 681 [4.a] (ed. Société genevoise de droit et de législation, Geneva); Aubert-Piguet, *supra* n. 40, at pp. 1502 et seq.
43. Cf. s. 1.2. *supra.*
44. Cf. Salome Stähelin, *Das Streikreicht in unerlässlichen Diensten* at p. 162 (Helbing & Lichtenhahn, Basel/Genf/München 2001).
45. Stöckli, *supra* n. 8, at Art. 357a para. 46.
46. Federal Supreme Court, 18 June 1985, BGE 111 II 245 [E. 4.c].

One such example could be the entire workforce of a nuclear power plant going on strike. In view of the risks for the population and the goal to be achieved, a complete shutdown of work in this constellation could hardly ever be proportionate.

2.2 Essential Services in the Strict Sense of the Term

2.2.1 Core Area

There is no uniform definition of essential service in Switzerland. The Federal Supreme Court held that the right to strike for public employees may not lead to the elimination of public service in necessary areas, such as the guarantee of public order, the protection of property, firefighting or care in hospitals. Compliance with the principle of proportionality, however, forbids denying the right to strike under the pretext of minimum service to public employees whose presence is not mandatory.[47]

It follows from doctrine and case law that in the core area of indispensable services, i.e., where directly vital services are provided, the permissibility of prohibitions on strikes is recognized.[48] This core area includes activities that affect the state's monopoly on the use of force and ensure public safety (e.g., police, army, customs, fire department),[49] the health care system (in particular health care and emergency services),[50] and hazardous establishments (e.g., nuclear plants).[51] In these vital areas, the duty to perform work stems from the public interest, regardless of whether it is performed in the public or private sector.[52] A strike in these areas would be an immoral means of exerting pressure.[53]

In these core areas, too, it is examined in each case carefully for which persons restrictions on the right to strike or even a ban on strikes is permissible. For example, the Federal Supreme Court had to rule on a clause of the Personnel Act of the Canton of Fribourg, which provided for a ban on strikes for all healthcare personnel, in the context of an abstract review of norms. Due to the lack of a limitation to personnel whose presence is absolutely necessary to preserve the life and health of patients, the Court declared the clause inadmissible.[54] According to the decision, the following arguments, among others, were put forward in favour of a strike ban during the parliamentary debates:

- a duty of health personnel to show appreciation for better working conditions than in other cantons and in the private sector;
- the duty to ensure optimal service at all times;
- to have the possibility to receive 'normal' care at any time.

47. Federal Supreme Court, 23 March 1995, in La Semaine judicaire (SJ) 1995, at p. 681, [4.a] (ed. Société genevoise de droit et de législation, Geneva).
48. Stähelin, *supra* n. 44, at p. 113.
49. Aubert-Piguet, *supra* n. 40, at p. 1502; Stähelin, *supra* n. 44, at pp. 116-128.
50. Aubert-Piguet, *supra* n. 40, at p. 1503; Stähelin, *supra* n. 44, at pp. 128-133.
51. Aubert-Piguet, *supra* n. 40, at p. 1503; Stähelin, *supra* n. 44, at pp. 133-140.
52. Stöckli, *supra* n. 8, at Art. 357a para. 46.
53. Stöckli, *supra* n. 8, at Art. 357a para. 46.
54. Federal Supreme Court, 9 October 2018, BGE 144 I 306 [4.4.4].

However, the Federal Supreme Court rejected these arguments and held that the restriction imposed by a general ban on strikes for all healthcare personnel is not in reasonable proportion to the public interests put forward and thus violates the principle of proportionality.[55]

2.2.2 *Further Areas*

In addition to the core area, there are areas that are of great importance for ensuring the basic needs of the population.[56] Here, an absolute ban on strikes might not be constitutional, but the right to strike can be limited by the obligation to provide emergency services.[57] Energy supply can be mentioned as an example.[58] Thus, a strike that would result in a permanent and complete cessation of electricity supply would be disproportionate, whereas a strike that would ensure a general supply of electricity with certain restrictions, for example, for private households during the night hours, might be lawful. Furthermore, emergency services are also mentioned in connection with ensuring uninterrupted operation in installations whose shutdown would cause disproportionate or irreparable damage to the owner.[59] In a similar vein, it is also added that a strike violates the principle of fair labour dispute management if absolutely essential maintenance work is omitted.[60]

It follows that the emergency service must provide the services necessary to ensure basic needs, as well as those necessary for safety reasons.[61] If such services were omitted, the exercise of the right to strike would be disproportionate.

With regard to the definition of the content and extent of an emergency service, there are hardly any legal regulations in Switzerland that could be invoked. Some scholars are of the opinion that social partners should determine how an emergency service must be structured and which areas are affected by it.[62] The Canton of Fribourg provides in the State Personnel Act that,[63] in the event of a strike, the State Council (the cantonal government) shall decide in which areas minimum operations must be provided. In order to guarantee minimum operations, employees shall report to their superiors before the strike begins and organize themselves under the responsibility of the head of service. In the event of disagreement, this person shall determine which employees must ensure minimum operations.

55. Federal Supreme Court, 9 October 2018, BGE 144 I 306 [4.4.3.4].
56. Aubert-Piguet, *supra* n. 40, at p. 1503; Stähelin, *supra* n. 44, at pp. 162 et seq.
57. Stähelin, *supra* n. 44, at pp. 162 et seq.
58. Aubert-Piguet, *supra* n. 40, at p. 1503; Stähelin, *supra* n. 44, at pp. 145-149.
59. Aubert-Piguet, *supra* n. 40, at p. 1503.
60. Ullin Streiff & Adrian von Kaenel & Roger Rudolph, *Arbeitsvertrag: Praxiskommentar zu Art. 319-362 OR* at Art. 357a para. N7 (7th ed., Schulthess Juristische Medien AG, Zurich/Basel/Genf 2012).
61. Stähelin, *supra* n. 44, at pp. 162 et seq.
62. Aubert-Piguet, *supra* n. 40, at p. 1503; Stähelin, *supra* n. 44, at pp. 163 et seq.
63. Article 75c Gesetz über das Staatspersonal des Kantons Freiburg vom 17 October 2001, Systematische Sammlung des Kantons Freiburg (SGF) 122.70.1.

2.3 Situations of Acute National or Local Crisis

Also, in the situation of a national or local crisis, the above-mentioned principles apply in full in Switzerland. However, the relevant laws of the Confederation and the cantons generally provide a legal basis authorizing the executive to provide for restrictions or the abolition of the right to strike.[64] In part, this possibility is limited to actual exceptional situations.[65] In a crisis, the executive authorities could make greater use of these powers, provided that the further conditions (in particular, the risk to the population) stipulated in the relevant laws are met.

As ultima ratio, the Federal Council may, in direct application of Article 185 of the Constitution, issue ordinances and rulings in order to counter existing or imminent threats of serious disruption to public order or internal or external security. Such ordinances must be limited in duration. However, the hurdle for this is very high and is unlikely to be easily overcome in the context of the right to strike. In the event of a strike in an area where life and health of the population are threatened, an emergency situation could arise that would legitimize the intervention of the Federal Council.[66]

3 COMPENSATORY GUARANTEES FOR WORKERS DEPRIVED OF THE RIGHT TO STRIKE

In Swiss doctrine, the view is sometimes expressed that, in the case of restrictions on the right to strike or bans on strikes, compensation in the form of a conciliation or arbitration guarantee must be provided.[67] In general, the Federal Act on the Federal Conciliation Board for the Settlement of Collective Labour Disputes (EES) provides for the possibility of the Federal Council to establish a Federal Conciliation Board on a case-by-case basis to mediate in collective disputes that extend beyond the borders of one canton (Article 1(1) of the EES). However, this possibility is not to be seen directly as a counterpart to a ban on strikes since the Federal Council only has the option of setting up the conciliation body and because, according to Article 1(2) of the Executive Ordinance on the EES,[68] a request from both parties is required; thus, no conciliation or arbitration guarantee is provided. Federal personnel law also does not provide for a corresponding guarantee, neither in Article 24 of the Federal Personnel Act nor in Article 96 of the Federal Personnel Ordinance. In the absence of a Swiss law on strikes,

64. E.g., Art. 24(1) Bundespersonalgesetz; Art. 12(2) Personalgesetz des Kantons Bern vom 16 Sep. 2004; § 46 Personalgesetz des Kantons Luzern vom 26 June 2001.
65. E.g., Art. 68(8) Gesetz über das Staatspersonal FR.
66. Cf. Urs Saxer, *St. Galler Kommentar, Die Schweizerische Bundesverfassung,* Arts 173 para. 1 lit. a-d, 180 para. 2, 184, 185, at Art. 185 para. 59 (Bernhard Ehrenzeller et al. eds, 4th ed., Dike Verlag AG, Zurich/St. Gallen 2023); Jörg Künzli, *Basler Kommentar, Bundesverfassung,* Arts 107, 175, 176, 181, 182, 184-186, at Art. 185 para. 36 (Bernhard Waldmann, Eva Maria Belser & Astrid Epiney eds, Helbing & Lichtenhahn, Basel 2015).
67. Aubert-Piguet, *supra* n. 40, at p. 1503; cf. Jean-Fritz Stöckli, *Das Streikrecht in der Schweiz,* in Basler Juristische Mitteilungen (BJM) 1997, pp. 169-188, at p. 184 (Basler Juristenverein (ed.), Basel).
68. Vollzugsverordnung zum Bundesgesetz vom 2 September 1949 über die eidgenössische Einigungsstelle zur Beilegung von kollektiven Arbeitsstreitigkeiten, SR 821.421.

there is thus no uniform, generally applicable legal basis providing for such conciliation or arbitration guarantees for employees affected by the ban on strikes.

4 CONCLUSION

In Switzerland, the right to strike is derived from Article 28 of the Federal Constitution and applies in principle to all employees in the public and private sector although it cannot be exercised individually. However, there is no specific law on strikes, so that restrictions on the right to strike are only regulated by law in isolated cases and otherwise result from the generally applicable principle of proportionality. Due to the fact that strikes rarely occur in everyday working life in Switzerland, many questions regarding necessary services have not yet been fully clarified. Among other things, it is unclear for which services the Federal Supreme Court draws the line between permissible prohibitions on strikes, permissible restrictions on the right to strike, and the unrestricted right to strike. However, previous case law has shown that the Federal Supreme Court makes assessments on a case-by-case basis and does make distinctions between the individual areas within the sector in potentially life-threatening areas.

CHAPTER 37

Restrictions on the Right to Strike in Turkiye

Kadriye Bakirci[*]

1 GENERAL INFORMATION

In Turkiye, workers are classified as self-employed (independent) or dependent workers.

Dependent workers are employees working under a private law employment contract either in the public or private sector; public (civil) servants; and other public officials who work under an administrative law employment contract in the public sector. Different strands of legislation apply to these three groups of (dependent) workers.

Labour/employment law only applies to employees working under a private employment contract in the public or private sector. On the other hand, the relationship between public servants and other public officials and the State is not a private contractual relationship. Therefore, they fall under the scope of a special section of public law (administrative law).

There is no provision within the legislation for the right to strike for public servants and other public officials. The right to strike is recognized only for employees in the Constitution of Turkiye (1982) and statutory law. However, the right to strike of employees is not absolute. Some permanent and temporary bans on the right to strike and suspension of the strike of employees exist in the public and private sectors.

* This research is supported by the Scientific and Technological Research Council of Turkiye's international post-doctoral research grant.

1.1 Legal Basis of the Right to Strike

The legal basis of the right to strike is the international conventions, the Constitution of Turkiye, statutes, and case law, in a hierarchical order.

International conventions regarding basic rights and freedoms are the highest source of legal order stated in Article 90(5) of the Constitution. According to this article, 'International conventions which are duly put into effect have the same effect as domestic laws ... In case of conflicts between international agreements duly put into effect regarding basic rights and freedoms and domestic laws, the provisions of international conventions shall prevail due to different provisions on the same issue.'

The first international instrument that acknowledges the right to strike explicitly is the UN Convention on Economic, Social, and Cultural Rights (ICESCR) (1966). According to the Convention, 'The States Parties to the present Covenant undertake to ensure ... the right to strike, provided that it is exercised in conformity with the laws of the particular country' (Article 8(d)).

Right to strike has been developed at the international level by the International Labour Office (ILO) supervisory bodies but is not explicitly provided nor regulated in the ILO Constitution nor any of the ILO Conventions or Recommendations.[1] The ILO's Committee of Experts on the Application of Conventions and Recommendations (CEACR) and the Committee on Freedom of Association (CFA) have over the years derived a right to strike from Article 3 of the ILO Convention concerning Freedom of Association and Protection of the Right to Organize (No. 87) (1948). Article 3, subparagraphs (1) and (2) of the Convention, provides that 'Workers' and employers' organizations shall have the right to draw up their constitutions and rules, to elect their representatives in full freedom, to organize their administration and activities, and to formulate their programmes. The public authorities shall refrain from any interference which would restrict this right or impede the lawful exercise thereof.' The right to strike is recognized by the ILO's supervisory bodies as an intrinsic corollary of the right to organize protected by the Convention, deriving from the right of workers' organizations to formulate their programmes of activities to further and defend the economic and social interests of their members.[2] Furthermore, in examining prohibitions on the right to strike, the CEACR has also invoked Articles 8 and 10 of the Convention.

Article 11(1) of the European Convention on Human Rights (ECHR) provides that 'Everyone has the right to freedom of peaceful assembly and to freedom of association with others, including the right to form and to join trade unions for the protection of his interests.' In *Demir and Baykara v. Turkey* (2008) case,[3] the European Court of Human

---

1. Gernigo, B., Odero, A. & Guido, H., ILO Principles Concerning the Right to Strike, ILO, Geneva, 2000, 21, https://www.ilo.org/sites/default/files/wcmsp5/groups/public/%40dgreports/%40jur/documents/genericdocument/wcms_453508.pdf (accessed 30 July 2025).
2. International Labour Conference 81st Session 1994, Report III (Part 4B), General Survey of the Reports on the Freedom of Association and the Right to Organize Convention (No. 87), 1948 and the Right to Organize and Collective Bargaining Convention (No. 98), 1949, Geneva 1994, https://www.ilo.org/public/libdoc/ilo/P/09661/09661(1994-81-4B).pdf (accessed 30 July 2025).
3. ECtHR, *Demir, and Baykara v. Turkey*, Application No. 34503/97, 21 November 2006.

Rights (ECtHR) confirmed that there is an inherent right to collective bargaining protected by Article 11 ECHR, within the right to freedom of association. Only interference that is strictly necessary for a democratic society can be justified. Therefore, it is a landmark case in the international development of freedom of association. It gave new content to Article 11 rights in the context of collective bargaining. Shortly afterwards, in the *Enerji Yapi-Yol Sen v. Turkey* (2009)[4] case, the ECtHR adopted a similar approach concerning industrial action. The ECtHR indicated that the right to strike was implicit in Article 11 of the ECHR, in reliance on ILO standards.

The ICESCR, observations, and views of the CEACR and the CFA, and the judicial rulings of the ECtHR are binding sources of law in Turkiye under the Constitution of Turkiye Article 90(5).

At the EU level, the right to strike is enshrined in Article 28 of the European Union Charter of Fundamental Rights (ECFR) (2000). The Revised European Social Charter (RESC) (1996) was a source of inspiration for the ECFR. Article 28 provides that 'Workers and employers, or their respective organizations, have, by Union law and national laws and practices, the right to negotiate and conclude collective agreements at the appropriate levels and, in cases of conflicts of interest, to take collective action to defend their interests, including strike action.' As a candidate for EU membership, Turkiye is required to harmonize its legislation with the EU's acquis communautaire.[5]

Turkiye ratified the European Social Charter of 1961 and the RESC which also explicitly recognizes the right to collective action, including the right to strike (Article 6(4)). The semantics of Article 6 of the RESC is much broader. The provision suggests that strike action is one among other species of collective action. However, Turkiye has not accepted Articles 5 and 6 of both Charters. Turkiye also did not ratify the COE Additional Protocol to the European Social Charter Providing for a System of Collective Complaints of 1995.

The main national sources of the right to strike are the Constitution of Turkiye, the Employee Trade Unions and Collective Bargaining Act (No. 6356) (2012), Public Officials Trade Unions and Collective Bargaining Act (No. 4688) (2001), and case law.

1.2 Main Features of the Regulation

Although the right to strike is not absolute and could be subject to certain conditions and restrictions, Turkish law is too restrictive on the right to strike, especially in the public sector.

Under international, regional, and EU law all workers are entitled to the right to strike. However, the Constitution of Turkiye recognizes the right to strike as a collective right of employees working under a private law employment contract either in the

4. ECtHR, *Enerji Yapi-Yol Sen v. Turkey*, Application No. 68959/01, 21 April 2009.
5. *See* EU-Turkey Joint Consultative Committee, Trade Union Rights Situation in Turkey, Joint Report, 32nd meeting, 7-8 November 2013, https://eur-lex.europa.eu/legal-content/EN/TXT/PDF/?uri=OJ:JOC_2015_242_R_0006&from=ENchrome-extension://efaidnbmnnnibpcajpcglclefindmkaj/https://eur-lex.europa.eu/legal-content/EN/TXT/PDF/?uri=OJ:JOC_2015_242_R_0006&from=EN (accessed 30 July 2025).

public or private sector but does not recognize it for public officials (public servants and other public officials who work under an administrative law employment contract in the public sector). The Constitution states that 'Employees have the right to strike during the collective bargaining process if a disagreement arises' (Article 54(1)).

Act No. 6356 states that the expression 'strike' means any concerted cessation by employees of their work with the object of halting the activities of a given establishment or of paralysing such activities to a considerable extent or any abandonment by employees of their work by a decision taken to that effect by an organization (Article 58(1)). Lawful strike means any strike called by employees by Act No. 6356 with the object of safeguarding or improving their economic and social position and working conditions in the event of a dispute during negotiations to conclude a collective labour agreement (Article 58(2)). An unlawful strike means any strike called without fulfilling the conditions for a lawful strike (Article 58(3)).

According to the definition of Article 58, all collective work stoppages or disruptions other than those organized in case of disagreement during collective bargaining and/or do not aim to conclude a collective labour agreement to defend employees' economic interests or aim to enforce a collective agreement, such as slowdowns, solidarity strikes, political strikes, general strikes, and collective actions, should be deemed unlawful.

However, the ILO's supervisory bodies consider that the right to strike should not be limited solely to industrial disputes that are likely to be resolved through the signing of a collective agreement.[6] Any work stoppage, however brief and limited, may generally be considered a strike. Regarding various types of strike action denied to workers, the CFA considers that these restrictions may be justified only if the strike ceases to be peaceful.[7]

In its 2012 General Survey, the CEACR noted Article 58 of Act No. 6356 and requested the Government of Turkiye to indicate how protest action, sympathy strikes, and other means of legitimate industrial action are protected in line with the 2010 Constitutional amendment.[8]

6. ILO Governing Body, 317th Session, Geneva, 6-28 March 2013, Committee on Freedom of Association, Report No. 367, Case No. 2814 (Chile) Definitive Report, March 2013, para. 354, https://www.ilo.org/wcmsp5/groups/public/---ed_norm/---.relconf/documents/meetingdocument/wcms_208542.pdf (accessed 30 July 2025); *See also* ILO Freedom of Association: Digest of Decisions and Principles of the Freedom of Association Committee of the Governing Body of the ILO Geneva, International Labour Office, 5th (revised) ed., 2006, para. 531, https://www.ilo.org/sites/default/files/wcmsp5/groups/public/%40ed_norm/%40normes/documents/publication/wcms_090632.pdf (accessed 30 July 2025).
7. ILO, Compilation of Decisions of the Committee on Freedom of Association Right to Strike, para. 783, https://www.ilo.org/dyn/normlex/en/f?p=NORMLEXPUB:70002:0::NO::P70002_HIER_ELEMENT_ID,P70002_HIER_LEVEL:3945366,1; International Labour Conference 81st Session 1994, Report III (Part 4B) (accessed 30 July 2025).
8. ILO, Direct Request (CEACR) – adopted 2015, published 105th ILC session (2016),Freedom of Association and Protection of the Right to Organise Convention, 1948 (No. 87) – Türkiye (Ratification: 1993), https://www.ilo.org/dyn/normlex/en/f?p=1000:13100:0::NO:13100:P13100_COMMENT_ID:3255738 (accessed 30 July 2025).

In Case No. 3011 (Turkiye) of 2013,[9] the CFA requests the Government of Turkiye to review together with the social partners section 58(2) of Act No. 6356 and Article 54(1) of the Constitution of Turkiye so that lawful industrial action is no longer limited to strikes linked to a dispute during the collective bargaining process, to ensure that the relevant provisions are brought into harmony with the principles of freedom of association.[10] The case involved the Turkish Civil Aviation Union (Hava-Iş Sen) member employees slowing down the operations at Turkish Airlines' workplaces to protest a legislative attempt to remove aviation employees' rights to strike. Turkish Airlines fired 316 of its personnel over the partial slowdown that forced the national flag carrier to cancel at least 128 domestic and international flights.

Concerning this collective action, different divisions of the Court of Cassation reached different and conflicting conclusions. The Court of Cassation 22nd Division concluded that the collective action of Turkish Airlines employees was unlawful, arguing that it was politically motivated.[11] However, the Court of Cassation 7th[12] and 9th[13] Divisions decided that dismissals were unlawful and employees should be reinstated.

According to the CFA, while purely political strikes do not fall within the scope of the principles of freedom of association,[14] trade unions should be able to have recourse to protest strikes, in particular where aimed at criticizing a government's economic and social policies.[15] The right to strike should not be limited solely to industrial disputes that are likely to be resolved through the signing of a collective agreement; workers and their organizations should be able to express in a broader context, if necessary, their dissatisfaction as regards economic and social matters affecting their members' interests.[16]

Strikes and protests that occurred in the Turkish metal industry in 2015 also raised questions about whether these strikes were 'lawful' or 'unlawful' and what the employers' rights would be when faced with such cases. 'Wildcat' strikes and protests of 2015 which were sudden, unexpected, and out of the procedure laid down by Act No. 6356 were initiated due to low wages. However, these strikes and resistance movements were not only against the employers but also against Turkish Metal Union

9. ILO, Report in Which the Committee Requests to Be Kept Informed of Development – Report No. 372, June 2014, Case No. 3011 (Türkiye) – Complaint date: 4 March 2013 – Follow-up, https://www.ilo.org/dyn/normlex/en/f?p=1000:70006:0::NO:70006:P70006_COMPLAINT_TEXT_ID,P70006_PARAGRAPH_NO:3173671,648 (accessed 30 July 2025).
10. ILO Governing Body 325th Session, Geneva, 29 October-12 November 2015, 376th Report of the Committee on Freedom of Association, Case No. 3011 (Türkiye), para. 151, https://www.ilo.org/sites/default/files/wcmsp5/groups/public/%40ed_norm/%40relconf/documents/meetingdocument/wcms_424082.pdf (accessed 30 July 2025).
11. Court of Cassation, 22nd Division, 14 May 2013, 2013/7515, 2013/10949.
12. Court of Cassation 7th Division, 12 April 2013, 2013/10927, 2013/6401.
13. Court of Cassation 9th Division, 4 February 2014, 2013/9629, 2014/3169; Constitutional Court of Turkiye, Application No. 2013/6932, 6 January 2015, para. 26/c.
14. ILO, Digest (1996), paras 528, 573, 901, 1245.
15. ILO, Digest (1996), para. 531.
16. ILO, Digest (1996), para. 529.

(Turk-Metal Sen) that was organized in these workplaces.[17] In cases related to these collective actions, different divisions of the Court of Cassation decided that the collective actions did not comply with the principle of proportionality, and they gave the employer the right to terminate employment contracts of employees with just cause.[18]

Act No. 6356 does not allow strikes that aim to solve a legal conflict such as to enforce collective labour agreements. According to the CFA, the solution to a legal conflict as a result of a difference in interpretation of a legal text should be left to the competent courts. The prohibition of strikes in such a situation does not constitute a breach of freedom of association.[19]

One of the ECtHR's decisions, *Dilek and Others v. Turkey* (2008),[20] raised the question of whether the Court's protection extends from a right to strike to a more comprehensive right to take collective action. In this case, several public servants had left their posts for a couple of hours to protest against the working conditions applicable to them. The Government of Turkiye and the applicants disagreed on whether the action concerned could qualify as strike action. However, the ECtHR did not enter into such a debate, considering the question of the definition of strike action to be irrelevant insofar as the action concerned constituted a 'collective action within the context of the exercise of trade union rights' in the generic meaning of the term.[21]

Similar views were expressed by the ECtHR in *Tek Gida v. Turkey* (2017),[22] a case involving a private employer. The employer dismissed several employees who were union members to prevent the number of such employees in its workforce from reaching the threshold for collective bargaining recognition. Although the dismissed employees were awarded substantial compensation for wrongful dismissal, they complained that the dismissals had the effect of eradicating trade unionism at the employer's factories and that the State's failure to safeguard the right to organize amounted to an infringement of Article 11 right.

In some other judgments involving Turkiye[23] also, the ECtHR did not address the issue of the right to strike and assess whether the recognition of such a right was an essential element of the right to form and join trade unions. In the cases concerned,

17. Celik, A., 'The Wave of Strikes and Resistances of the Metal Workers of 2015 in Turkey', Vol. IV,(10), Centre for Policy and Research on Turkey, London, 2015, pp. 21-37, https://www.researchgate.net/publication/325795423_The_Wave_of_Strikes_and_Resistances_of_the_Metal_Workers_of_2015_in_Turkey (accessed 30 July 2025).
18. Court of Cassation 9th Division, 9 May 2016, 2016/17006, 2016/15566. Court of Cassation 9th Division, 29 June 2016, 2016/1791, 2016/15580, Court of Cassation 9th Division. 19 April 2016, 2016/8279, 2016/1149.
19. ILO, Digest (1996), paras 532, 192, 897; *see also* Court of Cassation 9th Division, 21 June 1994, 1994/1728, 1994/9862.
20. ECtHR, *Dilek and others v. Turkey*, App Nos 74611/01, 26876/02, 27628/02, 30 January 2008.
21. *Dilek and others v. Turkey* (2008), para. 6.
22. ECtHR, *Tek Gida v. Turkey*, Application No. 35009/05, 4 April 2017.
23. ECtHR, *Karacay v. Turkey*, Application No. 6615/03, 27 March 2007; ECtHR, *Urcan and others v. Turkey*, Application Nos 23018/04, 23034/04, 23042/04, 23071/04, 23073/04, 23081/04, 23086/04, 23091/04, 23094/04, 23444/04 and 23676/04, 17 July 2008; ECtHR, *Saime Ozcan v. Turkey*, Application No. 2953/04, 15 September 2009; ECtHR, *Kaya and Seyhan v. Turkey*, Application No. 30946/04, 15 September 2009; ECtHR, *Dilek and others v. Turkey*, 2008.

public servants had been absent from their work to participate in a demonstration in support of a claim for better working conditions. In all cases, the restriction based on the statutory prohibition of public servants having recourse to collective action was considered to be disproportionate.

In Turkiye, only trade unions have the right to call a strike (Act No. 6356, Article 41). Non-union bodies, federations, or confederations of employees, and employees themselves are not allowed to call and launch a strike. However, over the years, the CFA made clear that strike action is a right that workers and their organizations (trade unions, federations, and confederations) are entitled to enjoy. The prohibition on the calling of strikes by federations and confederations is not compatible with Convention No. 87.[24]

Unlawful strikes are subject to dismissal and heavy fines. Under Act No. 6356, if a strike was declared unlawful by the Government or the competent court, the employer may, without any liability as to notice or compensation, terminate the employment contract (Article 70(1)). The Act provides administrative fines against unlawful strikes and violations of the guarantees for employees provided by the Act (Article 78).[25]

In Case No. 3011 (Turkiye) of 2013,[26] because of the alleged excessiveness of fines provided for in section 78(1) of Act No. 6356, the CFA requested the Government of Turkiye to consider reviewing the system of fines in line with its conclusions, in consultation with the social partners.[27]

In the view of the CEACR, regardless of the legality of the strike action, any sanctions imposed should not be disproportionate to the seriousness of the violations committed.[28]

24. ILO, Compilation, para. 757; *see also* European Committee of Social Rights, Conclusions, France, Decision Date 31 March 2000, Cycle XV-1, http://hudoc.esc.coe.int/eng/?i=XV-1/def/FRA/6/4/EN, E.T. 12 April 2019 (accessed 30 July 2025).
25. Article 1, subpara. (d), of the ILO's Abolition of Forced Labour Convention, 1957 (No. 105), prohibits any form of forced or compulsory labour 'as a punishment for having participated in strikes'.
26. ILO, Case No. 3011 (Türkiye) – Complaint date: 4 March 2013, Turkish Civil Aviation Union (Hava-Is) and International Transport Workers' Federation (ITF), https://www.ilo.org/dyn/normlex/en/f?p=NORMLEXPUB:50001:0::NO::P50001_COMPLAINT_FILE_ID:311 (accessed 30 July 2025); ILO, Report in Which the Committee Requests to Be Kept Informed of Development – Report No. 372, June 2014. Case No. 3011 (Türkiye) – Complaint date: 4 March 2013 – Follow-up, https://www.ilo.org/dyn/normlex/en/f?p=1000:70006:0::NO:70006:P70006_COMPLAINT_TEXT_ID,P70006_PARAGRAPH_NO:3173671,648 (accessed 30 July 2025).
27. ILO, Governing Body 325th Session, Geneva, 29 October-12 November 2015, 376th Report of the Committee on Freedom of Association Case No. 3011, October 2015, para. 151, https://www.ilo.org/sites/default/files/wcmsp5/groups/public/%40ed_norm/%40relconf/documents/meetingdocument/wcms_424082.pdf (accessed 30 July 2025); ILO, Nomlex, Freedom of association cases, Case No 3011 (Türkiye) https://www.ilo.org/wcmsp5/groups/public/---ed_normComplaint date: 4 March 2013 (accessed 30 July 2025).
    https://normlex.ilo.org/dyn/nrmlx_en/f?p=1000:20060:0:FIND:NO:20060:P20060_COUNTRY_ID,P20060_COMPLAINT_STATU_ID:102893,1495811 (accessed 30 July 2025).
28. ILO, Observation (CEACR) – adopted 2020, published 109th ILC session (2021). Abolition of Forced Labour Convention, 1957 (No. 105) – United States of America (Ratification: 1991).
    https://www.ilo.org/dyn/normlex/en/f?p=NORMLEXPUB:13100:0::NO:13100:P13100_COMMENT_ID,P13100_COUNTRY_ID:4046588,102871:NO (accessed 30 July 2025).

2 PERMITTED RESTRICTIONS

The right to strike may be restricted or banned only about public servants exercising authority in the name of the State, in essential services in the strict sense of the term, and in situations of acute national or local crisis, for a limited period and to the extent necessary to meet the requirements of the situation.[29]

2.1 Certain Categories of Public Servants

Taking into account the importance of ensuring the continuity of the functions of the three branches of the State (the legislative, executive, and judicial authorities), the CEACR and the CFA consider that States may restrict or prohibit the right to strike of public servants 'exercising authority in the name of the State'. It may not be extended to cover public servants in general or public employees engaged in state-owned commercial or industrial enterprises.[30]

Because of the above distinction, any legislative restrictions should define as clearly and narrowly as possible the class of public servants whose right to strike is restricted. The determination of such public servants should be made based on the nature of the tasks that they perform and the likely impact of disruption to that service in the event of a strike.[31]

Under the Constitution of Turkiye, 'The fundamental and permanent functions required by the public services that the State, state economic enterprises and other public corporate bodies assigned to perform by principles of general administration, shall be carried out by public servants and other public officials' (Article 128(1)). Turkish law does not recognize the right to strike for public servants and public officials employed under administrative law contracts in the public sector, regardless of whether they exercise authority on behalf of the State.

Article 27 of the Civil Servants Act No. 657 (1965) prohibits public servants from organizing, declaring, publicizing, participating in, supporting, or provoking the continuation of a strike. Similarly, Article 14 of Statutory Decree No. 399 (1990), which regulates the personnel regime of state economic enterprises and repeals certain

29. International Labour Conference 109th Session, 2021, Application of International Labour Standards 2021 Report III /Addendum (Part A) Addendum to the 2020 Report of the Committee of Experts on the Application of Conventions and Recommendations, https://www.ilo.org/sites/default/files/wcmsp5/groups/public/%40ed_norm/%40relconf/documents/meetingdocument/wcms_771042.pdf (accessed 30 July 2025).
30. ILO, Digest (1996), paras 537, 532; International Labour Conference, 96th Session, 2007, Report of the Committee of Experts on the Application of Conventions and Recommendations, Report III (Part 1A), General Report and observations concerning particular countries, para. 169, https://www.ilo.org/public/english/standards/relm/ilc/ilc96/pdf/rep-iii-1a.pdf (accessed 30 July 2025); *see also* ILO, Report in Which the Committee Requests to Be Kept Informed of Development – Report No. 344, March 2007, Case No. 2365 (Zimbabwe) – Complaint date: 9 July 2004 – Closed, para. 1446, https://www.ilo.org/dyn/normlex/en/f?p=1000:50002:0::NO:50002:P50002_COMPLAINT_TEXT_ID:2908909 (accessed 30 July 2025).
31. ILO, Labour Legislation Guidelines, Chapter V Substantive Provisions of Labour Legislation: The Right to Strike, 2001, https://www.ilo.org/legacy/english/dialogue/ifpdial/llg/noframes/ch5.htm (accessed 30 July 2025).

provisions of Statutory Decree No. 233, imposes the same prohibitions on public officials employed under an administrative law contract. In addition, Act No. 657 (Article 28) and Decree No. 399 (Article 19) prohibit also public servants and other public officials from deliberately and collectively withdrawing from public service or not coming to their posts or taking actions that will result in slowing down or disrupting State services and works. Decree No. 399 Article 19 further prohibits public officials working under an administrative law employment contract to make collective oral or written applications or complaints.

These laws which forbid strikes by public servants and other public officials do not meet the standard set out by the ILO supervisory bodies, ICESCR, and the ECtHR.

In *Enerji Yapi-Yol Sen*, while ECtHR acknowledged that the right to strike was not absolute and could be subject to certain conditions and restrictions, it held that a ban applied to all public servants was too wide a restriction. That case concerned a prime ministerial ban on public sector employees taking part in a national one-day strike.

In its 2012 General Survey, the CEACR requests the Government of Turkiye to review the legislation concerning public service workers with the relevant social partners with a view to its amendment to ensure that the ban on industrial action is limited to public servants exercising authority in the name of the State and those working in essential services.[32]

Act No. 657 (Article 125) and Decree No. 399 (Articles 44-45) provide disciplinary sanctions, and Penal Code (No. 5237) (Article 260) provides penal sanctions against public servants and public officials who take part in collective or industrial action.

However, the CEACR indicates that public servants who are not exercising authority in the name of the State should be able to carry out their activities, including industrial action, without sanction.[33] In cases of peaceful strikes, the CFA has stated that 'no one should be deprived of their freedom or be subject to penal sanctions for the mere act of organizing or participating in a peaceful strike'.[34]

In *Urcan v. Turkey* (2008)[35] and *Saime Ozcan v. Turkey* (2009),[36] teachers who had participated in industrial action were given prison sentences, which, in the case of Ms Urcan, was suspended, and, in the case of Ms Ozcan, was subsequently set aside. In both cases, the ECtHR upheld the complaints under Article 11, rejecting the Government's arguments that Article 11 permitted it to choose how the freedom of association was to be protected and that these could include means other than industrial action.

In *Karacay v. Turkey* (2007)[37] and *Kaya and Seyhan v. Turkey* (2009),[38] disciplinary warnings for participating in industrial action were held by the ECtHR to amount to unjustified violations of Article 11. In these cases, the detriment imposed was described

32. ILO, Direct Request (CEACR) - adopted 2015, published 105th ILC session (2016).
33. ILO, Direct Request (CEACR) - adopted 2015, published 105th ILC session (2016).
34. ILO, Compilation, paras 970, 972, 974.
35. *Urcan v. Turkey*, Application Nos 23018/04, 23034/04, 23042/04, 23071/04, 23073/04, 23081/04, 23086/04, 23091/04, 23094/04, 23444/04 and 23676/04, 17 July 2008, para. 34.
36. *Saime Ozcan v. Turkey*, Application No. 22943/04, 15 September 2009.
37. *Karacay v. Turkey*, Application No. 6615/03, 27 June 2007.
38. *Kaya and Seyhan v. Turkey* (2009).

by the ECtHR as at the minimum, being in the form of a disciplinary warning, yet the ECtHR found that this was an action that interfered with the right to freedom of association in a way that was not proportionate and justified.

The analysis in *Karacay* has been consistently followed in later cases that any form of sanction on individual strikers interferes with Article 11 ECHR.

In *Enerji Yapi-Yol Sen,* the case concerned the members of the trade union Enerji Yapi-Yol Sen who ignored the prohibition and were disciplined. The ECtHR held that the disciplinary action was 'capable of discouraging trade union members and others from exercising their legitimate right to take part in such one-day strikes or other actions aimed at defending their members' interests' and amounted to a threat to rights guaranteed under Article 11. The strike ban was not in response to a 'pressing social need', and the Government of Turkiye had thus failed to justify the need for the impugned restriction in a democratic society.

In *Ognevenko v. Russia* (2019),[39] the ECtHR concluded that disciplinary sanctions 'inevitably had a "chilling effect" on trade union members taking part in industrial action'.

Most of these ECtHR cases involve public sector workers. However, the ECtHR's judgment in *Tek Gida* is important to show there is no material difference in the positive obligation of the State to address concerns about Article 11 ECHR and its duty not directly to interfere with workers' rights. This supplements the overreaching point that the State owes a positive obligation to secure the effective enjoyment of rights for individuals under Article 11 ECHR through effective and clear judicial protection.

In its many judgments, the Constitutional Court of Turkiye has referred to the judgments of the ECtHR. In the *Selda Demir Taze* case, the Court, citing the ECtHR decisions, held the disciplinary reprimand, however minimal, was disproportionate because it was liable to deter legitimate participation in union-organized industrial action. The claim involved a warning issued for participation in a two-day strike organized to protest against a draft bill on primary education and training by the public servant's trade union. The Court emphasized that the freedom of association and the right to the union are among the freedoms enshrined in the Constitution as a basic value and embodying democracy and that they form one of the basic values of a democratic society. According to the Court, how the unions express their opinions within the framework of a union-related activity also benefits from the safeguards afforded by the right to a union, even if not acceptable to the competent authorities. The Court indicates that democracy, by its very nature, provides an opportunity for public discussion and resolution of matters and that individuals exercising their right to a union will also benefit from the safeguards afforded for the basic principles of a democratic society, such as pluralism, tolerance, and open-mindedness, as in the field of the freedom of expression.[40]

39. ECtHR, *Ognevenko v. Russia*, Application No. 44873/09, 20 November 2018, para. 83.
40. Constitutional Court of Turkiye, Application No. 2013/8463, 18 September 2014, para. 52; Constitutional Court of Turkiye, Application No. 2013/8463, 18/9/2014; Constitutional Court of Turkiye, Application No. 74552/01, 5 March 2007, para. 36.

2.2 Essential Services in the Strict Sense of the Term

The ILO's supervisory bodies have taken the position that it is admissible to limit or prohibit the right to strike in essential services in the strict sense of the term, defined as those the interruption of which would endanger the life, personal safety, or health of the whole or part of the population in which restrictions or even a prohibition may be justified, accompanied, however, by compensatory guarantees. What is meant by essential services in the strict sense of the term depends to a large extent on the particular circumstances prevailing in a country. Moreover, this concept is not absolute, in the sense that a non-essential service may become essential if a strike lasts beyond a certain time or extends beyond a certain scope, thus endangering the life, personal safety, or health of the whole or part of the population.[41]

On the other hand, in the view of the CFR and CEACR, a 'minimum service' could be appropriate as a possible alternative in situations in which a substantial restriction or total prohibition of strike action would not appear to be justified and where, without calling into question the right to strike of the large majority of workers, one might consider ensuring that users' basic needs are met or that facilities operate safely or without interruption.[42]

In this respect, the CEACR recalled that the maintenance of minimum services in the event of strikes should only be possible in certain situations, namely:

(1) in services the interruption of which would endanger the life, personal safety, or health of the whole or part of the population (essential services in the strict sense of the term);
(2) other services in which strikes of a certain magnitude and duration could cause an acute crisis threatening the normal conditions of existence of the population;
(3) in public services of fundamental importance; and
(4) to ensure the security of facilities and the maintenance of equipment.[43]

According to the CEACR, the minimum services imposed should meet at least two requirements:

> 1) must genuinely and exclusively be minimum services that are limited to the operations which are strictly necessary to meet the basic needs of the population or the minimum requirements of the service while maintaining the effectiveness of the pressure brought to bear; and
> 2) since this system restricts one of the essential means of pressure available to workers to defend their interests, their organizations should be able, if they so

41. ILO, Compilation, para. 837.
42. ILO, Compilation, para. 867; ILO, Observation (CEACR) – adopted 2022, published 111th ILC session (2023), http://www.ilo.int/dyn/normlex/en/f?p=1000:13101:0::NO:13101:P13101_COMMENT_ID:2173135 (accessed 30 July 2025).
43. ILO, Observation (CEACR) (2023).

wish, to participate in defining such a service, along with employers and the public authorities.[44]

The Constitution of Turkiye does not recognize the right to strike for public servants, and other public officials without making any distinction whether they are working in essential services.

The Constitution provides that the circumstances and workplaces in which strikes and lockouts may be prohibited or postponed shall be regulated by law (Article 54(3)). Concerning public and private sector employees, Act No. 6356 places a permanent ban on the right to strike in particular activities and services, usually defined as essential services (Article 62). The Act does not establish a definition of essential services but includes a list of activities deemed to be essential services in which work stoppages are not permitted. According to the Act, it is unlawful to call a strike in the following works: life and property rescue services; funeral services and cemeteries; city water supply networks, electricity, natural gas, petroleum production, refining and distribution, as well as petrochemical work beginning from naphtha or natural gas; workplaces directly operated by the Ministry of National Defense, the General Command of the Gendarmerie, and the Coast Guard Command; and fire services and hospitals operated by public institutions (Article 62/1). It is unlawful to call a strike in the sea, air, rail, and road vehicles, which have not finalized their journey in places of domestic destination (Article 62/2).

However, according to the CFA, the petroleum sector and oil facilities, distribution of fuel to ensure that flights continue to operate in the gas sector, and filling and selling gas canisters do not constitute essential services in the strict sense of the term.[45]

Act No. 6356 provides for the maintenance by a defined and limited category of employees of minimum service when a total and prolonged stoppage in a lawful strike might result in serious consequences for the public. According to Article 65, employees excluded from participating in a lawful strike are as follows:

(1) A sufficient number of employees, whose activities are unrelated to the production or sale of goods, shall be required to work, and the employer shall be obliged to employ them in order to: maintain the continuity of operations that must be sustained for technical reasons; ensure workplace safety and prevent damage to machinery, installations, equipment, raw materials, and finished or semi-finished products; and ensure the protection of animals and plants.

(2) The type and number of employees, including substitutes, to be excluded from a strike shall be announced in writing within the workplace by the employer or his/her representative during the six working days following the commencement of collective bargaining, and a copy of the announcement shall be notified to the employees' trade union that is a party. If an objection to this notice is not submitted to the competent court within six working days,

44. ILO, Observation (CEACR) (2023).
45. ILO, Compilation, para. 842.

the notice shall become final. Where an objection is submitted, the local court shall decide within six working days. This decision is final.

(3) If the employees to be excluded from a strike have not been determined for any reason during the time limit fixed within the legal time, the employees' or employers' trade union may request the competent authority to determine the number of such employees even after the expiry of the time limit. The competent authority shall determine this as soon as possible and notify the parties. Where necessary, the competent authority may ex officio determine this. Any of the parties may lodge an appeal with the competent court against this determination within six working days.

(4) The employees that will continue working in the workplace during the strike shall be determined ex officio by the competent authority and shall be notified in writing to the employer and employees concerned within three working days following the date that the competent authority is informed on the decision to call a strike and lockout. This provision shall not apply to the chairman and members of the executive board of the employees' trade union and its branch who work in the relevant workplace and are a party to the collective bargaining.

(5) The employer may recruit new employees, with the written permission of the competent authority, instead of the employees who do not work for any reason from among those who cannot participate in the strike.

In its 2012 General Survey, the CEACR requests the Government of Turkiye to take steps to review section 65 of Act No. 6356 in consultation with the social partners to ensure that workers' organizations can participate in the determination of a required minimum service at the workplace, and that, failing agreement, the matter may be referred to an independent body that has the confidence of the parties. The Committee considers that to promote the participation of the union in the determination of a minimum service in the event of industrial action, it would be important for the Government to provide for such participation in the law rather than granting this authority unilaterally to the employer. The Committee, therefore, requests the Government to take steps to review this provision in consultation with the social partners with a view to its amendment and to provide information on any developments in this regard.[46]

Act No. 5188 on Private Security Services (2004) also prohibits private security personnel from participating in strikes (Article 17). Private security personnel who breach the ban to participate in a strike are subject to an administrative fine of TRY 1 billion, and their work licence is cancelled. Such persons cannot work as private security personnel thereafter (Article 20(c)). Private security personnel are considered public servants for the Penal Code (Article 23(1)).

Capital Market Act No. 6362 (2012) Article 137(2) provides that strike and lockout are not allowed in services carried out by exchanges and other organized

46. ILO, Direct Request (CEACR) – adopted 2015, published 105th ILC session (2016).

marketplaces, central clearing institutions, central securities depositories, and the Central Registry Agency Incorporation, which are established and are performing their activities according to the Act.

2.3 Situations of Acute National or Local Crisis

The CFA considers a general prohibition of strikes can be justified 'in the event of an acute national emergency'.[47] This concept applies only in exceptional circumstances, for example, against the backdrop of an attempted coup d'Ètat against the constitutional government, which gave rise to a state of emergency.[48] The CEACR also considers the prohibition of recourse to strike action can be justified in case of an acute national crisis and then, only for a limited period and to the extent necessary to meet the requirements of the situation. The Committee has emphasized that 'this means genuine crises, such as those arising as a result of a serious conflict, insurrection or natural disaster in which the normal conditions for the functioning of society are absent'.[49]

According to the Constitution of Turkiye, in times of war, mobilization, or a state of emergency, the exercise of fundamental rights and freedoms may be partially or entirely suspended, or measures derogating the guarantees embodied in the Constitution may be taken to the extent required by the exigencies of the situation, as long as obligations under international law are not violated (Article 15(1)).

Act No. 6356 allows temporary bans (Article 62(2)) and suspension of strikes (Article 63) in situations of acute national or local crisis.

Act No. 6356 Article 62(2) provides that where the life of the community is paralysed by a natural disaster, the President of the Republic may prohibit strikes and lockouts in the workplaces located in such areas as may be necessary, provided that it will be effective for as long as the situation continues. The strike and lockout shall be implemented within 60 days after the prohibition is lifted, provided that the opposite party is informed 6 working days beforehand.

Act No. 6365 Article 63(1) allows the President to suspend a strike for 60 days by way of a decree. According to the article, a lawful strike or lockout that has been called or commenced may be suspended by the President for 60 days with a decree if it is prejudicial to public health or national security. The suspension shall come into force on the date of publication of the decree.

The 'suspension of a strike' in Turkiye turned into a routine habit and is not an exceptional situation.[50]

47. ILO, Compilation, para. 824.
48. ILO, Freedom of Association: Digest of Decisions and Principles of the Freedom of Association Committee of the Governing Body of the ILO Geneva, 4th (revised) ed., 1996, paras 528-530.
49. International Labour Conference 81st Session 1994, Report III (Part 4B), para. 152.
50. Celik, A., 'Trade Union Rights in Turkey: A Gloomy Picture', Vol. 23(3), International Union Rights, 2016, p. 5, https://www.jstor.org/stable/10.14213/inteuniorigh.23.3.0003 (accessed 30 July 2025); Celik, A., 'The Right To Strike Under Threat In Turkey', 2016, https://www.academia.edu/10399817/The_Right_To_Strike_Under_Threat_In_Turkey (accessed 30 July 2025).

In Case No. 3084 (Turkiye), the CFA stated that responsibility for suspending a strike on the grounds of national security or public health should not lie with the Government but with an independent body that has the confidence of all parties concerned.[51]

In this case, the complainant trade union (Kristal-Is Union) alleged that Article 63 of Act No. 6356, in general, and the Government's Decree No. 2014/6524 of 27 June 2014, which suspended a strike in the glass industry for a period of 60 days on grounds of public health and national security, in particular, are not in conformity with Conventions No. 87 and No. 98. The CFA stated that section 63 of Act No. 6356, which allows the Government to suspend a strike and impose compulsory arbitration on the grounds of national security or public health, is not in itself contrary to freedom of association principles as long as it is implemented in good faith and by ordinary meaning of the terms 'national security' and 'public health'. The Committee observes, however, that the Government indicates no reason why a strike in the glass industry might be considered harmful to national security and public health. The Committee further considers that the repeated application of this provision to prevent strikes in sectors such as the glass industry, which do not appear to have any direct connection to national security or public health, might amount to a systematic violation of the right to strike.

In 2015, the Constitutional Court of Turkiye concluded that it was not proven that the order suspending the strike, in this case, met a pressing social need and that this order 'was not necessary for a democratic society'. Consequently, the Constitutional Court held that there was a breach of the applicant's right to form trade unions guaranteed in Article 51 of the Constitution.[52]

In its Report 2021, the CEACR requests once more that the Government of Turkiye ensure that section 63 of Act No. 6356 was not applied in a manner to infringe on the right of workers' organizations to organize their activities free from government interference. The Committee further notes with concern that in 2017, five strikes were suspended, including in the glass sector on the grounds of threat to national security, while in 2015, the Constitutional Court of Turkiye had found a strike suspension in the same sector unconstitutional. The Committee notes that while the legislation indicates that the measure of suspension should be limited to strikes that may be prejudicial to public health or national security, it has been interpreted in such a broad manner that strikes in non-essential services have also been effectively prohibited. It informs in this respect that in January 2019 a strike called by the International Transport Workers' Federation-affiliated railway union (Demiryol-Is Sen) in Izmir has been postponed under these laws. The Committee requests the Government to provide its comments thereon. Considering that strikes can be suspended only in essential services in the strict sense of the term, for public servants exercising authority in the name of the State

---

51. ILO, Case No. 3084 (Türkiye) – Report No. 374, March 2015 Complaint date: 15 July 2014, Complaint against the Government of Turkey presented by the Kristal-Is (Trade Union of Glass, Cement, and Soil Workers of Turkey) is supported by the IndustriALL Global Union, https://www.ilo.org/sites/default/files/wcmsp5/groups/public/@ed_norm/@relconf/documents/meetingdocument/wcms_357167.pdf (accessed 30 July 2025).
52. Constitutional Court of Turkiye, Application Nos 2014/12166, 2/7/2015, para. 83.

or an event of an acute national crisis, the Committee requests the Government to ensure that the above is taken into consideration in the application of section 63 of Act No. 6356.[53]

In addition, the CFA emphasizes that economic consideration should not be invoked as a justification for restrictions on the right to strike;[54] however, when a service that is not essential in the strict sense of the term but is part of a very important sector in the country is brought to a standstill, once again, measures to guarantee a minimum service may be justified.[55]

3 COMPENSATORY GUARANTEES FOR WORKERS DEPRIVED OF THE RIGHT TO STRIKE

The ILO's supervisory bodies have taken the position that where the right to strike is subject to restrictions or a prohibition, in certain enterprises or services considered essential, or for certain public servants exercising authority in the name of the State, the workers should be afforded adequate protection to compensate for the restrictions imposed on their freedom of action. Such protection should include, for example, impartial conciliation and eventually arbitration procedures that have the confidence of the parties with which workers and their organizations could be associated. Such arbitration awards should be binding on both parties and once issued should be implemented rapidly and completely.[56]

Under the Constitution of Turkiye (Article 53/4) and Act No. 4688 (Articles 33, 34), in case of failure of collective bargaining negotiations in the public sector, the chair of Public Employers' Delegation (the Minister of Labour) on behalf of the public administration and the chair of Public Servants' Unions Delegation on behalf of public officials can apply to the Public Officials Arbitration Board. The Board's decisions are final and have the same effect and force as the collective agreement.

Act No. 4688 Article 29 provides that the Public Employer's Delegation shall be chaired by the vice-president or minister appointed by the President of the Republic and shall consist of representatives of ministries and public institutions and organizations designated by the President of the Republic.

53. International Labour Conference 109th Session, 2021.
54. ILO, Committee on Freedom of Association, Report No. 362, Case No. 2841 (France), November 2011, para. 1041, https://www.ilo.org/dyn/normlex/en/f?p=1000:50002:0::NO:50002:P50002_COMPLAINT_TEXT_ID:2912582.ILO, Committee on Freedom of Association, Report No. 367, Case No. 2894, March 2013, para. 339 https://www.ilo.org/sites/default/files/wcmsp5/groups/public/@ed_norm/@relconf/documents/meetingdocument/wcms_208542.pdf (accessed 30 July 2025).
55. ILO, Committee on Freedom of Association, Report No. 367, Case No. 2894, March 2013, para. 339, https://www.ilo.org/sites/default/files/wcmsp5/groups/public/@ed_norm/@relconf/documents/meetingdocument/wcms_208542.pdf (accessed 30 July 2025).
56. ILO, Compilation, para. 853; ILO, Direct Request (CEACR) – adopted 2019, published 109th ILC session (2021). Freedom of Association and Protection of the Right to Organise Convention, 1948 (No. 87) – Tajikistan (Ratification: 1993), https://www.ilo.org/dyn/normlex/en/f?p=1000:13100:0::NO:13100:P13100_COMMENT_ID:4018145 (accessed 30 July 2025).

In its comment, the CEACR notes that under sections 29 and 34 of Act No. 4688, 7 of the 11 members of the Public Officials Arbitration Board including the chair are designated by the President of Turkiye and considers that this selection process could create doubts as to the independence and impartiality of the Board. The Committee, therefore, requests the Government to take the necessary measures for restructuring the membership of the Public Officials Arbitration Board or the method of appointment of its members to more clearly show its independence and impartiality and to win the confidence of the parties. The Committee notes that the Government confirms that in addition to the Head of the Board, its 5 other members with knowledge in public administration, public finances, and public personnel regime, as well as 1 member among the academics proposed by the competent confederations, are appointed by the President. The Committee requests the Government to consider reviewing, in consultation with the social partners, the method of appointment of the Board member to more clearly show its independence and impartiality and to win the confidence of the parties.[57]

Concerning employees, the Constitution of Turkiye provides that in cases where a strike or a lockout is prohibited or postponed, the dispute shall be settled by the Supreme Arbitration Board at the end of the period of postponement. The disputing parties may apply to the Supreme Arbitration Board by mutual agreement at any stage of the dispute. The decisions of the Supreme Arbitration Board shall be final and have the force of a collective labour agreement (Article 54(4)). The organization and functions of the Supreme Arbitration Board shall be regulated by law (Article 54(5)).

Under Act No. 6365 Article 51, either of the parties may apply to the Supreme Board of Arbitration within six working days in disputes concerning the workplaces or the activities where it is prohibited to call a strike, decisions of the Supreme Board of Arbitration shall be final and have the same effect and force as the collective labour agreement.

In addition, Act No. 6365 Article 63(2) provides that after a suspension decree has entered into force, a mediator designated according to Article 50 shall make every effort for the settlement of the dispute during the suspension period. During the suspension period, the parties may also agree to refer the dispute to a private arbitrator. According to Act No. 6365 Articles 63(3) and 51 if an agreement is not reached before the expiry date of the suspension period, either of the parties may apply to the Supreme Board of Arbitration within six working days. Decisions of the Supreme Board of Arbitration shall be final and have the same effect and force as the collective labour agreement.

4 CONCLUSION

Turkiye is obliged to recognize the right to strike under the ICESCR Article 8/d. The observations and views of the CEACR and the CFA, as well as the judicial rulings of the

57. ILO, Observation (CEACR) - adopted 2019, published 109th ILC session (2021), Right to Organise and Collective Bargaining Convention, 1949 (No. 98) - Türkiye (Ratification: 1952), https://www.ilo.org/dyn/normlex/en/f?p=NORMLEXPUB:13100:0::NO::P13100_COMMENT_ID,P13100_COUNTRY_ID:4023183,102893 (accessed 30 July 2025).

EctHR, are binding and constitute sources of law in Turkiye. Turkiye is also under the obligation to harmonize its legislation with Article 28 of the ECFR.

However, as explained above, Turkish legislation concerning the right to strike is not in conformity with either international or European law. Only some recent Constitutional Court and Court of Cassation rulings conform with the ECtHR judgments. According to these precedents, even if the legislation limits the right to strike, the Courts shall take a deeper look at the circumstances, proportionality, and extent of the strike before ruling it 'unlawful' outright.

Since the right to strike for the protection and betterment of workers' economic and social interests is considered to be part of their democratic rights under international and European norms, Turkiye has to review its Constitution and its statutes with the relevant social partners and amend it to meet the UN, ILO and European standards.

CHAPTER 38

Restrictions on the Right to Strike in the United Kingdom*

Catherine Barnard

1 GENERAL INFORMATION

The UK's attitude to strike action is ambiguous at best and hostile at worst. The approach of the courts largely follows suit. Much depends on the colour of the government: the Conservatives are typically hostile; Labour is more sympathetic. The question of prescribing minimum service requirement for essential services is a case in point. Up until 2023, there had been no legislation prescribing minimum service levels in the public sector when strikes occur; this had been largely left to voluntary agreement between management and labour. However, the Strikes (Minimum Services Level) Act 2023 was introduced by the Conservatives to address what was seen as excessive industrial action in the public sector. For a government so hostile to matters European, it was somewhat surprising to see the government calling in aid the precedent of EU states for adopting the legislation. In fact, the UK law was much less well considered than national laws of other Member States and certainly inferior to ILO standards. It was also deeply unpopular with trade unions. So when Labour came to power in July 2024, it pledged to repeal the 2023 Act and the secondary legislation adopted under it; this has now been put in train by Clause 21 of the Employment Rights Bill 2024 and may become law in the Autumn of 2025.

This chapter will consider the UK's foray into regulating minimum services levels. It will examine the Strikes (Minimum Service Levels) Act 2023 in the broader context of an understanding of UK collective labour law. The chapter is structured as

* Some of the text in this chapter first appeared as an explainer and a blog written with Joelle Grogan https://ukandeu.ac.uk/where-does-the-strikes-bill-put-the-uk-relative-to-other-european-countries/ (accessed 12 May 2025); https://ukandeu.ac.uk/explainers/strikes-essential-services-and-minimum-service-levels/ (accessed 12 May 2025).

follows. Section 2 provides some historical context on the regulation of industrial action in the UK. Section 3 looks at the specific question of the provision of minimum service level in essential services considering both the ILO requirements and then the provisions of the Strikes (Minimum Service Levels) Act 2023. Section 4 then looks at the criticisms levelled at the Act and notes the Labour government's plans to repeal it. Section 5 concludes.

2 STRIKING IN THE UK

2.1 Legal Basis of the Right to Strike

As is well known, the UK is an outlier across Europe in its approach to strike action.

First, in the absence of a written constitution, there is no constitutional 'right to strike' under UK law. Strike action was long considered unlawful under the common law due to its interference with the employer's property rights. However, legislation passed in 1906[1] provided immunity to trade unions from certain legal action in civil law provided a number of conditions were satisfied. This *immunity*-based, as opposed to rights-based, approach to the regulation of strike action has shaped judicial interpretation of strike action: essentially, strikes are considered unlawful unless all the conditions for granting immunity are satisfied. One failure of a substantive or procedural nature, the details of which are now found in Part V of the Trade Union and Labour Relations Act 1992 (TULR(C)A 1992), and the immunity is lost.[2] Trade unions then become liable for damages for committing economic torts such as inducing breach of contract and, more likely, are subject to an injunction restraining them from calling their members out on strike (and risk being in contempt of court if an injunction has been granted by a court restraining the strike action).

The UK's immunity-based approach sits uncomfortably with its commitments under Article 11 ECHR.[3] This provides that everyone has the *right* to freedom of peaceful assembly and to freedom of association with others, including the right to form and to join trade unions for the protection of their interests and, following *Enerji Yapi-Yol*, the right to strike.[4] The UK's ambivalence to Article 11 can be seen in the Court of Appeal's decision in *Metrobus Ltd v. Unite*,[5] a case concerning whether the notice of a ballot was defective. The Court held that 'it would not be prudent' to follow

1. The Trade Disputes Act 1906. In the nineteenth century, the criminal law had also been central to restraining industrial action. For a fuller discussion, *see* the classic Lord Wedderburn, *The Worker And the Law* 3rd ed (Pelican S, 1986).
2. Or if the action falls outside the statutory framework, there is also no immunity: *Rookes v. Barnard* [1964] AC 1129.
3. https://ks.echr.coe.int/documents/d/echr-ks/guide_art_11_eng (accessed 12 May 2025).
4. In *Enerji Yapi-Yol Sen v. Turkey* (Judgment of 21 April 2009), the ECtHR appeared to accept that there was a right to strike under Art. 11, albeit a right that could be subject to certain conditions and restrictions; cf. *RMT v. UK* (Application No. 31045/10, 8 April 2014) where the Court said that while 'strike action is clearly protected by Art. 11', it did not accept that strike action was an 'essential element' of Art. 11; *see also Association of Academics v. Iceland* [2019] IRLR189.
5. [2009] IRLR 851 although cf *RMT v. Serco; ASLEF v. London and Birmingham Railway Ltd* [2011] IRLR 399.

Enerji Yapi-Yol Sen. Maurice Kay LJ then (correctly) summarized the position in English law:

> In this country, the right to strike has never been much more than a slogan or a legal metaphor. Such a right has not been bestowed by statute. What has happened is that, since the Trade Disputes Act 1906, legislation has provided limited immunities from liability in tort. At times the immunities have been widened, at other times they have been narrowed. Outside the scope of the immunities, the rigour of the common law applies in the form of breach of contract on the part of the strikers and the economic torts as regards the organisers and their union. Indeed, even now the conventional analysis at common law is that by going on strike employees commit repudiatory breaches of their contracts of employment ... It helps to keep this history and conceptual framework in mind when construing and applying the detailed provisions of the statute.

This quote gives a flavour of the hostility of the common law to strike action (and also concern about international interference with the operation of the common law in matters relating to industrial action).

Second, the British system of industrial relations has long been based on the principle of collective laissez-faire, meaning that the state traditionally abstains from getting involved in industrial relations, leaving this to management and labour to determine. However, following the winter of discontent,[6] Margaret Thatcher became Prime Minister in 1979 with a mandate to address 'Too many strikes'.[7] This led to the introduction of significant regulation of all aspects of industrial action, including removing immunity from certain types of strike action, including secondary action,[8] and imposing strict notice and balloting requirements[9] before trade unions could benefit from the immunity from strike action.

The Labour government of 1997-2010 did not reverse the Tory policy; the subsequent coalition government[10] and then Conservative governments continued to add further restrictions on strike action, most notably through the Trade Union Act 2016 which imposed balloting thresholds before strike action could be lawful in both the public and private sectors and then the Strikes (Minimum Service Levels) Act 2023 which, for the first time, introduced a power for government ministers to set, by Regulations, minimum service levels in listed sectors.[11] These regulations enabled employers to issue 'work notices' to require minimum service levels to be delivered in the specified sectors. The Act also restricted the protection of trade unions from legal action, as well as removing the automatic protection of employees from unfair dismissal if the minimum services were not delivered. This was largely done by amendments to TULR(C)A 1992.

---

6. https://www.bbc.co.uk/iplayer/episode/b007nn9k/andrew-marrs-history-of-modern-britain-4-revolution (accessed 12 May 2025).
7. https://www.margaretthatcher.org/document/110858 (accessed 12 May 2025).
8. Section 224 TULR(C)A 1992.
9. Sections 226-234A TULR(C)A 1992.
10. *See, e.g.*, https://www.gov.uk/government/publications/carr-review-of-the-law-on-industrial-disputes (accessed 12 May 2025).
11. Section 234B(1) TULR(C)A 1992.

As noted above, within the first hundred days of being in power, the Labour government fulfilled its commitment to introduce a major piece of employment legislation, the Employment Rights Bill. Of particular relevance to the purposes of this chapter are the plans to repeal key parts of the Trade Union Act 2016, replacing the double majority threshold for a successful ballot for strike action (*see* below) with a simple majority threshold, and repealing the Strikes (Minimum Service Levels) Act 2023.

2.2 The Regulation of Strike Action in the UK

As indicated above, the rules on strike action are laid down in the Trade Union and Labour Relations (Consolidation) Act 1992. The Act requires that strike action must be taken 'in contemplation or furtherance of a trade dispute' between the workers and their employers (the so-called golden formula).[12] A trade dispute is defined in section 244. It includes disputes over terms and conditions of employment, the physical conditions in which any workers are required to work, and termination or suspension of employment or the duties of employment of one or more workers.

These substantive conditions are supplemented by onerous procedural conditions. These include the balloting of trade union members before industrial action, and detailed notification requirements of both the ballot and industrial action to employers. In the Trade Union Act 2016, additional requirements were imposed, including a turnout threshold of 50% of members voting in any ballot, and for 'important public services', 40% of the workforce had to vote in favour of any industrial action (in addition to the simple majority of voters voting in favour).[13] The Employment Rights Bill 2024 will remove these thresholds. However, the other substantive and procedural conditions will remain.

If these substantive and procedural requirements are satisfied, the 1992 Act protects trade unions from being sued by employers for certain economic 'torts' (i.e., legal wrongs), including inducing workers to breach their contract of employment. Employees taking industrial action can claim at least 12 weeks 'automatic' protection from dismissal when taking industrial action lawfully called by their trade union.[14] The law further protects workers who are peacefully picketing, which involves protesting, communicating, or persuading workers to abstain from working at or near their workplace, subject to certain limits.

Some forms of industrial action are not protected. For example, 'secondary' or 'sympathy' strikes (i.e., workers employed by employer A striking against employer A

12. Section 219 TULR(C)A 1992.
13. For criticism, *see* M. Ford QC & T. Novitz, An Absence of Fairness: Restrictions on Industrial Action and Protest in the Trade Union Bill (2015) 44 ILJ 522 https://doi.org/10.1093/indlaw/dwv029 (accessed 12 May 2025). For further critique of the Trade Union Act, *see also* R. Dukes and N. Kountouris, Pre-strike Ballots, Picketing and Protest: Banning Industrial Action by the Back Door? (2016) 45 ILJ 337 https://doi.org/10.1093/indlaw/dww026 (accessed 12 May 2025) and K. Ewing and J. Hendy, The Trade Union Act 2016 and the Failure of Human Rights (2016) 45 ILJ 391 https://doi.org/10.1093/indlaw/dww027 (accessed 12 May 2025).
14. Section 238A TULR(C) (1992).

in sympathy with a group working for employer B) are not protected under UK law. Violence, intimidation or harm to individuals or property are also not protected. Certain workers are not permitted to take industrial action, including the police, prison officers and non-civilian officers in the army.

However, until 2023, there was no legal obligation on trade unions to establish a minimum service level in certain sensitive sectors. In other words, there was no minimum level of functioning that workers had to guarantee during industrial action, although in fact voluntary agreements were often put in place, especially in respect of the health service, to ensure sufficient levels of service. The Strikes (Minimum Service Level) Act 2023 changed this.

3 'MINIMUM SERVICE LEVEL' IN 'ESSENTIAL SERVICES'

3.1 The Background to the Strikes (Minimum Service Levels) Act 2023

As the previous section has shown, despite the increasingly strict requirements for lawful strike action in the UK, there had been no statutory requirement for a minimum service level in essential services. Traditionally, minimum service levels were provided, but this had been delivered by voluntary agreement between the employers and the unions, consistent with the collective laissez-faire tradition of UK labour law.[15] There is also a criminal offence in section 240 TULR(C)A 1992 of intentionally endangering life or causing serious injury to a person by going on strike, but there have been 'no prosecutions under this offence, likely due to the very high bar to secure a conviction'.[16]

However, following a wave of strike action in the public sector in 2022-2023,[17] the government decided the voluntary system was insufficient.[18] It had already introduced a Bill on minimum service levels in the transport sector, the Transport (Minimum Service Levels) Bill, in the Autumn of 2022.[19] This was part of the 2019 Conservative *manifesto* to ensure a minimum service operated during transport strikes.

However, the government decided that in the light of strikes not just in the transport sector but also in the health service (nurses, junior doctors, and consultants) and in education (schools and universities), a transport-specific Bill did not go far

15. https://publications.parliament.uk/pa/jt5803/jtselect/jtrights/1315/report.html (accessed 12 May 2025).
16. https://publications.parliament.uk/pa/jt5803/jtselect/jtrights/1315/report.html (accessed 12 May 2025).
17. According to research by the Resolution Foundation (https://www.resolutionfoundation.org/publications/labour-market-outlook-q2-2023/ (accessed 12 May 2025)), 'In the 12 months to May 2023, 3,9 million working days were lost to strikes (compared to an average of 450,000 per year during the 2010s), more than at any point since 1989. This 2023 high point is remarkable given the decline in union membership which has taken place over the past few decades – only 22% of employees were in a union in 2022, down significantly from 39% in 1989.' *See also* The Strikes (Minimum Service Levels: NHS Ambulance Services and the NHS Patient Transport Service) Regulations 2023 (legislation.gov.uk), para. 7.2.
18. *Ibid.*
19. https://ohrh.law.ox.ac.uk/challenging-the-right-to-strike-the-uk-transport-strikes-minimum-service-levels-bill/ (accessed 12 May 2025).

enough. It therefore replaced the Transport Bill with the Strikes (Minimum Service Levels) Bill[20] to apply across a number of sectors: health services; fire and rescue services; education; transport; decommissioning of nuclear installations and management of radioactive waste and spent fuel; and border security. The government justified the new Bill on the basis of ensuring that 'striking workers don't put the public's lives at risk and prevent people getting to work, accessing healthcare, and safely going about their daily lives'.[21] It also relied on the pressing social need for minimum service levels:[22]

> Fundamentally, strike action in the sectors outlined in the Bill can disproportionately impact the public, with recent strike action demonstrating this. People have been prevented from accessing work, children have missed out on learning and patients have missed out on healthcare. Businesses have also suffered as a result of strike action too and this has had a significant impact on our economy. The disruption from strike action has cost the economy over GBP 6 billion. This stems from all strike action, not just transport strikes.

The Bill was subject to significant criticism, not just by academics but also by the Joint Committee on Human Rights (*see* section 4).[23] It was also subject to extensive 'ping-pong' between the Houses of Commons and the Lords, largely over the scope of the powers the government had given itself. However, when the Bill became the Strikes (Minimum Service Levels) Act on 20 July 2023, its content remained largely unchanged.

Before considering the details of the legislation, the position taken by the International Labour Organization (ILO) towards minimum service levels at the time of strikes will be outlined. This provides context for an understanding of the Act and the criticism it was subject to.

3.2 The International Background

By definition, minimum service levels can reduce the effectiveness of strikes: workers required by law to work are unable to take part in industrial action. Where the minimum service level is not met, this can also have negative consequences on workers and trade unions, for example, by removing the legal protection they enjoy during lawful industrial action (such as protection from dismissal). This limitation on the rights of workers is justified by the public need for essential services. So how does the ILO approach the question of minimum service levels?

The right to strike is protected by International Labour Organization (ILO) Convention 87 (on Freedom of Association and the Right to Organise) which the UK

20. The Act applies only to Great Britain (England, Scotland, and Wales): s. 4 of the Strikes (Minimum Service Levels) Act 2023.
21. https://www.gov.uk/government/news/government-introduces-laws-to-mitigate-the-disruption-of-strikes-on-the-public (accessed 12 May 2025).
22. https://publications.parliament.uk/pa/jt5803/jtselect/jtrights/1315/report.html (accessed 12 May 2025).
23. Tenth Report of Session 2022-2023, Legislative Scrutiny: Strikes (Minimum Service Levels) Bill 2022-2023 (HC 1088 / HL Paper 157) on 6 March 2023.

has ratified. However, ILO Conventions are not legally binding in the UK (and so not enforceable in UK courts), although the European Convention on Human Rights is part of UK law by virtue of the Human Rights Act 1998, and UK courts must interpret UK law in the light of its ECHR obligations. The European Court of Human Rights has endorsed the ILO standards.[24]

The ILO recognizes there can be limits on strike action in essential services but emphasizes that 'the service required must genuinely and exclusively be a minimum service', and it must be 'strictly necessary to meet the basic needs of the population … while maintaining the effectiveness of the pressure brought to bear' by the strike.[25] Essential services in the strict sense of the term have been defined by ILO as:

(1) services provided by public servants exercising authority in the name of the state (such as the police or prison officers);
(2) for services the interruption of which would endanger the life, personal safety, or health of the whole or part of the population; and
(3) in the event of an acute national emergency.

While countries vary in their definition of what constitutes an 'essential service', they are typically services such as fire and emergency services, electricity and water supply, and the police and armed forces.

The ILO also emphasizes the need for bilateral negotiations on the content of minimum service levels prior to the strikes 'so that all parties can examine the matter with the necessary objectivity and detachment'. The ILO says that 'Any disagreement should be settled by an independent body, like for instance, the judicial authorities, and not by the ministry concerned.' So how did the British legislation address the question of the minimum service levels in the Act?

3.3 The Strike (Minimum Services Level) Act 2023

The Strike (Minimum Services Level) Act 2023 provided that the minimum service level would be specified by the relevant minister via 'minimum service regulation' (i.e., secondary legislation – rather than primary legislation which is made by Parliament). Before setting the minimum service level, the minister was required to *consult* 'such persons as [s/he] considers appropriate'.[26] There was no requirement to *negotiate*, let alone reach an agreement with trade unions. The regulation setting the minimum standard was laid before Parliament, but Parliament was not able to amend or change the minimum service level.

When a minister set a minimum service level, an employer could then give a 'work notice' to a trade union taking planned strike action.[27] This had to be given at

24. *Ognevenko v. Russia*, 20 November 2018, https://hudoc.echr.coe.int/eng#{%22itemid%22:[%22001-187732%22]} (accessed 12 May 2025).
25. https://www.ilo.org/static/english/dialogue/ifpdial/llg/noframes/ch5.htm#4 (accessed 12 May 2025).
26. Section 234F(1).
27. Section 234C.

least seven days before the strike could start.[28] The work notice identified workers required to work during the strike in order to reach the minimum level of service set by the minister as well as specify the work required to be carried out by them during the strike in order to ensure those levels of service are provided.[29] The notice could not list more people than were 'reasonably necessary' to provide the level of service.[30]

In deciding whether to identify a person in a work notice, the employer could not have regard to:

1) whether the person is or is not a member of a trade union;
2) whether the person has or has not;
   a. taken part in the activities of a trade union; or
   b. made use of services made available to the person by a trade union by virtue of the person's membership of the union; or
3) whether or not:
   a. a matter has been raised on the person's behalf (with or without the person's consent); or
   b. the person has consented to the raising of a matter on the person's behalf,

by a trade union of which the person is a member.[31]

There was nothing, however, to prevent an employer from requiring senior trade union officials to work (and therefore get paid) but not the members (who would not get paid). This could sow division in the union. The Joint Committee on Human Rights, when commenting on the Bill, put it this way:[32]

> The way in which the Bill would bring minimum service levels into effect, through a work notice issued by an employer backed by an obligation on trade unions to ensure members comply with that work notice, amounts to a serious interference with Article 11 rights. It could result in employers requiring strike leaders to work, and in unions being forced to persuade their own members to break their own strike.

Before giving the work notice, the employer was required to consult with the union and have regard to its views.[33] There was no obligation to negotiate or to come to an agreement with the trade union.

Under the Act, trade unions were obliged to take 'reasonable steps' to ensure their members complied with the work notice.[34] If a trade union failed to do so, then protection for legal strikes fell away. This meant that employers could seek damages against the trade union and could also dismiss workers who failed to comply with work notices during industrial action. Specifically, in respect of the trade union, the Act provided that 'any loss that would have been suffered even if the union had taken the

28. The Act also contains provisions on the variation of work notices: s. 234C(9)-(11).
29. Section 234C(4).
30. Section 234C(5).
31. Section 234C(6).
32. https://publications.parliament.uk/pa/jt5803/jtselect/jtrights/1315/report.html (accessed 12 May 2025).
33. Section 234C(8).
34. Section 234E.

reasonable steps mentioned in that paragraph is to be disregarded in calculating any amount to be awarded against the union by way of damages'.[35]

Various regulations were adopted under the Act. For example, The Strikes (Minimum Service Levels: NHS Ambulance Services and the NHS Patient Transport Service) Regulations 2023[36] introduced minimum levels of service for ambulance services and the NHS Patient Transport Service provided by ambulance trusts. As the Explanatory Memorandum explained, 'The levels of service are set so that on each day of strike a response is provided to emergency 999 ambulance calls, healthcare professional (HCP) calls, requests for Inter-Facility Transfer (IFT) and Non-Emergency Patient Transport Services (NEPTS) on days of strike action.' The instrument applied to the 10 National Health Service (NHS) ambulance trusts in England and the Isle of Wight NHS Trust. Regulation 4 made provision in relation to emergency (999) calls to the ambulance service, so that the minimum service level (MSL) was that 'on each day of strike, where a work notice is issued:

(a) All emergency calls are answered and triaged as they would be if the strike was not taking place, and
(b) an appropriate clinical response is organized and provided for calls triaged or escalated to life threatening, or for which there is no reasonable clinical alternative to clinical assistance being provided at the scene of an incident or by transporting the patient to a healthcare facility (or both), as it would be if a strike were not taking place that day'.[37]

4 CRITICISMS OF THE ACT

So why was the Act so controversial?

Trade unions argued that the Bill, now Act, was flawed for three reasons.

First, they said that the scope of sectors included in the Act was too broad.[38] For example, 'health services' and 'transport services' could relate to any aspect of work in either. 'Education services' is also not confined to services provided to those aged under 17 (as was the case with the 2016 Act) and could include primary, secondary or university sectors or any related work sector. The Act also did not state that the services had to be 'essential', and so it was at the discretion of the minister which services in the

35. Section 234E(2).
36. SI 2023/1343 (The Strikes (Minimum Service Levels: NHS Ambulance Services and the NHS Patient Transport Service) Regulations 2023 (legislation.gov.uk)) and the explanatory memorandum The Strikes (Minimum Service Levels: NHS Ambulance Services and the NHS Patient Transport Service) Regulations 2023 (legislation.gov.uk). *See also* Written statements – Written questions, answers and statements – UK Parliament. For another example, *see* SI 2023/1335 The Strikes (Minimum Service Levels: Passenger Railway Services) Regulations 2023 (The Strikes (Minimum Service Levels: Passenger Railway Services) Regulations 2023 (legislation.gov.uk)) and the accompanying guidance Strikes (Minimum Service Levels: Passenger Railway Services) Regulations 2023 – guidance on the regulations (publishing.service.gov.uk).
37. The Strikes (Minimum Service Levels: NHS Ambulance Services and the NHS Patient Transport Service) Regulations 2023 (legislation.gov.uk), para. 6.5.
38. https://www.ft.com/content/b4440533-9a0b-4693-bf86-8ec960cf4bf4 (accessed 12 May 2025).

designated sectors could be included. So, as we saw with the ambulance regulations, they cover not just emergency transport but also non-emergency patient transport services (NEPTS). As Novitz says, 'The failure to limit these sectors to "essential services" recognized in the ILO amounts to a significant breach of Article 11 of the ECHR. This follows from the judgment of the European Court of Human Rights (ECtHR) in *Ognevenko*.'[39]

Second, the Act gave the minister the power to act unilaterally to impose minimum service levels. There were two dimensions of this. On the one hand, the unilateral powers were not constrained by a requirement of reasonableness: so the minimum could be a very high number. Second, unlike the ILO requirements, there was no requirement for an agreement between workers and employers.[40] Unions argued, therefore, that the MSL Bill compared unfavourably with the policy in the Transport (Minimum Service Levels) Bill, where employers and workers were required to negotiate an agreement on what the minimum service level should be.

The UK's position was also out of line with much of the rest of Europe: in 85% of European countries which have legislated for it, minimum service levels involve an agreement between trade unions and employers.[41] An agreement between employers and trade unions on minimum service levels can be a condition of a lawful strike (as in Hungary). In other cases, the minimum can be set by primary legislation (i.e., by Parliament), but how this is achieved is left to agreement between trade unions and employers. The reasoning is that workers and employers are best placed to understand a minimum level of service and how it may be achieved.

The Transport Bill also made provision for the resolution of disputes over the minimum service level through the Central Arbitration Committee (CAC). However, there was no role for the CAC or any other dispute resolution mechanism in the Strikes (Minimum Service Level) Act 2023. The Act did not indicate how a trade union could challenge a minimum service level or a work notice and did not provide a role for an independent body, such as the Central Arbitration Committee, in dispute resolution. This compares unfavourably with the position in the majority (69%) of European countries where a dispute between a trade union and an employer over a minimum level of service should be resolved by either an independent body or through arbitration. In some states, notably Germany, the dispute can ultimately be resolved by a court.[42]

The government insisted that the 'approach within this Bill was compliant with Convention rights and that the Government were right 'to take a more direct approach in setting minimum service levels which enables minimum service levels to be

39. https://ukandeu.ac.uk/minimum-service-levels-legislation-in-conflict-with-strikers-and-with-europe/ (accessed 12 May 2025); *Ognevenko v. Russia*, 20 November 2018, https://hudoc.echr.coe.int/eng#{%22itemid%22:[%22001-187732%22]} (accessed 12 May 2025).
40. https://ukandeu.ac.uk/minimum-service-levels-legislation-in-conflict-with-strikers-and-with-europe/ (accessed 12 May 2025).
41. https://ukandeu.ac.uk/where-does-the-strikes-bill-put-the-uk-relative-to-other-european-countries/ (accessed 12 May 2025).
42. https://ukandeu.ac.uk/where-does-the-strikes-bill-put-the-uk-relative-to-other-european-countries/ (accessed 12 May 2025).

implemented more quickly, reduces the cost and administrative burden on employers and unions, and protects the lives and livelihoods of the public sooner'. The government also said that it had been 'clear that it will not introduce regulations to apply minimum service levels where it considers existing voluntary arrangements are necessary, adequate, and sufficient. We therefore encourage trade unions to ensure that voluntary arrangements are agreed prior to taking strike action'.[43] The government minister (Kevin Hollinrake MP Parliamentary Under Secretary of State – Department for Business and Trade) also said that any regulations under the Act would comply with Article 11 ECHR:[44]

> The regulations made under this Bill must be compliant with Convention rights, including Article 11, … . This is because section 3 of the Human Rights Act (HRA) 1998 requires subordinate legislation (and primary legislation) to be read and given effect in a way which is compatible with Convention rights and as such provides protection against arbitrary interference with Article 11. Any regulations will be clear as to the scope of minimum service levels. The amendment is therefore duplicative in nature and is therefore unnecessary.

He also said:

> I would like to reassure the Committee that ministers will carefully consider the compatibility of future regulations with Convention rights and international obligations before they are laid in Parliament.

Those international obligations include the post-Brexit UK/EU trade agreement and the Trade and Cooperation Agreement, where the UK committed itself to respecting labour standards, including 'as defined by the fundamental ILO Conventions'. As already indicated, there is a debate as to whether the Strikes (Minimum Service Levels) Act 2023 could be understood as undermining that commitment.[45]

Third, trade unions argued that the Act obliged workers to work and could force trade unions to penalize members who did not follow work notices. This could undermine trust between unions and their members and serve as a 'chilling factor' on industrial relations. Further, as noted above, the work notices could be used to create divisions in the union, requiring senior union officials to work but not other members of the union.

It was not just the trade unions which expressed concerns about the Act. Others have also spoken out. For example, Keith Ewing and John Hendy criticized the Bill/Act as imposing disproportionate penalties against trade unions for a failure to force members to work and argued that the Act did not have adequate safeguards against potential abuse.[46] Employers objected too. The Chartered Institute of Personnel and

43. https://publications.parliament.uk/pa/jt5803/jtselect/jtrights/1315/report.html (accessed 12 May 2025).
44. https://publications.parliament.uk/pa/jt5803/jtselect/jtrights/1315/report.html (accessed 12 May 2025).
45. https://committees.parliament.uk/writtenevidence/118654/pdf/ (accessed 12 May 2025), para. 36.
46. https://www.ier.org.uk/comments/strikes-minimum-service-levels-bill-and-the-ilo-a-reply-to-sunak/ (accessed 12 May 2025).

Development said that many employers had raised concerns about the 2023 Act: 'this law would not enhance employment relations or protect the public and that it could undermine trust between trade unions and employers'.

The Joint Committee on Human Rights said it was worried that the requirement for 'trade unions to take "reasonable steps" to ensure their members comply with a work notice issued by an employer does not provide the clarity needed to guarantee that trade unions and employees will know when this duty has been met and when it has not'. They suggested that 'Given the serious consequences of a failure to meet this duty, greater clarity is needed in the Bill. As drafted, the provision requiring trade unions to take "reasonable steps" may fall foul of the requirements of Article 11.'[47]

The government disagreed, arguing that a reasonableness standard is common in UK legislation. The Bill Minister, Lord Callanan, said:[48]

> First and foremost, a trade union should not call a union member identified in a work notice as required to work on a particular day out on strike that day. The trade union could also encourage those individual members to comply with the work notice and make it clear in their general communication with members that where members are named in a work notice, and therefore required to work on a particular day, they should attend work on that strike day.

The government subsequently published a draft code of practice on reasonable steps for consultation.[49]

The Joint Committee on Human Rights was also concerned that 'the Bill was passed through the House of Commons before an impact assessment was published and that, once published, the impact assessment has been rated as "not fit for purpose" by the Regulatory Policy Committee [RPC]'. The government justified this on the grounds of speed and said that there would be a detailed analysis to be conducted at the secondary legislation stage.[50] The Joint Committee was also worried that penalties imposed on trade unions and workers for failing to comply with the requirements of the Bill and of any work notice issued by an employer were severe and could amount to a disproportionate interference with Article 11. The government disagreed: If measures that provided less incentive were implemented, there would be a significant risk the minimum service levels would not be achieved, and strikes in services where minimum service levels are applied would continue to impact the public disproportionately.

Finally, constitutional lawyers – and members of the House of Lords – also expressed concerns about the broad 'Henry VIII' power in the body of the Act itself. This means that the Secretary of State had the power, by secondary legislation, to amend primary legislation (i.e., Acts of Parliament).[51] For example, Lord Thomas said

47. https://publications.parliament.uk/pa/jt5803/jtselect/jtrights/1315/report.html (accessed 12 May 2025).
48. Stated in Parliament on Tuesday 21 February; cited in https://publications.parliament.uk/pa/jt5803/jtselect/jtrights/1315/report.html (accessed 12 May 2025).
49. Consultation on 'reasonable steps' in relation to minimum service levels – draft code of practice (publishing.service.gov.uk) (accessed 12 May 2025).
50. https://publications.parliament.uk/pa/jt5803/jtselect/jtrights/1315/report.html (accessed 12 May 2025).
51. Section 3 says: 'Power to make consequential provision.

'This Bill is Henry VIII on stilts.' He also expressed concerns about the impact of the Bill on devolution 'One of the great virtues of this House is that it attaches great importance to accountability. By transferring responsibility for minimum services, the Bill is taking it away from those who are accountable to the people of Wales and Scotland. It is quite wrong that we should proceed on this basis.'[52] The government rejected these arguments.

The incoming Labour government did, however, heed these criticisms. In August 2024, it announced:[53]

> The policy of this government is that minimum service levels (MSLs) unduly restrict the right to strike and undermine good industrial relations. The introduction of the 2023 Act was met with widespread condemnation from employers and trade unions. Many employers across different sectors pointed to its unworkability and impact on employers' and trade unions' abilities to negotiate and come to resolutions on disputes.

Clause 61 of the Employment Rights Bill (ERB) delivers this. Until the ERB became law, the 2023 Act still applied, but the government, returning to the more laissez-faire roots of collective action in the UK, said that 'in this interim period we strongly encourage employers to seek alternative mechanisms for dispute resolution, including voluntary agreements, rather than imposing minimum service levels. The government encourages employers to engage in negotiation and discussion with trade unions, ensuring industrial relations are based around good faith negotiation and bargaining'.[54]

5 CONCLUSIONS

The Strike (Minimum Services Level) Act 2023 was a major piece of legislation which was consistent with the direction of travel taken by successive Conservative governments of imposing ver greater restrictions on the ability of workers to strike. It would have put the courts at the frontline of having to square the very difficult circle of respecting parliamentary sovereignty while ensuring compliance with the UK's international obligations, especially under the ECHR. The Labour government's plans to repeal the 2023 Act means that there will be a return to the pre-2023 Act position based

---

(1) The Secretary of State may by regulations made by statutory instrument make provision that is consequential on this Act.
(2) Regulations under this section may amend, repeal or revoke provision made by or under primary legislation passed –
   (a) before this Act, or
   (b) later in the same session of Parliament as this Act.'

52. https://hansard.parliament.uk/lords/2023-03-23/debates/BB8B9845-B835-4C5A-8B74-F374D1FFA475/Strikes(MinimumServiceLevels)Bill (accessed 12 May 2025), col. 1866.
53. Update on minimum service levels and the Conduct of Employment Agencies and Employment Businesses (Amendment) Regulations 2022 – GOV.UK (www.gov.uk) (accessed 12 May 2025).
54. Update on minimum service levels and the Conduct of Employment Agencies and Employment Businesses (Amendment) Regulations 2022 – GOV.UK (www.gov.uk) (accessed 12 May 2025).

on voluntary agreements on service provision. This is part of its more cooperative stance with the trade unions:

> The upcoming Employment Rights Bill will remove barriers to effective collective action and strengthen the rights of working people by empowering workers to organize collectively through trade unions. We believe this will help to usher in a new era of partnership that sees trade unions, employers and government working constructively together in co-operation and through negotiation.[55]

55. Update on minimum service levels and the Conduct of Employment Agencies and Employment Businesses (Amendment) Regulations 2022 – GOV.UK (www.gov.uk) (accessed 12 May 2025).

CHAPTER 39

Restrictions on the Right to Strike in Ukraine

Mykhailo Shumylo & Yana Simutina

1 GENERAL INFORMATION

1.1 Legal Basis of the Right to Strike

To date, Ukraine has ratified all main international standards on collective bargaining and strikes, such as the International Covenant on Economic, Social and Cultural Rights (Article 8) and the International Covenant on Civil and Political Rights (Article 22) were ratified on 12 November 1973; ILO Convention No. 87 concerning Freedom of Association and Protection of the Right to Organize was ratified on 14 September 1956; ILO Convention No. 98 concerning the Right to Organize and to Bargain Collectively was ratified on 14 September 1956; ILO Convention No. 154 concerning Collective Bargaining was ratified on 16 May 1994; ILO Convention No. 105 concerning the Abolition of Forced Labour, which prohibits the use of forced or compulsory labour 'as a punishment for having participated in strikes', was ratified on 5 October 2000.

At the European level, Ukraine ratified Article 6 paragraph 4 (right to collective action) of the Revised European Social Charter of 1996 with no reservations (ratification: 21 December 2006, entry into force: 1 February 2007) and Article 11 (right to organize) of the European Convention of Human Rights (ratification and entry into force on 11 September 1997).

At the national level, the right to strike in Ukraine is included in the corpus of constitutional rights and enshrined in the Constitution of Ukraine.

Article 44 of the Constitution guarantees the right to strike with some restrictions as follows:

> Those who are employed have the right to strike to protect their economic and social interests. The procedure for exercising the right to strike is established by law, considering the necessity to ensure national security, health protection, and the rights and freedoms of other persons. No one shall be forced to participate or not participate in a strike. The prohibition of a strike is possible only based on the law.

The Labour Code of Ukraine (LC), adopted in 1971, did not contain references to the right to strike until 2015 when the emergence of the right to strike appeared in Article 2-1 in the context of the prohibition of discrimination in the workplace.

Notably, the right to strike at the level of the law for the first time was fixed in 1989 in the Soviet period. Before, the Soviet legislation did not contain a direct ban on strikes. However, there was no legal regulation due to the ideological bias of the Soviet regime, which denied the struggle of social classes inside the country, and strikes were referred to as exclusively 'bourgeois phenomenon'.

It is one of the special laws, namely the Law on the Procedure for Resolving of Collective Labour Disputes No. 137/98, dated 3 March 1998 (LPRCLD), which provides rules on the procedure for exercising the right to strike (Articles 17-28). Although the right to strike is enshrined in the Constitution of Ukraine and recognized by law, it is strictly regulated and de facto makes it difficult to exercise this right due to the excessive overregulation and bureaucratization of the procedure. The procedures preceding a strike for initiating a collective labour dispute, handling, and resolving it are complicated and burdensome for the workers. These procedures take several weeks and require a great deal of paperwork. Most importantly, if any action is not carried out in time, or even one document (demands, minutes of a workers' meeting, etc.) is incorrect, the whole procedure may be considered illegal. Statistics evidence this. In 2019, there were 18 strikes and 86 social protests registered; in 2020, only 8 strikes and 110 social protests; in 2021, 11 strikes and 59 social protests.[1]

It is also worth mentioning a state intervention in the collective labour disputes and strikes' procedures. In 1998, the National Mediation and Conciliation Service of Ukraine (NMCSU) was established in Ukraine as a state agency, with one of its tasks, *inter alia*, to facilitate the settlement of collective labour disputes. This governmental body approved the Regulation on the Procedure for Conducting a Strike as a Last Resort for Settlement of a Collective Labour Dispute and Conciliation Procedures during a Strike No. 131 dated 18 November 2008, which details the provisions of the LPRCLD in terms of rights and obligations of employees and employer during a strike, and the body (person) leading the strike. The Regulation provides the procedure for considering and resolving a collective labour dispute and the NMCSU's assistance in resolving a collective labour dispute during a strike, certain aspects of declaring a strike illegal, the responsibilities of the parties to collective labour disputes, and participation in conciliation procedures, as well as the procedure for calculating time limits.

---

1. Report on the results of the activities of the National Mediation and Reconciliation Service for 2021 [In Ukrainian], available at: https://nmcs.gov.ua/media/files/externaldocument_File_J2BLOSsQRh/звіт%202021.pdf (accessed 31 July 2025).

1.2 Main Features of the Regulation

The definition of strike can be found in Article 17 of the LPRCLD. It defines a strike as a temporary collective voluntary suspension of work by employees (absence from work, failure to perform their labour duties) of an enterprise, institution, or organization (structural unit) to resolve a collective labour dispute. A strike is used as the final means (when all other options have been exhausted) to resolve a collective labour dispute (conflict) in connection with the refusal of an employer or an authorized person, employers' organization, or association of employers' organizations to meet the demands of employees or their authorized body, trade union, trade union association or its authorized body. Following from abovementioned, a strike is directly related to a collective labour dispute and cannot be applied outside of it.

Excessive representativity or the minimum number of employees is required to hold a lawful strike. Thus, the decision to call a strike at an enterprise shall be taken at the proposal of the elected body of the trade union or other representative organizations of employees by a vote of the general assembly (conference) of the employees and shall be considered adopted if a majority of the employees or two-thirds of the delegates at the conference vote in its favour.

This norm has been the subject of criticism by the ILO Committee of Experts on the Application of Conventions and Recommendations (CEACR), which recommended that 'if the national legislation requires a vote before a strike is held, it should ensure that account is taken only of the votes cast and the majority is fixed at a reasonable level'. It requested the Government of Ukraine to take the necessary measures to amend Article 19 of the LPRCLD accordingly.[2]

A similar observation was made by the European Committee of Social Rights (ECSR) in Conclusions 2018 – Ukraine on Article 6 paragraph 4:

> With regard to the entitlement to take collective action, the Committee previously noted that Art. 19 of the LPSCLD provides that a decision to call a strike has to be supported by a majority of the workers or two-thirds of the delegates at the conference vote in its favour. The Committee asked for explanations as to how this procedure operates. ... The Committee asked for information on what a conference means and how many workers are required to attend. ... Meanwhile, it reserved its position on this point.[3]

A strike is led by a body (person) appointed by the general assembly (conference) of employees when deciding to call a strike. The body (person) leading the strike must notify the employer, employers' organization, or association of employers' organizations in writing no later than 7 days before the strike and, in case of a decision to strike at continuously operating production facilities – 15 days in advance.

2. Observation (CEACR) adopted 2018, published 108th ILC session (2019), available at: https://www.ilo.org/dyn/normlex/en/f?p=1000:13100:0::NO:13100:P13100_COMMENT_ID:3962360 (accessed 31 July 2025).
3. ECSR, Conclusions 2018 on Art. 6 para. 4 Ukraine, available at: http://hudoc.esc.coe.int/eng?i=2018/def/UKR/6/4/EN (accessed 31 July 2025).

The employer, employers' organization, and association of employers' organizations shall, as soon as possible, notify suppliers and consumers, transport organizations, as well as other interested enterprises, institutions, and organizations of the decision of employees to go on strike.

The employer, the local executive authority or body of local self-government, and the body or person leading the strike must take the measures necessary to ensure the viability of the enterprise, to preserve property, to secure observance of the legal and social order, and to prevent any threat to the lives and health of people and the environment during the strike.

According to Article 22 of the LPRCLD, political strikes declared with the requirement to change the constitutional system, state borders, and administrative-territorial structure and claims that violate human rights are unlawful. Moreover, certain procedural requirements must be satisfied for the strike to be lawful. Also, it is not allowed to announce the strike during the implementation of conciliation procedures.

The decision to declare a strike illegal shall be made only by a court. The court must consider the case on this application, including the terms for preparing the case for trial, no later than within seven days.

A court decision to declare a strike illegal obliges the strike participants to decide to terminate or cancel the declared strike and employees to start working no later than the next day after the day a copy of the court decision is delivered to the body (person) leading the strike.

The legislation does not provide solidarity strikes. There are no explicit legal provisions on other types of collective action, such as warning strikes, sit-ins, go-slow actions, rotating strikes, work-to-rule, and blockades. Article 19 of LPRCLD provides that when conducting meetings, rallies, and pickets outside the enterprise, the body or person leading the strike must notify the local executive or local authority regarding the event planned no later than three days in advance.

Employees participating in a strike have a number of guarantees. Thus, participation in a strike, except for strikes declared illegal by a court, is not considered a violation of labour discipline and cannot be the basis for disciplinary action. However, employees who participate in a strike are not paid for the time they are on strike. Employees who did not participate in the strike but were unable to perform their work duties due to it shall be paid salaries in amounts not lower than those established by law and the collective agreement concluded at the enterprise for the period of downtime through no fault of the employee. It is the employer's responsibility to keep records of such employees.

There is also a guarantee for employers. Any loss or damage caused to an employer by an illegal strike shall be compensated by the body authorized by the employees to conduct the strike, up to the value determined by the court and within the limits of its funds and property.

The legal consequences of employees' participation in an unlawful strike and liability for violation of legislation on collective labour disputes are generally defined by LPRCLD. For example, organizing or participating in a strike declared illegal by a court is a violation of labour discipline.

On the question of employer's liability, the LPRCLD stipulates: 'An employer who has violated the laws of Ukraine, as a result of which the conditions for a strike have been created, and the strike has ended with full or partial satisfaction of the employees' demands, shall compensate the strike participants for losses in the amount determined by the court (within the limits of the funds and property belonging to him).'

The concept of a lockout is not defined in Ukrainian law. In the meantime, Ukrainian law contains an indirect prohibition on the use of strike-breakers during strikes, as stated in Article 36 of the Law of Ukraine 'On Employment of the Population' (2012), which states that business entities providing employment agency services are not entitled to provide employees to an employer to replace its employees who are on strike or engaged in other collective action.

2 PERMITTED RESTRICTIONS

2.1 Exclusions from the Right to Strike: Public Servants; Essential Services

It is worth emphasizing that the right to strike in Ukraine currently is denied to all public servants and restricted to employees in essential services. In the event of a state of emergency, strikes may be prohibited. Strikes are unconditionally prohibited under martial law.

As mentioned above, Article 44 of the Constitution says: 'The prohibition of a strike is possible only based on the law.' This provision is further detailed in Article 24 of LPRCLD. Thus, strikes shall be prohibited if the cessation of work by workers creates a threat to the lives and health of people or the environment; or impedes the prevention of natural calamities, accidents, disasters, epidemics, and epizootics or the elimination of their consequences. Employees (except technical and maintenance personnel) of prosecution authorities, courts, military forces, state authorities, security and law-enforcement bodies are banned from striking.

At the same time, there are currently more than 20 specific laws for certain categories of employees or sectors where the right to strike is mentioned in the context of its restriction.

An explicit ban on strikes exists for:

- Judges and employees of the Judicial Guard Service (Article 54 of the Law on the Judiciary and Status of Judges (2016) states that a judge cannot belong to a political party or trade union, show affection for them, participate in political actions, rallies, strikes. In addition, Article 162-1 of this Law stipulates that trade unions of the Judicial Guard Service and their members are prohibited from organizing or participating in strikes).
- Prosecutors (Article 18 of the Law on the Prosecutor's Office (2014) prohibits prosecutors from belonging to a political party or participating in political actions, rallies or strikes).
- Military personnel of the Armed Forces of Ukraine (Article 17 of the Law on the Armed Forces of Ukraine (1991) prohibits the organization of strikes by service members and reservists while performing their duties in the military reserve and

participation in them. Employees of the Armed Forces of Ukraine may not organize or participate in strikes).
- Military personnel of the National Guard of Ukraine (Article 11 of the Law on the National Guard of Ukraine (2014) prohibits the organization of strikes by service members of the National Guard of Ukraine and participation in them).
- Military personnel of the State Border Guard Service of Ukraine (Article 15 of the Law on the State Border Guard Service of Ukraine (2003) prohibits the organization of strikes by service members and employees of the State Border Guard Service of Ukraine and participation in them).
- Police (Article 61 of the Law on the National Police (2015) prohibits police officers from organizing and participating in strikes. Article 104 prohibits police trade unions and their members from organizing or participating in strikes).
- State Criminal Executive Service (Article 15 of the Law on the State Criminal Executive Service of Ukraine (2005) prohibits the organization of strikes by ordinary and senior officers and other employees of the penal service and participation in their conduct).
- Citizens sent for alternative (non-military) service (Article 8 of the Law on Alternative (Non-Military) Service (1991) provides that a citizen sent for alternative service has no right to participate in strikes).

According to the Law on Civil Service No. 889-VIII, dated 10 December 2015, a civil servant has no right to call a strike nor to take part in it. This means that a ban on strikes applies to all categories of public servants without any exception. According to the National Agency for Civil Service, by 31 March 2023, the number of civil servants in public authorities was 166,253.[4]

In the ILO Observation CEACR – adopted 2018, published 108th ILC session (2019) – the Committee had previously requested the Ukrainian Government to list specific categories of public servants whose right to strike is restricted or prohibited by the Law on Civil Service, pursuant to section 10(5) of which, civil servants are prohibited from exercising the right to strike. Recalling that the right to strike in the public service may be restricted or prohibited only for public servants exercising authority in the name of the State, the Committee requested the Government to clarify which categories of civil servants exercise authority in the name of the State and whether some or all civil servants are prohibited from exercising the right to strike and to amend the law accordingly.[5]

With regard to the public servants, in its conclusions (Conclusions on Article 6 paragraph 4 2010, 2014, 2018), the ECSR found the situation in Ukraine not to be in conformity with Article 6 paragraph 4 of the European Social Charter on the ground that all civil servants are denied the right to strike. The report indicated that the legislation had not changed during the reference period. However, it stated that the National Civil Service Agency of Ukraine is considering the possibility of ratifying the

4. Statistical data on the number of civil servants by 31 March 2023, available at: https://nads.gov.ua/storage/app/sites/5/DIYALNIST/KSDS/Інфографіка_1кв_2023.pdf (accessed 31 July 2025).
5. Observation (CEACR) adopted 2018, published 108th ILC session (2019), available at: https://www.ilo.org/dyn/normlex/en/f?p=1000:13100:0::NO:13100:P13100_COMMENT_ID:3962360 (accessed 31 July 2025).

ILO Convention No. 151 on the Protection of the Right to Organize and the Procedure for Determining the Conditions of Work in the Civil Service.[6]

In addition to the general ban to strike for all civil servants without any exclusion, several special laws directly prohibit the right to strike for employees of particular state authorities with special legal status. Such restrictions are imposed on the following:

- Employees of the Bureau of Economic Security of Ukraine (Article 20 of the Law on the Bureau of Economic Security of Ukraine (2021) prohibits employees of the Bureau from being a member or participating in the establishment or activities of political parties, organizing or participating in strikes).
- Employees of the National Anti-Corruption Bureau (Article 13 of the Law on the National Anti-Corruption Bureau (2014) prohibits employees of the National Bureau from being members or participating in the establishment or activities of political parties, organizing or participating in strikes).
- Local self-government officials (Article 12 of the Law of Ukraine on Service in Local Self-Government Bodies (2001) prohibits local self-government officials from being organizers or direct participants in strikes and other actions that impede the exercise of powers by state authorities or local self-government bodies).[7]
- Members of the Accounting Chamber (Article 19 of the Law on Accounting Chamber (2015) stipulates that a member of the Accounting Chamber may not belong to a political party or participate in political actions, meetings, rallies, marches, and demonstrations, as well as strikes).
- Military personnel, civil servants, and other employees of the State Service for Special Communications and Information Protection of Ukraine (Article 12 of the Law on the State Service for Special Communications and Information Protection of Ukraine (2006) prohibits military personnel, civil servants, and other employees of the State Service for Special Communications and Information Protection of Ukraine from organizing and participating in strikes).

A legal definition of essential services (services, the performance of which is provided by state authorities, local governments, institutions, enterprises, and organizations of any form of ownership, the failure, interruption, and violation of the provision of which leads to immediate negative consequences for national security) is enshrined in the Law on Critical Infrastructure No. 1882-IX, dated 16 November 2021. The essential services listed in this law are as follows:

- management and provision of essential public (administrative) services;
- energy supply (including thermal energy supply);

6. 10th National Report of Ukraine on the implementation of the ESC, July 2018, p. 51, available at: https://rm.coe.int/10th-national-report-on-the-implementation-of-the-european-social-char/16808e45b9 (accessed 31 July 2025).
7. On 2 May 2023, the Parliament adopted a new Law on Service in Local Self-Government Bodies, which will come into force six months after the date of termination or cancellation of martial law in Ukraine. The new law does not contain provisions restricting the right of local self-government officials to strike.

- water supply and sanitation;
- food supply;
- health care;
- pharmaceutical industry;
- vaccine production, sustainable functioning of bio-laboratories;
- information services;
- electronic communications;
- financial services;
- transport support;
- defence, national security;
- law and order, administration of justice, detention;
- civil protection of population and territories, rescue services;
- space activities, technologies, and services;
- chemical industry;
- research activities.

Nonetheless, considering the importance of the concept and types of essential services for the right to strike, the provisions of the Law on Critical Infrastructure and the LPRCLD still need to be harmonized.

In addition, some particular laws prohibit the right to strike for workers who provide services that can be defined as essential services in the strict sense of the term.

They can be divided into two groups. The first group includes services with an explicit ban on strikes in all circumstances:

- Emergency rescue services (Article 116 of the Civil Protection Code of Ukraine (2012) prohibits ordinary and senior civil protection officers and other employees of emergency rescue services from organizing or participating in strikes).
- Personnel of nuclear facilities and facilities intended for radioactive waste management (Article 35 of the Law on the Use of Nuclear Energy and Radiation Safety (1995) provides that personnel of nuclear facilities and facilities intended for radioactive waste management do not have the right to strike).

The second group includes services where employees are not strictly forbidden to strike, but in cases when strikes pose a threat to sustaining livelihoods:

- Employees of electricity companies (Article 13 of the Law on the Electricity Market (2017) prohibits strikes at electricity companies in cases where they may lead to a disruption of the sustainability of the united energy system of Ukraine).
- Personnel of heat supply facilities (Article 30 of the Law on Heat Supply (2005) prohibits strikes at heat supply facilities in cases where they may lead to disruption of the stability of heat supply to consumers during the heating season).

- The staff of the electronic communication services provider (Article 24 of LPRCLD prohibits participating in strikes if such actions lead to the termination of the functioning of electronic communication networks or the provision of electronic communication services, which creates obstacles to ensuring national security, healthcare, human rights, and freedoms).

Furthermore, the Mining Law of Ukraine (1999) prohibits strikes for employees at mining companies unrelated to public servants or essential services. Article 49 provides additional requirements for persons working in particular hazardous underground conditions and peremptorily states that strikes and hunger strikes are prohibited in underground workings. Remarkably, this provision appeared in the national legislation as a response to miners' repeated 'hunger strikes' in the 1990s.

With regard to the essential services, the ECSR recalled that restricting strikes in sectors that are essential to the community is deemed to serve a legitimate purpose since strikes in these sectors could pose a threat to public interest, national security and/or public health (Conclusions I (1969), Statement of Interpretation on Article 6 paragraph 4). However, simply banning strikes even in essential sectors, particularly when they are extensively defined, is not deemed proportionate to the specific requirements of each sector. At most, the introduction of a minimum service requirement in these sectors might be considered in conformity with Article 6 paragraph 4. As there is no provision for the introduction of a minimum service, and strikes are simply prohibited for certain categories of employees, the Committee found that the situation is not in conformity with the Charter.[8]

2.2 Evolution of Restrictions on the Right to Strike in Ukraine

Ukrainian legislation has been modified to remove restrictions on the right to strike in the transport sector. Before the Law on Transport amendments in 2022, the right to strike at transport was restricted. This restriction resulted in the ECtHR judgment *Veniamin Tymoshenko and Others v. Ukraine* No. 48408/12, 2 October 2014. In this judgment, the ECtHR noted that the prohibition of strikes at transport enterprises provided for in Article 18 of the Law 'on Transport' violates the right to freedom of association guaranteed by Article 11 of the ECHR. The ECtHR noted that the cases in which a strike by transport workers is prohibited under Article 18 of the Law of Ukraine on Transport are more restrictive than those provided for in Article 24 of the LPRCLD, which covers labour disputes in all sectors. In particular, in addition to cases where a strike poses a threat to human life or health, it is also prohibited for employees of transport enterprises in cases 'related to the transportation of passengers, maintenance of continuously operating industries'. Thus, the court emphasized the need to bring the Law of Ukraine on Transport in line with the Constitution and the LPRCLD.[9] It took the

8. ECSR, Conclusions 2018 on Art. 6 §4 Ukraine, available at: http://hudoc.esc.coe.int/eng?i=2018/def/UKR/6/4/EN.
9. ECtHR, *Veniamin Tymoshenko and others v. Ukraine*, Application No. 48408/12, 2 October 2014, paras 80-86, available at: http://hudoc.echr.coe.int/eng?i=001-146671 (accessed 31 July 2025).

Parliament eight years to implement this ECtHR decision into national legislation. The new version of the Law on Transport, amended in 2022, refers to the general procedure set out in the LPRCLD and does not provide additional grounds for transport workers.

Generally, it can be argued that Ukrainian legislation restricting the right to strike is being liberalized. In addition to the transport sector, the liberalization process is also evidenced by the proposals of the government working group on drafting a new law on Collective Labour Disputes. The particular changes would narrow the circle of employees currently prohibited from strikes and introduce special conditions (minimum service requirements) for the exercise of the right to strike for specific categories of employees in essential services. The general ban on organizing and participating in strikes is proposed to be retained for prosecutors, judges, civil servants of category 'A' (senior civil service corps only), police officers, military personnel of the Armed Forces of Ukraine, the State Border Guard Service of Ukraine, the Security Service of Ukraine, ordinary and senior officers of the Civil Protection Service, the National Anti-Corruption Bureau of Ukraine, ordinary and senior officers of the State Criminal Executive Service.

2.3 Situations of Acute National or Local Crisis

Article 64 of the Constitution of Ukraine indicates that under martial law or a state of emergency, certain restrictions on rights and freedoms may be established, indicating the duration of these restrictions. The rights and freedoms provided by the exhaustive list of Articles of the Constitution cannot be limited. Constitutional rights in the field of labour are not included in this list. Therefore, any restrictions or changes in labour legislation under martial law that worsen the situation of employees are allowed. This fact was important after the beginning of the Russian Federation's full-scale aggression against Ukraine in February 2022.

Article 19 of the Law of Ukraine on the Legal Regime of Martial Law (2015) prohibits strikes, mass gatherings, and actions under martial law. If a regime of martial law is declared, an automatic prohibition of strikes applies until it is repealed.

Article 16 of the Law of Ukraine on the Legal Regime of the State of Emergency (2000) includes a ban on strikes among the measures aimed at preventing riots or criminal offences, protecting public health, or protecting the rights and freedoms of others. If a state of emergency is declared, the Parliament or the President of Ukraine may prohibit strikes from being conducted for a period not exceeding one month. A joint act of the Parliament and the President of Ukraine must approve an extension of such prohibition.

3 COMPENSATORY GUARANTEES FOR WORKERS DEPRIVED OF THE RIGHT TO STRIKE

Restrictions on the right to strike for employees in certain types of activity do not mean they do not have the tools to protect their rights. For example, Article 25 of the LPRCLD stipulates that in cases of legislative restrictions on the right to strike and when the recommendations of the NMCSU on resolving a collective labour dispute (conflict) are not taken into account by the parties, the NMCSU shall apply to the court for resolution of the collective labour dispute (conflict). It is a compensatory guarantee for employees whose right to strike is restricted, as otherwise collective labour disputes cannot be considered by the court, as these categories of disputes are not subject to court jurisdiction and alternative, non-judicial remedies should be applied.

4 CONCLUSION

The right to strike is one of the fundamental labour rights recognized internationally and enshrined in the national legislation of the vast majority of countries. Ukraine is no exception. Regulatory and legal consolidation of the right to strike in Ukraine has a long history of formation and development. Its evaluation went through several stages – from complete prohibition to constitutional recognition. Even though the right to strike is enshrined in the Constitution of Ukraine and recognized by law, it is strictly regulated and de facto makes it difficult to exercise this right due to the excessive overregulation and bureaucratization of the procedure.

The right to strike might be temporarily restricted in acute national or local crises for the sake of national security and the preservation of the State. One of the unconditional consequences of the introduction of martial law is the prohibition of strikes and other collective actions, which directly follows from the Law of Ukraine 'on the Legal Regime of Martial Law'. The limitations of labour rights established by the said law are based on the norms of the Constitution of Ukraine.

The legal regulation of strikes in Ukraine needs to be improved, considering the principles developed by the ILO Supervisory bodies and the practice of the ECSR. The ECtHR's case law has had a positive impact on national labour legislation in this sphere. However, despite some progress in bringing national legislation in line with international standards (removal of the ban on the right to strike in the transport sector), the problem of compliance with ILO standards in terms of restrictions on the right to strike for all civil servants and certain public sector employees remains unresolved. The prohibitions in such cases have to be considered excessive. In this regard, any legislative restrictions should clearly and narrowly define the class of public servants whose right to strike is restricted. The determination of such public servants should be based on the nature of the tasks they perform and the likely impact of disruption to that service in the event of a strike.

The narrowing of the categories of employees who are prohibited or restricted from taking part in strikes should become a positive trend in Ukrainian legislation and demonstrate the growing importance of ensuring that the majority of workers have the right to strike.

BCLR - BULLETIN OF COMPARATIVE LABOUR RELATIONS

Vol. Author/Title/Year/ISBN

1. Roger Blanpain, *Individual Employment Contracts: Collective Agreements,* 1970.
2. Roger Blanpain, *Social Planning,* 1971 (ISBN 90-312-0018-2).
3. Roger Blanpain, *Guaranteed Income Funds,* 1972 (ISBN 90-312-0019-0).
4. Roger Blanpain, *Employee Participation at the Level of the Enterprise,* 1973 (ISBN 90-312-0020-4).
5. Roger Blanpain, *Vastheid van Betrekking: Staking en Bezetting,* 1974.
6. Roger Blanpain, *Labour Law and Industrial Relations (International Bibliography),* 1975 (ISBN 90-312-0023-9).
7. Roger Blanpain, *Multinational Enterprises,* 1976 (ISBN 90-312-0024-7).
8. Roger Blanpain, *Worker's Participation in the European Company,* 1977 (ISBN 90-312-0044-1).
9. Roger Blanpain, *Women and Labour,* 1978 (ISBN 90-312-0077-8).
10. Roger Blanpain, *European Conference on Labour Law and Industrial Relations: Multinational Enterprises,* 1979 (ISBN 90-312-0091-3).
11. Roger Blanpain, *Job Security and Industrial Relations,* 1980 (ISBN 90-312-0147-2).
12. Roger Blanpain, Greg Bamber & Russell Lansbury, *Technological Change and Industrial Relations: An International Symposium,* 1983 (ISBN 90-312-0205-3).
13. Roger Blanpain, James Janssen van Raay & A. Moulty, *Worker's Participation in the European Community: The Fifth Directive,* 1984 (ISBN 90-654-4187-5).
14. Roger Blanpain, *Equality and Prohibition of Discrimination in Employment,* 1985 (ISBN 90-654-4215-4).
15. Roger Blanpain, *Restructuring Labour in the Enterprise: Law and Practice in France, F.R. of Germany, Italy, Sweden and the United Kingdom,* 1986 (ISBN 90-654-4283-9).
16. Roger Blanpain & E. Kassalow, *Unions and Industrial Relations: Recent Trends and Prospect: A Comparative Treatment,* 1987 (ISBN 90-654-4294-4).
17. Roger Blanpain & Marco Biagi, *Trade Union Democracy and Industrial Relations,* 1988 (ISBN 90-654-4394-0).
18. Roger Blanpain & Jelle Visser, *In Search of Inclusive Unionism,* 1990 (ISBN 90-654-4439-4).
19. Roger Blanpain, *Flexibility and Wages: A Comparative Treatment,* 1990 (ISBN 90-654-4461-0).

20. Roger Blanpain, Stephen Frenkel & Oliver Clarke, *Economic Restructuring and Industrial Relations in Industrialised Countries,* 1990 (ISBN 90-654-4488-2).
21. Roger Blanpain & Friedrich Fürstenberg, *Structure and Strategy in Industrial Relations,* 1991 (ISBN 90-654-4559-5).
22. Roger Blanpain, Amira Galin & Ozer Carmi, *Flexible Work Patterns and Their Impact on Industrial Relations,* 1991 (ISBN 90-654-4572-2).
23. Roger Blanpain, *Workers' Participation: Influence on Management Decision-Making by Labour in the Private Sector,* 1992 (ISBN 90-654-4600-1).
24. Roger Blanpain, Brian Brooks & Chris Engels, *Employed or Self-Employed,* 1992 (ISBN 90-654-4613-3).
25. Roger Blanpain & Tiziano Treu, *Industrial Relations Developments in the Telecommunications Industry,* 1993 (ISBN 90-654-4642-7).
26. Roger Blanpain & Marco Biagi, *Industrial Relations in Small and Medium Sized Enterprises,* 1993 (ISBN 90-654-4696-6).
27. Roger Blanpain & Marco Biagi, *Participative Management and Industrial Relations in a Worldwide Perspective,* 1993 (ISBN 90-654-4769-5).
28. Roger Blanpain, Jacques Rojot & Hoyt N. Wheeler, *Employee Rights and Industrial Justice,* 1994 (ISBN 90-654-4804-7).
29. Roger Blanpain & Ruth Ben-Israel, *Strikes and Lock-Outs in Industrialized Market Economies,* 1994 (ISBN 90-654-4841-1).
30. Roger Blanpain, Kazuo Sugeno & Yasuo Suwa, *The Harmonization of Working Life and Family Life,* 1995 (ISBN 90-411-0064-4).
31. Roger Blanpain & Laszio Nagy, *Labour Law and Industrial Relations in Central and Eastern Europe,* 1996 (ISBN 90-411-0298-1).
32. Roger Blanpain, *Labour Law and Industrial Relations in the European Union,* 1997 (ISBN 90-411-0527-1).
33. Taco Van Peijpe, *Employment Protection under Strain,* 1998 (ISBN 90-411-0528-8).
34. Roger Blanpain, Takashi Araki & Ryuichi Yamakawa, *The Process of Industrialization and the Role of Labour Law in Asia,* 1999 (ISBN 9-041-1104-7-X).
35. Roger Blanpain & Marco Biagi, *Non-standard Work and Industrial Relations,* 1999 (ISBN 90-411-1117-4).
36. Roger Blanpain, *Private Employment Agencies: The Impact of ILO Convention 181 (1997) and the Judgment of the European Court of Justice of 11 December 1997,* 1999 (ISBN 90-411-1118-2).
37. Roger Blanpain, *Multinational Enterprises and the Social Challenges of the XXIst Century: The ILO Declaration on Fundamental* Principles *at Work, Public and Private Corporate Codes of Conduct,* 2000 (ISBN 90-411-1280-4).
38. Roger Blanpain, Ryuichi Yamakawa & Takashi Araki, *Deregulation and Labour Law: In Search of a Labour Concept for the 21st Century,* 2000 (ISBN 90-411-1370-3).
39. Roger Blanpain, *The Council of Europe and the Social Challenges of the XXIst Century,* 2001 (ISBN 90-411-1543-9).

40. Roger Blanpain, *On-Line Rights for Employees in the Information Society, Use & Monitoring of E-Mail & Internet at Work,* 2002 (ISBN 90-411-1626-5).
41. Roger Blanpain, *The Evolving Employment Relationship and the New Economy: The Role of Labour Law & Industrial Relations,* 2001 (ISBN 90-411-1691-5).
42. Roger Blanpain, *Involvement of Employees in the European Union, Works Councils, Company Statute, Information and Consultation Rights,* 2002 (ISBN 90-411-1760-1).
43. Michele Colucci, *The Impact of the Internet and New Technologies on the Workplace: A Legal Analysis from a Comparative Point of View,* 2002 (ISBN 90-411-1824-1).
44. Roger Blanpain, *White Paper on the Labour Market in Italy: The Quality of European Industrial Relations and Changing Industrial Relations,* 2002 (ISBN 90-411-1841-1).
45. Roger Blanpain, Russell D. Lansbury & Young-Bum Park, *Impact of Globalisation on Employment Relations: A Comparison of the Automobile and Banking Industries in Australia and Korea,* 2002 (ISBN 90-411-1850-0).
46. Roger Blanpain & Antoine Jacobs, *Employee Rights in Bankruptcy: A Comparative-Law Assessment,* 2002 (ISBN 90-411-1942-6).
47. Roger Blanpain, Takashi Araki & Shinya Ouchi, *Corporate Restructuring and the Role of Labour Law,* 2003 (ISBN 90-411-1949-3).
48. Roger Blanpain, *Collective Bargaining, Discrimination, Social Security and European Integration,* 2003 (ISBN 90-411-2010-6).
49. Roger Blanpain & Luis Aparicio-Valdez, *Labour Relations in the Asia- Pacific Countries,* 2004 (ISBN 90-411-2239-7).
50. Roger Blanpain & Ronnie Graham, *Temporary Agency Work and the Information Society,* 2004 (ISBN 90-411-2252-4).
51. Roger Blanpain, *The Actors of Collective Bargaining: A World Report,* 2004 (ISBN 90-411-2253-2).
52. Roger Blanpain & Michele Colucci, *The Globalisation of Labour Standards: The Soft Law Track,* 2004 (ISBN 90-411-2303-2).
53. Roger Blanpain, Takashi Araki & Shinya Ouchi, *Labour Law in Motion: Diversification of the Labour Force & Terms and Conditions of Employment,* 2005 (ISBN 90-411-2315-6).
54. Roger Blanpain, *Smoking and the Workplace,* 2005 (ISBN 90-411-2325-3).
55. Roger Blanpain, *Confronting Globalization: The Quest for a Social Agenda,* 2005 (ISBN 90-411-2381-4).
56. Roger Blanpain, Thomas Blanke & Edgar Rose, *Collective Bargaining Wages in Comparative Perspective: Germany, France, the Netherlands, Sweden and the United Kingdom,* 2005 (ISBN 90-411-2388-1).
57. Roger Blanpain & Anne Numhauser-Henning, *Women in Academia & Equality Law: Aiming High - Falling Short?,* 2006 (ISBN 978-90-411-2427-6).
58. Roger Blanpain, *Freedom of Services in the European Union: Labour and Social Security Law: The Bolkestein Initiative,* 2006 (ISBN 978-90-411-2453-5).
59. Roger Blanpain, Frans Pennings & Nurhan Sural, *Flexibilisation and Modernisation of the Turkish Labour Market,* 2006 (ISBN 978-90-411-2490-X).

60. Roger Blanpain & Boel Flodgren, *Corporate and Employment Perspectives in a Global Business Environment*, 2006 (ISBN 978-90-411-2537-X).
61. Roger Blanpain, Shinya Ouchi & Takashi Araki, *Decentralizing Industrial Relations and The Role of Labor Unions and Employee Representatives*, 2007 (ISBN 978-90-411-2583-3).
62. Roger Blanpain, *European Framework Agreements and Telework: Law and Practice: A European and Comparative Study*, 2007 (ISBN 978-90-411-2560-4).
63. Roger Blanpain, Jim Kitay, Leanne Cutcher & Nick Wailes, *Globalization and Employment Relations in Retail Banking*, 2007 (ISBN 978-90-411-2620-1).
64. Roger Blanpain, Russell Lansbury, Jim Kitay, Nick Wailes & Anja Kirsch, *Globalization and Employment Relations in the Auto Assembly Industry:* A *Study of Seven Countries*, 2008 (ISBN 978-90-411-2698-6).
65. Roger Blanpain & Michele Tiraboschi, *The Global Labour Market: From Globalization to Flexicurity*, 2008 (ISBN 978-90-411-2722-8).
66. Roger Blanpain, Michele Colucci & Frank Hendrickx, *The Future of Sport in the European Union: Beyond the EU Reform Treaty and the White Paper*, 2008 (ISBN 978-90-411-2761-7).
67. Roger Blanpain, Linda Dickens, *Challenges in European Employment Relations: Employment Regulation, Trade Union Organization, Equality, Flexicurity, Training and New Approaches to Pay*, 2008 (ISBN 978-90-411-2771-6).
68. Roger Blanpain, Hiroya Nakakubo & Takashi Araki, *New Developments in Employment Discrimination Law, 2008* (ISBN 978-90-411-2782-2).
69. Roger Blanpain, Andrzej Marian wiątkowski, *The Laval and Viking Cases: Freedom of Services and Establishment v. Industrial Conflict in the European Economic Area and Russia*, 2009 (ISBN 978-90-411-2850-8).
70. Roger Blanpain, William Bromwich, Olga Rymkevich, Silvia Spattini, *The Modernization of Labour Law and Industrial Relations in a Comparative Perspective*, 2009 (ISBN 978-90-411-2865-2).
71. Roger Blanpain, Juan Pablo Landa & Brian Langille, *Employment Policies and Multilevel Governance*, 2009 (ISBN 978-90-411-2866-9).
72. Roger Blanpain, European Works Councils; *The European Directive 2009/ 38/EC of 6 May 2009, 2009* (ISBN 978-90-411-3208-6).
73. Roger Blanpain, William Bromwich, Olga Rymkevich & Silvia Spattini, *Labour Productivity, Investment in Human Capital and Youth Employment: Comparative Developments and Global Responses*, 2010 (ISBN 978-90-411-3249-9).
74. Greg J. Bamber & Philippe Pochet, *Regulating Employment Relations, Work and Labour Laws: International Comparisons between Key Countries*, 2010 (ISBN 978-90-411-3199-7). General Editor: Roger Blanpain.
75. Roger Blanpain, Desislava Nikolaeva Dimitrova, *Seafarers' Rights in the Globalized Maritime Industry*, 2010 (ISBN 978-90-411-3349-6).
76. Roger Blanpain, Hiroya Nakakubo & Takashi Araki, *Regulation of Fixed- Term Employment Contracts*, 2010 (ISBN 978-90-411-3356-4).

77. Roger Blanpain, William Bromwich, Olga Rymkevich & Iacopo Senatori, *Rethinking Corporate Governance*, 2011 (ISBN 978-90-411-3450-9).
78. Roger Blanpain & Frank Hendrickx, *Labour Law between Change and Tradition: Liber Amicorum Antoine Jacobs*, 2011 (ISBN 978-90-411-3424-0).
79. Roger Blanpain, Thomas Klebe, Marlene Schmidt & Bernd Waas, *Trade Union Rights at the Workplace*, 2012 (ISBN 978-90-411-3460-8).
80. Roger Blanpain, William Bromwich, Olga Rymkevich & Iacopo Senatori, *Labour Markets, Industrial Relations and Human Resources Management: From Recession to Recovery*, 2012 (ISBN 978-90-411-4004-3).
81. Roger Blanpain, Hiroya Nakakubo & Takashi Araki, *Systems of Employee Representation at the Enterprise: A Comparative Study*, 2012 (ISBN 978-90-411-4080-7).
82. Roger Blanpain & Frank Hendrickx, *Temporary Agency Work in the European Union and the United States*, 2013 (ISBN 978-90-411-4769-1).
83. Roger Blanpain, Toker Dereli, Y. Pınar Soykut-Sarıca & Aslı en-Tabaı, *Emerging Patterns of Work and Turkish Labour Market Challenges under Globalization: Readings on Labour and Employment Relations*, 2014 (ISBN 978-90-411-4983-1).
84. Roger Blanpain, Pablo Arellano Ortiz, Marius Olivier & Gijsbert Vonk, *Social Security and Migrant Workers: Selected Studies of Cross-border Social Security Mechanisms*, 2014 (ISBN 978-90-411-4770-7).
85. Roger Blanpain & Nikita Lyutov, *Workers' Representation in Central and Eastern Europe: Challenges and Opportunities for the Works Councils' System*, 2014 (ISBN 978-90-411-4746-2).
86. Roger Blanpain, Ulla Liukkunen & Chen Yifeng, *China and ILO Fundamental Principles and Rights at Works*, 2014 (ISBN 978-90-411-4984-8).
87. Roger Blanpain, *The Use of Languages and Employment Relations*, 2014 (ISBN 978-90-411-5606-8).
88. Roger Blanpain, Hiroya Nakakubo & Takashi Araki, *Protection of Employees' Personal Information and Privacy*, 2014 (ISBN 978-90-411-5608-2).
89. Roger Blanpain, Jan Wouters, Glenn Rayp, Laura Beke & Axel Marx, *Protecting Labour Rights in a Multi-polar Supply Chain and Mobile Global Economy*, 2015 (ISBN 978-90-411-5662-4).
90. Roger Blanpain & Stefania Marassi, *Globalization and Transnational Collective Labour Relations: International and European Framework Agreements at Company Level*, 2015 (ISBN 978-90-411-4748-6).
91. Roger Blanpain, Frank Hendrickx & Petra Herzfeld Olsson, *National Effects of the Implementation of EU Directives on Labour Migration from Third Countries*, 2016 (ISBN 978-90-411-6257-1).
92. Roger Blanpain, Frank Hendrickx & D'Arcy du Toit, *Labour Law and Social Progress: Holding the Line or Shifting the Boundaries?* 2016 (ISBN 978-90-411-6747-7).

93. Roger Blanpain & Frank Hendrickx, *Reasonable Accommodation in the Modern Workplace: Potential and Limits of the Integrative Logics of Labour Law*, 2016 (ISBN 978-90-411-6258-8).
94. Roger Blanpain, Frank Hendrickx & Bernd Waas, *New Forms of Employment in Europe*, 2016 (ISBN 978-90-411-6239-7).
95. Roger Blanpain, Frank Hendrickx, Hiroya Nakakubo & Takashi Araki, *The Notion of Employer in the Era of the Fissured Workplace: Should Labour Law Responsibilities Exceed the Boundary of the Legal Entity?*, 2017 (ISBN 978-90-411-8470-2).
96. Elena Sychenko, *Individual Labour Rights as Human Rights: The Contributions of the European Court of Human Rights to Worker's Rights Protection*, 2017 (ISBN 978-90-411-8629-4).
97. William Bromwich & Olga Rymkevich, *Improving Workplace Quality: New Perspectives and Challenges for Worker Well-Being*, 2017 (ISBN 978-90-411-8628-7).
98. Sarah De Groof, *Work-Life Balance in the Modern Workplace: Interdisciplinary Perspectives from Work-Family Research, Law and Policy*, 2017 (ISBN 978-90-411-8630-0).
99. Sylvaine Laulom, *Collective Bargaining Developments in Times of Crisis, Second Edition*, 2025 (ISBN 978-94-035-0628-9).
100. Frank Hendrickx & Valerio De Stefano, *Game Changers in Labour Law: Shaping the Future of Work*, 2018 (ISBN 978-90-411-9953-9).
101. Ivana Palinkaš, *The Legal and Institutional Framing of Collective Bargaining in CEE Countries: Between Europeanisation and Decentralisation*, 2018 (ISBN 978-90-411-9199-1).
102. Jeremy Waddington, *European Board-Level Employee Representation: National Variations in Influence and Power*, 2018 (ISBN 978-90-411-9202-8).
103. Jan Pichrt & Kristina Koldinská, *Labour Law and Social Protection in a Globalized World: Changing Realities in Selected Areas of Law and Policy*, 2018 (ISBN 978-94-035-0093-5).
104. Matthew W. Finkin, *American Labor and the Law: Dormant, Resurgent, and Emergent Problems*, 2019 (ISBN 978-94-035-0654-8).
105. Giuseppe Casale & Tiziano Treu, *Transformations of Work: Challenges for the Institutions and Social Actors*, 2019 (ISBN 978-94-035-0891-7).
106. Miguel De la Corte-Rodríguez, *EU Law on Maternity and Other Child-Related Leaves: Impact on Gender Equality*, 2019 (ISBN 978-94-035-1452-9).
107. Valeria Pulignano & Frank Hendrickx, *Employment Relations in the 21st Century: Challenges for Theory and Research in a Changing World of Work*, 2020 (ISBN 978-94-035-1764-3).
108. Matteo Bottero, *Posting of Workers in EU Law: Challenges of Equality, Solidarity and Fair Competition*, 2021 (ISBN 978-94-035-2860-1).
109. Bernd Waas & Christina Hießl, *Collective Bargaining for Self-Employed Workers in Europe: Approaches to Reconcile Competition Law and Labour Rights*, 2021 (ISBN 978-94-035-2373-6).

110. Mathias Wouters, *International Labour Standards and Platform Work: An Analysis of Digital Labour Platforms Based on the Instruments on Private Employment Agencies, Home Work and Domestic Work*, 2022 (ISBN 978-94-035-4024-5).
111. Luca Ratti, *In-Work Poverty in Europe: Vulnerable and Under-Represented Persons in a Comparative Perspective*, 2022 (ISBN 978-94-035-4996-5).
112. Silvia Rainone, *The Role of the Court of Justice in EU Labour Law: A Case Study on the Transfer of Undertakings Directive*, 2023 (ISBN 978-94-035-2896-0).
113. Frank Hendrickx, Elena Gramano & David Mangan, *Privacy@work: A European and Comparative Perspective*, 2023 (ISBN 978-94-035-3106-9).
114. Elena Sychenko & Adalberto Perulli, *Employment Law and the European Convention on Human Rights: The Research of the Recent Jurisprudence of the ECtHR Related to Employment Law (2017-2021)*, 2023 (ISBN 978-94-035-3556-2).
115. Ilda Durri, *Casual Work Arrangements and Platform-Based Work: The Casual Work Agenda as a Way to Enhance the Labour Protection of Platform Workers*, 2023 (ISBN 978-94-035-3107-6).
116. Charalampos Stylogiannis, *Collective Labour Rights for Self-Employed Workers: A Human Rights-Based Approach of Platform Work*, 2023 (ISBN 978-94-035-0667-8).
117. Heather Kurzbauer, *Employment Vulnerabilities in the World of Orchestral Musicians: Symphonic Metamorphoses*, 2023 (ISBN 978-94-035-2737-6).
118. Natalie Videbæk Munkholm, Vincenzo Pietrogiovanni & Karsten Engsig Sørensen, *Managers in European Law: Rights and Duties of Executive and Non-executive Managers in a European Perspective*, 2024 (ISBN 978-94-035-3286-8).
119. Frank Hendrickx & Christina Hiessl, *The Meaning of Work: A Labour Law Perspective*, 2025 (ISBN 978-94-035-0579-4).
120. Bernd Waas, *Restrictions on the Right to Strike: International Law and National Laws in Europe*, 2025 (ISBN 978-94-035-2519-8).

www.ingramcontent.com/pod-product-compliance
Ingram Content Group UK Ltd.
Pitfield, Milton Keynes, MK11 3LW, UK
UKHW020130290926
15471UKWH00003B/388

9 789403 525198